THE FOUNDERS

THE FOUNDERS

The Origins of the ANC and the Struggle
for Democracy in South Africa

André Odendaal

Democracy, underpinned by a dignified universalism, came to South Africa in 1994, at great cost, and we remember those who paved the way for it. The oppressed people of this country thereby showed – once again – that 'Time is longer than rope'.

First published by Jacana Media (Pty) Ltd in 2012

10 Orange Street
Sunnyside
Auckland Park 2092
South Africa
+27 11 628 3200
www.jacana.co.za

© André Odendaal, 2012

ISBN 978-1-4314-0291-5

Cover design by publicide
Set in Sabon 10.5/15.2pt
Job no. 001781
Printed by Ultra Litho (Pty) Ltd, Johannesburg

See a complete list of Jacana titles at www.jacana.co.za

Contents

PART TWO: THE CREATION OF WIDER NETWORKS

PART THREE: WAR AND CHANGE

PART FOUR: UNIFICATION

Introduction

'Equal rights for all South of the Zambesi' is the motto that will yet float at the masthead of this new ship of state which has been launched under the Union, and no other will be permanently substituted while there is one black or coloured man of any consequence or self-respect in the country, or any white man who respects the traditions of free Government – so help us God.

– *Izwi Labantu*, 16 February 1909

In 1910 a new country came into being: the Union of South Africa. Several million people with dozens of identities, some of which defied easy description, fell within its boundaries. They were speakers of Xhosa, Zulu, Tswana, Sotho, English, Dutch and many other languages, but now they were also all South Africans. However, the constitution of the new South Africa barred the majority of the country's inhabitants from being voters and citizens. A.K. Soga, feisty editor of a small-town newspaper, *Izwi Labantu*, warned, in the prophetic words quoted in the epigraph above, that until all South Africans were recognised as citizens, the country would never be at peace with itself.

Soga drew on the wisdom and experiences of his remarkable family and equally remarkable peers when he penned his warning to the colonial rulers. His father was the distinguished Tiyo Soga, the first university student and ordained Christian minister produced by the indigenous people in southern Africa. His mother was an 'upright and thrifty'

Scotswoman, Janet Burnside. His grandfather, 'old Soga', was a councillor to Chief Sandile of the Ngqika, who died fighting for his king in the last war of dispossession. Ambushed by African allies of the colonial forces, this ironsmith of note reputedly gave his killers his own weapon, telling them to do a clean job.[1]

A.K. Soga belonged to the class of pioneering intellectuals and activists who emerged from the 1860s onwards to lead the struggle for the political rights of their people in the new colonial societies of southern Africa. As the indigenous people lost their independence and land, these new-style Africans, sometimes called 'school people' or *kholwa*, because they were generally mission-educated Christians, developed a range of political goals and strategies. Finding themselves within the same boundaries and under the same government and social order as their conquerors, they adopted the language, codes and methods of the colonisers and set up their own newspapers and political organisations, made use of the common franchise in the Cape and petitioned parliament. In plotting their way forward, they drew on a mixture of ideas, combining homegrown African humanism – or *ubuntu* – with western democratic notions and Christian beliefs to shape a new political vision for the future.[2] They warned that the African people – defeated and now a subject people – had to take on the colonisers at their own game if they were to survive in the new colonial world. For this, they needed to adapt to western-style constitutional politics. 'Take paper and ink [and] fire with your pen,' Isaac Wauchope exhorted them.[3] Their efforts were to lead to the founding of the South African Native National Congress, later renamed the African National Congress, in 1912.

The dream A.K. Soga and his peers harboured of 'equal rights' in their own country seemed a mere pipedream when the ANC was born on 8 January 1912. Even after 50 years had passed, Soga's prediction seemed improbable: colonialism and segregation had by then evolved into a violent system of institutionalised racism called apartheid. Then, remarkably, in one of the most dramatic turn-abouts in global politics during the twentieth century, South Africa became a democracy. On 27 April 1994 people stood patiently in long queues as all South Africans voted for the first time. Shortly thereafter, Nelson Mandela moved seamlessly from being the world's most famous prisoner to President of South Africa. Soga's stubborn prediction of 85 years earlier had come true. The preamble of the Constitution of this new ship of state was written as if its drafters had him and his colleagues in mind:

We ... adopt this constitution as the supreme law of the Republic so as to –

Heal the divisions of the past and establish a society based on democratic values, social justice and fundamental human rights;

Lay the foundations for a democratic and open society in which government is based on the will of the people and every citizen is equally protected by law;

Improve the quality of life of all citizens and free the potential of each person; and

Build a united and democratic South Africa able to take its rightful place as a sovereign state in the family of nations.

May God protect our people.[4]

As President Mandela took the salute at his inauguration, the world celebrated South Africa's 'miracle' transition to democracy. But democracy was not the outcome of a miracle; it was the product of centuries of lived experience, innovation and struggle, often dispersed and contradictory, in the most trying historical circumstances, on the part of those who had been dispossessed. The party that Mandela led, 'the Struggle' that he symbolised and the values he espoused, all had their roots deep in history. Though the ANC, the oldest surviving political organisation on the African continent, was founded in 1912, its origins go back decades further. A rich body of intellectuals, activists and organisations had paved the way from the 1860s onwards. They did so in complex, multi-dimensional ways – as the lives of the Soga family show – articulating a new model for 'race relations' and political participation in southern Africa. They were Africans 'always in the process of becoming', who had to 'negotiate different historical contexts in all their vexed complexities', as one writer has noted.[5]

This book sets out to identify those pathbreakers who first developed the framework, form and content of the freedom struggle in South Africa, and seeks to put their lives and actions in context. They are still virtually unknown – unlike those who sowed the seeds of revolutionary movements in, say, America and India – but they were the very founders of the ANC and, indeed, the originators of the ideas, shaped in an African context, that ultimately led South Africa to democracy. Although the demands of the early leaders and organisations mostly fell short of universal adult suffrage, they were the direct precursors of the later struggle for equal rights for all. [6] The structures they created, the methods they followed and the ideas they articulated continue to influence us. One cannot understand South Africa today without knowing about them.

The Founders grew out of my master's dissertation, published in 1984 as *Vukani Bantu! The beginnings of black protest politics to 1910*, and my 1983 doctoral dissertation on 'African political mobilisation in the eastern Cape, 1880–1912'.[7] In these studies, I provided the first detailed descriptions of the earliest African political organisations in South Africa, particularly in the eastern Cape, and showed how they increasingly banded together, in response to the process of unification from 1902 onwards, to form the ANC.[8] In a review of *Vukani Bantu!*, one scholar noted that this book 'is by far the fullest study of African politics over those early years for which the evidence has been considered, until recently, to be too fragmentary for useful analysis [and] in this supposed archival desert [the writer] has brought alive plants whose extinction had been more or less taken for granted'.[9] He continued, 'The hitherto neglected early history of the black man's struggle for political equality is here brought to life. By using untapped archival sources and vernacular newspapers, the author has succeeded in tracing and following some very obscure political movements. He has brought the story to the point at which these organisations can be related to each other, and has demonstrated connections between them which previous scholars like Walshe, Roux, Benson, and Karis and Carter were unable to make.'

Subsequent studies covering the same broad field have drawn directly or indirectly from the above-mentioned works, and the knowledge they provided has now been absorbed into both general histories and specialist monographs, as well as the internal narratives of the ANC and its alliance partners.[10]

Since my two works first appeared in the early 1980s, new multi-disciplinary academic currents have come to the fore, in post-colonial and post-modern studies, feminism, cultural theory, and historical anthropology. Moreover, a host of impressive books, many based on these new approaches, have been written on the responses of Africans to Christianity and colonialism, which have considerably deepened our knowledge of the subject. I have found this scholarship exhilarating to read, including, for example, recent studies by Jeff Guy, Tim Couzens, James Campbell, John and Jean Comaroff, Veit Erlman, Jeff Opland, Abner Nyamende, Lungisile Ntsebeza, Mcebisi Ndletyana, Park Mgadla and Stephen Volz, Charles Villa-Vicencio and Peter Grassow, and Paul Landau and Roger Levine. Besides their new theoretical and conceptual insights, they have been particularly helpful in deepening my understanding of pre-1900 developments outside the eastern Cape, and in helping me trace the connections of people involved in the first organisations to the very beginnings of indigenous Christianity. They have also reinforced the understanding, now widely held, that history is not so much about what happened as about how individuals and groups construct or imagine history. I am impressed, moreover, by the nuance they have introduced in respect of such matters as language and voice and 'facts' and 'events', and by the retreat from old approaches that emphasised fixed dichotomies such as those between the 'political' and 'non-political', or 'tribal' and 'modern'. In this book I attempt to include some of this new material and some of these new perspectives, without reinventing the original narratives. Hopefully, many of the recent studies broadly complement or affirm, rather than negate, the importance of my research.

At the same time, *The Founders* remains essentially a work, fashioned out of detailed empirical research, that tells the story about a remarkable body of South Africans who even today are generally unknown. It is an organisational or 'family' history that seeks to construct a group biography of the first generations of activists and political bodies in South Africa. It examines the areas and networks in which they operated, their concerns and the factors that propelled them to start working together. It self-consciously attempts to record names, personalities and organisations that populated this network. It is a history with specific, limited aims. As James Campbell has noted, studies of this kind 'inevitably intersect with dozens of historiographical debates' and, like him (though without the same skills), I am 'content to address such issues implicitly' rather than as a main concern.[11] Above all, I see its value in restoring the African voice and identity, as a pre-condition for informed analysis of this period and its politics.

For me, the key that unlocked the remarkable story of early African politics was the earliest newspapers published for black audiences in South Africa. The contents of these pioneering publications, usually around four to eight pages in length, were often half in English and half in an indigenous language. The English sections, which were usually the part accessed and used by academic historians, often dealt with mainstream colonial politics and the 'native question'. Struggling through the Xhosa sections with my imperfect knowledge of the language, I came upon a treasure house waiting to be explored. For here were a myriad of reports on the activities of the new intellectuals and activists – on everything from local politics to teachers' meetings, debates, choirs, sports, weddings, funerals and even names of hotel guests – written by the actors themselves, in their own language. I was fortunate to discover early on in my own research and career what scholars currently emphasise: that understanding language is 'key to the translation, exchange and transmittal of ideas' in the colonial context, and key to restoring rounded African lives and ideas to the historical record.[12]

Conducting research on the early indigenous intellectuals also helped shape my identity and life in profound ways. As a child of the eastern Cape, I was filled me with amazement when I first encountered the source material. Here was a world I knew nothing about, though I had grown up in that very region. It opened wide my eyes and helped to change fundamentally the way I looked at myself and my country. It also enabled me to be truer in important ways to my own sense of identity and humanity, among other things by becoming involved in a modest way in the 'struggle'. The title of *Vukani Bantu!* (Rise up, you people!), derived from an exhortation by the early activists described here, and chosen after taking advice from a petrol pump attendant, reflected something of the personal journey I undertook. In 1984 I concluded that book by writing that 'the National Congress started by those visionaries in top hats and tails ... seventy-five years ago has come a long way' and wondered whether, when the ANC reached its centenary, it would be 'as guerrilla or government'. That question has now been answered. Democracy came quicker than most expected in the early 1980s. Now, completing this work nearly three decades later, at a time when the ANC is in government, I have been privileged to be able to reflect once again on the stories of the founders and the contemporary meanings of their ideas and struggles. It is my hope that the little-known past described here will inspire those both inside and outside the ANC who read it to proceed into the future more enlightened and more emboldened in the pursuit of human dignity and democracy in an unequal, unsettled world.

PART ONE

ROOTS

1

The crucible
of colonialism

They were conquerors, and for that you want only brute force –
nothing to boast of, when you have it, since your strength is just
an accident arising from the weakness of others. They grabbed
what they could get for the sake of what was to be got. It was just
robbery with violence, aggravated murder on a great scale, and
men going at it blind – as is very proper for those who tackle a
darkness. The conquest of the earth ... is not a pretty thing when
you look into it too much. What redeems it is the idea only. An idea
at the back of it.

– Joseph Conrad, *The Heart of Darkness*

The African National Congress, or the South African Native
National Congress, as it was first called, emerged from the crucible of
colonialism in the early years of the twentieth century. By then, European
powers had been engaged in conquering and colonising large parts of the
globe for almost five centuries. In the process, indigenous people had been
subjugated, enslaved, deprived of their land and freedom, even in places
exterminated, all in the name of western civilisation and 'progress'. This
process of coercion, justified by ideologies of racism and often explained in
religious terms, continued in institutional forms in colonial territories and
became part of the very fabric of life under colonialism. In 1982, in the last
decade of apartheid, the ANC publicity secretary, Thabo Mbeki, noted:

South Africa was conquered by force and is today ruled by force. At moments

3

when White autocracy feels itself threatened, it does not hesitate to use the gun. When the gun is not in use legal and administrative terror, fear, social and economic pressures, complacency and confusion generated by propaganda and 'education', are the devices brought into play in an attempt to harness the people's opposition. Behind these devices hovers force. Whether in reserve or in actual employment, force is ever present and this has been so since the white man came to Africa.[1]

Today, the entire global system of politics and economics has been shaped by Europeans and their descendants. Every day, in every aspect of our lives, as we absorb great chunks of media posted at dizzying speed in the postmodern digital world and watch live invasions of countries from Iraq and Afghanistan to Libya, this is impressed on us.

Starting with the Spanish and Portuguese journeys of 'discovery' in the 1400s, countries and continents were systematically colonised and reshaped by people from Europe. As David Landes has explained in *The Wealth and Poverty of Nations*, Europe could use new navigational techniques to travel 'anywhere' and, with their superior technology, 'now held a decisive advantage in the power to kill'. Ninety per cent of the Mexican Indian population, more than 20 million people, were killed 'by the white man and his fellow-travelling pathogens (smallpox, influenza etc.)'.[2] Roughly 20 million Africans were captured and transported as slaves from Africa to service the sugar and cotton plantations of the New World, as many as half of them dying en route. In 1800, the 500 British slave ships made up a third of the British merchant navy, and the products of the slave plantations in the Caribbean accounted for 80 per cent of British imports. Around this time, too, some 75,000 elephants were slaughtered every year and 100 tons of ivory were imported into Britain as part of its African trade. The harshness of this model of 'progress' has prompted one historian to say that the 'pianos and cutlery of England' were stained with the blood of Africans.[3]

In the nineteenth century, powerful new nation-states emerged in tandem with the Industrial Revolution. This gave rise to a New Imperialism, as a result of which Britain and other European powers carved up Africa.

In the nineteenth century Britain became the undisputed global super-power. With India as the 'jewel in the Crown', it controlled dozens of colonies and dependencies across the globe. This expansion was made possible by the technological advances that enabled Britain to become the first industrialised nation in the world, and it was driven by the quest for political influence and the search for new markets and raw materials.[4]

In America, westward expansion and the colonisation of the continent came to be guided by the notion of 'manifest destiny', which justified conquest as part of a divine plan. After the discovery of gold in California and the 1849 rush, the Union expanded and 'in a single bound' its frontier reached the Pacific. The pressured Indian societies in-between were completely subjugated and deprived of both their land and their means of subsistence – more than 9 million bison were systematically slaughtered in the early 1870s, following the discovery of a commercial process for making buffalo leather.[5]

During the era of European expansion, the world came to be defined in the image of Europeans. In the 1500s, the Belgian 'father' of cartography, Gerhard Mercator, was faced with the problem that 'a two-dimensional outline requires some distortion'. Being a confident European, his answer was to put Europe at the centre of the world: 'Thus the northern hemisphere occupies two-thirds of traditional maps, the southern hemisphere, twice the size, shrinks into the remaining space. Hence Greenland seems about the same size as Africa, whereas in fact Africa is about 14 times larger.' Far from being objective measures of space and territory, maps of the New World reflected colonial thinking. Africa became diminished in the very way it was viewed. Europeans also congratulated themselves on having 'discovered' and given names to the places that came to be inscribed on their maps – such as East London, Berlin, Queenstown and King William's Town in South Africa, and New England, New Amsterdam (later New York) and New Orleans in America – even though people were already living there when they arrived and had names of their own for these localities.[6] In addition to the pain they caused, the conquerors also negated language and its meanings.

The conquistadores and colonisers drew on the religion of Christianity and, later, secular ideas of progress and individual rights. These strands of thinking were not antithetical to the process, but a corollary of it. As one historian has noted, 'England's expansion overseas was both commanded and justified by God.' The seventeenth century, when modern America and South Africa were first colonised, 'was an age when all men defined themselves, their society, their activities, and their institutions in terms of God; when the meanest plowboy could feel himself to be, like the sparrow, the immediate object of God's concern'.[7] But the colonised people fell outside the pale of the plowboy and the sparrow. They were deliberately excluded as 'savages' and 'barbarians', thus making it admissible for unchristian violence and conquest to be visited on them.

This kind of thinking also showed itself among great Enlightenment figures in America and Europe. While the philosophers and political architects of the American Revolution, like Jefferson and Washington, spoke about the rights of man, they remained slaveholders and firmly excluded slaves and Native Americans from the family of free Americans. They were not unusual among Enlightenment intellectuals in their views.

The particular paths of political expansion and economic development taken by Britain and America in the nineteenth century reinforced ideas about the inferiority of 'native' peoples and grew into a strong socialised system of belief in western superiority. In this age of progress, science was used to justify racism. People were categorised within a hierarchy of social progress, with Anglo-Saxons at the top of the ladder of civilisation and others lower down. The 'darker races' were regarded sometimes as being closer to animals than to other human beings. In 1863 the *Edinburgh Review* noted: 'There is no vast difference between the intelligence of a Bosjeman [Bushman] and that of an oran-utan, and the difference is far greater between Descartes or Homer and the Hottentot than between the stupid Hottentot and the ape.'[8]

The writing of the much admired British statesman Winston Churchill gives an insight into the depth and tenacity of Social Darwinism in western thinking. Observing the slaughter of wave upon wave of Sudanese Mahdist fighters by the recently invented machine gun at Omdurman in 1898 – 11,000 were killed and 15,000 wounded – the young Churchill wrote:

'These extraordinary foreign figures ... march up one by one from the darkness of barbarism to the footlights of civilisation ... and their conquerors taking their possessions, forget even their names. Nor will history record such trash.'[9] A recent biography of Churchill has underlined the relish with which he supported 'jolly little wars against barbarous peoples'. He thought Indians were 'beastly people with a beastly religion', couldn't abide Africans, recommended poison gas in Kurdistan to 'spread a lively terror' and, generally, did not doubt that 'the Aryan stock is bound to triumph'.[10] But the 'jolly little wars' that Churchill spoke about did not have jolly consequences for the colonised majorities.

The shaping of South Africa and other countries amid the clamour of Christianity, civilisation and 'progress' was in fact accompanied, step by step, by systematic violence over a long period. And the power and the paradigms that grew out of the five hundred years of conquest remain substantially intact in today's globalised world. Trying to make sense of the more intangible transnational power of the industrialised North in the twenty-first century, Hardt and Negri speak about its being still 'continually bathed in blood' in practice, but still 'always dedicated to peace – a perpetual and universal peace outside of history'.[11]

Already by the end of the eighteenth century, the westernmost outliers of the independent southern African chiefdoms had come into contact with the advancing tide of white settlers in what is today known as the eastern Cape. For more than a century these borderlands saw an accelerating process of interaction between the two, one that was often violent and brutal. At length, by military conquest in what has been called South Africa's 'Hundred Years War' and by other means, economic, social and cultural, Africans were absorbed and incorporated into the colonial state and their independence came to an end.

The eastern Cape was but one of many regions where interaction between settler society and the indigenous pastoral societies of Africa developed. But because it was the earliest and the longest-lasting, it was here that the class of new Africans, educated and christianised, first emerged and that the first African organisations were established to protect and advance African rights in the encroaching white colonial order. Some African chiefdoms managed to avoid falling under direct colonial rule by accepting British sovereignty. Under the statesmanlike rule of Moshoeshoe, the Sotho carved out for themselves a separate status as a British Protectorate, which in the 1960s gained independence and emerged as the kingdom of Lesotho. A similar status was acquired by some of the Tswana chiefdoms, which are the direct forebears of the present-day Republic of Botswana. But most of the other African chiefdoms in the subcontinent fell victim to direct colonial rule with increasing rapidity towards the end of the nineteenth century.

Indeed, it was the discovery of diamonds and gold in the interior and the subsequent mineral revolution in the late 1800s that set in train a wholesale process of conquest and incorporation. This saw the Zulu of Cetshwayo, the Pedi of Sekhukhune and many other societies steamrollered into submission, generally with the aid of British troops. For Britain played a shaping role in the pacification, reorganisation and unification of southern Africa at the end of the nineteenth and beginning of the twentieth centuries, all in the service of the new mining economy, which required for its efficient operation political stability, geographical unity and a cheap labour force, all under the British flag.

After the mineral discoveries, independent African territories fell one by one. Many submitted 'voluntarily' to their pacification, but this process can be fully understood only against the background of a century of conflict and the use of force.[12] Annexation merely legalised a gradual process of expanding British rule. Those who refused to bend the knee were conquered militarily.

By the time the Boer republics were defeated in 1902, southern Africa was already producing a quarter of the world's gold. Though Johannesburg had barely celebrated its fifteenth birthday, it was already a key part of the global economy. The world market was controlled from London and, in keeping with the sovereignty-based New Imperialism, Britain set about consolidating the various territories into one South Africa, which could become part of 'a configuration of states which in their internal developments were expected to complement the economy of Great Britain'.[13]

In 1910 the new white dominion was inaugurated as the Union of South Africa. It was in fact the terms of this union, which secured white interests, including those of the recently conquered Boers, at the expense of black, that formed the immediate cause of the formation of the ANC in 1912. Waking up to find themselves pariahs in the land of their birth, to adapt the memorable phrase of Sol Plaatje, a founding member of the ANC, African people throughout South Africa realised that the Union had come about to their detriment and that the avenues for advancement in the new society were closing. They formed the ANC in direct response to this.

Colonialism and conquest brought about immense changes in the African societies of southern Africa, impacting radically on their economies, cultures, thoughts and ways of life. A crucial part in this process of incorporation and change was played by European missionary societies, particularly through the churches and schools they set up. Dotted around the African landscape like small English villages,[14] the mission stations were in a physical sense enclaves of colonialism in African lands, outliers and harbingers of the colonial tide that would sweep through the entire subcontinent, and incubators of the new ideas and ways of life that would transform the local people – vehicles, as the missionaries saw them, through which 'heathens' and 'barbarians' would be brought from darkness into the light of Christianity and civilisation.

As in so many other ways, the eastern Cape led the way, inasmuch as missionary work began here at an early stage. What is more, the encounter here with missionary Christianity as well as the African response was to be emblematic of the experience elsewhere in southern Africa. Instructive in this regard is the missionary venture undertaken in 1816 by a group under the aegis of the London Missionary Society, consisting of James Read senior, Joseph Williams, Dyani Tshatshu, and a contingent of Khoikhoi Christians, who founded a short-lived mission in Xhosaland near present-day Fort Beaufort. Dyani Tshatshu was 'the first member of the Xhosa aristocracy to live voluntarily among the encroaching Europeans'. The son of Chief Kote Tshatshu of the Ntinde Xhosa, who lived in the environs of modern-day Port Elizabeth, he was educated at the Bethelsdorp mission station. Living on and off with James Read for ten years, Dyani became a Christian and was taught to read and write.[15] By his early twenties, he had been initiated formally both into Xhosa manhood and into European ways. On 1 April 1816, dressed in a specially tailored suit, he set out with the first party of missionaries allowed by the colonial government to travel beyond the Fish River, across which some 20,000 Xhosa had been driven in a recent war. Guided on their way by Khoi from Bethelsdorp, 'who have been for most of their lives in residence among the Caffres', the party started preaching to groups of Xhosa soon after crossing the river. 'Our brother Tzatzoo,' Read observed, 'prayed for the first time, in that language, which seemed to have a good effect.'[16]

After twenty days' journey they reached the village of the influential Makhanda kaNxele, who had met the pioneering missionary the Rev. Johannes van der Kemp, had worked in Grahamstown and had visited Bethelsdorp. Over six feet tall, Makhanda was a commoner whom Ndlambe of the Rharhabe made a chief in the same year that Read and his party met him.[17] On 21 April 1816 Tshatshu and Makhanda preached in front of one thousand people in the village. The Xhosa 'prophet' mixed Christian messages with African 'religion and idiom'; as the missionaries noted, a form of indigenous Christianity had already taken root among the Xhosa.

At Makhanda's village, the party met, as well, Ndlambe and various other chiefs, including Dyani's father and Chief Kama of the Gqunukhwebe, who (as Read had already noted in 1810) 'had always ... much regard for the word of God'. After discussion, the missionaries were invited to set themselves up in Ndlambe and Ntinde territory. But they pushed on, looking to settle amongst Ngqika's people, as they had been instructed by the colonial government. At length, Ngqika gave them permission to select a spot next to the Kat River, about 15 miles from his own Great Place, near present-day Fort Beaufort.[18]

One of Ngqika's advisers was Ntsikana, who soon gathered around him a group of followers practising their own form of indigenous Christianity. Reputed to have developed his ideas independently of the missionaries, Ntsikana composed a number of powerful hymns, which remained special to African Christians for decades afterwards. One of these, *Ulo Thixo omkulu ngosezulwini* (He, the great God in heaven), was often sung at congresses of the ANC. He became the source and fountainhead of an adaptive form of African response to Christianity, which welcomed the new ideas and ways on the Xhosa's own terms. In this, he stands opposed to Makhanda, the great 'warrior-prophet', who in the end sought to attack and root out the invading settlers and became a symbol of uncompromising resistance to colonialism.[19]

The mission station set up on the Kat River in 1816 did not last long. When war broke out between the Ngqika and Ndlambe in 1818, the mission was abandoned. But the engagement of the Xhosa with Christianity was to grow, even if hesitantly and haphazardly from then on, and an increasing number of African Christians followed in Dyani Tshatshu's footsteps. For his part, Ntsikana and his followers continued to practise their new religion. Before he died in 1821, he encouraged them to settle at a new mission station set up by the Rev. John Brownlee of the Glasgow Missionary Society at Tyhume in 1820. The gathering of Ntsikana's followers at what was later known as Old Lovedale produced in time a nucleus of Christian thinkers and activists, with an attachment to the Ngqika royal house, who would in succeeding decades make an impact on the politics as well as religious life of the Cape, the most notable being Tiyo Soga. Sons and grandsons of Ntsikana, Makhanda and Chief Kama would also become leaders in the new style of constitutional politics that emerged in the second half of the nineteenth century. When Imbumba Yama Nyama, the first modern nationalist organisation in southern Africa, was formed in 1882, it drew its name from Ntsikana's exhortation that Africans remain inseparably united. Ntsikana himself was specifically cited as an inspiration:

> They are white under the soil
> The bones of the thing [son] of Gaba
> Grass has grown over that grave
> Of the great hero of the nation
> Yet he is still alive, he still speaks.[20]

From such small beginnings, the missionary enterprise was to grow dramatically throughout the rest of the nineteenth century. The biggest missionary presence in the eastern Cape and southern Africa was established by the Wesleyans. Starting with the Wesleyville mission near Grahamstown (among the Gqunukhwebe), founded in 1823, the Wesleyans set up a chain of missions that eventually stretched along the length of south-east Africa, linking Mount Coke near King William's Town (among the Ndlambe), Butterworth (among Hintsa's Gcaleka) and Clarkebury near the Mbashe River (among the Thembu), and reaching as far as Edendale, outside Pietermaritzburg, in Natal. Other mission societies were equally influential. The Scottish Presbyterians opened the Lovedale Institution in 1841: it became the most famous educational missionary school and training college in the subcontinent. In addition, the Presbyterians established important missions at Burnshill and Pirie, at Mgwali (among the Ngqika) and at Blythswood near Butterworth. The Anglicans entered the mission field a little later, setting up St Luke's near East London (among Chief Mhala's Ndlambe), St Mark's near Queenstown (among Sarhili's Gcaleka) and St Matthew's at Keiskamma Hoek (among the Mfengu). Similar enterprises by these and other mission societies spread throughout the subcontinent in the course of the century.

For the first 40 years in the eastern Cape, the missionaries struggled to make headway. Mission stations were destroyed in successive frontier wars and the number of converts remained low.[21] The major turning point for the missionary project came with the cattle-killing tragedy in 1856–7. As a result, the authority of the chiefs and traditional beliefs was drastically reduced and the impoverished and homeless people became receptive to missionary influence. Missionary education in the Cape also began to receive government backing for the first time, thanks to Sir George Grey, and educational opportunities for African children increased. New schools were opened and existing facilities, such as those at Lovedale, were improved.[22] From being 'feeble and despondent', Christianity in Xhosaland became 'aggressive and triumphant'.[23]

By 1884, more than one hundred mission stations dotted the landscape of the eastern Cape.[24] Attendance at mission schools in the Cape rose from 2827 pupils in 1856 to 15,568 pupils in about 700 schools in 1885.[25] The numbers of Africans passing secondary and tertiary level also showed a steady increase. By 1887 more than 2000 Africans had received a secondary education at Lovedale alone. They became teachers, ministers, law agents, magistrate's clerks, interpreters, carpenters, storemen, transport riders, blacksmiths, telegraph operators, printers, clerks and journalists.[26] Educated and equipped to fit into western society and eager to advance within the new colonial world, these people naturally began to aspire to share in the life of the colony. Their mission education taught them to 'speak' in the language of Christianity, to understand the nuances of western constitutional politics and, in a cultural sense, to employ the protocols of 'civilisation', on which the missionaries laid such stress.

The network of believers or 'school people' that emerged from these mission stations and schools was to influence the intellectual history and political life of South Africa profoundly. It was from within their ranks that alternative political narratives began to develop, challenging the colonial order. Friendships and associations started at the schools, and extended beyond and after, helped give coherence to African opinion throughout the region. Eventually, frustrated by the limitations and constraints of the missionary-mediated world, the school people began to mobilise independently in order to give voice to their own opinions and aspirations.

It was from the mission stations of the eastern Cape and their surrounding catchment areas that the first proto-nationalist political organisations emerged. And this applied in time to the rest of southern Africa as well. One has only to consider the Dubes of Inanda, the Lutulis of Groutville, the Kumalos and Msanes of Edendale, the Morokas of Thaba Nchu, the Mosheshes of Lesotho, the Molemas of Mafikeng, and the Sandiles, Sogas and Umhallas of Mgwali and St Mark's, to understand how the mission stations and schools became the breeding grounds for twentieth-century African nationalism.

2

Africans in a colonial order

For some of those who were its subjects and objects, [colonialism] was about domination and violence, invasion and exploitation, even genocide; for others, an ongoing struggle in which they sometimes gained and sometimes lost; for yet others, an ambiguous process of making themselves and their worlds anew – and, in varying degree, on their own terms. For some, it appeared to be primarily about the material conditions of existence, about the sale of their labor, the seizure of their lands, the alienation of their products; for others, it was equally an encounter with European knowledge and techniques and modes of representation. For some it was all of these things, for others it was few of them. But for everyone it involved a distinctive experience: the experience of coming to feel, and to re-cognise one's self, as a 'native'.

– Jean and John Comaroff, *Of Revelation and Revolution*

The cultural demands of the missionaries with their churches, schools and strict codes of behaviour, which equated 'traditional' with 'uncivilised', were only some of many pressures for change facing Africans. Deprived of their independence and in many instances their land, Africans now lived within the same boundaries and under the same governments as their conquerors, and they had to come to terms with this political fact as well. The formation of colonial states (and eventually the Union of South Africa in 1910) incorporating the numerous pre-colonial independent chiefdoms led to a vast increase in social scale and the broadening of the whole scope of politics. For Africans, formal power now lay not at the relatively nearby Great Place, but at the magistrate's courts in the towns and centres set up by the colonists and, through them, with the colonial governments in Cape Town, Pietermaritzburg, Bloemfontein and Pretoria, all of which were by 1902 accountable to the British Colonial Office at 13–14 Downing Street in London.

By and large the creation in the Cape Colony of magistracies ensured that colonial rule was imposed on the subject people without disturbing traditional relations completely. Colonial administrators appointed headmen, who were often traditional chiefs, or else, especially in the eastern Cape, elected councillors. These became what John Lonsdale has called 'political communicators' between the colonial authorities and traditional communities. The headmen maintained order and supervised the day-to-day running of their locations. They retained limited powers such as the right to allocate certain forms of land and allow or refuse permission for newcomers to reside in their locations – often circumventing the authority of the magistrates in the process. The new headmen fulfilled corrupted versions of the pre-colonial chiefly roles. Though their authority was profoundly compromised and they were subject to the new magistrates, nevertheless they sometimes became powerful local leaders. This system of quasi-indirect rule mitigated to some extent the effects of Africans losing their independence and political freedom. It also made it easier and cheaper for the colonisers to rule. In this way government control extended to the lowest levels of African society even though most African communities did not have face-to-face relations with the white administrators.[1] As late as 1884 a headman in Kamastone near Queenstown could still tell visiting officials, 'Some of us have never seen a magistrate here'.[2]

Where the colonial authorities deposed sitting chiefs and councillors, as often happened after wars or disputes over land and other rights, competing authorities and antagonisms emerged in the new districts, often complicating local politics. The conflict between the uSuthu royal faction led by King Dinuzulu and his 'prime minister', Mnyamana of the Buthelezi clan (forefather of Chief Mangosuthu Buthelezi), and the pro-British Mandlakazi faction led by Zibhebhu during the Zulu civil war of 1879–84 is just one of numerous examples of this.[3] In *Long Walk to Freedom*, Nelson

Mandela recounts how his father, Gadla Henry Mphakanyiswa Mandela, was arbitrarily removed as a headman in later years by the magistrate. He too was a 'kingmaker' and senior councillor to the royal house during the time of the Thembu paramount Dalindyebo and the regent Jongintaba. Like Mnyamana Buthelezi, he occupied a position similar to that of prime minister. When summoned by the magistrate, Mandela senior refused to come. He believed: 'When it came to tribal matters, he was guided not by the laws of the king of England, but by Thembu custom. The defiance was not a fit of pique but a matter of principle ... When the magistrate received my father's response, he promptly charged him with insubordination. There was no enquiry or investigation; that was reserved for white civil servants. The magistrate simply deposed my father, thus ending the Mandela family chieftainship.'[4] The consequences of such action were often serious for the headmen involved. Mandela senior lost his title and his 'fortune', being 'deprived of most of his herd and land, and the revenue that came with them'.

Three sources of local power thus coexisted for African communities under the new colonial order: the old, legitimate but crumbling chiefly authority, a new set of local leaders recognised by the colonial government, and the local magistrate. When the colonial parliaments and Native Affairs departments, in turn, overruled magistrates or introduced new measures with which their officials on the ground did not agree, local politics were further complicated.

As a result of these changes in authority, the new laws imposed on Africans, the loss of land and the many other ways in which people had to adapt to colonial rule, situations arose ripe for conflict and contestation: within chiefdoms, between chiefdoms, and at many levels between Africans and the colonial authorities.

The complexity of inter-African relations in the period of change accompanying colonialism was well demonstrated when the Mfengu, originally refugees from Natal chiefdoms scattered by the Mfecane, became allies of the Cape in the War of 1835. At the same time that the Xhosa paramount Hintsa was killed in degrading circumstances by British forces under Colonel Henry Somerset, 17,000 Mfengu, led by the missionary John Ayliff, were resettled around Peddie on land taken from the Xhosa.

They not only served as a buffer between the Xhosa and the settlers, but sided militarily and otherwise with the colonial forces in the Cape–Xhosa wars of 1846, 1850–3 and 1877–8. For their support they received land in the Victoria East, King William's Town and Queenstown districts, and in the Wittebergen Reserve (later the Herschel district). In the 1860s, as the frontier shifted and land and population pressure increased, 30,000 Ciskeian Mfengu were removed to 'Fingoland' across the Kei, an area comprising the Butterworth, Nqamakwe and Tsomo districts in former Gcaleka Xhosa territory. Mfengu also settled in other Transkeian areas such as Thembuland and East Griqualand.[5] The collaborative role played by the Mfengu in these wars shaped a style of politics that, as we shall see, put great store on loyalty to the British Empire. On the other hand, those sections of the Xhosa who had been on the receiving end of colonial conquest subsequently adopted a more nationalistic approach to political issues.

Under colonialism Africans were subjected to new forces and challenges and they responded in multiple ways to minimise the negative effects and protect their interests. This book is concerned primarily with the emergence of those who came to adopt a constitutional approach to politics, seeking to participate in local community and wider colonial debates by means of political interest groups, newspapers and electoral politics from the second half of the nineteenth century onwards. The lead here was taken by the new class of mission-educated 'school people', often working closely with peasant farmers and with chiefs and headmen who saw opportunities in participating within the system.

While the political activities of these new-style activists and intellectuals followed a distinct pattern – often directing concerns about 'matters of state' (in English) to newspapers and parliament – their politics were also intertwined with 'popular' responses to pressing local issues, which often emanated from the particular experience of colonialism and of change in their region or locality. Grassroots mobilisation, chiefdom politics, spontaneous reactions to major events, and fading attempts at maintaining independence became interconnected with the new modes of expression.

Regional specificities influenced the shape of late-nineteenth-century constitutional politics. The consequences of the Nongqawuse cattle-killing movement of the mid-1850s, for example, had a dramatic effect on the way people in the lands of the Xhosa responded to the unfolding process of colonisation. In immediate terms it led to their forcible integration into the Cape economy and society. With hardly any bargaining power left, they entered the colonial world on terms set by the colonists.[6] The way in which Africans were assimilated into colonial society after war and conquest also shaped a particular politics among them in this region. As J.M. Coetzee has observed:

The cattle-killing may have marked the end of Xhosa military power, but it was by no means the end of the Xhosa. With the hold of tradition broken, individual Xhosa were released to sink or swim in the colonial economy. Many sank, some swam … From [the missionary institutions] for advanced education began to emerge a new Xhosa elite, 'Christian, articulate, model Victorian gentlemen in their conservatism, respectability and sobriety' … Westernised by force as the Zulu never were, the Xhosa were to provide black South Africans with political leaders for the new age they were entering, including most of the founding fathers of the African National Congress.[7]

In Zululand, Bechuanaland and the Transkei, the mode of incorporation was different, and different ways of political mobilisation emerged as a result. Having lost confidence in their ability to assimilate large African populations *en bloc*, colonial governments set much of these areas aside as demarcated reserves in which African land was inalienable, a pattern of landownership that has remained in force to the present.[8] Although the chiefs in these areas were incorporated into the administrative system, they retained more of their authority than some of their counterparts elsewhere. Chiefly authority remained relatively strong (though debased) and chiefs retained a degree of autonomy within a system of indirect rule.[9] This system came to be associated with Theophilus Shepstone, who was in charge of Natal's 'native policy' from 1846 to 1875.[10]

The varied ways Africans responded to colonial encroachment and control often laid down guidelines and patterns for the future. On one side of the spectrum, there were those individuals and groups who totally rejected the encroaching colonialism. Holding a more centre position were those who argued for careful accommodation and acceptance of change, but on African terms. Finally, there were those who openly identified with and enthusiastically supported the new order. All these responses, never compartmentalised and fixed, were to play themselves out in complex and ambiguous ways during the course of the late nineteenth century, giving shape to new forms of politics. For each response there emerged people who came to symbolise or represent the traditions or positions involved.

From 1815 onwards, for instance, the Ngqika 'prophet' Ntsikana formulated a type of indigenous Christianity, drawing on concepts, symbols, myths, legends and rituals of African tradition and relating them to the experience of his people. As Janet Hodgson has pointed out, Ntsikana was in favour of accommodation and growth; this involved acceptance of the coming of the Europeans and adoption of their faith on the Xhosa's own terms. He propagated evolutionary change from within, through a selective acceptance of the incoming culture. Later generations of African politicians perpetuated this tradition, and drew inspiration from him.

Ntsikana's approach gave legitimacy to Ngqika's policy of allying himself with whites against his hostile uncle Ndlambe, who had refused to accept Ngqika's kingship. On the other hand, Ndlambe's 'war doctor', Makhanda or Nxele, spawned a tradition of militancy which wholly rejected the white man and his culture. Makhanda had also come into contact with the missionaries and experimented with Christianity. But with the Ndlambe facing hostility from Ngqika and the colony, he imagined a tribal god that was stronger than the white man's god, reverted to polygamy because this god said the Xhosa should multiply, and advocated a return to traditional practices of worship.[11] After Makhanda led a force of almost 10,000 men in a memorable (and near successful) attack on Grahamstown, he was captured and sent to Robben Island by the British. He died in 1820 while trying to escape and became a symbol of militant black resistance, which later generations of freedom fighters evoked. As the ANC turned to militancy and then armed struggle in the twentieth century, it glorified the resistance of Makhanda and other pre-colonial leaders like Hintsa, Sekhukhune, Moshoeshoe and, later, Cetshwayo and Bambatha who resisted colonialism with force.

A third tradition of politics, that of working closely with the colonists, was typified by the refugee Mfengu as well as by individual Xhosa like Dyani Tshatshu, son of Chief Kote Tshatshu of the Ntinde. Having taken up arms against the Xhosa and settled on their lands, the survival and well-being of the Mfengu depended on collaboration with the colony. Likewise, Dyani Tshatshu effectively removed himself from Xhosa society to live with the missionaries, acting as an interpreter and facilitator between them and African communities.

These different responses constantly evolved and changed as the process of colonial rule unfolded in the nineteenth and twentieth centuries. And the individuals caught up in these changes faced many, often contradictory, challenges. Dyani Tshatshu was expelled from the church and returned to assume the role of chief of the Ntinde from his father; after supporting the colonial forces in one war, he was dispossessed of large portions of his land after taking sides against them in another. The early Tshatshu and the late Tshatshu operated within different but interconnected paradigms. A look at African politics during the twentieth century will also make this clear. Although the Mfengu are sometimes typecast as collaborators, many individual Mfengu became involved in radical struggles. They included the religious leader Enoch Mgijima, whose followers, the Israelites, were massacred at Bulhoek in 1922, and such revolutionary nationalist and socialist members of the ANC and Communist Party as Govan Mbeki and his son Thabo. Likewise, there were Ndlambe, Thembu, Zulu, Southern Sotho, Tswana and Pedi who could draw on a tradition of armed resistance to colonialism, while other clansmen collaborated actively with the apartheid state in 'homeland' or Bantustan politics during the twentieth century.

The formal system of colonial government in the different regions of what became South Africa was another vital factor in shaping modern African politics. In the Cape in the nineteenth century, the constitution and political system allowed limited participation for Africans and gave black people some space for action, of which they took advantage. The constitution of the colony, promulgated in 1853, provided for a qualified non-racial franchise. Every male citizen over the age of 21 years who owned property worth £25, received a salary of £50 per annum or else a salary of £25 and free board and lodging was entitled to vote.[12] This constitution became widely regarded as a model for participation by colonised people in multi-racial societies. Indeed, according to Noël Mostert, this was one area where post-abolitionist and humanitarian sentiment combined momentarily with British national interest to deliver something ahead of its time in the colonial world.[13]

At mid-century Governor Sir George Grey made strenuous attempts to assimilate the Xhosa into the colonial system. Rather than trying to exclude or segregate Africans permanently, 'who must [then] always remain a race of troublesome marauders', he encouraged acculturation and poured money into the building of schools, hospitals, roads and other public works on their behalf, gave land grants to individual Africans, and provided the missions with government aid.[14] Explaining his motives for this, Grey said:

We should try to make them part of ourselves, with a common faith and common interests, useful servants, consumers of our goods, contributors to our revenue; in short, a source of strength for this colony, such as Providence designed them to be ... Should this plan be carried out, our ultimate frontier defence would be a fertile and populous country, filled with a large population, partly European, partly native; the Europeans reared in the country, acquainted with its inhabitants, and their mode of warfare; the natives, won by our exertions to Christianity, trained by us in agriculture and in simple arts, possessing property of their own, and a stake in the country, accustomed to our laws, and aware of their advantages, – attached to us from a sense of the benefits received, – respecting us for our strength and generosity.[15]

But Grey's paternalist vision of assimilation never became the orthodoxy in southern Africa. Instead, the Natal system of aggressive segregation and the master–servant model of the Boer republics came to shape South Africa in the twentieth century. In Natal, which came under British control in the early 1840s, Africans could in theory vote, as in the Cape, but in practice they were deliberately excluded. In the Afrikaner republics of the Highveld – the South African Republic and the Orange Free State – there was no pretence about political, economic and social equality. In the former, the underlying principle, entrenched in the constitution, was 'geene gelijkstelling van gekleurden met blanke ingezetenen ... noch in Kerk noch in Staat'

21

[no equality between people of colour and white inhabitants in either church or state].[16] Similarly, in the Orange Free State only whites could become citizens of the country. The indigenous people had no political rights; their main function was to provide labour. This attitude would be supported by British capitalist interests, particularly after the discovery of diamonds and gold, which led to a high demand for cheap labour.[17]

From the very limited base of opportunity in the new colonial order, Africans in the different southern African territories began to articulate their views and mobilise within the colonial political systems. In the process, as Paul Landau has observed, 'colonialism encountered not some inertial substance but ongoing efforts to organise and create using any means proven effective, running up from a past outsiders knew little about'.[18] This political assertiveness was particularly evident in the Cape Colony. The limited rights Africans enjoyed there not only raised hopes that colonial society would gradually open up to allow for greater participation as Africans proved their fitness to participate on equal terms with whites, but also stimulated formal mobilisation in constitutional politics much earlier on than elsewhere in South Africa. By the 1860s there were clear signs of this new movement, especially in the eastern Cape, to which we now turn.

3

Tiyo Soga and voices
from the 1860s

This 'Morning Sir' of the Xhosa people whenever they see a white
face is very annoying.

– Tiyo Soga, 1864

Initially, formal African political activity in the Cape Colony took
place mainly within the framework of magisterial rule, mirroring the new
geography of colonial authority. Both pre-colonial leaders, who often
still enjoyed considerable popular legitimacy and authority, and newly
appointed government headmen (sometimes the same 'old' leaders) fell
under colonial officials, who were in turn accountable to the Native Affairs
Department and other branches of government in Cape Town.

Gradually, headmen began to broaden their political focus and develop
an interest beyond the local magisterial level. During official visits of the
Governor and other high-ranking dignitaries to the frontier, headmen
would take part in welcoming ceremonies and were introduced to them.[1]
Some even travelled to Cape Town and saw at first hand the workings
of government in the capital. In 1860 Chief Sandile of the Ngqika, for
example, was invited to accompany Prince Albert and Governor Sir
George Grey by boat to Cape Town and was fêted there. A prominent
Mfengu headman has left an enthralling account of a similar journey, made
a decade later. After travelling by sea to Cape Town, he was received by
the Secretary for Native Affairs, the Prime Minister and the Governor,
introduced to the printing press at Saul Solomon's famous printing works,
and shown through parliament and 'the treasure house containing the

money of the whole country, in which were heaps of money'. He was impressed by the European way of life: 'These things of the English made me to think that it was through education that they do such great wonders. Fellow countrymen, let us strive for learning – let us give our children up to it.'[2] In time, headmen and other political communicators started bypassing magisterial authority to approach the government directly and even challenged the competency of local officials, often using law agents and sympathetic missionaries as intermediaries.[3]

The loyalists in the Mfengu districts in the Transkei provide a ready example of pre-colonial leaders and new-generation colonial headmen working willingly within the colonial system. After Fingoland had been established in the Transkei in 1865, upwards of 100 headmen held regular meetings with the magistrate, they collected a voluntary tax to administer the district, they contributed large amounts of money to build the educational institution of Blythswood, based on the lines of the famous Lovedale Institution in Alice, and they began to organise and participate in events such as Native Agricultural Shows.[4] All these activities drew them closer into the orbit of the colonial world.

Although change led to a decline in the influence of traditional headmen deriving their status from the chief, both they and government-appointed headmen would play a crucial role in African politics throughout the period of this study.[5] With the patronage they had at their disposal, their local influence was substantial; they continued to perform the vital function of 'political communicators' between the authorities and their people; and, as representatives of a wider community, their co-operation was much sought after by the new educated political elite emerging from the mission stations, seeking a base for economic opportunity, for social mobilisation – in church and school sites – and for political action.

In the 1860s, literate 'school people' emerged as a distinct stratum of society in the eastern Cape and started to make their voices heard. The most famous of them was Tiyo Soga. After being sent to Scotland for two stints of study between 1847 and 1857, he graduated from Glasgow University and returned home as an ordained Presbyterian minister, with a Scottish wife on his arm. As the couple disembarked at Port Elizabeth they were stared at. But Soga now had a status which could not be ignored: he was a man of the cloth. Soga developed a high profile in public life. He preached in white congregations in several towns and received attention from the colonial press. While unappreciated by most conservative colonists, church officials and newspapers, he developed extensive contacts in liberal circles in the colony, notably with the parliamentarian Saul Solomon, owner of both the *Cape Argus* and *Port Elizabeth Telegraph*. Soga was paraded by the church hierarchy as a model of what the missionaries wanted to achieve. In addition, his father having been a councillor to the Ngqika chief, traditional leaders now looked to him to act as an intermediary with the British and colonial authorities. When Prince Albert visited the eastern Cape in 1860, Soga read a message of welcome and loyalty to him. The Ngqika ruler Sandile asked Soga to accompany him when the Xhosa chiefs met Albert and to travel with him and the Prince to Cape Town by boat. During their stay there, Sandile visited his daughter and three sons, and the children of other chiefs at Zonnebloem College. He recounted to them how he had seen the Prince of England scrubbing decks with British soldiers on the boat, and exhorted them to work hard at their education.[6]

Soga came to fill a role as a skilled communicator similar to that of Dyani Tshatshu in the early nineteenth century. After returning to South Africa, he settled down as a missionary among his own Ngqika people, who had been impoverished by the cattle-killing. He based himself at Mgwali, where he built a stone church, which still stands today. There was a difference now in the way he conducted himself as a Christian and minister, which helps explain his influence and ideas. Whereas before, missionaries had insisted that people like Soga had to distance themselves from traditional African culture and society to prove themselves 'civilised', Soga said he was 'not afraid now of getting on well with my countrymen here'. As a result, 'I have their confidence thoroughly'. In this shift in nuance, one can trace the germ of the new style of African politics, in which western-educated individuals identified themselves with their African roots and started articulating new ideas about how best Africans could protect their interests within the relentlessly expanding colonial system.[7]

Donovan Williams has described Soga as a figure of crucial importance for the intellectual and political history of South Africa, as a precursor of African nationalism. An educated Christian missionary living in a disputed frontier zone, he was a man of two worlds in whom western, Christian values coexisted uneasily with his African heritage. He resolved these conflicts by committing himself firmly to Christianity and the Victorian ideals of progress and advancement, but at the same time he retained loyalty and respect for his 'nation' and tried to preserve its territorial and cultural integrity.[8] He was proud of who he was and where he came from. As his early biographer, John Chalmers, said:

Tiyo Soga had an honest pride in his manhood as a pure Kafir. He was disposed to glory in his Kafirhood. He did not bow down before any one, because of his own black face. Burns's song, 'A man's a man for a' that', was a great favourite with him. Hence he was not disposed to demean himself, when treated slightingly or shabbily, by a fearful or slavish submission. He seemed at such times to grow taller before you, as if he would say 'I am also a man! a gentleman! a Christian!'[9]

Soga chided Christians who believed that mission people should hold themselves aloof from traditionalists, and lacked respect for them and the chiefs. [10] He said chiefs received their authority from God and should be respected in the same way as white leaders.[11] Moreover, Africans should not be unduly submissive to whites: 'Raise your hats to chiefs and to respectable dignified people. To white gentlemen bow gently your heads even though you do not utter a word. Do this to white people who deserve this. This is very pleasing. But we do not advise that you do this even to poor whites of no repute who are no better than yourselves. This "Morning Sir" of the Xhosa people whenever they see a white face is very annoying.'[12]

Soga's most powerful political statement was made in the *King William's Town Gazette* on 11 May 1865. Reacting to a piece by a fellow missionary, who declared that the 'Kaffir race' was doomed to extinction because of its indolent habits and backwardness, he responded in an article entitled 'What is the destiny of the Kaffir race?' Soga rejected the thesis put forward in the missionary's article and criticised him for doing 'monstrous injustice to a class of natives who amidst much that is against them have been striving to rise and to improve'. Moreover, he added in reply,

I find the family of the Kaffir tribe extending nearly to the equator; along this line I find them taking the north eastern coast of Africa, the dominant and the governing race; they are all one in language and are one people – Now I venture to say that if this includes all these tribes the process of its extinction will take very long indeed – Africa was of God given to the race of Ham. I find the Negro from the days of the old Assyrians downwards, keeping his 'individuality' and 'distinctiveness' amid the wreck of empires, and the revolution of ages. I find him keeping his place among the nations, and keeping his home and country ... I find him opposed by nation after nation and driven from his home. I find him enslaved ... I find him exposed to all these disasters, and yet living – multiplying 'and never extinct' ... I believe firmly that ... neither the indolence of the Kaffirs, nor their aversion to change, nor the vices of civilization, all of which barriers the gospel must overthrow, shall suffice to exterminate them as a people.[13]

According to Williams, this was the first expression of an 'Africa-consciousness' by a black writer in southern Africa and it made Soga one of the pioneers of Pan-African thought, along with contemporary West African nationalists such as J.A. Horton, James 'Holy' Johnson and E.W. Blyden.[14] In his writings, Soga emphasised pride in the African past, the dignity of African leaders and people, belief in the territorial and cultural integrity of African societies, a common African identity or nationhood transcending old distinctions, and a divine, predestined mission which the 'sons of Ham' had to fulfil in Africa.[15]

Soga has been described as someone who 'saw no contradiction between his Xhosa-ness and adherence to British civic nationality', though his approach to colonialism and the 'civilising project' has also been qualified as one of 'subversive subservience' and 'intimate enmity'.[16] Whichever way one sees it, this University of Glasgow graduate as well as a small circle of like-minded peers developed a template of ideas and responses that succeeding generations of mission-educated Africans would draw upon.

Although framing his arguments within a missionary discourse, and not as an independent nationalist, Soga gave voice to a strong belief in the integrity and inherent value of African societies. In his day he was an individual exception, rather than someone representing a politically mobilised constituency. But in articulating some of the attitudes and ideas that had been generated in the Cape borderlands since the first contacts between black and white, he paved the way for the later educated and christianised Africans, facing the challenge of making sense of the conflicting worlds of which they were part.

Within the framework of his Christian beliefs and western education, Soga remained respectful of the African community from which he had emerged. He encouraged the following generations to do so as well. In a tract entitled 'The inheritance of my children', which he wrote just before his early death at the age of 41, he left his children 62 guidelines to help them through the difficulties of life. In the first of these he wrote:

You will ever cherish the memory of your mother as that of an upright, conscientious, thrifty, Christian Scotch woman. You will ever be thankful for your connection by this tie to the white race. But if you wish to gain credit for yourselves – if you do not wish to feel the taunt of men, which you sometimes may well feel – take your place in the world as coloured, not as white men; as Kafirs, not as Englishmen – For your own sakes never appear ashamed that your father was a Kafir, and that you inherited some African blood. It is every whit as good and as pure as that which flows in the veins of my fairer brethren.[17]

This was advice his children followed. At least two of his sons, J.H. Soga and A.K. Soga, became active in organised politics in the late nineteenth and early twentieth centuries.[18]

Tiyo Soga was one of a small group of literate contemporaries who, by the 1860s, were beginning to find their voice and express themselves publicly as a group for the first time. In 1860 African Christians in King William's Town were among those formally welcoming Prince Albert and shortly afterwards they started contributing written pieces to the first newspaper of substance in Xhosa, *Indaba* (The News), published monthly at Lovedale from August 1862 to February 1865. *Indaba* became a vehicle for the first literate generation of Africans to articulate their aspirations and ideas in a public forum in their own language. Although *Indaba* was missionary-orientated and tried to avoid 'local and party politics' as far as possible, it did provide mild coverage of contemporary political events. It reported on the Cape parliament, the role of which 'most of our readers understand, though some perhaps but imperfectly', it explained laws affecting Africans passed by parliament and it touched on other general political matters, as well as overseas news.[19] In the correspondence columns, African readers raised religious issues such as the relationship between Christians and chiefs, as well as the topics of education, liquor, agriculture, medicine, justice, 'tribal' history, and the value of a community newspaper. These touched the heart of the whole process of change, and give us insight into the political ideas of the earliest literate Africans.

In the first issue, Soga welcomed the appearance of the newspaper and exhorted people of different chiefdoms and clans to use it as a repository to preserve their history: 'Why should we not revive and bring to light this great wealth of information? Let us bring to light our ancestors: Ngconde, Togu, Tshino, Phalo, Rharhabe, Mlawu, Ngqika and Ndlambe. Let us resurrect the ancestral spirits of the Xhosa and Fingo nations to bequeath to us a rich heritage. All anecdotes connected with the life of the nation should be brought to this big corn pit, our national newspaper the Indaba (The News).'[20] In addition to translating Bunyan's *Pilgrim's Progress*, writing hymns and helping translate the Bible into Xhosa, Soga also collected material for a book on Xhosa history. His biographer noted how he was sometimes up after midnight in a hut, 'note-book in hand', learning from 'wrinkled countrymen of his own' about the past: 'He knew all the brave warriors of his race; and when he met them his face brightened up, and he would say, "That is So-and-so"; I shall draw him out, and you will hear his adventures.'[21]

While Soga was the most prominent writer in *Indaba*, a number of other correspondents had a notable influence on future generations as well. Among the contributors was Ntsikana's son, William Kobe Ntsikana, who had been a correspondent in the pages of the early Lovedale newspaper *Ikwezi* in the 1840s.[22] His son, bearing the same names, became in turn a leading political figure in the 1880s. Another writer, Simon Peter Gasa, remained involved in public life for so long that he himself was able to make the jump eventually to organised politics: 40 years later, in the first decade of the twentieth century, he became a member of the Transkeian Territories General Council and of the executive committee of the Inter-State Native College Scheme for African higher education, which led to the formation of Fort Hare University.[23] Ntibane Mzimba, influential in the Free Church's Lovedale congregation in Alice, and father of the religious separatist leader Pambani Mzimba, also wrote for the newspaper.[24] Another correspondent was Govan Koboka.[25] The son of one of Chief Maqoma's former councillors, he became an interpreter and medical intern, dispensing medicines and acting as a surgical dresser at Grey's Hospital in King William's Town, and later was prominent and politically active at Lovedale.[26] Other contributors included Gwayi Tyamzashe, John Muir Vimbe, John Mazamisa, Rob Mantsayi and Barnabas Sokabo. These men were mainly ex-Lovedalians, engaged in occupations connected with missionary life such as teachers, evangelists, interpreters and students. They came from all over the eastern Cape and belonged not just to the Ngqika Xhosa, but also to the Mfengu, Thembu and other southern Nguni groups.

This formative group of public intellectuals writing in *Indaba* in the 1860s could claim connections to the very beginnings of Christianity among Africans and their influence would be felt later in the first political organisations as well. The lineage of the Ntsikanas went back to the time of the first visit of *uNyengane* (Dr Van der Kemp) to Xhosaland in 1799. After Ntsikana's death, his followers continued his work at the Tyhume mission of the Rev. John Brownlee (known as Old Lovedale), where the first printed work in Xhosa was published in 1824. The Soga family was close to the family circle of Ntsikana, and remained so at least until Tiyo's death. The Mzimbas apparently were also part of a group of believers that emanated from Old Lovedale.[27] And the influence and activity of the *Indaba* circle reached forwards too, into the era of African politics in the last decades of the nineteenth century. Gasa, Mazamisa, Koboka and Sokabo all became politically active when Africans started asserting themselves in colonial politics, and men like Mzimba, Vimbe and Tyamzashe remained prominent in community affairs until at least the mid-1880s.[28] Like Soga, these correspondents had a history and their names were to recur in history.

It was in the 1860s, too, that a new generation of literate intellectuals were educated at Lovedale and the other educational institutions in the closely linked mission belt in Xhosaland – what colonists now commonly called the 'Border'. As with the *Indaba* circle, the enrolment lists of the eastern Cape mission schools show the most intimate connection between the earliest literate Africans and later African politics. Many of the students educated at Lovedale in the 1860s became prominent when western-style politics burst on the scene in the 1880s. William Gqoba, John Knox Bokwe, Elijah Makiwane, Pambani Mzimba, Andrew Gontshi, W.D. Soga and Pambani Figlan, who went on to achieve public prominence later,* were all students on the banks of the Tyhume during that decade.[29]

By the 1860s Africans had also begun to mobilise at the ballot box. As early as 1860, less than a decade after the introduction of the franchise at the Cape, the return of William Stanton to parliament for the Somerset East constituency was attributed to the fact that 'all the black voters deserted the old missionary interest and one and all voted for him'. In 1869, the support of the Mfengu voters in Fort Beaufort enabled George Wood to win the Legislative Council seat for that constituency. The first attempt to have Africans enfranchised on a large scale occurred when Mfengu headmen applied to have 600 of their followers registered in 1866. Here was another sign of political awakening, though school people as a general rule still did not participate in electoral politics, despite the fact that many possessed the necessary property and income qualifications.

The new-style political activity was not confined to the old mission belt. In the Wittebergen Reserve (later Herschel) in the north-eastern Cape, John Parkies, an interpreter and aspirant law agent, led protests against the reserve superintendent in the mid-1860s. He was said to be a troublemaker, 'constantly writing … political letters', according to Cape officials. In 1869, 125 residents of the Reserve sent a petition to parliament on behalf of the 18,000 'British subjects', complaining about the 'arbitrary rule' they were subjected to, though 'entitled to be ruled by British law'.[30] By that time there were already several hundred people who had been baptised and taught to read and write in the Bensonvale mission, the main station

---

* Other students included Joel Ndungane, Daniel Mzamo, Charles Ntozini, William Seti, Nkohla Falati, Peter Tyamzashe, Seti Makiwane, Samuel Mzimba and M.N. Galela.

at Wittebergen. According to Jeff Peires, the literacy rate was higher here than in many of the older eastern Cape missions. 'Only Healdtown and Peelton served a more literate community. The mission library subscribed to 15 publications in addition to which seven private individuals subscribed to periodicals of their own choosing. 25 were able to read English, most were multilingual in English, Afrikaans, isiXhosa and Sesotho.'[31] The local missionary noted that 'they have a taste for reading and purchased books as far as they could afford to do so'. The Bensonvale library was also better stocked than those of some of the older mission stations, which, Peires notes, 'subscribed to only one periodical, the mission publication *Indaba*'. The views of Tiyo Soga and his peers were, therefore, being read throughout the region as the school people started to give voice to their opinions on religious, educational and political matters.

Between the beginnings of Christianity and education among the Xhosa from the 1810s onwards, the first articulations of African opinion in the 1860s and the start of African political mobilisation in the 1880s, there exists a definite link. And, if by the 1860s the earliest expressions of new forms of African political consciousness had become evident amongst a small group of literate Africans, the 1870s was the decade when this group swelled to the extent that it became a clearly discernible stratum of Cape society and started to define its role in the colonial system, paving the way for political mobilisation on a significant scale. The death of Dyani Tshatshu in 1868 and that of Tiyo Soga in 1871 served almost as a symbolic transition from the early phase of Christian evangelism to the new one in which educated Africans would start challenging their missionary mentors and the subservient role in society which most colonists expected them to adopt.

4

The first generation
of activists, 1870s

From the very outset the natives knew that it has been the intention of the present Government to disarm every black man, merely because he is black, to gain popularity from a section of the colonists, whose aim it is to reduce the natives to nonentity for its own selfish ends. Let the press, politicians, and constituencies guard against this despotism.

– John Tengo Jabavu, 1878

By the 1870s the response of Africans to missionary educational institutions had altered noticeably. After the cattle-killing and a period of relative quiet in the border areas after the previous Cape–Xhosa war in 1850–3, and as the period of contact with Europeans lengthened, African resistance to missionary education declined. As Sheila Brock noted, 'Education became desirable as a means of advancement and social acceptance and often as a means of playing the European at his own game'.[1] In the three decades before 1870, a total of 380 pupils had enrolled at Lovedale; in the next decade, almost a thousand did so.[2] Facilities improved with the increase in numbers. Similar expansion took place at Healdtown, St Matthew's and other educational institutions. Though still far outnumbered by 'red blanket' people, the number of school people grew steadily: in 1882 they comprised one-fifth of the total African population in King William's Town.[3]

The enrolment lists of the main educational institutions in the 1870s reflect the direct link between the growth in African education and the beginnings of African political mobilisation. Indeed, nowhere else in the history of South Africa, except perhaps at Stellenbosch University with its connection to Afrikaner nationalism, can the 'old school tie' have played such a part in group politics as it did at Healdtown and Lovedale (and, later, Fort Hare). These institutions came to fill the same kind of grooming role among Africans in southern Africa that Oxford and Cambridge did for the ruling class in England.

Among the 52 male students at Healdtown in one year alone – 1875 – were many who were soon to become well-known names in African politics: James and Meshach Pelem, John Tengo Jabavu, Jonas Goduka, Silas Molema, Charles and James Pamla, Richard Kawa and Boyce Kota.[4] A decade later, they would be leading the first political organisations; young men, many still in their twenties, with a mission in life. Saul Msane, Enoch Mamba, Gana Kakaza and George Pamla also studied at Healdtown in that decade.

During the same period, an equally impressive cohort of young leaders-in-waiting was entering nearby Lovedale: Edward Tsewu, Isaac Wauchope, Walter Rubusana, Isaiah Sishuba and many others who became prominent in politics.[5] The so-called Kafir Institution in Grahamstown, run by the Anglicans, produced Thomas Mapikela, William Philip and the later ANC president Josiah Gumede. The Institution was subsequently moved to St Matthew's College, Keiskamma Hoek ('chased out of Grahamstown by the Grahamstown whites', according to Jeff Peires).[6]

The names of these new-style Africans are given here as markers for what lay ahead in politics, in the eastern Cape and elsewhere. As the examples of Silas Molema (from Mafikeng in Tswana territory), Saul Msane (from the prominent Edendale mission community in Natal) and S.M. Phamotse (from Basutoland) show, they came from throughout southern Africa to attend the prestigious schools in the south. In this way intellectual, church and political networks across regions and territories came into being. Josiah Semouse demonstrated the hunger the new generation had for education by walking for eleven days from Basutoland to register at Lovedale in the early 1880s. The prosperous Fenyang and Makgothi families from Thaba Nchu on the southern Highveld took a slightly easier route – after the railway line from East London reached the banks of the Orange River, their sons went in horse-drawn Cape carts to Aliwal North and then caught the train from there – but the desire for education among the school people was everywhere evident and it would connect the students and their families in powerful ways in future.

In order to cater for these students and the 'many thousands' of other Africans able to read their own language, a new English–Xhosa monthly newspaper, the *Kaffir Express*, also known in the vernacular as *Isigidimi sama-Xosa*, was started at Lovedale in October 1870.[7] It was edited by the Lovedale principal, Dr James Stewart. The Xhosa columns were entrusted to African students, who translated some of the English columns and provided other news of interest.[8] Among Stewart's chief helpers were Elijah Makiwane (assistant editor) and John Knox Bokwe (clerk).[9] The aim of the newspaper was to create an African reading public and introduce them to wider subjects, such as the Franco-German War and the discovery of diamonds in South Africa – the topical news of the time – as well as to promote in a nonsectarian way the cause of missions generally.[10]

Although *Isigidimi* was controlled by missionaries and steered a supposedly non-political course, it did reflect African opinion. In the correspondence columns, literate Africans from throughout South Africa discussed a wide range of issues: education, religion, the liquor question, the validity of traditional customs such as lobola and circumcision, and other matters.[11] These were important topics for the emerging class of educated Christians. Through the pages of the paper they developed writing skills and were introduced to public debate. More letters were always received by the paper than could be published, and sometimes special supplements were printed to accommodate all the correspondence. Issues with more than ten letters were not uncommon.[12]

That literate Africans were becoming a settled stratum of society, with its own continuities and character, was demonstrated by the fact that a number of the contributors to *Indaba* between 1862 and 1865 were still penning their opinions in *Isigidimi* a decade later. Among them were W.K. Ntsikana Gaba, S.P. Gasa, John Muir Vimbe, Peter Masiza and Gwayi Tyamzashe. Tyamzashe, in addition, demonstrated the mobility that became a feature of the lives of the educated class. By 1874, he had moved to Kimberley as the first African minister on the diamond fields. Though he wrote about the Sodom and Gomorrah conditions existing there, this did not stop him from purchasing a licence to prospect.[13]

New contributors to the newspapers came to the fore as well, including K.N. Boza (the regular Port Elizabeth correspondent), Nkohla Falati (grandson of Ntsikana), Peter Rwexu and Isaac (Wauchope) Citashe, then a bright student in mathematics and member of the Literary Society at Lovedale. Wauchope, whose grandmother had been a member of Dr Van der Kemp's mission station at Bethelsdorp, volunteered to join the first party of Lovedale missionaries to Nyasaland (present-day Malawi) in 1876.[14] After an eventful journey by sea from Port Elizabeth to Durban and thence up the coast to the Quelimane River in Mozambique, the party made their way to Nyasaland, where Wauchope contracted fever and nearly died.[15]

Conditions and attitudes had changed since Tiyo Soga and his contemporaries first articulated their views in *Indaba*. As a result of the increasing ascendancy of white supremacist policies and the deepening of white control over Xhosaland, the younger group of literate and christianised people began to challenge old assumptions and examine the role of the missionaries in a more critical way. They found it impossible to achieve 'the inner poise and singleness of mind' characteristic of the earlier group.[16]

Their mixed reactions to colonialism were reflected within the first few issues of *Isigidimi*. In a letter filled with Africanist overtones in January 1871, 'Kokela', a correspondent from Gcalekaland, idealised the African societies of the past and lamented the radical changes that had taken place in them since the advent of the missionaries. Africans were no longer independent as in the past and they were forsaking their traditional dignity and customs, as well as losing old attributes such as physical courage and oratorical skills. Kokela also criticised the missionaries for destroying the purity of the Xhosa language by trying to standardise 'Fingo' and Xhosa into a single language, and for teaching English, Roman and Greek history at the expense of African history. Appealing to all who could read or write to preserve African history for future generations in pure Xhosa, he set the ball rolling by sending in a genealogy of Xhosa chiefs.[17]

Kokela's anti-colonialist Africanist approach met with a scathing response from another correspondent, who believed in the advantages of acculturation and the superiority of western civilisation. 'Fundani Makowetu' (Be learned, my countrymen), who described himself as 'a member of the going-astray-generation', countered that 'to be under the English is more advantageous'. He felt that Africans had still not advanced enough and that African independence retarded progress. Moreover, it was important to learn about the history of the English, Greeks and Romans, as they had 'done something for the world', which could not be said of those mentioned by Kokela.[18] Supporters of both viewpoints continued the debate until Dr Stewart, whose sympathy and that of the newspaper were 'entirely with the party of progress', put an end to it.[19]

Even though most letters in *Isigidimi* reflected the missionary viewpoint, it is clear that by the 1870s the expansion of white power and the hardening of colonial attitudes on the 'native question' had begun to cause many literate Africans to challenge the missionary assumption that Christianity and European ideas represented civilisation and progress in contrast to the supposed barbarism and darkness of traditional African values. Indicative of the new attitudes emerging were the explicitly 'political' letters – on topics such as the Xhosa chief Maqoma's 'involuntary return to Robben Island' – which Africans sent to *Isigidimi*, but which the editor declined to publish.[20]

By the end of its first year, *Isigidimi* had over 800 subscribers, 500 of whom were Africans. The newspaper had been started on the calculation that with 50 mission stations providing 20 subscribers each, the total African circulation would be at least double that. But only Port Elizabeth, with a total readership of over 100, Lovedale, Burnshill and Healdtown yielded that number.[21] Nevertheless, *Isigidimi* grew steadily year by year. In July 1873 the *Kaffir Express* and *Isigidimi* became separate newspapers, both doubling in length, and at the beginning of the following year Elijah Makiwane began to edit *Isigidimi*, though under supervision.[22] He thus became the first African newspaper editor in South Africa. The needs of the African reading public later increased to the extent that *Isigidimi* was published bi-monthly from mid-1879.

At the same time that the new intellectuals showed an interest in the press, they developed organisational and procedural skills as members of professional, official and voluntary bodies, which proved useful in preparing them for politics. The students sent out from the mission schools to every part of the eastern Cape as ministers, catechists and teachers all acquired organisational responsibilities and became accountable to various authorities. The Bishop of Grahamstown, for example, described a quarterly meeting in August 1871 of African teachers in the St Mark's district where Nathaniel Umhalla, Peter Masiza and 20 others 'each in succession either read his journal (some in Kaffir, some in English), or else gave an account *viva voce*, with statistics of what work was going on at the several kraals where they were stationed'.[23] To give another example: from 1871, there was an 'Annual Meeting of the Wesleyan Native Ministers in the Graham's Town District'.[24] In some areas, such as Lesseyton near Queenstown, Africans enjoyed a measure of local self-government. Government regulations provided for a five-man management committee elected annually by the erfholders at a public meeting.[25] The committee appointed its own salaried African treasurer and voted sums of over £100 for the improvement of the location.[26] Africans were also beginning to play a part in voluntary organisations. In 1872 an interdenominational Fort Beaufort Native Total Abstinence Society was formed with just under 40 members.[27] At the Lovedale Literary Society, Pambani J. Mzimba and Elijah Makiwane debated the question 'Has the reign of Napoleon I been beneficial to France?'[28] All these activities prepared Africans for involvement in colonial politics.

The new forms of consciousness and activity extended more and more to the field of electoral politics as well. The granting of responsible government to the Cape Colony in 1872 and the subsequent emergence of political parties stimulated interest in politics and the vote.[29] In 1873, 100 Mfengu were registered as voters at Oxkraal in the Queenstown district. The local church minister asked the Secretary for Native Affairs to make special provision for a polling station to be set up in the area.[30] The Mfengu of Oxkraal accounted for over 10 per cent of the total votes (930) in the Queenstown constituency.[31] With the registration of increasing numbers of African voters, political candidates had perforce to seek their favour. In 1874 the local magistrate declared that the Mfengu in the Victoria East constituency (under which Lovedale fell) were 'beginning to understand that a man with a vote is of more importance than one who does not possess that advantage'. Previously, Africans in the district had tended not to lay claim to the franchise, although about 700 qualified for it, but in 1873 no less than 280 sent in claims to be registered. In a decision which caused 'some discontent' among them, the registration court upheld the objections of European voters and disallowed the applications on technical grounds. Had the Victoria East Mfengu succeeded with their applications they would have determined the outcome of the 1874 election, as the total number of electors in the constituency stood at only 365, of which less than half actually voted.[32] Meanwhile, at Healdtown Charles Ntozini, one of the first Africans to learn the printing trade and work for colonial newspapers, had gone around the school shouting 'Vote for Mr Ayliff' and had ferried voters to the polling booth with his horses and cart.[33] Because Mr Ayliff was the son of the 'Mfengu Moses', the Rev. John Ayliff, who had brought the Mfengu into the Promised Land of the colony, the Mfengu voted for him.[34] But though African voters were uniting at local level, they had not yet developed the cohesion needed to exert pressure on parliament to protect broad African interests. However, this would come soon.

These first tentative steps at involvement in the social and political life of the Cape were symptomatic of the growing adaptability of Africans in fitting into colonial society and of their hopes and expectations of eventually playing an active role in the colonial world. This could also be seen in the ordination of an increasing number of Africans to the ministry from 1871 onwards, including Charles Pamla, Charles Lwana, Boyce Mama, Gwayi Tyamzashe, Pambani Mzimba and James Dwane.[35] Within the Cape civil service, educated commoners and sons of chiefs such as Edmund Sandile and Nathaniel Umhalla began to be appointed to interpreters' and clerks' posts.[36] In the economic sphere there was growing prosperity among an emerging African peasantry, adapting to the market economy. The 1870s witnessed a virtual 'explosion' of peasant activity in the eastern Cape as Africans bought or leased land in their hundreds, took to sheep farming and wool production on a large scale, and produced a considerable agricultural surplus.[37] In all spheres, Africans were adapting to the Cape Colony's institutions, systems and norms.

However, at the very stage that Africans first entered the colonial world in the 1870s, their long-term prospects of occupying an extended role in the ostensibly liberal, non-racial Cape political system began to diminish. There were two important reasons for this. Firstly, as a result of the mineral discoveries, South Africa underwent a permanent socio-economic revolution which was to change the nature of liberalism at the Cape and lead to increasing restrictions on African political and economic advancement.[38] Secondly, a series of wars broke out throughout South Africa between African societies clinging to their independence and Imperial and colonial forces seeking finally to crush black resistance and impose firm European control. These conflicts had a polarising effect on relations between black and white people at the Cape. The first of these was the Cape–Xhosa war (the War of Ngcayecibi) of 1877–8 between the Gcaleka, supported by a portion of the Ngqika, and Cape forces aided by 'loyal' Mfengu, Thembu and Ngqika. This was followed in 1879 by the destruction of the Zulu kingdom, the subjugation of the Pedi and the unsuccessful revolt of Moorosi's Phuthi chiefdom in southern Basutoland. The following year the Gun War erupted in the wake of Sotho resistance to the disarmament policy of the Cape government. Similar causes also led to a rebellion in Thembuland and other parts of the Transkei, during which the rebels sought to join up with the Sotho.[39] With the exception of the Sotho, who successfully defended their right to keep their guns and their country, these conflicts had predictable results: African people lost more land and power and became impoverished.[40]

The wars, as well as government policy during this period, caused considerable dissatisfaction among educated Africans in the eastern Cape, who were growing acutely aware of the overall discrepancy between Christian values and western political ideals and the realities of white conquest. Most Cape Africans remained loyal to the government during the War of Ngcayecibi, though they were critical about the way the campaign was waged. Only a few Christians and educated people joined the rebels. The most prominent had close connections with the traditional leadership. One of them, Dukwana, the son of Ntsikana and Tiyo Soga's former close confidant, was a lay preacher at Mgwali, described as 'the orator of the Ngqika – second only to Tiyo Soga in his moral influence over the people'. Others who went over to the rebels were the sons of

Chief Sandile, Gonya (Edmund) and Mlindazwe (Bisset), who worked as clerk and interpreter respectively in local government offices. Nathaniel Umhalla, son of the Ndlambe chief Mhala and brother of the rebel leaders Makinana and Ndimba, tried to maintain a precarious neutrality.[41] But he and the two Sandiles were captured, and Dukwana and a number of other school people from Mgwali were killed in the fighting. Before he died, Dukwana continued to preach in the field, declaring that it was not against Christianity and civilisation that he had rebelled, but against the government, which was destroying the national existence of the Ngqika.[42] Chief Sandile and Tiyo Soga's father, who had been neither educated nor converted, were also killed by the colonial forces.[43]

These events starkly illustrated the dilemma of the school people. Educated, christianised and adapted to dominant European ways, but tied by blood, background and concern for their kinsmen to African society, they were caught up in a web of complex ambiguities. For Umhalla and others committed to the new ways, the war was a traumatic experience, both psychologically and materially. The Mfengu were in an analogous position. They had sided with the government forces and, as Michael Spicer has pointed out, were even perhaps responsible for provoking the war, with an eye to gaining more land.[44] But in the post-war settlement they were placed on a par with the enemies of the colony. The much-resented Peace Preservation Act of 1878 compelled all Africans, whether they had been loyal or not, to hand in their arms. According to the *Christian Express*, the way the Act was implemented did 'more to create anger, disaffection, and a sense of injustice among the natives than any single thing of the kind has ever done'. It led to large-scale discontent and called forth the first major protest petitions by Africans to the Cape parliament since its inception in 1854. Chief Mbovane Mabandla from Middledrift, hereditary chief of the Bele Mfengu, a prominent spokesman for decades in eastern Cape affairs, was one of those who led the protests.[45]

The Peace Preservation Act contributed directly to the political mobilisation of school people in the next few years. One of them later declared, 'I thank Mr Sprigg [Cape Prime Minister] who opened the eyes of our nation which was sleeping and saying "no everything will be fine". He is the one who [made sure] our eyes are open. We see that if we do not wake up and stand up for our rights none will do it for us.'[46] John Tengo Jabavu, a 19-year-old Mfengu who was to become a household name in the Cape Colony over the next three decades, reflected African awareness about the motives behind the Act in two letters published in the *Cape Argus* in December 1878. 'From the very outset the natives knew that it has been the intention of the present Government to disarm every black man, merely because he is black, to gain popularity from a section of the colonists, whose aim it is to reduce the natives to nonentity for its own selfish ends. Let the press, politicians, and constituencies guard against this despotism.'[47]

While the Peace Preservation Act (and other class legislation like the Vagrant, Branding and Pass Acts) heralded the beginning of a statutory onslaught on African rights in the Cape Colony, the propaganda attack on the class of 'school Kaffirs', which went back to the days of Dr John Philip and had been simmering in the preceding few years, also escalated to a new level of intensity after the war.[48] Taking advantage of the presence of some school people on the side of the enemy, the colonial press challenged the whole system of mission education. After a copy of *Pilgrim's Progress* with the name of a Lovedale student inscribed on the inside flyleaf had been found on the body of Dukwana Ntsikana, the *Standard and Mail* remarked that the book should be kept 'as a standing advertisement of missionary labour'.[49] Commenting on the perceived disloyalty, the *Grahamstown Journal* asked: 'Does not the defection of this Dukwana sustain the great complaint of the colonists, that the missionaries spoil the natives by petting them, by making too much of them, by shutting their eyes against their faults, and by taking their part when they are in the wrong? For years this man, in his office as elder, has sat in Church Courts with an equal power of vote on all the affairs of the Church with the grey-haired, Scottish pastors, who, for learning, wisdom, and piety, are not surpassed by any in the colony. There is the secret of the mischief.'[50]

Similar views were expressed by other frontier newspapers.[51] The missionaries rejoined by criticising colonist attitudes and leaning the *Christian Express* in a more political direction. In a series of articles on the crisis in colonial politics, it warned that Africans in the Cape were now 'more desponding, hopeless and intractable than they have been for

42

a generation previously'. The disaffection that existed among both loyal Africans, who were 'puzzled, bewildered and irritated', and those who were disloyal was sowing seeds for future revolt.[52]

By the beginning of the 1880s, a hundred years after the opening of the Cape–Xhosa frontier, disillusionment and resentment were widespread among Africans of all classes in the eastern Cape. The colonial historian George McCall Theal, then in government service in the area, noted: 'There never was a period in South African history when the repugnance to civilised government was so great. They seem to have lost all faith in European honesty, truth and justice. They are quiet, not because they regard us with affection, but because they see no chance of successful resistance – they offer a passive resistance which no people on earth know better how to carry out.'[53]

For educated and Christian Africans, the realities of white conquest were turning their dream of equality and Christian brotherhood in a state imbued with mid-Victorian liberal values into a nightmare. A different kind of reality had been brought home to them by their experience of war, dispossession of land, loss of independence, population pressure and economic impoverishment, followed by the 'taking away of the guns' (the Peace Preservation Act) and other racially discriminatory legislation.

Against this background, the aspiring African middle class, which had hitherto been openly uncritical of white rule and at pains to stress their collaborative role, now began to mobilise politically in a concerted way to fight for the protection of African rights. As a result, during the 1880s the registration of voters snowballed, African political and other voluntary organisations emerged, an African-run newspaper was started and the first generation of new-style political activists came to the fore, representing the African voice. One of the new leaders, Isaac Wauchope, then a clerk and interpreter in the Port Elizabeth magistrate's court, summed up in typical Xhosa idiom the aims and essence of the new approach:

Your cattle [rights] are gone, my countrymen!
Go rescue them! Go rescue them!
Leave the breechloader alone
And turn to the pen.

Take paper and ink,
For that is your shield.
Your rights are going!
So pick up your pen.
Load it, load it with ink.
Sit on a chair.
Repair not to Hoho [Sandile's mountain refuge],
But fire with your pen.[54]

The new educated class realised that the future of Africans in a common society was being challenged. Having developed western skills and gained confidence in numbers, they emerged from under the missionary wing to meet this challenge. Their strategy was constitutional – to 'fire' with the pen to protect their rights. Armed resistance and other violent forms of opposition to white expansion had proved futile. A new way had to be sought. From 1879, throughout the eastern Cape they began to organise politically to express this dissatisfaction and promote African interests.

5

'Deeper than
his civilisation'

I am going about from place to place, suspicious of being sought after.
– Nathaniel Umhalla, 19 January 1878

As African societies were drawn more tightly into the colonial
orbit in the nineteenth century, individual Africans underwent remarkable
personal journeys. Roger Levine has given us a sense of the challenges and
contradictions facing Dyani Tshatshu between his birth in 1804 and 1868,
when he died, expelled by the church he had so believed in and crushed
by the state he had tried to accommodate. Donovan Williams has provided
an insight into the remarkable life of Tiyo Soga life between 1829 and his
premature death from consumption in 1871. These were 'new Africans',
taking a road where none had trod before. By 1880, after 80 years of
contact with the European colonisers, not only had the cohort of believers
and school people represented by Tshatshu, Soga and others grown into a
distinct segment of colonial society, numbering several tens of thousands, but
many of them were frustrated and ready to speak out independently in an
overtly political way.

Before we describe this unfolding process of political mobilisation, it is
necessary first to examine more closely who these people were and how they
were equipped as individuals to take their place in a changing world. In
this chapter, we borrow heavily from the work of three scholars – Janet
Hodgson, Christopher Saunders and Noël Mostert – to look at the shaping
experiences of one such person.[1] In this way we can better understand how
the new-style political activists had been shaped, what kind of world of ideas

they occupied, and what responsibilities they were busy assuming. By the 1880s, the person we shall investigate was spelling his name as Nathaniel Cyril Umhalla.

The biographical narrative starts with the apocalypse of the cattle-killing in 1856–7. This was meant to herald the arrival of a new world for the Xhosa. For Nathaniel Umhalla and his father, Chief Mhala of the Rharhabe branch of the Xhosa, a son of Ndlambe, it did indeed bring change that was scarcely believable and far different from what was anticipated. Both the lives of the father, who can be said to have represented the old ways, and the son, who represented the future, were radically disrupted. Both embarked on journeys that would take them far away from the familiar world at the Great Place, near modern-day East London.

Described as a 'great hater of the English', Chief Mhala had tried to coexist with the powerful foreigners for strategic reasons. In 1858, following the cattle-killing, he was one of several chiefs brought before kangaroo courts and sent to the notorious prison of Robben Island. Mhala was court-martialled and found guilty of treason on evidence which the Cape Attorney-General at the time agreed 'would have failed to convince any who are strangers to South Africa' and 'could scarcely have been deemed conclusive'. The colonial rulers wanted to make a political example of those opposing them and remove Mhala and several other chiefs from their positions, even if this meant subverting justice. Mhala was transported hundreds of miles away from his homeland, by boat, and incarcerated on a cold island in the sea. The descriptions left to us by observers show something of the humiliation, terror and deprivation that accompanied the process.

When the soldiers brought him down to the beach, they put him under a crane, and told him they were going to hang him. They actually put a rope around him to frighten him, but an officer stopped them. When they got aboard ship ... Mhala suddenly gave three most dreadful yells ... the deposed chief was terrified at the appearance of the waves as they broke outside, and he fancied the sea was coming in upon him. This made him cry out for fear ... Mhala was very low-spirited, and sat on deck looking wistfully at the land that was once his own.[2]

Mhala's son was sent to Cape Town by boat as well, but his was a different

kind of journey. The young Mhala, still in his teens, was accompanied by
no less a person than the Governor of the Cape, Sir George Grey. Drawing
on his experiences in New Zealand, Grey's plan was to 'civilise' the Xhosa
and assimilate them into the colonial order. After the cattle-killing, he could
proceed forcefully with this 'dispersion and breaking down of the Xhosa
social structure'. Among other things, he decided to set up a special college
in Cape Town to educate and anglicise the sons of chiefs. He persuaded the
chiefs of the western Xhosa and their councillors to allow their children to
be given a British education there. Among those who agreed were Sandile,
Maqoma, Mhala, Xhoxho and Tshatshu. Grey promised to look after the
students personally and to let them return home on completion of their
studies.[3] Although the chiefs had previously resisted, they were now 'keen
to come to terms'. They also saw the value of having their sons skilled in the
new ways. In effect the children became diplomatic hostages.

In February 1858 Grey boarded HMS *Hermes* in East London en route
to Cape Town, accompanied by 35 'princes and princesses' from the main
Xhosa clans and chiefdoms. There were only three girls, among them
Emma, daughter of Sandile. Unbeknown to the Governor, all except one
of the boys were 'lesser sons', because it was the duty of the eldest sons
and heirs to receive and nurture the traditions of the chiefdom. Grey also
persuaded the Sotho chief Moshoeshoe and the Rolong chief Moroka to
send their sons to his new school.

The first location of the new college was the home of the Bishop of
Cape Town. Later, the school moved to a former wine-farm, Zonnebloem,
on the edges of what would become District Six in Cape Town. These sites
were chosen because they were 'within reach of the highest civilization
in South Africa and yet separated from the contamination of the Town'.[4]
Of the 'little savages', as some called them, the worst was expected. Their
warden, the clergyman son-in-law of the Bishop of Cape Town, expected
his new pupils to be 'a compound of the wild beast and of the spirit of
evil, with passions uncontrolled, and full of that mixture of duplicity and
cruelty which is generally considered the characteristic of those who for
long years have sat in darkness'.[5] They created a sensation in Cape Town
and were stared at when they went to church in the cathedral. Yet, to
the surprise of their teachers, the new pupils soon 'turned out to be as

intelligent as any similar group of English children and remarkably well behaved'. Their superiors did not know that an African upbringing placed great emphasis on respectfulness to elders, good manners and obedience. Soon there was a 'perfectly well-ordered school, containing many boys of exceeding promise'.[6]

All the children had received a traditional upbringing. They would have been 'skilled in herding cattle and goats and proficient in stick fighting'. They would have sat on the edges of the *imbizo* of the Nguni, the *kgotla* of the Tswana and the *pitso* of Moshoeshoe's mountain kingdom, observing (like Nelson Mandela in later years) the discussions and manners of their elders, from whom they would have heard stories of the great exploits and heroic deeds of the African past.[7] Now, in foreign surroundings many hundreds of miles from home, these young Africans were to be turned into black Englishmen and -women.

Janet Hodgson, the historian of the college, has documented in sensitive detail how the young people set out on their new lives, and how their 'African identities were soon submerged'. The first step in the acculturation process was to wear the correct dress:

They were fitted out in western clothing; the girls in flannel petticoats, dresses, aprons and shoes, and the boys in flannel shirts, duck or moleskin trousers, caps and blucher boots. They were also introduced to all the paraphernalia of western living such as soap, scouring, blacking, wax candles and sheets, and their diet was comparable to any similar English boarding establishment ...

The pupils were soon regimented into a strictly supervised routine, their day being ordered by the ringing of a bell. Their time was taken up by instruction and improvement and there was little room for play ...

Their lessons were largely taken up with learning the three Rs and religious instruction. The boys were divided into three classes and the top group soon forged ahead. By the end of the first year they were tackling English grammar and composition and were able to do difficult sums in the first rules of arithmetic. They all had difficulty with English reading, however, and this continued to be their main weakness.[8]

[Soon] the curriculum was expanded to include Geography, English History and the elements of Euclid. Greek and Latin followed a few years later. [The system was] based on the time-honoured theory that Classics and Mathematics were the best instruments for training the mind.[9]

Every day at Zonnebloem, as the sons of Maqoma, Mhala and Xhoxho went to school at their little 'Eton in Africa', they could see across the waters the island in the Bay where their fathers – whom they were not allowed to visit – were imprisoned.

As at any British public school, provision had to be made for the healthy physical development of the children. For physical exercise, 'drilling' was introduced in the second year. Teachers reported that some of the elder boys 'did not yield quite so cheerfully' to this discipline.[10] They also did not appreciate the manual work they were expected to do. In African culture, this work was done by women.

Soon, the sons of the chiefs were playing cricket as well. The college authorities introduced the game in 1861 and reported 'a subsequent keenness' for it, which the college was happy to encourage. By 1864, the year in which over-arm bowling was finally permitted in England, Zonnebloem College had two teams. The 'Firsts' played their first games away in Rondebosch in August 1864 and Wynberg in February 1865.[11] The little princes were, indeed, cricketing pioneers. Cricket was then still in its infancy at the Cape, though becoming popular thanks 'to its promotion as a fashionable form of recreation' by Sir George Grey's successor, Governor Sir Philip Wodehouse.

When the college students went on a special ten-day outing to Stellenbosch in July 1865, two of the pupils, Nathaniel Cohon and 13-year-old Walter Monde, documented the visit in writing. Written at the same time that the older *Indaba* circle were putting pen to paper in the eastern Cape, theirs was among the earliest published writing in English by black South Africans. They went by train, which must have been very exciting, as the Cape Town–Wellington route, the first railway line in Africa, had been open for only a little over a year and a half. Walter Monde continued with the story:

We arrived at Stellenbosch about one o'clock; and about half past one we had our dinner, and before dinner we saw some young men going to play quoits, and we went to them and knew one out of them and we looked at them playing and thought they can play that kind of game pretty well, and then after we had seen them playing, we went into the house and had our dinner there in the hall, and after we had our dinner, we went outside, and Stellenbosch people were very anxious to see us; great many of them went out from their houses to look at us; and it seemed to us that they never saw People [Africans] before, especially Malays and Hottentots, and we went on looking what kind of place it is, and I myself thought it was a pretty place full of trees along the sides of the Streets and water running along the sides of the Streets, and we went and saw the Dutch Church, and we admired it very much indeed, and I am sure it is the best Dutch Church that I ever saw in my life, and after going around the Town, we came back and saw the same young men that were playing quoits, but this time we saw them playing Cricket our favoured game and they kindly asked us if some of us would play, and we were very much obliged to them and some of us played with them, and when play was finished their Captain came and asked if we would like to have a match with them, we said yes we would try.[12]

The sons of chiefs at Zonnebloem more or less trod where none of their compatriots had gone before. Lifted out of their familiar world for up to 12 years, they developed ideas and ways of thinking which were new among their people. And, although their African identities would remain primary (even if more complex) – they regarded Maqoma as heroic as Napoleon or the Duke of Wellington – these pupils in many ways assumed the identity of black Englishmen. They were baptised as Christians and the names they adopted emphasised the point: George and Jeremiah Moshesh, Samuel Moroka, Edward Maqoma, Edmund Sandile, and, spectacularly, Boy Henry Duke of Wellington Tshatshu. There were three Georges among them – named after the Governor himself, whom they called 'uncle' and who used to visit regularly and play chess with them.

Nathaniel Umhalla was about 15 when he went to Zonnebloem. His teachers described him as someone 'who had inherited considerable intellectual ability from his father'. He showed such 'exceptional talent' that he was permitted to attend a drawing class at the Cape Town School of Art.[13] After eight years of schooling in Cape Town, he was sent to St Augustine's Anglican missionary college in Canterbury, England, in 1866 to further his studies. Before going overseas, Nathaniel returned home for a holiday. We are told that 'he resisted all his father's efforts to persuade him to become a heathen again, even refusing the tempting offer of being made a chief'. He spent two years in England where he visited the House of Commons. 'He was said to have been much impressed with the debating skills of Gladstone and Disraeli, and to have become a firm believer in British democracy.'[14] His 'piety, gentlemanly manners, diligence and commendable progress with his studies' were much commented upon in England.

After his return to South Africa in December 1868, Umhalla became a 'catechist-teacher' and then assistant to the Rev. H.T. Waters, head of the St Mark's mission in the Cofimvaba district near Queenstown (the later birthplace of Chris Hani). The Anglicans reached deep into Xhosa society from their centre at St Mark's; the mission station had about 50 outposts and 30 schools, some up to 80 miles from the main location.[15] Umhalla emerged as an important figure here. An 'admirable' reader of English, he became headmaster and took the English and Xhosa services when Waters was absent. He was described as the most 'enlightened native' on all the Anglican missions.

In November 1869, Umhalla participated in a Zonnebloem College reunion at St Mark's: church services were held and various educational activities were organised, as well as 'several games of cricket' and an athletics meeting, which included a 'ball throwing contest'.[16] Twelve ex-pupils attended, including Edmund Sandile. The following year, in November 1870, Umhalla played for the St Mark's side against the white Queenstown Club together with several other ex-Zonnebloem pupils.[17] He had by now developed a life-long love for this British game. According to the *Queenstown Free Press*, 'It was a novelty in these parts for our swarthy brethren to put themselves against Englishmen in a game of skill – especially cricket in which Englishmen take credit for being the most proficient in the world, and it therefore did not surprise us to see such a throng of ladies, gentlemen, children and natives as were never on our cricket ground before, turn out on this occasion to witness the sport'.[18]

The local Queenstown people were clearly impressed, particularly as the visitors, who lived a 'considerable distance apart', had not been able to prepare or play together for several months. Moreover, the spirit on both sides was good: 'There was no temper shown, no impatience, no complaints on the part of anyone; everyone behaved himself as a gentleman.'[19] Not everyone shared these positive feelings, though. The *Free Press* noted:

Among the talk upon this unusual event we were surprised to hear some intelligent men, at least they call themselves such, shake their heads at it, and speak as though they thought the European were demeaning themselves in playing such a game. We cannot see it, and most attribute such feelings to the abominable prejudice which would raise impassable barriers between one race and another. Occasionally friendly games like that on Wednesday would, we are sure, promote kindly feelings between Kafirs and English, and from all we saw and heard of those native players we certainly think there was nothing derogatory in Englishmen playing with them.[20]

Far from being inferior, the African players were in many respects more sophisticated than their white opponents, according to the *Free Press*. Not only did they have skilled bowling styles, and not only were they 'far removed from the raw Kafirs', they were also better educated and more well-travelled than the local cricketers: 'In fact, they are men, who as far as book learning goes, are far better educated than many of their opponents. Several of them have been to England, and others have lived in Cape Town.'[21]

Though he had been described as the most 'enlightened native' on the Anglican missions, Umhalla's white colleagues reported him to the church authorities for a 'defect which deterred him from being an earnest missionary to his brethren'. Whatever the fault he was supposed to have committed – and charges like these were often culturally biased – his white missionary superiors thought he might be better suited for a government position. After being charged with 'gross misconduct', Umhalla moved to King William's Town and became an interpreter in the magistrate's court. This was described as 'an ill-paid post of great responsibility'.[22] Umhalla became an important public figure and one of the pioneers of cricket in that town.

After refusing to support the colonial war against the Ngqika in the War of Ngcayecibi in 1877–8, Umhalla became one of the first black citizens of the Cape Colony to be charged with treason. In the aftermath of the conflict he was arrested and put on trial. A diary he had kept during the war was used as evidence. It showed the difficulty Umhalla had of reconciling his inner conflicts of identity. When war broke out, white colonists and officials suspected that Umhalla was sympathetic to his rebel brothers and that he might be in touch with them. He declared his loyalty, but 'to deport him out of harm's way' the government instructed Charles Brownlee, the Secretary for Native Affairs, to order him to Cape Town.[23] After agonising over the matter with confidants like Charles Ntozini and Daniel Dwanya, Umhalla's concern for the 'preservation of my people' exceeded the call of duty, and he resigned his position in the government service.[24] Thereafter, returning to his people at Mncotsho near the small town of Berlin 'to the surprise and joy of all', he maintained a precarious neutrality. He did not join his brothers in the fighting, but went into hiding, because he feared what the government might do to him, 'going from place to place' until he was arrested two months later.[25]

In his diary, Umhalla used the discourse learned at school, in college and in the government offices in King William's Town to describe his experiences. His strong commitment to Christianity shines through in the regular invocations and prayers to his God.[26] He also acknowledged his preference for western life: 'I am sure Kafir life is no life; it is actually being dead whilst one lives. Nothing to elevate or enervate the soul, nothing to animate the mind or quicken the intellect.'[27] Yet it is clear that his sympathy lay with his people and that he was deeply attached to them. He wished to see the people remain united, whether in war or peace, so that they could achieve the best possible post-war settlement; when the war option was chosen he was hurt by the suffering he saw; he made contact with men who were active in the war; he spoke of the 'enemy' (meaning the colonial forces) and of African 'patriots'; he prayed 'God bless the Kafir, and may he nerve our army for the fight'; he took part in a *sangoma*'s dance as 'a political step'; and he criticised missionaries who were at the same time 'political intriguers'.[28]

When the *Cape Times* commented on Umhalla's diary, 'Deeper than his civilisation is his genuine Kafir nature',[29] it was stating in its own terms a truism about the whole class of school people. Notwithstanding their receptiveness to western ideas, they were much closer to their communities and much more respectful of African culture than has been realised. The *Cape Times* was correct in one important respect: Umhalla and his peers were deeply African. They were born into African societies, their families often remained largely 'traditionalist', they lived and worked among 'tribal' people after graduating from the mission schools, they shared common hardships with their kinsmen, and often adhered to old customs which missionaries regarded as heathen and obnoxious.

The strong pull of traditional customs such as circumcision on the educated elite was graphically described by one of Umhalla's colleagues, the great Xhosa writer and poet S.E.K. Mqhayi:

I knew how hateful the circumcision school was to the ministers, but I had determined to be expelled [from Lovedale] rather than not become 'a man'. In my own mind I felt that I was going to be a worker for my own people in my own country, a worker for the Gospel, for social service, in politics, and in educational matters; and it was clear to me that I could not accomplish my work if I did not become a man as they were. At last on the 6th March, 1894, the assegai did its work. When the assegai has made its cut, the operator tells you to say, 'I am a man.' There were 25 of us, but 10 of these used to come up secretly at night owing to their fear of the ministers, and then go back home at day time to put on their old rags. When we came out of the school – J.K. Bokwe – spoke to me most severely for trying to get education and then going back to heathen customs.[30]

Nathaniel Umhalla, deeply schooled in western ways and still self-consciously a 'chief', was arrested and charged with high treason and murder. At his trial in July 1878, the first charge was withdrawn and he was acquitted of the second. Judge Dwyer declared: 'Colour does not prevent you rising to the highest position in the state.' But when he applied to be restored to his old position, he was turned down. The Governor rejected a personal appeal made by the Bishop of Grahamstown on Umhalla's behalf, on the grounds that he was unrepentant and had been neglectful of any sense of duty to the government and, therefore, he could not recommend him for 'any of the many positions for which he is otherwise by nature and education so well fitted'.[31] Like Dyani Tshatshu 40 years before, Umhalla was rejected by colonial society when he chose to assert his African identity. In the 1880s, Umhalla was living in King William's Town and ready to become a spokesman for his people. He would help form a Native Congress and edit a newspaper. At the point when we take up the next part of the narrative, this treason triallist of 1878 was also the captain of the King William's Town cricket team: in 1883 he led the town in the first-ever inter-town match against their rivals from East London, who were known by the anglicised name of the Gaika Cricket Club. The Ngqika may have only recently been vanquished, but they were playing cricket, learning to read and write at school, praying in church, and getting ready for the next stage of the struggle to retain their dignity in a society that did not respect it. Nothing could better explain the dynamic, often seemingly contradictory nature of *usoGqumahashe* (Nathaniel Umhalla) and his peers and their politics than this delightfully ironic image of African men in white flannels and a team with a 'tribal' name.

6

Isigidimi and the Native Educational Association

It seems we march to our very grave
Encircled by a smiling gospel.

– Jonas Ntsiko ('Hadi Waseluhlangeni'), 1884

T he impulse for political mobilisation among Africans in the eastern Cape came from the newspaper *Isigidimi sama-Xosa*. It provided a central forum for school people in the mission heartland who were becoming increasingly politicised, to air their views and co-ordinate strategies. By 1879 the busy correspondence columns of *Isigidimi*, which now appeared bi-monthly, were reflecting the new, more assertive mood of the educated stratum, calling into question government policies and emphasising the need for direct political action.

In a letter to the newspaper in mid-1879 Shad B. Mama, a government interpreter from the Gqunukhwebe community at Middledrift, who later became a law agent, criticised the treatment meted out to Gcaleka and Ngqika women and children held during the recent Cape–Xhosa war. The letter was later read in parliament where it created 'some sensation'.[1] In another letter Mama exhorted his countrymen to start asserting themselves in colonial life: it was high time they became not only ministers but judges, lawyers and magistrates as well.[2] J.T. Jabavu, a young school teacher from Somerset East,[3] went even further, declaring the time had come for black people to elect their own spokesmen to parliament. For the 'nation' to rise it was important that they had a say in government. There were many educated men capable of representing their race. Other correspondents like Simon Peter Sihlali were more cautious in their pronouncements, because 'we do not have the brains and wisdom yet', but they agreed that the time had come for Africans to prepare themselves to shoulder greater responsibilities and combine to protect their interests.[4]

Jabavu's views need elucidation. Besides being the first person to use the press to call on his fellow Africans to mobilise politically, he was the most regular of the early *Isigidimi* correspondents and went furthest in outlining the political aims and strategies of the new-style intellectuals. Jabavu's point of departure was that Africans had to mobilise and help themselves, because whites did not want the 'nation' to rise and instead sought to deprive them of their rights. Africans had to accept responsibility for their own future. Instead of living in the past, they had to look to the future and obtain a say in the running of the country. They could achieve this in several ways. Firstly, they had to learn to use the vote intelligently, as well as elect their own people to parliament. The statistics for frontier constituencies like Victoria East and Queenstown showed that this was by no means a pipe-dream. Secondly, Africans had to read the colonial newspapers so that they could become familiar with developments in colonial politics. By doing so, they would be able to identify the dangers facing Africans and then meet them. Thirdly, they had to work with local 'friends of the natives' and keep sympathetic people in England informed about the situation in the colony. Until Africans understood colonial politics and exercised their constitutional rights, they would never be happy under British rule. It was up to the educated elite to lead the way, as the mass of people were ignorant of their rights. They had to act like true patriots, who would die for their people if necessary. They would have to take issue with whites in the newspapers and challenge magisterial actions with which they disagreed, not just acquiesce passively, as they had done in the past. Jabavu envisaged progress and freedom for Africans in the Cape if they proceeded along these lines.[5]

Jabavu's references to 'patriots', 'my people' and the 'black nation', and his determination and concern for his people, reveal the African bias of his views and ambitions. His interest in politics had developed when, after leaving Healdtown, he went in 1877 to teach in Somerset East, where he apprenticed himself to the local *Somerset Courant* in his spare time in order to learn the printing trade. Through reading the exchange copies of colonial newspapers in the *Courant*'s office, he soon became engrossed in colonial politics.[6] As he put it, 'From a provincial newspaper office I have been fortunate to acquire some knowledge of Constitutional Government, and since, I have felt a great anxiety for the incapability ... of my countrymen to use their constitutional rights which have, all the time, been assumed by their white fellows'.[7] Soon he was writing pieces for the Somerset East *Advertiser*, *Isigidimi* and the *Cape Argus*, one of the leading newspapers in the colony.[8] The Healdtown Wesleyan missionaries with whom he was closely associated threatened him with church censure if he persisted with his political articles, but although he was reluctant to upset them,[9] Jabavu's involvement in politics grew. His articles continued. Through them he began to develop links with liberal colonial politicians like Saul Solomon and in May 1880 he started a long correspondence with the secretary of the Aborigines Protection Society, F.W. Chesson, in London, to ensure that the African viewpoint would be heard in Britain.[10] This was only the beginning. In 1881 Dr James Stewart of Lovedale approached Jabavu to become the full-time editor of *Isigidimi* in succession to Elijah Makiwane, who had in the meantime become a church minister.[11] Jabavu accepted, and thus began a career as newspaper editor which was to last four decades.

Jabavu went to Lovedale determined to use *Isigidimi* for 'educating the people to their rights under the Queen's sway'.[12] He succeeded to a large extent. His editorials emphasised the need for African advancement and combination.[13] He used the newspaper to influence the African vote and publicise African organisations. He increased general news coverage and encouraged political debate in the correspondence columns. *Isigidimi* became the recognised 'mouthpiece of the nation',[14] a forum for school people to swap ideas and keep in touch with each other across regional divides. In general, Africans in the 1880s grew much more critical towards the political, educational and religious status quo. Meshach Pelem, a young Healdtown-trained teacher, for one, set in motion a new, at times heated debate about education when in 1881 he criticised the manner in which missionaries controlled African education and proposed that black communities should work together to form their own independent, nondenominational schools.[15] The debate was still continuing two years later.[16] Pelem was supported in his views on missionary education by his elder brother, James, but was strongly opposed by a section of opinion led by Isaac Wauchope.[17]

Isigidimi's columns were also used to express disappointment with the churches which missionaries had established among Africans. One of the newspaper's most respected correspondents, the noted writer Jonas Ntsiko, a catechist at St John's Anglican mission in Umtata, who styled himself 'Hadi Waseluhlangeni' (The harp of the nation) wrote:

Some thoughts till now ne'er spoken
Make shreds of my innermost being;
And the cares and fortunes of my kin
Still journey with me to the grave.
I turn my back on the many shames
That I see from day to day;
It seems we march to our very grave
Encircled by a smiling gospel.
And what is this Gospel?
And what salvation?
The shade of a fabulous ghost
That we try to embrace in vain.[18]

The views and opinions reflected in *Isigidimi* began to be translated into political action. From the late 1870s onwards, people from Lovedale, where the newspaper was produced, and the surrounding mission areas came together in a range of new voluntary associations. With church ministers and teachers to the fore, these gave impetus to a process of political mobilisation which soon galvanised the school people throughout the region. The first, most lasting and most broadly representative of the early bodies was the Native Educational Association (NEA). It was based in the 40-mile stretch from King William's Town and Peddie to Alice and Fort Beaufort, which became the heartland of the new politics in the 1880s. *Isigidimi* faithfully recorded the NEA's progress, thereby establishing a tradition in which new organisations emerged, accompanied by newspaper mouthpieces to publicise and promote them.

The origins of the NEA went back to 1876 when John W. Gawler, the respected 'head native teacher' at St Matthew's College,[19] initiated a teachers' association for the Alice district. Gawler was the grandson of Makhanda, and he owed his Christian names to the fact that his father Mjuza had been a policeman under the white magistrate Gawler. Like many other sons of pre-colonial chiefdom elites, he had been sent to obtain a western education, had gone on to accept Christianity and adopt a European name.[20] The body started by Gawler led a precarious existence for a couple of years, and it seems never really to have got off the ground. It was re-established as the NEA in 1880, and then began to grow in strength from 1882 after adopting an elaborate constitution and after *Isigidimi* began publicising its activities.[21] The first president of the organisation was Jesse Shaw, a white herbalist from Fort Beaufort who was closely involved with Africans.[22] He was elected after Gawler had applied for recognition to the Superintendent-General of Education. Dr Dale agreed on condition that a European was at the helm.[23] Gawler then assumed the post of secretary and treasurer.

Soon after arriving at Lovedale, J.T. Jabavu was made vice-president of the NEA. He was largely instrumental in revitalising the organisation. He gave full coverage of meetings in his newspaper, played a key part in drawing up the constitution, occupied the chair on numerous occasions,[24] and insisted on organisational efficiency. Under the regime of secretary-treasurer Gawler, organisation had apparently been lax.[25] He was replaced as treasurer by J.K. Bokwe and brought to account in his secretarial duties.

Bokwe held the post of treasurer for more than a decade. His private papers reflect the difficulty he had in keeping the NEA's finances liquid.[26] It stayed out of the red, but only just. In 1885 it had a balance of 12s 6d after expenses of only a few pounds; members owed £56 in unpaid subscriptions, which were 5s per annum.[27] Though there were notable exceptions, this state of affairs was symptomatic of the financial difficulties facing most of the African organisations that emerged in the next 30 years.

Nevertheless, the NEA grew from a small body revolving around the mission axis of Lovedale–Healdtown–St Matthew's into a wider organisation representing the whole eastern Cape. In 1885 its membership stood at 110,[28] including people from throughout the region. One of its meetings in 1887 was attended by individuals from Port Elizabeth, Somerset East, Cradock, Grahamstown, Fort Beaufort, Victoria East, Peddie and King William's Town as well as observers from the Transkei.[29] Many of the most prominent mission-educated leaders in the eastern Cape belonged to the NEA. In the first 15 years of the organisation's existence, the position of president was occupied by Elijah Makiwane, Pambani Mzimba, William Kobe Ntsikana and J.S. Dlakiya. Benjamin Sakuba was secretary from 1884 to 1888 and Walter Rubusana succeeded Jabavu as vice-president in 1887.* All these people represented a cross-section of the emerging educated class. Initially, membership was restricted to those in the teaching field, but it was later opened to other people as well. Because of its original composition, most members were churchmen and teachers, but they were subsequently joined by tradesmen, businessmen, interpreters, wagon-makers, labour agents and educated headmen.[30]

NEA meetings were held half-yearly during the school holidays. The biggest were attended by up to 60 or 70 members, though usually the attendance was about half that. Proceedings at first were in English but Xhosa was later allowed. Meetings were held at Fort Beaufort (to suit the president, who was conspicuously absent at other venues) and mission centres such as Burnshill, Macfarlan, Debe Nek, Pirie and Peelton.

The NEA and other early organisations have been typecast as small, uncoordinated groups that soon expired,[31] but this underestimates the level of networking and organisational depth that existed. Newspaper reports in Xhosa of more than 30 NEA meetings from 1881 to 1900 indicate how consistent and durable African organisation actually was in the early period.[32] Although their activities went virtually unnoticed in the colonial press, vernacular reports confirm a long tradition of organisation and politics with its own particular dynamics.

The guiding principles of the NEA, as enunciated in the constitution, were 'to take a special interest in all educational matters, in schools, in teachers and all others engaged in similar work, the aim of which is the

---

* Among prominent members up to 1887 were Thomas Bottoman, Nicholas Bovula, James Pelem, Nathaniel Umhalla, Ebenezer Mhlambiso, Skepe Nzeku, Solomon Maqina, Andrew Gontshi, Peter Tyamzashe and the Revs. Eben Magaba, Peter Kawa, Boyce Mama and William Philip.

improvement and elevation of the native races; to promote social morality and the general welfare of the natives'.[33] At first, politics were not discussed. When the president suggested in 1882 that the NEA should write a native history of the country (which would include the various wars of conquest) from the African viewpoint, drawing on accounts by elders, Gawler said he feared this would be seen as a political step and put the NEA under suspicion.[34] But the NEA soon developed from a professional body into a general political movement. By the time the government started cutting back on teachers' salaries in line with a general attack on African education, this change in focus was becoming obvious. An NEA committee reported: 'What will move us, and what will make us have our rights is to have people on our side in parliament – members must try to help here.' There was a pressing need to ensure the registration of people who qualified as voters.[35] The NEA also expressed its dissatisfaction with the pass laws and proposed that Africans serve on juries to ensure fair justice.[36] At a meeting in January 1884, Paul Xiniwe from Port Elizabeth read a paper stressing that the time had come for Africans to sit in parliament.[37] From this time onwards the NEA continued to show an interest in wider politics. An NEA deputation met the Cape Prime Minister, Gordon Sprigg, in 1887 and raised matters such as parliamentary representation for Africans in the newly annexed Transkeian districts, liquor prohibition in African areas and the pass laws. No educational issues were discussed on that occasion.[38]

In asserting themselves politically, the younger generation appeared to be moving too fast for some of the older, more conservative members. Elijah Makiwane, who succeeded Jesse Shaw as president in 1885, stated in his inaugural address that Africans at that stage were still inferior to Europeans, and dwelt at length on the problem of young men, 'and more particularly those connected with the Association', who claimed to be equal to them. 'The rising generation forgets,' he said, 'that the natives are an inferior race.' It was foolish for a people who had just recently come into contact with 'civilisation' to compare themselves with a nation which had produced Shakespeare, Bacon and Milton and which had the knowledge to build railways and make wire fences.[39] Makiwane's ideas reflect the extent to which the Victorians' conception of themselves as leaders of civilisation and as pioneers of industry and progress moulded the ideas of many of their protégés.[40] Jabavu certainly was not comfortable with this conventional, missionary line of thinking. By 1887 he was trying to have a new constitution accepted that would widen the scope of the NEA and make it politically more effective.[41] He suggested that branches be formed in different areas, which would then recruit members from the local community and elect delegates to attend the regular NEA meetings.[42] The proposals were investigated by a committee and turned down.[43] Perhaps frustrated by the inability of the NEA to move in a more political direction, and angered by what he regarded as a personal snub, Jabavu cut his links with the NEA.

The operational structure suggested for the NEA by Jabavu was soon adopted by other, more explicitly political bodies operating independently of missionary institutions. As these organisations emerged, the NEA gradually reverted to its role of a teachers' association and in 1906 it finally became the South African Native Teachers' Association (SANTA).[44] Many prominent teachers and intellectuals, including those who became actively involved in politics, remained NEA members, as the subsequent election of people such as Walter Rubusana and Jonathan Tunyiswa as president demonstrated.[45]

The NEA was not the only example of mobilisation in the area in the early 1880s. Many aspirant politicians took their first steps in bodies like the Lovedale Literary Society, the Healdtown Mutual Improvement Association and the Healdtown Teachers' Association, a general association formed in 1881 and which by 1885 had more than 200 members.[46] Jabavu proved himself an outstanding debater in the Lovedale Literary Society. The issues he and his contemporaries discussed in the Society during his first year at Lovedale included: 'Should native marriages be recognised before the law?' (debate with Samuel Mzimba, 18 November 1881); 'The lack of fixity and aim in the life of educated native young men' (10 February 1881); and 'Is it useful at the present time to carry on a native press?' (Affirmative, J. Knox Bokwe, negative, J.T. Jabavu, 3 March 1882).[47]

When students graduated and left institutions like Lovedale and Healdtown, they set up similar organisations in their new postings, such as the Burnshill Young Men's Mutual Improvement Association and the D'Urban Teachers' Mutual Improvement Society in the Peddie district.[48]

This Society discussed matters such as the registration of Africans as voters, while members were also encouraged to read newspapers and acquaint themselves with public affairs.

Explicitly political groups were formed as well at local level in the old mission areas. By 1883, an 'organisation to try to uplift the black nation' existed in the Victoria East district, where Lovedale was located. It held regular meetings and included some prominent people as members. A committee comprising representatives from seven areas in the district was also elected.* This kind of local organisation, based on delegates representing various parts of the districts, was the prototypical building-block for the regional political network that would be built, from the bottom up, throughout the eastern Cape in the 1880s. The issues discussed as well as the composition of members were also typical: the organisation looked at matters such as the registration of voters, tax grievances, the reinstatement of the Xhosa chieftaincy and the transfer of the Transkei to Imperial rule.[49]

Two other early organisations are worth noting. In 1884 the Stockenstrom Original Africander Association was formed in the Victoria East district to promote education and professional advancement and to ensure vigilance in political and public matters. It hoped eventually to develop into a wider 'Native South African Association', co-operating with people from as far afield as the Transkei, East Griqualand, Basutoland and the diamond fields.[50] Then in February 1885 the Peddie Native Association, or Manyano Lwabantsundu, was started.[51] Also known as the Fingo Association, it seems to have consisted of an alliance of the local school people and headmen. After the member of parliament, James Rose-Innes, addressed Peddie headmen and people about the land question in 1886, the Association's secretary, Shad B. Mama, communicated the views of the people to him.[52] Rose-Innes in turn recognised the Association's leaders as the main local spokesmen.[53] In order to protect local Africans from pressure from land-hungry whites, they sought 'tribal title' and full access to their land, which had been given to the Mfengu by treaty in 1845,

---

* The area representatives were Andrew Fadana (Gaga), A. Balfour (Alice), R. Fini (Gqumahashe), M. Bolosha (Roxeni), M. Vokwana (Mxelo), a Mr Mbikwana (Nxukwebe) and a Mr Jonas (Sheshegu). Members included Pambani and Samuel Mzimba, James Bovula and J.T. Jabavu, who joined in March 1884.

though parts of it had been taken over by encroaching white farmers.[54] Among those involved was the Rev. Samuel Mvambo, who was involved in several other wider initiatives.[55]

Towards the end of 1884 delegates from various towns and districts started an initiative to form an African branch of the British imperialist lobby group, the Empire League, in the Alice–King William's Town–Peddie triangle.[56] In order to discuss the idea, Mbovane Mabandla, influential hereditary chief of the Bele Mfengu living in the Tyhume valley near Middledrift, organised two large and 'thoroughly representative' meetings of people from several districts. The first of these was held at Macfarlan on 10 March 1885 and the second at Ntaba-ka-Ndoda (Mountain of Man) on 17 April.[57] It was decided to communicate with the League with a view to forming an affiliated African organisation, and with Africans in other areas to spread the movement.

This meeting expresses its strong opinion in favour of the Imperial government taking over and administrating as a Crown Colony all the native territories beyond the Cape Colony; as the anomaly of their administration by a Parliament in which they have no representatives is productive of mischief, and the colony is, moreover, at present unable to protect them from possible filibustering expeditions.

The meeting having in view the fluctuations of native policies to which natives have been victims ever since the introduction of Responsible Government, would rejoice if the Cape Colony would revert to the form of Government which previously existed, and would respectfully urge the Imperial Government to consider this matter.[58]

The upshot of the meeting was not the formation of an African Empire League, but the immediate dismissal of Mabandla as headman by the government.[59] This action against 'the recognised head of the largest section of the Fingo nation' created a sensation among Africans and led to strong protests from Mabandla's councillors and others.[60] The magistrate in King Williams Town, R.J. Dick, who was commissioned to investigate Mabandla's case, reported in his favour.[61] The Secretary for Native Affairs thereupon ordered that Mabandla be reinstated, but then countermanded the decision after further charges were brought against both the chief and Dick by C.A. King, the local government official at Middledrift.[62] The controversy dragged on for more than a year, even reverberating in parliament, before Mabandla was eventually reinstated.[63] It highlighted three recurring themes in African politics at the time: the dissatisfaction of Africans with colonial rule, their efforts to preserve African territorial integrity and autonomy by seeking indirect Imperial rather than direct colonial rule, and the sensitivity of the authorities (and the missionaries) to the new forms of African assertion.

The meetings that were held in connection with the Empire League illustrate the dynamics of the new approach to politics by Africans throughout the eastern Cape and the foundations upon which it was based. They were not just one-off occurrences, but part of a longstanding process of regional politics. In organising the meetings Mabandla, following in the footsteps of his father, who had been headman before him for 48 years, used traditional lines of political communication when he invited other traditionally recognised leaders, such as William Shaw Kama of the Middledrift Gqunukhwebe, Ebenezer Mhlambiso from the Amatole Basin and Mbem Njikelana from Keiskamma Hoek, and educated opinion-formers from the surrounding areas.[64] From the start, educated people, in spearheading new forms of politics, worked closely with traditional political leaders.

The last organisation of note to be established in this period was the King William's Town Native Vigilance Association, set up in 1887. Continuity in leadership with previous bodies was emphasised by the election of William Mtoba and Green Sikundla as chairmen. Sikundla had chaired the two Empire League meetings in 1885.[65] The secretary of the new Association was the newspaper editor J.T. Jabavu, who played a powerful part in publicising and co-ordinating its activities.[66] The Native Vigilance Association subsequently played a key role in attempts to form an umbrella political body for the whole eastern Cape.

The emergence of these first organisations in the missionary heartland and the increasingly political role of *Isigidimi* were only two aspects of a broader process of political mobilisation under way in the eastern Cape in the early 1880s. It is to this wider picture that we now turn.

7

Imbumba Yama Nyama, 1882

How come they take our name and call us kaffirs – when they
arrived Africa was already standing?
  – Thomas Mzozoyana, referring to the Afrikaner Bond, 1883

After the Native Educational Association, the next most
important organisation to emerge was Imbumba Yama Nyama (the South
African Aborigines' Association), which was formed in Port Elizabeth in
September 1882. Imbumba was an explicitly political organisation that
aimed to unite Africans politically so that they could work together 'in
fighting for national rights'. The name of the organisation was taken from
the words of the famous prophet Ntsikana, who had warned Africans to
be *imbumba yamanyama* or inseparably united.[1] Called Imbumba yomfo
ka Gaba in one report, it also drew inspiration from him:

They are white under the soil
The bones of the thing [son] of Gaba
Grass has grown over that grave
Of the great hero of the nation
Yet he is still alive, he still speaks.[2]

The chief instigators of the new organisation were Simon Peter Sihlali,
W.P. Momoti, Meshach Pelem and Isaac Wauchope, who were among
the foremost correspondents debating 'national' issues in *Isigidimi* during
the early 1880s. In August 1882 Sihlali, the first and at that stage the

only African to pass the Cape of Good Hope University matriculation examination, and Momoti wrote from Graaff-Reinet, asking Wauchope and other Port Elizabeth community leaders to organise a meeting where an African union could be formed. They responded positively to the idea and on 26 September 1882 Imbumba was constituted.[3]

The only people from outside Port Elizabeth to attend the inaugural meeting were the two men from Graaff-Reinet and a solitary representative from Uitenhage. The organisers expected Meshach Pelem (from Middelburg), the Rev. James Dwane (Grahamstown) and Thomas Mzozoyana (Colesberg) to be present as well, but they failed to arrive. The meeting appointed a provisional executive to run Imbumba until branches were operative and an annual meeting could be held to elect office-bearers and adopt a constitution. The provisional executive consisted of Sihlali as president, Momoti as his deputy, and the Rev. Daniel Mzamo of the local Anglican Church (a 'nephew' of the Natal Hlubi chief Langalibalele) as chaplain.[4]

Imbumba was formed largely in response to the Afrikaner Bond, a white farmers' organisation represented in parliament, which many Africans perceived as a threat to their interests. Known in Xhosa as *Imbumba Yama Bhulu*, the Bond demonstrated to Africans the usefulness of mobilising ethnic power. In mentioning the Bond's hostility to African education and its effectiveness as a body, Sihlali asked: Where is our Bond? Imbumba members later claimed that their organisation was the true Afrikaner Bond,[5] while the Afrikaner farmers' association was merely the Boeren Bond. Thomas Mzozoyana asked: 'How come they take our name and call us kaffirs – when they arrived Africa was already standing?'[6]

Mzozoyana's statement was one of many that reflected strong nationalist feelings among members of Imbumba and other leaders at this time. Rather than adapting meekly to the colonial order, Africans responded deliberately to military conquest, disarmament and subsequent class legislation to ensure that their voice would be heard in the country. The language and symbols of politics within Imbumba (and *Isigidimi*) make this abundantly clear. When they 'saw the guns of war finishing off people of different tribes', the new politicians started the organisation 'to fight battles in writing rather than guns'.[7] This theme of 'fighting with the pen' recurs constantly. The new-style activists proclaimed a new form of resistance to white power. For it to be effective, they had to tackle the white man at his own political game. It was important therefore, in the words of Sihlali, to uplift 'the nation' and unite the feuding 'family of Africa'. According to Wauchope, the hitherto antagonistic Xhosa, Mfengu, Zulu and Sotho had to form a unity that nothing could dissolve.[8]

Not only did the new leaders use the symbols of the past but their appeals to the people were in traditional idiom (such as praise poems). They respected the chiefs, who were the cornerstones of traditional society, and sought to co-operate with them. Paul Xiniwe, who was active in both the NEA and Imbumba, told a Sotho member who declared his intention of starting a branch in Basutoland when he returned there, 'you must start with Masupha'.[9] Masupha, son of Moshoeshoe, was for many years the focus of dissatisfaction with colonial rule in Basutoland.[10] Imbumba also sought the release of the Ngqika, Thembu and Gcaleka chiefs imprisoned after the wars of previous years. The *Christian Express* noted that these men were often prayed for in public as well.[11]

Although the level of adaptation varied, the new generation, like Ntsikana, Soga and Umhalla before them, saw themselves primarily as Africans. They were Africans rooted in their African past and present and seeking a better African future. Though they spoke out of 'politeness' in the moderate language of constitutionalism, because they still needed to prove their suitability for acceptance within the colonial order, this did not detract from their basic African consciousness and aims, as the vernacular reports of early African political activities make clear.

The constitution of Imbumba set out ten main objectives. They were to discuss and protect the rights of all Africans in South Africa with regard to legislation, land and education, in the last respect particularly by translating works into Xhosa; to encourage 'the nation' to become voters; to support the 'national newspaper', *Isigidimi*; to monitor the actions of the local municipality of Port Elizabeth; to encourage 'the nation' to become eligible for positions on the town council and in parliament; to promote constitutional activities such as petitioning the authorities and using the press; and, finally, to end denominational and ethnic divisions among Africans.[12]

Imbumba got off to a promising start. It was welcomed by Jabavu and readers of *Isigidimi*.[13] Branches were started in Port Elizabeth, Graaff-Reinet and Colesberg, and Africans from several other districts in the eastern Cape and Transkei expressed an interest in establishing branches there too. Numbers rose from 40 at the launch to over 300 by May 1883.[14] A notable new recruit was the Rev. Pambani Mzimba from Lovedale, who was also prominent in the NEA. Isaac Wauchope described him as one of those ministers who were not scared of coming down from the pulpit and getting their gown and white tie dirty to lift their people from the mud.[15]

Most of the activity occurred in Port Elizabeth, the second oldest, biggest and economically most flourishing town in the eastern Cape, which had a relatively large and stable resident African population. As early as 1878 petitioners (not connected with *Imbumba*) who had 'been born and resided all their lifetime in Port Elizabeth' were already making representations to the government.[16] Subjected to the cosmopolitan influences of the town and detached to some extent from 'tribal' life, these people adapted more easily to the new ways than those in the outlying rural areas. There were several early indications of this. Port Elizabeth provided by far the largest readership for *Isigidimi* in the 1870s,[17] and by the end of that decade the first cricket clubs, benefit societies, mutual improvement associations and temperance organisations had emerged there. Black Port Elizabeth residents had also built substantial houses and several churches and schools for themselves.[18] By the time Imbumba was formed, Isaac Wauchope was already renowned for his involvement in local disputes 'caused by the government and the town council'.[19] There was thus a basic foundation from which political organisation could proceed. Those involved in Imbumba comprised the permanent and semi-permanent part of the town's population. Reflecting the class stratification that was already taking place among Africans, Wauchope contrasted them with the 'riotous Kaffir beer-brewing portion', who were migrants working mainly as labourers at the docks and living under abject conditions.[20]

The branch of Imbumba in Port Elizabeth met regularly, often once a month for several months running.[21] In 1883 it had close on 100 members.[22] The 13-person local committee elected at the inaugural meeting was headed by Isaac Wauchope (chairman) and the Rev. Samuel Mvambo (secretary).

Indicative of his status, Wauchope was also secretary of the Ethiopian Benefit Society and 'Grand Secretary' of the local True Templar temperance organisation.*/23 Frank Makwena, who became Imbumba vice-president in 1884, captained the combined Port Elizabeth cricket side against the local white Port Elizabeth Cricket Club in 1885 and later started the Basuto Pioneering Trading Company.[24]

The leaders of Imbumba did not operate in a vacuum. They were involved in articulating community concerns, albeit mainly sectional ones, and were part of an educated stratum tied together by a whole network of involvements and activities.[25] Church ministers were particularly important in the early mobilisation, as they could provide facilities and support. The Rev. Daniel Mzamo (founder of the Ethiopian Benefit Society) was also a leading Imbumba member; his successor as minister of the local Anglican congregation, the Rev. Daniel Malgas, later gave support too; but, much to the disappointment of leaders of Imbumba, the local Wesleyan minister, the Rev. Peter Mpinda, remained aloof from the organisation and withheld his church's facilities from it.[26]

The link between the temperance movement and Imbumba seems to have been more than coincidental. After the International Order of Good Templars (IOGT) introduced the cause of temperance in southern Africa in 1851, African and coloured Christians participated within church groups and the IOGT until the first black temple, the Ark of Refuge Temple, was founded in Port Elizabeth in 1875.[27] As the number of black templars grew, a separate Independent Order of True Templars (IOTT) was formed for them in 1879. Within three years the interdenominational IOTT had a membership of 3500, grouped into 40 temples throughout the eastern Cape. A large majority of the members were coloured people.[28] The IOTT operated more in the urban centres such as Port Elizabeth, Uitenhage, Graaff-Reinet and Grahamstown, the venues for the first ten annual conferences from 1879 onwards.[29] These towns also constituted the basic geographical framework in terms of which the pioneering Imbumba functioned in the early 1880s. Moreover, the leadership in both groups overlapped to a large

---

* The other executive committee members were George Qaba, Peter Manse, William Mnga, J. Morley, William Zwartbooy, Peter Rwexu, Daniel Ntsiko, Philip Job, Joseph Ngaba, J. Changana and William Nonkasa.

extent. The important names in Port Elizabeth were Isaac Wauchope and Daniel Mzamo, in Graaff-Reinet Simon Peter Sihlali and W.P. Momoti, and at Lovedale Pambani Mzimba and J.K. Bokwe.[30] They were also among the most prominent people associated with Imbumba and the NEA. At the same time the participation of so many churchmen also highlighted the important role of the missions and churches in building the early political networks.

The Port Elizabeth Imbumba involved itself in a wide range of local issues. It brought African dissatisfaction with municipal laws to the attention of the town council; it attended licensing board sittings to oppose applications to open canteens near African areas; it asked for the establishment of a Native Management Board; it saw to the registration of voters; and it opposed moves by the council to have a bill passed to remove the largest African location, the Native Strangers location, to a site away from the town – an early step towards urban segregation in the Cape.[31]

On the electoral front, when the date for the sitting of the registration court drew near, Imbumba organised a general meeting and distributed registration forms, which resulted in 100 people applying to become voters. During the parliamentary election at Uitenhage in 1884, Imbumba also encouraged the black 'agents' there to rally the African vote behind the sitting member of parliament, John McKay, who had sympathetically handled a number of representations from Imbumba. McKay was, however, defeated.[32]

The branch with the highest membership was Graaff-Reinet, the home town of one of the chief organisers of the body, W.P. Momoti. By mid-1883 there were 140 members, many of whom were Dutch-speaking coloured people.[33] From the beginning, the founders of Imbumba were also in touch with community leaders in Colesberg. By 30 October 1882 a branch had been formed there, with Moss Swanepoel as president and Thomas Mzozoyana as secretary. Charles Ntozini, formerly of Healdtown, whose work as a printer had taken him to Colesberg, also played a leading role in the branch.[34] When the Prime Minister, Thomas Scanlen, visited Colesberg, he was waited upon by an Imbumba deputation, whose main concern was African education.[35]

Imbumba held its first annual congress in Port Elizabeth on 4 July 1883.

Delegates from the three branches were present, and reported on their areas. A number of committees were formed to oversee various matters, such as the registration of voters, location grievances and education, and passed several resolutions for submission to parliament. In one of these, Imbumba requested that the franchise qualifications should not be raised in order to deny the vote to blacks.[36]

The meeting also decided to approach the NEA with a view to amalgamating the two groups and any other associations to ensure an effective African voice.[37] It must have become clear by this stage that Imbumba was not making inroads into the main areas of African settlement in the eastern Cape. Although tentative steps had been taken to form branches in places like Queenstown, Peddie and Alice,[38] Imbumba took root only in a few urban centres in the region: this made it an organisation on the outside looking in. At a time when railways were just beginning to snake their way into the eastern Cape, local community groups were still too area-bound in both a physical and political sense to feel obliged to travel to far-off places like Port Elizabeth for political conferences.

Imbumba leaders tried to surmount this problem by bringing under one umbrella all organisations already existing, as well as by attempting to form new branches. The plan was that Imbumba would be a kind of nerve centre for the regional affiliates, and would reach out to its members by holding meetings on a rotating basis at places like Grahamstown, Alice, Peddie and King William's Town.[39] The idea was sound but the time not yet ripe. The result was that Imbumba became just one of a number of still relatively uncoordinated groups in the eastern Cape. The 1884 annual conference in Cradock emphasised the point. The only people to attend from outside Cradock were the two Port Elizabeth delegates, Frank Makwena and Paul Xiniwe. In consequence, Imbumba, with its assertive voice and national aspirations, did not succeed in becoming the cog around which the new politics in the eastern Cape could revolve. It faded from the scene after a few years. Nevertheless, the NEA and Imbumba had made the point that, for the new-style activists to be successful, they would need to be organised at regional and country-wide levels as well.

What were the reasons for the failure of Imbumba to achieve its goals? For one thing, its base lay outside the main areas of African settlement. For another, a rift developed between the organisation and J.T. Jabavu, editor of *Isigidimi*, which left Imbumba without a voice in the press. *Isigidimi* ended up openly deriding the Imbumba, which in turn decided to stop using the newspaper as a mouthpiece.[40] Was this linked to the personality of Jabavu, who was in later life described as prickly and unforgiving of opponents? Or was it related to wider ideological or ethnic factors and, possibly, to competition between Imbumba and the NEA, which operated in neighbouring districts? Shortly after the 1884 annual conference in Cradock, the Imbumba official Joseph Ngaba suggested that the various existing organisations should amalgamate under its aegis. He made the point that the NEA could not become as effective as Imbumba as a political body, for it had several weaknesses: teachers were not necessarily best suited for politics; women were not suitable either; the NEA's white president would be at a loss when they discussed the position of chiefs; the NEA's use of English prevented 'our red people' from participating; and Dr Dale would disapprove of his teachers moving beyond the educational field into politics (while Imbumba would grant teachers and other civil servants the anonymity they needed within a general organisation).[41]

This type of criticism was not unfounded and it may well have induced the NEA to open up its membership, allow the use of Xhosa and become more political. However, it also put paid to the idea of amalgamation between these two important early bodies. Imbumba was clearly more African-focused and radical than the NEA, which was restricted by its links to the educational institutions and had a more moderate approach. Both bodies were important, however, as launching pads for the new directions in politics. The differences between the two bodies also provided another lesson: the politics of the emerging middle class were not homogeneous. From the start, internal differences and changing alliances, based on a range of issues – from regional and ethnic distinctions, religious denominationalism and socio-economic divisions to personality factors – showed themselves in organisations and electoral politics. Such differences were to play an important role in African politics as the century wore on.

8

New organisations
in Thembuland

Oh! Africa until when will people die without anyone to speak for
them.

— Henry Vanqa, 1884

The failure of Imbumba to grow quickly into a strong,
representative eastern Cape organisation, as had been intended, meant
that organisational politics initially developed mainly along local and,
therefore, largely ethnic lines. Besides Port Elizabeth and the Eastern
Province districts, where Imbumba gained some foothold, and the mission
heartland around the commercial centre of King William's Town, where
the Native Educational Association operated, new organisations were also
formed in the early 1880s in the Thembu areas of Glen Grey, Emigrant
Thembuland and Thembuland proper, as well as the Mfengu and Ngqika
districts in the southern Transkei.

The first bodies to emerge in the Thembu areas were the South African
Native Association (SANA) and the Thembu Association, both based in the
Glen Grey district, where the colonial Thembu were engaged in resisting
attempts by colonists to have them removed to the Transkei so that the
district could be opened up for white settlement.[1] SANA seems to have been
a cross-ethnic organisation for the local school people, and was formed by
them as part of the same deliberate process of mobilisation involving the
NEA and Imbumba. It drew on the same ideas and was also known in
Xhosa as the *Mbumba*. In fact, if allowance is made for loose translations
and second-hand reports in the archive, these two organisations could just

as well have had the same names in English – the first-mentioned Imbumba
was described as the South African Aborigines Association, the other as
the South African Native Association.

Were they started as part of the same initiative? Were they even part
of the same organisation? The answer to the first question seems to be an
emphatic yes. In the case of the second, there are some tantalising leads,
but no conclusive evidence. Meshach Pelem, who was marginally involved
in Imbumba while teaching in Middelburg, was the brother of James
Pelem, one of the mobilisers in Glen Grey. Both were Healdtown old boys
and among the most militant and controversial of the intellectuals writing
in *Isigidimi* in the early 1880s. Other evidence comes from a report by
Boyce Kota in September 1883 that attempts were being made to spread
Imbumba to Queenstown. In mid-1884, SANA office-bearers approached
both the NEA and Imbumba with a view to closer co-operation and
affiliation.[2] Both bodies responded positively, but we know nothing more.
This was proof at least of SANA's close identification with other groups.
Mobilisers taking part in the same broad debate were emerging in every
area of the eastern Cape with a commonality of purpose.

The president of SANA, or the Glen Grey *Mbumba*, was David
Malasi; the vice-president, Richard Kawa. Both were teachers. Malasi was
simultaneously president of the Glen Grey Teachers' Association (known
in Xhosa as the Thembu Teachers' Association).[3] Kawa, a Mfengu born
in Peddie and educated at Healdtown in the early 1870s, was a notable
among the school elite. On graduating first class, he was appointed second
head teacher (the highest position for an African) at Healdtown in 1876.
He had a formative influence on the careers of Jabavu and other students.
After participating in the Cape–Xhosa War of 1877–8 on the side of the
colonial forces, he resigned from Healdtown in 1879, hoping to study to
become a medical doctor. Though he began his studies, this goal proved
too ambitious and he ended up teaching at Mount Arthur in the Glen Grey
district, where he reconnected with his old schoolmate from Healdtown,
James Pelem.[4] The Mount Arthur mission was also run by the Wesleyans
and, as the eastern Cape historian Jeff Peires has commented, one's school
and one's church denomination mattered at that time. 'If you had schooled
at Healdtown, you were effectively closer to a teacher at Mount Arthur

than one who was a Presbyterian down the road'.[5]

Like the NEA and Imbumba, SANA was strongly opposed to the hardline 'native' policy of the Sprigg government.[6] It also saw the Afrikaner Bond as a threat. At meetings people were informed about Bond intentions to disenfranchise Africans and were urged to register as voters so that they could have a say in who was elected to parliament.[7] But, in the words of its organisers, SANA was 'only a small organisation', and it seems to have merged with the Thembu Association, which had popular support.

The Thembu Association grew out of the resistance of the estimated 20,000 Glen Grey inhabitants to the renewed calls by land-hungry colonists to have them removed to the Transkei after the rebellion of 1880–1, in which a portion of the district had taken part. The Association was to a large extent a populist movement, led by an alliance of educated leaders and traditional headmen. After 25,000 morgen of land, about a tenth of the district, had been alienated and sold to the Imvani Indwe Railway Company in December 1882,[8] and white farmers moved into a fertile part of Glen Grey, the Thembu began to mobilise in order to resist the dismemberment of the district.

James Pelem, Ngqika by birth, emerged as a key figure in this struggle. He addressed several petitions to the government as secretary of mass meetings. At one of these, in August 1883 the Thembu elected a delegation to go to Cape Town to press the government for reassurances that the people's land would be secured for them and that no more would be alienated. Over £100 was collected for the delegation, which consisted of Petrus Mahonga (chairman), James Pelem (secretary), Thomas Zwedala, the Rev. E.J. Warner (the local Wesleyan missionary) and S. Mpila (later replaced by Samuel Sigenu).[9] Mahonga, Sigenu and Zwedala were important local headmen, the last-mentioned becoming a major figure in local affairs for the next 20 years. Here was a clear case of established local communicators bypassing the resident magistrate, who they felt was hostile to their interests,[10] and co-operating with the school people (and the local missionary) to make political demands. The Thembu Teachers' Association also delegated Pelem to call on the Superintendent-General of Education, Dr Langham Dale.[11]

At their meeting in Cape Town the deputation received a reassurance from the government that the people's land rights would be respected and that they would be consulted on key issues in public meetings. However, nothing would be done about those already removed. At two meetings attended by 600 and 1000 people respectively, the Thembu expressed appreciation of the reassurances they had been given, but requested the government to reconsider its refusal to relocate the dispossessed Thembu.[12] They also noted that the presence of whites in the district increased pressure on land and would lead to friction.

Meetings continued to be held on a regular basis for several years, usually at Mount Arthur. In 1884 those connected with the meetings grouped themselves formally into the Thembu Association, headed by Petrus Mahonga, Samuel Sigenu, Thomas Zwedala, Henry Vanqa and others.[13] From the start there was fairly close co-operation between SANA and the Thembu Association. In May 1884 committees from the Thembu Association and SANA met to discuss mutual issues, and it seems they merged soon afterwards. In November, Kawa and Zwedala wrote to the government as members of a Thembu Association Committee; nothing more was heard of SANA after that year. From that time Malasi and Kawa became regular co-signatories of petitions to the authorities with Zwedala and other Thembu Association leaders.[14]

At the joint talks the two bodies occupied themselves with much the same issues as African organisations elsewhere. They viewed with concern a number of recent court cases which they felt highlighted the unequal justice that Africans were subjected to and passed a resolution calling for black people to be allowed to sit on juries. Reporting on this decision, Henry Vanqa exclaimed, 'Oh! Africa until when will people die without anyone to speak for them.' The meeting also decided to see to the registration of as many voters as possible and expressed the wish that if, as appeared inevitable, the land of the Transkeian Thembu was annexed, it should fall under British rather than Cape control.[15] As a result of the success achieved by the Sotho in resisting the Cape's expansionist aims and maintaining a degree of self-government, there was a strong feeling among eastern Cape Africans at this time that Britain should take over the control of 'native affairs' from the Cape.[16] The disastrous way the Cape government had handled the disarmament measures was one of the main reasons. To show its support for this view, the Thembu Association decided in February 1885 to start an African branch of the Empire League.[17] However, although they communicated with members of parliament about this, the branch did not materialise.[18] Africans saw indirect British rule as a means of preserving their land and a measure of self-government.

The crucial issue of land continued to be the main concern of the Thembu Association into the second half of the decade. Under pressure from white farming interests, the government again tried in 1885 to persuade Africans from Glen Grey to move to the Qumbu and Tsolo areas in the Transkei, which had been confiscated from rebels during the 1880–1 disturbances. Although a small group of headmen agreed to move to Qumbu with their followers, the majority refused.[19] When the Secretary for Native Affairs, J.A. de Wet, decided to intervene personally in November, he met with firm resistance from Sigenu (who became chairman of the Thembu Association), Zwedala and Pelem, acting as spokesmen for the 600 people present. De Wet berated the Thembu for listening to these 'political agitators' and not working through their magistrate. He said although they had a legal right to hold meetings, they were 'not far enough advanced to act as white people in political matters' and therefore 'it is better for you to be led by white men who can be trusted'. He singled out Pelem in particular, declaring him a political adventurer who was 'always looking for something on which to vent his eloquence – I warn Pelem that unless he settles down and leaves the people to themselves he will be removed from the district'.[20] De Wet's tirade at once acknowledged the effectiveness of Thembu resistance and highlighted government dislike of the new breed of political activists that was emerging. The authorities could do little to men like Pelem, who as private citizens and voters enjoyed the protection of the law, though they did try to exert pressure on headmen and other civil servants.[21]

The Glen Grey land question remained a burning issue for many years and the Thembu continued to agitate for the rights to their land, being supported by local missionaries and merchants.[22] The Thembu Association remained prominent. By co-operating with traditional leaders and headmen, the activists in Glen Grey succeeded in establishing a popular base for political action.

In Emigrant Thembuland, to the east across the Indwe River in the Transkei, new-style organisations emerged among the landowning peasantry, who were 'amongst the most progressive and thriving natives in South Africa'.[23] In the 1870s, the four Emigrant Thembu chiefs, Gecelo, Sitokhwe, Ndarhala and Matanzima, under pressure from magistrates and missionaries intent on breaking their power, had given the modernisers large tracts of ground for individual use.[24] This had led to the emergence of a small new class of 'progressive farmers'.[25] Mankayi Rengqe, one of the most prosperous, had been Sitokhwe's chief councillor until 1876. During the war of 1877–8, he had accompanied the magistrate Charles Levey with a force of his followers to help capture the Gcaleka chiefs Edmund and Matanzima Sandile at Sitokhwe's Great Place, an action which virtually ended the war.[26] On the recommendation of Levey, Rengqe was made independent of Sitokhwe and placed in charge of the northern portion of his territory to act as a counterweight to the chief.[27] Rengqe's farm was a model of progress. The *Frontier Guardian* reported that his flocks, herds, homestead, outbuildings, orchards and cultivated lands would put many a white man to shame. One of his pet projects was a water furrow of three miles from the Indwe River to his agricultural lands. Rengqe was also said to be a 'highly polite and intelligent man, with a mind much more capable of grasping the political situation than many so-called Europeans'.[28] Wealthy farmers like Rengqe also sent their children to school at Zonnebloem in Cape Town, where they could mix with white children.[29]

The emergence of a landowning elite led to resentment among traditionalists who felt the consequences of increasing pressure on the land. This was exacerbated by the fact that many of these black farmers were Mfengu. In 1880 a rebellion broke out involving two of the four chiefs, Sitokhwe and Gecelo. The farmers' property was attacked, and they in turn rallied to the side of the government.[30] In the aftermath of the rebellion Sitokhwe and Gecelo lost their land, while Matanzima Sandile and Ndarhala, who had remained loyal, were confirmed in theirs. Emigrant Thembuland was then divided between the districts of Elliot (for white farmers) and Cofimvaba (the preserve of Matanzima and Ndarhala), with Xalanga in between. In a move meant to create a buffer to protect Elliot from Thembuland, the entire Xalanga district was divided into small farms and distributed to peasant farmers, entirely free of any traditional authority.[31]

The 'modernising' farmers were situated mainly around Xalanga or Cala in the north; some individuals could also be found around St Mark's mission station in the Cofimvaba district. They all played key roles in the new politics. Even before the land allocation mentioned, these leading farmers had been organised as early as 1876 by the magistrate into an Emigrant Thembuland Native Agricultural Society.[32] At the third annual meeting in 1879 he reviewed the progress the Society had made:

Four years ago, there were but eight square houses in the District, this year there will be seventy when a few, which are in course of construction, are completed. For every bag of wheat sown four years ago, ten are now sown. At the formation of this Society – about thirty water-courses had been taken out, now there are nearly two hundred. The amount of ground brought under cultivation has increased by about 100 per cent. Not 20 per cent of the people formerly came to the office clothed, now not ten per cent come unclothed. I have also noticed a marked improvement in the building of the huts. All this you have achieved not by force, but by being advised and guided. I am glad to be able to say that this Society has been mainly instrumental in bringing about this improvement.[33]

He also explained how it worked:

Every man, before he can become a member of it, must be proved to be of good character, and the owner of a square house of the value of about £40. We have a Committee of management, who reside in different parts of the District, and whose duty it is, by their example and advice, to show to the more ignorant of their fellow countrymen, how to take out water-courses, to cultivate the soil, to sow grain and to improve themselves generally, and at every annual meeting to report what success they have obtained.[34]

On the list of committee members of the Society, Mankayi Rengqe's name appeared first. Underlining the Society's close connections with the authorities, the magistrate acted as chairman and the Governor, Sir Bartle Frere, was the honorary president.[35] The Society flourished. In 1883 it built its own hall, with a library attached, at a cost of £340, which was hired by white colonists for concerts and other purposes.[36] The chairman in 1883 was the magistrate, Charles Levey; his deputy was Mankayi Rengqe. Members, who totalled almost 70 in number, included Solomon Kalipa, Pambani Figlan and Lot Mama.[37]

However, the Xalanga progressives soon turned from the hunters into the hunted as land-hungry colonists began to eye their land, and consequently they began to mobilise politically. After the 1880–1 rebellion white squatters moved onto the rebel lands and settled among the loyalists, whose removal they soon demanded. Friction resulted. On the recommendations of the Thembuland Commission of 1883, the government set aside the northern side of the district for whites (in what was called Cala) and the southern side for Africans. Black landowners, therefore, had to move south of this dividing line and accept much smaller farms, on average no more than 500 morgen in extent, although some had held more than 1000 morgen before. The new land was also granted on tenuous 'tickets of occupation', as distinct from the more favourable title given to the white settlers.[38] In an effort to preserve their land rights, Xalanga landowners adopted the same tactics as their Glen Grey neighbours. They requested the government to include Emigrant Thembuland in the envisaged annexation of the Transkeian territories to Britain.[39] However, when Thembuland was annexed in 1885 they came firmly under Cape control.

The Xalanga people accepted the system of 'tickets of occupation' only when the government threatened to forfeit their claims and assign their land to other approved claimants.[40] However, in 1886 they formed themselves into an Umanyano lwase Batenjini (Thembuland Union), which was really the political arm of the Agricultural Society, and through it they continued to make 'frequent expostulations' against the system, asking for proper title deeds and surveys and expressing a willingness to meet the full costs of these.[41] However, their activities had little effect. Despite almost constant representations at all levels of government during the intervening years, the Xalanga landowners still did not have title deeds to their land by the time of Union in 1910, when they came under still further pressure.[42]

The main communicator for the Xalanga Umanyano was its secretary, the Healdtown-educated Pambani Figlan, who was said to be the spokesman for a 'large number of natives'.[43] Other prominent members were Mankayi Rengqe and Solomon Kalipa (the two most senior headmen in the district), Timothy Makiwane and Robert Madliva.[44] While the first two could not sign their own names, the others had been educated at Healdtown or Lovedale. Once again, here was an instance of the mission-educated people co-operating with traditionalists and spearheading a new form of protest and resistance. The activities of the Xalanga farmers also provide an excellent case-study in class formation in African society. The landowning elites – both Mfengu and Thembu, headmen and commoners, educated and non-literate – perceived their interests to be the same and faced a common resentment from ordinary Thembu, who were becomingly increasingly alienated from the land.

The Umanyano people were closely involved with later efforts to provide an effective African voice in the eastern Cape. As a body, it continued to function as a local mouthpiece well into the twentieth century, even if in an informal guise. For a long time, the names Rengqe, Kalipa, Figlan and Madliva headed the numerous petitions to the authorities from this close-knit community, which also strongly resisted attempts by outsiders to buy land amongst them.[45]

In Thembuland proper, where the colonial advance came later and was less penetrating than in the other areas, no new-style organisations were established in the period under discussion. However, during the last few years of Thembu independence, when annexation to the Cape loomed inevitably nearer and traditional leaders and political methods were patently powerless to stop this process, a Healdtown-trained Thembu minister, the Rev. Nehemiah Tile, emerged to lead a final, futile bid to preserve Thembu independence. A fervent Thembu nationalist and close adviser of the paramount Ngangelizwe, Tile stepped into the limelight in 1883 when he became the leading political spokesman for the 'Tembu Nation'. He directed a number of petitions to the government on behalf of the 'Lord Ngangelizwe',[46] and when the Secretary for Native Affairs held a meeting with the Thembu in June 1884, Tile was their spokesman. De Wet regarded the fact that an 'agitator' like Tile assumed a role usually taken by chiefs and councillors as an insult to the government.[47] The demands articulated by Tile were for the reunification of the Thembu nation and 'the consolidation of their traditional lands from the sea to Glen Grey, the removal of the magistrates, whose role in weakening traditional authorities was resented, indirect imperial rather than direct colonial rule, recognition of the Lord Ngangelizwe's paramountcy and the restoration of his traditional powers'.[48]

Tile's political activities soon brought him into conflict with both the authorities and the Wesleyan Church. Possibly under pressure from the government, the church confronted him with charges of stirring up hostility to the magistrates, addressing a public meeting on the Sabbath, not keeping his missionary superior informed of his political activities and donating an ox at the traditional circumcision of Ngangelizwe's great son, Dalindyebo.[49] Tile responded by leaving the church and forming an indigenous Thembu church, which institutionalised Thembu nationalism in a modern form. The church was adapted to the heritage of the Thembu. The paramount chief was acknowledged as its head, following the precedent of the English sovereign as head of the Church of England.[50] As the *Isigidimi* columns showed, mission-educated Africans throughout the eastern Cape were at this time increasingly critical of the role of missionaries in the whole process of white conquest. But this did not mean a rejection of education and Christianity. The new class wanted to acquire the benefits of western 'civilisation' while preserving their own cultural and territorial integrity, as Tile's petitions on behalf of the Thembu demonstrated. While they desired the greatest possible degree of autonomy and the strengthening of traditional authority, they also wanted help from the government 'to fill up our country with Education'.[51] This was in the well-tried tradition of selective accommodation of western culture.

Although the Thembu Church was clearly a radical innovation and a landmark event, Tile's ideas and aims were not, as some historians have claimed,[52] unusual for this time. Although his church is recognised as one of the first breakaways from mainstream Christianity in what came to be known as the Ethiopian movement, Tile's activities must be seen within the context of related developments that were taking place in the nearby Xalanga and Glen Grey districts and in African politics regionally. Meshach Pelem had called for a kind of educational separatism in the press in 1882 and Imbumba, formed in the same year, was clearly an important assertion of African political identity. Simultaneously, emerging leaders in Emigrant Thembuland and the areas surrounding King William's Town sought to preserve their lands and autonomy by looking to come under indirect British rather than direct Cape rule. Tile was not alone in his aims. While seeking a place for themselves in a common Cape society, the new-style political activists in the eastern Cape at the same time wished to preserve the independence of chiefdom authorities as far as possible.[53]

Under pressure from the government, Ngangelizwe and, later, Dalindyebo, who succeeded him, were forced to disclaim their support for Tile, despite their sympathies with his aims.[54] Tile continued to oppose colonial intervention right up to the formal annexation of Thembuland in 1885. When he was arrested for inciting chiefs to refuse to pay hut tax to the magistrates, he declared that the fear of banishment, imprisonment or death would not deter him from doing what he considered to be his duty to his chief and people.[55] Until shortly before his death in 1891, the chief magistrate was still describing him as the initiator of all the 'agitations' at Dalindyebo's Great Place.[56]

Nelson Mandela, growing up three decades or so after the Thembu lost their independence, has left us with a graphic description of the importance that the Great Place retained in the lives of the Thembu after colonisation and of the atmosphere that Tile and the school people from surrounding areas must have experienced there.

My later notions of leadership were profoundly influenced by observing the regent and his court. I watched and learned from the tribal meetings that were regularly held at the Great Place. These were not scheduled, but were called as needed, and were held to discuss national matters such as a drought, the culling of cattle, policies ordered by the magistrate, or new laws decreed by the government. All Thembus were free to come – and a great many did, on horseback or foot ...

On these occasions, the regent was surrounded by his amaphakathi, a group of councillors of high rank who functioned as the regent's parliament and judiciary. They were wise men who retained the knowledge of tribal history and custom in their heads and whose opinions carried great weight ...

Everyone who wanted to speak did so. It was democracy in its purest form. There may have been a hierarchy of importance among the speakers, but everyone was heard: chief and subject, warrior and medicine man, shopkeeper and farmer, landowner and labourer. People spoke without interruption and the meetings lasted for many hours. The foundation of self-government was that all men were free to voice their opinions and were equal in their value as citizens. (Women, I am afraid, were deemed second-class citizens.) ...

Only at the end of the meeting, as the sun was setting, would the regent speak. His purpose was to sum up what had been said and form some consensus among the diverse opinions. But no conclusion was forced on people who disagreed. If no agreement could be reached, another meeting would be held. At the very end of the council, a praise-singer or poet would deliver a panegyric to the ancient kings, and a mixture of compliments to and satire on the present chiefs; the audience, led by the regent, would roar with laughter.[57]

While politics at the Great Place remained important to Africans for many years after the advent of colonial rule, the power of the chiefs was severely circumscribed by European conquest in the nineteenth century, which radically changed the political, social and economic patterns of centuries for Africans. Increasingly the magistrates and their courts in the new towns became the focus of politics and the new literate generation of activists started taking the lead, often working with chiefs like the mission-educated Dalindyebo.

9

Mobilising along the Kei

Is it right for educated young men to marry uneducated girls?
– Butterworth Mutual Improvement Society debating topic, 1885

The Mfengu districts of the southern Transkei, to the east and south of the Thembu areas, were formerly home to the Gcaleka Xhosa of Sarhili. In the aftermath of the cattle-killing, the Gcaleka were brutally expelled and, in 1865, their lands were allocated to 30,000 Mfengu from the Ciskeian districts of Victoria East and Peddie. Magistrates came in and set up the new colonial districts of Tsomo, Nqamakwe and Butterworth, which they collectively called Fingoland. The neighbouring Idutywa district was established to accommodate the Xhosa unbelievers who had refused to kill their cattle and joined the colonial side instead; it included many Mfengu and will be dealt with here.[1]

If the new style of politics in the Thembu areas revolved around conquest as work-in-progress, in the southern Transkei the issues were more settled and straightforward. The welfare of the Fingoland inhabitants depended on the politics of collaboration. In 1865 a colonial representative, Walter Currie, warned the Mfengu chiefs and headmen that if 'you throw the Government away, you throw your country away at the same time. The Kaffirs [Gcaleka] will be too glad to take advantage of every false step you take.'[2] The Mfengu were well aware of this. When the Cape–Xhosa war broke out in 1877, their two leading headmen, Veldtman Bikitsha and Menziwe Luzipho, were prime targets for Xhosa attacks. Veldtman in turn rallied the Mfengu behind the Cape government. For his loyalty he was given a farm and the permanent rank of Captain of the Fingo Levies. (This reward carried with it the prerogatives attached to rank and, when he visited England for the Queen's jubilee in 1897, he was given a grand uniform for the occasion.)[3]

With Veldtman Bikitsha as their acknowledged leader, the Transkeian Mfengu showed themselves to be model subjects. The loyalists in the Fingoland districts provide a good example of traditional leaders adapting readily to the colonial presence and working within the system. Co-operation between headmen and colonial authorities was put on a more formal footing with the formation of the Fingoland District Society in February 1882. The Mfengu agreed voluntarily to pay 2s 6d per head each year towards a central fund, matched on a £ for £ basis by the government, which would be controlled by the Society and spent on such purposes as the construction of roads and local government. Under this arrangement the magistrates at Tsomo, Nqamakwe and Butterworth met once a month with local headmen to discuss expenditure. A general committee composed of the chief magistrate, the Fingoland magistrates and ten headmen from each district came together quarterly to decide on the more important issues and the general running of the Society.[4]

At the same time that the Mfengu headmen were drawn closer into the colonial administrative framework, educated preachers, teachers and government officials in the districts also began to group themselves into organisations to work closely with the authorities. By 1882 a Transkeian Teachers' Association (TTA) was operating under the presidency of the Rev. E.L. Coakes, a high-ranking Anglican missionary.[5] Like the pioneering Native Educational Association on the other side of the Kei River, the TTA met twice a year, but, unlike its counterpart, it kept strictly to educational matters. Among its members were many whose names would come to feature prominently in politics: W.F. Bassie and P.D. Tshacila (successive secretaries), Nkohla Falati (grandson of Ntsikana), Joel Madubela and Theodore Ndwandwa (Veldtman Bikitsha's son-in-law, interpreter and right-hand man, who was also linked to J.T. Jabavu by marriage).[6] Although the teachers' organisation was based mainly in Fingoland, members were drawn from other Transkeian districts such as St Mark's, Cala, Kentani and Engcobo as well.[7] The TTA became an established part of life in colonial Transkei and was still holding regular meetings at the time of Union in 1910.

With the blessing of local missionaries and the TTA, Joel Madubela started a Butterworth (later Transkei) Mutual Improvement Association early in 1884.[8] The aim of the organisation was to promote African education and advancement, being based on a similar body at Healdtown, where Madubela and others had studied. The Association was unashamedly elitist. The proceedings of the half-yearly meetings were in English,[9] tea meetings, concerts and recitals were held, and papers were presented on topics such as 'Is it right for educated young men to marry uneducated girls?' and 'Which work is more prosperous for a man to do, agency or clerkship?' Religious and educational issues were also popular while discussions on such topics as Robert Browning's poetry and phonography were not out of order.[10]

Notwithstanding the gusto with which western ideas were absorbed, this organisation was meant specifically for Africans, and its rules and ethos reflected this. When a white man applied for membership, he was turned down.[11] In order to 'grow politically', members were encouraged to continue learning until they became magistrates, judges, attorneys and lawyers and not just teachers, for which their education had geared them.[12] An attempt to change the organisation's name to the Mutual Improvement Christian Society was strongly resisted.[13] And when the Victorian theme of the Europeans' thousand-year start on Africans in the march of civilisation cropped up in discussions, it was dismissed angrily by M.N. Galela and others who declared that colour distinctions were invalid: there were educated blacks and still many uneducated whites.[14]

The president of the Mutual Improvement Association was George Pamla, member of a prominent school family. After graduating from Healdtown in 1873, he taught in the Queenstown and Mount Frere districts before taking up a post as head teacher in Butterworth in 1881.[15] Within the Association teachers once again predominated, but there were also agriculturists and others. As with the TTA, members were drawn from Idutywa, Engcobo and St Mark's in addition to the three Fingoland districts, and there was overlapping membership between this and other bodies. Several leaders of the TTA also belonged to the Association, among them Enoch Mamba, Patrick Xabanisa and Joel Madubela, who were later to become leaders in political affairs.*

The Association also sought closer ties with its counterparts. George Pamla attended an NEA meeting in Grahamstown in January 1887 with this aim in mind.[16] A few months later, the organisation decided to change its name to the Transkei Native Educational Association and assume a more political function. The secretary was instructed to warn the chief magistrate of Fingoland, Captain Matthew Blyth, not to be surprised if it discussed politics.[17] Later that year a report noted that the organisation had affiliated to the NEA.[18]

The first explicitly colonial-style political organisation in Fingoland was founded only in 1887. This was the Manyano nge Mvo Zabantsundu (Union for Native Opinion). The chief magistrate reported that it had been holding meetings in the Nqamakwe and Tsomo districts, spreading propaganda among the 'semi-educated class' by claiming that 'they are an oppressed people and that the actions and intentions of both the Government and its officers in these Territories is nothing but evil'.[19] At a meeting with the headmen and people of Nqamakwe in June, he described the Manyano in a typical over-reaction as proceeding 'like a snake in the grass' and warned the Mfengu 'to guard against being misled by mischievous educated rascals, who have their own selfish ends to serve'. 'Representation was a thing that is as high above the heads of the natives as the moon.'[20] The magistrate existed for receiving people's grievances, Blyth said, but in fact the Manyano was set up as a watchdog body to enable Africans to assert their rights independently of the magistrates.

There were three important reasons for the formation of the Manyano. Firstly, by 1887 Fingoland was the only important African area under colonial rule where no political organisation had emerged, and the local Mfengu were fully aware of the fact.[21] Moreover, in that year the Cape parliament passed the first legislative measure aimed at restricting the African franchise and the newly annexed Transkeian territories also gained a seat in parliament for the first time.[22] As in the eastern Cape

---

* Other BMIA members were M.N. Galela (vice-president), Solomon Maqina (secretary), Patrick Xabanisa (assistant secretary), Joel and John Madubela, Enoch and Paul Mamba, Jeremiah Mazamisa, Charles Bikitsha, Theodore Ndwandwa, Richard Ndungane, J.J. Vili, William Daniel and W. Bassie.

districts, Africans could vote for a candidate of their choice to represent the new local constituency. These factors brought home the need for a local organisation.

The Manyano's main promoter was Andrew Gontshi, a 31-year-old, Lovedale-educated Ngqika who owned a farm in the neighbouring district of Kentani, and worked as a law agent in Fingoland.[23] He was the first African in the Cape to follow this occupation and the first to sit on a jury.[24] Gontshi travelled throughout Fingoland and as far as St Mark's and Engcobo to promote the Manyano.[25] He pleaded for black unity, arguing that the Xhosa, Mfengu and Thembu were united by their colour, and that education showed the futility of tribal jealousies.[26] However, although the organisation aimed to unite and represent the whole Transkei, it remained essentially a Mfengu organisation centred on Nqamakwe.

The president of the Manyano was John Mazamisa, an educated headman from the district, who along with Tiyo Soga had been one of the contributors to *Indaba* newspaper in the early 1860s. The secretary was the Rev. J.J. Sikwebu.[27] Some meetings of the Manyano were attended by almost 100 people. Gontshi gave an indication of the body's composition when he said there were many intelligent people in its ranks who owned land and had spent much money on building houses.[28] Headmen featured prominently among them, especially men like Mazamisa, Lambata Mgidi and K. Dingiswayo. Some of the most active school people in the Manyano besides Gontshi and Sikwebu were the Rev. S. Mzamo, Pato Lusaseni and Campbell Kupe, who was to lead Manyano and Mfengu opposition to government administrative and land measures in the 1890s.

In view of the fact that headmen, teachers and other African civil servants began to encounter problems by participating in politics around this time, Gontshi made contact with James Rose-Innes, an advocate and member of parliament for Victoria East, for clarification of their political rights. Rose-Innes assured them that Africans were fully within their right to participate in politics.[29] The way was now open for the Manyano to operate without fear of official retribution.

In addition to his work in the Manyano, Andrew Gontshi was also responsible for the formation of a political organisation in his home district of Kentani, the last of the Transkeian Territories stretching along the colonial border from Glen Grey to the Indian Ocean. After the 1877–8 war the defeated Ngqika had been moved en masse across the Kei River into this former Gcaleka territory, including those who had never participated. It was among them that Gontshi, who was granted a farm when the land was apportioned in 1883, began to organise.[30] He was prompted to do so by two letters that appeared in *Isigidimi* in late 1884. A correspondent writing under the pseudonym 'Tand Uhlanga' (Lover of the nation) described the progress of the neighbouring Mfengu and Thembu agriculturists and compared this with the backwardness of the Ngqika. The educated men, whom he compared to sly 'river dwarfs', prospered at the expense of those who were not educated.[31] Gontshi – to whom the charge of indolence clearly did not apply – thereupon convened a meeting of leading Transkeian Ngqika at his house on New Year's Day, 1885.[32] It was attended by Chief Feni (Fynne) Tyali and some minor chiefs as well as a sprinkling of 'progressives': J. Peters, the teachers W.F. Bassie and Ludidi Gongwana, the 'agriculturalists' Charles Nkente and W. Bombo, the carpenter J. Kota, and Tiyo G. Soga, a clerk in Kentani and a relation of his famous namesake. They decided unanimously to form Intlanganiso Ye Nqubelo Pambili Yama Ngqika or the Association for the Advancement of the Ngqika.[33] The co-operation of the chiefs gave the new body a solid local base. Its origins can be detected in the representations made through Gontshi to the government by Feni Tyali and Nowawe Sandile, widow of Chief Sandile, on behalf of the 'Gaika headmen and people in the district'.[34]

The Association's task was not made easier by a crippling drought. Gontshi estimated in 1885 that it had claimed about 80 to 90 per cent of the Ngqika's cattle. Nevertheless, he reported, there was some progress. In this respect he mentioned particularly the progressive farming methods of A.K. Soga, son of the revered Tiyo Soga.[35] After going to school and, later, university in Scotland like his father, he joined the civil service, working in the Native Affairs Department, and subsequently became an acting magistrate. The Soga family had lived in the area since the late 1860s, when Sarhili of the Gcaleka requested that Tiyo Soga start a mission at Tutura, eight miles from his Great Place. Soga was also buried there in 1871. For Sarhili, this invitation had been a political move to shore up his remaining authority after two-thirds of his land had been carved up into Fingoland and other districts. The Sogas had moved to Tutura before the post-1878 removal of the Ngqika to this area. (Tiyo had, in fact, strongly opposed colonial suggestions already in the 1860s to move Ngqika communities here, knowing it would create tension between the different chiefdoms.) His biographer has described how Soga in 1868 was 'occupied with putting up accommodation for a large family, which had been accumulating over eleven years'. Alan (aged 6 at the time) and two elder brothers were sent off to boarding school at Lovedale. Their parents, unhappy with the discrimination the boys would suffer if they sought to further their education in the Cape Colony, then packed the three off to Scotland in 1870, at great expense. Explaining this, Tiyo Soga said he could never subject them to 'an ordeal such as I have been through'.[36]

By 1887 the attention of Gontshi's Association was focused firmly on political matters such as parliamentary representation, and it began to open up links with similar bodies elsewhere. In July a deputation from the Association attended an NEA meeting at Peelton mission station near King William's Town.[37] It was probably from his base as president of the organisation that Gontshi launched the Manyano in that year to unite African opinion in the Transkei. By 1887 several new names had come to the fore in the Association. The secretary was R. Robinson Mantsayi, son of one of the contributors to *Indaba* in the 1860s. Another member of the Ntsikana–Soga line, Alexander Dukwana Ntsikana was also an Association member and chaired one of the meetings in Gontshi's absence. Another prominent organiser was Nzanzana Mqhayi, great-uncle of the famous Xhosa writer S.E.K. Mqhayi.[38] The 'Poet of the Nation' himself lived at Nzanzana in Kentani as a boy before he 'cast off his sheep's blanket' and was sent to Lovedale.[39] Here, again, we see old connections reaching back many years that operated among educated Christians as they started mobilising politically in the Cape Colony in the 1880s.

Political organisations emerged in all the southern Transkeian Territories during the 1880s. Similar developments did not occur in the rest of the Transkei until later, when they were brought firmly under Cape control, although educated Africans had already begun to apply new forms of political activity there. An outstanding example was Umhlangaso J.S. Faku, the Lovedale-trained 'prime minister' of the still independent Mpondo chiefdom. In trying to preserve Mpondo independence against Cape encroachment, Umhlangaso made skilful use of the press to put across the Mpondo point of view in disputes with neighbouring chiefdoms and the Cape government.[40] Much like Tile's efforts on behalf of Dalindyebo, here was additional proof that independent African societies started to employ western-style political methods in the 1880s *before* they came under white control.

10

Using the ballot box

When the election came the natives held meetings among themselves, and fully discussed their grievances, and the kind of man they required. There were 'local' meetings and there were general meetings. Questions affecting the district and questions affecting the colony – such as education – were gone into. Amongst other things it was agreed ... that the natives were not to bind themselves to any candidate until such a candidate was heard when addressing his countrymen, and when addressing the natives.

– J.T. Jabavu, 1885

African voters were a factor of some importance in electoral politics in the Cape Colony from the commencement of representative government and an elected parliament in 1853.[1] As previously noted, parliamentary candidates were returned in Somerset East and Fort Beaufort during the 1860s as a result of the support of black voters and there were other signs of early involvement, too. In the 1870s the introduction of responsible government led to the formation of a party system and elected representatives. The Afrikaner Bond emerged to lobby on behalf of farmers' interests and to contest elections. Among Africans, interest in electoral politics increased as the numbers and confidence of school people grew and competition for the support of voters became fiercer. Nevertheless, by the end of the 1870s the overall number of African voters was still relatively low. They had not yet combined or developed common strategies

Table 1: White and black voters in six eastern Cape constituencies, 1882–6

	Whites		Africans		Total		% of Africans	
	1882	1886	1882	1886	1882	1886	1882	1886
Aliwal N.	1020	686	260	800	1280	1486	20.31	53.84
F. Beaufort	1019	1432	160	400	1179	1832	13.57	21.83
KWT	1306	2001	370	1300	1676	3301	22.10	39.38
Queenstn	1860	2069	220	1700	2080	3769	10.58	45.10
Victoria E.	538	503	90	520	628	1023	14.33	50.83
Wodehouse	1376	1386	50	1325	1424	2711	3.51	48.87
Total	7117	8077	1150	6045	8267	14122	13.91	42.81

to make broader political demands.

All this changed in the 1880s as Africans began to assert themselves in a concerted way in colonial politics and sought to have a say in the running of the country. Leaders of African opinion exhorted their countrymen to become enfranchised, organised the registration of voters, scrutinised the records of candidates, began to make tougher demands on them, aspired to send Africans to parliament and generally started co-ordinating their political activities. The upshot was a dramatic growth in the number of African voters and in their political awareness. In the six 'frontier' constituencies in the eastern Cape – Aliwal North, Fort Beaufort, King William's Town, Queenstown, Victoria East and Wodehouse – African voters increased sixfold from 1150, or 14 per cent of the total vote in 1882, to 6045, or 43 per cent in 1886. The number of white voters in these constituencies rose by only 914 to 8077 in the same period.[2] The accompanying table gives a breakdown of the figures for each of these constituencies.

Clearly, African voters had become a key part of electoral politics in these constituencies. There were also sizeable African voting communities in Uitenhage and Port Elizabeth; and African voters were to become an important factor in the constituencies of Tembuland and East Griqualand, created in 1887, after the Transkeian Territories were annexed to the Cape.[3]

At the most, then, Africans could influence 14 seats; the rest lay outside their main areas of settlement in the eastern Cape. Still, mobilised African voters had the potential to become an important political factor in the colony. From this would develop a form of politics that eventually undermined the very foundations of white rule. The impulse for electoral mobilisation came from the press and fledgling political organisations, and from white politicians who began to realise the potential of the African vote and seek African support. As we have already noted, from 1879 Jabavu and other *Isigidimi* correspondents started hammering home the theme that to protect their precarious position in Cape society, Africans should make use of their constitutionally guaranteed franchise rights and even send men of their own colour to parliament.

As early as 1881 it was rumoured that Isaac Wauchope, soon to be one of the driving forces behind the black 'Bond', or Imbumba, would stand for parliament in Uitenhage at the next election.[4] Subsequently Jabavu was approached to stand in Victoria East but decided in the end not to do so.[5] Correspondents also mentioned people such as Elijah Makiwane, Gwayi Tyamzashe and William Shaw Kama, the Christian chief of the Gqunukhwebe, as suitable candidates.[6] However, no African candidates entered the field in the elections in 1884. The new generation decided that rather than take that step at this stage, they should back sympathetic 'friends of the natives'. Once this *modus vivendi* was established, the idea of Africans sending an African representative to parliament receded into the background. It became the norm for Africans to elect sympathetic whites to represent them instead. It took three decades before an African, Walter Rubusana, stood for and won a legislative position in the Cape Provincial Council.[7] But by then Africans had been barred from the highest legislative body in the country, the Union of South Africa parliament.

The 1884 election was the first in which the new African political class deliberately mobilised electorally, worked out a broad strategy and tried to co-ordinate the African vote throughout the eastern Cape. Much of the activity centred on Lovedale, where Jabavu used *Isigidimi* to promote joint action in the various constituencies and successfully mobilised local African voters to return the candidate of their choice to parliament. Towards the end of the previous year Jabavu had brought the forthcoming elections to the notice of Africans in the first of two open letters in *Isigidimi*. In them he pleaded for an end to apathy and encouraged people to use their votes in a critical, constructive way. He said they had a right to sway the vote and determine their own futures. If they did not wake up, they would suffer the same kind of disabilities as after the previous elections in 1879, when the parliament then elected subjected them to disarmament and pass measures, helped polarise blacks and whites, and was responsible for waging war against African people. Spelled out here were the recurring grievances among Africans in the early 1880s. Moreover, the few 'friends of the natives' were not standing again for parliament or else were under pressure from unashamed white supremacists. It was, therefore, important that Africans should elect the right people to stand for them.[8]

In Victoria East, which included Alice and part of the Peddie district, Jabavu championed the cause of James Rose-Innes, whom he described as a liberal in the mould of Saul Solomon. Jabavu regarded Rose-Innes as an ideal candidate because 'he hates the way we are treated' and, as an advocate, he could defend African rights with eloquence.[9]

Jabavu addressed meetings in several places in the constituency and, together with other local spokesmen, canvassed actively on behalf of Rose-Innes.[10] Working in conjunction with people such as Elijah Makiwane and Pambani Mzimba at Lovedale and leaders of the local Native Association (of which he became a member only in March 1884), he succeeded in uniting the 100 or so African voters from Alice solidly behind Rose-Innes. The plan was that they would give him both votes they were entitled to cast, a tactic called 'plumping'. Among the 31 electors who signed the requisition inviting Rose-Innes to stand were Govan Koboka, John Knox and Candlish Bokwe, who were prominent at Lovedale, and Andrew Fadana and A.N. Jonas, committee members of the local Native Association.

On election day in 1884 the local activists manned polling booths throughout the district to see that this plan was implemented.[11] As a result of plumping, Rose-Innes was returned to parliament ahead of six other challengers. The unanimity with which Africans voted for him created a sensation in the opposing camps.[12] Although Africans held a shade less than 15 per cent of the vote, they had acted in a calculated and concerted manner to return the candidate of their choice. Their success heralded a new era of African involvement in Cape electoral politics.

There was also much excitement about the elections in the Aliwal North constituency, which included the largely African district of Herschel. The number of voters here was somewhere between the 1882 figure of 260 out of a total of 1280 and the 1886 figure of 800 out of a total of 1486.[13] The candidates were J.W. Sauer and D. de Wet, supporting the government of Thomas Scanlen, and H. Tamplin, an advocate from Grahamstown who supported Gordon Sprigg, author of the Disarmament Act. In the election campaign, the 'liberal' Sauer was backed by Jabavu as well as the local Africans, to whom he was known as 'Government Sauer'; he would represent them in parliament for nearly 30 years. Tamplin made an early start to his campaign by calling together all the headmen in Herschel. He won the support of about 70 Africans under Augustus Bell, a headman and local agent for *Isigidimi*.[14] However, Tamplin was no match for Sauer, whose meeting with the local electors drew between 1500 and 2000 people. On polling day a 'great gathering of Basutos and Fingos, mounted and on foot', descended on the mission village of Bensonvale to vote for him.[15]

When Tamplin entered the Aliwal North contest, *Isigidimi* warned voters not to be misled by his promises, because he was a supporter of Sprigg and was on record as saying that Africans should be taxed more heavily.[16] Joel Gundwana, one of Sauer's principal backers and, like his rival, Bell, a headman and an *Isigidimi* agent and correspondent, remarked that Jabavu's advice had helped foil Tamplin's bid.[17] Jabavu criticised Augustus Bell for not heeding his advice and remained unimpressed when Bell explained why he had done so.[18] No longer could white candidates in the eastern Cape exploit African voters and ignore their interests.

After the election Jabavu claimed that sympathetic candidates were returned 'in every contest we interested ourselves in'.[19] Though an exaggerated claim, he was probably referring to the Victoria East, Aliwal North and King William's Town contests. In King William's Town both the candidates he had supported, F. Dyer and W.J. Warren, were elected. Dyer received 225 votes from Africans and 447 from whites, Warren 219 and 375, and the defeated candidate 5 and 268 respectively.[20] The pattern of African voting suggests calculated local action. Grahamstown was another constituency where a candidate preferred by Jabavu was returned.[21] In Uitenhage, as we have seen, Imbumba succeeded in getting about 100 people to apply for registration as voters and encouraged the local people to vote for the sitting member, John McKay (also recommended by Jabavu in *Isigidimi*), but he was defeated.[22] In Oxkraal and Kamastone near Queenstown, an important centre in African politics from the start, an

Isigidimi correspondent noted approvingly how Chief Zulu had canvassed 266 people in one day to apply for registration.[23]

The 1884 election marked a new phase of African involvement in Cape electoral politics. For the first time the new generation of politicians used the press to influence voters and co-ordinate action. They looked critically at the contestants, devised electoral strategies and pursued them aggressively to return sympathetic candidates whose access to the political centre they now put to their advantage. Having been sent to parliament by the Victoria East voters, Rose-Innes became the focus of African attention throughout the eastern Cape. Africans in and beyond his constituency saw him as a symbol – their own representative whom they had sent to parliament.[24] They regularly referred matters to him and held him up as an example of what could be achieved, confirming their earnestness about the new approach to politics. Henceforth, African participation was to be an important factor in Cape politics.

White colonists for their part were quick to point to the Victoria East result as an example of the thoughtless exercise of the 'blanket vote', the result of missionary manipulation. Opposition to the vote for Africans intensified. The defeated member for Victoria East, John Watson, ominously remarked that he would endeavour to have as many Africans as possible removed from the voters' lists.[25] In parliament, calls for the restriction of African political rights began during the 1884 session and intensified thereafter.[26] But the stereotype of politically naive and easily manipulated Africans was unfounded. African and missionary attitudes in the Victoria East election had not coincided. Dr Stewart of Lovedale, who clashed with Jabavu for actively involving himself in the contest, was soon lamenting the fact that local Africans had sent Rose-Innes to parliament instead of Watson, who would have been better disposed towards the interests of Lovedale.[27] As for the 'blanket vote' charge, Jabavu dismissed it with contempt. If the vote in Victoria East had been a blanket vote because Africans voted *en bloc*, what was the uniform support Afrikaners gave to the Afrikaner Bond? Jabavu argued that from 'tribal' experience Africans were natural politicians and they had voted in an intelligent and independent way:

The truth, however, is that in the Victoria East district you have a large number of intelligent natives. Some of these had their training in Kafir courts, or inkundla, and can grasp a political situation much more intelligently than some whose right has not been questioned. The other voters have received their training in some of the Institutions and in the towns. Well, then; when the election came the natives held meetings among themselves, and fully discussed their grievances, and the kind of man they required. There were 'local' meetings and there were general meetings. Questions affecting the district and questions affecting the colony – such as education – were gone into. Amongst other things it was agreed, though not by formal resolution that the natives were not to bind themselves to any candidate until such a candidate was heard when addressing his countrymen, and when addressing the natives. The 'man' was to be estimated, his opinions carefully noted on both occasions, and minutely compared ... men who could be relied upon were sent to take 'notes' and report (at the meetings). These reports were compared and it was only then that a decision was arrived at. All this was done without the help of those dreaded influential missionary wire-pullers, and as the discussion was very free it will appear that the native voters deserve to be called 'independent electors'.[28]

Many white critics did not credit Africans with political initiative of their own, or recognise that African politics had its own particular dynamism. Yet, as the elections of the 1880s showed, the opposite was in fact true.

11

Launch of the
'national newspaper', 1884

I am thankful to you, son of Jabavu ... You have defeated the
government and its armies, destroyed its war chariots, scattered its
horsemen. The tails of the Pondo cattle you have saved.

– 'Ntlola-Yo-Hlanga', 1887

In order to give direction to the unfolding process of political
mobilisation, properly represent African views and protect their rights, the
new intellectuals began to feel the need for an independent newspaper.
The missionary-controlled *Isigidimi* no longer satisfied their needs. As
Booi Kwaza, a leading member of the Cradock branch of Imbumba, put it,
Africans had to rely on a newspaper controlled by 'foreigners'; the time had
come for them to establish their own press.[1] So much criticism was levelled
against *Isigidimi* that the renowned correspondent Hadi Waseluhlangeni
compared it to a warrior whose enemies had hurled so many spears into
his body that he looked like a porcupine.[2] *Isigidimi*'s shortcomings as a
medium for the expression of African opinion were highlighted when it
refused to publish an article by Hadi, pseudonym for Jonas Ntsiko, in May
1884 on the grounds that it attacked British rule in South Africa.[3]

While criticism against the newspaper was directed mainly at its being
part of the system of colonial control, there were some who did not see
eye to eye with its young editor, J.T. Jabavu. Though it had initially set
out to promote *Isigidimi* as the 'national newspaper', Imbumba decided
to stop using it as a mouthpiece because of the hostile press it started
receiving from Jabavu after one of its officials had criticised the National

Educational Association, of which he was part.[4] Jabavu was, however, no puppet of Lovedale. He was strong-headed and frustrated as well by the controls exercised by the missionaries. At first he had been relatively free to write what he liked, but, after complaints from whites about *Isigidimi*'s 'political tendency', Dr Stewart warned Jabavu to be more moderate. Stewart found it necessary to 'eviscerate' a 'very political' article which in particular criticised the Prime Minister, Gordon Sprigg, and the governor, Sir Bartle Frere. Later, John Chalmers, Tiyo Soga's biographer and former colleague, wrote to Stewart saying he was disgusted with *Isigidimi*, which in his view was far too political, 'Jabavu-ish' and Methodist. And, he added, 'I do wish the editor would have that conceit knocked out of him of introducing Latin and English so extensively.'[5] When Jabavu used *Isigidimi* to comment on the parliamentary elections and support the candidature of James Rose-Innes, sharp differences arose between editor and patron.[6] According to Jabavu, his political involvement almost cost him his 'daily bread'.[7] Faced with the alternatives of suppressing his views and carrying on at Lovedale or setting out on an independent course, he handed in his resignation on 29 May 1884, three months before his contract was due to expire.[8] While Jabavu stayed until September, there was considerable acrimony between him and Stewart, similar no doubt to the alienation that was commonly occurring between many politicised Africans and the missionaries.[9]

Now 24 years old, recently married and matriculated, Jabavu had to look elsewhere for a suitable career. Several avenues beckoned. He already owned a farm in the Peddie district and could go back to teaching, but his sights were set higher. First he considered taking up law, then decided that his real calling was journalism.[10] He investigated the possibility of setting up an independent African newspaper. For some time this had been one of the aims of the emerging intellectuals. Meshach Pelem, for example, had written to Jabavu while he was still with *Isigidimi*, encouraging him to start a newspaper to give expression to the feelings of the African people, and remarking that for a man of his talents to remain fettered at Lovedale was like being buried alive.[11]

Jabavu drew up detailed plans for an independent newspaper, but was faced with the obstacle of finance. An opportunity presented itself after he had displayed his considerable political talents in the 1884 election as a canvasser for James Rose-Innes. Impressed by his plans and his ability, Richard Rose-Innes, James's brother, and James Weir, both from King William's Town, agreed to enter into a joint guarantee for Jabavu at a local bank.[12] Weir was a merchant and Richard Rose-Innes a lawyer with an extensive African clientele. Regarding them as liberals in the tradition of Saul Solomon, Jabavu had no difficulty in supporting their political cause against the views of the majority of white colonists. They, in turn, were no doubt impressed after the election in Victoria East by the potential of African voters and of an independent black newspaper.[13]

The way was now open for Jabavu to go ahead with his plans. He toured the eastern Cape to drum up support for the venture and wrote to local people, public figures and sympathisers, informing them of his plans and asking for aid.[14] As if to rub salt in the wounds, he also placed a full-page advertisement in *Isigidimi* to publicise *Imvo* among Xhosa readers.[15] A printing contract was entered into with the *Cape Mercury*.

The first issue of Jabavu's new newspaper was scheduled to appear on 27 October 1884, but it was stopped by its promoters because it treated missionaries 'after a free-lance fashion'. This led to a showdown between Jabavu and the managerial board. He insisted that he was 'not their tool' and must be free to conduct the paper as he pleased.[16] This event illustrated the dilemma for Africans of co-operating with whites. Having determined for nationalistic reasons to mobilise politically, they were confronted with the need for compromises through their alliances with white politicians and sympathisers.

Jabavu made his point and on Monday 3 November 1884 the first issue of his new *Imvo Zabantsundu* (Native Opinion) appeared. This was a landmark occasion in the political history of South Africa. It won for its brilliant founder, editor and proprietor a place in South Africa's history and renown in the eastern Cape. Edited by Jabavu for almost 40 years until his death in 1921, *Imvo* rapidly became a widely respected institution in African society and in colonial politics.

The founding of *Imvo* was an integral part of the wider process of African mobilisation within the colonial system in the 1880s – another reflection of the assertiveness that was everywhere becoming evident on the part of Africans. It took place alongside and in tandem with the emergence of new organisations, the rise of interest in parliamentary politics and the growth of critical attitudes towards the role of the church and education. A concomitant mobilisation was also taking place in the economic and professional spheres, as the launching of *Imvo* reflected. The new generation used the press to call on their countrymen to become not just teachers and clerks, but shopkeepers, lawyers, wagon-makers, builders, journalists, printers, butchers, hoteliers and farmers – all occupations traditionally reserved for whites. In doing so, they were expressing a real determination to advance and 'develop the nation'.[17]

The themes of mobility and advancement can be seen at work in individual lives. Andrew Gontshi, who, as we have seen, founded two Transkeian political organisations, began his career as an interpreter and clerk. By 1880 he had become a law agent. At the end of 1881 he was supporting moves to form an organisation that would help Africans start their own businesses by providing loans. The body would also submit political grievances to the government.[18] Even though the envisaged organisation did not materialise, Gontshi proceeded on his own initiative. He opened a shop, which failed, and then started farming, all the while continuing with his law agency work.[19]

Other political figures also began to launch new enterprises and seek professional qualifications. The energetic Paul Xiniwe, whom we have come across in his work in the NEA and Imbumba, was persuaded by Jabavu to leave his teaching post in Port Elizabeth and follow him to King William's Town, where in 1887 he opened the first hotel for Africans in the colony.[20] Xiniwe soon expanded his business activities and became one of the leading entrepreneurs who emerged from the eastern Cape mission schools. He later opened a temperance hotel in King, costing around £2000. It was described as 'in every sense of the term, a grand hotel', and became a favourite venue for social and political gatherings.[21] Far from being isolated cases, these initiatives were part of a whole process of social, political and economic mobilisation that was taking place as Africans self-consciously adapted to the challenges of colonial society.

Imvo's broad political significance can also be gauged from its links with various local agents and representatives in the eastern Cape and further afield. Most of its agents were community leaders whose names appear frequently in this book.[22] They included Paul Xiniwe and George Qaba, both local Imbumba leaders, in Port Elizabeth; the Rev. Benjamin Dlepu, chairman of the Cradock branch of Imbumba; John Gawler, founder of the NEA, who lived in Keiskamma Hoek; and David Malasi, president of the Thembu Teachers' Association and the South African Native Association, in Glen Grey.* Further afield, Charles Ntozini, one of the earliest politically active mission people, now living at Jagersfontein, was the agent on the diamond fields; while Saul Msane, who later became a leader of the Natal Native Congress and South African Native National Congress, represented *Imvo* at Edendale in Natal. Other agents included the respected Rev. Boyce Mama and Thomas Mqanda at Peddie; and Jonathan Tunyiswa at Mount Coke, near King William's Town. Mqanda and Tunyiswa would found and lead for many years the South African Native Congress, about which more anon.

Imvo was not only welcomed with open arms by the new elite, but indeed was planned in collaboration with them, as Jabavu's pre-launch meetings in various parts of the eastern Cape make clear. The activists of the early 1880s responded enthusiastically to the new lines of communication and the new forum for political expression opened by Jabavu, sending in regular reports of social and political activities in their various districts and reacting to news and views published in *Imvo*. In a short time the new newspaper brought together the fragmented pattern of African politics in the eastern Cape into a much more cohesive whole. As well as adding to the confidence and effectiveness of the emerging elite, it became a potent unifying force among Africans.

As a result the new-style activists started to be noticed in colonial society, and not always with approval. The *Alice Times* commented that 'simultaneous with the starting of the Native newspaper, *Imvo*, has arisen among native circles a class of educated or semi-educated young men –

---

* Among the other *Imvo* agents were James Maqubela, also of the SANA, from Dordrecht; Pambani Figlan, secretary of the Manyano of the Xalanga landowners; and his brother, James, at Burnshill; Theodore Ndwandwa, Veldtman's right-hand man, at Butterworth; Joel Gundwana and Augustus Bell, leaders of opposing camps in the 1884 parliamentary election, in Herschel; Richard Nukuna of the Queenstown Native Vigilance Association; J.W. Sondlo, secretary and treasurer of the local village management board, at nearby Lesseyton; and Walter Rubusana, vice-president of the NEA in 1887, at Peelton.

both Kafirs and Fingoes – who aspire to be the leaders of Native thought and opinion'.[23] Of course, the school people and their backers outside the mission stations had cultivated these aspirations for some time, and it was their aspirations that had generated *Imvo*, not the other way around. The *Alice Times* added that, having climbed to 'their present proud elevation' on the ladder of their basic education, the new men had kicked it away 'and now stand without leading strings on their dizzy height'.[24]

What was really at issue in this piece, written by a missionary, was the loss of missionary control over the school people. From the start there was a simmering feud between *Imvo* and *Isigidimi*. In 1885 a major debate on native education erupted, with Dr Stewart and Lovedale on one side and Jabavu and a vocal section of mission school graduates on the other. At the heart of the debate was the contention of Stewart and other missionaries that classics-based education among Africans had been a failure and that in the 'native mind' it had produced a positive evil.[25] What they were in effect promoting was an inferior education based on the assumption that 'the first need of the Kafir people is not the vote, nor a few matriculation passes, but the Gospel of Christ' and the evangelisation of their countrymen.[26] Discriminating on the grounds of colour not merit, this was unacceptable to Africans. Without Latin they could not matriculate or proceed to university like white pupils and would therefore be fitted only for positions of subservience in colonial life.[27] They vigorously attacked the missionary thesis. 'Lovedalian', an *Imvo* correspondent from Kimberley (probably Meshach Pelem or the Rev. Gwayi Tyamzashe), described Stewart's statement as a clear case of *suppressio veri et suggestio falsi*. Going back 20 years, he listed the names of people who had studied classics at Lovedale and who now held respectable and responsible positions, and asked what positive evils and failure study of the classics had produced in them.[28]

The emergence of *Imvo* as an independent, assertive African mouthpiece undoubtedly put missionary paternalism under the microscope and brought into much clearer relief the missionary–African relationship. *Imvo* enabled Africans to express their point of view for the first time and exposed missionary interests as divergent from those of Africans in a way *Indaba*, *Isigidimi* and other newspapers could never have done. That their interests did clash is certain. Dr Stewart, for instance, was much more concerned about the effects of the emergent political and educational organisations, the formation of *Imvo* and the demand for equal educational opportunities than colonial hostility to African rights, which was the central concern of the new generation.[29]

The sensitivity of both camps to the question of control or independence was deepened by the feud that developed between *Imvo* and *Isigidimi*. When *Imvo* was launched, it met with an extensive and generally welcoming response from the colonial press; *Isigidimi* remained, however, silent, 'neither expressing praise nor dispraise'.[30] The two newspapers lost no opportunity to cast aspersions at each other.[31] Underlying these clashes were deeper tensions between the missionaries, and what they stood for, and the class of people they had created and the role that educated Africans desired for themselves in colonial society. It was a battle *Imvo* soon won. While subscribers 'came in shoals and the demand for *Imvo* increased rapidly',[32] *Isigidimi* went into rapid decline. Its readership dropped significantly and it reverted to monthly publication instead of fortnightly. After William Gqoba, the noted writer who had succeeded Jabavu as editor, died in 1888, *Isigidimi*'s missionary sponsors decided to close the newspaper after 19 years, as it was no longer paying for itself.[33] The 'Xhosa Messenger' had lost its voice.

Once it got off the ground, *Imvo* provided a link not only between literate Africans, but also between them and traditional leaders. Chiefdom authorities were kept informed by the newspaper, even if this required having someone read it to them, and used its columns to state their case and report on their activities. The example of Umhlangaso J.S. Faku, so-called 'prime minister' of the independent Pondoland, illustrates this well. A subscriber to *Imvo*, he regularly protested about actions of the Cape government in letters to *Imvo* and published proclamations on behalf of the Mpondo rulers in its pages.[34] According to Faku, *Imvo* was 'the national newspaper'.[35] Paramount Dalindyebo of the Thembu similarly requested the newspaper to publicise certain matters relating to his people.[36] The colonial government was well aware of the importance of *Imvo* as an opinion-former and disseminator of news in the traditionalist rural areas. At a meeting with Dalindyebo and the Thembu in 1885, for example, the Secretary for Native Affairs took the trouble to refute certain 'erroneous' ideas that might have been created by *Imvo*.[37]

One of the outstanding features of the first few years of the newspaper's existence was its defence of the territorial integrity of the Transkeian chiefdoms, particularly the efforts of the Mpondo to preserve their independence against colonial encroachment. Towards the end of 1886, when war between the Mpondo and the Cape seemed a distinct possibility, Jabavu highlighted the situation and wrote several editorials criticising 'the unyielding spirit of the Cape Ministry'.[38] When a peaceful settlement was eventually achieved, a correspondent wrote in Xhosa praise fashion: 'I am thankful to you, son of Jabavu that you have defeated the enemy of the Pondos. You have defeated the government and its armies, destroyed its war chariots, scattered its horsemen. The tails of the Pondo cattle you have saved; the souls of a thousand Pondos you have saved; the land of the Pondos you have saved; today there reigneth peace in Pondoland and this has been done through you in this paper of yours.'[39]

In addition to its concern for African independence, the new 'Native Opinion' aired and sought redress for a wide range of African grievances. These included the pass laws, location regulations, liquor laws, the administration of justice in the courts and 'anti-native' legislation emanating from parliament. The newspaper also contributed in no small way to the dramatic increase in African voters between 1882 and 1886. Jabavu spurred on various communities to register as many people as possible to become voters and was unceasingly vigilant about any attempts to disenfranchise Africans.[40]

Just as important as the raised level of consciousness was the unity *Imvo* helped engender. It widened the focus of Africans by bringing Cape politics to the attention of local interest groups and encouraging them to act in a co-ordinated way. Not only did it link community leaders, agents, reporters and correspondents directly, but by energetically analysing colonial politics from the African viewpoint and communicating this to its readers, it forged new views and a bond between people across old 'tribal' and parochial lines. Unlike *Isigidimi*, *Imvo* was not merely a restricted forum for the opinions of school people only, but a purposely created political vehicle designed to serve the interests of all classes of Cape Africans.

The newspaper was distributed throughout the Cape Colony and

Transkei, as well as in the Orange Free State, Basutoland, Natal and the South African Republic. When gold was discovered on the Witwatersrand, agents there distributed the paper in the new mining centres. Jabavu's main line of communication was the network of mission stations, churches and schools, the 'old school tie', his former *Isigidimi* contacts, the emergent political organisations and leaders, and chiefly authorities. He had distribution points in virtually every local community in the eastern Cape. Community leaders acted as his agents: they had to ensure circulation in their areas, canvass new subscribers and chase up those whose payments were overdue, and represent readers' complaints to the editor.[41] Public meetings were held periodically in some places for these purposes.[42]

Finances were always a problem. Richard Rose-Innes explained that many readers 'expected never to be asked to pay'.[43] Even the Native Affairs Department had to be reminded that it was not keeping up with its payments.[44] Soon the guarantors found to their dismay that the bank overdraft was approaching four figures: something had to be done. Accordingly, they appointed an accountant and bookkeeper and placed Jabavu on a small monthly salary, 'which he cheerfully accepted'. Eventually, financial stability was restored. As promised, the guarantors thereupon handed back full control of the newspaper to the proprietor.[45]

Imvo's agents were also prominent amongst the correspondents on whom *Imvo* largely depended for its community news. The paper never had a large staff and was therefore heavily reliant on voluntary contributions and the use of material from exchange copies of colonial newspapers. At first Jabavu employed his brother-in-law, Benjamin Sakuba, as a sub-editor, but he left in 1887 to start a business of his own.[46] He seems to have been replaced by W.D. Soga, who was prominent in the King William's Town Native Vigilance Association from its inception in 1887.[47]

The paper had no shortage of voluntary contributions. The Xhosa columns were filled with letters and reports of meetings and social activities. These covered every conceivable event, from tea meetings, concerts and weddings to religious gatherings, teachers' and farmers' meetings, and political events. Even the names of the guests who stayed every month at Paul Xiniwe's hotel were noted. The pages of the newspaper provide a treasure house of information on the social history of the new intellectuals and activists. The English columns, which concentrated more on colonial and wider local politics, provided an interface between African and white opinion in the Cape. With the founding of *Imvo*, these frontiers had moved firmly away from Lovedale and the missionaries to King William's Town and Jabavu.

In sum, *Imvo* made an immense impact on colonial politics. Firstly, it circumscribed and gave momentum to the whole process of African political mobilisation which had been gathering pace since the beginning of the 1880s. Secondly, it brought Africans firmly into the system of colonial, particularly electoral, politics. And, thirdly, it drew grudging acknowledgement from the colonial establishment of the importance of Africans as a constituency. If parties and politicians from then on treated questions of importance to Africans with impunity, it was at their peril. By *Imvo*'s third birthday Jabavu could state without fear of contradiction that, as the standard-bearer of 'Native Opinion', his newspaper was now a power in the land.[48]

12

The Union of Native Vigilance
Associations, 1887

... about the severest blow that has ever been aimed at Native
rights since representative institutions were introduced into this
country.

– *Imvo Zabantsundu*, 23 March 1887

Despite the centralising influence of the 'national newspaper',
Imvo Zabantsundu, the emergent political leaders in the eastern Cape had
difficulty in constructing a representative region-wide body that could co-
ordinate and give direction to their activities and organisations in a formal
manner. By the mid-1880s, there was a readiness for political combination
which needed to be translated into reality. Africans were everywhere
mobilising politically and beginning to exert their rights independently of
missionary and magisterial control. Activists and intellectuals, operating
in strong school and church networks, had common aims, and envisaged
co-operation with their counterparts, but were still largely area-bound.

As we have seen, at least ten new organisations now existed. Among
them, Imbumba Yama Nyama operated in Port Elizabeth and the
eastern districts, the South African Native Association and the Thembu
Association in Glen Grey, the Manyano nge Mvo Zabantsundu (Union of
Native Opinion) in the southern Transkei, and the King William's Town
Native Vigilance Association. Initially, the only really operative region-
wide organisation was the Native Educational Association, which did not
claim for itself an explicitly political role.

The lively debates of the day increasingly pointed to the need for a strong umbrella body to consolidate the mobilisation process of the early 1880s. Leaders of public opinion and the newspapers, first *Isigidimi*, and then *Imvo*, continually emphasised this. In 1886 the call for a representative regional organisation was once more pursued seriously by the old Healdtown stalwart Richard Kawa, who meanwhile had moved back to his home district of Peddie, and by his former school friend and political ally in Glen Grey, James Pelem. Writing in *Imvo* under the heading 'How about us going to Cape Town?', Kawa said Africans should set up a meeting where they could discuss matters such as land and franchise rights and send delegates to raise them with the government in Cape Town.[1] Pelem supported the proposal and suggested that a meeting be held in King William's Town in January 1887 for this purpose. He listed a whole host of familiar community leaders who should attend.[2] Boyce Mama from Peddie, Nathaniel Umhalla, and Pato Lusaseni from Nqamakwe added their support for the idea.[3] However, even though *Imvo* was still publishing the names of people Pelem wished to see attend up to a fortnight before the scheduled date,[4] the meeting did not come off. Nevertheless, according to Nathaniel Umhalla, some people did get together to discuss Pelem's plans and formed a committee to see if these could be implemented. Some outstanding leaders were represented on this committee: Jabavu, Makiwane, Mzimba, Kawa, Umhalla, the Rev. Charles Pamla and Pelem himself.[5]

John Tengo Jabavu now came to the fore. First, he tried to extend the scope of the NEA into a more representative and politically effective movement.[6] Reacting to growing hostility to black interests in parliament, he declared in August 1886: 'Our voice should be heard. While there is no common understanding between us there is no hope, and no time should be lost to establish it. The Native Educational Association which should take its undoubted place as the guiding star of the native people should take up this subject without delay, and devise means whereby a Union of the Natives for political and general purposes might be formed.'[7] At an NEA meeting in Grahamstown in January 1887, he proposed a new constitution providing for the formation of local branch associations, which would be represented annually at a central NEA conference.[8] In this way the organisation would become more effective and representative instead of relying on a scattered individual membership. The meeting appointed a committee to investigate Jabavu's proposals and instructed it to report at the next gathering in July.[9] But for some unexplained reason this meeting turned down the new constitution submitted by the committee under Jabavu.[10]

Though, organisationally, nothing concrete had yet emerged, the idea of co-operation and unity was slowly gathering force. Africans in the eastern Cape were becoming increasingly mobile and showing a willingness and ability to work together. Inter-town and inter-district co-operation became an increasingly regular feature in all spheres of life: church conferences, annual meetings of the Independent Order of True Templars, and regular inter-town cricket tournaments, which started in December 1884 between Port Elizabeth, East London, King William's Town and Grahamstown.[11] All these and similar developments showed that local groups were beginning to link together to create a new integrated framework for regional co-operation.

What finally provided the trigger for a regional organisation, encompassing under its wing all existing groups, was the Parliamentary Voters Registration Act passed by parliament in September 1887. Known by Africans as *Tung' umlomo* (The sewing up of the mouth), this Act extended the franchise to the newly acquired Transkeian Territories, but changed the rules by invalidating tribal tenure as a basis for the property qualification.[12] As most Africans in the Transkei held land on tribal or communal tenure, this was a direct threat to their interests.[13] *Tung' umlomo* was the culmination of several years of efforts on the part of colonists to have African voting rights restricted.[14] White fears of being swamped at the polling booth had been heightened by the successes already achieved by Africans in electoral politics and by the threat posed electorally by the annexation of areas with large African populations to the Cape, such as Thembuland in 1885.

From the moment the government signalled its intention in March 1887 to introduce such a measure, *Imvo* protested vigorously. For several months its editorials and articles concentrated on the bill, which was 'about the severest blow that has ever been aimed at Native rights since representative institutions were introduced in this country'.[15] According to *Imvo*, having taken away their weapons under the Disarmament Act, Sprigg now sought to remove even their constitutional weapons.[16] Urged on by *Imvo*, African communities in more than 15 of the main towns in the eastern Cape organised meetings to discuss the legislation.*

Reports of the protest movement provide a glimpse of the political network that had developed in the eastern Cape since the new-style activists began organising at the turn of the decade. Meetings were held throughout the region, the names of their organisers usually familiar from organisational politics before, and the subsequent reports sent to *Imvo* demonstrated both the extent of communication that existed between leaders in various areas and the sense of unity that prevailed. Besides meetings at district level, there were also gatherings in local areas where African populations were concentrated, indicating that they were outgrowths of community feeling. In the Queenstown district, for example, the people at the Oxkraal and Kamastone locations, Glen Grey, Lesseyton and Queenstown itself mobilised locally and sent representatives to joint district meetings.[17] At Oxkraal and Kamastone alone, 600 people signed a petition to parliament opposing the bill.[18] In East London a deputation of people representing various parts of the district waited on the local member of parliament to express disquiet at the new legislation.[19] Similarly, meetings organised by the newly established King William's Town Native Vigilance Association in May, July, and September were attended by delegates from never less than eight areas in the district.[20]

But the new political communicators did not operate in isolation from the rest of the African population. They worked at grassroots level within and on behalf of African communities. An impressive 19-page petition sent by the King Native Vigilance Association to parliament was signed by just under 1000 people from various part of the district.[21] Fully four-fifths of the signatories were non-literate people and their crosses were witnessed by their literate compatriots. Similarly, the East London delegation that lobbied the local member of parliament included members 'not professing to enjoy the privilege of registered voters'.[22] The new forms of mobilisation

* These included Port Elizabeth, Cradock, Herschel, Grahamstown, Seymour, Stockenstrom, Fort Beaufort, Healdtown, Peddie, King William's Town, East London, Queenstown, Whittlesea (i.e. Oxkraal and Kamastone), the Fingoland districts, and the Thembu areas of Glen Grey, Dordrecht, Cala and Engcobo.

thus encompassed a wider field than just registered voters and school people.

The main thrust of the campaign against the Voters Registration Act came from Port Elizabeth and King William's Town, where Jabavu was active. The campaign really started in earnest at a meeting in Port Elizabeth on 16 July 1887, which resolved to request the Governor not to give assent to the proposed bill. Failing this, it suggested that four delegates supported by a petition should be sent to England to put the matter before the British government and people.[23] Five days later, the King William's Town Vigilance Association came out in support of the proposed actions.[24] One of its members, Philip Mali, justified the idea of a delegation on the basis of pre-colonial political traditions: according to Xhosa precedent, the mandate at Hintsa's Great Place could not be set aside by the courts of Ndlambe or Ngqika. There was always a court of appeal from the decision of Ndlambe's court to the court of Hintsa.[25]

Jabavu then made a special trip to Port Elizabeth to co-ordinate protests with activists there.[26] They had set up a Native Committee to organise the deputation and to keep the Colonial Office in London informed.[27] The secretary of the committee was Frank Makwena, who had been vice-president of the now defunct Imbumba. Though the organisation had expired, its former leaders, like Isaac Wauchope, Peter Rwexu and George Qaba, were still directing political affairs in Port Elizabeth.[28]

As a result of his visit, it appears that agreement was reached that Jabavu – through *Imvo* – would take the lead. Mobilisers from Port Elizabeth now started directing their correspondence through Jabavu, a useful middle-man with experience and contacts. He probably also finalised with them 'The Petition of the South African Natives to the Queen', which was printed in *Imvo* early in August 1887, and subsequently adopted in each of the eastern Cape districts.[29] Following his Port Elizabeth visit, Jabavu attended a meeting organised by various interest groups in the Queenstown district to discuss the Act.[30] A broad campaign was taking shape. Besides making representations to both the Cape and British governments, Africans at the same time also made contact with sympathetic opposition members from the eastern Cape constituencies and other 'friends of the natives' at home and abroad.[31] As early as March, Jabavu wrote to F.W. Chesson of the

Aborigines Protection Society, saying, 'We are marshalling the local forces, but we fear the battle will have to be fought out in England'.[32] In addition to writing regularly to Chesson, Jabavu kept a small group of Liberal MPs and British newspapers informed about local developments, mainly by sending them copies of *Imvo*.[33] He hoped that the overseas lobby, strengthened by the envisaged deputation, would be able to counteract the 'duplicity' of the reports emanating from the Cape Governor and ministers,[34] and cause the British government to refuse assent to the Act.

The decision to take the struggle to England marked a new departure in African politics. The gravity with which the new leaders viewed a future without full constitutional rights and protection and the intractability of the colonial government led them to register the fullest protest possible. Here again they were asserting their political independence and confidence. No longer were they satisfied with mere reassurances from colonial missionaries, officials and politicians.

At the end of August the campaign took a further step forward when Jabavu, no doubt acting in concert with various local groups, issued a notice convening the first-ever regional conference of political organisations in the eastern Cape.[35] The aim was to discuss *Tung' umlomo* as well as other matters, including the formation of a permanent umbrella organisation to look after African interests.[36] The date for the conference was set first for 20 September and later for 6 October 1887 in King William's Town.[37]

This conference was a historic event in African politics. It was the first combined political meeting of Africans in the eastern Cape, and reflected a hitherto unequalled sense of unity among them. It was attended by about 100 people, including between two and four official delegates from no less than 13 eastern Cape districts. Elijah Makiwane, the respected elder statesman and past president of the NEA, was in the chair.[38]

The list of delegates to the meeting provides an indication of the important and continuing role in local politics of the various organisations whose emergence has been traced in this book. There were many familiar faces. The old Thembu Association stalwarts Samuel Sigenu, Thomas Zwedala and James Pelem represented Glen Grey; while Mankayi Rengqe and Solomon Kalipa, undisputed leaders of the flourishing local landowning community, represented Cala. Green Sikundla and William

Mtoba, the first two presidents of the King William's Town Native Vigilance Association, were delegated by that district. The affiliations of delegates from other districts were perhaps more obscure, but no less instructive. One of the delegates from Peddie, Thomas Mqanda, was active in local politics and later became a major political figure as president of the South African Native Congress.[39] P.D. Tshacila from Engcobo was secretary of the Transkei Teachers' Association and the Engcobo Native Vigilance Association.[40] Much would be heard in future also of his colleague J.Z. Tantsi. The Queenstown delegates, Joshua Sishuba (headman from a prominent Mfengu clan in Oxkraal), Harry Mtombeni (a Kamastone-based law agent) and J.W. Sondlo (secretary and treasurer of the Lesseyton Village Management Board), were well-known community leaders.[41] The Grahamstown representatives were Robert Xholla and Samuel Danga, both still prominent there in the 1900s.[42] In addition to the official delegates, major figures such as Nathaniel Umhalla, William Ntsikana, Benjamin Sakuba and Paul Xiniwe attended the meeting, and there were no doubt many others – people like Walter Rubusana and Jonathan Tunyiswa, for example. Letters and telegrams of support were also read from communities which did not manage to send delegates. This was undoubtedly a deeply representative gathering and a sign of the level of organisation existing throughout the eastern Cape and southern Transkei by 1887.

The two most important absences were representatives from Port Elizabeth, whose leaders were nevertheless still in touch with Jabavu, and the newly formed Manyano in Fingoland.[43] Though the Voters Registration Act extended the franchise to Africans in the Transkei for the first time, while simultaneously restricting the qualifications for Africans in general, the Manyano decided by a large majority at a meeting on 30 September not to join in the protests against it.[44] Its leading figure, Andrew Gontshi, even supported the Act, saying that nowhere did it discriminate specifically against black people; in his view it ensured that only 'advanced' people would vote and not those who were unfit to do so, such as the mass of 'red' people.[45] Gontshi's views were at odds with the overwhelming weight of opinion in the Transkei and the colony. They were even opposed within the two organisations he had helped start: Pato Lusaseni was among those in the Fingoland Manyano who disagreed with his position, and Alexander

Dukwana Ntsikana from the neighbouring Kentani-based Association for the Advancement of the Ngqika attended the conference in King William's Town, though he was not listed as an official delegate.[46]

In an attempt to put African organisational politics on a more formal, effective and co-ordinated footing, the historic King William's Town conference resolved to form an Imbumba Eliliso Lomzi Yabantsundu, or Union of Native Vigilance Associations. Affiliated local groups in every district were to form branches to guard African interests at a local level, in what would be called an Iliso Lomzi or Native Vigilance Association. Existing local structures were to serve as the basis for them. They were to be co-ordinated through *Imvo* and a King William's Town-based executive committee under Jabavu as secretary-general. In this role Jabavu was empowered to summon a meeting of the general body whenever the need arose. He would be assisted by his committee, consisting of Nathaniel Umhalla, Cobus Mpondo, Paul Xiniwe and Benjamin Sakuba.[47]

The King William's Town conference reviewed the situation created by the Voters Registration Act, which had come into force on 1 September, and confirmed the decision to send a four-man delegation to England. The nominees put forward by the district meetings and the general conference included J.T. Jabavu, Elijah Makiwane, Isaac Wauchope, Andrew Gontshi, Samuel Sigenu, Solomon Kalipa, James Pelem, Daniel Dwanya, Nowawe (widow of the Ngqika chief Sandile) and the Rev. James Read. The nomination of Nowawe, Andrew Gontshi (although he had not attended) and Read, son of James Read, who had set up the first mission near Ngqika's Great Place, together with Dyani Tshatshu, in 1816, was a recognition of the continuing influence of a 70-year-old tradition and network connecting Ntsikana, Tiyo Soga and the Ngqika chieftaincy.

When the time for elections came, the people who received the most votes were Jabavu, Read and the Glen Grey leaders Pelem and Sigenu.[48] The conference decided that the delegates should leave for England as soon as practicable after the framing of the new voters' lists for the 1888 elections, when it could be clearly ascertained that the new Act had deprived large numbers of Africans of their franchise rights. In the meantime, funds would be collected and an all-out effort made to register all those people who qualified as voters.[49] The conference resolved, furthermore, that if the definition of tribal or communal tenure was used indiscriminately to disqualify African voters, test cases would be brought before the Supreme Court to challenge the disqualifications.

When the King William's Town conference ended, the leaders immediately got down to the tasks they had set themselves. The shiny new logo of Imbumba was soon being conspicuously displayed on the letterheads of the indefatigable J.T. Jabavu.[50]

13

Vigilance Associations challenge
Tung' umlomo

We therefore pray your most Excellent Majesty that in the event
of the said measure, which is most obnoxious and quite adverse to
our best interests as Natives, passing both Houses of Parliament,
Your Majesty will exercise Your Royal Prerogative in our favour.
– Petition of Native Inhabitants of the Location of Oxkraal, 1887

For more than a year after the King William's Town conference of
October 1887, the leaders that emerged at the meeting busied themselves
with important matters: the proposed delegation to England, the formation
of local Native Vigilance Associations, the sitting of the voting registration
courts and the campaign for the 1888 general elections, which were just
around the corner. *Imvo*, the 'national newspaper', exhorted people to
action and reports about local efforts came streaming in.

The overseas delegation did not materialise. Although Jabavu pressed
ahead with arrangements, and some £300 was reportedly collected in
various areas, it soon became clear that the idea was not feasible.[1] Not all the
African groups and leaders agreed with this step and influential 'friends of
the natives' both at home and abroad counselled against a deputation. Glad
to have acquired the franchise for the first time, the Fingoland Manyano
across the Kei, for example, decided not to join in the campaign.[2] Then,
differences between Nathaniel Umhalla and Jabavu over the appeal to the
Crown became a public issue.[3] Soon afterwards, the respected Charles
Pamla, the first African minister ordained in the Cape Colony, created a
furore within African politics when he told Prime Minister Sprigg in an

interview that he quite agreed with some points of the Registration Act and assured him he had given no support to the appeal to England.[4] Coming at such a sensitive time, Pamla's well-publicised actions gave the government's plans much-needed legitimacy. Jabavu and many others regarded them as an ugly betrayal of African interests.[5] More significantly, James Rose-Innes informed Jabavu at the end of October 1887 that although he disagreed strongly with the alteration to the franchise, he 'could not possibly be a party to any agitation which would have for its object the interference of the Home Government with the liberty of the parliamentary government of this country'.[6] At the same time, both the British Secretary of State and F.W. Chesson of the Aborigines Protection Society warned that no good would be done by the proposed deputation.[7] Jabavu and his colleagues in the new Union of Native Vigilance Associations reluctantly dropped the idea.

In accordance with the resolutions of the King William's Town conference, the focus shifted to the formation of local Native Vigilance Associations, whose immediate objective was to secure the registration of as many African voters as possible for the forthcoming elections. Known in Xhosa as Iliso Lomzi, or literally 'eye of the house', a vigilance committee was set up in each of the main areas and from these sprang several permanent Native Vigilance Associations to safeguard local rights. The new associations confirmed the intention of local activists to co-operate henceforth on a formal and regular basis.

A good example of the post-conference focus on setting up vigilance associations is provided by the Herschel district, which had not attended the King William's Town deliberations. Formerly known as the Wittebergen Reserve, this diamond-shaped district, tucked into the north-east corner of the Cape where its borders with the Orange Free State and Basutoland met, was inhabited by a mixed population of Hlubi, Tlokwa, Sotho, Thembu, Mfengu and 'Bruinmenschen', totalling 25,000 in 1891.[8] Jabavu's first visit to Herschel in November 1887, shortly after the King William's Town conference, symbolically incorporated the district into the eastern Cape network of politics. He was given an enthusiastic welcome by a cavalcade of 50 horsemen at the end of a day-long journey on horse-back from Aliwal North.[9] His visit came at the invitation of local leaders (who had asked him to represent them at the conference) to inform and advise them about the current political situation. Two meetings were organised for the locals to hear Jabavu, each attracting in the vicinity of 500 people.[10] They were held at the Wittebergen and Bensonvale mission stations, whose light, Jabavu remarked, was beginning to chase away the surrounding darkness in an area where the 'emblems of civilisation' were to be seen only here and there.[11] This comment revealed much about the political and economic development of the Herschel district. New-style politics took root around the mission stations – there was a third important one, St Michael's, at Dulcies Nek – and radiated out from them into the surrounding areas. The missions were also the foundation upon which a prosperous peasantry emerged in Herschel during the late nineteenth century. As Colin Bundy has shown, many of the most prosperous farmers lived around the mission stations, lying as they did in the fertile lowland areas of the district and situated as they were on the main transport routes.[12] This upper stratum of peasants took the lead in local politics.

The chairman for at least three years of the Iliso Lomzi which emerged in Herschel after 1887 was Joel Gundwana.[13] An early correspondent in *Isigidimi* and one of J.W. Sauer's main supporters in the 1884 election, he remained a leading local spokesman until Union in 1910.[14] His main opponent in 1884, and for some time subsequently, was the headman Augustus Bell from Dulcies Nek. In 1890 Gundwana offered to resign because of Bell's opposition to him, but 'the chief and community' dissuaded him from doing so.[15] The chief in question, probably the influential Mehlomakulu, had led the Hlubi into Herschel after the establishment of the Orange Free State in 1854.[16] He supported the new forms of politics and, as head of the largest group in the district, his voice clearly carried great weight.[17] Mehlomakulu's sons also participated in the activities of Iliso, as did other active chiefs and headmen who all exerted considerable local power. A correspondent from Dulcies Nek complained in *Imvo* in 1898 that, on ignoring the chief's directive on how to vote, he came back to find his lands confiscated.[18]

The fact that Joel Gundwana was said to be much liked by the chiefs perhaps had something to do with his political standing.[19] One of the grievances against the local magistrate mentioned to Jabavu was that only headmen were allowed to speak at meetings called by him; this entrenched their power.[20] Working together with the progressive headmen and chiefs was a tiny educated elite centred on the missions or magistracy. They included the law agent Shad B. Mama, the Rev. A. Masiza and the teachers S.T. Mdliva and Abram Parkies. These teachers were no doubt members of the Herschel Teachers' Association (established in 1888), which met in turn at the three mission stations on a regular basis.[21]

As the meetings of Iliso, the considerable electoral campaigning, and the existence of the teachers' association all show, politics in Herschel, as in other areas, were based on a common pattern and network of activity.[22] Permanent vigilance associations like the one at Herschel emerged in King William's Town, Queenstown and many other places in 1887. They served as prototypes for hundreds of similar local bodies which came into being throughout South Africa, as far afield as Rhodesia, the Transvaal and Natal, in the succeeding decades. Their designation, shape and aims became institutionalised in African politics in the twentieth century.

When the registration courts sat in 1888 to ratify the new voters' lists, a concerted attack was launched on the African franchise. In some areas wholesale objections were made against all the Africans who applied for the franchise, based on three main arguments: the communal tenure disqualification, insufficient property values and the claim that some Africans were aliens under the terms of the Cape constitution because they were born outside the colony as it existed then.[23] The Afrikaner Bond, which had the most to fear from the African vote and waged a deliberate campaign against it, was usually responsible for raising these objections.[24] But local African spokesmen were well prepared to counter them. Encouraged and guided by *Imvo*,[25] they co-ordinated registration applications, hired the services of lawyers and succeeded in getting hundreds of local Africans to attend the sessions. In Queenstown, leaders from various parts of the constituency met in December to discuss strategy and progress.[26] The following month they presented the applications of Africans in their respective field-cornetcies before the registering officers.[27] Dissatisfied with some results, they turned out in force at the final hearings before the civil commissioner early in February 1888. The hearings lasted a week, with local attorneys, assisted by spokesmen like Harry Mtombeni, James Pelem and Richard Nukuna, leading the defence. The *Imvo*'s correspondent described Mtombeni as a man among men for successfully repulsing the Bond's challenge to 84 out of 90 claims from Whittlesea. Around 700 Africans attended the sessions, including most of the headmen from Glen Grey.[28]

This pattern repeated itself elsewhere. In Herschel legal representation was sought and at least 600 people came to substantiate their claims before the registering officer against Bond objections early in January.[29] When the provisional lists came before the magistrate in February, some 700 or 800 people attended.[30] Even the unannounced postponement of the sitting for a week, which caused hundreds of people to descend on the magistracy in vain at a busy time for crop-growing peasants, did not deter them.[31]

In Glen Grey the president of the Thembu Association, Samuel Sigenu, and about 60 other residents who fell within the Wodehouse constituency were present. David Malasi reported that although there were many prominent and wealthy Thembu present, only the names of about 20 of those who owned private property and western-style houses were entered.[32] In East London, where there had been only one African voter before, local action resulted in about 100 new people being registered.[33] In King William's Town, Jabavu, in his capacity as secretary of the Native Vigilance Association, retained the lawyer Richard Rose-Innes to challenge the rejection of 235 African claims by various field-cornets in the compilation of the provisional lists. They succeeded in getting 71 of these claims recognised.[34] Similar action was taken in other areas: the Peddie people hired the Grahamstown barrister H.J. Tamplin; the Cala people retained a lawyer from East London; and Richard Rose-Innes appeared on behalf of locals at the Alice registration court.[35]

Jabavu co-ordinated activities and campaigned tirelessly, both in the field and through his newspaper. For several months the registration issue was the main preoccupation of *Imvo*. Jabavu complained about the heavy legal expenses connected with the campaign.[36] No doubt some of the money collected for the Imbumba deputation to England was used to defray costs.[37]

As a result of the Voters Registration Act some 20,000 voters, or 25 per cent of the electorate, were struck off the lists. Most of these were African and coloured people.[38] In the eastern Cape, where Africans exerted the greatest influence, the drop in voting numbers was 33 per cent overall. The biggest decrease was in the Wodehouse constituency, which included a large part of the future Glen Grey constituency, from a total of 2711 to 1425. In the so-called Tambookie and Umhlanga locations alone, the numbers dropped from around 400 to the 20 or so mentioned by David Malasi.[39] The decrease in the other main constituencies was as follows: Queenstown, 1153; King William's Town, 1049; Victoria East, 317 (all Africans); Fort Beaufort, 583; and Aliwal North (Herschel), 408.[40] Despite this, Africans still constituted important minorities in these voting districts.

In the general election held during the second half of 1888, several seats were decided in favour of 'liberal' candidates by the African voters. In King William's Town, W.J. Warren headed the poll with 943 votes, of which 726 were cast by Africans.[41] Colonial newspapers also attributed to the African vote the return of J.S. Mackay in Uitenhage, Joseph Orpen in Wodehouse, and J. Laing and C.W. Hutton (one of the most outspoken critics of the Voters Registration Act) in Fort Beaufort.[42] The Herschel Africans also played a large part in the return in the Aliwal North seat of liberal, anti-ministerial and anti-Bond candidates: at the two polling stations of Herschel and Bensonvale, J.W. Sauer received 275 out of a total of 555 votes, and E. Orsmond 266 out of 488. The Bond candidates, on the other hand, did not get a single vote at Bensonvale and only eight between them at Herschel.[43] These results confirmed the importance of the new politics among Africans in the eastern Cape.

The 1888 election was the first since Jabavu had started *Imvo*. He involved himself in the campaign with gusto and gave full coverage to developments. Both *Imvo* and *Isigidimi* welcomed the results, and their views on which candidates should be elected were similar,[44] and seemed generally to reflect the broad opinions of the African electorate. However, the election also revealed differences among Africans that would have negative effects in both the immediate and long term.

In King William's Town, Nathaniel Umhalla and Charles Pamla split the African vote by encouraging a group of around 60 voters to support a member of the Sprigg ministry, Colonel Schermbrucker, against the liberal opposition candidates, W.J. Warren and Richard Solomon (nephew of Saul Solomon), who were supported by Jabavu and *Imvo*. Although Warren was returned, Schermbrucker pipped Solomon by just 44 votes for the second seat. His winning total was made up of 874 white and 60 African votes, compared with Solomon's 727 African and 167 white votes.[45] The voting in King William's Town had been preceded by an intense period of electioneering in which senior figures, such as Elijah Makiwane, J.K. Bokwe, Isaac Wauchope, Walter Rubusana and W.K. Ntsikana, sided against Pamla and Umhalla, who were clearly in a minority.[46]

In Queenstown the African vote was split in a similar way. Before the election two meetings of representatives from various parts of the constituency were called to decide on combined action. The final gathering was attended by over 500 people, including Jabavu, who had travelled from King William's Town.[47] But no agreement was reached as to which candidates to support. Instead of combining with the rest of the African voters, James Pelem and a bloc of around 100 Glen Grey people supported the Sprigg candidate, John Frost, who was already assured of victory because he could count on the vote of both the English and Afrikaner voters. According to *Imvo*, this let in the Afrikaner Bond candidate for the second seat, which Africans could have captured for one of the two candidates most sympathetic to their interests if they had combined.[48] Here, then, were some early signs of division within African politics, products of particular local, social and political impulses, which were to crystallise out later in more serious fractures.

The momentum of the politically hectic years of 1887 and 1888 was carried on into 1889. Africans took part in elections for the Legislative Council, the upper chamber of parliament. And when parliament tried to push through new pass laws, protest meetings were held in various districts.[49] A delegation consisting of Jabavu and two of his allies, Elijah Makiwane and Isaac Wauchope, travelled to Cape Town to protest on behalf of those who would be affected, the first time Africans from the eastern Cape had taken such a step.[50] To their satisfaction, the bill was withdrawn.[51] Africans were now a force in Cape politics.

The campaign against the Voters Registration Act, culminating in the King William's Town conference and the formation of the newest and largest Imbumba in October 1887, was a landmark in African organisational politics. Great strides had taken place since the early *Isigidimi* correspondents had started urging Africans to mobilise politically at the beginning of the decade. Political organisations had emerged throughout the eastern Cape, Africans had begun their own independent newspaper and they had made an impact on Cape electoral politics. Now, aroused as never before, they were co-operating on a formal basis for the first time and signalling, with the creation of Imbumba, their intention to consolidate this unity in the future. *Tung' umlomo* did not muzzle eastern Cape African voters, as intended. Instead, it made them more vocal and active than ever before in colonial politics. The African voters were a vibrant factor in the 1888 election and, even though thousands were struck off the voters' roll by the 1887 legislation, intense registration efforts brought the numbers back to the previous level by 1891.[52]

Despite the parliamentary attack on the African franchise, which in many ways was an acknowledgement of the vigour and potential of the new constitutional approach to politics, African involvement in Cape politics grew. In the short space of a few years in the 1880s, mission-educated African intellectuals and activists had laid the foundations for a new strategy of political assertiveness and resistance to white domination – firing with pens and words rather than arms – and were determined to build on these foundations to ensure a place for themselves in colonial society.

14

'A Native Bill for Africa'

... the measure prejudices the rights and property of Your Majesty's subjects and is inconsistent with Your Majesty's treaty obligations with large numbers of Natives who are now forced to surrender their rights to lands occupied by their fathers and themselves ... and to pay a labour tax such as is at best a qualified slavery.
– Petition against the Glen Grey Act, *Imvo Zabantsundu*, 1894

In the early 1890s the pace of politics in the eastern Cape quickened. Following the Voters Registration Act of 1887 and the Franchise and Ballot Act of 1892, which further eroded the rights of black voters, in 1894 the Cape government once again hauled out the legislative heavy artillery and aimed it at the colony's black population, whose interests the tenacious but pressured African voters sought to represent. In that year, Cecil John Rhodes, the Prime Minister and arch-imperialist, piloted through parliament the Glen Grey Act, which he called his 'Native Bill for Africa'.

The Act, named after the district where Rhodes's plans were first introduced, had three key components. Firstly, it aimed to break up the traditional system of communal tenure by surveying and allocating land in individual allotments. These would be held on strict conditions, allowing for forfeiture and alienation in the case of 'non-beneficial occupation'. One of those who felt the harsh end of this particular whip was the Congress leader and longstanding Glen Grey spokesman, James Pelem, who had his land taken away in 1903 and was declared bankrupt. Secondly, the

Act imposed a labour tax on all males who did not own allotments and had not been employed outside the district for a specified period every year. This mechanism was intended to push Africans without title off the land and onto the labour market. Thirdly, the Glen Grey Act created a system of district councils with limited powers in which Africans would be represented. Because the law had been amended to disenfranchise Africans who held title to land under communal tenure, the representation offered on the district councils was a quid pro quo for the removal of the common right to be represented in the Cape parliament. In this sense the Act was a step towards the formal segregation and apartheid of later years. Rather than encouraging individual advancement regardless of colour in a common system, it sought to channel Africans as a group into segregated political structures. As Lungisile Ntsebeza remarks, the Council system, according to its architect, Rhodes, was intended 'to keep the minds of natives occupied' and 'to employ their minds on simple questions in connection with local affairs'.[1]

By directly attacking the land base and political rights of Africans, the Glen Grey Act aroused considerable resentment. Jabavu declaimed furiously against it in *Imvo*, and organised a large meeting of the local Native Vigilance Association, which added its voice of condemnation and forwarded a petition to the Imperial government.[2] He exhorted Africans all over to follow suit.[3] In the eastern Cape the most intense political activity since *Tung' umlomo* seven years earlier ensued. Petitions written in terms similar to the one from King William's Town were sent to the British Colonial Office from more than 30 towns in the eastern Cape, as local groups followed *Imvo*'s lead.[4] The campaign also had reverberations in the Cape parliament, where Jabavu was both roundly criticised and defended.[5]

In Glen Grey itself, which was an African reserve, local residents had long feared moves by white farmers and the government to dispossess them of their land, and had organised accordingly. The main voice here was the Thembu Association: from 1889 its chairman was David Matsolo, its vice-chairman Chief Somerset Mlanjeni and its secretary James Pelem.[6] David Malasi was still prominent and for many years he was described as the chief co-ordinator of those voters who fell within the local Wodehouse constituency.[7] The Association was responsible for convening large meetings in the district from time to time.[8] These were well supported by the local headmen and often attracted hundreds of people, giving politics in Glen Grey a distinctly populist flavour.*

In the early 1890s divisions appeared between the mission people on the Wesleyan missions and the rest of the district. After the Secretary for Native Affairs had agreed to give individual title in Glen Grey, a large number of people in the principal Wesleyan mission stations, backed by the influential local missionary, E.J. Warner, successfully applied for them. Their lands were surveyed and a village management board was introduced at the main mission station of Mount Arthur.[9] But the people at Bengu and Macubeni as well as 'other civilised and industrious natives', led by Pelem and Daniel Dwanya from St Mark's, who had 'spent much money and labour and have made considerable improvements on their land', found the conditions unfavourable and did not take up the offer.[10] Their interests began to clash with those of the Wesleyan mission residents, and local divisions once again played into differences between J.T. Jabavu and others.

In March 1892 the Wesleyan mission people met and deputed Hendrick Kalipa, the Rev. Johannes Mahonga and Jabavu to meet with government officials in Cape Town on behalf of the district.[11] This raised an immediate outcry, as parts of the district as well as the Thembu Association chairman had not been invited. 'In the name of thousands of the Thembus, who are in dark clouds on this subject', David Malasi immediately demanded a full district meeting so that the deputation's intentions could be clarified and discussed.[12] When the deputation went ahead without heeding this call, Malasi informed the government that it was not representative.[13] A counter-delegation consisting of Malasi, Pelem, the law agent Daniel Dwanya, and two headmen was dispatched to Cape Town.[14] Although sometimes co-operating, from this time on these would be the two main interest groups in Glen Grey district, conveniently distinguished after the Glen Grey Act as those representing the Old and the New Survey.[15]

As a result of the Glen Grey Act, some 7500 small plots were surveyed

* Other leading spokesmen to emerge here were Hendrick Kalipa and Thomas Zwedala (Macubeni), Stephen Kalipa and Solomon Teka (Agnes), Benjamin Mgcodo (Zwaartwater), Henry Zuba (Mount Arthur), Komana Sibeko (Buffelsdoorns), Laso Ngqungqa (Cacadu) and David Malasi.

and allotted to holders on an individual basis, though for the purpose of the franchise the land was deemed to be held under communal tenure.[16] In compensation for their deprivation of the franchise, a Glen Grey District Council was established to administer local affairs. It consisted of 12 members, half being nominated by the Governor and half by the 18 location boards set up to represent the land-holders in the district.[17] Though dissatisfied with many of the Act's provisions, local leaders of public opinion, prominent since the 1880s, were soon dominant in the new institution. Considering also the fact that they were usually the biggest beneficiaries in the allotment of ground, their presence on the council confirms Colin Bundy's argument that the Glen Grey system gave the upper stratum of peasants – headmen, bureaucrats, farmers – institutional form.[18] Longstanding members of the District Council in the ten years after its inception included such well-known names in eastern Cape politics as Hendrick Kalipa and Thomas Zwedala, Edmund Mahonga (sometime president of the Glen Grey Teachers' Association), Thomas Sondlo, Abram and Hendrick Vanqa, and Hans Matsolo. Stephen Kalipa became the council's inspector of roads, the lively David Malasi its collector of road rates, and, in later years, Richard Nukuna, former secretary of the Queenstown Iliso Lomzi, its salaried burrweed inspector.[19] All had been active in organisational politics before the introduction of the council, and their names would recur in subsequent years.

Rhodes was determined to use the Glen Grey Act as the model for administering areas with large African populations, and it was soon extended to the five southern Transkei districts of Butterworth, Nqamakwe, Tsomo, Idutywa and, later, Kentani.[20] As in Glen Grey district, a number of the most prominent local communicators were absorbed onto the councils: in Butterworth Veldtman Bikitsha; in Nqamakwe John Mazamisa; in Idutywa Enoch Mamba; in Tsomo William Njikelana; and in Kentani Kondile Tokwe. At first the introduction of the Council system in Fingoland caused much dissatisfaction. Even model colonial subjects like Veldtman Bikitsha were uneasy about it.[21] After the government had pushed through the Act by proclamation without consulting the local people, a protest movement was organised, led by a committee representing the 'Fingo nation' under Campbell Kupe, one of the founders of the Manyano in 1887.

The resident magistrate of Nqamakwe described the protest as 'decidedly representative' of the majority of Africans in the Nqamakwe, Tsomo and Butterworth districts.[22] A series of meetings was held, representations were made to government, and people withheld payment of the general levy.[23] It was a popular response, critical of the role of headmen and not supported by them.[24] But as the Act became a *fait accompli*, opposition to the extension of the Glen Grey Act gradually subsided and the new system was accommodated within the established network of Fingoland politics.*

Glen Grey was but one of the districts of Thembuland that had come under colonial rule in 1885. Like the district that formed the pilot project for Rhodes's new scheme of 'native administration', the whole area of what was popularly known as *Batenjini*, stretching from Queenstown to the Great Place at Mqhekezweni, began to experience new forms of political organisation. Activists and interest groups from a wide area around Queenstown, the new economic and administrative hub of this important eastern Cape sub-region, had long enjoyed close links. In 1887 they, too, formed a Native Vigilance Association.[25] Like its counterparts in King William's Town and Herschel, Queenstown's Iliso Lomzi was well grounded and based on long-existing networks. Prior to 1887 no formal umbrella organisation had existed in the town, but the passage of the Voters Registration Act formally brought together representatives from the Oxkraal and Kamastone locations, the Hackney, Shiloh, Lesseyton and St Mark's mission stations, Tarkastad, Glen Grey, Cala, Engcobo and Queenstown itself.[26]

According to the breakdown of voters in Queenstown, Oxkraal and Kamastone had some 400 African voters in 1887, Glen Grey an equal number, while there were less than 50 in Queenstown and nearby Lesseyton.[27] As the Glen Grey people already had their Thembu Association, they did not want to be submerged in a body centred on Queenstown.[28] It was accordingly agreed that the three areas would organise separately and come together

---

* Though the Council system was also meant to be extended to the Xalanga district, this only happened in the 1920s because of the complexity of local land matters and relationships.

periodically to co-ordinate their actions. This was a practical arrangement in view of the distinct concentrations of Africans and the distances separating them. A separate Iliso Lomzi was also formed at Hewu and Whittlesea during the excitement of 1887. Although people here participated enthusiastically in the broader-based Queenstown Iliso, it was felt (as in Glen Grey) that a local body was needed for local matters as well.[29]

With its bloc of several hundred African voters, Oxkraal and Kamastone locations formed an important area in African politics. Most of the residents were Mfengu who worked the land, all but two of the voters being classified as 'farmers' (peasants) in the 1903 voters' roll. Their main spokesmen were Iliso people – such as the Sishubas and the Mtombenis – who included both long-standing headmen and younger, educated people.[30]

Meetings of the co-ordinating Queenstown Iliso were held on a quarterly basis for several years. The convener and secretary was the well-connected Richard Nukuna, a local boarding-house owner, *Imvo* agent and sports personality.[31] Those prominent in the Iliso included the Revs. Jonas Goduka and Samuel Mvambo, who represented the town itself, Harry Mtombeni from Hackney, John Sishuba from Kamastone, James Pelem from Glen Grey, John Sondlo from Lesseyton, Sol Kalipa from Cala, Daniel Dwanya from St Mark's and J.Z. Tantsi from Engcobo. In close touch with them was J.T. Jabavu, the secretary-general of Imbumba, who attended meetings in Queenstown regularly from 1887 onwards. This was a reflection of the increasingly important role played by this extended area in the unfolding 'national' movement in the 1890s.[32]

Electoral issues were the Iliso's main concern, but local matters such as roads, quitrent payments and management were also considered. Iliso spokesmen were in the forefront of moves to have local village management boards instituted.[33] Not surprisingly, when they were introduced Harry Mtombeni became chairman of the Hackney board and John Sishuba of the Kamastone one.[34]

Despite regular meetings to discuss joint action, divisions reflecting wider organisational and ethnic splits in the eastern Cape revealed themselves from the start and voting unity was never assured in Queenstown.[35] Right up to the time of Union the two main areas, Glen Grey and Whittlesea, almost invariably ended up disagreeing on at least one of the candidates. At an Iliso meeting in 1891, deadlock was reached as to which candidates to support in the Legislative Council elections and a showdown followed. After the meeting decided to leave the matter to a committee, the visiting Jabavu and one of the Kamastone Sishubas refused to abide by the decision, and demanded that the issue be put before the meeting again. This provoked the chairman, Daniel Dwanya, to walk out, followed by James Pelem, Richard Nukuna and others. The meeting was continued in their absence with Hendrick Kalipa in the chair.[36] These kinds of local differences were precursors of the formal divisions that would emerge in eastern Cape politics.[37]

In the adjoining Transkeian Territories, where two new constituencies of Griqualand East and Tembuland were created after incorporation in the Cape, the 1888 elections gave Africans in Thembuland proper their first taste of electoral politics. The voters there soon asserted themselves, returning J.C. Molteno and Richard Solomon in 1894 and 1899, respectively.[38] Cala provided the bulk of African voters in the Thembuland constituency – no less than 443 out of a total of 735 in 1902[39] – and this district, with its African enclave of Xalanga, continued to be an important centre in Transkeian and eastern Cape politics. The main Cala politicians in the 1880s, men such as Mankayi Rengqe and James Dwane, were still taking the lead there in the 1890s.[40] Further evidence that the whole area was beginning to fit into the pattern of eastern Cape politics was provided by the formation of an Iliso Lomzi in neighbouring Engcobo district after the 1887 King William's Town conference. This Iliso was based among the Qwati clan of the Thembu living in the district and had the active support of Chief Dalasile.[41] The secretary was P.D. Tshacila, who had been an agent and communicator for the Thembu chiefs in the area for some years.[42] Other prominent members were J.Z. Tantsi, who became a leader in the separatist Ethiopian Church; Thomas Poswayo; and Simon Peter Sihlali, founding president of Imbumba Yama Nyama in 1882.[43]

New-style politics in the Thembu areas were still closely linked to chieftaincy politics. In 1888 voters at Clarkebury would not commit themselves until a decision had been taken at the paramount Dalindyebo's Great Place. Dalindyebo was said to be the head without which the Thembu body could not act.[44] In 1890 the main Thembu spokesmen in political organisations in Glen Grey, Cala and Engcobo went in a body to pay their respects to their chief at his court at Mqhekezweni, where Nehemiah Tile of the Thembu Church took a prominent part in the proceedings.[45] In 1899 a big meeting of spokesmen from various areas in the Thembuland constituency met at Mqhekezweni to discuss voting unity and a regional organisation for the Transkei.[46] But the new forms of colonial politics spread slowly beyond the southern Transkei. In 1899, five years after it had become the last independent southern Nguni chiefdom to be incorporated in the Cape, there was still not a single African registered voter in Mpondoland.[47]

In overview, the Thembu areas on both sides of the Indwe River, stretching from the commercial centre of Queenstown to the Great Place at Mqhekezweni, became key bases for the new-style politics of the 1880s and 1890s. The people of *Batenjini* showed as well as anywhere else how the new forms of politics reached down to grassroots level. In every district a complex local pattern was woven around the market place, magistracy, chief or headman's *imbizo*, polling booth, town hall, church and school. Traditional leaders, literate and non-literate peasants, wage-earning labourers and an emerging middle class interacted in various ways and in various degrees. Local activities were in turn linked to wider educational, economic, social and cultural spheres as well. The Cape's annexation of Thembuland in 1885 and the struggles of people in Glen Grey and the districts surrounding Queenstown to retain their land and political rights made this a key area in the politics of the 'nation'. As we shall see, *Batenjini* became a major catchment area for both the South African Native Congress and the broad Ethiopian church movement in the 1890s. It played an important role in forging relations between the two and in promoting the ensuing co-operation and fusion of ideas that propelled organised African nationalism in South Africa.

PART TWO

THE CREATION OF WIDER NETWORKS

15

The South African Native Congress, 1890–1891

Not all the natives are blind followers of a certain native leader.
– James Pelem to Cecil John Rhodes, 1895

The internal stresses and divisions in African politics revealed by the 1888 elections were soon institutionalised in the formation of Ingqungqutela, or Congress, to rival Imbumba, or the Union, led by J.T. Jabavu. The new organisation was started by leaders who had different interests and different ideas about the way the broad political movement should be directed. In particular, they saw the need for a body that was more representative and accountable in a formal way, and aimed as well to give it a southern African reach, as its name, the South African Native Congress, emphasised. Its formation indicated that African politics were becoming more dynamic and varied, as a result of new factors and influences, such as the increasing leverage of Africans voters, and the resultant attention given to them by Cape politicians.

The leading initiator of the Congress was Jonathan Tunyiswa, a young school teacher from Mount Coke near King William's Town. He was one of a group who wished to see Imbumba meeting annually in conference, as had been envisaged at its founding, so that it could articulate African views in a representative way like the Afrikaner Bond. Writing in *Imvo* in August 1889, he asked what had happened to Imbumba, and called for a conference to be held that year. There were many problems facing the black 'house' that needed to be confronted, he wrote.[1] But no such conference was held. Despite repeated approaches taken in this regard,

Jabavu made it clear that he did not support the idea.[2]

Tunyiswa persevered with his attempts. On 2 May 1890 he organised a small 'committee' meeting at the King William's Town library to discuss a more representative new African organisation along the lines of the Bond. Two members of the five-man Imbumba committee elected in 1887 attended. One was the respected Nathaniel Umhalla, who had clashed with Jabavu;[3] the other was the local entrepreneur Paul Xiniwe. Also present were William Kobe Ntsikana (president of the Native Educational Association), H. Mboni and the Rev. William Philip from East London. Though the old guard of Jabavu, Wauchope and Makiwane were invited, they did not attend. To enable them to be present it was decided to hold a further meeting, which occurred later in May.[4] Again they did not attend.* One of those who did join was the blind poet Jonaş Ntsiko ('Hadi Waseluhlangeni'), who had studied with Umhalla at Zonnebloem and in England. At this meeting a decision was taken to go ahead all the same with plans for a new organisation.

Tunyiswa accordingly issued a notice calling the people of King William's Town and the neighbouring districts of East London, Stutterheim, Peddie and Alice to a meeting on 7 July 1890 to discuss the formation of a Native Congress.[5] The appeal was thus addressed to the heartland of the new politics – an area with traditionally close lines of communication, where the first African organisations had emerged in the proximity of King William's Town and the leading mission stations.[6] Tunyiswa's call met with a good response. After Ntsikana, Tunyiswa and Umhalla had explained the aims, this third meeting, attended by 58 delegates, agreed to form a new Congress and draw up a constitution for the body.[7] However, progress was slow and it took 18 months before the Congress was finally constituted.

After the meeting in July 1890, lively views for and against the envisaged body were expressed by correspondents in *Imvo*. The majority opposed it on the ground that it was a divisive move that undermined the position of Jabavu, with his proven record as spokesman for Africans, as well as his newspaper and the 1887 Imbumba, which it was claimed was still in existence as an organisation.[8] Jabavu himself remained aloof,

* Green Sikundla, president of the King William's Town Iliso Lomzi, Mbem Njikelana, Peter Tyamzashe and W.D. Soga were also present at the second meeting.

neither approving of nor openly criticising the plans. He did not wish to give his personal, organisational or press support to what in effect was a rival initiative.[9] Though Jabavu soon announced that the whole matter of a new Congress was at an end, in March 1891 Tunyiswa published a manifesto on behalf of his committee, reiterating the original plans.[10] This manifesto was distributed extensively, far beyond the five districts involved the previous year, and preparations were made for an inaugural conference.[11] Inundated by enquiries, Jabavu was pressed into publishing an open letter to his followers, dissociating himself from the Congress.[12]

The inaugural conference of the new South African Native Congress (SANC) was held at Lose in the King William's Town district on 30 and 31 December 1891. It was a widely representative gathering, drawing in 34 people from 15 eastern Cape towns. The delegates included two of the committee of five elected at the founding conference of Imbumba in 1887: Nathaniel Umhalla and Benjamin Sakuba from Uitenhage, who was also secretary of the NEA and the King Native Vigilance Association. (Another of the 1887 five, Paul Xiniwe, later associated himself with the Congress but was, at the time of its formation, in England with the African Native Choir.) James Pelem from Glen Grey, one of the most forceful proponents of a regional organisation since the early 1880s, was present too, as were Tunyiswa, W.D. Soga, Ntsikana and Mboni, the key promoters of the Congress idea from the very beginning, together with Umhalla. From the surrounding districts came, among many others, Walter Rubusana and the councillors of Chief Kama from Middledrift.[13] From further afield came a number of Fingoland leaders as well as the Rev. Elijah Mqoboli, Isaac Tshwete from Herschel and Shad Mama from Basutoland.

When the conference opened, Nana Ganya, the chief templar of the King William's Town IOTT, was made chairman. One of the pressing points of the discussions was the relationship between this organisation and Imbumba. Tunyiswa stressed the link, indeed 'showed' that the bodies were the same, and claimed he had been given the task of convening meetings by Jabavu. Some delegates were then sent to ask Jabavu to attend so that this could be corroborated, but he refused to comment.[14] Finally, the constitution was accepted and the South African Native Congress came into being.

An executive was formed to run the Congress. Thomas John Mqanda, a farmer, headman and prominent Methodist from Peddie, who had been unable to attend, was elected president, while Tunyiswa and Soga were made secretaries and Nana Ganya treasurer. The rest of the first executive committee consisted of Umhalla, Stephen Xo from Wartburg, D. Marela (representing the Middledrift Gqunukhwebe), Mboni, Pelem, Richard Nukuna from Queenstown, and Jonathan Nangu and Pato Lusaseni from Fingoland.* Besides the King William's Town heartland, therefore, Glen Grey, Queenstown and the Mfengu districts of the southern Transkei were also represented on the first executive.[15]

The inaugural conference of 1891 passed three resolutions for submission to the Secretary for Native Affairs. The major one noted with alarm the electoral changes proposed by the Afrikaner Bond, which threatened black franchise rights, and asked the government not to support them. Before the meeting ended, Queenstown was decided upon as the venue for the next meeting.[16]

Though Congress eventually became a major factor in Cape African politics, it took some time before it established itself as a real force. Not until the SANC started its own newspaper six years later did it seriously begin to rival Jabavu and *Imvo* in influence. While he and his newspaper enjoyed real recognition throughout the Cape in the 1890s, the SANC remained virtually unknown in the broader public life of the colony. Nevertheless, it had a definite influence on the emergent national movement. Henceforth, there would be two distinct political streams in the region. Even if it did not at first enjoy a high profile as an organisation, it widened the scope of African politics in the eastern Cape by providing an ideological and organisational base for leaders and intellectuals such as Umhalla, Pelem and Rubusana. Moreover, its very name was aspirational, pointing to the creation of a wider inter-territorial unity: South Africa at that stage was still two decades away from being born.

* The others present included Solomon Maqina (Fingoland), John Jonkers (Burgersdorp), Attwell Maci (Peelton), Bikani Soga (King William's Town), David Dwashu (Zelini), Julius Ngxamgxa (Wartburg, the alternative choice for president) and members of the Mama and Tele families from Middledrift.

At first Jabavu was tolerant of the moves to form the SANC. He said he was not interested in joining, but that those involved were free to organise as they wished.[17] Imperiously supreme until the late 1890s, he continued to operate in a manner that had become accepted since the foundation of *Imvo*. Acting as a pressure body in white colonial politics and as a watchdog and disseminator of public opinion among Africans, *Imvo* continued to represent 'native opinion' and remained the lynchpin of black politics. From the King William's Town Native Vigilance Association, Jabavu received the organisational authority and support he needed. Moreover, if crises arose he could summon the umbrella body, Imbumba. He was there to inform and lead African opinion.

Some groups in the eastern Cape found this arrangement in many ways beneficial. It was a tidy way of being linked to a political centre without the extra demands of active, full-time organisation on a wider, regional scale. Materially, they would have been hard pressed to find the funds needed for this kind of politicking. Time was a factor as well. It was not easy to communicate across an extensive region like the eastern Cape. Though there was a railway system running through the eastern Cape and Transkei, the most common mode of transport was still by horse. Even into the twentieth century, people invited to attend conferences sometimes explained that they were unable to do so because of the 'scarceness of horses in this bad year'.[18]

Jabavu and his newspaper provided the means for Africans to bridge these distances. In fact, various local groups had institutionalised his central role as guardian when they empowered him at the 1887 conference as secretary-general to decide when to call meetings of Imbumba. *Imvo* was thus really more than a newspaper: it was 'the mother of all the associations', as one correspondent put it.[19] The mandate given him in 1887, and the different ways this was understood, lay at the heart of the differences between Jabavu and the SANC.

In the decade after 1887 Jabavu enjoyed his greatest influence in both colonial and African politics. He became a national figure, probably the most famous mission-educated African since Tiyo Soga. His views were noted and discussed in the Cape press and parliament and he was influential in colonial politics, in particular as a thorn in Rhodes's side

when the Prime Minister sought to implement the Glen Grey Act and
annex Pondoland in the mid-1890s.[20] Jabavu was a potent friend or else
opponent of frontier parliamentary candidates, whose record in respect of
Africans he closely scrutinised in *Imvo*. Without any doubt, he influenced
Cape elections, being instrumental for example in the nomination and
return of J.C. Molteno in the Tembuland constituency in 1894.[21]

Jabavu shaped public opinion generally through his newspaper;
campaigned fearlessly in person in electoral politics; led deputations to
local and central authorities; was the driving force behind the regular
mass meetings of his organisational base, the King William's Town Native
Vigilance Association; and, in times of crisis such as when the Glen Grey
Act came before parliament, exhorted other local groups and organisations
to mobilise together and present a united front.

After a decade in the editor's chair of the only independent newspaper
in southern Africa, Jabavu had become the leading spokesman for African
opinion. But, useful though his role was, it meant that African politics
was directed from a small centre. When the process of African political
mobilisation expanded and outlying districts began to be organised, it
became increasingly difficult to accommodate disparate ideas and interests
in this way. As the scope of African politics widened, so did its complexities.
It was in this context that the fledgling Congress group emerged and soon
developed into a serious rival.

16

'The Congress'
versus 'The Union'

[The South African Native Congress's] organisation is not yet
complete; still, it is already a power for good in the country, and
will undoubtedly assume the position of the representative Native
Association of the future.

       – Walter Rubusana, 1900

The formation of the South African Native Congress in 1891
introduced a second Nguni bull with distinct patterns on its hide into the
camp of eastern Cape politics. The SANC soon came to challenge Jabavu,
seeking to become the main voice for African public opinion. Indeed, its
formation led to a lasting split between the Congress group and the Jabavu
camp. The result was that politics in the region became polarised until long
after Union in 1910. From the 1890s, what can be termed Ingqungqutela
(or 'The Congress') challenged Imbumba ('The Union') head on.

The rivalry between the Congress and the Union was many-sided and
assumed many dimensions, not least personal. Though Jabavu himself
was still only in his early thirties and the SANC's Nathaniel Umhalla, for
example, was much older, the generational aspect was often referred to
in *Imvo*'s discussions of Congress. 'Elders' complained in the paper of
the Congress's activities and Jabavu himself referred to them as 'young
bloods', people who still needed to be schooled.[1] In general, Jabavu did
not take kindly to criticism and was unforgiving of his enemies. According
to his son, he 'lacked the power to reconcile himself with his opponents in
frank discussion', ignoring, condemning, ridiculing or antagonising them

instead.[2] Jabavu's aristocratic pride was a fault on which contemporaries were generally agreed.[3]

Economically and organisationally, too, Jabavu must have realised that the new body represented a potent challenge to his power base and his business interests in the form of *Imvo*. Initially, however, Congress did not present much of a real threat to Jabavu. Very little is known about the SANC in the years after its inaugural conference in December 1891, though there is a definite, if thin, line of continuity with conferences held in Queenstown in July 1893, and at the Wartburg mission station in the Stutterheim district in May 1895.[4] With some reason, therefore, Jabavu was able to portray the Congress as an insignificant body, representing only the few people who had started it.[5]

Nevertheless, the Congress leaders – Nathaniel Umhalla, James Pelem, Jonathan Tunyiswa and others – had support bases that could not be ignored, including the Native Educational Association, more than half of whose executive members were involved in the SANC's formation.* Bolstered by the support it received, the Congress set about establishing a mouthpiece for its opposition to Jabavu. In 1895 Pelem wrote to Cecil Rhodes, then Prime Minister, saying that many educated Africans were opposed to *Imvo*'s policy, but had no vehicle to express their opposition. He proposed that Rhodes establish a Xhosa-language newspaper 'and nominate me as its proprietor and editor'.[6] Pelem's approach was in keeping with attempts by the Congress group to start a paper to promote their views. Though rumours about the appearance of a paper to rival *Imvo* began to circulate as early as 1891, it was only in 1897 that it materialised.[7] In that year a group of Congress officials launched an appeal to the African community to raise £500 for a company, the Eagle Press Printing Co., that would run their newspaper.† Despite the 'ravages of Rinderpest', Africans responded with just a little under the required sum.[8]

---

* They were William Philip (vice-president), W.K. Ntsikana (immediate past president), Jonathan Tunyiswa, Peter Tyamzashe and Mbem Njikelana. By 1894 Tunyiswa and H. Mboni had joined Njikelana, Tyamzashe and Ntsikana on the teachers' executive. Ntsikana, Tyamzashe and Philip were still there in 1898 when another Congress insider, Walter Rubusana, became NEA president, with Tunyiswa as vice-president.

† Among them were Paul Xiniwe, Rob Mantsayi, Walter Rubusana, Peter Kawa, William Kobe Ntsikana, W.D. Soga and the president, Thomas Mqanda.

The remainder of the capital needed to start up the newspaper seems to have been provided by Rhodes. With the 1898 elections approaching, the former Prime Minister was in search of new allies after the realignment in Cape politics following the disastrous Jameson Raid, in which Rhodes had played a part. Rhodes nominated an associate of his, the MP C.P. Crewe, to take charge of the paper's financial affairs. Eventually, the African directors clashed with Crewe: in 1900 Rubusana reported him to Rhodes for being arrogant and attempting to assume functions not concerned with finance.[9]

Izwi Labantu (The Voice of the People) was launched in East London in November 1897. Its appearance was a historic step in the unfolding of a national political movement in South Africa. It was only the second independent African newspaper after *Imvo*, appearing 13 years to the month after *Imvo*'s birth. *Izwi* gave those intellectuals and activists with a more African-centred approach to politics a forum in which to conduct debate and air their views. Its appearance was also a welcome addition to an industry serving African readers in their own languages, and a major step forward in the development of Xhosa literature. Two important missionary newspapers had recently been shut down – *Isigidimi* in 1888 and *Inkanyiso lase Natal* in 1896 – and so *Izwi* helped fill a literary vacuum for the school people.

Within a short time *Izwi*, like *Imvo*, started to be read outside the eastern Cape heartland of African politics. This helped connect intellectuals in different parts of southern Africa and indirectly paved the way for broader political co-operation. Within a few years a whole range of similar independent (and struggling) newspapers appeared across the subcontinent – from Pietermaritzburg and Pietersburg to Cape Town, Inanda, Mafeking and Maseru – giving common shape and voice to the spreading process of political mobilisation. As with *Izwi*, these newspapers tended to emerge in tandem with political organisations and develop a symbiotic relationship with them.

The first editors of *Izwi* were Nathaniel Umhalla and George Tyamzashe, a young Lovedale alumnus from a well-known family, who had cut his teeth at *Imvo* under Jabavu.* Within a year, Umhalla's position as editor

* The Tyamzashe family counted among its members Lovedale-educated Gwayi Tyamzashe, the pioneering minister and newspaper commentator (going back to *Indaba* in the 1860s

was taken over by the Scottish-educated Alan Kirkland Soga, son of the famous Tiyo Soga. Sent to Scotland in 1870 at the age of seven for his schooling, he later studied law in Glasgow (apparently without qualifying). On returning home, he began work as a civil servant in the Native Affairs Department and, after passing the law examinations, became an acting resident magistrate. But racial discrimination blocked his progress. 'Prompted by back-stairs influence and the "color-line" at the hands of his Chiefs in the service', Soga was moved sideways to the Labour Department at the instigation of Cecil John Rhodes. After resigning 'in disgust', he switched to journalism and politics and became a skilled commentator on South African affairs. During the course of the next decade, he would establish himself as one of the most notable spokesmen for Africans in the Cape.

In 1900 George Tyamzashe was replaced as editor by Richard Tainton Kawa, who had started his career as the senior 'native' teacher at Healdtown but had subsequently fallen out with the Methodists. He later wrote a history of the Mfengu, *Ibali lamaMfengu*, which Jeff Peires has described as containing 'some of the most penetrating critiques of colonialism ever produced by a colonial beneficiary'.[11] As editor, Richard Kawa was in turn followed by J.N.J. Tulwana and the renowned Xhosa writer and poet Samuel Edward Krune Mqhayi.[12] Born in 1875 near Alice, Mqhayi has been described as the 'father of Xhosa poetry'. He provided a link between the traditional Xhosa oral poetry sung by the *iimbongi* or praise singers and modern poetry, by committing *izibongo* to writing.[13] Many of these praise poems were printed in *Izwi*.[14] Steeped in Xhosa tradition and history, he came to be acknowledged as *imbongi yesizwe* (the Poet of the Nation). His writing also reveals much about the broad conceptions and ideas that powered the early SANC.[15]

In 1901 Paul Xiniwe was made sporting editor of *Izwi*. Another regular contributor (and SANC member) was Walter Rubusana, who later published a book based on early writings in that newspaper, namely *Zemk' Iinkomo Magwalandini* (1906). For this and his work on the translation of

---

and *Isigidimi* in the 1870s); Peter Tyamzashe, a leading member of the Native Educational Association from Mngqesha; and, in generations to come, the composer Benjamin Tyamzashe and the journalist and ICU activist Henry Tyamzashe.

the Bible into Xhosa, he was awarded an honorary doctorate by an African American college.[16]

With a newspaper to publicise their activities and some distinguished staff members and correspondents, the Congress group set about actively developing the SANC as well as local Native Vigilance Associations, which were meant to ensure its representative character.[17]

The realignment in Cape politics, which had coincided with the founding of *Izwi*, put Jabavu in a quandary. In electoral politics Jabavu had consistently supported independent, liberal 'friends of the natives' against colonial hardliners. As Jabavu saw it, the anti-African lobby consisted of the followers of Sir Gordon Sprigg, who as Prime Minister had taken away the guns (and dignity) of Africans by means of the Disarmament Act in 1878, and attempted to deprive them of their constitutional weapons by means of the Voters Registration Act in 1887.[18] Jabavu's other opponent was the Afrikaner Bond, which since its foundation in 1880 had regularly attacked African education and franchise rights.[19] In the 1890s, Jabavu also turned against the jingoism and racism of Rhodes and Dr Jameson, who co-operated politically with the Bond, though their interests were Imperial rather than South African. For him, the loose group of 'friends of the natives' came closest to representing the idealised Christian and British values of equality and 'progress' that educated Africans wished to see entrenched and extended at the Cape. It was logical that Jabavu should support them.

However, when the Jameson Raid led to Rhodes's resignation as Prime Minister and shattered the alliance between Rhodes and the Bond, a new political realignment resulted. One of its outcomes was a two-party system based mainly on racial, English–Afrikaner lines. On one side there was the South African League (later the Progressive Party), on the other the Afrikaner Bond. Jabavu's champions James Rose-Innes, J.W. Sauer and John X. Merriman and other liberal 'friends of the natives' fell out over which side they should align themselves with. Rose-Innes sided with the League, while the other two took an anti-jingoist position and decided to co-operate with the Bond in what later became the South African Party. This put Jabavu in a quandary, as Africans had always opposed the Bond. He chose to continue supporting the 'friends of the natives' on both sides. This decision was made easier for him because the Bond began for the first time to woo black voters, and because Sauer and Merriman were dependent on African support in their eastern Cape constituencies.[20]

The stand adopted by Jabavu in this realignment complicated African politics, though it was perfectly logical and consistent. Both Rhodes and Sprigg, the League leaders, hardly had a record worth supporting. They exhibited strong white supremacist ideas and between them were responsible for the Disarmament, Voters Registration and Glen Grey Acts, the three laws that struck most fundamentally at African rights and were most vigorously opposed by them. Jabavu emphasised that, in backing Merriman and Sauer, he was continuing to support the best men, not the principles of the Bond.[21] This policy received wide support, though it also met with strong opposition.

The SANC, newly vitalised by the founding of *Izwi Labantu*, strongly backed the League, which through Rhodes partly financed the newspaper, and made its first concerted attack on Jabavu. The SANC capitalised on the traditional African fear and mistrust of Afrikaner domination and provocatively claimed that Jabavu was handing Africans over to the mercy of the unscrupulous 'Boers'.[22] The battle was fought on three levels: through the press, the holding of separate conferences, and active campaigning by party agents on both sides.

In July 1898, in view of the forthcoming general elections, the SANC held an electoral convention in Queenstown, which leading spokesmen from various parts of the eastern Cape attended. The conference was chaired by 'Bishop' James Dwane, newly installed as head of the separatist AME Church in southern Africa. It predictably resolved to support the South African League.[23] Thereafter, the revitalised Congress and its mouthpiece went on the offensive. Fierce discussion took place in the press, as *Izwi* and *Imvo* took opposing sides.[24] During the election campaign the SANC president, Thomas Mqanda, and other leaders such as Rubusana and W.D. Soga acted as electoral agents, travelling to various parts of the colony to put forward the Congress and Progressive view.[25] Mqanda and Rubusana were active as far away as Aliwal North, where they spoke against J.W. Sauer's candidature. Jabavu likewise visited several voting districts to oppose the League.[26] It was the first time that African agents had been active on such a wide scale in Cape elections.

So seriously did Jabavu take the Congress challenge in 1898 that he convened a conference of Imbumba in the same month as the SANC conference in Queenstown. This was the first formal, region-wide meeting of the organisation since its formation 11 years earlier. Forced into a defensive conclave, it met at Indwe on 20 July 1898, and decided to advise Africans to stick to proven 'friends of the natives' in the elections.[27] Merriman and his running mate in the local Wodehouse constituency were given the opportunity to address the meeting.[28]

The composition of the delegates to the conference showed where Jabavu's main support lay in the eastern Cape. Especially important was his home district of King William's Town, as well as his Fort Beaufort, Kamastone, Cala and Fingoland connections. These areas, constituting an arc of Mfengu settlement, would consistently support him in the years ahead. The delegates from Jabavu's strong home base were J.K. Bokwe, who had left Lovedale in 1897 after 35 years there to join Jabavu as proprietor of *Imvo*, and Green Sikundla, leader of the local Native Vigilance Association at its inception in 1887. Nearby Fort Beaufort was represented by Peter Congwane, chairman of the local village management board, and the Rev. Isaac Wauchope,[29] one of the outstanding early African figures, who had been ministering at Blinkwater near Fort Beaufort since his ordination at Lovedale in 1892.* Another important area of support was the Kamastone location near Queenstown, where John Sishuba was spokesman for the large bloc of local voters. He would become one of Jabavu's chief

---

* Delegates included Chief Ebenezer Mhlambiso (Amatole Basin), Charles Lwana (Keiskamma Hoek), the Rev. J. Sikwebu (secretary of the Iliso Lomzi in Peddie), H. Myoli (Stutterheim), J.M. Mkobeni (Breidbach), J. Vantyi (Pirie), S.H. Mnyanda (Xugwala), T. Putu (Mt Coke), Mbem Njikelana (Debe), M. Tonga (Peelton), C.P. Matyolo (a shoemaker from King William's Town) and a Mr Poswa (Mngqesha). Among the observers were W.D. Soga of the SANC, Pambani Figlan, Sol Kalipa, Landule Ngcwabe, Jeremiah Mtila, T. Makiwane, J. Somtunzi and a Mr Mxaku.

lieutenants in the following years.[30] The delegates from Queenstown were E.L. Qwelane, an insurance agent,[31] and the Rev. Benjamin Dlepu, active in politics since the formation of the original Imbumba in 1882. From nearby Glen Grey came Hendrick and Stephen Kalipa, the former a member of the local District Council. Next-door Cala was strongly represented by the Revs. John Manelle and Eben Magaba and the headmen Mankayi Rengqe and Duncan Makohliso, two leading figures in this relatively well-off, well-organised area. S. Milton Ntloko, another close lieutenant of Jabavu, came on behalf of adjoining Fingoland. Finally, Dordrecht and Indwe, the venue for the conference, were represented among others by Enoch Mamba.[32] Mamba was the only delegate to oppose the argument in favour of the 'best man' candidates, and was solidly in favour of Rhodes and Sprigg.

In the following year, 1899, Jabavu once more convened Imbumba – this time to counter the SANC in the mini-election held in April that year as a result of a new delimitation.[33] At its meeting on 30 August at Pirie, Jabavu again emphasised that the gathering was part of the original Imbumba, and said it had been called because 'native agents of League candidates [the Congress leaders] have made futile efforts to personate this body'. It was decided to extend the scope of Imbumba by drawing up a constitution and ensuring as many centres as possible were affiliated so that Africans could present a united front. Jabavu noted that, in recent visits to Fort Beaufort, Whittlesea, Herschel and various parts of Thembuland, including the Great Place of Dalindyebo, he had encountered unanimous support for such a move. 'Organisation for the future' was identified as a priority, and Isaac Wauchope was tasked with the writing of a constitution. Clearly, Imbumba was now following the example of the Congress and was seeking to respond to the organisational challenge it presented.[34]

The meetings of both the Congress and the Union in 1898 confirmed a further fundamental divide between them: the ethnic divisions between the two camps. Though these divisions were far from absolute, they were clear and unquestionably rooted in historical experience. The SANC had developed from a Rharhabe (Ndlambe, Ngqika, Gqunukhwebe) and

Thembu base, while the *Imvo* group relied mainly on Mfengu support. Moreover, the SANC with its national orientation was linked directly to a patriotic strain of Xhosa Christianity going back to the very first contacts with missionaries in 1799. This is borne out by the leadership roles played in the Congress by Nathaniel Umhalla, the grandson of Ndlambe, and by the Soga and Ntsikana families, with their 70-year-old tradition of combining Christianity with loyalty to the Ngqika royal house. Support for the SANC also came from the Gqunukhwebe under their Christian chiefs at Middledrift; as the westernmost Xhosa, they had interacted with both Khoikhoi and whites from early on.

An analysis of the leadership structures, conference venues and areas of support of the SANC and Imbumba in the 1890s and 1900s confirms this analysis.[35] Of the 30 known SANC executive members from 1891 until 1913, 22 lived in traditional Rharhabe areas of settlement: Tutura and East London through to Berlin, King William's Town, Peelton and Toise River. Moreover, of the known conference venues between 1891 and 1909, more than half were in the adjoining Thembu areas of Queenstown, Glen Grey and Lesseyton. Thembuland became a stronghold for both Congress and the religious separatist movement. The influential James Pelem was one of the prominent SANC supporters here. After Thembuland, the Ngqika mission stations of Wartburg and Mgwali followed as popular SANC conference venues, while King William's Town was also a centre of activity because most executive committee members lived in that district.

The structural foundation of the SANC was thus mainly based on the Rharhabe–Thembu axis. Noticeably under-represented in the organisational structure of branches, office-bearers and conference venues were the traditional Mfengu areas in Fingoland and along the old Ciskeian frontier from Peddie to Oxkraal near Queenstown. On the other hand, a similar analysis of the rival Imbumba group under Jabavu shows a predominantly Mfengu influence along this very axis.[36]

Historically, the Mfengu had been allies and beneficiaries of colonial rule, whereas the Ngqika, Ndlambe and Thembu had been subjugated and dispossessed. These different historical experiences were reproduced in the early political movements, too, and helped shape the strategies and ideological content of these organisations. While from the start the new political elite had purposely tried to diminish 'tribal' and denominational tensions, wider social strains were inevitably reflected in the new forms of constitutional politics, as the scope of African politics widened in the eastern Cape.

In the 1900s, separate ethnic commemoration festivals further institutionalised these historic, ethnic, political and organisational differences. In 1908 the Mfengu observed for the first time a Fingo Emancipation Day, celebrating the Mfengu release from Gcaleka 'slavery' and their coming under British rule in 1835. This project had been led by the veteran Mfengu leader, Captain Veldtman Bikitsha, who had taken part in the original exodus from Gcalekaland to the colony.[37] On behalf of the Mfengu he headed a deputation to the Governor, asking that provision be made for a commemorative day.[38] The government consented and local authorities were instructed to arrange for Mfengu school children and civil servants to attend the celebrations.[39]

The Mfengu insisted that their commemoration of Fingo Emancipation Day (held annually on 14 May) was 'in no way antagonistic to the other nationalities whose friendly relation [they wished] ... very much to retain, and to whom they are indebted to their kindness and rescue from starvation prior to becoming British subjects'.[40] The project was at least partly inspired by concern at the deteriorating position of Mfengu in colonial society and by the desire to have the government officially acknowledge their past services and safeguard past agreements.[41] However, it aroused considerable resentment among people of other groups.[42] After representations by Chief Dalindyebo and the Thembu, the celebrations were restricted to the Mfengu districts of the Ciskei and Transkei and one or two other places.[43]

On the appointed day, 14 May 1908, the Mfengu celebrated the first Fingo Emancipation Day at numerous well-attended meetings throughout the eastern Cape and as far afield as Kimberley, where Isaiah Bud Mbelle was prominent.[44] The Mfengu political elite controlled the proceedings. At Peddie, where some 3000 people gathered at the spot where the Mfengu had pledged their loyalty to Britain after the exodus, the Native Vigilance Association was directly responsible for organising the celebrations.[45] Participants here included numerous political activists, including the

SANC president, Thomas Mqanda, Richard Kawa, and local chiefs and headmen.* The active role of the SANC president in celebrations that *Izwi* and many Congress members found offensive reflects the fact that ethnicity and political affiliation did not always coincide. Others present who defied easy boundaries were the religious separatist leaders Pambani Mzimba and Benjamin Dlepu. For Mzimba to be part of a commemoration of 'Fingo emancipation', while at the same time supporting the Congress and heading a large separatist church, was an astonishing personal achievement and an example furthermore of the complexity and diversity of African experiences at the time.

The introduction of Fingo Emancipation Day led to calls for a similar festival for the Xhosa communities. Writing in *Izwi*, George Nzungu proposed that the Xhosa have their own day in honour of the 'saint' and prophet Ntsikana, who had told Africans to become 'an inseparable union'.[46] By drawing inspiration from Ntsikana, who professed Christianity 20 years before the Mfengu migration, the Xhosa could also stress a deeper, older tradition of African Christianity. According to Nzungu, they would, moreover, be able to hold their heads high with the Irish, who had their St Patrick's Day, and the English with their St George's Day. The first annual Ntsikana Remembrance Day was held on 10 April 1909.[47] Some 1500 people from various districts attended the meeting in the King William's Town district. In charge of the proceedings were Walter Rubusana, J.K. Bokwe, Nathaniel Umhalla, Meshach Pelem, Bertram Xiniwe (son of the late Paul) and the organiser, George Nzungu.[48] Pelem, the SANC vice-president, was the first chairman of the Ntsikana committee.

The two celebrations continued for well over half a century until 1973 when, paradoxically, they were discontinued in line with the Bantustan government's 'Ciskeian nationality policy', aimed at reconciling the Xhosa and the Mfengu.[49]

---

* Also present in Peddie were Benjamin Dlepu, William Rulashe, William Bekwa, Mark Mpahla and the veteran Rev. Charles Lwana. The main Transkeian organisers were Veldtman, Theodore Ndwandwa, L.W. Mazisa and Patrick Xabanisa (for many years the regional chairman). Also involved were J.D. Gulwa (Lovedale), S.T. Danga (Grahamstown), Harry Mtombeni (Hackney) and John Sishuba (Kamastone).

In the last years of the nineteenth century, the divisions between the SANC and Jabavu's Imbumba began to assume strong ideological dimensions. Reflecting Rharhabe–Thembu experiences, the SANC had a more African-oriented approach to politics, concerned with the grassroots and local experience, whereas Imbumba, representing the mission-trained old guard and collaborationist Mfengu, had a more assimilationist, meritocratic and class-oriented approach. Talented people in Imbumba like Jabavu, Wauchope, Bokwe and Makiwane had made a real impact in several spheres on the white colonial establishment and consequently became more enmeshed within it.

Developments in the mid-1890s highlighted the different cultures of politics. In 1896 a rinderpest epidemic swept through the subcontinent, killing around 80 per cent of cattle in the eastern Cape alone and destroying the economic independence of thousands of Africans, who were pushed into labour migrancy, in much the same way as the cattle-killing had done.[50] This economic disaster, coming on top of the political threats posed by the Glen Grey Act, seriously undermined the long-term prospects of Africans in colonial society. Feeling the pinch of colonialism, many Africans responded by withdrawing, psychologically if not physically, from the new order. What was described as a wave of African 'race' consciousness swept throughout southern Africa around the turn of the century. It was manifested most conspicuously among Christians and the educated elite by the formation of separatist churches, which broke away from the paternalistic control of the mission churches to form self-reliant African bodies responding to African needs. Similar responses occurred, as we shall see, in the educational and economic spheres as well. Long-evident Africanist ideas now came to the surface among christianised and educated Africans, and activists and intellectuals from different territories started working together to give political content to these notions.

The SANC strongly supported the separatist church movements. It defended the so-called Ethiopians, and the separatists participated actively in the political organisation's structures. The SANC also set up an independent higher education scheme to fund an African-run college, the Queen Victoria Memorial Scheme. Jabavu and the Imbumba camp, on the other hand, rejected these movements as radical, confrontational and counterproductive. Working within structures acceptable to white colonists, such as the Inter-State Native College Scheme and the established mainstream churches, they actively opposed the more Africanist projects.[51]

Generationally, too, the Imbumba group represented older, more moderate views; the SANC, younger and more radical ones. The Mfengu, at the heart of Imbumba, had been the first Africans in the Cape to be enfranchised. Many Mfengu voters by the end of the century belonged to an older generation who had enrolled before the franchise qualifications were tightened in 1887 and 1892; while most of the Xhosa voters were of a younger generation, who had qualified under the later, more stringent laws. The older category of voters comprised mostly rural peasants with access to land, while the younger people were better educated and professionally more qualified.[52] Jabavu's principal non-Mfengu supporters – Wauchope and Bokwe, for example – were of the old missionary school. In all, his support base consisted of the minority Mfengu, school notables and white politicians.[53]

The emergence of two clear camps in eastern Cape politics – Ingqungqutela and Imbumba – helped shape the evolution of the new-style African politics in South Africa at the end of the nineteenth century. While these differences were never absolute – a myriad of cross-cutting alliances influenced by a whole range of social and personal factors bridged the basic divides, thus enabling political opponents to work together in religious, temperance, sports and other bodies – the two distinct camps, both aspiring to represent the African voice in the eastern Cape and beyond, remained competitive and politically hostile towards each other well into the twentieth century.

17

The 'Believers' and
the British in Natal

We bear earnest witness that this cutting off of the Zulu, without
our having been given a single opportunity of answering or being
listened to, we do not willingly accept. We desire that these words
may not be obliterated, but always remain known for ever and ever.
– Martin Lutuli on behalf of Shingana kaMpande, 1886

In Natal, as in the eastern Cape, a new stratum of Christian and
educated Africans emerged in the second half of the nineteenth century.
Numbering about 10,000 by the 1880s, they were often referred to as
kholwa (believers) and were initially based mainly around the mission
stations.[1] One prominent centre was the Wesleyan mission of Edendale
outside Pietermaritzburg, which the missionary James Allison and his
congregation of one hundred families had set up in 1851 on land they had
themselves bought. Some of the earliest expressions of African political
assertion in Natal came from here. Johannes Kumalo, the main spokesman
at Edendale, is reported to have protested at a meeting of 'civilised natives'
in 1863 that although the *kholwa* had left 'the race of our forefathers'
and started imitating the English, they still were not treated fairly before
the law: 'Look around you. You have an English house, English tables,
chairs ... Everything round us is English but one, and that is the law. The
law by which our cases are decided is only fit to be eaten by vultures.'[2]
The other important elder at Edendale was Stephen Mini, the Christian
chief. According to one historian, the Kumalo, Mini and Molife families
were among Natal's oldest and wealthiest Christians and 'for a long time

dominated local politics'. In 1867 the Edendale people were wealthy enough to buy the farm Driefontein near Ladysmith, upon which a new mission was started, and the Africans became the 'major suppliers of foodstuffs' for the towns surrounding the two settlements.

In addition to these Wesleyan centres, the Congregationalist American Board of Missions set up a belt of stations along the coast, stretching from Amanzimtoti in the south, to Inanda near Durban and Groutville (present-day KwaDukuza) further north. From these emerged important dynasties of school people like the Dubes and Lutulis, as well as many prominent leaders of public opinion. These mission stations and their schools, such as Adams College and Inanda Seminary for girls, were as integral to the process of political mobilisation in Natal as Lovedale and Healdtown were in the Cape.[3]

A large section of the new *kholwa* class of Christians comprised non-literate peasants living on the mission 'reserves'. Their chiefs and headmen became influential in Natal African politics, providing legitimacy and support for the educated activists, whose vision and skills drove the first proto-nationalist organisations. Tracing these kinds of linkages is important in understanding the emergence of the new politics.

But what were the formal political avenues open to this emerging class of christianised and literate Africans in Natal? After Britain annexed Natal in the early 1840s, a system of segregation was developed by the longstanding Secretary for Native Affairs, Theophilus Shepstone. In Natal, Africans were governed by 'native law' and were not eligible for the franchise.[5] Theoretically, mission-educated Africans with the necessary qualifications could participate in colonial politics, and their rights were constitutionally entrenched, but in practice they were excluded from effective participation in the social and political structures of Natal society. According to the provisions of the 1856 constitution, all men above the age of 21 years who possessed any immovable property worth £50 or rented property to the yearly value of £10 were eligible for the vote.[6] However, steps were soon taken to restrict the African franchise. The most important measures in this respect were two Acts of 1864 and 1865. The former laid down the conditions under which Africans could be exempted from the operation of 'native law', while the latter stipulated how Africans might become enfranchised. An African wishing to be exempted from 'native law' had to petition the Governor, giving particulars about his family, property and chief, and furnishing proof of his ability to read and write. An unmarried woman needed a European of good standing to support her exemption application as well.

Letters of exemption were not automatically acquired once these stipulations had been fulfilled: it was in the Governor's discretion to grant or refuse an application.[7] If exemption was granted, qualified Africans had to wait for a further period of seven years, and show that they had resided in Natal for 12 years, before they could petition the Governor for the franchise. Petitions for the franchise had to be accompanied by a certificate signed by three registered European voters and endorsed by a justice of the peace or resident magistrate. Once again, it was in the Governor's discretion to grant or refuse the application.[8] In fact, such applications usually proved to be a futile exercise. The South African Native Affairs Commission found in 1903 that in the 38 intervening years only two Africans out of a total estimated African population of 904,041 had acquired the vote in Natal.[9] Exemptions were also sparingly granted: by 1904 an estimated 5000 people, including the progeny of exempted men, were living under the exemption law.[10]

However, the authorities remained hostile to the exemption measures, which they saw as undermining the pseudo-traditionalism that formed the basis of 'native policy' in the colony. The government tried to avoid treating exempted Africans as a special category of people and usually referred to Africans in blanket terms. Exemption was defined in the narrowest terms: exempted Africans were freed from the operation of customary law only, and not from many of the discriminatory restrictions applying to Africans in general.[11]

For the small, emerging middle class of ministers, teachers, journalists, shopkeepers, farmers and *kholwa* chiefs in Natal, the position they found themselves in was unenviable. They had embraced new ideas and practices but were not accepted by colonial society. They were regarded as outsiders by both traditional Africans, whose way of life they had in many respects abandoned, and the colonists, whose way of life they wished increasingly to emulate. To the *kholwa*, this was a painful and frustrating dilemma.[12] The allegiances of the *kholwa* would be tested to the limit during the Anglo-Zulu War of 1879 and in the civil wars that racked Zululand throughout the 1880s. A number of Christian communities, whose futures depended on their show of loyalty to the colony, supported British and colonial forces against the Zulu kingdom in 1879. Some Edendale residents, for example, were among those who 'cast their lot with British efforts to crush the Zulu'.[13]

A number of *kholwa,* on the other hand, gave their support to attempts to preserve the territorial and political integrity of the Zulu kingdom. Bishop J.W. Colenso and his assistants at Bishopstowe worked on behalf of the uSuthu royal faction during the civil war, while Martin Lutuli from Groutville became secretary to the young prince Dinuzulu in the mid-1880s, as the royal house tried desperately to maintain its position. Lutuli was involved in major negotiations on behalf of the uSuthu, including meetings at Government House in Pietermaritzburg. He was present when the British plan for the dismemberment of Zululand was conveyed to the king's closest advisers. As members of an oral culture, the Zulu had conventionally conveyed their positions through the spoken word, which the colonial authorities could manipulate and misinterpret. Now Martin Lutuli put down for posterity what Shingana kaMpande, trusted adviser to the king, dictated to him: 'We bear earnest witness that this cutting off of the Zulu, without our having been given a single opportunity of answering or being listened to, we do not willingly accept. We desire that these words may not be obliterated, but always remain known for ever and ever. We return now to the Zulus, that we may tell them what we have heard, and they also will answer for themselves.'[14] At the moment of defeat and conquest, the Zulu had found a new written voice – and the new struggle that lay ahead would revolve largely around the skills of literacy and western political protocols.

Lutuli was helped by a young teacher from the Amanzimtoti Institute, Josiah Gumede, who had grown up and studied in the Cape and who later became president of the ANC in 1927. The young Gumede served as a messenger for the king and acted, moreover, as a negotiator on the king's behalf in meetings with representatives of the Transvaal Boers, who were eyeing the Zulu country. Far from distancing themselves from 'traditional' authority, he and Lutuli 'befriended and acted as indunas' or advisers to Cetshwayo's successor. As Gumede's biographer has noted: 'He had gained first-hand experience of the realities of whites' coercion and dispossession of the Zulus' land. He experienced the frustrations and difficulties which confronted the Zulu royal house. The Boers' occupation of nearly five-sixths of Zulu territory instilled a sense of bitterness in him towards the Boers. At the same time Gumede felt the British offered little, if any, help to prevent the disintegration of the Zulu socio-economic and political stability... Gumede never approved of the British annexation of Zululand.'[15] After their assignment in Zululand, Josiah Gumede and Martin Lutuli, now friends for life, returned to their posts at the Amanzimtoti Institute and the Umvoti mission reserve, respectively, having begun a journey of political activism that would stretch over many decades.

As in the Cape, the mission-educated *kholwa* began to assert themselves in the 1880s, using the new discourses of Christianity, western education and British and American political ideas in pursuit of their aspirations as Africans in colonial Natal society. The pioneering organisation in this respect was the Funamalungelo (Seeking Civic Rights) Society, started in 1888. It soon gained a mouthpiece in the missionary-owned *Inkanyiso* newspaper, which followed less than a year later. The initiator of Funamalungelo was Johannes Kumalo, a spokesman for the Edendale and Driefontein communities, who had long been active and influential among Natal Africans. Kumalo explained that the aim of the Society was to provide the means for exempted Africans to 'get to know and understand one another; as well as learn something of their position as exempted Natives; and above all to improve themselves so as to attain the highest state of civilisation'.[16] Its focus was primarily on increasing black landownership, electoral politics and civil rights.[17] Like the Native Educational Association in the Cape, Funamalungelo was centred on key mission stations, in its case Edendale and Driefontein.

Complementing the work of Funamalungelo, a Zulu–English monthly newspaper was started in April 1889. This was *Inkanyiso* (The Light), which was printed in Pietermaritzburg on a new press provided by the Anglican Society for the Propagation of the Gospel. Like *Isigidimi*, based at Lovedale, which people throughout South Africa were reading by the 1880s, *Inkanyiso* was meant to be a voice for the missionaries and the newly christianised Africans. A prospectus stated that 'we wish to give publicity to our thoughts, in the hope that, as our English friends become more acquainted with "Native Opinion", a better understanding between us may be created'.[18] The newspaper also helped promote debate among the *kholwa* and recorded their activities, including meetings of the Funamalungelo Society. In 1891, *Inkanyiso* changed its name to *Inkanyiso lase Natal* and became a weekly. Its circulation reached 2500 by September that year and reports in the mid-1890s indicate that exempted Africans had become firm supporters of both the paper and Funamalungelo. A notice of a meeting of the Society in Edendale in 1894 described the main topic as the 'elevation [of Africans] to a proper state of civilisation and the best means of arriving at it'.[19] It was also reported that 'white friends who had studied the Native interest and bore it at heart attended a meeting of the society and took part in the discussions'.[20] In 1895 a Zulu syndicate bought out *Inkanyiso lase Natal*. The first black-owned newspaper in Natal, *Inkanyiso* was thereafter published and edited by Solomon Kumalo, a member of the Driefontein–Edendale community. According to Switzer, it became a 'relatively vociferous protest paper'.[21]

In 1896 the Funamalungelo Society was chaired by Simeon Kambule. His grandfather had been the first headman at Edendale, his father had died while trying to rescue the injured British commander during conflict with the Hlubi in 1873, and he himself had fought on the side of the British in the Zulu War in 1879. 'If any family could be said to define Zulu Christian achievement in Natal it was the Kambules,' one historian has commented.[22] As chairman of the Society, he petitioned the government for clarification of the status of exempted Africans, and requested exemption from the discriminatory laws affecting them, but the petitions brought no relief.[23] Exempted Africans continued to be dissatisfied with their position in Natal society.

Both Funamalungelo and *Inkanyiso* were signs of an emerging independence and activism among the *kholwa*. In this they were sustained and informed by their links with the eastern Cape. A number of prominent figures in Natal were educated at mission schools like Lovedale and Healdtown, among them Bryant Cele, Saul Msane, Cleopas Kunene,

Mark Radebe and Josiah Gumede. Before *Inkanyiso* was started, local intellectuals sent reports of their activities to *Imvo*. Saul Msane, who was born at Edendale (and later married into the Mini family), became the Edendale agent for *Imvo* on his return from Healdtown. He and others wrote letters to that newspaper and *Imvo* also carried news about the first stirrings of constitutional politics in Natal, such as the petition by 'Exempted Natives' of 1890, which included the names of Lutuli and Mini.[24]

Church networks, especially among the Wesleyans, were also important vehicles for the cross-pollination of ideas and the growth of broader networks. J.T. Jabavu's brother Jonathan was transferred by the Wesleyan Church from the Cape to Natal around 1890. Soon, he was reporting back on the existence of both an Edendale Mutual Improvement Association, of which he was chairman, and a Vigilance Association (Iliso Lomzi) – this shortly after the historic King William's Town conference of 1887 had decided to establish Native Vigilance Associations in the Cape. Church conferences also provided important opportunities for networking. In 1890 and 1891 Stephen Mini met with Cape and Orange Free State church leaders and laymen like J.T. Jabavu and Thomas Mqanda, president of the newly formed South African Native Congress, at two Wesleyan conferences.

By the mid-1890s the *kholwa* were becoming involved in some tough political contestations, which went beyond the prim Christianity and political tameness of the early *Inkanyiso* and Funamalungelo Society. In 1895 John Dube, who had returned to the colony in 1892 after spending seven years in America, wrote to *Inkanyiso*, complaining that magistrates were abusing their authority by forcing Africans who came to them to 'crawl on their hands and knees ... The native Christians ... are not excluded in this practice, and should they attempt to walk on their feet like men, policemen are ordered to force them to kneel down.'[26] At the same time, the itinerant Josiah Gumede, then acting as paid secretary and spokesman for Chief Ncwadi of the Ngwane at Bergville, was involved in organising petitions to have the local magistrate removed for his bias against the chief and the oppressive way in which he exercised his authority.[27]

Other independent initiatives also came to the fore. In 1896 Solomon Kumalo and Dr John Nembula were involved in efforts to start an African

Christian Union – a radical self-help scheme with the motto 'Africa for the Africans', begun by the controversial missionary Joseph Booth. At the outset the initiative generated much excitement among *kholwa* leaders, but in the end they decided at a large meeting not to go ahead with it.[28]

A further sign of growing self-assertion was the expression of religious independence. While the African Methodist Episcopal Church, which had spread rapidly through the rest of southern Africa, was banned by the government in Natal, other independent churches established themselves in the colony, to the dismay and alarm of the authorities. In 1901 the Secretary for Native Affairs listed three separatist churches calling themselves Congregationalist, Presbyterian and 'the Church of the Native Races'. These bodies, he said in an interview, 'preached a doctrine that the native was the proper owner of Africa and that he should throw off all European control and claim his own'. One preacher, Johannes Zondi, had been sentenced to three months' imprisonment for sedition. When released, 'he started forthwith with his old propaganda', only to be arrested and 'punished' once more, before continuing again, undeterred, with his work. One breakaway from the American Congregationalists in Noodsberg, led by P. Mkeza, set up eight missions in Natal and Zululand in the late 1890s. The main secession from the Presbyterian Church was the Presbyterian Church of Natal, begun by Thomas Sibisi, who established branches in Estcourt and Msinga.[29]

According to the authorities, the increasingly assertive political activists in Natal espoused the 'same doctrine' as the Ethiopian churches. Their major concern, it was reported in 1901, was a new Natal Native Congress, already set up the previous year, which sought to become 'the mouthpiece of the native peoples of the Colony'. It would put politics in Natal on a different footing as the new century began and would have a great impact on the politics of the country.

18

Bloemfontein, 'Black Mountain' and Basutoland

His Honor the President says: 'The days of slavery are gone' ... a slave means one wholly under the will of another. Now, Mr Editor, a native has no voice in politics here – not even in things concerning themselves. They have to do the will of a white man, and the will they must do; and what return do they get for their servitude? Nil.
– W.M. Somngesi, Rouxville, 1892

In the area that today makes up the Free State province of South Africa and the independent kingdom of Lesotho, the first new-style political organisations emerged for Africans only in the early 1900s, but their roots lay in the nineteenth century. Three centres were of particular importance for the evolution of this new politics: Bloemfontein, Thaba Nchu (Black Mountain) and Basutoland. All three became bases for the emergence of proto-nationalist political organisations run by mission-educated leaders.

Though its founding predates the establishment of the Orange Free State in 1854, Bloemfontein grew in size and importance after it became the capital of the new Voortrekker state. Within the republic relations between white and black were conducted as between *bazen tegenover dienstknechten* (masters and servants).[1] The republican constitution stipulated that only whites could become citizens of the country.[2] Ordinances effectively excluded blacks from owning land and also specifically closed the possibility that the few existing black landowners could vote by declaring that they 'zullen nimmer als burgers worden beschouwd' (will never be regarded as citizens), although they were liable to be called up for military service.

Laws made it illegal for black males to live or travel in the republic without a pass; from 1895 women were included in this prohibition. Municipal locations were strictly controlled: inhabitants had to register, and only those who worked for whites or had fixed jobs were allowed to reside in them. Rigid social segregation was maintained. *The Friend* summed up the feelings of the white colonists, both Boer and British, when it wrote in 1884, 'The native is a child, a minor to our law, so that they have to rest satisfied with the laws made for him by the white man.'[3]

For much of the nineteenth century a prominent feature of the southern Highveld was the absence of centralised political authority or any dominant chiefdom or ethnic grouping. People's identities remained fluid as a result of the *difaqane* or great dispersal, following the rise of Shaka's Zulu kingdom. The great scattering of people, compounded by early colonial intrusion, led to a high degree of dislocation and mobility, as scattered individuals and groups fled the violence and sought safety and land in the region. Among them were the Griqua communities, established north of the Orange (now Gariep) River at Philippolis and Griquatown. According to Paul Landau, 'They developed a nonracialized Christian elite, which mixed Sechuana-, Khoe- and Dutch-speakers together', and helped spread literacy and Christianity north of the Vaal River.[4]

Given the restrictive policies of the republic, the size of the educated class of black Free Staters remained small and the emergence of formal political associations was retarded. The social and political developments that had occurred among Africans in the Cape and, to a lesser extent, in Natal were not paralleled in the Free State until after the South African War. This is not to say that there was an absence of political awareness or activity prior to the Free State becoming a British colony. People who were to emerge later as leaders of the first political organisations established themselves early on as leading men in the towns of the republic as well as in the Thaba Nchu reserve.

Waaihoek township in Bloemfontein consisted of a diverse range of people, reflecting the fluid identities of the region. To facilitate the administration of the township, 'block men' were appointed to represent a group of dwellings and matters affecting residents were referred to them. In May 1882 the inhabitants of the Waaihoek township chose Jacob Lavers, later president of the Orange River Colony Native Vigilance Association, as a field cornet. In 1891 Jan Mocher, another long-serving leader of the same organisation, was elected to the same position.[5] Both men were to become prominent in early political organisations in the region. The biggest complaint of the residents was the stringent application of the pass laws. Wives of the householders were involved in civic affairs as well: in 1899 they presented an illuminated address to President Steyn.[6]

After a visit to Bloemfontein in 1894, J.T. Jabavu pronounced approvingly on this system of local government, and noted that Waaihoek had its own 'town hall and a council of its own composed of Natives, which is presided over by the Mayor'. He also observed that there were 'good and decent buildings' in the township.[7]

With the discovery of gold on the Witwatersrand, the Free State began to be drawn more firmly into a wider world. This was graphically symbolised by the extension of the railway from the Cape, which reached Bloemfontein in 1890 and soon joined that city to Johannesburg and Pretoria. The traffic of people and ideas began to flow with increasing strength towards the Free State from both directions.

Links with Cape society, which predated the coming of the railway, provided an important stimulus to the growth of new forms of politics in the republic. Because the government provided a tiny grant of £125 per year for African education in the 1880s, those wishing to study further had to travel south to the eastern Cape to attend the mission institutions there. Probably the best-known African Christian in Bloemfontein was Gabriel David, who in 1867 went to study at the Anglican institution in Grahamstown. On finishing his studies in 1871, he was sent to Bloemfontein to assist the minister in charge of the new 'native mission' being established there. After 19 years, he was ordained in 1890, 'the first Tswana to receive the Anglican priesthood'. He was based at St Patrick's Church, 'the centre of the native work' of the Anglicans in the Free State.[8] By 1885 there were 200 black Christians in Bloemfontein. Just as in the Cape, the political ideals of the early educated Africans in the Free State and Basutoland were shaped largely by Christian beliefs and values. The first presidents of the two African political associations to emerge after 1900 in the Orange River Colony were both Christian ministers.

The circulation of ideas from the Cape was also assisted by and through the press. *Imvo Zabantsundu* was disseminated in the Free State and Africans from the republic reported regularly about conditions in the country in its columns. One such correspondent was W.N. Somngesi of Rouxville, who in 1891 described the Free State as a slave state.[9] In the following year Somngesi entered the broader political debate by writing a letter to the *Cape Mercury*, in which he rebutted points made by the President of the Orange Free State in an article on 'The Native Question'. The letter was later reprinted in the Bloemfontein newspaper *De Express*. Repeating his *Imvo* theme, Somngesi declared:

His Honor the President says: 'The days of slavery are gone, and let us be thankful that it is so.' I may ask first, what is a slave? A slave is any one in bondage. Are the natives free in the Free State? Are the native ministers and other respectable people not bound to carry passes, which they are bound to pay for? Are the natives free to go and see their friends who are living on farms close by? I say no. It does not matter whether your friend was dying on a farm, you dare not pass the boundaries of the town commonage without a sixpenny pass. Native preachers dare not forget their passes on Saturdays if they have to go out preaching on Sundays – pas op, for a fine of £3 or one month's imprisonment with hard labour. Do they not pay a poll tax, and [get] nothing in return done for them; whilst the white man is free from the tax, and his children's schooling supported by Government?

Secondly, a slave means one wholly under the will of another. Now, Mr Editor, a native has no voice in politics here – not even in things concerning themselves. They have to do the will of a white man, and the will they must do; and what return do they get for their servitude? Nil.

Thirdly and lastly, a slave means one who has lost all power of resistance. What I have said on the first and second points will explain the third, and I will, therefore, dwell no longer on this painful subject of 'The Native Question', with the prayers and hopes that the Lord will hasten the time when all nations will be entirely freed from bondage.[10]

In addition to the flow of ideas and people from the Cape, traffic from the north started to pour into the Free State especially after the coming of the railways. A new message began to bleed into the northern parts of the territory. From its source in Pretoria, the separatist church movement, known as Ethiopianism, soon flowed across state boundaries and reached its greatest popularity in the Free State. As its historian, James Campbell, has said: 'By the beginning of the South African War in October 1899, AME churches had been established in towns and cities all across the republic. In Bloemfontein, the capital and a burgeoning rail center, the church attracted several hundred adherents, including an entire congregation of former Anglicans. In Kroonstad, further up the line of rail, African Methodism seems virtually to have swept the location. By mid-1899, the Kroonstad AME Church boasted a substantial brick building, day and night schools, regular weekly classes, and an active women's prayer union.'[11] According to Campbell, the success of this movement was that it linked town and countryside in ways that 'recognised and spoke to the varied experience and eclectic consciousness of Free State Africans'. Eighty to ninety per cent of Africans in the region lived on rural farms, as labour tenants and sharecroppers, and their fortunes were closely connected to and affected by economic developments in the South African Republic. The separatist churches became strong in places like Parys, Kroonstad, Viljoensdrift and Vredefort, where sharecropping was widely practised.

The person responsible for the initial foray of the Ethiopians into the Free State was Jacobus Gilead Xaba, who came from one of the Edendale *kholwa* landowning families. After studying at Healdtown in the eastern Cape, he was posted to Heilbron in the Free State as a Wesleyan preacher and teacher. But he fell out with his white superior and was suspended. He then joined the Ethiopians and 'became the movement's most ardent and effective evangelist'. Benjamin Kumalo, who was also from a well-known *kholwa* family in Natal, and had studied at Lovedale, later took over from Xaba as head of the church in the Free State.[12] Another key AME Church leader was Marcus Gabashane, long-time resident of Thaba Nchu, who, as an itinerant preacher, succeeded in drawing away many congregants from the established churches, especially the Wesleyans.[13]

In 1898 the African American Bishop Henry Turner of the AME Church visited Bloemfontein and met with government officials during a six-week tour of South Africa to consolidate the new southern African branch of the church. His visit was another sign that Free State Africans were not separate from, but instead part of, an increasingly coherent movement of Africans throughout the subcontinent, working together in the social, educational, religious and political spheres.

The second area of importance for the nascent African nationalist movement was the independent enclave of Thaba Nchu, lying between Bloemfontein and Basutoland, where in 1834 Wesleyan Methodist missionaries had helped settle the Tswana-speaking Seleka Rolong under their chief Moroka. Thaba Nchu became known as a stronghold of education and Christianity. Moroka, who remained in office for over half a century, sent four sons to study in the Cape – one, Samuel, to Zonnebloem, from where he went to the Anglican missionary college of St Augustine's in Canterbury. By the end of the 1870s the Methodists had more than one thousand members at Thaba Nchu and the Anglicans about half that number.

After Chief Moroka's death in 1880, a bitter succession dispute developed between his mission-educated sons, the heir apparent, Tshipinare Moroka, and the Zonnebloem-trained Samuel Moroka, which eventually turned violent and led to Tshipinare's death. This provided the Free State republic with the excuse to annex Moroka's country in 1884 and banish Samuel permanently from the area.

Before he died, Tshipinare had the whole Moroka territory surveyed, with a view to providing legal title to the land in the form of individual deeds. The intention was that he and his allied chiefs would hold the land inalienably on behalf of their subjects. But with his death and the annexation by the Free State, large parts of the land were in effect alienated and privatised. The republic acquired control over a sizeable portion of Moroka's country while some of the chiefs sold their new farms to whites and moved away. By 1900 the situation on the ground was as follows: there were 54 farms owned by the landowning Rolong elite; two 'native locations' at Seleka and Thaba Nchu; and a number of white- and government-owned farms, the latter occupied by former British soldiers demobilised after the South African War.[14]

The African landowning elite that emerged in Thaba Nchu were to produce important political leaders in the twentieth century. Prominent among them were Joel Goronyane, Moses Masisi and John Mokitlane Nyokong, who in 1899 petitioned the Free State President in regard to land rights in the Moroka district as 'voormannen der Barolong natie'.[15] All three were in the forefront of setting up newspapers and organisations in the early years of the twentieth century. John Nyokong was a wealthy landowner, who complained to a government commission that 'as owner of the farm Maseru, he had been completely frustrated by official instructions not to use his own expensive harvesting machinery purchased for one thousand pounds except under the supervision of a white engineer whom he could not afford to employ throughout the year'.[16] His grandson, James Moroka, studied at Edinburgh University and qualified there as a doctor, before becoming the fifth ANC president in the late 1940s.

Other notable political figures closely connected to this elite were Jeremiah Makgothi, brother-in-law of Moses Masisi, and W.Z. Fenyang. Makgothi, born in 1860 to Christian parents, was sent to study at Lovedale between 1875 and 1883. When he returned home, he became headmaster of the first boarding school in Thaba Nchu for African boys and helped translate the New Testament into Serolong, some forty years after Robert Moffat had published his Tswana translation. His granddaughter, the Soweto Committee of Ten activist of the 1970s, Ellen Kuzwayo, recalled how the family used to travel the 30 miles from their farm to Thaba Nchu in the 'Cape carriage, drawn by four beautiful stallions'.[17] The value attached to education by the Thaba Nchu elite and their relative wealth can be seen from the fact that in 1908 no less than 14 of their children were studying at Lovedale.[18]

The third centre of political activity in the region was the mountain kingdom of Basutoland, where Moshoeshoe had welded together groups of disparate refugees from the Mfecane, who in time became known as the

Sotho. One of the great statesmen of the nineteenth century, Moshoeshoe was the only African leader on the southern Highveld able to protect the integrity of his land and carve out a relatively autonomous state for his people.

This mountain kingdom underwent a process of missionisation similar to that happening elsewhere in the region. French missionaries from the Paris Evangelical Missionary Society formed a close alliance with Moshoeshoe as he consolidated his diverse following into a 'nation' with its own territory. Education and literacy started to take root. From the start, developments here were closely connected to what was happening in the territories abutting it.[19] Until well into the twentieth century Basutoland was expected to become part of South Africa, and people from the kingdom played an important part in developing an overarching sense of national unity in the subcontinent as well as helping forge the networks that would ultimately lead to the formation of the modern ANC.

Something of the mobility of the educated class and their links with the neighbouring colonies and states can be gleaned from the reminiscences of Josiah Semouse, who was born in Basutoland and later became a member of the African Native Choir, which toured Britain in the 1890s.

I was born in 1860, at Mkoothing, in what is known as one of the conquered territories (Basutoland). My parents being Christian people, I was naturally so brought up; I first attended school at a small village called Korokoro, where my father was appointed local preacher, and there I learnt to read and write my own language. Then I went to the Morija training institution, about thirty-six miles from my home. I heard from a native teacher that there is a school in Cape Colony, called Lovedale, which is famous for the practical knowledge that it imparts to its pupils. But, a few months after, war broke out between Basutoland and the Cape Colony about the order of disarmament. I took part against the British during this war, but I was not happy, because I did not know the English language then. When this war was over, which was decided in our favour, I left Basutoland for Lovedale, travelling day and night; I slept for a few hours till the moon came out, and then pursued my course, till I reached my destination in eleven days, the whole distance being about 600 miles. At Lovedale, I received both education and civilization, then one day, in March 1886, the principal of the college received a telegram from Kimberley to say that there was a vacancy in the office there for an honest, educated man. I was sent to fill up the vacancy, and I remained there till the end of March 1891, when I received an esteemed offer from the manager of the African Choir to join the choir for England.

As Semouse's testimony shows, close ties were maintained by the Sotho with Lovedale and eastern Cape institutions. Shad B. Mama, one of the main correspondents in *Isigidimi* in the early 1880s and a loyal South African Native Congress supporter, moved to Basutoland by the 1890s; he still regularly attended conferences of the Congress. Its secretary, Dr Rubusana, noted that the SANC was in contact with 'native chiefs and leading men' in Basutoland'.[20] Sotho intellectuals became closely involved in the broad regional process of political mobilisation, one of the more prominent being the ex-Lovedalian Simon Phamotse, who began the *Naledi ea Lesotho* newspaper in the 1900s.

By the end of the nineteenth century, Africans from the Free State formed part of an increasingly coherent political and social movement stretching across the territories of southern Africa. That their focus, contacts and aspirations went beyond the republic and, indeed, southern Africa was demonstrated in a direct and unusual way when in late 1899 a team 'consisting of the best footballers available amongst the natives of the Orange Free State' undertook a tour to England. It was the first-ever international football tour from South Africa. In the categories of the time, the team consisted of 'Basutos', with the exception of two 'Hottentots'.* Even though the listed names are distorted by English ignorance, they do tend to support the argument of scholars about the mixed and fluid nature of identities in Free State society. The first match was against Newcastle United at St James Park and the South Africans lost 6–3 in front of a crowd of 6000. From the perspective of the globalisation of sport and the

---

* The team consisted of Adolph (goal), Abel Botloks and August Daniells (backs), Apollis, Solomon and Broffit (half-backs), S. Korje and D. Lakey (right wing), J. Twayi (captain, centre) and J. Martin and Thloka (left-wing forwards).

mega soccer leagues of today, the teams the Free Staters played against are astonishing. Their opponents included Liverpool, Manchester United, Aston Villa, Tottenham Hotspur, Arsenal, Sunderland, Nottingham Forest, Derby County, Sheffield United and West Bromwich Albion in England, Glasgow Celtic and Hibernian in Scotland, and Belfast Celtic in Ireland. The matches were watched by large crowds. However, it soon became apparent that the South African footballers were woefully mismatched. The tour turned into a characteristic Victorian side-show in which people from the colonies were displayed and regarded by the Victorians as the 'exotic other', reinforcing the ideas of the day about the place of Africans in the scale of civilisation.[21]

The captain of the 1899 football team was Joseph B. Twayi, who in the next few years became a leading member of the Orange River Colony Native Vigilance Association.[22] In the press, the footballers were described as 'a gentlemanly lot, well conducted, and are of no mean intelligence'. 'They can all speak English fluently – some of them are capable of writing and conversing in four different languages, including English and Dutch. They all have a trade – some are clerks, others grocer's assistants, tailors and carpenters.' According to a report, the aim of the visitors was 'to show the British public how far they are advanced in the beloved game of soccer'. But the real significance of the tour for those involved would have been the political and social message it sent out. The new Africans once again sought to signal their determination to take their place in colonial society and show how far they had progressed in terms of their fitness to belong.

The football team was in England when the South African War broke out in October 1899 and the players lost no time in declaring publicly their loyalty to Britain. A new era was at hand, and these Free Staters must have looked forward to it with great expectations.

19

Diamonds and the expansion
of political networks

There is no town like Kimberley in the whole of South Africa. They work day and night. Many nights pass sleepless because of the noise and smoke all night long. Sunday is little recognised ... I have never seen a city as bad as Kimberley. And its laws are also bad. Black people are ... chased around like locusts and put in jail when they have no pass ... The diamond diggers work naked, their bodies exposed to the sun. After work you are searched, searched thoroughly, turned upside down in a disgraceful manner.

– Josiah Semouse, January 1887

The lands to the west of the Boer republics of the Orange Free State and the Transvaal were for long occupied by Tswana-speaking people and mixed groups of Khoisan origin such as the Griqua and Korana, who became powerful because of their access to horses, firearms and wagons. Following well-established African trade and communication routes, incoming Europeans opened up the 'missionary road' to the north, along which a steady traffic of goods and ideas travelled backwards and forwards. Mission stations were started at places such as Philippolis, Griquatown, Kuruman and Mafikeng. The settlement of Mafikeng, on the Molopo River, was set up by Chief Molema, head of the Christian section of the Tshidi Rolong, who established a thriving Christian community there. He was later joined by his half-brother, the paramount Montshiwa Tawana, after suffering defeat at the hands of the Transvaal Boers. At first Montshiwa complained that the Christians 'were obeying the book more than the King', but by the 1880s he 'had appointed a "royal chaplain", made Methodism into his 'state religion' and ensured that prayers were said at his *kgotla* or court before all public ventures.[1] Both his and Molema's factions of the Rolong were to play an important part in the development of African organisational politics in South Africa. Chief Molema's son Silas set up the first school in the region in 1878 after completing his studies at Healdtown in the eastern Cape. He also started the first independent Tswana-language newspaper. Mafikeng later developed into an important colonial settlement, a stop-over on the railway line to Rhodesia, and site of a famous siege during the South African War.

Several other *dikgosi* such as Sechele Motswasele of the Kgabo Kwena around Molepolole and Khama of the Ngwato were responsive to the Christianity of the missionaries, and grew strong through alliances with them. Sechele, baptised in 1848, became 'a leading patron of Christianity in the mid-nineteenth century'.[2] Khama Sekgoma was baptised at the age of 20 after coming into contact with Livingstone; he was described as 'among the noblest trophies won by Christianity from out of unbroken heathenism'. Becoming chief in 1872, Khama was able, by working closely with the missionaries, to protect his land from being taken over by Cecil John Rhodes and hostile Boer neighbours. The *Christian Express* at Lovedale praised his 'aristocracy of character' and put him on a par with Moshoeshoe as a statesman.[3]

It was the evangelical and educational work of the missionaries that gave rise to a new class of literate, Christian Africans in the interior. By 1880, 'there were several thousand Batswana attending schools and churches affiliated to various mission organizations in the interior of southern Africa'. As in the eastern Cape and Natal, these literate, mission-educated Africans started contributing to missionary publications, such as the *Mahoko a Becwana* newspaper, published in Kuruman, and began to redefine themselves in a changing cultural milieu. Other contributions to the paper were made by the *dikgosi* themselves, either writing directly or through secretaries and representatives. Their correspondence revealed the dynamic interaction between traditional figures of authority and the growing number of mission-educated intellectuals, as the networks of literacy and the new ways spread steadily throughout southern Africa.[4]

The trajectory and pace of development in the interior changed dramatically when diamonds were discovered near Hopetown in 1867. Within a few years Britain had annexed the diamond-bearing territory and called it Griqualand West, despite protests by the Boer republics, the Tlhaping, Griqua and Korana alike. In a short time the population on the diamond fields grew to 30,000. Most of the African immigrants came initially from the eastern Cape and Basutoland, though soon Africans from throughout the subcontinent started streaming there in search of money and guns.

New Rush, renamed Kimberley, became a centre with a polyglot of cultures and people, who were bound together in new ways. One of the newcomers was the recently ordained Lovedale graduate, the Rev. Gwayi Tyamzashe from Peelton near King William's Town, who arrived in 1872 with the purpose of setting up a new congregation for the Presbyterians of the Free Church of Scotland. Tyamzashe compared New Rush – the 'crowding of its streets, and the noise of the machinery and workmen' – with what he had heard of the great metropolis, London. He was not impressed with the behaviour of the fortune-seekers: 'I observed that nearly every evening was devoted to private and public amusements, insomuch as there seemed to be no room left for the great work for which we had come.' The 'rough life' lived by both white and black inhabitants made him feel that 'this place was only good for those who were resolved to sell their souls for silver, gold, and precious stones ... [or] the pleasures of a time'.[5]

Soon, permanent churches, schools, hospitals and other public buildings replaced the temporary structures of the first rush. Three major developments marked Kimberley's physical growth: the laying out of a permanent water supply from the Vaal River in 1881, the completion of the railway line from Cape Town in 1885, and the introduction of the compound system in 1887, which made possible the rigid control of African labour, as large business monopolies emerged in the diamond-mining industry.[6]

Most of the new arrivals at the diamond fields were workers living in poor conditions in the compounds, but there were also a good number of mission-educated school people and artisans from the eastern Cape, who followed in the footsteps of Tyamzashe and lived in the town. With their unique qualifications they generally occupied the most sought-after and best-paid jobs available to black residents. Among the early settlers who later became well-known Kimberley citizens were the Wesleyan lay preacher Johannes Kozani from Grahamstown, Joseph Moss and the ex-Lovedalian Jonas Msikinya, who became interpreter at the Beaconsfield magistrate's court in 1879. Around 1880, a group of Lovedale students were recruited through the school's principal as staff at the expanding post office in Kimberley – these were prestigious postings denoting 'progress' at a time of revolution in communications. In the early 1880s eastern Cape activists involved in the first political organisations, like Meshach Pelem, made their way north, too. The historian Brian Willan has observed how bullish about the future and 'invigorated by the air' of this 'supremely British place' the educated incomers were. They started numerous churches, clubs, choirs and societies, which operated as part of a 'network of regular activities and involvement'. And, as on the mission stations of the eastern Cape, the ideas of 'progress' and 'civilisation' remained important lodestars for the school people here.[7]

Music became an integral part of life on the diamond fields. As early as April 1878 a group called the Kimberley African Amateur Minstrels gave a performance in the town, 'the earliest African musicians to perform as a group'.[8] David Coplan explains that for the ethnically diverse elite there, 'Music became a bond of interest and association and a means of expressing social aspiration'.[9] 'Almost every school prizegiving, organisation meeting or other occasion included musical entertainment.' Sport was also popular in the town. There were two cricket clubs for Kimberley's Africans, the Duke of Wellington CC (known simply as 'Duke') and the Eccentrics CC. The local derby was a big social occasion and was often held as the main entertainment on Christmas Day. In line with the cosmopolitan environment, the local African cricketers also played against Indian, 'Malay' and coloured teams. There were several rugby clubs and three tennis clubs, namely Blue Flag, Champion and Come Again. Women were welcomed as members and played in the competitions as well.[10]

The educated class, who assumed a position of social dominance and leadership in Kimberley, revelled in this new and burgeoning world.

According to Willan, 'Anybody who was anybody sought to become involved in running [a] club even if they did not actually play the game.' This was how the upwardly mobile Sol Plaatje, brought up on a German mission station, became joint secretary of Eccentrics CC in 1895 at the age of 19. The president was the post office employee Boyce Skota, 'a very religious and real upright Christian gentleman', whose son later became secretary-general of the ANC. The vice-president was the Basutoland-born boarding-house keeper, Patrick Lenkoane. Legendary for his sense of humour, he was described as 'one of the leading citizens among his people'. The local Anglican and Methodist ministers were both honorary officials, the latter being Jonathan Jabavu, brother of the famous John Tengo.

In this cosmopolitan milieu, focused on innovation rather than tradition, people readily crossed boundaries and embraced change. Sport, for instance, was played across religious and ethnic divides. The Griqualand West Coloured Cricket Union, started in 1892, represented all black cricketers in the area; while the rugby board, formed in 1894, used the word 'Colonial' rather than the more conventional 'Coloured' in its title, the first recorded instance of a non-racial approach to sport in South Africa. *Imvo* newspaper noted that it did not discriminate on the basis of *bala, luhlanga, lulwimi, nalunqulo* (colour, nationality, language or religion).[11]

This transcendence of divides was reflected, too, in personal relations. For several years Isaiah Bud Mbelle, a Xhosa-speaking Mfengu from Burgersdorp, shared a house in the Malay Camp with the young Tswana-speaking Rolong Sol Plaatje. In the course of time, Mbelle's sister Elizabeth came to visit and fell in love with her brother's housemate. When she and Plaatje decided to get married, both sets of parents were scandalised. But the couple went ahead nevertheless: yet another example of how the younger generation was self-consciously crossing old boundaries and shaping new directions.[12]

Numerous influences from diverse quarters were at work. The popular troupe, the Jubilee Singers, touring under the direction of Orpheus McAdoo, who had studied with Booker T. Washington, visited several times from the United States in the 1890s and introduced Kimberley residents to African American ideas and inspirations. One of its members, Will Thompson, settled in the city and became involved in its cultural life. Similarly, a West African, W. Cowen, gave a public address on 'Civilisation and its advantages for the African races'. A John Cowen was one of a group of ten who requested funds from De Beers for building an African branch of the YMCA in 1896; the other nine described themselves as 'Fingoes', Xhosa, Mpondo, Sotho and 'Becuana'. Willan argues that this was a deliberate strategy to show their broad representivity and universal outlook – people were stretching identities beyond old confines.

The human traffic from all parts of southern Africa came and went, connecting the school people in wider networks. Charlotte Manye proceeded from Kimberley to perform and study in Britain and America for a whole decade. Alice Kinloch, described as coloured, met her Zulu husband in Kimberley before ending up in London, where she helped form the African Association in 1897. Robert Grendon, a teacher of Irish–Herero extraction at the Beaconsfield high school, who had himself been educated at Zonnebloem College in Cape Town, and had helped set up the *Inkanyiso* newspaper in Natal, went on to become a poet and tutor to children of the Swazi king.[13]

By the 1890s the African population in Kimberley was over 8000 in size, among them a 'considerable number of educated natives', many of them Mfengu, trained at Lovedale and belonging to the Wesleyan Church. This educated stratum of black residents lived in ethnically mixed suburbs where they were able to buy property. Gwayi Tyamzashe lived a few houses away from Plaatje and Mbelle's shared digs in Malay Camp, while the Rev. Jonathan Jabavu lived in Green Point. The elite also filled the best jobs open to Africans in the town: interpreters at the magistrate's court, clerks, post office employees, teachers, ministers, entrepreneurs. Their earning power ranged from Isaiah Bud Mbelle's annual salary of £250, making him the best-paid black civil servant in the Cape, and Sol Plaatje's £78 per annum, to the wages of those who 'found employment in the stores from five pounds to six pounds per month'.

Politics in Kimberley were dominated by the figure of Cecil John Rhodes, whose company De Beers virtually ran the town. Rhodes first became Prime Minister of the Cape in 1890. While educated Africans in Kimberley participated in electoral politics, they did not mobilise in explicitly political organisations, as in the eastern Cape, perhaps because they defined themselves in this cultural melting pot more as individuals of the middle class than in ethnic terms. The most notable organisation for local Africans was the South African Mutual Improvement Association, which in a very moderate way discussed topical issues and debated how Africans could 'advance' themselves. In 1892 the Coloured People's Progressive Party of South Africa was formed, by Robert Grendon among others, to oppose the Franchise and Ballot Act, which Rhodes's government had introduced to further restrict the African franchise. The party claimed to speak 'on behalf of the coloured inhabitants of Griqualand West'. Two of its members, Hadjie Ozier Ally, the chairman, and John Tobin, would later become well known in Cape Town politics.[14] Africans, like Johannes Kozani, were also involved.

In 1895 the Rev. Jonathan Jabavu and other local leaders went in numbers to support Samuel Cronwright-Schreiner, husband of the writer Olive Schreiner, when he gave a public talk in which he attacked Rhodes's 'retrogressive legislation on the Native question'. Kimberley's Africans, it seems, were content to work with prominent local liberals such as Cronwright-Schreiner, Advocates Richard Solomon and Henry Burton (who helped them win several cases challenging discrimination), and Percy Ross Frames, one-time chairman of De Beers and a former Lovedale student himself. They were, according to one local leader, 'a magnificent group in whose hands the Natives of Kimberley entrusted their interests'.[15]

After the Jameson Raid, when old political alliances fell apart in the Cape, Rhodes came under increasing attack from the 'friends of the natives' who had previously been his allies. When the South African League, a body established to defend British involvement in southern Africa, came out in support of Rhodes's Progressive Party, the 'B' branch (for coloured people) in Kimberley put pressure on Rhodes to explain his position subsequent to the Jameson Raid. Addressing 'a number of African and Coloured meetings and deputations' before the 1898 elections, he gave them the assurance that his policy was 'equal rights for all civilised men south of the Zambesi'. These words of Rhodes's became the rallying cry for the new-style African politicians, a demonstration of the bargaining power that the electoral system gave them after 1896.[16]

By bringing together people from all over southern Africa in a melting pot of cultures and ideas, Kimberley paved the way for organisations with wider reach and subcontinental ambitions. It was in Kimberley that the first national associations in rugby, cricket and soccer, for both black and white, were all established. The whites-only South African Rugby Football Board led the way in 1889, its first president being the 'friend of the natives' Percy Ross Frames.[17] The South African Cricket Association was formed early the next year, with the Currie Cup its tournament trophy.[18] Local black enthusiasts soon emulated the example of the white cricket and rugby players. Enjoying access to the same powerful mining patrons that encouraged the white organisations, black sports administrators in Kimberley drew up plans to start national rugby and cricket bodies and competitions for those sportsmen excluded from them. The person at the head of these efforts was the captain of the Rovers Native Rugby Football Club and secretary of the Griqualand West cricket and rugby boards, Isaiah Bud Mbelle, a young man 'of immense ability and wide-ranging talent' who had been educated at Healdtown.[19] In July 1897 Mbelle and his colleagues persuaded Rhodes to present 'all the Coloured Sporting People of South Africa with a Silver Cup, valued at Fifty Guineas, for Competition amongst themselves on the same lines as the Currie Cup'.[20] In August of that year, the South African Coloured Rugby Football Board was formed, with Robert Grendon its first president and Mbelle its first secretary.[21] Mbelle also persuaded David Harris of De Beers, a member of the Cape parliament, to donate a trophy worth 100 guineas to black cricketers. On 1 November 1897, Harris informed Bud Mbelle that he had consulted with the Randlord Solly Joel, and 'I have this day ordered from England a suitable silver trophy, and on its arrival I shall be glad to hand it over to the Griqualand West Colonial Cricket Union, as a Barnato Memorial Trophy'.[22]

The first cricket tournaments reflected the inclusive goals of the early black administrators. While Western Province had mainly Muslim players, Griquas consisted of both Africans and coloureds, and the eastern Cape teams were made up entirely of Africans. By 1903 they had combined to form the South African Coloured Cricket Board, with Daniel Lenders as president.[23] This move towards unity showed that 'non-Europeans' were determined to work together and, moreover, that African administrators were in the forefront of the early development of sport in South Africa. On both these levels, Kimberley contributed significantly to the growth of national unity in the social sphere, as a precursor of formal political unification in South Africa.

As Kimberley developed into an economic magnet attracting people from throughout the subcontinent, Britain set about reshaping the areas in the hinterland of the fabulously rich new town to suit its interests. To counter the territorial ambitions of the Transvaal, which was eyeing the Tswana chiefdoms to the west of its borders, the British government sent the Warren Expedition north in 1884 to 'pacificate the territory' and 'reinstate the natives on their lands'.[24] Meshach Pelem was one of those who accompanied the expedition north from Kimberley.[25] The outcome was the declaration in 1885 of the new Crown Colony of British Bechuanaland, incorporating the southern Tswana areas west of the Boer republics and up to the Molopo River (including Mafikeng). At the same time, the lands of the Tswana north of the Molopo River up to the Limpopo River were declared a British Protectorate, giving *dikgosi* such as Khama and Sechele undefined autonomy under British protection.

In the next decade, the Bechuanaland Protectorate came under pressure from imperialists like Rhodes, who were intent on pushing north in the search for wealth and extending British influence. The territorial and political autonomy of the Protectorate was finally guaranteed in 1895, following representations by a delegation to London of the *dikgosi*, including Khama, Sechele and Bathoen. In the same year, the Crown Colony of British Bechuanaland was finally transferred to the Cape. At the time of its incorporation British Bechuanaland contained the largest concentration of Africans in the Cape outside the Transkeian Territories and the eastern Cape[26]. As a result of this relatively late imposition of colonial rule, and the initial policy introduced there of indirect rule, participation in electoral or protest politics took place under the guidance of the still widely prevalent authority of the *dikgosi*. The extent to which chiefdom politics continued to dominate in British Bechuanaland can be gauged by the fact that there were only about 100 Africans from the area on the Cape voters' roll in 1904 and only 88 in 1908.[27] According to the rather condescending Sol Plaatje, this was a fair estimate of the number of people capable of participating in electoral politics in an informed way.[28]

Though the Bechuanaland Annexation Act had left the status of the Tswana chiefs largely untouched, in the first decade of the twentieth century the Cape authorities attempted to weaken the powers of the chiefs and gradually subordinate them to magisterial rule. Colonial officials saw the relative autonomy of the chiefs as an unwelcome anomaly in the Cape system of 'native administration'.[29] This gave rise to considerable dissatisfaction, at the centre of which stood Badirile Montsioa of the Tshidi Rolong, grandson of the famous Montshiwa Tawana, who had ruled for nearly fifty years from 1849 to 1896. Badirile strenuously resisted the encroachment of white authority and consequently endured a stormy relationship with the Cape government.[30]

Outside Kimberley, educated Africans in this vast new territory of the Cape Colony worked in liaison with the chiefs rather than forming separate political organisations. As Plaatje reported to the South African Native Affairs Commission, there were no vigilance associations in Bechuanaland, but whenever any issue affecting Africans arose the educated class immediately advised the chief about the matter and asked him to take steps. Badirile Montsioa explained: 'The older headmen of the tribe are a number of primitive men who know nothing about South African politics, which appear to be difficult to be understood by the white people themselves. If anything affecting the welfare of the nation is under consideration, we have enlightened men among ourselves whom we consult under such circumstances, and their counsel may be relied upon to be better than that of a solicitor, as their interests will be at stake.'[31]

There was thus close co-operation between chiefly and western-educated elites to preserve from further encroachment the rights and autonomy the Rolong still possessed. A good example of this was the support Sol Plaatje received from the educated *kgosi* Silas Molema, who was also secretary and chief adviser to the paramount Badirile Montsioa.[32] In 1898, Plaatje moved from Kimberley, where he worked as a messenger at the post office, to take up the better-paying job of clerk and interpreter to the civil commissioner in Mafeking. According to his biographer, Plaatje would not have got the position without a nod from Molema. Soon afterwards, war broke out and Plaatje, close to the British administration during the siege of Mafeking, wrote his famous war diary. In April 1901 the proprietor of the local *Mafeking Mail and Protectorate Guardian*, N.H. Whales, started an English–Tswana newspaper called *Koranta ea Becoana* (*The Bechuana Gazette*). Plaatje and Molema were closely involved in the plans and, after twelve numbers of the paper had been published, Molema purchased it from Whales later in that year. *Koranta* was the first African-owned Tswana-language newspaper. The shareholders included various *dikgosi*, notably Bathoen Gaseitsiwe of the Ngwaketse.[33] From this base, Sol Plaatje launched a career that was to make him a South African literary and political legend.

By 1900, the northern Cape had become a key part of the political and economic life of southern Africa. Its main centre, Kimberley, which produced more than half the revenue of the Cape, was an incubator of new forms of experience and organisation, drawing people and ideas from all over southern Africa. In this way it also helped build wider networks and larger ideas, anticipating the emergence of the Union of South Africa. Educated Africans were part and parcel of this process and would play an important role in the emergence of a national movement for Africans in South Africa. When the modern-day ANC was formed in 1912, Plaatje would be elected its first secretary, with George Montsioa, the English-educated grandson of the venerable Chief Montshiwa, as his assistant.

20

Gold and a
new nationalism

Our [church] district meetings have been separated from the
Europeans since 1886 ... [They] were held in a more or less barbaric
manner. We are just like a lot of Kaffirs before the landdrost for
passes. What the white man says is infallible.

– Mangena Mokone, 1892

Deep in the interior of southern Africa, north of the Vaal River,
a new colonial state, the South African Republic or Transvaal, came into
being in 1854. Like its sister republic to the south, the Orange Free State,
it had no pretence about allowing political, economic and social equality
between black and white. But republican authority was fragile and weak
in many parts of the country, with the presence of large African chiefdoms
within its borders, which retained a degree of autonomy. It took a British
army, in the years after Britain first annexed the Transvaal in 1877, to
defeat Sekhukhune, the Pedi chief.

Because colonialism came later and often remained tenuous in the
Transvaal, the integration of Africans into colonial society was initially
slower than in other parts of southern Africa. As elsewhere, missionary
societies played an important role in the process of cultural mingling,
though, because of Boer hostility to the British, it was European rather
than British missionaries that came to dominate in the Transvaal. The
Berlin Mission Society was the biggest missionary body in the republic. By
the 1870s it was operating in a large swathe of territory from Heidelberg,
Middelburg and Lydenburg in the south-east up to the territories of the

Pedi, Lobedu, Venda and Tsonga further north.[1] The Botshabelo mission of the Berlin Society near Middelburg had the largest school in the republic; numbers of students there grew from 420 in 1867 to 1480 in 1880. Like Lovedale in the eastern Cape, it was regarded as a model mission station in the subcontinent.

By the 1880s, there was a sizeable number of African Christians in the Transvaal.[2] As John and Jean Comaroff have shown, they responded in many-sided ways to the message of Christianity, which kept being reworked in the engagements between Europeans and the indigenous people. For example, *Kgosi* Mokgatle of the Fokeng, who had welcomed the Hermannsburg Mission Society into his territory in the late 1860s, bought land for a mission from the republican authorities, provided horses for the missionaries to do their rounds and encouraged people to become Christians, even though he himself did not convert, out of respect for the traditionalists within the chiefdom (until shortly before his death at the age of 91). All the same, some 50 of his relatives had converted by the 1880s and two of his sons, Paul and Bloemhof Mokgatle, were sent abroad, with the approval of President Paul Kruger, to study in the Netherlands in 1887.[3]

After the first British annexation, the Wesleyans also entered the mission field, establishing a new Transvaal and Swaziland circuit of the church and opening the Kilnerton Institute, the first African teacher-training institution in the republic, on a farm just outside Pretoria, in 1883. A 32-year-old minister of Pedi origin, accepted two years before on probation, was sent up from Durban to Pretoria to help the white superintendent set up the new institution. His name was Mangena Mokone. Working under supervision, he 'opened the church and school at Kilnerton, building the fittings for each with his own hands'.[4]

Mokone started work at Kilnerton at roughly the same time that the careers of Walter Rubusana (who was ordained as a Congregational Church minister in 1883) and J.T. Jabavu (who set up *Imvo* in 1884) were launched further south. Like them, he would become one of the most influential African Christians of his age. He had hoped to study at the Wesleyan seminary at Healdtown, but the church felt his Dutch and Pedi language skills and knowledge of the Transvaal made him an ideal candidate to be sent to Kilnerton instead.[5] But even from Pretoria he kept in touch with political developments further south, by subscribing and writing to *Imvo*, which charted the struggles of the African elite in the eastern Cape.[6]

Once formally ordained in 1888, Mokone travelled throughout the republic on behalf of the Wesleyans, opening missions in the Waterberg and Makapanstad. He also worked briefly in Potchefstroom and the new mining town of Johannesburg. As in the Free State, restrictive government policies kept the size of the educated class of Africans small and retarded the emergence of African political associations and vernacular newspapers. One Wesleyan field-worker, Philip Mushi, who was given 30 lashes in public by an official, complained that 'the Dutch they are very sharp with our people'.[7] All the same, the Transvaal republic was to be a nursery for the most dynamic social movement to emerge among African Christians across the subcontinent in the last decade of the nineteenth century.

With the discovery of gold on the Witwatersrand, the South African Republic underwent a convulsion. The mining town of Johannesburg soon grew in leaps and bounds. Within ten years it was bigger than Cape Town and its population reached 102,000 in 1896.[8] Within a few years, this new conglomeration of humanity was linked by railway to all the major port cities of South Africa and from there, by ship, to the wider world.

Among those who descended on the goldfields were educated Africans from the rest of southern Africa. As in Kimberley, they would have occupied the most sought-after positions open to Africans. By 1895 there were no fewer than 65 Wesleyan lay preachers in Johannesburg, and a count the next year showed that 4500 Christian Africans lived 'within three miles of the Johannesburg market'.[9] At first, Africans lived in informal settlements on either side of Market Street, but, in keeping with the pattern of urban segregation emerging elsewhere in southern Africa, they were gradually moved to 'locations' on the periphery of the growing city. In 1889 a location for 'Coolies, Arabs and coloured people' was set up in Newtown. Plots of land were sold by auction and, by 1893, 2000 Africans and many more Indians were living here. The expansion of the railway yards led to the alienation of the African portion of this location and Africans were forced to move to a new location in Braamfontein. However, the census of 1896 showed that most Africans managed to remain in the city – only one in seven of the 14,195 Africans counted were living in the location.[10]

If the white Uitlanders felt aggrieved because of their treatment at the hands of the Kruger government, Africans were far worse off in every respect. As Keith Beavon has noted: 'By 1900 almost all the aspects that until the 1990s were to characterize the apartheid city of Johannesburg were already in place. Africans had to carry passes, they were prohibited from walking on the pavements, they were excluded from public places, they were not permitted to use the regular intra-urban public transport, and they were largely confined to the single sex "barracks" of the mines, the "Kaffir location", and the servants' quarters of the opulent whites. Their access to liquor had been constrained, they laboured long and hard for very low wages, and they had no political rights.'[11] Despite these choking restrictions, the educated class of Africans carved out for themselves economic opportunities and socialised and mobilised in dynamic ways. The 1904 census put their numbers at 25 per cent of the permanent black population of 24,348. This meant that there were more than 6000 registered school people in the city at the time. It was from this group that political leaders were drawn and political organisations subsequently emerged.

In his study of how the socio-economic circumstances of the city shaped various forms of popular music, David Coplan details the creative avenues developed by educated Africans in *eGoli*. The Wesleyans, for example, set up bands of preachers who made their entrance to the mining compounds, 'singing, shouting, and moving to the rhythm of their song'. In the locations, the Salvation Army held services for large numbers of people, where the 'wonderful singing was quite a feature'. Attracted by the local audiences, the American entrepreneur Orpheus McAdoo brought his singing troupe, the Jubilee Singers, four times to Johannesburg in the 1890s. In this environment of renewal, hope and adversity, new musical forms started emerging. In 1897 a young school teacher and composer from the eastern Cape, Enoch Sontonga, living in the Nancefield location, composed an African anthem that would become famous: *Nkosi Sikelel' iAfrika* was the title he gave it.[12] In time it became the ANC anthem.

The eastern Cape mission presence in Johannesburg could also be seen in the growth of cricket clubs. Over New Year in 1897/98, the Doornfontein Standard CC played three matches in a few days – against Bloemfontein CC at Kroonstad, the local Ottomans CC and Elandsfontein Diggers CC from Germiston. There were around ten 'native' cricket clubs in Johannesburg in 1898, when they came together to form a Transvaal Union. We know of their existence because the migrants at the goldfields regularly sent reports of their activities for publication in *Imvo* and *Izwi*.

These social activities were a far cry from what white employers and mining bosses expected of Africans in the new town. As early as 1891, roller skating was a popular attraction and there was a tennis court in Doornfontein specifically for Africans. In 1897 no less than 882 licences were granted for the operation of African 'eating houses', the local version of white society's pubs and theatres. At these establishments, which operated from six in the morning to nine at night, waitresses did their best to attract customers: 'The girls study effect. They dress to kill … They pose themselves as gracefully as possible and devote the greatest share of attention to the patron with the largest purse.'[13] Some moralists complained that Africans 'were being spoilt by the loose, rough, godless life' (*worden bedorwen door het losse, ruwe, goddelose lewen*): in 1897 a law was passed to stop black men and white women from engaging in 'immorality'. White newspapers noted the unwelcome influence of the 'Lovedale Institute', 'Exeter Hall' inclinations and 'Uncle Tom's Cabin ideas' in Johannesburg: 'The worst classes are without doubt the so-called educated natives; they dress in fine raiment, strut about the streets … side by side with white ladies, and consider themselves in every way equal to white men.'[14]

That Africans had no social or political rights in the republic did not deter them from engaging politically with the authorities. In 1896 Mangena Mokone petitioned the government about the pass laws, speaking for people who were carpenters, general dealers and owners of coffee shops and boarding houses.[15] Topping the list of signatures on another petition in that year was a familiar surname – Mzimba (perhaps the Cape-based leader Pambani Mzimba, who is known to have visited Johannesburg on church matters).[16] In 1898 stand-holders in the 'Kaffir Location' sent several petitions complaining of 'the ill-treatment we have suffered from time to time under the laws and officials of the Transvaal Government' to the Cape Government Labour Agent in Johannesburg.[17] The influence of Cape activists was soon evident, and the Aborigines Protection Society in Britain, in touch with African leaders throughout southern Africa, also protested on their behalf against the pass laws and other injustices meted out to local Africans. By the 1890s Africans in the republic were becoming part of the new-style politics in the subcontinent.

The most significant movement among educated, Christian Africans in the 1890s originated not from Johannesburg but from the Kilnerton Institute and nearby Marabastad, a 'location' in Pretoria, the capital of the Boer republic. At its head was the energetic, multilingual Wesleyan minister Mangena Mokone, who was appointed principal of the Kilnerton Institute in 1892, a decade after helping establish it as the first teacher-training college in the republic. From the start, he hit his head against the glass ceiling of racial discrimination. He found that, though he was the principal, 'I was not esteemed as one who belongs to it or has any say'.[18] Mokone's return to Kilnerton in 1892 brought to a head his frustration with the white church hierarchy. White ministers earned more than their black colleagues; they held separate circuit conferences, and did not bother to let their black colleagues receive the minutes; unlike the latter, they were given housing, transport ('ox-wagons') and furniture; they lived away from their congregations, not with them; and they treated their African colleagues poorly and did not give them the recognition they deserved. According to Mokone, 'We are called "Revs" but we are worse than the boy working for the missionary'. And, at the segregated district meetings for black ministers, where a white chairman ran proceedings, 'We are just like a lot of Kaffirs before the landdrost for passes. What the white man says is infallible'.[19]

By October 1892 Mokone had had enough. He resigned from Kilnerton and the church and started preaching as an independent Methodist in a hut in Marabastad, before erecting his own church building. Having been established only four years previously, Marabastad – which reputedly gave birth to the fusion music called *marabi* – was the first formal, government-approved 'location' in the republic, with a mixed population. At the opening of Mokone's new church, a banner was hung over the altar with the words of Psalm 68: 31 on it: 'Princes shall come out of Egypt; Ethiopia shall soon stretch forth her hands unto God.' Mokone named his church the Ethiopian Church, or *iTiyopia* in the vernacular, after this biblical reference.[20]

Mokone and his followers interpreted the Psalm as a promise of the evangelisation of Africa. The church was to be open to all Africans and it was to be run by African leaders.[21] Though the term 'Ethiopian' had been popular among African Christians at least as far back as 1867, when Tiyo Soga quoted the same text in his letter on 'The survival of the black race', Ethiopia now acquired a whole new meaning. The subversive message sent out by the Ethiopians was that they were proud of their African consciousness and identity, despite the fact that white missionaries and colonialists regarded African culture as inferior, and were confident enough both to appropriate and reinterpret aspects of universal culture and to lead their congregations themselves. Western-educated intellectuals like Mokone began to rewrite the colonial narrative in an African idiom in such a way and on such a scale that it could not be reversed by the colonial establishment.

James Campbell has written extensively on the emergence of the Ethiopian Church and his account provides the basic narrative of its development traced here. The first to join Mokone as the new Ethiopian Church slowly extended its support base was the Cape-born Samuel Brander, with 60 of his followers. He was an Anglican preacher from the Waterberg district, who had lived on the diamond fields for a decade. Next, three eastern Cape churchmen working in Johannesburg joined as well: S.J. Mpumlwana, Abraham Mngqibisa (a Wesleyan originally from Fort Beaufort and father-in-law of Enoch Sontonga) and Jantje Zachariah Tantsi (from the Thembu area of Engcobo). The well-connected Tantsi brought a wealth of political experience and a string of eastern Cape connections with him and immediately came to the fore in Mokone's new church. Other important recruits were the Orange Free State-based Jacobus Xaba, 'the movement's most ardent and effective evangelist', who had been educated at Healdtown, though he came from the Edendale mission in Natal, and the 63-year-old Marcus Gabashane from Thaba Nchu. A 'Samuelite', who had followed Samuel Moroka out of Thaba Nchu when the latter was exiled, Gabashane first spread the Word in the western Transvaal before embarking on a 'one thousand-mile trek up the entire length of the Bechuanaland Protectorate'. He was given support at various stages by Samuel Moroka himself, who would remain an Anglican.[22]

By 1894 Mokone's Ethiopians had built their first church on the goldfields; within five years nearly a dozen churches sprouted in Newtown, Vrededorp and Fordsburg in the heart of Johannesburg and the surrounding mining towns. In 1894, too, the church also held its first annual meeting. Drawing on Tantsi's eastern Cape networks, Mokone thereafter led a delegation to the eastern Cape in late 1894 or 1895 to recruit members and build alliances. Here the party met with Jonas Goduka, who in 1891 had succeeded Nehemiah Tile as head of the Thembu Church. Goduka turned down the offer to join forces but he did issue a joint call with Mokone for new recruits. From this emanated the next tier of Ethiopian Church leaders. Several other well-connected people in the school community joined Mokone, including the Lovedale-educated Benjamin Kumalo, Isaiah Sishuba from the Queenstown district, and H.R. Ngcayiya, who was closely connected with Tantsi and later became a founder member of the ANC. From the start, the new churches' leaders were well connected with the broader mission-school elites and, indeed, formed part of the new educational, religious and political networks.

The process of recruitment in the Ethiopian Church showed the easy connectivity that existed between African Christians in different parts of South Africa by the 1890s. Mokone knew personally all the initial recruits (barring perhaps Gabashane) from his church work, and he now began to draw in the next generation of leaders from established eastern Cape school and political circles.[23] The biggest catch was James Mata Dwane, one of the most respected figures in the eastern Cape. Dwane's father was connected to the royal house of the Ntinde Xhosa but 'transferred his allegiance' to Chief Kama of the Gqunukhwebe, 'whose love and respect he enjoyed all his life'. The young Mata was born in Kamastone near Whittlesea in 1848; the family moved with Chief Kama to Middledrift in 1855 after the Gqunukhwebe were rewarded with land there for their loyalty to the colony in the War of Mlanjeni. Converted at the age of 19, he lived for a while with a white missionary family, before starting his studies in 1867 at the newly opened Healdtown Institution for the training of Wesleyan teachers and ministers. In 1872 he gave up teaching so that he could return to Healdtown and study for the ministry. On completion, he began circuit work in Port Elizabeth in 1875 and was ordained there in January 1881. When the pioneering Imbumba Yama Nyama was formed in Port Elizabeth in the following year, the newly ordained Dwane was mentioned as an interested party in Grahamstown. By 1885 he was superintendent minister of a circuit in the Cala district – at exactly the time that Nehemiah Tile was busy organising his Thembu Church in this region.[24] The energetic Dwane was thus close to some of the key early developments in eastern Cape politics. He soon became a highly regarded church and political leader in the region.

Mokone's delegation met Dwane in Queenstown in 1895.[25] Dwane accepted their overtures and was immediately given a leadership role in the Ethiopian Church. Indeed, he soon took over the leadership of the church from Mokone. In a real sense the Mokone–Dwane alliance represented a symbolic marriage between the eastern Cape elite and emerging leaders of public opinion in the other colonies. It also represented a big step forward in the creation of a genuinely national movement of educated and christianised Africans in southern Africa.

In the same year as the meeting with Dwane, Mokone came to hear of the independent black-controlled African Methodist Episcopal (AME) Church from a South African student studying in the United States, Charlotte Manye. The daughter of a Tlokwa father and Mfengu mother, she grew up in the 1880s in Uitenhage and Port Elizabeth, where Isaac Wauchope and Paul Xiniwe were among her teachers. After school, Manye moved with her family to Kimberley, where she started teaching. She soon came to the fore with her magnificent voice and strong personality. A member of the pioneering African Native Choir, which toured the British Isles, she lived there for more than two years before travelling with a reconstituted choir to Canada and the United States in 1893. After the choir was left in the lurch by its promoter in Cleveland, she and several other choir members were offered scholarships at Wilberforce University in Ohio, the AME's leading educational institution in America. This large church, founded by a former slave in reaction to colour discrimination in the Methodist Episcopal Church in the United States, encouraged black assertiveness.

In a letter home, Charlotte Manye gave details about the church and its work; this letter was shown to Mokone when he made a family visit one day. In May 1895 Mokone began corresponding with the AME Church in the United States with a view to closer co-operation.[26] In 1896 he and his fellow Ethiopian Church leaders were invited to attend the AME Church's annual convention in Philadelphia. In response, it was resolved to send Mokone, James Dwane and Jacobus Xaba to America to seek affiliation to the AME Church. Each delegate had to raise his own passage.[27] After being sponsored by the Matsolo brothers from Glen Grey, Dwane was the only one of the three who succeeded in reaching America. Here he was well received at special functions organised by the AME Church in Philadelphia and Atlanta. It was agreed to proceed with the amalgamation of the two churches and, in a major move, the Americans appointed Dwane as General Superintendent of the new AME Church in South Africa, with authority to ordain ministers, pending the arrival of an accredited American bishop. This meant that the Ethiopian Church was now formally absorbed into the AME Church and that Dwane, rather than Mokone, became the new head of the local branch.[28]

Shortly after Dwane's return in 1897 from his lengthy trip abroad, leaders of the former Ethiopian Church met at Lesseyton near Queenstown, where their new head formally 'reobligated' 20 of them into the AME Church. The church was divided into two main sections: the Transvaal Conference (including the Orange Free State and Basutoland) and the South African Conference, which in effect covered the Cape Colony. The position of the South African province of the church was consolidated when in March 1898 Bishop Henry Turner of the AME Church visited South Africa. A strong supporter of the recolonisation movement, which promoted the idea that African Americans return to the continent, Turner received a huge welcome and achieved some startling results in his visit of six weeks. He proceeded triumphantly from Cape Town through Bloemfontein to Johannesburg, where the touring Jubilee Singers from America were among those to welcome him, before meeting President Paul Kruger in Pretoria. During Turner's visit, large AME Church meetings were held in Pretoria and Queenstown. After receiving the endorsement of both the Transvaal and South African Conferences, Turner consecrated James Dwane as Mission Bishop of South Africa. Dwane, whom Campbell has described as 'self-possessed, eloquent, by far the best educated of the Ethiopian ministers', had now assumed a national profile.[29]

Dwane and his church put great store on setting up independent educational institutions. Though land was purchased in Queenstown for a centre for higher learning, the plans did not materialise, but the impetus eventually led to the establishment of the AME's Bethel Institute in Cape Town (run by Francis Gow, a West Indian married to an American woman) and its northern counterpart, the Wilberforce Institute at Evaton near Johannesburg.[30]

The AME Church meetings held in Pretoria and Queenstown during Turner's visit marked the beginning of a huge surge in growth and the church became increasingly national in character. Soon the membership had reached 10,000, gathered in 73 congregations. By 1900 the Transvaal Conference of the church consisted of four districts, namely Pretoria, Johannesburg, Potchefstroom and the Orange Free State, each divided into circuits and stations. The Pretoria district stretched from the capital through Sekhukhuneland and modern-day Polokwane to Bulawayo in Rhodesia; while the Potchefstroom district reached as far north as Tati in modern-day Botswana. The South African Conference, or the Cape branch, was made up of five districts: Queenstown, Pondoland, King William's Town, Port Elizabeth and Cape Town. This organisational grid overlay the networks already created by the established mission churches in southern Africa and by the emerging political bodies. It was the inter-meshing of these networks and structures that would provide the impetus for a national political movement, bringing activists and intellectuals (with their grassroots support) in different parts of the subcontinent closer together.[31]

⬇

Ethiopianism spread rapidly throughout southern Africa in the 1890s. While Mangena Mokone's Ethiopian Church became the most important, it was not the only separatist church that emerged in these years, though it gave its name to the broad movement of religious separatism and African consciousness that swept throughout the country. The independence these churches offered from white control and the possibilities inherent in the American connections made the Ethiopian movement attractive to educated Christians, just at a time when it seemed they had reached a cul de sac in their advancement within the colonial order. The new churches became a mould into which all sorts of aspirations flowed.

Besides the AME Church, two of the most important were begun by eastern Cape men. Edward Tsewu, a contemporary of Elijah Makiwane and Pambani Mzimba, who had been trained as a teacher at Lovedale and ordained as a minister of the Free Church in 1883, was working among migrant labourers in Johannesburg when he broke away to form his own Independent Presbyterian Church.[32] During Bishop Turner's visit to South Africa in 1898, he joined forces with the new AME Church.

Soon after Tsewu's breakaway, Pambani Mzimba, the first African to be ordained by the Free Church, seceded with his large Lovedale congregation to form the Presbyterian Church of Africa. Within five years the number of Mzimba's adherents was conservatively estimated at 17,000, growing to 52,352 in 1910.[33] Though most were resident in the eastern Cape, including the Transkei, he also attracted more than 10,000 followers in Natal, more than 1000 each in the Transvaal and Orange River Colony, and pockets of support in Cape Town, the northern Cape and Bechuanaland. This secession at Lovedale, the very heart of the whole missionary enterprise in southern Africa, by one so widely respected, shocked the white missionary establishment.[34]

The new church movements of the 1890s were a natural consequence of the emergence of a new class of mission-educated Africans. Growing in confidence, numbers and skills, African religious leaders began to challenge the paternalism, discrimination and chauvinism in the established churches by withdrawing and forming self-reliant African churches with distinctive

African characteristics, better able to relate to African needs. In doing so, they displayed the selective adaptation to European religion and culture advocated by such early figures as Ntsikana and Makhanda. Within their own churches they were able to reassert their former independence, while at the same time retaining the elements of western religious practice and thought they valued.

The separatists caused an upheaval in the work of the missionary churches. As they drew thousands of members away from the established churches and undermined their influence, numerous disputes arose about legality, governance, membership, facilities and finances.[35] Within white society as a whole there was a massive backlash, reaching near hysterical proportions. Especially in Natal, administrators, missionaries and colonists raised the exaggerated spectre of an anti-white Ethiopian movement which aimed to drive the white man into the sea.[36] Colonial governments and white opinion-formers expressed alarm at the political implications of this 'race' consciousness and religious rebellion.

As for the new educated class, Ethiopianism caught their imagination. Complementing the role of the new political organisations that had begun to emerge, the independent churches articulated dissatisfaction with white rule, propagated African assertiveness, mobilised financial and other resources, and put in place facilities such as church and school buildings, thereby establishing the framework for permanent bodies.[37] Through the churches, long-articulated African ideas and notions of African unity were given organisational content and became more visible in the politics of the educated activists.

21

The emergence of a national movement

> I am not an Ethiopian, but I could just as well be one because, the
> Ethiopian says our nation must help itself since no white man will
> lift up the black nation. Frenchman are uplifted by Frenchmen,
> Italians are uplifted by Italians, every nation is uplifted by its
> educated members. Africa will also be helped by educated Africans
> who will work hard and give themselves, with their little education
> to the nation.
>
> – Walter Benson Rubusana, 1906

From the various political and social activities already described, there emerged in the late 1890s a functional national movement connecting activists and interest groups in all the various colonies and states in southern Africa. It was built on the marriage between a quickly spreading religious separatist movement and the constitutional politics of the pioneering black elite in the eastern Cape and elsewhere. Though the first steps were tentative, this development was to have a major, long-term impact on South African society.

There has long been a debate about whether the separatist church movement of the late nineteenth century was linked to the politics of an emergent nationalism. The proposition that there was a link has been put forward by various historians, tending to use generalised arguments in view of the limited understanding until now of the early political organisations themselves. James Campbell and others have more recently rebutted this view. Influenced by academic orthodoxies that stress the narrow and conservative nature of the 'petition-and-plead' politics of the mission-educated elite, Campbell has seen in religious separatism a different kind of political response, which tended to be manifested in rural populism and social movements separate from the constitutional politics that we have dealt with in this book.[1]

The strength of Campbell's study lies in the depth of focus given to the growth of Ethiopianism in the Transvaal and Orange Free State. On the basis of his evidence, he found it difficult to make a direct connection between the religious and political movements. While he recognised the involvement of separatist church leaders in the growing political movement after the South African War and in the formation of the South African Native National Congress in 1912, he dismissed the notion that there was a dynamic relationship between them in the earlier period.

From the evidence of the eastern Cape in the 1880s and 1890s, I should like to argue differently. It seems to me that there were in fact very real connections between Ethiopianism and the emerging political movement, that they evolved in tandem and that there was a direct, mutually reinforcing connection and synergy between the two. Ethiopianism was both a launching pad for the new forms of organisational politics and a complementary, parallel process. Outside the Cape Colony, in the states where Africans were denied any political rights, Ethiopianism sometimes perhaps became the primary vehicle for political expression. In general, religious mobilisation helped generate an integrated political movement on a national basis through the spread of universal Christian ideas, through church networks and through co-operation across regional and ethnic bounds. And, at the same time, many of the same actors and leaders were involved in the twin processes.

The most obvious and earliest example of this 'marriage' between religious separatism and political organisation is Nehemiah Tile's Thembu Church, which has already been referred to. Although there had been earlier expressions of independence, this was the first organised and sustained separatist church initiative. Tile's Church was established at a time when the Thembu were still nominally independent but in reality were experiencing the last days of their independence. From the start of his career, Tile was a thoroughgoing activist, who showed real political acumen in trying to defend the territorial and political integrity of the Thembu chiefdom under the paramount Ngangelizwe and his son and successor, Dalindyebo. His aim was to ensure a united, relatively autonomous Thembu territory under indirect British rule (much like nearby Basutoland) instead of direct Cape rule.[2] Tile's activities, his tactics and the timing of his petitions, were linked to the broader process of political mobilisation taking place in the eastern Cape and need to be seen in that context.

At more or less the same time that he set up his church, the pioneering South African Native Association and Thembu Association were being constituted in nearby Glen Grey and Emigrant Thembuland and were confronting the government on land issues. The Thembu Association at Glen Grey and the Thembu Church were both part of the same political world, in some ways not very far apart from each other.[3] And even after Thembuland was annexed to the Cape in 1885, Tile continued with his political work. During the intense campaigning by Africans against the Voters Registration Act in 1887, Tile was active in the protests in Cala, Glen Grey and Thembuland, writing and speaking on behalf of the young, mission-educated paramount, Dalindyebo, who maintained close ties with the new style of politics and the new educated constitutionalists. He was also in touch with leaders such as Veldtman Bikitsha in other districts.[4]

From the very first secession, there thus existed an intricate inter-connectedness between religious separatism, expressions of African nationalism, local politics and the emerging African leaders and organisations. Broadly speaking, the independent religious leaders and new-style political activists were part of the same continuum, not opposite responses. This was plain in the eastern Cape from as early as the 1880s and 1890s and, to a lesser extent, in Natal, though in the Transvaal and the Orange Free State the connections would become obvious only after 1900, when religious leaders became prominent in forming proto-nationalist political organisations once these became tolerated under British rule.

Between Tile and Mangena Mokone, the founder of the Ethiopian Church in 1892, there are direct and indirect links, as we have seen. Indeed, according to a history of the separatist movement written in 1904, Mokone was directly inspired by Tile. For one thing, J.Z. Tantsi, Mokone's lieutenant in the Ethiopian Church, hailed from the very areas in which

Tile had worked and was deeply enmeshed in the organisations, such as the Native Vigilance Associations, emerging there from the mid-1880s onwards. In October 1887, for example, Tantsi was a delegate for Engcobo when the second Imbumba (or Union of Native Vigilance Associations) was started in King William's Town – the first genuinely region-wide political body in the eastern Cape. One of those involved with Tantsi in the Queenstown Association was Jonas Goduka, a Wesleyan schooled at Healdtown, who became successor to Tile as leader of the Thembu Church. Goduka and two of his 'moderators', David Dalamba and the Rev. James J. Vili, a committee member of the Native Vigilance Association in the Umtata district, became supporters of the South African Native Congress, in this way confirming the active link between the religious separatists and the political constitutionalists.[5] Goduka's church went on to celebrate a lifespan of a hundred years and, like Tantsi, he worked confidently in the interlinked worlds of church and politics for decades.[6]

It was Goduka whom Mangena Mokone travelled to meet in person and discuss church matters. In return, Goduka sent one of his colleagues, P. Kuza, 'to help Mokone with his work in Pretoria'.[7] Later, Mokone asked Jacobus Xaba, the Healdtown-educated head of the Ethiopian Church in the Free State, to meet with Goduka on his behalf to propose an amalgamation of their churches. Though Goduka decided against union, the two bodies agreed to co-operate even though they remained separate. Goduka and Mokone jointly called on African Christians to join them, and a group of eastern Cape leaders promptly did so. This first stage in the formation of alliances thus brought partners for the Ethiopians in an area that had both a long history of political mobilisation and nearly a decade's experience of African nonconformism.

The second phase of the alliance between Mokone's Ethiopians in the north and eastern Cape leaders involved the co-option of the Rev. James Dwane, who became a leader in the Ethiopian Church in 1895. Dwane was one of the most senior school people in the eastern Cape. The alliance was more than coincidental: Mokone knew he was acquiring someone with both a proven track record and a solid support base.[8]

Dwane had a strong support base in the Thembu areas. As superintendent minister of the Wesleyan Church in the Cala district from the mid-1880s onwards, he was involved in the evolution of the new-style politics there. In 1891, for instance, he presented an illuminated address to the Governor on behalf of the 'Indwana committee of the South African Native Vigilance Association'. The annual meetings of the Queenstown circuit of the Wesleyan Church gave Dwane further opportunities to work together with many prominent members of the political elite in the eastern Cape, such as J.T. Jabavu and Jonathan Tunyiswa, secretary of the SANC.[9] Some of his strongest supporters lived in Glen Grey.

Dwane's other support base lay across the mountains in Middledrift. His principal backer, Ngangelizwe Kama, was both the chief of an important section of the Gqunukhwebe and the colonial headman in what was called Kama's Location in that district, who also took part in the work of the King William's Town Native Vigilance Association.[10] Kama was part of a long-established lineage of Christian chiefs prominent in the educational, church and political matters close to the hearts of the school people. The Rev. James Read had noted as early as 1810 that Chief Kama, who married one of Ngqika's daughters, 'had always ... much regard for the word of God' and Ngangelizwe's father, William Shaw Kama (named after the missionary who set up a mission among the Gqunukhwebe in 1823), was ordained as a minister before becoming chief in the 1880s.[11]

Dwane had been born and grew up among the Gqunukhwebe and his sister married Kama's brother. In 1894 he went to England on a fundraising tour for his congregation, but when the Wesleyan Church insisted that he hand over the money he had collected, he broke with them and was joined by Kama. Dwane then obtained a position with Jabavu as 'co-editor' of *Imvo* with the purpose of pursuing his educational plans. But first a request by the brothers Hans and David Matsolo from Bengu near Queenstown that he start a separate black church, and then the proposal from the deputation sent by the Ethiopian Church in 1895, changed his life.[12] In the 1890s, as we have seen, he became the leader of the new AME Church, into which the Ethiopian Church was now folded, and increasingly assumed the role of a national figure.

All the while that Dwane was becoming upwardly mobile in the church, he remained in close touch with his political network in the eastern Cape. Before joining the Ethiopians, he consulted both Chief Kama and Daniel Dwanya, a political colleague in both Thembuland and Middledrift, who was a longstanding SANC supporter. At the time of Dwane's visit to America in 1896 to formalise the union between the Ethiopian Church and the AME Church, he listed among his supporters such prominent political figures as 'King' Sigcau, 'King' Dalindyebo, 'King' W.S. Kama, 'King' Ebenezer Mhlambiso, as well as James and Meshach Pelem, David Malasi, Paul Xiniwe and W.D. Soga.[13] These were traditional leaders of the Mpondo, Thembu, Gqunukhwebe and Mfengu and some of the most influential members in key early political organisations.

The third important assertion of church independence in the Cape during the 1890s was the shock breakaway of the Rev. Pambani Mzimba from the prestigious Lovedale Presbyterian congregation in 1898. Like the earlier breakaways and subsequent partnerships, Mzimba's secession involved an alignment between the Transvaal and eastern Cape. The Transvaal connection was made through the person of Edward Tsewu, a Lovedale-trained minister who had moved to Johannesburg after Mzimba helped start a congregation there in 1891. When Tsewu became involved with the Ethiopians in 1896, Mzimba was sent up to *eGoli* to help settle matters and, according to Switzer, 'he undoubtedly made contact with the leaders of the Ethiopian Church at that time'.[14] The upshot was that Tsewu started his own Independent Presbyterian Church on the Witwatersrand, which was followed soon afterwards by Mzimba's breakaway. The loss of these two longstanding colleagues would have come as a double blow to the Lovedale establishment. Tsewu would also start a new political party in Johannesburg after the British took over the Transvaal, called Iliso Lomzi, borrowing a name commonly used in the eastern Cape, and he would become a founder member of the South African Native National Congress in 1912.

According to the assistant chief magistrate of the Transkei, Mzimba's

Presbyterian Church of Africa was 'almost entirely restricted to the Fingo tribes some of which are to be found in every district'.[15] Judging from the localities in which congregations emerged and the character of the leadership, this seems to have been more or less true for the Cape section of the church.[16] The members who seceded from the Lovedale congregation with Mzimba were all Mfengu; Xhosa members of the church, who were in the minority, stayed loyal to the last one.[17] This Mfengu–Xhosa division had political implications too, as we have seen. Jabavu and his Imbumba colleagues were primarily Mfengu. Their areas of settlement in the eastern Cape coincided largely with Mzimba's church strongholds: from Chief Mbovane Mabandla's location in his home district near Alice, where Lovedale was located, to the Butterworth and Nqamakwe districts in Fingoland and to Hewu near Queenstown. But Mzimba and his church bucked the trend of ethnic mobilisation in eastern Cape politics. Both he and Mabandla, his main backer, supported Congress in the 1900s. This underlines the essentially nationalist nature of both the separatist church movement and the Congress, which in a real sense became the political wing of the Ethiopians.[18]

In electoral politics, while SANC leaders generally were staunchly Progressive, not all Congress voters supported this pro-British, pro-imperialist party. Mzimba was among those who, together with Jabavu, voted instead for the 'friends of the natives' in the South African Party. One of Mzimba's ministers, J. Jolobe, informed John X. Merriman in 1903 that 'the ministers and members of the ... church are strong and staunch supporters of the S.A.P. all over'.[19] Mzimba himself was probably the key African figure in the electoral politics of Victoria East. A candidate who had been assured of the African vote in the constituency was described as a 'Mzimbaite'.[20] Mzimba's name also headed a list of 'the most influential natives' in the constituency drawn up for electoral purposes by Richard Rose-Innes, who had been involved in politics there since 1884, when his brother was sensationally returned to parliament by African voters to represent them.[21]

Besides Mzimba and Mabandla, many of the Presbyterian Church of Africa's leaders were involved in the new political organisations. Campbell Kupe, who supervised the work of the church in the southern Transkeian districts of Nqamakwe and Butterworth, was involved with the Manyano nge Mvo Zabantsundu from its inception in 1887 and during the 1890s led the opposition against the Glen Grey Act in Fingoland.[22] The long-serving secretary of the Native Educational Association, W.W. Stofile, was in charge of the church's East London and King William's Town districts.[23] Another of Mzimba's ministers, Reuben Damane, was a 'leading spirit' in the considerable opposition raised against the implementation of the Glen Grey Act in the Qumbu district in 1903–4.[24] The respected and politically active Rev. Benjamin Dlepu also joined the church.[25] Leadership in the new politics and the new church movement overlapped seamlessly.

In a short time, Pambani Mzimba 'came to be recognized even in political circles as a man to be considered'.[26] He and his Presbyterian Church of Africa spread quickly from the Cape to the other colonies and helped promote the idea of African unity, independence and self-assertion.

In a revealing incident, Mzimba was taken to court after his secession by the Lovedale mission, demanding the return of property, money and records. Mzimba was supported by Chief Mabandla and opposed by his former close colleague Elijah Makiwane.[27] After Makiwane complained to the government in the early 1900s about harassment of members of the established churches in the location,[28] his mission house was burnt down.[29] The dispute dragged on for several years, with the government eventually intervening in an effort to end it.[30] Speaking from his own experiences, Makiwane remarked tellingly: 'Those who refuse to join this movement are now called white men or Britons. I have myself been so called on several occasions and the meaning is that those who have not joined have not been true to their nation, because the movement is regarded as the building up of the Africans as people. To be called Mlungu [white man] is therefore considered a great reproach.'[31]

James Campbell has emphasised the 'intense localism' and rootedness of popular struggles and politics that accompanied the 'Ethiopianism' of the AME Church into the rural areas of the Free State, Transvaal and Bechuanaland in the 1890s and 1900s, as if to counterpose this with the overly formalistic politics of the supposedly elite and submissive eastern Cape voters and early organisations.[32] But the religious schisms and differences in the eastern Cape showed something different, as the incident just recounted reveals. James Dwane was involved in similar dramas. When Ngangelizwe and his councillors at Middledrift finally decided to set aside a piece of land for Dwane (now with the Order of Ethiopia) to build a college, high passions were engendered. George Songqo Kama, who disputed Ngangelizwe's right to the chieftaincy, opposed the plans for the college.[33] After a court case in which the latter failed to have the former declared illegitimate, and therefore deprived of this inheritance, armed followers of Ngangelizwe set out to attack George. Fortunately, he was out.[34] The chief and his followers were arraigned and found guilty of rioting and public violence.[35] Though Dwane was at first implicated, he was later exonerated of blame. The whole affair took place at the expense of the Middledrift community: the court case cost more than £2000 in fees and the government took advantage to further undermine what autonomy the chiefs and headmen still enjoyed.[36]

These cases involving prominent eastern Cape intellectuals and leaders illustrate the power struggles and differences that often occurred in local politics as headmen, magistrates, missionaries and constitutionalists jostled for influence and support. All this goes to show that polite petitions to the Queen were but one aspect of a multi-pronged form of politics and, in this case, religious issues were the trigger for the eruption of scarcely restrained local tensions. The fact is that some mainstream political leaders and organisations in the eastern Cape enjoyed a close and continuing relationship with the Ethiopian movement.

The alliance between the Ethiopian church movement and the network of eastern Cape political groups led in time to the formation of what became known as the Congress movement in South Africa. In particular, the partnerships formed by James Dwane and Mangena Mokone, and by Edward Tsewu and Pambani Mzimba, connected geographically dispersed support bases in the separatist church to the well-established political organisations of the eastern Cape. This gave both momentum and reach to the latent force of African nationalism, which now became visible, functional, formally organised and expressed in an inter-territorial form for the first time.

From its formation in 1890, the SANC had clear 'national' aspirations based on an African-centred approach to politics. Though at first its profile was low, from 1897, when the Congress set up its own newspaper, and the political temperature rose throughout southern Africa, the SANC started asserting itself and spreading its influence. Alliances emerged between the political and church movements. Important Ethiopian leaders participated in the SANC, and Congress in turn strongly supported and defended Ethiopianism at a time when opposition to the religious separatists was reaching near hysterical proportions among white colonists and governments. The SANC declared that the separatist movement was a healthy symptom of independence and progress on the part of Africans, springing from impulses created by the introduction of western education, religion and civilisation among them. Separatists were not anti-white, but stood for black assertion; and they pursued their aims in a legal, constitutional manner. The whole alarmist outcry against Ethiopianism on the part of the colonists and the press was unjustified, in Congress's view. It also complained to the Cape Prime Minister about 'the manifestly unfair treatment' to which several of the separatist leaders were subjected.[37]

The event that cemented the relationship between the evolving national religious separatist movement and the evolving national political movement was the meeting of the SANC in Queenstown in July 1898. Fresh from having been confirmed a month or two before as the General Superintendent of the AME Church in South Africa, James Dwane attended and chaired the SANC meeting, thereby symbolically and practically linking the political and religious movements.

Though political movements do not come into being in an instant, there can be no mistaking the significance of the conference in Queenstown. If there was a moment when an organised, functional African nationalism can be said to have come into existence in South Africa, this was it. The independent churches identified themselves here with the eastern Cape-based SANC in its bid to activate a still vaguely defined national movement in politics that would transcend colonial boundaries. Dwane's elevation to the chair in Queenstown formalised the marriage, while the presence of fellow church leader Pambani Mzimba, who had broken away from the Lovedale missionary heartland scarcely three months before (shortly after Dwane had visited him as a house guest),[38] further underlined the relationship.

From 1898 onwards, aspiration, opportunity and action converged to make possible the first concrete steps of a national movement in South Africa. The South African War that followed helped in its own way to export the prototypical politics and organisations of the Cape to the rest of South Africa. From that time, the SANC began to spread in influence and reach to other parts of South Africa. As its name, pronouncements and activities showed, the SANC aimed to speak on behalf of all Africans throughout South Africa, and it came to have a direct influence on the development of organisational politics in the other colonies. Walter Rubusana declared that although the Congress's 'organisation is not yet complete, still, it is already a power for good in the country, and will undoubtedly assume the position of the representative Native Association of the future'. He and other leaders travelled extensively to promote the SANC, and *Izwi*, which was read as far north as the Witwatersrand, carried full-page advertisements of its constitution.[39]

When groups in Bloemfontein and Johannesburg presented petitions to the new British authorities immediately after the South African War ended in mid-1902, *Izwi* reported that 'we' (i.e. *Izwi* or SANC people) had helped draw these up. The newspaper was confident that African people in the new colonies would soon have their own congresses and it invited them to work with the SANC towards this end.[40] Three representatives from the Transvaal duly attended the SANC annual conference at Lesseyton near Queenstown in September 1902. They were the AME leader J.Z. Tantsi, Charlotte Manye and Daniel Ketse.[41] In May 1903, SANC members, including Tantsi and his separatist church colleague H.R. Ngcayiya, were responsible for the formation of the Transvaal Native Congress in Johannesburg.[42] Ngcayiya, an activist in Queenstown from the 1880s, later became an executive member of the Orange River Colony Native Vigilance Association (later Congress), as did his fellow AME leader

Benjamin Kumalo. Moreover, a Bloemfontein representative attended the 1903 SANC annual conference in Glen Grey. The chiefs and educated elites in British Bechuanaland, that part of the colony outside the eastern Cape with the largest concentration of Africans, were also well disposed towards the Congress, and attempts were made to spread the SANC's influence further afield, to Natal, the Orange River Colony, Basutoland and Rhodesia, mainly through its Queen Victoria Memorial Scheme.[43]

As we shall see, the new regional Congresses and other developments in the early 1900s were in important ways an extension and reinforcement in the political realm of both the original SANC and the Ethiopian movement. The loosely allied political and church groupings – while expressing themselves in very different ways in various parts of southern Africa – provided an umbrella for an assertive form of modern politics that gave as much priority to the 'nation' as to working with colonial authorities. In addition to the well-established inter-territorial structures, created by the churches above all – the South African Wesleyan conference had been in existence since 1883 – the patronage and support provided by sympathetic chiefly leaders were also vital. From the start, as James Campbell has demonstrated, traditional leaders supported the Ethiopian movement, in a process filled with 'paradoxes within paradoxes'. In 1901, for instance, twelve chiefs, including 'virtually all the major paramount chiefs in southern Africa', were on hand in Cape Town to welcome the new AME Bishop, Levi Coppin, on his arrival from America.[44] The protocols of unity engaged in by the chiefs and new leaders affirmed the idea of unity and of an African-centred approach to politics that would defend and promote Africans within the colonial order. From these disparate struggles and this loose sense of unity came the first steps of a new national movement.

The new railway line from the Cape to the new metropolis of Johannesburg, along which people and ideas started moving forwards and backwards, provided the spine for the new national movement. It enabled local issues and activities to be linked to centralising ideas and forces at a time of dislocation and trauma as well as opportunity for Africans throughout southern Africa. This national movement thus took shape on the back of the revolution in transport and communication following the mineral discoveries. While connections had been present from early on, it now became much easier to travel and communicate across territorial boundaries. The railway and telegraph lines allowed the elite to deposit suitcase loads of new ideas at every siding and station from the early 1890s onwards. At the same time, the Imperial project of subjugating the independent African chiefdoms, under way between 1870 and 1900, infused this process with gravity. It sharpened understandings and created a sense of urgency for activists engaging with developments both politically and ideologically. Leaders of well-established political organisations and the separatist churches realised the urgent need as never before to work together to advance broad African interests.

From 1898 onwards, a South Africa-wide network of African organisations came into being with a presence throughout the country. What also emerged was a form of politics that would become distinguishable as the 'Congress tradition'. This aimed to unite Africans against the harshness of colonialism, while balancing 'national' African aspirations with broader, inclusive notions drawn from Christianity, political liberalism and African humanism. This tradition came to be hegemonic within the ANC in twentieth-century South Africa.

By 1900, the basic ideas, leadership and structures of a new national movement were in place. The tentative but clear linkage of activists across South Africa would be further cemented by political developments after the South African War, when all the different territories were brought under British rule for the first time. The subsequent process of political unification, achieved in the formation of the Union of South Africa in 1910, paved the way for the formal establishment of a single national organisation, the South African Native National Congress, in 1912.

22

Women in the struggle

I wish there were more of our people here [in the USA] to enjoy
the privileges of Wilberforce [University] and then go back to teach
our people so that our home can lose that awful name, 'the Dark
Continent', and be properly called the continent of light.
                                        – Charlotte Manye, 1894/5

Women have generally been absent from South African
narratives of nationalism and the nascent struggles for democracy before
1912. It has been accepted that those who started 'the Struggle' and the
ANC were men, the 'founding fathers' to use the language of patriarchy,
and that women's involvement in politics postdates 1912.

In academic studies as well as in the ANC's celebratory accounts
during its centenary celebrations in 2012, the women's 1913 anti-pass
demonstrations in Bloemfontein and the formation of the Bantu Women's
League in 1917 are regarded as the tentative entry points of women into
the grand narrative of nationalism.[1] Through this organisation, which
later became the ANC Women's League, women enjoyed only 'auxiliary
membership' of the ANC – until the 1940s they were treated as a separate
category without voting rights. Charlotte Maxeke (born Manye) stands
out as the only notable woman in the roll-call of ANC pioneers until the
mass struggles of the 1950s, which saw the formation of the Federation of
South African Women in 1954, the historic women's march to the Union
Buildings in 1956, and popular protests by women in Cato Manor and
elsewhere.[2]

This 'invisibility' of women in politics and the story of politics can be explained by the patriarchal systems operating in both African and colonial societies, as well as the bias of a male-dominated historical profession in South Africa. In the last few decades, the advent of an academic concern with gender and an increase in the number of women historians and social scientists have alerted us to the limitations of outmoded, patriarchal understandings of the past. In a path-breaking paper, Helen Bradford not only decried the omission of women from history and history-writing but went on to show that South African historical works are suffused with 'androcentric' approaches, with the result that 'our historical vision is so impaired as to be unacceptably inaccurate'. A key insight of hers is that generalised narratives and language have consciously or unconsciously structured ways of thinking: 'On the one hand, men are largely gender neutral, conceptualized not as men but as people, linked with categories like economics, politics or race. On the other hand, women are gendered beings, with an implicit or explicit emphasis on their sexual attributes and their familial relationships with men.'[3]

Though this book is not a properly gendered history, the present chapter attempts to make a start at redressing the exclusion of women from the narratives of nationalism before Union by examining the ways in which they contributed to the social and political developments that form the core of this study. Even if the organisations described here were for men only, it is possible to show that women were indeed part of the tapestry of politics from the beginning.[4]

In her history of social dislocation and missionary activity in Xhosaland in the nineteenth century, Natasha Erlank has pointed out that 'The possession of power in these chiefdoms rested on a series of inequalities which had their origin in the control men had over women'. Women were 'considered inferior to men', though they were 'nevertheless in possession of a certain gentle authority'. They had a status 'symbolically equivalent to that of cattle', because wealth in African societies was measured in cattle and cattle were used as a way of transferring women from one family to another on marriage. While there were aspects of these customs and rituals that brought stability and protection to both the communities and to the individual women concerned, the underlying fact remained that women were, institutionally speaking, perpetual minors: 'Women could only ever be exchanged, they could not exchange cattle themselves or own cattle.'[5]

Similarly, in Britain during the nineteenth century, patriarchal norms clearly defined gender roles. Men were seen as providers and leaders, while women were regarded as the 'weaker sex', whose role it was to act as nurturers and procreators, responsible for child care and the household. These gender differences were 'scientifically' rationalised during the Victorian period.[6] As Kathleen McCrone has explained: 'traditional Victorians summoned all the power of custom, religion and science at their disposal in defence of existing social arrangements. They insisted that God and nature had imbued women with qualities of mind and body that destined her for specific tasks, such as being man's helpmate, nurturing his children, and protecting the sanctity of his home.'[7]

If the restrictions on women emanating from this approach are reduced to one sphere of life – in this case, recreation and sport – one can see how severe they were. In Victorian eyes, the ideal woman was 'antithetical to sport'. 'Passive, gentle, emotional and delicate, she had neither the strength nor the inclination to undertake strenuous exercises and competitive games.' Science was invoked to support this thesis. Two physicians, Edward Clarke and Henry Maudsley, whose views became widely influential, maintained that women were biologically weaker than men, and, if they exercised, their health would be ruined: 'if women and girls behaved abnormally by acquiring a masculine type of education, their vital energy would be sapped and their health ruined ... they would lose their natural grace and gentility and be turned into coarse, imperfectly developed creatures who would produce degenerate off-spring or none at all.'[8] This view remained the orthodoxy for many years. Unchallenged, it 'represented a potentially fatal blow to the ambitions of women in every direction except the domestic', as McCrone has pointed out. The notion of the naturally frail woman was turned into a virtuous stereotype – and an industry. So-called scientific facts about women's frailty led to an excessive belief in the benefits of spas, prescriptions and treatments. Women's conditions became medicalised, and doctors and moralists thrived as women's complaints were turned into a 'medical-business complex'.[9]

In important respects, then, women in African societies shared much in common with European women. However, as Natasha Erlank has argued, colonial conquest, and the intensifying loss of cattle that accompanied it, not only destabilised long-held African customs and undermined the security these gave individuals, both men and women, but also made attractive to vulnerable African women the European notion of marriage based more on individual choice and the opportunities that conversion and missionary education offered them.[10] African women came to play key roles on the mission stations and their experiences in negotiating complex new paths in a changing world were just as remarkable as those of men. One of the most outstanding figures was Sandile's daughter, commonly called Princess Emma, who together with the children of other Xhosa chiefs studied at Zonnebloem College after its opening in 1858. Her exceptional life and journey, straddling the 'traditional' and colonial worlds, has been beautifully documented by Janet Hodgson. The first African woman in the Cape to privately own land and sign an antenuptial contract, she taught at a church school in Grahamstown after completing her studies at Zonnebloem and later married Chief Sitokhwe of Emigrant Thembuland. As his wife, she enjoyed an elevated status because of her education. She wrote letters in English to the colonial authorities on behalf of her husband at a time when his chiefdom was under great pressure and also handled his business affairs. Emma's half-sister Victoria (named after the British queen) lived with Tiyo Soga and his family for four years before marrying Chief Umhlangaso of the Mpondo, the last independent Nguni ruler in southern Africa, who, as we have seen, employed a secretary and used *Imvo* in his political campaigns.[11]

Princess Emma's story illustrates the relevance of women's experiences to the politics that form the subject of this book. During the political ferment in Glen Grey in the 1880s and 1890s, she found herself at odds with the powerful Mahonga family. The Rev. Johannes Mahonga, head of the Wesleyan mission at Seplan and grandson of a loyalist supporter of the magistrate E.J. Warner, had been awarded land at Seplan by Emma's husband, Chief Sitokhwe, under pressure from Warner. The land Mahonga took possession of and rented out (as an absent landowner initially) was more than that agreed to by Sitokhwe. After the chief's death, Emma contested the Mahongas' ownership of the land. A government land commission took her side and, after it had settled the Seplan mission land issue, Emma moved there. Freed by her husband's death to practise Christianity once again, she in fact became a member of Johannes Mahonga's congregation.[12]

By the 1890s many more women had followed in the footsteps of Princess Emma. While creating opportunities for individuals, the mission schools at the same time reinforced Victorian conventions about the role of women in politics and society. The best the mission-educated young woman could wish for in career terms was to be a teacher. Otherwise, domestic labour was the norm – either as wives or as domestic servants in the employment of colonial whites. Girls were generally trained to fit 'respectably' into the colonial order, and taught to fulfil expected gender roles. As black women, they belonged not only to the 'weaker sex', but also to an inferior 'race'. The Bishop of Grahamstown reported in 1885 that the girls at St Matthew's College were instructed every day 'in all the duties of domestic life, such as washing, ironing, sewing, cooking and baking' by a Miss Lucas. Great trouble was taken to keep them 'pure'.[13]

Seventy years later, not much had changed. In the 1950s, 'The curriculum at Lovedale and other mission schools prepared girls for a life of servitude and domestic labour, reinforcing colonial values and gender stereotypes. The home and mother-craft syllabus included instructions on how to wash a hairbrush and comb and clean silverware, the subject of hygiene was "taught from a book compiled in England and based upon a life as remote as the moon" … The widely used Laundry and Housewife Primer advised the students on appropriate shoes – "in the country, very strong ones and lighter type for town wear", warning that "fancy feathers never wear well". Several pages of the slim volume were devoted to the setting of tables in the manner appropriate for breakfast, supper, dinner and afternoon tea as well as the correct method of waiting at table.'[14] All the same, these Africans, like their male counterparts, were never wholly constrained by the expectations of the missionaries or of colonial society. They, too, became part of the new social networks and politics of identity from the very start, even if their formal involvement was not encouraged.

One sign of an active political consciousness was the correspondence entered into by women with African newspapers. In 1884, an unnamed 'lady reader' from Somerset East wrote to *Isigidimi*, criticising men who said women should not be involved in public life. 'This is an old mistake, to believe that there are some matters which the ladies cannot listen to ... Nothing becomes strong without them.' Getting 'amaledi' involved could only strengthen an organisation, she declared. The correspondent also noted that while the pioneering Native Educational Association (NEA) allowed the participation of women, Imbumba Yama Nyama did not; in her view, this was probably why the NEA was stronger than Imbumba.[15]

Besides being allowed to participate in bodies such as the NEA, women played an active role in political campaigns. When the Queenstown Native Vigilance Association held a successful meeting at Lesseyton in August 1887 to protest against the Peace Preservation Act, which imposed disarmament on all Africans, a newspaper reported that 'Lesseyton women also deserve gratitude for what they did on that day, which we will never forget'.[16] However, the other side of the coin was the comment made at the same meeting in relation to subscribers to the 'national newspaper', *Imvo*, who did not pay: 'One who subscribes and doesn't pay shall have a skirt on like a woman [laughter].' As the report makes clear, women were seen by men as junior partners and auxiliaries in politics.

A 'Petition of Native Women' from King William's Town to parliament in 1889, calling for the prohibition of liquor in the Cape, was typical of the supportive role played by them. The petitioners described themselves as people who 'although physically weak, are strong of heart to love our Homes and our Native Land'. They strongly opposed 'Alcoholic Stimulants which craze and cloud the brain, make misery for man and all the world, and most of all for us, and for our children'. The content and tone of the petition accorded with the views of both missionaries and school people about the evils of liquor and the genteel, nurturing role of women in society. Among the 35 pages of signatures attached, names such as Mzimba, Figlan and Xiniwe indicate that the partners and families of local political figures were involved.[17]

The social activities of the mission-educated women followed a similar path to those of men. In 1884 the wives of the leaders of Port Elizabeth's black community set up a tennis and croquet club. At the helm of the ladies' croquet club were Mrs Wauchope (secretary), Mrs Malgas (treasurer and umpire) and Mrs Rwexu (umpire). The elaborate constitution of this club (written in Xhosa) appeared in the missionary newspaper, *Isigidimi*.[18] Local women also became active tennis players, playing mixed doubles with the men.[19] These were among the earliest women's sports clubs in South Africa.[20] Through their participation, women made a clear statement about their role, as they saw it, in colonial society.[21]

When Port Elizabeth hosted the Kimberley 'native team' for the first time in January 1888, the cricket match was played at the white Union CC grounds, where it cost 6d to sit on the pavilion. The local community 'fully supported the game'. 'For the first time in the history of matches in the area married men brought their wives and single men brought their partners', according to a newspaper report. The reporter believed this should be applauded, 'as it is a symbol of change in our communities'.[22]

In other spheres of life, too, women involved in the 'modernising' project played an active, participatory role – they were not mere adornments. An outstanding example was the life of Nokutela Dube, wife of John L. Dube, the founding president of the ANC. As Heather Hughes has pointed out, Nokutela Mdima was an ambitious and talented woman, who enjoyed a remarkable career in her own right. For 30 years after her marriage to John Dube in 1894, she was constantly at the side of her famous husband, as co-builder of their educational and political projects. The daughter of a notable school family, she was said to speak 'good English with a deliberation that is charming' and 'her manner is grace itself'. She shared platforms with her husband in places from Durban to New York and London, when it was still a rarity for an African woman to do so, helping to raise thousands of dollars for their educational work. She not only had a beautiful soprano voice, but became adept at making speeches. She was, moreover, an able pamphleteer and school teacher, set up the famous Ohlange choir, which travelled regularly to Johannesburg and other centres in South Africa, composed many songs, and, together with her husband, produced the first book of Zulu secular songs in a modern idiom. All in all, Nokutela Dube was 'a most admirable role-model of African womanhood'.[23]

There were a number of other exceptional people in the ranks of educated Victorian women. Charlotte Manye, who spent ten years abroad before returning home as the first African woman graduate in southern Africa, has already been mentioned in this book for her part in initiating links between the Ethiopian Church and the AME Church in the United States. Her subsequent career in politics and education is fairly well known, including the fact that Chief Dalindyebo of the Thembu allowed her to attend the discussions at his Great Place, usually reserved for men.[24]

Less well-known is the role that Alice Kinloch from Kimberley played in the establishment of the African Association, which prepared the way for the Pan-African movement of the twentieth century. According to the historian David Killingray, it was she, the Trinidadian Henry Sylvester Williams and Thomas J. Thompson who were responsible for founding the Association in London in 1897. On 15 October of that year, she wrote that 'with some men of my race in this country, I have formed a society for the benefit of our people in Africa ... To-night the initiation of "The African Association" takes place ... I am trying to educate people in this country in regard to the iniquitous laws made for blacks in South Africa.' Sylvester Williams later explained that 'the Association is the result of Mrs Kinloch's work in England'. At the founding meeting, Kinloch was elected treasurer of the body.

The African Association's main aim was to convene a conference of the 'African race from all parts of the world' so that British public opinion could be made aware of the adverse conditions under which black people lived, in South Africa and elsewhere. The historic Pan-African Congress of 1900, held in Manchester, stemmed directly from the Association, although Alice Kinloch did not attend, as she had by then returned to southern Africa.[25] Living at one time at 172 Buckingham Palace Road in London with her Zulu husband, Kinloch was also active as a speaker and pamphleteer during her stay in England. 'Alice spoke at the Writers' Club, London, and was encouraged ... to tour areas of northern England on behalf of the Aborigines Protection Society, from 3 to 5 May 1897, speaking at meetings in Newcastle-upon-Tyne, York and Manchester on "the cruel and violent measures by which the native races of South Africa are being deprived of their lands and liberty".'[26]

According to Killingray, Kinloch returned to South Africa in February

1898, first living in the Transvaal, before she moved to Verulam in Natal in 1899 to farm. She continued to be active in support of the African Association, now under the chairmanship of H. Mason Joseph from Antigua, whose task it became to prepare for the proposed Pan-African conference.[27] In letters to Harriette Colenso, she complained about the lack of local support for the movement: 'I have sent you per post a Report and the rules of "The African Assoc." which will explain the interest we have in it. I really thought Mr Williams had sent you all particulars concerning it last year. We have been invited to the conference but shall not be able to be present. We have tried to get some of our people in the Cape Colony interested, but they are so taken up with Messrs Rhodes & Co etc, that they fail to see the usefulness of such an organisation. We don't know anyone in this part except a brother who is not interested. The West Africans have responded most generously.'[28]

While Charlotte Manye and Alice Kinloch were unusual for their explicit political involvement, women were, it is clear, close to the politics of the emerging organisations in South Africa by the final years of the nineteenth century. In one powerful example from 1899, Deena Rubusana wrote to the mayor of East London, requesting him to meet with a delegation of women about their dissatisfaction with conditions in the East Bank location. They were received in the Council Chambers. Supported by Nozimanga Hanisi and Annie Feni, who both spoke, Mrs Rubusana read a petition and raised their grievances, which included high rentals, the summary eviction of householders, and the power of the superintendent and headman 'to violate the privacy of our homes'. Mrs Rubusana maintained the correspondence for over two months, showing real grit in pursuing what the mayoral office referred to as 'native grievances'.[29]

Deena Rubusana, Nokutela Dube, Charlotte Manye, Alice Kinloch and other contemporaries were strong personalities in their own right. Something of the social milieu in which they operated is revealed by Margaret McCord's biography of Katie Makanya, Charlotte's sister.[30] Many of those who became involved in political or semi-political matters were often linked to leading figures by ties of education, blood, friendship or marriage. Theirs was a close-knit network of peers and associates, who often intermarried, and became involved in a range of common, overlapping activities. Heather Hughes, in discussing the role played by Nokutela Dube, notes that both her and her husband's families had 'long been intertwined in the small world' of a particular missionary movement. Political leaders often became 'family' through cross-marriage. James Dwane married Klaas Mayekiso's daughter in the Glen Grey district; Elizabeth Bud Mbelle married Sol Plaatje; Kate Xiniwe married W.D. Soga; Paul Xiniwe married Eleanor Dwanya, sister of Daniel, and an impressive list of political figures attended their wedding as guests, including Chief William Shaw Kama, John Knox Bokwe, Peter Rwexu, W.N. Somngesi, Isaac Wauchope and J.T. Jabavu.[31] Jabavu himself was married to Elda Sakuba, whose brother was politically active, and whose uncle was Theodore Ndwandwa, right-hand man of the influential Veldtman Bikitsha in Fingoland.[32] Women took it upon themselves to fulfil a complementary role to that of the menfolk. Together, school people of both sexes were self-consciously engaged in carving out a new role for themselves in southern Africa: their goals were shared as much by the women as the men.

All the same, formal politics was very much a man's world. As Hughes has noted, both Dubes 'saw as part of their mission the elevation of the status of women', yet there was no question of Mrs Dube being regarded as his political equal. A few months after Charlotte Manye returned from a decade abroad with a Bachelor's degree, she attended the South African Native Congress's 1902 conference and delivered an impressive address. However, it was decided that, even though 'the hand that rocks the cradle rules the world', the time was not yet ripe to allow women to become members. With her stage personality and educational achievements, Manye remained in the public spotlight for many decades, though never as an official member of the Congress.

One of the first manifestations of African women organising independently in the first decade of the twentieth century was the Manyano movement. Starting in Natal in the early 1900s, it emerged from an older tradition of women's prayer groups. In 1907 a conference was held at Edendale, attended as well by some women from the Transvaal. One of those present at Edendale, Mrs S. Gqosho, wife of a Wesleyan minister in Potchefstroom, helped organise the Native Women's Christian Union in her home town the following year. Some 150 delegates attended 'to consult over matters affecting their class'. In time, the Manyanos grew into a powerful national movement. As one of its members explained, the organisation gave women 'recognition as being of equal value before God with the men'.[33]

In the same year as the Potchefstroom conference, A.K. Soga made a full-page call in *Izwi Labantu* to 'The Coloured women of South Africa' on behalf of the SANC's Queen Victoria Memorial Committee, calling on them to help form women's-only branches and collect money for this higher education project. He declared that women were needed to assist. 'Poetry and art, music and culture, industry and economy, the management of the home and family life, these and other social, religious and educational duties fall within the scope of women's mission,' he added. The Memorial Scheme was 'an ideal and incentive upon which to concentrate their energies and devote their efforts'. The branches would fall under the direction of a 'Lady president' (a position held subsequently by Kate Xiniwe); clause 6 of the memorandum, dealing with 'male friends', specifically warned against men interfering in their work. Soga concluded, 'There must be some motive in life and no nobler object or worthier ideal presents itself to the women of Africa than to work for the elevation of the people'.[34]

Meanwhile, women in East London, working in tandem with Dr Walter Rubusana, marched in protest about their conditions. Washerwomen were losing work because Indian and Chinese people had 'practically monopolized all the washing of the town', the rates for hut sites and trading licences were too high, and the 'native residents' had to pay levies at the market and were not permitted to trade in firewood among themselves. Four to five hundred women, who 'maintained orderly rank and demeanour', marched to the City Hall, where Rubusana spoke on their behalf.[35] *Izwi* commented, 'Such a movement on the part of the women may be interpreted according to what one chooses, but we prefer to regard it as a sign that women are beginning to assert themselves and, like their fairer sisters the suffragettes in England and women all the world over, they will eventually force governing bodies to sit up and take notice'.[36] In solidarity with their East London sisters, women in Queenstown, helped by another SANC leader, the Rev. Eben Koti, marched on the mayor's office, complaining about local hardships: they did not have money to travel to Johannesburg to find work and life was made difficult for them by increased taxes for water and the selling of milk. They declared that the chiefs had helped them in the past; now the mayor was in that position, and they needed his support.[37]

While African women did not feature in the main narrative of political mobilisation before Union – white women formed the first suffragette body only in 1911[38] and won the right to vote only in 1930 – they did play political roles from an early stage, mostly behind the scenes. As the momentum of politics quickened in the first decade of the century, they slowly became more visible and articulate. Within a few years, women in Bloemfontein would open a new chapter in their political struggles when in 1913 – in scenes contemporary with the suffragette campaign in England and the Gandhian passive resistance struggles in South Africa – they protested against the pass laws and were sent to prison.

23

Black economic empowerment

I Afrika yeya ma Afrika (Africa is for the Africans).
                                        – George A. Ross, 1893

The economy was yet another sphere in which Africans began to organise in the late nineteenth century. Colonialism undermined the subsistence economies of the indigenous pastoral societies and drew them into the market economy of the Cape in various ways. On one hand, a relatively prosperous and independent African peasantry emerged, buying or leasing land, engaged in sheep farming and wool production, producing a considerable agricultural surplus, and generally adapting positively to economic changes and market opportunities.[1] On the other, the industrial revolution that followed the discovery of diamonds and gold led to the creation of a huge wage-earning working class, increasingly denied access to land.[2]

It was the peasantry and growing middle class emerging from the mission stations, particularly in the eastern Cape and Natal, that laid the foundations for the new forms of African constitutional politics. During the last quarter of the nineteenth century the political rights and economic security of these people came under increasing attack, statutory and otherwise. When laws were passed restricting the franchise in the Cape Colony in 1887 and 1892, Africans mobilised politically to meet the challenge. As Stanley Trapido has noted, 'the defence of the franchise was closely related to the defence of the peasantry'.[3]

It is beyond the scope of this book to analyse in depth the position of Africans in the economy, but it is noticeable how soon the new educated stratum started organising and participating in the economic sphere, as a way of strengthening their position in colonial society. By 1881 Andrew Gontshi, the founder of two early Transkeian political organisations, was supporting moves to form a body to help Africans start their own businesses.[4] One of the express aims of the first African political organisation, Imbumba Yama Nyama, founded the following year, was 'to hold on to the ground of our fathers by buying land in these bad times'.[5] In 1884 the first independent African newspaper was launched. Opinion-formers began to encourage Africans to buy property, start businesses and attain professional qualifications in order to ensure a sound African economic base. For this purpose they formed themselves into economic interest groups: mutual aid organisations, burial societies, companies, farmers' associations and the like. As early as 1877 an Ethiopian Benefit Society had been formed in Port Elizabeth with the aim of collecting money for mutual aid and burial purposes. In 1885 it had a bank balance of over £400 and at one stage it had more than 100 members. People like Daniel Mzamo, Peter Rwexu and Isaac Wauchope were prominent in its activities.[6] By 1891 there were already seven black-owned shops and a butcher in Port Elizabeth.[7] Another conspicuous example was the flourishing Emigrant Thembuland Native Farmers' Association. Under its auspices the 'rich' Thembuland farmers held shows and meetings, promoted progressive farming ideas, and pursued their interests generally.[8] There were also early farming associations amongst the Gqunukhwebe at Middledrift, at Kubusi near Stutterheim, Engcobo and Peddie.[9] Important political figures like Mankayi Rengqe, Sol Kalipa, Pambani Figlan, J.T. Jabavu and Thomas Mqanda were involved in these groups.

The first steps to unite Africans in the eastern Cape in a common economic organisation came with the formation of the African and American Working Men's Union (AAWMU) in the early 1890s. Port Elizabeth people, who had started the first sports clubs, temperance bodies, benefit societies and the pioneering Imbumba Yama Nyama, again took the lead. In 1891 two well-known local spokesmen, George A. Ross and Moses Foley, together with Ozias Henderson and Henry Phipps, African Americans living in Port Elizabeth, revealed their business plans.[10] The Union intended to start black-run businesses and help create jobs for local Africans. Five thousand shares were advertised at £1 each. Efforts were made to involve other areas: the promoters addressed meetings in Uitenhage, Grahamstown, Kimberley, Aliwal North and King William's Town, and were in contact with people from as far afield as Basutoland, Bechuanaland and Natal.[11] By April 1892 the Union had shareholders in 16 centres.[12] By September only 2300 shares remained to be sold.[13] Over £1600 had already been collected by the end of the year and some £500 of this was expended on preliminary organisation.[14] A board of directors, which met every week, was elected.[15] Early in 1893 the AAWMU opened in Port Elizabeth the first of what it hoped would be many shops throughout South Africa. It was staffed and had been built entirely by blacks on a site bought by the Union after difficulties had been encountered in trying to hire premises.[16] Stocks were ordered directly from overseas, among them clothes and equipment for sports clubs and church ministers.[17] The Union also intended buying from its African clientele wool, hides and foodstuffs and exporting them. The aim was to corner from white wholesalers and retailers the African market, which amounted to about half of the colony's trade returns.[18]

The Union was a success, even if a modest one. In the first half of 1894, cash sales in the shop brought in a shade under £1500.[19] The after expenses balance stood at £630 in December 1894.[20] The Union was still running its own shop, employing staff and holding regular meetings of shareholders in the early 1900s.[21]

The formation of the AAWMU was closely linked to the process of political mobilisation then occurring. It was started by political leaders in Port Elizabeth, and enjoyed the active support of the chairman of the local Iliso Lomzi, Benjamin Dlepu.[22] Reports of its meetings and a letter to the *Imvo* by its chief organiser show its unmistakably Africanist character. It stood for race pride and dignity, race combination and race advancement in a colonial society that discriminated against black people. Despite age, ability or experience, Africans were still called John, Jack or Jim and held the most menial jobs. As Benjamin Dlepu said, 'Even white boys call us "boy"'.[23] Membership was expressly for blacks only.[24] There were no class distinctions: it was open to rich and poor, educated and non-literate.[25] Its aim was the development of the 'nation'.[26] The organisers exhorted Africans to start businesses to 'free ourselves from slavery' (Rwexu) and 'gain respect for ourselves' (Foley).[27] Ross urged his fellow men and women to stand on their feet and work for the nation. Through the Union, Africans would show *i Afrika yeya ma Afrika* (Africa is for the Africans).[28] Here, contemporaneous with the separatist church movement, which made the slogan famous, was the rallying cry of Pan-Africanism. African imagery and history were evoked in their prospectus: the land of their forefathers had been taken away and, with it, their dignity. Long ago, men used to fence their homesteads to prepare for their sons: the Union would also fence homesteads for its children so that they could become 'people among people'. Peter Rwexu also emphasised a broader transatlantic bond. The Union's American members were tied by blood to Africa; they were 'Xhosa' who had been enslaved in Africa and taken to America.

Following the AAWMU, a number of similar co-operative economic ventures were started, apparently inspired by it. In 1894 *Imvo* reported that a company based on the model of the AAWMU was being floated in Natal.[29] Apparently because of a rift within the AAWMU, Frank Makwena, a Sotho living permanently in Port Elizabeth, who had been vice-president of the Imbumba Yama Nyama, started the Basuto Pioneering Trading company around 1896.[30] It had committees or agents in Port Elizabeth and various Basutoland towns. Despite its strong Sotho character, it was open to all black people in South Africa.[31]

Another direct outflow of the AAWMU was the African Trading Association started at King William's Town, the inland commercial centre of the eastern Cape, by people who felt the AAWMU in Port Elizabeth was too remote.[32] The initiative for the Association was taken by Paul Xiniwe, whose business ventures in King William's Town and East London included a hotel, a boarding house and several stores.[33] Its aim was to provide a central fund to help Africans buy land and start their own businesses. Xiniwe's plans captured the imagination of a large cross-section of eastern Cape political leaders. Three well-attended meetings were held in King William's Town.[34] Captain Veldtman, Pambani Figlan and Patrick Xabanisa were prominent attendees from the Transkeian Territories and Thembuland, while Joseph Moss (reputed to be the richest African in Kimberley), the chiefs Ebenezer Mhlambiso, W.S. Kama and Mbem Njikelana, and various South African Native Congress stalwarts also gave support.[35]

The fate of the African Trading Association is not known. It does not appear to have been a success, despite the influential backing it received, because in 1901 Xiniwe and the Rev. Edward Tsewu were again trying to launch an African Trading Association. They sought £5000 to start stores in various parts of the eastern Cape. While Tsewu went on to establish the Transvaal Landowners' Association, the fate of Xiniwe's initiative is unknown; it could have perished after his death at a relatively early age in 1902.

The Transkeian politician S. Milton Ntloko advertised shares in a Tsomo-based Transkei Pioneer Company in 1898. Its objective was to alleviate the land shortage for blacks by buying, leasing or selling property.[36] Walter Rubusana was the chairman of a similar company, the Ark of Refuge Society, in East London.[37] He was also a director of the Eagle Press Printing Company, formed by the SANC leaders to start the *Izwi* newspaper in 1897, and one of the developers of the Goddarton township scheme in East London in the 1900s.

All these enterprises reflected the efforts of the new generation of politicians in the eastern Cape to provide a solid economic base for Africans in colonial society. Their activities were closely linked to the process of political mobilisation. Similar developments occurred in other parts of southern Africa as well. There were several hundred 'coffee houses' for blacks in Johannesburg in the 1890s, and the entrepreneurial success of the affluent Edendale and Driefontein communities in Natal is well known.[38]

The rise of the eastern Cape and Transkeian peasantry in the late nineteenth century has been well documented. In 1904, there were 3544 African farmers in the Cape out of a total of 40,942.[39] In 1906 Africans bought 16,500 acres of land in the Peddie district alone.[40] Statistics for neighbouring districts showed similar increases.[41] At the same time, the number of whites on the land was decreasing. As the Prime Minister, John Merriman, observed: 'We drove out the tide but it is slowly coming back and may flood us out some day. The worst is that what is a danger to us Europeans from the Native point of view represents an effort to raise themselves to a higher plane than that of mere communal tenure, and marks a distinct advance in civilisation – two opposite tendencies which will be hard to reconcile without however dealing with matters of high policy which touch the very heart of our existence.'[42] Indeed, this was a telling assessment. Increasingly in the twentieth century, as Africans sought more land and a greater role in the Cape and, later, the South African economy, white economic interest groups opposed them. In response, successive white governments imposed drastic statutory restrictions on African economic advancement and curtailed the kind of entrepreneurship that had been displayed early on.

24

Playing the white man at his own game

Already all sorts of guesses are indulged in as to the probable motives of the sons of Ham in taking to this English time-honoured pastime. 'Mimicry', 'travesty of civilization' and expletives of a like character have been hinted as the possible causes, but our countrymen have gone on the even tenor of their way without noticing their critics ... the natives do not only mean to persevere in playing at cricket, but are resolved to proceed from conquering to conquest so far as the cricket world is concerned.

– *Imvo Zabantsundu*, 3 November 1884

While previous chapters have demonstrated the essential Africanism inherent in the early ideas and organisations of the mission-educated African Christians, this chapter reveals the lasting influence of British culture and ideas on them. Their politics and their strategies for the future were, indeed, premised on a fusion of what they saw as the best of their lived experiences and history as Africans and the imported vision of human emancipation embodied in the Bible and political liberalism.

Africans became ardent sports followers, particularly of cricket, which was regarded as the most 'gentlemanly' of Victorian games. Love of the game, it was believed, would demonstrate their ability to assimilate European culture and behave like gentlemen, and, by extension, show their fitness to be accepted as fellow citizens in Cape society. By this means the school people could pay homage to the leading ideas of 'civilisation', 'progress', Christianity and Empire, which were so important to colonists.[1]

At the mission schools, recreation became a matter of supreme importance. Many of the traditional pastimes of Africans were deemed 'incompatible with Christian purity of life' and had to be abandoned by those embracing the new religion of the missionaries. Provision was therefore made in the school programme for 'healthy exercise and the profitable employment of leisure'.[2] Drill became a regular feature on timetables and sports like cricket and football were introduced.[3]

As with politics, Lovedale and Healdtown became the main nurseries for African cricket over the years. Inter-college matches came to assume the same importance as they did at British public schools and the local whites-only boys' schools. In fact, in 1891 Lovedale played Dale College from King William's Town and beat them by 15 runs, a result that is hard to grasp in view of the country's subsequent history.[4] In 1884 there were no less than five clubs centred on Lovedale. These were the 'European' club, the Oriental CC (for students), the Brotherly United CC (for those working at Lovedale), Gaika's Imperial CC (the 'location' club) and True Blue CC (for coloured people). From schools like Lovedale and Healdtown, thousands of departing students took with them their skills and talents, setting up clubs and becoming involved in spreading the game wherever they settled. In Port Elizabeth, for example, ex-Lovedalians challenged the rest in 1883 and easily beat them.[5]

The development of organised cricket in black communities closely followed that of the segregated cricket establishment in many respects; step by step from its introduction into schools (in the 1850s), the formation of clubs (1860s), and the introduction of inter-town competitions (1880s), leagues and provincial competitions (1890s), to the formation of a national controlling body (1900s). Nowhere was this enthusiastic growth more evident than in the eastern Cape. By the 1880s, following white precedent, there were thriving clubs and regular competitions in almost all areas in the region.[6] As in politics, a distinct tradition of sport developed in the eastern Cape and cricket clubs soon became an integral part of the new community networks and activities.

The first regular reports of Africans playing cricket can be found in *Isigidimi*. This missionary newspaper reported, for instance, on the first inter-town match between Champions CC of King William's Town and

Gaika [Ngqika] CC from East London on the Queen's birthday, 24 May
1883. The King William's Town team won, but when they went by train
to East London for the return match in September the tables were turned.[7]
From then on, matches between teams from these towns became regular
features, played mainly on public holidays. In the 1883 East London game,
Walter Rubusana was one of the umpires; special mention was made in
the newspaper report of how well he did the job.[8] The captain of the King
William's Town was Nathaniel Umhalla, who had only recently emerged
from the traumatic experience of being charged with treason.

Cricket was placed on a more co-ordinated footing in the mid-1880s.
In 1884 teams from the main eastern Cape centres of East London, King
William's Town, Queenstown, Grahamstown and Port Elizabeth organised
the first official inter-town tournament, based on similar inter-town
tournaments for the best white sides in South Africa.[9] This was a remarkable
achievement if one considers that white cricketers were holding only their
third inter-town tournament in nearby Port Elizabeth in the same month.[10]
From this time on, tournaments of all sorts became commonplace.

The King William's Town Champion CC, captained by Nathaniel
Umhalla, which won the first tournament, gave an indication of the
proficiency of Africans at the game when they subsequently defeated
one of the white King William's Town club sides, which included several
players who had participated in the white tournament.[11] At about the
same time, the Port Elizabeth Africans twice beat the white Cradock side.[12]
These victories were by no means the exception.[13] No wonder that the *Port
Elizabeth Telegraph* observed that the game 'seems quite to hit the Kaffir
fancy'.[14]

Commenting on the King William's Town match, the *Cape Mercury*
remarked that it was significant 'to all those who take an intelligent interest
in the progress of the country'. Evoking images of peace less than a decade
after the last of the wars of dispossession, the newspaper said that the
game reminded it of an old song:

And men learn't wisdom from the past,
In friendship joined their hands;
Hung the sword in the hall;

the spear on the wall,

And ploughed the willing lands.

The newspaper added: 'those who play together will not object to work together, and the manly fellows who donned the flannels last week will have a heartier feeling of respect for their dusky conquerors than they had before.'[15] A delighted *Imvo* commented that such cricket matches were 'calculated to make the Europeans and Natives have more mutual trust and confidence than all the coercive and repressive legislation in the world'.[16] When the Port Elizabeth Africans followed by beating the white Cradock town club early in 1885, *Imvo* exclaimed: 'It is enough to say that the contest shows that the native is a rough diamond that needs to be polished to exhibit the same qualities that are to be found in the civilised being, and that he is not to be dismissed as a mere "schepsel" [creature], as it has been the habit of the pioneers to do so hereto.'[17]

The launch of *Imvo* in November 1884 revealed just how popular cricket had become among eastern Cape Africans. In the very first edition, Jabavu devoted his editorial notes to the game:

To our Colonial English contemporaries, the playing of the game of cricket by natives would seem to be regarded as a strange phenomenum [sic]; and already all sorts of guesses are indulged in as to the probable motives of the sons of Ham in taking to this English time-honoured pastime. 'Mimicry', 'travesty of civilization' and expletives of a like character have been hinted as the possible causes, but our countrymen have gone on the even tenor of their way without noticing their critics … the natives do not only mean to persevere in playing at cricket, but are resolved to proceed from conquering to conquest so far as the cricket world is concerned.[18]

Over the years, hundreds of cricket reports appeared in *Imvo* (even during winter), under the title *Ibala labadlali* (sports field or 'patch of the players'). By 1887 the paper had appointed a sporting editor.[19] The Dyer & Dyer merchant house soon began placing advertisements in *Imvo*, directed specifically at African cricketers and clubs, offering cricket kit of every variety.[20] *Isigidimi* noted that the educated and christianised school people 'tina mpi imnyama igqobokileyo' – had left behind the old tribal ways, but had not yet also adopted the new, in particular the leisure activities of cricket, lawn tennis, croquet, hunting and dancing of the English. The paper fostered interest by, for instance, placing news of a century by 'Dr Grace' against Australia,[21] and giving advice on how cricketers could best protect their bats in hot climates, where they broke easily. The suggested remedy: *'uyifake kunye namafuta embizeni, uyibilise ke yonke lonto kunye'* (You put it together with fat [oil] into a pot and bring everything to a boil together).[22] In time, cricket became not only the favourite sport in the African communities of the eastern Cape, but an integral part of their lifestyles.

Sport served an explicitly political function for the school people from the beginning. They saw it as an important part of the self-conscious process of modernisation in which they were involved. Early political leaders were almost invariably also leaders and members of the first sports clubs. This showed their commitment to community development, at a time when people were organising at every level and starting to build a whole new framework of interrelated activities based on western and colonial models.

Sport was also one of the ways in which they could celebrate lofty British notions over colonial prejudice. In shaping their vision for the future, the new elite idealised British values. This was partly tactical, so as to win support for British intervention, and partly aspirational, so that their own visions for the future of the colony could be held up publicly as a goal. Despite the many contradictions, they glorified things British. When the first English cricket side under Major Wharton toured South Africa in 1888/89, black spectators cheered them on against the local white sides in an obvious political commentary. In the report on the match by the tourists against the King William's Town-based Cape Mounted Rifles team, *Imvo* noted, 'It is singular that the sympathies of the Native spectators were with the English'.[23]

As important as the games were the social activities connected with cricket. Sports on public holidays such as Empire Day and Christmas were almost inevitably followed by social functions. Here the aspiring black middle class could display their elegance and accomplishments. These events differed little from those that catered for white society. Often, functions were held in the local town hall, with the mayor or other dignitaries in attendance. At one typical event in Kimberley, a splendid dinner was put before the guests, followed by a programme of musical entertainment and speeches. It started off with a toast to the Queen and ended with a rendering of 'God Save the Queen'. Finally the proceedings were brought to a close with speeches, hymns and a benediction.[24]

Sport, as well as the related social activities, provided the school people with a training ground for participation in the new society. In typical Victorian fashion it offered both a personal and political lesson. As a member of the African Political Organisation emphasised, when speaking on the topic of a sound mind in a social body, sport and politics were closely linked:

Great lessons can be learned ... on the cricket and football fields – two forms of sport of which our people are passionately fond. No one who is not punctual, patient, accurate and vigilant, can ever expect to become a consistently good batsman. Both batsman and spectators know that; and yet do we carry those moral lessons into our private or public life? Patient, of course we are: but are we punctual and vigilant? ... are we as watchful of our public welfare as the batsman is of every ball – even those which the umpire declares to be wide? If we were, much of our present trouble would have been forestalled.[25]

Membership and rank in sports clubs were signs of social success: they enhanced the respectability and status of political figures. Besides being a pillar of middle-class respectability as an editor, politician, long-serving Wesleyan church steward and templar, J.T. Jabavu was president of two of the sports clubs in King William's Town, the Frontier Cricket Club and the Oriental Lawn Tennis Club.[26] In the 1890s he presented the Jabavu Cup for inter-town cricket competition in the eastern Cape.[27] Committee members of the Frontier Cricket Club in the 1890s included Paul Xiniwe, W.D. Soga, Nathaniel Umhalla, John Knox Bokwe and James Dwane.[28] Political differences do not seem to have been a major factor here. Sol Plaatje's newspaper, *Tsala ea Becoana*, seemed to corroborate this when it declared that the Mfengu and Xhosa should learn to co-operate in politics in the same way they did in sport.[29]

While cricket was by far the most popular sport, the aspiring black middle class also took, to a lesser extent, to sports like tennis, croquet, football and rugby. According to the Rev. Elijah Makiwane, writing in 1888, in 'almost all the towns [of the eastern Cape] there are cricket clubs which are in a more or less thriving state, and at Port Elizabeth and a few other towns, there are also croquet and lawn tennis clubs', which generally included both men and women.[30] Football among Africans took root in the 1890s, also initially in Port Elizabeth.[31] Rugby, or *mboxo* (the thing that is not round), followed later in the decade and became the next most popular game in the eastern Cape after cricket. Today, the eastern Cape is still the only region in the country where rugby has a popularity rivalling soccer among Africans.[32]

As in cricket, the first black teams were probably institutional, based at Lovedale, Healdtown and the Anglican Institution in Grahamstown. According to one source, it was the headmaster of the last-mentioned school, the Rev. R.J. Mullins, who introduced rugby to black players.[33] The first adult rugby club was the Union Rugby Football Club, formed in Port Elizabeth in 1887. Among those involved were leading figures in the local Native Vigilance Association. At first, Union's opponents were the town's coloured rugby teams, which formed themselves into a Port Elizabeth Coloured Rugby Union in 1892; but in 1894 a second African club, Orientals, was established, followed by the Morning Star, Rovers, Frontier and Spring Rose clubs.[34] Union and Orientals became the strongest teams, and their matches and colours were modelled on the rivalry between the main white clubs, Crusaders and Olympics.

Rugby contests between different towns in the eastern Cape took place well before the turn of the century. By 1904 the level of organisation and enthusiasm had reached the stage where the first inter-town tournament could be organised in Port Elizabeth. Teams from Grahamstown and East London participated. Following the inauguration of the tournament, an Eastern Province Native Rugby Union was formed in 1905. Its first president was Tobias Mvula, a delegate from Port Elizabeth to South African Native Congress conferences.

With the opening up of the diamond and gold fields in the last quarter of the nineteenth century, the new sports began to take root in the interior as well, mimicking the process of economic and political integration that the mineral discoveries had unleashed. Cape migrants in these new centres were prominent in organising clubs and events there and they reported on these developments in the pages of *Imvo*. In Kimberley, cricket and rugby flourished, with local Africans playing with and against 'Malays' and coloured sportsmen who had carried the games with them from Cape Town. Kimberley became the new sports capital of southern Africa.

Contests began across territorial boundaries. In 1888 a Kimberley team travelled down to the coast to play Port Elizabeth at cricket for the first time.[35] From 1890 onwards, teams from the South African Republic took on Kroonstad and other towns in the Orange Free State. By 1898 there were around ten 'native' cricket clubs in Johannesburg.[36] Regular contests now occurred between teams from the two republics and sides from the eastern Cape and the diamond fields.[37] The new railway spread sport, as it did politics.

In Natal, Edendale (and, later, Adams College) became the main base for cricket.[38] The team lists were full of prominent *kholwa* figures with surnames like Msimang, Mtimkulu, Xaba and Kumalo, who played a large role in the politics and social life of that colony.[39] Cricket was also played at the Ohlange Institute, founded by John Dube, but perhaps because of the American influence soccer became more popular here and, indeed, throughout Natal.

In Bloemfontein there were seven cricket clubs by 1907. Oriental, captained by J.B. Twayi, was reported to be the strongest club in the city. Matches with white teams apparently also occurred.[40] Tennis, golf and football were played, too. Describing life in Bethulie in the southern Free State in 1911, the magistrate wrote that 'Natives go in for tennis, football and cricket whilst nearly all the younger population attend school. Nearly all are church goers.'[41] Cricket was also played in the Rolong enclave of Thaba Nchu and in neighbouring Basutoland. At Thaba Nchu in the 1900s, teams drawn from the prosperous, highly politicised landowning elite played against their white neighbours, perhaps former British soldiers who had been granted land in the area after the South African War. Commenting on these matches, which the Africans won more than once, *Tsala ea Becoana* remarked that whites held themselves socially aloof in order to command respect from blacks, but 'the fact is no Natives respect their European neighbours as much as the Barolongs at Thaba Nchu who twice beat the whites in fair games of cricket. In other parts, where the whites will not play them, the coloureds boast that the whites are afraid of them.'[42]

Running parallel to the process of political mobilisation and unification, the spread of sport throughout southern Africa led to the formation of the first regional and national bodies for black sportspeople. In 1897 the South African Coloured Rugby Football Board was formed and in 1903 the South African Coloured Cricket Board. Remarkably, the latter was only the second national cricket association to be established in the world, predating the Australian Cricket Board and – by several decades – the West Indian, New Zealand and Indian controlling bodies. The involvement of both African and coloured sportsmen in these new national boards also predated formal co-operation between African and coloured organisations in the political arena. Though political union was still nearly a decade away, emerging black leaders were already defining themselves as South African and seeking to cross assumed boundaries in more ways than one.

25

Part of a global dialogue

I may forget the railroads, I may forget the Steam Engines, but
I will not forget what I have seen here [in the British Houses of
Parliament] tonight. I have seen a company of men not taller than I
am meet here and touch the spring that moves the world.

– Dyani Tshatshu, 2 August 1836

Noël Mostert has argued that what happened in early South
Africa was crucial in shaping global history and ideas: not only because of
the now widely accepted thesis that all humans originated on the African
continent, but also because of what happened in the 'human collision'
in the eastern Cape in the nineteenth century. Indeed, he contends, the
interactions in this region – 'the product of two of the greatest human
odysseys and endeavours, the terrestrial one of Africa and the maritime
one of Europe' – also produced 'an enlarged global consciousness', which
challenged and helped transform western thinking.[1]

The reason for this, according to Mostert, was the circumstances
that prevailed in southern Africa in comparison with North America,
where the process of colonial conquest was overwhelming, optimistic
and unquestioning of itself. In the mixing bowl of the eastern Cape,
where resistance to colonialism was much stronger, a number of unique
forces and factors were stirred together – Enlightenment ideas, religious
sensibilities, the politics and profit motive of colonialism, and African
agency – during a particular period of globalisation, to produce a new
moral frontier internationally. In the early nineteenth century, when anti-
slavery abolitionist ideas and strong evangelical religious convictions
became focused on the Cape frontier, the outcome was 'a commitment to

240

create a universal conscience concerning questions of race and to establish a censorious vigilance over the fate of indigenous societies grappling with colonial intrusion'. 'The frontier line of the Cape accordingly assumed, as the nineteenth century advanced, a commanding role in the moral struggle for the soul of the new British empire ... [and it] became a microcosm of the tension between high-minded conscience and self-interest which accompanied the nascent industrial age and its expanding commerce.'[2]

From the start, the remarkable group of Africans emerging from the many mission stations and schools in south-east Africa sought to become active participants in this global debate and helped contribute to the new patterns of thought that emerged from it. Influenced by the trinity of African humanism or *ubuntu*, the egalitarian message of Christianity and mid-Victorian political liberalism, and proceeding from a newly constructed base of schools, churches, newspapers and organisations at home, they engaged with metropolitan debates, positioning themselves to intervene as effectively in them as possible. In the process, their struggles and activities acquired an international dimension, which became a strong feature of twentieth-century political resistance in South Africa.

Cosmopolitanism was one of the goals, and attractions, of the new African politics. The school people relished the opportunities of becoming acquainted with the wider world and finding the means to engage with it through education, work and politics in the new colonial states. They adapted readily to cosmopolitan ideas and ways of life, and interacted easily with people and ideas overseas. Many travelled abroad, studied abroad and formed close ties with people overseas. Tiyo Soga married a Scots woman; Pambani Figlan an Irish woman. Southern Africans eagerly followed global politics and debates and welcomed outsiders into their circles and organisations.

This openness to mixing was nothing new for Africans. For centuries, their societies had been noted for being open and welcoming and for incorporating outsiders. Many European and Asian shipwreck survivors, dumped on the eastern shores of South Africa from the 1600s onwards, were taken in by African communities. Coenraad de Buys, a colourful Dutch-speaking buccaneer and polygamist, was accepted into Xhosa society, becoming for a time Ngqika's adviser and interpreter.[3]

241

The movement of people and ideas also flowed in the other direction: Africans had for centuries visited Europe and America. In 1613 a Khoikhoi man with the name of Coree, living in the vicinity of Table Bay, was enticed onto an English boat and forcibly transported to England, where he lived for nearly a year in the household of Sir Thomas Smythe, governor of the British East India Company.[4] Often under duress, other Africans were taken to Europe and put on display as specimens of the exotic savages that the Europeans were taming and civilising as their conquest of the world proceeded. Sarah Baartman, the Khoi woman displayed as the 'Hottentot Venus', is perhaps the most famous example.[5] She was exhibited in Piccadilly, where it cost 2s for spectators to view her. 'One pinched her, another walked around her; one gentleman poked her with his cane, and one lady employed her parasol to ascertain that all was "Nattral". This inhuman baiting the poor creature bore with sullen indifference.'[6] At the time of the Anglo-Zulu War, a Canadian showman calling himself the 'Great Farini' imported Zulu men and women to perform war dances in a commercial exhibition that moved from London to Paris and then to New York.

While Europeans and Americans were inventing the 'savage' or celebrating 'empire' in this way, African leaders and mission-educated intellectuals from southern Africa began visiting these countries for other purposes. Between the 1830s and 1900 several hundred Africans travelled to Britain and the United States for educational, religious or political reasons, in the process experiencing the life and ideas of the great metropolitan centres directly. From these experiences and engagements arose new ideas which refined or challenged, through an African lens, the dominant western perspectives on the development of the world order. The visitors also set about constructing a counter-narrative of the African as someone who could, if given the opportunity, take his place with anyone else in the 'civilised' world. They 'countered negative stereotypes with their intelligence and industriousness, self-consciously framing their continued acquisition of education, Christianity and entrepreneurial capitalism as part of the larger goal of collective racial uplift of their "benighted" brethren in Africa'.[7]

From early in the nineteenth century, Africans became involved in political missions to the centre of power in the British empire. As we have seen, the first venture of this kind to London was made in 1836 by Dyani Tshatshu, the Christian chief from Xhosaland, and Andries Stoffels, an elder from the Kat River settlement, who travelled with Dr John Philip to testify before the House of Commons Select Committee on Aborigines about the unfair treatment meted out to the Xhosa on the Cape frontier. Tshatshu was questioned for two and a half days. He presented himself in the dual role of an 'assistant missionary' and a 'Caffre chief', speaking on religious matters as well as in defence of Xhosa interests on the frontier. As missionary, he argued that Christianity would bring light to his countrymen and that it needed to be encouraged in an unqualified way. As a chief, he criticised the 'iniquities of the last war' and the attitudes of both the British authorities and white settlers towards the Xhosa.[8]

Constantly in the spotlight, Tshatshu and his colleagues became media celebrities in Britain, while at home the colonial press vilified them for allegedly misleading a gullible British public. The most popular figure in the party, Tshatshu became a sought-after speaker, drawing thousands to his meetings during his sustained travels through England and Scotland. Tshatshu's vision for the future was of a southern Africa governed in a constitutional way – a goal that succeeding generations of mission-educated Africans would in time wholeheartedly endorse: 'He told the English that men should come and teach the Caffres, and make for them Colleges, and teach them Greek, and Latin, and Hebrew, and English, and then the Caffres would have a House of Commons, and a House of Lords, and then they will only fight like the English with a newspaper ... Then will come the time when the assegai will be put down, and nations will only fight with the book and paper.'[9]

By the end of the century, political missions to Britain had acquired fresh purposes. As the new style of politics emerged among the educated class of Africans, their spokesmen, recognising where the centre of power lay in the empire, began to appeal over the heads of the colonial governments to London, lobbying the Colonial Office, petitioning the British parliament and working with sympathetic British MPs and interest groups like the Aborigines Protection Society in London. Both new-style African politicians and traditional chiefs, seeking to protect their authority against colonial encroachment, travelled to Britain on formal political missions. Among the most famous was the deposed Zulu king Cetshwayo, who in 1882 went to London to request that he be allowed to return to Zululand. Cetshwayo was 'installed in a house in Kensington and taken on tours of the capital, drawing admiring crowds wherever he was recognised'. Though his political ends were not achieved, the personal triumph he enjoyed was due in a large degree to the support networks provided in England by the family of Bishop Colenso and other 'friends of the natives', including the Aborigines Protection Society.

A more successful mission was undertaken in 1895 by three Tswana *dikgosi*, Khama, Bathoen and Sebele, who undertook a six-month-long journey to Britain in a bid to prevent Cecil Rhodes and his British South Africa Company from annexing Bechuanaland. At first, the Colonial Secretary, Joseph Chamberlain, refused to see them but, helped by their London Missionary Society connections, they embarked on an extensive speaking tour, which publicised the Company's harsh practices. Chamberlain climbed down and the Tswana were given the Protectorate status they sought.[10]

These delegations to London had common themes and purposes. African leaders appealed to a British sense of 'fair play' as the noose of colonialism tightened around them and they were threatened with the dispossession of land and power. In the process, they recognised the importance of the constitutional politics in which the new-style activists so fervently believed, and sought to align themselves with it. Indeed, in many of the missions involving chiefly rulers, the new class of mission-educated people played supportive roles. As we shall see, deputations to London acquired growing importance for both new- and old-style leaders in the early part of the twentieth century, as the rights of Africans came increasingly under threat in the move towards unification in South Africa.

During the late nineteenth century the international contacts and experiences of the growing body of mission-educated Africans widened. This deepening of exchanges was part of their increasing politicisation and self-conscious efforts to create opportunities that could enhance African agency and construct new narratives about African people that would counter European stereotypes and prejudices. As J.T. Jabavu said of a proposed cricket tour by Africans to England in 1884, it 'would also afford our friends there the opportunity of realising the tone that European civilisation gives to the society of Africans'.[11] Even if some Europeans continued to see them as 'trophies' or exotic specimens, mission-educated Africans proceeded in their own way to redefine their identities and find roles for themselves in the globalising world of which they now formed part.

One of the most remarkable cultural exchanges involved the African Native Choir – also styled the Jubilee Chorus by its members and the Kaffir Choir by the white entrepreneurs promoting it – which arrived in London in the British summer of 1891. Within four days of disembarking, the choir participated, together with over 28,000 visitors and singers, in the final event of the Jubilee celebrations for Queen Victoria at the Crystal Palace. Their participation earned them an invitation to perform for the Queen at her summer palace of Osborne on the Isle of Wight. A glittering audience was present: 'ladies in silken gowns, soldiers in uniform, Scots in green and yellow kilts, Indians wearing turbans, a West African boy in a scarlet tunic and twenty or thirty Englishmen in black frock coats and trousers.'[12] Paul Xiniwe, one of the members (and Jabavu's assistant at *Imvo*), introduced the choir to the Queen. Among the items performed was John Knox Bokwe's composition *Vuka Deborah*. In the first half, clothed in 'tribal' dress, the choir sang African folksongs. In the second, the choristers wore 'their Christian clothes' and performed in English. This was a complex interplay of identity and ritual, which challenged stereotypes and allowed for multiple readings and multiple meanings to be created. Some British journalists, having previously deemed Africans 'so undeveloped as to be thought scarcely worthy of association with music', expressed surprise at the quality of their singing. One critic put a Xhosa solo on a par with Rossini's *Cujus animam*, saying that it was 'difficult to accept it as a specimen of native music at all'.[13] David Coplan, the historian of African music in South Africa, has commented:

the choir divided their programme between British-style secular items and African songs arranged for four-part Western harmony. Likewise, they performed partly in Western formal evening dress and partly in indigenous African 'native' costume of the period. While missionaries back in South Africa were scandalized by the use of indigenous fashion, British audiences and commentators (then as now) had serious difficulty deciding whether they preferred their visiting Africans 'civilised' or 'uncivilised'. They were in any case explicitly disturbed by the multi-layered ambiguous cultural politics ingeniously expressed by this mixing of dress codes. The performers themselves, of course, took nothing but easy confidence and pride in their sartorial code-switching.[14]

After the royal command performance, the African Native Choir sang at many high-society events, such as a garden party given by the philanthropic Baroness Burdett-Coutts at her home in Hampstead. Then, during the winter of 1891/92 the choir spent five months on the road, touring the north of England, Scotland and Ireland. In the summer of 1892, they were back in the capital again, singing 'almost every afternoon or early evening ... at the great houses around London'. Their base was a boarding house in Finsbury Park.[15]

The choir had been assembled by a Kimberley entrepreneur, James Balmer, as a way of making money from the exotic talent of people from the colonies. Working under the direction of a Cape Town music teacher and pianist, the 16-member choir included in its ranks some respected school people, most of whom had eastern Cape connections. Paul Xiniwe, ex-Lovedale, was accompanied by his wife, Eleanor, and two nephews, John Xiniwe and Albert Jonas. Then there were the Manye sisters, Charlotte and Katie, whom Xiniwe had taught at school in Uitenhage before they moved to Kimberley, where Charlotte herself became a teacher. Others with Lovedale connections* included Wellington Majiza, Josiah Semouse

* Four other eastern Cape people were in the party – John Mbongwe from Burgersdorp, George McClellan from Graaff-Reinet, Anna Gentle and Johanna Jonkers. Among the three people making up the Kimberley component were Neli Mabandla and a woman described as Martha, granddaughter of the Ndebele chief Lobengula.

(a telegraph operator in Kimberley), John Hadebe (who, a fellow chorister noted, 'talked only of books'), Sannie Koopman and Francis Gqoba (probably related to the former *Isigidimi* editor).

The members of the choir remained in England for about a year, with the exception of the Manye sisters, who stayed for more than two, before Charlotte proceeded to America and Katie returned to Kimberley. Though the tour was a financial failure for the promoters, the experiences of the troupe must have been incalculable for their future development.[16]

In 1892 a second choir from southern Africa arrived in London. This was the Zulu Choir, formed by Saul Msane, who had been educated at Healdtown and later became a leading ANC figure. The choir also included the future ANC president Josiah Gumede, who resigned his teaching job at Amanzimtoti to undertake the trip, and Solomon Kumalo. Members were drawn almost exclusively from the well-off *kholwa* from the Driefontein–Edendale communities, who dominated Natal African politics from the 1860s to the 1890s. After two months of training at Driefontein and a preparatory southern African tour, Msane's party arrived in London on 1 May 1892. The choir spent the summer in London with daily shows – called 'From the wilds to Westminster'– at the Royal Aquarium. The programme followed the same lines as the African Native Choir's performances: African songs and dress in the first half; 'Christian clothes' and English-language songs in the second. But the Zulu Choir was reported to have met with less success than its predecessor and most members returned home in March 1893.[17]

The insistence by the white impresario that the choristers put on 'tribal' dress as part of the show – to pander to the prejudices of British audiences about 'savages' from Africa – led to problems on two levels. Firstly, Msane and the choir came under strong criticism from the Natal newspaper *Inkanyiso lase Natal* and black Christians at home, who expressed disgust that the choir could perform traditional Zulu songs and wear 'tribal' dress. The same critics also insisted that Msane and the choir should not have even gone to England: 'Do Natives know the dangers of an idle life at sea? Do the girls, or their parents, realise what it means to pass twelve months in the company of a lot of single men, amidst the excitements of a life such as theirs will be?' Such behaviour could subvert their Christianity and put at risk the purity of the young people in the party.

Choir members themselves appear to have felt that the promoters had gone too far in trying to commercialise and exoticise this tour. The most politically active among them – including Msane and Gumede – broke away from the choir, claiming that the manager was compromising their reputation as educated Christians. Msane's group was left stranded in London, but they reconstituted themselves as the Zulu Christian Choir and toured the British Isles in this guise until August 1893, by which time they had collected enough money to return to Natal. Msane and Gumede themselves would have been intent on using the tour to demonstrate to the British the 'progress' made by Christian Africans in the colonies: they had a clause inserted in their contracts that they 'shall not be required to commit any act contrary to their profession of Christianity'.[18] What the controversy showed was that the colonials were not passive objects, but sought to turn the tour to their own purposes.[19]

Running parallel to the process of political mobilisation within southern Africa, these cultural experiences involved a high degree of African agency. Although external actors, entrepreneurs and models like the American Jubilee Singers may have helped inspire or even realise their travels abroad, it was the school people, drawing on their own networks and resources, who grasped the opportunities and created their own successes. They were living embodiments of the virtues of self-help and 'improvement', of 'progress' and 'civilisation', as well as of the struggle against racism and stereotyping. Their performances were in this sense as political as the journeys by political, religious and educational leaders overseas to raise awareness of the situation of their people back home.

Until the last decade of the nineteenth century, Britain was the main reference point for the pioneering African activists and intellectuals, setting out to stake their claim in the global world. It was to Britain that a number of early figures went to study, the most notable being Tiyo Soga, who as an 18-year-old was taken in 1847 by the Rev. John Chalmers from Lovedale to further his education in Glasgow. Soga stayed abroad for two years, a solitary African 'in the western metropolis of Scotland' before he returned, homesick, to the eastern Cape in 1849. After two years, he went back to Scotland, where he qualified as a minister of the United Presbyterian Church and was ordained in Glasgow in December 1856. Soga was a good student, respected by his peers and 'the best men in the community', and was constantly in demand at soirées. By the time Soga left, he commented, 'Scotland ... I can never forget. I shall look back at it as my second home.'

After nearly seven years abroad, Soga arrived back in Port Elizabeth in mid-1857, making a startling impact from the moment he stepped ashore with his new Scottish bride:

You should have been with us this day to witness the wonder and amazement with which a black man with a white lady leaning on his arm seemed to be viewed by all classes! We were 'a spectacle unto all men!' In walking through the streets, black and white turned to stare at us, and thus was the case as often as we went out. It seemed to some to be a thing which they had not only never seen, but which they believed impossible to take place. From the remarks of some of my countrymen as they passed us, I at once understood that the report of our presence had gone far and wide. The day has really been one of the triumphs of principle.[20]

Back in South Africa, Soga was to become the most famous educated African of his day. In time Soga's own children would follow in their father's footsteps. John Henderson Soga was sent to Scotland at the age of three for medical treatment.[21] After schooling at Glasgow High and the Dollar Academy, he enrolled at Edinburgh University in 1886 and qualified as a minister of the United Presbyterian Church in 1893. His younger brothers, Alan Kirkland Soga, later editor of *Izwi Labantu*, and Jotello Festire Soga, also studied at Glasgow High School and the Dollar Academy. Jotello went on to qualify as a veterinarian in Edinburgh at the age of 21, returning to South Africa in 1886 to work for the Cape government. For twenty years – until his death from a drug overdose in 1906 – he remained the only Cape-born university-qualified vet in the colony.[22] The eldest son, William A. Soga, became a medical doctor after his studies at Glasgow University; both he and Jotello were also ordained as missionaries, with the aim of serving and healing the 'nation' through Christianity and 'progress' – the motto, almost, of the age.[23] The experiences of the Soga children are even more remarkable if one recalls that their illiterate grandfather was killed by colonial forces during the last Cape–Xhosa War in 1878 while they were being educated in Scotland.[24]

Others followed in the Sogas' footsteps to Britain, including a long line of former students from Zonnebloem, most notably Nathaniel Umhalla. All the individual journeys undertaken by these young Africans were exceptional for their time, and required considerable personal courage to complete. But from the mid-1890s Africans began to visit the United States in increasing numbers and American influences in southern Africa consequently grew. The immediate reason for the deepening contact was the alliance formed between the American-based AME Church and the Ethiopian Church in southern Africa from 1896 onwards. Though contacts with African Americans went back many years, the amalgamation of the churches came about through the initiative of Charlotte Manye, then studying at Wilberforce College in Ohio. It was her letters home that led to Mangena Mokone, based in Pretoria, linking up with the AME Church in the United States. Charlotte also encouraged some of her contemporaries in Kimberley to study at Wilberforce. In 1896 Chalmers Moss (ex-Lovedale) and Henry Msikinya (ex-Healdtown), sons of two of the most distinguished personalities in that town, joined her, followed soon afterwards by Charles Dube (brother of John), Theodore Kakaza (ex-Healdtown), Charlotte's future husband Marshall Maxeke (ex-Lovedale) and James Tantsi (ex-Zonnebloem). These students came from the cream of the new educated elite in southern Africa. Their school affiliations show just how firmly based the independent church movement became in the mainstream of educated black society.

Important independent church leaders such as James Tantsi, H.R. Ngcayiya, Marcus Gabashane, Isaiah Sishuba and Mangena Mokone sent their children or family to the States to study. This pattern became more pronounced in the first decade of the twentieth century, when people not linked to the separatist churches, such as the Montsioas from Mafikeng, the Moroka and Nyokong families from Thaba Nchu, and the Msimangs, Gumedes and Kuzwayos from Natal, sent family members to school and university in America and Britain. The trickle grew into a stream. By 1904 some 30 students were being sponsored by the AME Church alone.[25] The historian James Campbell, making a conservative estimate, has put the total number of South Africans who studied in the United States alone from 1894 to 1914 at between 100 and 150, about 50 of whom went to Wilberforce College.[26] Campbell has summed up the importance of these transatlantic study opportunities for the black elite:

the rush of students to the U.S. colleges bespoke enormous frustration with European missionary education, which had produced scarcely a dozen black matriculants in the previous fifty years. At the same time, however, elite Africans continued to subscribe to ... the idea that education was the key to individual and racial progress ... 'Negro' education emerged as a kind of panacea, which would wrench open all the doors that mission education had promised, but failed, to open. Everywhere, the departure of students for America was portrayed in providential terms, as the germinal event in the birth of a new African civilization.[27]

In the United States, the southern Africans studied at some twenty colleges and institutes, including Wilberforce in Ohio, Hampton in Virginia, Lincoln in Pennsylvania and the Tuskegee Institute in Alabama, Georgia, where the emphasis was more on industrial education and self-help, as propounded by its founder, the influential Booker T. Washington. One South African student, Pixley Seme, went on to distinguish himself at Columbia University in New York. At Wilberforce the students were in touch with some of the wealthiest and most informed African Americans in America, 'the cream of black Ohio society'. As Campbell explains, 'Without question, this was the most educated and affluent black community in America, and the South African students were quickly gathered into its fold.'[28] It was also a very politically connected university, overseen by the AME Bishop Benjamin Arnett, who was secretary of the National Convention of Colored Men and a confidant of the Republican President William McKinley, who came from Ohio. At Lincoln, the great Pan-Africanist intellectual W.E.B. Du Bois was among those who taught Charlotte Manye; he later wrote the foreword to her autobiography.

After relations had been established by the Ethiopians with the AME Church, contact between the United States and South Africa grew quickly.

James Dwane travelled to the States on a successful visit in 1896/97, Bishop Turner undertook a major tour of southern Africa in 1898, Dwane returned in 1899, and Pambani Mzimba – also granted an interview at the Colonial Office in London en route – brought with him eight young Africans to study at Lincoln University in 1901.[29] Among them were the sons of well-known eastern Cape families – Melrose Sishuba, John Sonjica and Gordon Dana. Within two years, nearly two dozen of these Presbyterian Church of Africa members were studying at Lincoln and Tuskegee. Some of them might have been among the 18 students reported by the *South African Spectator* in early 1904 as having embarked for America in one month alone.[30]

Dwane's visits to America as the representative of the Ethiopian Church demonstrated the highly political nature of the contacts with the United States. He was fêted by the AME Church leadership in Philadelphia and Atlanta, and during his two visits

he travelled through most of the southern states, visiting colleges, meeting politicians (including President McKinley), speaking everywhere to packed lecture halls. Adept at gauging the susceptibilities of his listeners, he held audiences spellbound with tales of his birth in a world 'enveloped in ignorance and darkness', of his youthful conversion, his struggle for education, his battles with white missionaries. Everywhere he stressed the need for an institution of 'higher learning' in South Africa, where Africans could be trained as ministers and teachers. African American audiences greeted him with hallelujahs; they penned poems about him and organized local 'Dwane Missionary Societies'. Southern whites, much to [Bishop] Turner's amusement, lined up to shake his hand and invited them into their homes, intimacies they scarcely could have imagined extending to their black neighbours.[31]

Meanwhile, a second front of contacts between the United States and southern Africa was developed by American Board missionaries and, in particular, by one of their most important protégés, John L. Dube. After spending five years working and studying in America between 1887 and 1892, Dube returned in November 1896 for a second visit to study for the ministry and raise funds to start his own school. He had been frustrated in his goal of taking over his father's old congregation at Inanda near Durban because of a lack of qualifications and set out to become formally ordained. Still only in his twenties, and accompanied by his new wife, Nokutela, Dube landed in New York and plunged straight into church and public affairs there. He soon made contact with Booker T. Washington, the most prominent African American leader at the time, and travelled down to his Tuskegee Institute, where he gave a rousing address at the commencement ceremony, followed by a talk also at Hampton College on his return journey.[32]

In the 1890s African Americans were examining and redefining their identities, roles and political philosophies in the aftermath of slavery, the Civil War and Reconstruction. Many of them perceived conditions for black people in America to be worsening rather than improving. In a highly publicised speech in Atlanta in September 1895, Booker T. Washington proposed that blacks follow a *festina lente* approach of self-help through industrial education, as the time was not yet ripe for them to agitate for social equality and integration. This speech was well received by the white establishment in America, and Washington's power and prestige grew as he became the conduit of patronage from the President and many business leaders and foundations. He had a close working relationship with President Theodore Roosevelt, advising his administration on African American issues; so influential was he that the phrase 'kitchen Cabinet' came to apply to his circle.

But African American intellectuals from the north, further removed from the underdevelopment of the south, criticised what they called the 'Atlanta Compromise'. Instead, they sought to obtain the vote and civil rights within an integrated political system, and eventually gave organisational content to their ideas through the launch of the Niagara movement in New York in 1903 and the National Association for the Advancement of Colored People in 1910.[33] The more radical position was led by people such as the Washington journalist John Edward Bruce and the Harvard-educated W.E.B. Du Bois, who in turn drew inspiration from earlier radicals and Pan-Africanists.

By the late 1890s John Dube and other South Africans visiting America had established links with leaders of African American opinion there.

Through these contacts they were able to engage with and understand at first hand the competing ideological positions and strategies that existed for African Americans. Dube himself was influenced in lasting ways by American ideas, projects and politics, and his experiences there were to profoundly shape African politics in South Africa in the long term. His extensive American networks sustained his work for decades in South Africa and made possible his distinguished career in politics and education.

People from southern Africa could readily identify with the experiences of enslaved Africans in America and find lessons for themselves in the search by African Americans for a place in the United States after the Civil War and Reconstruction. Their experiences in America had a profound impact on the nascent political, educational and church organisations and their members back in South Africa, not least by tending to edge them away from the integrative model of working with 'friends of the natives', derived from British and Cape liberalism, towards a separatist model of organising on the basis of a more African-centred, self-help approach.

By the end of the nineteenth century, Africans from South Africa were confidently travelling abroad and becoming part of the global dialogue about the future of an increasingly interrelated world, including the role of Africans within it. When W.E.B. Du Bois coined his famous aphorism at the first Pan-African Congress in 1900, 'The problem of the twentieth century is the problem of the colour line; of the lighter and darker races of man', he had been in touch with these new South Africans, indeed had taught some of them. From him and from their international experiences in general, they drew new ideas and lessons with which to fashion a vision for the future of their own country. The Rev. James Dwane from Middledrift in the eastern Cape embodied these developments in his life and career as much as anyone else. Not only had he travelled to England and twice visited the United States, meeting with the President, but in an attempt to give content to Psalm 68: 31 – 'Princes shall come out of Egypt; Ethiopia shall soon stretch forth her hands unto God' – he had also approached Cecil Rhodes for permission to extend the activities of his Ethiopian Church to the north of the Limpopo; he is even said to have communicated with King Menelik of Abyssinia in order to extend his church's work to Sudan and Egypt.[34]

These connections with the rest of Africa should not be overlooked. In the late nineteenth century, educated South Africans became mission workers in modern-day Mozambique and Malawi and were also part of the colonisation process in Rhodesia (Zimbabwe), accompanying the conquering 'pioneer column' as clerks, missionaries, interpreters and teachers. One of these was the father of Chief Albert Luthuli, who was himself born in Rhodesia. Correspondents from Rhodesia wrote regularly to *Imvo*, which also commented as a matter of course on developments in neighbouring territories, and J.T. Jabavu himself travelled to Bulawayo.[35]

The ventures, travels, sojourns and delegations abroad should be seen as an extension of the broad process of mobilisation occurring in various spheres of the lives of Africans; part of a self-conscious agenda of social and political advancement.[36] They also involved profound personal journeys. John Knox Bokwe has left a record of his three-week journey by sea to Britain in 1892, which gives some indication of what the adventurers experienced. After taking the train to Cape Town, he boarded the *Moor* and soon succumbed to sea-sickness and 'had to consider the "depths of the sea" and mediate deeply upon them'. He busied himself by setting poems to music and learning about 'the use the white man had made of the sun and the compass' to navigate. As far as the passengers were concerned, 'some were rough, some gentle'. One Transvaler, 'enraged at him suggesting a better move in a game of draughts', let Bokwe know that the Cape Colony was spoiling 'black men' by educating them. Fortunately, 'the rude formed a small class'. 'Several first-class passengers later showed interest in him, and when he fell sick, they came and asked after "John Kaffir".'[37]

The new elite of Africans were preparing themselves to become global citizens and shapers of a new society in South Africa. The cosmopolitanism of these early intellectuals guided their local struggles in important ways. At the level of individuals, four of the first five ANC presidents had travelled abroad for study or other purposes before 1900. More generally, the patient development of an international solidarity network by black

South Africans and their sympathisers over many decades forms at least part of the reason why the anti-apartheid struggle became one of the most important moral crusades since the abolition of slavery. Internationalism was deeply ingrained in the ANC from the beginning.

PART THREE

WAR AND CHANGE

26

The South African War, 1899–1902

... those who were ready to lose their lives and to sacrifice their all for the King, should all be treated alike as was the case in our own country with our own Kings. Even the humblest men in the country got the same mark of distinction as the greatest because they had all shared the dangers and risks of the war.

– Stephen Mini, Natal Native Congress, 1902

As Africans from southern Africa made increasing contact with the rest of the world by the end of the nineteenth century, southern Africa itself was being drawn forcibly into the embrace of the British Empire and the global economy by the prevailing superpower. The new century dawned with the region in the grip of the South African or Anglo-Boer War, an event that was to have a profound effect on African politics.

When hostilities broke out on 11 October 1899, politically active Africans generally supported Britain in the struggle against the South African Republic and the Orange Free State. They hoped that a British victory would result in the extension of idealised British liberal values to the Afrikaner republics. Applied to South Africa, these ideals were best exemplified by the non-racial constitution of the Cape Colony and Cecil John Rhodes's opportunistic promise of 'equal rights for all civilised men south of the Zambesi'.[1]

The pronouncements of Imperial officials both before and during the conflict gave strength to the hope that a new political dispensation awaited Africans in the event of a British victory. In October 1899 the

British Colonial Secretary, Joseph Chamberlain, declared, 'The treatment of the Natives [in the Transvaal] has been disgraceful; it has been brutal; it has been unworthy of a civilised Power.'[2] A few months later, Lord Salisbury, the Prime Minister, said there must be no doubt that, following victory, 'due precaution will be taken for the philanthropic and kindly and improving treatment of these countless indigenous races of whose destiny I fear we have been too forgetful'.[3] The High Commissioner in South Africa, Sir Alfred Milner, similarly assured a coloured deputation, 'It is not race or colour but civilisation which is the test of a man's capacity for political rights.'[4] Milner, in fact, had used the ill-treatment of black people in the South African Republic as one of the reasons for intervening in affairs there.[5]

Support for Britain was general among the African intelligentsia and the new African political organisations. *Izwi*, mouthpiece of the South African Native Congress (SANC), repeatedly praised Imperial officials like Chamberlain and Milner and vigorously endorsed Imperial intervention in South Africa on the ground that it would reverse increasingly reactionary trends in colonial attitudes towards Africans.[6] The newspaper envisaged that after victory had been achieved, the British government would 'purify our Courts and Temples, and that an era of peace and good government will be established for all time'.[7] The 'native question' would finally be settled.[8] *Izwi*'s editor, A.K. Soga, demonstrated his loyalty by serving as a trooper in Brabant's Horse for several months, before returning to resume his duties on the paper, seeing action on the front at Stormberg and Dordrecht.[9] Little wonder that his newspaper condemned the republics as wholeheartedly as it supported Britain. *Izwi* repeatedly listed 'Boer atrocities' on Africans and wrote of the 'narrow, prejudiced and inhuman tyranny of Boer Republicanism'.[10]

The SANC and *Izwi* also used the war issue to score party political points. It attacked 'mugwumps' like John X. Merriman in the South African Party (SAP) who were critical of Imperial intentions and cast doubts upon their patriotism.[11] Inevitably, this criticism brought the SANC into conflict with J.T. Jabavu and those who supported the SAP, especially its liberal wing of Merriman and J.W. Sauer. These 'friends of the natives' regarded the war as unjust and preferred to align themselves with the Afrikaner

Bond, rather than compromise with the Milner–Rhodes–Progressive Party axis, whose policies were geared to promoting capitalist interests and Imperial intervention.[12]

In other parts of South Africa as well, there was no ambiguity about whom the new political class supported. The pronouncements by Joseph Chamberlain and Lord Salisbury had buoyed politically active Africans and they in turn encouraged the British war effort. At its founding meeting on 1 June 1900, the Natal Native Congress gave considerable attention to the war and adopted several resolutions pledging loyalty to Great Britain. The first, to 'our beloved Queen', was carried by members standing and singing 'God Save the Queen', followed by three cheers. Chamberlain and Milner were thanked for their firm stand on Transvaal affairs, especially in respect of the liberty and rights of Africans, and the British government was asked to safeguard these rights in regard to education, provide a degree of direct African representation in the legislatures of the different states, and allow Africans the freedom to trade and acquire land. Finally, the hope was expressed that steps would speedily be taken to bring about a confederation of South African states after the annexation of the republics.[13]

In the republics themselves, the attitude of African spokesmen was broadly similar to their compatriots in the colonies of Natal and the Cape. On the outbreak of war, Joseph Twayi from Bloemfontein made it clear, while speaking in Oxford during his team's football tour of England, that Africans in the Free State supported a British victory and had a 'desire of serving the mother country'. *Pastimes* noted: 'After the match at Sunderland a few weeks ago, the kaffirs were invited to the Oxford Music-hall, where the captain (J. Twayi, centre-forward), in response to the enthusiastic reception accorded the team, made a short speech, and concluded by assuring the good people of the town that all intelligent natives of South Africa were loyal subjects of Her Majesty. This, it may be stated, brought the house down.'[14] Within months of British troops taking the republican capital, Twayi was part of a delegation which presented a 'loyal address' on behalf of the black inhabitants of the new colony to the British Military Governor, and was soon playing a prominent part in local politics.

Twayi's stand was symptomatic of wider allegiances among Africans in the republics. British troops who occupied Bloemfontein during the war were greeted with enthusiasm by Africans parading in the streets.[15] A house servant proudly announced, 'Now I am an Englishman.'[16] Similarly, when British troops occupied Johannesburg, many Africans destroyed their passes, believing that the republican pass laws had become obsolete. They expected immediate equality of treatment, while those in public employment sought an increase in wages to the pre-war level, with arrears. When it became clear that their expectations would not be met, some showed 'such a mutinous spirit' that the assistance of troops was necessary to arrest them.[17]

There was one notable exception to the display of unconditional support for the British cause among the emerging political leaders. To the dismay of many, J.T. Jabavu adopted an independent approach in *Imvo*. Although expressly loyal to Britain and 'wishing for the triumph of British arms', Jabavu disagreed with the need for war and criticised the 'war party', which had eagerly sought the 'war remedy' to further their own ends rather than attempting to avoid conflict through diplomacy. By the 'war party' he meant the Milner–Rhodes–Progressive Party alliance.[18] In adopting this line, Jabavu was undoubtedly influenced by his friends Merriman and Sauer, who regarded the war as unjust. Jabavu also endorsed the views of the anti-war, Liberal pro-Boer lobby in England and thus formed part of the broad anti-war movement that emerged in Britain and at the Cape.[19]

Despite his pro-SAP loyalties, very few had expected Jabavu and his newspaper to adopt an independent stance in a war between Boer and Brit. His position had serious implications for him personally and it exacerbated the divisions that had become apparent among political activists and intelligentsia in the eastern Cape in the late 1890s. The subtleties of Jabavu's broad South African views were lost in the passions of the moment. Although he emphasised that his criticism of the war did not affect his loyalty to Britain, Jabavu's antagonists accused him of behaving in a disloyal, if not treasonable, manner. He was subjected to virulent attacks by *Izwi* and other newspapers of the Argus group, which supported the Progressive viewpoint.[20] His stand cost him support among people who saw the issue in terms only of loyalty or disloyalty to the Crown.[21] In contrast, influential leaders like the Thembu paramount Dalindyebo and Captain Veldtman Bikitsha of Fingoland immediately offered the active support of their people to the war effort, while the rival SANC held a special meeting in King William's Town early in the war to convey its loyalty.[22]

Jabavu's views also caused his old friends R.W. Rose-Innes and James Weir, whose financial support had helped set up *Imvo*, to withdraw their subscriptions and general support for the newspaper. In a sequel, the Mercury Printing Press terminated its contract to print the paper. To cap it all, despite being more cautious and guarded after the promulgation of martial law, *Imvo* was banned by the military authorities in August 1901.[23] This banning was greeted with wholehearted approval by *Izwi*. 'Nemesis – which punishes the arrogant and tyrannical abuse of prosperity – has found out our native contemporary at last,' the paper declared with obvious satisfaction.[24] It now had the field to itself.

Coming so soon after the political realignment in Cape politics following the Jameson Raid, the war seriously affected the course of African politics. Jabavu's independent stand against the English political and financial establishment – represented by Rhodes, the Argus press, the Progressives, and the Imperial authorities – undermined his political and economic bases. Conversely, the hands of his rivals in the Congress were strengthened: they were able to take from Jabavu the moral high ground in electoral politics by offering African voters an attractive, even if crude, anti-Afrikaner, pro-British alternative.

Officially, the South African War was regarded as 'a white man's war'. It became the firm policy of the Imperial, colonial and republican governments to limit, as far as possible, African participation. None of them had any intention of endangering white control over Africans.[25]

The Cape government maintained that the arming of Africans would have an unfavourable effect on Africans. Consequently, Africans were not to be used for any offensive purposes whatever, but could be employed for defence purposes where conditions required.[26] The British government, which did not wish to offend colonial opinion, endorsed this policy.[27] Similarly, even after the fall of the major towns in the republics, the republican armies still in the field declined to arm potential African allies at the risk of undermining the security of whites in South Africa.[28] In reaction to the arming of Africans by the British in the besieged town of Mafeking, General Cronje wrote to the British commander, Colonel Baden-Powell: 'It is understood that you have armed Bastards, Fingoes and Barolong against us – in this you have committed an enormous act of wickedness … reconsider the matter, even if it costs you the loss of Mafeking … disarm your blacks and thereby act the part of a white man in a white man's war.'[29]

Notwithstanding this official stance on all sides, tens of thousands of Africans were in fact involved in the war, not only in non-combatant, but also combatant roles and as suffering bystanders. Their most significant contribution to the war was in the non-combatant field. Africans were used by both sides in such capacities as scouts, guides, runners, drivers, dispatch riders, grooms, cattle herders and trench diggers. High wages and high commodity prices provided an attractive economic incentive for collaboration.[30] Some African labourers earned 3s or 4s a day, as opposed to the modest 1s of the common British soldier.[31]

Africans also participated actively in the war, although this was officially frowned upon. African troopers in the Cape Mounted Rifles and Cape Police carried out arduous duties in the field.[32] African contingents were enrolled in the Transkei, while a force of 500 Zulu police was recruited to protect Zululand. Prominent Natal Native Congress supporters such as Stephen Mini, Simeon Kambule and Josiah Gumede joined the Natal Intelligence Department as scouts and patrolled the border and helped in the relief of Ladysmith. Gumede, who was the 'Chief of Native Scouts', served throughout the war and was afterwards involved in the Native Refugee Department, dealing with the reintegration of black survivors from the concentration camps. He and many others turned down the bronze medals given to Africans, as opposed to the silver medals received by whites, because 'they had all shared the same danger and risks of war'.[33] Africans also fought on the British side at Dordrecht and Sterkstroom, as well as at Mafeking,[34] where 300 Africans were formed into the 'Black Watch' during the siege.

Though official statistics are difficult to come by, Lord Kitchener admitted in March 1902 that over 7000 armed Africans were employed by the British army at that stage. Some estimates put the number at 30,000. After the war, when Africans were ordered to hand in all firearms, 50,488 weapons were surrendered in the Transvaal alone.[35]

Except in isolated cases, the republican forces did not arm Africans. General Smuts testified that Africans fought on the Boer side at Mafeking, but that they were armed without official knowledge.[36] Generals Buller and French also reported occasional instances of armed African participation on the side of the Boer forces.[37]

The last major category of Africans involved in the war was the bulk of the African population situated mostly in the rural areas, who found themselves unwittingly embroiled in the conflict and significantly affected by its course. Kitchener's 'scorched earth' policy, devastating land which could be useful to the enemy and clearing affected areas of inhabitants, had serious consequences for both black and white. Thousands of Africans on Boer farms (and many in African villages and settlements) had their homesteads burnt and were removed from the land. Most of the African males thus affected were pressed into service in the army, while the women and children were sent to concentration camps. By July 1901 there were 37,472 Africans in camps in the South African Republic and the Orange Free State, of whom more than 30,000 were women and children. Ten months later, the total had risen to a massive 107,344.[38] James Campbell has described these camps as 'fetid' places where 'starvation stalked' – the mortality rate in the Free State camps in 1901 was 436 per thousand. AME ministers and church workers such as Samuel Mabote, Nicholas Makone, John Kubedi and John Phakane ministered to people held there and buried the dead during this time of 'profound duress and disillusionment'. In this way they helped to spread the separatist church movement, which was to be closely involved in organisational politics in the former republics after the war.[39]

Republican incursions and military rule had a similarly disruptive effect on African communities and bit deep into their social and political fabric. Provisions and labour were commandeered and, in areas where firm control was established, republican 'native law' was declared. When in 1899 republican forces occupied Jamestown in the Cape, Commandant Olivier announced that African suffrage rights would immediately be revoked. Registered African voters were ordered to report to the landdrost, where their hands were specially stamped and they were issued with a pass. In this way Africans were deprived of their civil liberties and assimilated into a cheap or unpaid labour force.[40]

The significant involvement of Africans in the South African War raised on both sides the spectre of a 'native uprising'. The threat posed by Africans was in fact a major consideration in the decision by the republican representatives to surrender. In the discussions that preceded the Treaty of Vereeniging in May 1902, Boer leaders remarked that chiefdoms inside and outside the republics had almost all been armed and were fighting against the Boer forces: this had 'brought about an impossible state of affairs in many districts'.[41] Even at the Cape, government ministers expressed concern at the arming of Africans by the military authorities.[42]

Against this background of African loyalty, involvement and sacrifice in the war, Africans nurtured hopes of a post-war dispensation in which black political rights would be recognised and entrenched throughout South Africa. At the least they expected that the Cape franchise would be extended to the Transvaal and Orange River Colony. But already at an early stage of the war, the Imperial authorities moved to extricate themselves from the vague statements Salisbury and Chamberlain had made about the extension of African political rights in the event of a British victory. By March 1901 there was no longer any doubt that the British had revised their stance. Lord Kitchener, supreme commander of the British forces, informed the republican governments that in the event of peace it was not the intention of the British government to grant the franchise to Africans in the two former Boer republics before representative government was introduced. And if given, it would be limited 'to secure the just predominance of the white races'. The legal position of coloured persons would, however, be similar to that held in the Cape Colony.[43]

Kitchener's assurance formed the basis of the clause relating to the African franchise, which was inserted in the peace treaty at Vereeniging. Clause 8 stated simply, 'The question of granting the Franchise to natives will not be decided until after the introduction of self-government.'[44] No mention was made of Kitchener's promise to put coloured people on a level of equality with whites. This stipulation in the peace treaty was arrived at without pressure from the Boer representatives. As Milner told Generals Hertzog and Smuts, 'On this question I am at one with you.'[45]

The Treaty of Vereeniging came as a rude shock to Africans. Instead of their position improving, the status quo was maintained. They were aggrieved that the Boers, who had been 'enemies of the King and British principles' in a war, were favourably treated, while the interests of Africans, who had shown their loyalty by 'heart and deeds', were ignored.[46]

Why did Britain spurn an alliance with Africans during and after the war? As Donald Denoon has pointed out, despite the rhetoric of Imperial paternalism, the particular interests of Africans were incompatible with broad British interests. Britain needed the Afrikaners as a collaborating group in South Africa. Therefore, even while it was engaged in armed struggle with them, Britain did not want to close the avenues to future co-operation. Africans were regarded as of little real use as a political and economic collaborating group at that stage. To promote African interests would have been to alienate even further their European kith and kin in South Africa. As Denoon says, the task of Imperial officials was to manipulate South African affairs, not to precipitate social change. This approach explains the conciliatory terms of the peace treaty.[47]

Thomas Pakenham has nicely summed up the situation for Africans at the end of the war: with 12,000 fatalities, their political and economic aspirations unfulfilled, unsatisfactory post-war compensation payments and massive impoverishment in the wake of hostilities, Africans had clearly paid a heavy price in the so-called white man's war.[48]

27

New politics
in the Transvaal

Unless the interests of the Natives in the Transvaal Colony are
in some way protected by Your Majesty's Imperial Government
... the position of Natives in that Colony, under Representative
Government, will be a degrading and humiliating one, and one on
which your petitioners look with considerable alarm.

– Native United Political Associations of the Transvaal Colony,
1905

The South African War had a profound effect on the future direction
of southern Africa. With the demise of the Boer republics, the whole of
modern-day South Africa fell under British control. In the aftermath,
Britain set out to unite the various colonies in order to rationalise their
increasing inter-dependence in a broad political and economic framework.
In the process, African politics were tremendously stimulated. The educated
intelligentsia in the ex-republics, now British subjects, began to organise
constitutionally and seek access to the political centre. In the process they
created a network of organisations and newspapers stretching through the
colonies and beyond, including the neighbouring Protectorates.

At the same time, the various bodies representing African interests in
all the colonies of what was now called British South Africa began to set
common goals and seek ways of co-operating.[1] An important part in this
post-war political awakening was played by Cape activists, steeped in the
traditions of western-style constitutional politics. As we shall see, Cape
politicians, particularly in the South African Native Congress (SANC),

had a direct influence on the development of organisational politics in the other colonies. It was the symbolic political marriage between Ethiopianism and the SANC at the 1898 Queenstown conference, as well as the South African War which followed, that helped export the prototypical form of politics and organisation which had developed in the Cape Colony to the other territories. As a result, the eastern Cape-based SANC, spearheading the 'national' struggle, spread in influence and geographical reach to other parts of South Africa. As its name, pronouncements and activities showed, the SANC sought to speak on behalf of all Africans in South Africa. Immediately after the war ended and peace was declared in May 1902, it helped various groups in the former republics to organise.

What galvanised political activists into action almost immediately after the conclusion of the war was the South African Native Affairs Commission. The Commission was set up in 1903 to develop a 'common understanding on questions of native policy' in view of the anticipated federation of the British colonies in South Africa.[2] In the course of its proceedings it travelled extensively throughout South Africa to collect evidence before reporting in April 1905. Hundreds of spokesmen from all the colonies appeared before it to air their grievances and express their views on broad inter-colonial matters. Their main political demand was for the extension of the franchise and the Cape political system to the other colonies. They also emphasised land rights and greater economic and educational opportunities. From the start Africans reacted with scepticism to the Commission, fearing that it would recommend a policy of segregation, and a diminution of the political rights enjoyed by black people in the Cape.[3] Indeed, this is exactly what happened. In its report issued in 1905, the Commission noted with alarm the growing influence exerted by African voters in the Cape and concluded that the political system prevailing in that colony was 'sure to create an intolerable situation and is an unwise and dangerous thing ... pregnant with future danger'. While recognising that some form of representation was essential, it believed that this should be granted without conferring on Africans political power 'in any aggressive sense, or weakening in any way the unchallenged supremacy and authority of the ruling race'.[4] The omens for the future position of Africans in South Africa were not promising.

In the new British colony of the Transvaal, it was soon made clear to Africans after the war that continuity in the political life of the defeated republics would not be disrupted by the change in administration. The political colour bar was retained and the position of Africans remained fundamentally the same. Measures such as the republican pass laws continued to be applied, and neither the franchise, nor the widely envisaged transfer of Afrikaner land to Africans,[5] nor better economic opportunities, materialised. Africans soon realised that no major changes would be effected in their lives. Sir Godfrey Lagden, who became the Commissioner for Native Affairs in the Transvaal, was forcibly struck by the false hopes held by Africans and instructed his officers to impress on them that the Afrikaners would not be deprived of their land and that Africans should be respectful to whites.[6] According to Louis Botha, before this had been brought home to them the 'Kaffirs looked down upon the [conquered] Boers' and regarded themselves as equals under British rule.[7]

In some cases there was an actual deterioration in the position of Africans after the advent of British rule. According to a Wesleyan minister in Pretoria, some 'civil, self-respecting' Africans who spoke Dutch fluently and had seen the 'best side of the patriarchal government', now found themselves bound by such restrictions as the pass laws from which they had been practically exempt before.[8] Indeed, Lagden admitted that the pass laws were applied more vigorously than formerly, and conceded that this had given rise to African discontent.[9] Africans in the Transvaal also complained that land which had previously been their inalienable property was now being appropriated by whites.[10]

Moreover, there was considerable dissatisfaction in the field of labour. Africans on the Witwatersrand felt that after the war working conditions on the mines had deteriorated.[11] Having anticipated substantial social and economic reforms, workers were faced instead with a reduction in wages, and the prospect that there would be little chance of their position improving. This was brought about by the massive expansion of industry planned by the British government as the main component of its policy of post-war reconstruction in the Transvaal. In the rural areas, too, there was economic dissatisfaction and hardship. Most Africans in the former republics emerged poorer from the conflict. The British army's scorched-earth campaign had led to large-scale impoverishment, and the problem thereafter was exacerbated by slow and insufficient compensation payments.[12]

Disappointed by the terms of the peace, and faced with harsh post-war conditions and an unsympathetic new British administration, Africans in the Transvaal began to organise themselves into formal political associations to protect their interests and articulate their views for the first time.

The first organisation to come to the notice of the authorities was the Zoutpansberg Native Vigilance Association, founded in 1902. It soon broadened its activities and developed into the Transvaal Native Vigilance Association (TNVA), with P.A. Masibi at the helm.[13] In 1905 the president became the Rev. William Mpamba, formerly of Lovedale and Thembuland, who had pioneered the Presbyterian Free Church mission in the Zoutpansberg in the 1890s.[14] (One historian has described the TNVA as 'virtually an AME front', so Mpamba might by then have crossed the line to join the separatist church movement.)[15] Many of the principal chiefs of the region were members of the organisation. Though the authorities were unwilling to allow the TNVA to call them together for meetings, as this would give the Association 'an undesirable importance in the minds of the natives', it is clear that the TNVA maintained contact with chiefs in the northern Transvaal and they in turn co-operated with the body.[16]

The TNVA espoused the cause of political and civil rights for every 'civilised' man irrespective of colour, and the full privileges of British citizenship for all. One of its objects was to educate Africans in their rights. In this respect some success was achieved when complaints about the over-charging of Africans on the railways led to government investigations that resulted in an improvement in the situation.[17] The TNVA also made representation to the government on behalf of Africans who were being turned off land as the British administration began a serious attempt to implement the 1895 republican Squatters Law in order to promote 'closer settlement' and capital-intensive agriculture.[18]

To broaden the influence of the TNVA, it was decided in July 1903 to start a newspaper. As a result, the first African-owned and -controlled newspaper in the Transvaal, *Leihlo la Babathso* (The Native Eye), appeared under the editorship of Levi Khomo, with columns in Pedi, Sotho and English.[19] However, after a year it was discovered that Khomo had squandered the Association's hard-earned finances. The paper was obliged to close down a few months later.[20] When Simon Molisapoli, Khomo's successor as editor and TNVA secretary, attempted to convene a meeting to discuss this state of affairs, Lagden refused to sanction the gathering on the grounds that 'the public assembly of Africans from all parts of the colony was calculated to prejudice the peace, order and good government'.[21] The local *Zoutpansberg Review* criticised Lagden's step in the light of the findings of the South African Native Affairs Commission (of which Lagden was chairman), which had approved of the principle of African political activities being conducted openly.[22]

In the meantime, another African organisation appeared in the Transvaal. On 16 May 1903 members of the Cape-based SANC active in the colony formed a Transvaal branch in Johannesburg. Two SANC representatives were also reported to have held meetings in the Waterberg district and in Rustenburg, where they succeeded in forming another branch.[23] For a number of years the leading figure in the new Transvaal Native Congress (TNC) was the young tramming contractor in Johannesburg, Jesse M. Makhothe,[24] a Sotho who had been educated at Lovedale. Another prominent figure was the older, well-known Saul Msane, who hailed from Edendale in Natal and who had been educated at Healdtown. Msane, also a founder member of the Natal Native Congress in 1900, joined the TNC while working as a compound manager for the Jubilee and Salisbury gold mining company, and maintained his links with the NNC at the same time – the NNC entrusted him with promoting its Isivivane scheme for economic self-help in the Transvaal in 1907.[25] Msane later became secretary-general of the ANC and editor of its newspaper, *Abantu-Batho*.[26] According to Makhothe's evidence to the Native Affairs Commission, the TNC was multi-ethnic in composition, consisting of both educated Africans and some chiefs.[27] Its main aims, as set out in its constitution, were to protect and promote African rights particularly in respect of issues of land, education and religion, and lay grievances before the authorities.[28] Later meetings of the TNC were attended by delegates

The Rev. Tiyo Soga, the first university student and ordained Christian minister produced by the indigenous people of South Africa, who studied in Scotland in the 1840s and 1850s. (NLSA PHA)

The wages of colonialism: the 'hanging tree' in Salisbury (Harare), where resisters to Cecil Rhodes's British South Africa Company were executed. This photograph was used as the frontispiece to Olive Schreiner's indictment of the Company, *Trooper Peter Halkett of Mashonaland*. Schreiner and her brother Will also supported African protests against Union in 1909 and, generations later, another Schreiner, Jenny, was jailed for being part of the armed struggle of the ANC's Umkhonto weSizwe.

Changing worlds. Above: Xhosa chiefs imprisoned on Robben Island in
the late 1850s and 1860s, photographed by Gustav Fritsch. (NLSA PHA)
Below: Some of their sons were sent to study at Zonnebloem College in Cape
Town, where they were photographed in 1863. (Cape Archives)

New ways: the Rev. James Archbell preaching to his mission congregation at
Thaba Nchu with an African interpreter, as painted by Charles Bell in November 1834.
(*Museum Africa AM 2436*)

The Lovedale girls' school, c. 1890. (*Lovedale Missionary Institution, South Africa:
Fifty Views from Photographs*, 1894)

Dinner time at the Lovedale boys' boarding school. (*Lovedale Missionary Institution, South Africa: Fifty Views from Photographs*, 1894)

The carpentry workshop at Lovedale. (*Lovedale Missionary Institution, South Africa: Fifty Views from Photographs*, 1894)

Students at drill, Lovedale. (*Lovedale Missionary Institution, South Africa: Fifty Views from Photographs*, 1894)

Elijah Makiwane and Pambani Mzimba (on the left) with fellow students at Lovedale in the 1870s. Makiwane became the first editor of *Isigidimi sama-Xosa* and first president of the Native Educational Association. Mzimba became a supporter of the South African Native Congress and the founder of the breakaway Presbyterian Church of Africa. (*Lovedale Missionary Institution, South Africa: Fifty Views from Photographs*, 1894)

Pastor and deacons at the Umvoti (Groutville) church of the American Board of Missions in Natal, 1900. (ABC 78.4 vol. 3; by permission of the Houghton Library, Harvard University)

Imvo Zabantsundu.

(NATIVE OPINION.)

Authorised Medium for the Publication of Government Notices addressed to Natives throughout the Colony and the Territories.

[IXABISO 3d.]   KING WILLIAMS TOWN, NGOLWESI-NE, OCTOBER 17, 1889.   [No. 257

"Imvo."
(IN KAFIR AND ENGLISH.)
The Medium for reaching Native Con-
sumers in every District of the Colony.
EDITED BY
J. TENGO JABAVU.
PUBLISHED ✦ EVERY ✦ WEDNESDAY.
Subscription (in advance):
Twelve Months ... ... 15s. 6d.
Six Months ... ... 7s. 6d.
Deferred Payment ... ... 4s. per quarter.
ADVERTISING RATES—THE LOWEST.

Office of "Imvo Zabantsundu"
(NATIVE OPINION),
Kingwilliamstown, Cape Colony,

3 Sept., 1894

H. R. Fox-Bourne Esq
Sec. Aborigines' Protection So.
Broadway Chambers
Westminster, S.W.

Dear Mr. Fox Bourne

I have not availed
myself of the privilege of addressing
you for years, but now occasion
has arisen. To understand the
matter I beg leave to refer you to
the columns of "Imvo" 15 August
where you will see an article
introducing a Petition to the Queen,
& the grounds thereof are given in another
of 29 August. Carefully peruse both &
whether as a Society you could not influence
her Majesty's Gov't to have a proviso inserted
in the Glen Grey Act guardian Natives
in the matter of the ali...ation of their
...selves. This,
...allowing the
...strong opposi...t here. Question
...out among...Commons in
this subject.
...we taken the liberty
you a dozen copies of
the numbers of "Imvo" to
...ference is made in the
...you may send copies
Ripon, Lord Rosebery, Mr
...ston and any other states-
...influence, also have
...roduced to some of the
...paus of opinion, like the
...icle and others in the
...many lend us the powerful
of their advocacy. Natives
of sending a deputation to the
the subject of the Boer legislation
- success in this matter
~ very sincerely

Tengo Jabavu
J.

John Tengo Jabavu, pioneering newspaper
editor, who started *Imvo Zabantsundu* in
November 1884; it became the 'mother of
all associations' as Africans started
mobilising politically. (D.D.T. Jabavu,
The life of John T. Jabavu)

☀ IMBUMBA ✝ ELI ✝ LISO ✝ LOMZI ☀

(NATIVE VIGILANCE SOCIETY.)

J. TENGO-JABAVU,
SECRETARY.

King Williamstown, Cape Colony,

Oct, 20th 1896

Recvd 3.10
pm

His Worship
The Mayor
King Williamstown

May it please Your Worship,
This is
to request permission to use
the Market (Produce) Building
for a Native Mass Meeting
on the Rinderpest on Tuesday,
27 Oct, in the course of the
forenoon.

The matter is a most
important one, with which
the Burgesses are sure to be
in Sympathy

... been arranged
... Official and
... Parl' for the
... meet and
... ers to the Natives
... who, as you
... iderable stock —

... honour to be

Elijah Makiwane, John Tengo
Jabavu and Isaac Wauchope,
prominent political leaders of
the Native Educational Association and the Imbumba Eliliso
Lomzi Ontsundu (or Union of
Native Vigilance Associations),
in 1888. (D.D.T. Jabavu, *The life
of John T. Jabavu*)

Pioneering journalists. Solomon T. Plaatje, his wife Elizabeth and Silas Molema (front right) with other staff members of the *Becoana ea Koranta* outside the newspaper's printing office in Mafeking. (Reproduced with permission, courtesy of Molema-Plaatje collection, Historical Papers, University of the Witwatersrand Library)

A.K. Soga, editor of *Izwi Labantu*, published in East London from 1897 to 1909. (T.M. Skota, *African yearly register*)

F.Z.S. Peregrino, founder and editor of the Cape Town-based *South African Spectator*. (NLSA INIL 24184)

The Rev. John Knox Bokwe, churchman and composer of note, who trained at Lovedale, was a partner of J.T. Jabavu's and co-editor of *Imvo Zabantsundu*. (R. Shepherd, *Lovedale South Africa*)

Dr Walter Benson Rubusana, stalwart of the South African Native Congress and president of the South African Native Convention, who became the first and only African elected to the Cape Provincial Council (in 1910). (NLSA PHA)

Nathaniel Cyril Umhalla, educated at Zonnebloem College, Cape Town, and St Augustine's College in Canterbury, England, was a founding member of the South African Native Congress and editor of *Izwi Labantu*. (S.E.K. Mqhayi, *U So-Gqumahashe*, 1921)

Dr Abdullah Abdurahman, president of the
African Political Organisation. (UCT Library)

Alfred Mangena, leader of a dock strike
and of protests against forced removals
in Cape Town in 1901, who became the first
African advocate in South Africa
and a founding member of the ANC.
(T.M. Skota, *African yearly register*)

Daniel J. Lenders, vice-president
of the African Political Organisation.
(NLSA APO Album)

IKAYA ⸫ LABANTSUNDU

NE VENKILE

E QONCE.

SIYAWAZISA umai wakowetu akuba
livuliwe

IBHOTWE LAWO

Elinamacebe onke e Business.

Ivenkile kaloku inento yonke ngamananizala, sinokutengela sitengisele abakudan, bakufupi IQIYA zetu ze sifika sintle, zinkulu, kwanetyali zoblobo. ICUBA letu lama Mjondo nelama Xesibe libalulekile ngokulunga—silitumela nakwindawo esikude.

IMPAHLA YEBHOLA ne Tennis ne Foot Ball, itshipu kakulu. Icawadi zonke zesi Xhosa, sko namaculo ase Wesile. Ingoma esimnandi sifika i Kwata zonke. Kuko ne Sebe Lesihlangu elipetwe ngu Mr. C. P. Matyolo, ir geibi kakuhle.

PAUL XINIWE,

General Agent,
Market-Square.

IKAYA LASE MONTI SELIVULIWE.

Paul Xiniwe, member of the Native Educational
Association and of Imbumba Yama Nyama,
who became a prominent entrepreneur,
sportsman and leader of the African Native Choir,
which toured Britain in 1891–2. (T.M. Skota,
African yearly register)

GRAND CONCERT

BY THE

AFRICAN NATIVE CHOIR.

PROGRAMME

Part First.

1.	"INTLABA-MKOSI"	Kaffir
2.	"Q Qa Qa Qa,"	Kaffir

A short piece in the Kaffir tongue adapted to the music of Schumann's "Merry Peasant" giving a striking illustration of the *clicks* used in the native language. These *clicks* are considered to be the most charming part of the "*taal*" perhaps because of their being so difficult to acquire by Europeans.

3.	PART SONG	English
4.	"ULO TIXO MKULU"	Kaffir

This is the first piece of music known to have been sung by Christian Kaffirs. The words and music are the original composition of Ntsikana, the first convert among the Amaxosa tribe.

5.	"CHILDREN ASLEEP"	English
6.	"MOTJIEVERAKATANG"	Dutch-Hottentot

(A HUMOROUS HOTTENTOT SONG.)

This song is supposed to be a passage at arms between a native woman, who is very fond of talking, and some of her people who are taunting her for her propensity to chatter so incessantly.

7.	SELECTION	English
8.	"THE LORD'S PRAYER."	English

This number is given by request. When the prayer was sung by the choir before the Queen, Her Majesty was greatly affected.

Part Second.

9.	SELECTION	Kaffir
10.	"MOLO-KE-DA"	Kaffir

The natives of South Africa, when traveling in parties, have a singular habit of singing—keeping time to the melody with their feet. Standing upon a hill, you can hear their peculiar chant when the band is miles away.

Molokeda is a representation of the effect produced by the gradual approach and disappearance of one of these parties, who have just left their *Kraals* to go into the towns in search of employment.

Perfect stillness is kindly requested during the singing of this piece.

11.	*Quintette,*	"ON THE MOUNTAIN."	English
12.		"TYPICAL WEDDING SONG."	Kaffir

The song is purely Native, and the harmonies have not been in any way Europeanized; it is sung at the Wedding Feast by the friends of the Bridegroom. The Bride, whose sobs can be heard amid the general rejoicing, is finally led away by two of the guests to her husband's *mgwelo* which awaits her. At some of the marriages the festivities are kept up days and nights without cessation.

13.	"LUTUKELA"	Kaffir
14.	"SEND THE LIGHT."	English

The words and music of this piece were composed expressly for the European tour of the African Choir, by gentlemen in South Africa who were wishful the enterprise should be a success.

15.	"ONWARD CHRISTIAN SOLDIERS"	Kaffir and English

Bill for a performance of the African Native Choir.
(Courtesy of Professor Bernth Lindfors)

International contacts and influences. Bishop Henry Turner welcoming James Dwane and the Ethiopian Church into the African Methodist Episcopal Church, Atlanta, USA, 1896. (L.L. Berry, *A Century of Missions of the AME Church*)

W.E.B. Du Bois, Pan-Africanist, writer and teacher at Wilberforce and Atlanta universities, who taught a number of South Africans studying in the USA.

Booker T. Washington, founder of the Tuskegee Institute, whose views on black self-help through education also had a great influence on John Dube and many other South Africans.

AME Bishop Henry Turner and the Transvaal annual conference, Pretoria, 1898.
(Courtesy of Moorland-Springarn Research Center, Howard University)

The Rev. Pambani J. Mzimba, founder of the Presbyterian Church
of Africa. (T.M. Skota, *African yearly register*)

John Langalibalele Dube, founder and editor of *Ilanga lase Natal*, founder of the Ohlange Institute and first president of the ANC. (H. Hughes, *First president*)

Nokutela Dube, in the late 1890s. (Cherif Keita)

Ohlange Institute: a trade class. John Dube is on far right. (H. Hughes, *First president*)

Enclosure No. 4
S.N.A. 1161 1908

Ohlange Industrial School

Phoenix, April 20th 1908.

S. O. Samuelson Esq.
    P. M. Burg

Sir, I am directed by Rev. A. Mtimkulu
and others who have communicated with
the Minister for Native Affairs asking
him to give them a date when they
can discuss Native matters which are to
be submitted to Parliament, to appoint
a date and announce same in the Ilanga
I have selected May 1st and shall so
announce it in this week's Ilanga
unless I hear that that date is unagreeable
to the Minister for Native Affairs. If he cannot
meet the Kolwas on that date please wire
me and tell me when it would be convenient
for him to see us. I am sir your obedient servant
                                    John L. Dube.

Street scene in Johannesburg in the early 1900s, showing the effects of
both racial segregation and emerging class differences among black people.
One contemporary commentator remarked: 'The worst classes are without
doubt the so-called educated natives; they dress in fine raiment, strut about
the streets ... side by side with white ladies, and consider themselves in
every way equal to white men.' (*Graphic*, 17 March 1906)

Members of the Kimberley elite: Sol T. Plaatje (back left), Isaiah Budlwana
Mbelle (back right) and Patrick Lenkoane (seated right).
(Reproduced with permission, courtesy of Molema-Plaatje collection,
Historical Papers, University of the Witwatersrand Library)

The Inter-State Native College scheme eventually led to the formation of the
University of Fort Hare. The committee, 1905, with (in front)
Isaac Wauchope (left), J.K. Bokwe (right) and J.T. Jabavu (standing, third left).
(Cory Library for Historical Research)

193
19**2** 192 or 87
1904
REPRESENTATIVES AT—
EIDELBERG,
EREENIGING,

Native A
No.

POTCHEFSTR
KRUGERSDOR

Transvaal Basuto Committee.

Chairman:

Secretary: WILLIAM P. LETSELEBA.

Acting Sec. :

* * *

* * *

Johannesburg, 17th Feb 1

P.O. BOX 197.

The Honourable

O.R.C. Native Congress Executive Committee.

IN YOUR REPLY PLEASE REFER TO

1595

Bloemfontein, August 8th 190

Sir

I Have the honour to send you the following resolutions mentioned by us to H.E. when interview

1) We Shan H.

2) We

3)

20

AFRICAN NATIONAL POLITICAL UNION

HEAD OFFICE:—KILNERTON.

NATIVE
AFFA
100

No. 1238

PRETORIA

P.O. BOX 70.

15th April 09

Sub. Native Commissioner
Pietersburg
Sir

Could you kindly allow me to call a meeting of as ma

After intense mobilization after the South African War, the South African Coloured and Native Delegation travelled to London in 1909 to protest against the passage of the South Africa Act on behalf of a wide range of organisations. Back row (from left): Thomas Mtobi Mapikela (ORCNC); J. Gerrans (representing Tswana chiefs of Bechuanaland), Daniel Dwanya (SANC sympathizer and longstanding representative of Chief Kama of Middledrift), Daniel Lenders (vice-president of the APO). Front row (from left): Matt. J. Fredericks (APO secretary), Dr Abdullah Abdurahman (president of the APO), William P. Schreiner (ex-Prime Minister of the Cape), Dr Walter B. Rubusana (of the SANC and president of the South African Native Convention) and John Tengo Jabavu (president of the Cape Native Convention). (NLSA APO Album)

Founders of the South African Native National Congress. Pixley kaIsaka Seme (above), together with the leaders of the South African Native Convention and several of his overseas-trained legal colleagues, initiated the new 'Native Parliament' in January 1912 (R. Rive and T. Couzens, *Seme: The founder of the ANC*, Skotaville Publishers, 1991). Others prominent in initiating the movement were (below, from left) Thomas Mtobi Mapikela from Bloemfontein (treasurer), Walter Benson Rubusana from East London (vice-president), John Langalibalele Dube from Inanda (president), Saul Msane from Johannesburg, and Sol. T. Plaatje from Kimberley (secretary). (Reproduced with permission, courtesy of Molema-Plaatje collection, Historical Papers, University of the Witwatersrand Library)

from throughout the colony, stretching as far afield as Pietersburg.[29]

The Congress became one of two influential African organisations in the Transvaal before Union. The other was the Transvaal Basuto Committee. Its founding date is not certain, but in 1904 it was represented before the South African Native Affairs Commission by its chairman, Paulus Malatye, and eight members. In his evidence to the commission Malatye, who had been born and bred in the Transvaal, called for Africans to be permitted to own land and complained about the ill-treatment meted out to them in Johannesburg, especially the curfew regulations imposed on them. His complaint that the curfew interfered with their church work and attendance at concerts in the city indicates the involvement of educated Africans in the organisation.[30] The Basuto Committee also took an active interest in education, being at one stage the only body recognised by the government for the purpose of receiving contributions to the Inter-Colonial Native College Scheme.[31] Like all its counterparts, the Basuto Committee sought to protect African interests or, as it was expressed in the vernacular, to be 'the husband of the widows and the father of the blind'.[32] Emphasising that its concerns were not limited to Sotho people only, in 1905 William Letseleba, its secretary, approached the Secretary for Native Affairs with a view to bringing existing African organisations in the Transvaal under its aegis.

The Native Affairs Department believed that the Basuto Committee's request was motivated by its disagreements with another organisation, Iliso Lomzi, which officials said 'incurred the displeasure of the majority of the educated natives of Johannesburg'.[33] Iliso Lomzi lo Notenga (the Transvaal Native Landowners' Association) was led by Edward Tsewu, moderator of the Independent Presbyterian Church, who came from the eastern Cape and was well known in political circles.[34] Tsewu achieved prominence in 1905 when he successfully brought a court suit against the Registrar of Deeds involving African land rights. The exclusion of Africans from the right to acquire property in the Transvaal had for long been a major grievance. Matters came to a head when Tsewu – helped by fellow separatists Marshall Maxeke (husband of Charlotte Manye), James Tantsi junior and D.H. Hlati – contested the refusal by the Registrar of Deeds to register land in his name. In the event, the court decided that the relevant republican legislation was invalid and that there were no legal impediments to the registration of property in the name of Africans in the Transvaal.[35]

While the court decision was a triumph for Africans, it raised fierce opposition from white colonists. Sir George Farrar introduced a resolution in the Legislative Council aimed at reversing the court ruling. This was passed and embodied in a draft ordinance.[36] Africans then protested to the Colonial Office, and when it came before the new Liberal government in England, Lord Elgin refused to sanction the ordinance.[37] Though government officials believed he fell into disfavour with other organisations by claiming the 'entire credit' for the successful test case,[38] it was one of the biggest victories in the decade for the Transvaal activists and Tsewu remained in the forefront of politics.*

By mid-decade, the Transvaal colony was being led towards responsible government by Sir Henry Campbell-Bannerman's Liberal government.[39] In 1906 a committee under the chairmanship of Sir J. West Ridgeway was sent to South Africa to investigate an appropriate constitution for the two former republics.[40] During its stay of two months, the committee collected evidence from all interested parties. Among those who testified were Mangena Mokone, leader in South Africa of the African Methodist Episcopal Church, and a deputation from the Transvaal Native Congress.[41]

The Ridgeway Committee's recommendations were accepted by the British government. With regard to the question of the African franchise, the committee recommended that the matter should be left to the new self-governing states themselves to decide. Any attempt to dictate to white colonists would be bitterly resented and the best policy would be 'to trust to their sense of justice'. The committee was convinced that sooner or later the new legislatures would deal with African representation in a liberal spirit. However, the report added, 'It cannot be reasonably expected that the native population will ever be placed on an equality with the white population in the matter of franchise.'[42]

---

* Other leading members of the Landowners' Association were Tyesi Gunuza, D.H. Hlati and James Ngubane.

On 6 December 1906 the Transvaal was granted responsible government, and in June 1907 the Orange River Colony was given similar
status.[43] Prior to this, the prospect of responsible government presented
the fledgling African organisations with their first real opportunity to
make themselves heard. Realising that the inferior position they occupied
in the ex-republics would be permanently entrenched under responsible
government unless adequate safeguards were adopted, they appealed to
the Imperial government to protect their interests in the most concerted
campaign yet displayed on their part.

With constitutional change in the offing, a massive petition of Africans
was forwarded to the British government by the United Native Political
Associations of the Transvaal in April 1905. The petition referred to
the deterioration in the position and status of Africans since the British
occupation, and asked the Imperial government to reserve for consideration
all legislation affecting Africans under the new constitutional dispensation.
It was signed by no less than 46 chiefs and 25,738 others.[44] Typically,
Lagden played down the strength of feeling that existed. In his view the
petition 'was rapidly engineered by a few half-educated natives who are
connected with native newspapers ... [and] cannot be taken to have been
understood by or to represent the natives in general'.[45]

As its name suggests, the United Native Political Associations consisted
of a loose alliance of the main political organisations in the Transvaal,
namely the Transvaal Native Congress, the Transvaal Native Vigilance
Association, the Transvaal Basuto Committee and Edward Tsewu's Iliso
Lomzi. Later in the same year, the leaders of these four organisations
represented African grievances in a joint deputation to the Governor,
Lord Selborne, and the Lieutenant-Governor, Sir Arthur Lawley, on which
occasion they again emphasised the great importance Africans attached
to Imperial protection. The TNC appears to have played the leading
part in the alliance.[46] The TNC was also responsible for drawing up a
petition in 1906, urging the British government 'not by any means to hand
over Natives to the colonial legislators'. Congress was emphatic about
its demand for representation and was equally insistent that it was the
responsibility of Britain to see that this was granted.[47]

During this period of political excitement, yet another organisation emerged in the Transvaal. This was the African National Political Union (ANPU), which was formed early in 1906.[48] The aims of the ANPU were 'to unite all the natives of Africa into one body socially and politically' and to secure for them the same liberties enjoyed by other British subjects. The Union was led by Sefako Mapogo Makgatho, who later became the president-general of the ANC from 1917 to 1924.[49] Initially, he had sought to join the Basuto Committee, but on meeting with no response, he grouped his followers into a separate association.[50]

Although the ANPU was soon active throughout the Transvaal, its strongholds were at Mphahlele's Location near Pietersburg – where Makgatho, the son of a chief, was born – and in Pretoria, where he and the body's secretary, Phillip Maeta, were attached to the teaching staff of the Kilnerton Institution, run by the Wesleyan Methodist Church.[51] Besides Mphahlele, many other chiefs in the northern Transvaal became members of the ANPU. Records show that Makgatho and some of his followers were also involved at one stage or another in the activities of the Transvaal Native Vigilance Association,[52] the other political organisation with a stronghold in the northern Transvaal, where more than half the African locations in the Transvaal were situated.[53] The position here roughly paralleled that in British Bechuanaland where members of the educated class worked closely with the chiefs.[54]

All the new African bodies that emerged in the first decade of the twentieth century displayed a more or less common approach. They all resented the inferior status of Africans in Transvaal society and the Native Affairs Department files bear testimony to their persistent efforts to alleviate their position. They expressed grievances on such wide-ranging issues as taxation, passes, education, religion, trading rights, labour, land tenure, and ill-treatment in towns, where they were prohibited from using pavements and tram cars. The British High Commissioner, Lord Selborne, criticised this situation in a speech in 1909:

I will only ask the white men to consider whether they have ever calculated the cumulative effect on the Natives of what I may call the policy of pin-pricks. In some places a Native, however personally clean, or however hard he may have striven to civilise himself, is not allowed to walk on a pavement in the public streets;

in others, he is not allowed to go into a public car, or to pay for the privilege of watching a game of cricket; in others he is not allowed to ride on top of a tram-car, even in specified seats set apart for him; in others he is not allowed to ride in a railway carriage, except in a sort of dog kennel; in others, he is unfeelingly and ungraciously treated by white officials.[55]

Though the government in the new British colony may have been tolerant towards the development of African associations after the war, the status of Africans in the Transvaal remained much the same as before and their demands went largely unheeded.

28

New politics in the
Orange River Colony

Your petitioners believe that without some measure of representation in the legislatures of this Colony their interests will ever remain in jeopardy, and that however they may conform to the rules of civilised life they can never hope to enjoy those of its privileges as, for instance, liberty to trade and to own land, which are at present withheld from them.

– Orange River Colony Native Vigilance Association
petition to the King, 1906

As in the Transvaal, Africans were present on the pavements to welcome the conquering British troops to Bloemfontein and within months they were mobilising to secure their political future in the new Orange River Colony (ORC). Already in January 1901, while the war was still far from over, a deputation presented a 'loyal address' on behalf of the black people living in the colony to the British Military Governor. The delegation was headed by D.T. Matsepe, A.P. Pitso, Joseph B. Twayi (who had led the pioneering football team to England the year before), Jan Mocher (a Bloemfontein community leader or 'block man') and E. Slamat (whose name indicated a Muslim background). Bearing over 250 signatories including several Sotho, Rolong and other chiefs, the address declared that the British government was 'the only government to which a native can look for his common rights'. And, looking to the future, they confirmed their readiness to prepare for the introduction of civil government and, with it, 'those changes in the constitution of the late Orange Free State to which we most humbly and anxiously look forward.'[1]

As in the Transvaal, black leaders in the Orange River Colony envisaged greater freedom under British rule, but these illusions were soon dispelled. Under the British, Africans remained excluded from rights which they desired. Almost a decade later, there were still more than 30 laws that discriminated against them on the statute books of the colony.[2] Frustrated, yet allowed more freedom of expression than previously, they began to articulate their feelings.

The first organisation to come to the notice of the authorities was the Native Committee of the Bloemfontein District in 1902. This was composed of pre-war leaders or 'block men' in the Waaihoek township who had formed themselves into a 'reflection committee' to discuss questions of interest.[3] In March 1902 the committee presented an address to the Deputy Administrator, Sir Hamilton Goold-Adams, as well as two petitions, one of which was signed by 1479 people from the districts of Bloemfontein, Thaba Nchu, Kroonstad, Rouxville, Smithfield, Fauresmith and Zastron. The wide circulation of the petition and the issues it raised indicate that the committee was not merely concerned with local matters. In it, the petitioners requested the Imperial government to grant black people in the colony the same political, land, educational and commercial rights as other British subjects.[4]

The members of the Native Committee who met Sir Hamilton Goold-Adams included three of the war-time petitioners from the year before – A.P. Pitso, J.B. Twayi and E. Slamat – as well as people who would become prominent, namely Jacob Lavers and Peter Phatlane.* The membership of the deputation reflected the scattered and diverse ethnic composition of the black population of the colony outside the 'reserves' and included people from the Rolong, Mfengu, Thembu and 'coloured' population.[5] That people of mixed descent were members of the committee underlines this point. In the Orange River Colony all blacks were defined as 'coloureds' and no distinction was made between Africans and coloured people.[6] Because locations were ethnically mixed,[7] and the scattered African population did not have a strong sense of ethnic identity, co-operation among Africans and between Africans and coloureds was much easier to achieve than

* The other committee members were A. Louw, P. Motsufi, I. Motshelela and A. Jordaan.

elsewhere. The African Political Organisation (APO), formed in 1902 as a vehicle for coloured opinion throughout South Africa, had branches in Bloemfontein, Fauresmith, Jagersfontein and Reddersburg.[8] Though they reported to a different political centre – the APO headquarters in Cape Town – they stayed close to local African activists in the colony.

In May 1903 the Native Committee, now styled the Bloemfontein Native Vigilance Committee, was officially recognised by the government.[9] By the following year an Orange River Colony Native Vigilance Association (ORCNVA) was in existence. It appears to have been a loose alliance of vigilance committees from various towns in the colony, with the leaders of the Bloemfontein committee the driving force behind it. When the Association appeared before the South African Native Affairs Commission in September 1904, it was represented by such familiar people as Joseph Twayi, Jan Mocher, Jacob Lavers, Peter Phatlane and the AME Church leader Benjamin Kumalo.[10]

The ORCNVA was the first attempt to unite Africans on a colony-wide basis. It was based on the earlier Cape models represented by Jabavu's Imbumba and, more especially, the South African Native Congress. The Natal-born Kumalo had studied and lived in the Cape and, through his AME Church affiliation, was in touch with activists in the eastern Cape and other colonies. The leaders of the new body were typical in their class and occupational composition. Its delegates before the South African Native Affairs Commission consisted of two ministers of religion, two cartage contractors, a mason, a brickmaker, and a dray-cart driver.[11] The Association explained that although it represented 'progressive, enlightened' Africans, it also sought to encourage traditionalists to become 'civilised'. This term was defined in a wide sense: one did not have to be a Christian or be able to read or write to fall into this category.[12] The case of the longstanding local spokesman Jacob Lavers was given as an example. He could neither read nor write, but he lived 'like a civilised man' at home, was a successful businessman, and had become a leader in his community.[13] Defying colonial prejudices, the Association regarded most Africans in the colony as being 'civilised' according to these standards.[14]

In its view, all people who had attained a certain standard based on the voting qualifications in the Cape should be allowed the franchise and the related 'privileges of civilisation'. Failing this, it wished Africans to be represented by special representatives elected by themselves. Although it wanted no colour differentiation, it was satisfied that these representatives should be white until such time as relations between the races improved. 'Tribal' Africans should be governed by 'native law', but at the same time encouraged to advance to the status of 'civilised men'.[15] The ORCNVA was also dissatisfied that all Africans were treated the same, regardless of class. Under an ordinance of 1903 only ministers of recognised Christian denominations and teachers in approved educational institutions holding higher education certificates were exempt from 'native law'.[16] Ministers of African separatist churches were excluded from these provisions.[17]

An allied organisation formed by local leaders after the war was the Orange River Colony Native Teachers' Association, which started in 1903. The secretary of this body was also the secretary of the ORCNVA and made representations on behalf of both bodies to the government.[18] In its aims the Teachers' Association filled a similar role to that of the Native Educational Association in the Cape, which was still in existence after a quarter of a century and closely allied to the South African Native Congress.[19]

Although, unlike the other colonies, the Orange River Colony produced no African newspaper, the fortnightly paper from neighbouring Basutoland, *Naledi ea Lesotho* (Star of Basutoland), was circulated in the colony. *Naledi* was launched in 1904, with articles in both Sotho and English.[20] Because of Basutoland's close proximity to the other colonies, news from these areas appeared regularly in the *Naledi*.[21] Although it was not an organ directly representing the views of local groups, *Naledi* nevertheless kept people in the Orange River Colony in touch with African opinion in the rest of South Africa.[22]

As in the neighbouring Transvaal, the level of political activity in the colony intensified from 1905 onwards with the approach of responsible government. In an effort to guard their interests, Africans made representations before the Ridgeway Committee, approached the colonial authorities and petitioned the Crown. During the fortnight the Ridgeway

Committee was in the Orange River Colony, several African groups appeared before it, including the Native Vigilance Association and the AME Church as well as a deputation of the Rolong from Thaba Nchu.[23]

In another significant development the various local vigilance associations decided at their annual meeting in Bloemfontein on 16 June 1906 to revise the constitution of the Vigilance Association and form a permanent and more explicitly political organisation. As a result, the designation 'Vigilance' was replaced by 'Political' in the body's new name.[24] The government refused, however, to recognise the organisation unless it revised its name, regarding the use of 'Political' as 'injudicious and incorrect'.[25] The Governor also made several amendments to the constitution, which he stated were 'all in the direction of showing that the Natives wish to do everything in a constitutional manner'.[26] The Association was forced to comply. It dropped both words from the title and simply styled itself the Orange River Colony Native Association. In time, the word 'Association' was gradually superseded by 'Congress'.

Despite the change in name and the shift in emphasis, no major changes in policy and activity occurred. The composition of the organisation remained the same and it continued to pursue a moderate, strictly constitutional path in attempting to achieve its aims. Established figures like Kumalo, Lavers, Mocher, Phatlane and Twayi, together with emerging leaders like Elijah Tshongwana, Thomas Mapikela and H.R. Ngcayiya, continued to play a prominent part in its activities. The three last-mentioned spokesmen provide further examples of the deep influence of the pioneering activists and intellectuals from the Cape on the spread of the new styles of organising in southern Africa after the war. Thomas Mapikela, who had been educated at the Anglican Institution in Grahamstown, moved to Bloemfontein in 1892 and became a key figure for three decades in the Orange River Colony (later Orange Free State) Native Congress and in national politics.[27] Elijah Tshongwana, also formerly of Grahamstown and one-time secretary of the Mpondo paramount Marelane, became the secretary of both the Orange River Colony Native Congress and the Orange River Colony Native Teachers' Association in 1906.[28] The ubiquitous Henry Reed Ngcayiya from Thembuland, one of the genuinely national political figures of these decades, was on the executive committee as well.[29]

After responsible government was introduced in July 1907, the attention of Africans was concentrated primarily on two measures which were most opposed. These were the Rights of Coloured Persons in Respect of Fixed Property Act of 1908, which aimed at weakening the position of African sharecroppers on farms, and the cost-cutting decision to abolish the Native Affairs Department.[30] The ORC Native Congress and the African Political Organisation were joined in protest against these measures by two new organisations, the Becoana Mutual Improvement Association (BMIA), representing the Rolong in the Thaba Nchu district, and the Eastern Native Vigilance Association from Bethlehem, which represented those people directly affected by the worsening condition of people in the rural areas.[31]

Although the BMIA was a new structure with a new name, it was in fact deeply rooted in decades of politics in that district, and it soon moved to the vanguard in building a united front of political organisations across South Africa. At the head of the Association were the same people who had petitioned the Free State President as *voormannen der Barolong natie* in 1899, the Rev. Joel Goronyane, Moses Masisi and John Mokitlane Nyokong.[32] They and other members, such as W.Z. Fenyang and Jeremiah Makgothi (Masisi's brother-in-law), were well respected in African educational and political circles. Goronyane, the chairman, whose father had been a head teacher at Thaba Nchu in the 1860s, was headman of the Thaba Nchu 'native reserve',[33] and from this position of authority he made representations to the South African Native Affairs Commission and the Ridgeway Committee.[34] All the Association leaders were private landowners; Goronyane, for example, owned three farms.[35] Although 'mortgaged up to the eyebrows', these people were relatively wealthy and influential and were recognised as leaders of the 20,000 Rolong in the district.[36] They were also in close touch with prominent figures like John Mocher and Thomas Mapikela in Bloemfontein through church connections and other activities: when the new Wesleyan Church was formally opened in Bloemfontein in 1903, Nyokong was a special guest, speaker and donor.[37]

The Eastern Native Vigilance Association (ENVA), formerly the

Bethlehem branch of the ORCNC, also represented a rural constituency, but one without formal land rights. It spoke for people directly affected by the increasing attacks on independent sharecroppers on farms in the eastern districts of the colony after the granting of responsible government. The ENVA's goal was to secure the franchise based on the Cape system – it declared that all Africans were fit to vote – and, at the same time, it wanted Africans settled on reserves like Witsieshoek, where fixed tenure and farming land could be provided. This demand reflected its particular concerns about rural sharecroppers, who were becoming increasingly vulnerable.[38] As one historian has explained, 'Large highly skilled sharecropping families, long the backbone of agricultural production in the Free State, found old landlords unwilling to take them on ... Many were told to cull their herds or trek. Labour extractions intensified, and landlords increasingly demanded service from wives and children.'[39] The purpose of the proposed Fixed Property Act was to tighten control over these so-called squatters: tenants on farms now needed to sign contracts, and women and children had to be registered as workers. Moreover, the old practice of whites fronting for land purchases by Africans was specifically forbidden.[40] The ENVA called for the protection of farm labourers against ill-treatment, fair wages for children working on farms, and legal recognition of half-share agreements, as farmers sometimes did not honour their commitments and Africans were powerless to do anything about this. The increasing restrictions placed on African sharecroppers were preliminary salvos anticipating the passage of the cruel Land Act of 1913. Led by Obed Mokhosi (president), A.R. Goliath Rakhatoe and others, the ENVA would remain in the forefront of the African defence until then, and would also be involved in the founding of the ANC.[41]

The protests of both the ENVA and the Becoana Mutual Improvement Association against the Fixed Property Act were partly successful. On the advice of the Colonial Office, the government shelved the implementation of the Act, pending the decision of the four colonies concerning union.[42] In this and other ways, Africans sought to defend and extend their position in the post-war Orange River Colony, now under British rule, but showing little real change from before.

29

The Natal Native Congress

'This was no war, but a man-hunt.'
 – M.K. Gandhi on colonial reactions to the Bambatha rebellion

The new century started with a flurry of political activity in Natal. On 1 June 1900, representatives from a number of districts in the colony met in Pietermaritzburg to establish the Natal Native Congress (NNC). Mark Radebe, editor of *Ipepa lo Hlanga* and secretary of the new body, explained that 'it had occurred to several of the native people in different parts of the Colony' that the war in which South Africa was then embroiled required Africans to show their support for Britain and 'to consider the desirability or otherwise, of forming an organisation similar to the Indian Congress and the Farmers' Conference'.[1] Sixty delegates from various districts attended.* The Christian Chief Isaac Mkize from Cedara, who had taken the lead with Chief James Majozi to set up *Ipepa* in 1898, was once again one of the initiators and was elected as the NNC's first president.[2]

The goal of the new NNC was to become 'the mouthpiece of the native peoples of the Colony'. Although an organisation run by *kholwa*, it was open to all Africans, exempted or not, and a particular goal was to involve chiefs and their representatives. In a key address at the launch, Chief Stephen Mini from Edendale explained: 'Most of those present, if not all, were of the Amakolwa section of the native population. A few of them were exempted from Native Law, but he hoped no distinction would be made when they came to draw up the rules. He hoped representatives of

---

* They included delegates from Edendale, Cedara, Richmond, New Scotland, Inanda and Verulam.

all classes of natives would be admitted as members of Congress. They must be one, and the native chiefs must be consulted and asked to send representatives.'[3]

Within months of its formation, the NNC claimed to have 23 branches scattered through Natal. It continued to grow thereafter, becoming far more representative than the Funamalungelo, which still existed in the early 1900s. (In 1905, Funamalungelo unsuccessfully challenged a Native High Court decision that children of exempted fathers were not themselves automatically exempted.)[4] The mere fact that, first, the independent *Ipepa lo Hlanga* newspaper and, now, the Congress had been formed was a big step forward in political organisation both for the Colony of Natal and the rest of southern Africa. Launched one month before the first Pan-African Conference in Manchester, the NNC went on to celebrate its centenary in a democratic South Africa.

The new Congress sought to cultivate political awareness among Africans by educating them about their rights under the colonial system of government and laws and, most importantly, to act as a forum for articulating grievances. Some chiefs were in sympathy with the NNC, and though they failed to send representatives to meetings, they were kept informed of developments.[5] Looking to the future, the NNC identified education, representation in parliament, 'purchase of lands' and trade opportunities (*'ukuzitengisela kahle ezintweni zonke'*) as its priorities.[6]

Unlike the Cape, electoral politics simply did not exist for Africans in Natal, depriving them of a legitimate sphere in which to mobilise and influence public opinion. Though they looked for support from 'friends of the natives' in order to get their views heard within colonial politics, even sympathetic white Natalians believed that Africans 'should not fancy themselves as equals of the white man and expect the same rights as him'.[7] In general, though its means were moderate and constitutional, the NNC was regarded with suspicion and disapproval by white colonists and the government alike.[8] The Secretary for Native Affairs made it clear in the *Natal Witness* in 1901 that he saw Congress as espousing the 'same doctrine' as the Ethiopian churches: 'it is a fact that there is a widespread movement among the natives under the cloak of religion, having for its objective a political combination for the supremacy of the black race'.[9]

Though the government did not clamp down openly on the NNC, because it did not want to give its members 'the advertisement of martyrdom' and because action of this nature would have been irregular in terms of the privileges granted to exempted Africans,[10] it kept a close watch on the NNC's activities. When the Criminal Investigation Department was detailed to keep a check on it, African detectives reported that the NNC held private meetings, admission to which was reserved for holders of tickets issued by the Congress secretary, and they were, therefore, unable to ascertain what had taken place.[11] Chiefs, as servants of the state, were particularly vulnerable to government pressure and could be removed from their positions if found 'unsuitable to fill a position of trust under the government'.[12] This action was contemplated against Stephen Mini, a prominent member of the NNC and later its president, and his political activities probably also contributed to the rejection of his application for the franchise in 1905.[13]

The most prominent public figure to emerge from the ranks of the *kholwa* in the first decade of the century was the Rev. John Langalibalele Dube, who returned from studying in the United States just before the founding of the NNC. With a strong belief in the idea of 'Africa for the Africans' and in Booker T. Washington's notion of self-help through education, Dube started the first major independent, African-controlled school in South Africa, the Zulu Christian Industrial School (later Ohlange Institute) at Inanda, just north of Durban, where he was minister. Helped financially by his father's trusted friend and clan leader, Chief Mqhawe of the Qadi, he opened the school with much fanfare on 8 August 1900, during the annual conference of the African Congregational Church held nearby.

Besides Dube and Chief Mqhawe, the first trustees of Ohlange were Madikane Cele, the close confidant of the chief, who remained his *inceku* or adviser even after becoming a Christian and forgoing some of the traditional ways; Bryant Cele, a Congregational minister and vice-president of the NNC; and Dube's brother-in-law, John Mdima. From this base, aided by his American supporters and funders, some sympathetic local whites, and his own local network, John Dube launched a lifelong career in education and politics. Called *Mafukuzela* (The one who struggles against obstacles), he rose to an undisputed position of leadership in Natal and, later, South African politics, until by the time of Union he had the same kind of profile and influence as the Cape political leaders Jabavu and Rubusana.[14]

In April 1903 Dube started a new newspaper, *Ilanga lase Natal* (The Sun of Natal), which soon displaced *Ipepa lo Hlanga* as the mouthpiece for African opinion in the colony. *Ipepa,* begun in 1898 by the same people who had initiated the NNC, had a short but eventful life, meeting with white hostility from the start.[15] The *Natal Witness,* echoing government views, wrote in 1901: 'The articles therein are of the most seditious character, and if published in any other paper would probably put the editor and proprietor in gaol at short notice. They all tend in one direction – that the white man is a usurper, that the kafir is the proper owner of the land, and that he should claim his rights.'[16] At the end of 1901 the paper's directors were summoned before the Under-Secretary for Native Affairs. Chiefs Mkize and Majozi were given a 'friendly warning', whereupon they 'voluntarily' decided not to take out a licence for publication the following year. By this time, *Ipepa* had 550 subscribers. The most prominent people associated with the paper – such as editor Mark Radebe (described as a 'prominent businessman with premises in Commercial Road in the City') and Cleopas Kunene – were all from the Edendale–Driefontein–Pietermaritzburg area and had all studied at different institutions in the Cape.[17]

After being closed down in August 1901, *Ipepa* managed to revive itself, only to fall victim to Dube's *Ilanga lase Natal.* The field now belonged to *Ilanga* and its upwardly mobile editor. Dube's paper was printed initially on the same press as the *Indian Opinion* in Durban, but Dube later acquired a separate press from America for his Ohlange Institute. There he was helped by close colleagues at Ohlange such as Bryant Cele and Skweleti Nyongwana (both leading NNC officials), as well as Robert Grendon and his brother Charles Dube. The students in the industrial section 'staffed' the paper. Like *Ipepa, Ilanga* was regarded with suspicion by the authorities and kept under strict surveillance, as regular translations of the newspaper's Zulu columns in the Native Affairs Department files testify. By simply entering the colony's public debates, Africans were regarded as agitators and were putting themselves at risk.[18]

Dube was not much involved with the Congress to start with. The key leaders were Methodists and from Pietermaritzburg and the surrounding mission stations like Edendale and Driefontein. According to his biographer, he 'was not disposed to relate easily to such well-established social networks with their own acknowledged leaders and particular local interests'. Besides the newspaper rivalry between *Ilanga* and *Ipepa*, there were, then, denominational, regional and generational differences; moreover, the midlands people were mostly individual property-holders, while at Inanda and other areas land rights tended to be communal and less secure. In addition, Dube did not get on with NNC leaders such as Saul Msane and Martin Lutuli.[19] As a result, 'This faultline – coast versus midlands – would persist for decades in the regional Congress.'[20]

The outbreak of the Bambatha rebellion in February 1906 had a dramatic impact on both Natal and South African politics. When disturbances broke out in Richmond after the imposition of a poll tax on all adult males in the colony, martial law was proclaimed and armed forces were sent in to quell the unrest. The dissident Chief Bambatha and his followers retreated to the dense Nkandla Forest where they engaged troops in a guerrilla struggle. In June 1906 this resistance was crushed at Mome Gorge. Further outbreaks occurred in the Mapumulo division; these, too, were soon put down. The disturbances exacted a terrible toll: between 3500 and 4000 Africans were killed, in contrast to some two dozen whites.[21] M.K. Gandhi, who led an ambulance brigade of Indian stretcher-bearers, observed, 'this was no war but a man-hunt'.[22]

According to Shula Marks, the most important outcome of the rebellion was the national unity it engendered among Africans.[23] Throughout the region, Africans were outraged by the heavy-handed actions of the Natal government. In Natal itself, the position of the *kholwa* was questioned by both white colonists and authorities, even though the NNC was at no stage even remotely implicated in the rebellion. While many members of the Congress were not without sympathy for the rebels, the NNC and most educated *kholwa* tried to adopt a precarious neutrality. Indicative of the deep suspicion with which white Natalians treated the *kholwa* was the controversy that developed around *Ilanga*. After John Dube had used the exhortation *Vukani Bantu* (Rise up, people) in an editorial,[24] *Ilanga* was branded as dangerous, libellous, seditious and treasonable by the *Natal Witness*,[25] and Dube was summoned before the Governor and given a severe reprimand.[26]

However, *kholwa* were reportedly involved in the operations on both sides. On the one hand, some separatist Christian preachers were said to have accompanied Bambatha's forces into the field, among them two members of Pambani Mzimba's separatist Presbyterian Church. On the other hand, some *kholwa* actively supported the government forces: the Edendale community contributed the 'A' Squadron of the Natal Native Horse and Dube's patron Chief Mqhawe of the Qadi also eventually lent support to the colonial forces, under pressure.[27]

From the side of the rebels, their fence-sitting and collaboration gained for the *kholwa* the tag of *amambuka* (traitors), while there was a tendency on the part of whites to see every educated African as a dangerous Ethiopian ready to drive the white man into the sea.[28] It is against this background, and also in the light of his fear that he might lose prospective backers for his school at Ohlange,[29] that we must view John Dube's apology in *Ilanga* for giving the government cause to suspect his loyalty. He added, 'There are grievances to be dealt with, but I can fully realise that at a time like this we should all refrain from discussing them, and assist the government to suppress the rebellion.'[30] Dube's retraction met with scathing criticism from *Izwi*: 'We would rather lose a thousand papers than our self respect.'[31] This was easier said from the calm atmosphere of the Cape than done in the reality of rebellion-racked Natal.

To survive, Dube had to rely on a politically careful strategy. While he strove for black unity and believed that 'justice would be done only when the African ruled the country', a moderate approach in the meantime was the only feasible means of obtaining political leverage for Africans.[32] Even this did not put the authorities at ease. In August the Minister of Native Affairs suggested that *Ilanga* be suppressed,[33] but apparently Dube's status as an African exempted from 'native law' prevented this from happening. Pressured by his white backer, the wealthy sugar baron George Hulett, Dube went into temporary retirement from politics and concentrated his energies on his school. His case showed up the limits of the new politics and the constraints in which the *kholwa* operated. All the same, the new political class, in Natal and the other colonies, had become more politicised than ever. With Union approaching, they began to mobilise more intensely, even though with caution in Natal.

After the Bambatha, rebellion a number of issues kept Africans in Natal politically active. The arrest of the Zulu king Dinuzulu on charges of rebellion in 1907 caused considerable dissatisfaction in the colony. Then in 1908 the introduction in parliament of three Native Administration Bills, based on a report of the Natal Native Affairs Commission, caused widespread reaction. Opposition to the bills was led by *Ilanga*, the NNC and Iliso Lesizwe Esimnyama (Eye of the Black Nation), a new midlands-based organisation closely linked to Congress, which had emerged in 1907. Iliso was an attempt by *kholwa* to broaden political activity so as to include 'tribal' Africans. An observer at an Iliso meeting remarked, 'The desire of the *kholwa* (who were in charge of the meeting) was clearly to be at one with the rest of the Natives.'[34] Prominent Congress members such as Martin Lutuli, Mark Radebe, H.C.C. Matiwane, Abner Mtimkulu, Cleopas Kunene and J.T. Gumede were also involved in the formation of the new organisation.[35]

In an effort to publicise its activities, Iliso also discussed the possibility of forming a newspaper which would serve as a mouthpiece for Africans. This attempt to set up a new paper was probably related to the tensions between coastal and inland interests and a desire by the influential Pietermaritzburg-based people to find a voice for themselves once again after the demise of *Ipepa*. For his part, Dube was still not comfortable with the NNC: he approached the Minister of Native Affairs with a plan to launch an alternative Native Congress 'on a scale larger and under different conditions from the one we have had', and requested from him the names of all chiefs in Natal and Zululand so that he could contact them.[36] It is, therefore, not surprising that when the NNC appeared before the Natal Native Affairs Commission in April 1907, Dube did not represent that body. Yet by 1908 he had become secretary of the NNC, with S.E. Kumalo as the chairman, and was engaged in his first big political campaign against the Native Administration Bills.* An alliance of sorts had been formed. And out of this, Dube would emerge as the dominant political figure in Natal and a national leader.[37]

---

* Veterans like Mark Radebe, Stephen Mini, and Skweleti Nyongwana, the printer who helped set up *Inkanyiso* in 1889 and subsequently taught at Dube's school, were still taking the lead as well.

30

Gandhi and the
Natal Indian Congress

> Our sympathies go out to our oppressed fellow subjects who are
> made to suffer for the same cause that we suffer, viz., our slight
> pigment of skin.
>
> – *Naledi ea Lesotho*, 1908

Mohandas Gandhi stands alongside Martin Luther King and
Nelson Mandela as one of the great political icons and moral leaders of
the twentieth century. For two decades – before he was given the honorific
'Mahatma', or 'Great Soul', – Gandhi lived in South Africa. His struggles
paralleled those of the African founders described in this book. This
chapter, by way of an interlude, looks briefly at the early Gandhi and his
relations with African people, especially his one-time neighbour John Dube
and the Natal Native Congress.

From 1860 to 1890 large numbers of people came from India to work
and settle in Natal. Many of the indentured Indians stayed on in Natal
after their contracts ended, and became known as 'free' Indians. They
were joined by traders and merchants, the so-called passenger Indians,
who travelled at their own cost. Being relatively wealthy and wishing to
be treated as 'British' Indians, this group started lobbying, petitioning and
using the courts to promote their interests in colonial Natal in the same
way as the *kholwa*. Many of the wealthier Indians in South Africa were
initially Muslims from Gujarat, as taboos about food and crossing the *kala
pani* ('black water' or ocean) militated against voluntary travel abroad by
high-caste Hindus. (Gandhi himself had to resist strong family and caste

pressure to cross the seas for his studies and work.) On 22 August 1894, 34 years after the first arrivals from India, the Muslim merchants formed the Natal Indian Congress (NIC) in Durban.

The context of the NIC's emergence was the rapid rise of Indian immigrants to Natal and the attempts by the colonial authorities to reverse the inflow by restricting the rights that 'free' Indians had enjoyed until then in the colony. In 1895 the Natal government passed the Immigration Law Amendment Act in an effort to halt the inflow. Indentured Indians were now required to return to India on the expiry of their contracts or become re-indentured. All free Indian adults became subject to a 'residence tax' of £3 per annum. The Natal parliament made clear its intention through the Act: 'Indians were appreciated as labourers only and were not welcome as settlers and competitors.'[1]

The secretary of the new Congress formed to defend the interests of local Indians was an English-trained lawyer from Gujarat in north-west India, Mohandas K. Gandhi. Brought to Natal at the age of 23 in May 1893 to help as a Gujarati–English interpreter in a case between two local Indian businessmen, Gandhi was pitched straight into the thick of things. Ejected from court on his second day in Natal by the magistrate for supposedly showing disrespect by wearing a turban as headdress, he immediately penned a letter to the local newspaper on the issue, which set him on a course of regular correspondence with the press to protest against discrimination encountered by 'free' Indians, who were notionally British subjects.[2]

Like similar African bodies in the South African colonies, the NIC was initially an elite organisation concerned mainly with sectional interests as a means of gaining a toehold for wider participation. These were, however, very different sectional interests at first. The NIC was divided from its African counterparts by religion, culture and interest, and the two had little contact at first. But the mission-educated Christian intellectuals in Natal would have been aware of its formation, even if just from reports in the press, and took lessons from this. For many years, if not decades, the NIC had little interest in or contact with the political struggles of the *kholwa* or Africans in general, and Africans were at the same time mostly hostile to the Indian migrants as well. Initially, the Native Congress and the

Indian Congress made no effort to link up with each other.

Six years after starting the NIC in tandem with the Muslim merchants who had briefed him, Gandhi volunteered his support for Britain in the South African War. Like African political activists at the time, he did so in the hope that it would lead to a relaxation of restrictions imposed on 'British Indians' in South Africa, only to find that in the aftermath of war the British and colonial administrations would have none of it.

For a short while, Gandhi served as a non-commissioned officer in charge of a thousand Indian stretcher-bearers, witnessing action at Spion Kop. The ambulance corps consisted of both indentured and 'free' Indians and was multi-faith, with Hindus, Muslims and Christians all participating. The NIC leaders provided financial support. According to Gandhi's biographer Joseph Lelyveld, his purpose was to make the point 'that Indians, whatever the colour of their skins, saw themselves and should be seen as full citizens of the British Empire, ready to shoulder its obligations and deserving of whatever rights it had to bestow'.[3]

After the ambulance brigade was disbanded, Gandhi left for India in October 1901 with the idea of returning permanently to his home country. However, after peace was declared in May 1902, he was persuaded to return and represent the grievances of the Natal and Transvaal Indians to the British Colonial Secretary, Joseph Chamberlain, who was due to visit the country. Like Africans, Indians had their expectations of a better deal under a British-controlled South Africa dashed. The Natal delegation led by Gandhi met with Chamberlain but was received 'coldly'. They were told that 'if Indians wanted to live in an area dominated by Europeans they had best try to placate their immediate masters'.[4]

As conditions worsened for Indians under the British in the Transvaal, Gandhi decided to stay and take up the cudgels on their behalf. He opened a legal office in Johannesburg and soon afterwards launched a British Indian Association. For most of the next decade Gandhi was based in the Transvaal, though he also maintained his links with Natal.

Like their African counterparts, Gandhi and his fellow activists began a newspaper, so that they could have a mouthpiece for their political work. *Indian Opinion* was started in Durban on 4 June 1903. The new weekly appeared in English, Gujarati, Tamil and Hindi. Madanjit Vyavaharik, a printer and community activist, took the initiative in setting it up, and the first editor was Mansukhlal Nazar. Both were close to Gandhi. As a recent biographer has noted, 'The newspaper represented not so much Indian opinion as Gandhi's. He wrote for it every week, and it therefore contained the essence of his thoughts while he was working on the ideas that would make him world-famous.'[5] When the paper's founder returned to India, Gandhi took over financial control. When it got into financial difficulties, Gandhi decided to set up his first ashram on a hundred-acre farm at Phoenix just outside Durban and run it from there. His new neighbour was John Dube, the head of the newly founded Ohlange Institute.

There are two different views about the neighbours in Inanda. The first position, advanced today by the ANC and South African government, is that Gandhi and Dube were not only neighbours, but comrades in struggle, who should be celebrated together as founders of democracy. Nelson Mandela cast his vote at Ohlange during the first democratic election in 1994, in tribute to Dube, and today Ohlange and the neighbouring Phoenix are part of a heritage trail marketing this partnership. Based on later political alliances and post-democracy 'rainbow nation' perspectives, this interpretation conveniently ignores many nuances that make the story more interesting. It ignores, too, the polite indifference and even perhaps cultural incomprehension that may have existed between them.

The second view is that Gandhi failed to identify with Africans and, indeed, that he maintained a disparaging attitude towards them during his stay in South Africa. Both of these positions – the uncomplicated narrative of joint political struggle and the one that fixes early Indian attitudes of superiority towards Africans – need to be tested, explained and understood in the historical context of the early 1900s. A serious study of this topic is overdue.

Both Gandhi's and Dube's actions showed striking similarities at the time. Both mobilised as British subjects to enable their constituencies to be given the same rights as British subjects. Both joined the war effort to show their loyalty to the cause. Both were constrained by the 'ambiguities of dependence' arising from this approach. Both were spokesmen at this stage for small, educated or relatively privileged sectors of their communities, and were compromised in the process. But as the historians Ashwin Desai and Goolam Vahed warn, these compromises 'should not be read as complicity'. They argue:

The 'imperial subject' project aimed to expose the language of Empire, which stated that all were equal under its rule, as well as the racism and exclusionary policies of colonists. [However, the] limitations of this tactic were exposed as the system rendered all non-whites or blacks as 'uncivilized' or unworthy of inclusion in the decision-making body politic. For Datta, 'the South African War was the point where the "imperial subject" begins to disintegrate ... The imperial order became globally divided ... [as] the White "achievers" invoke[d] the simple world of White versus non-White to fix and immobilize the prospect of internal mobility within the scale of civilisation'. For some this would mark a turn from complicity to confrontation.[6]

That Gandhi, bearing the rank of sergeant-major, led a volunteer ambulance brigade which served as stretcher-bearers for the colonial forces in the Bambatha rebellion in 1906 is not too difficult to explain.[7] By volunteering for the brigade, Gandhi followed the traditional path of colonised elites aspiring to gain political rights in a common system. To be heard in the first place, they needed to demonstrate loyalty to the Crown, and then proceed with strategies to attain their goals: in this case, to have South African Indians recognised as British citizens, with the rights that this status conferred. In this respect, Gandhi's outlook and actions were virtually identical to the actions and strategies of some African leaders, who fought on the side of the government forces.

In the aftermath of the Bambatha rebellion, the two neighbours in Inanda remained unsatisfied with the broader political situation and with their personal inability to influence it. Both seriously rethought their positions and took on roles that started to reject the position of 'imperial subject' to which they had subscribed previously. Dube increasingly moved into an embrace with Zulu nationalism and the royal house (through his close links with the Zulu king Dinuzulu), even though his family had originally fled from the Zulu kingdom during the Mfecane.[8] Later, he took on the leadership of the national movement in South Africa. Gandhi, for his part, saw the suppression of the Bambatha uprising as a crude man-hunt rather than war. Afterwards, he began to develop his idea of satyagraha or soul force on which he would base his strategy of passive resistance.[9] According to a recent biographer, the South African War and the Bambatha rebellion also 'taught him the futility of venturing a full frontal military attack on the dominant nation'.[10] While still in South Africa, Gandhi progressed to radical, direct action and passive resistance strategies.

These lessons were among several that Gandhi learned in South Africa. Another was the firm belief in an Indian nationalism that transcended Hindu–Muslim divisions, which he acquired from associating extensively with Muslim businessmen in Africa and setting up the NIC with them. He was influenced as well by a number of nonconformist Christians, whose egalitarian writings and beliefs helped him to develop his position against the Hindu caste system. From 1901, when he deliberately broke class taboos by travelling third class through India and cleaning toilets at Indian Congress meetings, he began his various experiments with truth in South Africa.

Gandhi has been criticised for the supposed feelings of superiority he and other Indians showed towards Africans. Indian leaders successfully demanded that the Natal authorities should provide three entrances instead of two in public buildings, so that Indians would not have to share entrances with Africans.[11] These views remained for long. Gandhi's mouthpiece, *Indian Opinion*, talked of Indians being 'degraded by commerce with Kaffirs'.[12] In 1909 a well-known member of the Indian community declared in court that he objected to carrying a pass 'in civilised country as though he were a Kaffir'.[13] In the same year, a passive resister friend of Gandhi's wrote to him complaining about being 'locked up [in jail] with the Kaffirs'.[14]

There were feelings of prejudice in the opposite direction, too, as Dube's biographer has confirmed.[15] A report in *Izwi* from January 1908 stated that Africans could not be expected to regard the 'Indian question' with much sympathy: 'The countrymen of Gandhi are, like the Mohammedans and Malays, extremely self-centred, selfish and alien in feeling and outlook'.[16] A month later, the same newspaper placed without comment an extract from an American newspaper, in which it was said that Africans in South Africa had not forgotten that Indians had volunteered to serve with 'the

English savages of Natal who massacred thousand of Zulus in order to steal their lands'.[17] On the basis of such statements, recent writers have gone further and one, the biographer Joseph Lelyveld, has highlighted, as a central argument in his book, Gandhi's supposed antipathy towards Africans.[18]

While mutual prejudice undoubtedly existed, both the African leaders and Gandhi were committed to universal visions in politics and would come to seek ways of gradually tempering these notions of 'the other'. As Gandhi put it in a speech in Johannesburg in 1908, 'If we look into the future, is it not a heritage we have to leave posterity that all the different races commingle and produce a civilisation that perhaps the world has not yet seen?'[19] In the final analysis, both sides preferred to keep their struggles separate, lest their respective positions vis-à-vis colonial whites were imperilled. In fact, there was a good reason *not* to work together. To antagonise colonial administrators by raising broader issues other than those directly affecting Africans or Indians made little sense at the time. It was already an uphill battle just to have some of their demands recognised. As a result, Indians preferred to keep their own interests distinct from issues affecting Africans in general, and work 'quietly along their own lines'.[20]

What of the relationship between the two highly significant projects to be found right next to each other in Inanda from 1903 onwards? Dube's and Gandhi's biographers maintain that they hardly had any contact, and on one level this makes sense. The neighbours not only lived in a world where mixing was not encouraged, but also had very different cultural and religious outlooks. Whereas Dube's inspiration had been Christianity, self-help and black America, Gandhi came to his experiment with truth by way of Hinduism, Ruskin and Tolstoy.[21] But another reason why Dube and Gandhi did not meet more regularly was simply that Gandhi was physically absent from Phoenix for most of the time. He spent most of the first decade of the twentieth century living in Johannesburg, although his family remained at Phoenix. Still, it is remarkable that two such visionary experiments in community and political advancement such as Ohlange and Phoenix – each of which would in its own way have national and international repercussions – existed next to each other, but seem to have been so largely disconnected.

But there were also lessons learned from each other and some degree of co-operation. The formation of the NIC directly influenced the formation of the Natal Native Congress in 1900 and the first editions of Dube's newspaper were printed on *Indian Opinion*'s press in Durban (before it was moved to Phoenix). To take on the printing of a newspaper with political aspirations, running parallel with one's own, cannot be considered a small matter. We do know, too, that Gandhi listened to Dube give one of the most impressive speeches of his public life to an audience of international scientists at Mount Edgecombe, the home of Dube's patron, Marshall Campbell, in 1905. *Indian Opinion* described him as an African 'of whom we should know' and the newspaper also commented on various developments in African politics, from Walter Rubusana's and A.K. Soga's cross-questioning of the Cape Prime Minister in 1904 to Edward Tsewu's successful court challenge to the restrictions placed on African land rights in 1905, Alfred Mangena's actions against the Natal government in 1906 and Gandhi's support for the Inter-State Native College Scheme.[22] Later, John and Nokutela Dube supported Gandhi in London in 1909.

Despite not actively co-operating, African and Indian leaders did recognise their common lot and show a degree of solidarity in the first decade of the twentieth century. *Naledi ea Lesotho* expressed admiration for the passive resistance methods of the Transvaal Indians,[23] and *Indian Opinion* reciprocated by declaring, 'Our sympathies go out to our oppressed fellow subjects who are made to suffer for the same cause that we suffer, viz., our slight pigment of skin'.[24]

However, it is true that both African and Indian leaders remained shy of direct co-operation during the early 1900s. Although Indian activists foresaw that Closer Union would lead to the curtailment of the liberties of all 'non-whites',[25] they did not actively join African and coloured organisations in agitating against the draft South Africa Act. Gandhi was in London at the same time as the Coloured and Native Delegation in July 1909, and he did support them indirectly. But the struggles of Gandhi and the Indian organisations throughout the period under review remained largely focused on the past and present treatment of Indians, rather than on the wider issue of the prospects of Union and its effects on the black population. This approach was based on the argument that while the indigenous people had a right to demand political equality, the Indian settlers should for the time being concentrate on their civil rights, which were constantly in jeopardy.[26]

Just as the Bambatha rebellion threw African political activists and emerging organisations in Natal into a crisis of identity and survival in the mid-1900s, it did the same to Gandhi. The challenges the Indian communities in Natal and the Transvaal faced from the British and colonial authorities were, moreover, so harsh that they found their very right to live in southern Africa being questioned. However, the emergence of a determined Indian protest movement in the Transvaal and the moves towards the unification of the southern African colonies gradually started to bring Indians and Africans into the same orbit of colonial politics for the first time. They commented more and more on each other's struggles, and by 1909 some convergence in action had begun, as Anil Nauriya has documented. Under the leadership of Gandhi's son, Manilal, relations between Ohlange and Phoenix improved 'markedly' from 1913 onwards.[27] But it would be only in the 1940s, with the famous Doctors' Pact between Dr A.B. Xuma of the ANC and Yusuf Dadoo and Monty Naicker of the South African Indian Congress (SAIC), that the African and Indian struggles in South Africa truly started merging, leading to the formal partnership of the ANC and the SAIC as members of the Congress Alliance in the early 1950s.

31

Cape Town and
post-war politics

The black man who is still ashamed of his race and people is still
a slave.

– John Tobin, November 1903

Cape Town occupies an important place in the history of
African nationalism, even if those who are described as 'Africans' in
the peculiar lexicon of the country have always been a minority there.
As seat of government and of parliament, and the largest town and
commercial centre in the Cape Colony, Cape Town was the destination
in the nineteenth century of many Africans, who made their way there as
prisoners, petitioners, students, civil servants, labourers and others.

More permanent residents began arriving from the early 1800s. The
first large group of free Africans to settle in Cape Town were Mfengu from
the eastern Cape who came in the 1830s. There was also an influx from
that region after the cattle-killing episode.[1] The census of 1865 listed 674
Africans, among them the sons of eastern Cape chiefs who were studying
at Zonnebloem College. From the 1880s Africans were recruited in large
numbers to work in the docks as manual labourers. By 1890 they totalled
1000; by 1900, 1500. They were housed in a special docks 'location' where
the V&A Waterfront now stands. The other 8500 African residents were
spread out through the town, mainly in the 'Kafir haunts' in Papendorp
(Woodstock) and District Six, as well as in Simonstown and Camps Bay,
where there was a 'location' for 500 tramway workers.

By the turn of the century, the African population was well settled and starting to become politically assertive. In the 1890s there were several strikes and court cases involving the eastern Cape workers, who resisted low wages and fought for better working conditions.[2] By 1899 the educated elite were holding political meetings, sending petitions to government and organising socially, setting up six cricket clubs in the town. But Africans comprised only a small percentage of the total population at that time, and the pace in organisational and electoral politics was set by people in the coloured communities among whom they lived and with whom they sometimes co-operated.

The earliest political activity on a communal basis among Cape Town's 'non-Europeans' involved Cape Muslims, or 'Malays' as they were often labelled. By the mid-1870s, following the grant of responsible government to the colony, members of the Cape Muslim community were 'showing a keen interest' in both municipal and parliamentary politics, and colonial politicians actively sought the 'Malay vote'. Abdol Burns, a cab driver of Scottish descent, was the main spokesman at the time. 'No political meeting especially at election time was complete without a speech by Abdol Burns,' the *Cape Argus* noted. In 1884 a number of prominent Muslims, including the well-known Achmat Effendi, served on the electoral committee of a successful candidate for parliament; a decade later, Effendi himself stood for parliament, though he lost when a law was hastily passed forbidding cumulative voting, which would have secured him the seat.[3]

Individuals from coloured Christian communities were also active in electoral politics. However, as the goal of the coloured elite generally was to seek integration with white society rather than mobilise separately as an ethnic outgroup, it took some time before organisations in Cape Town emerged to represent them. This reluctance to organise politically on an ethnic basis by people seeking a home as individuals in white colonial society (with which they shared commonalities of language, religion and culture) changed during and after the South African War. A combination of economic and political factors led to a heightened sense of ethnic identification and the emergence of several specifically coloured organisations from 1901 onwards.

The idea that black Capetonians should mobilise politically in a more assertive way was given momentum late in 1900 by the arrival of F.Z.S.

Peregrino, an avowed Pan-Africanist. Born in Accra in 1851, he lived in Britain for 23 years before crossing the Atlantic to America, where he became editor of a newspaper in upstate New York. His son Francis J. Peregrino relocated to Cape Town in 1898, and Francis senior followed in November 1900 after spending four months in Britain around the time of the first Pan-African Conference in Manchester.[4]

Peregrino senior was a political showman. Within weeks of his arrival, he brought out the first issue of the *South African Spectator* on 1 December 1900, the third black-run newspaper in the Cape. He found himself a home in Oak Avenue, Newlands, set up office in the city centre and was soon in the forefront of local affairs. The most active seller of the newspaper was the influential and politically active John Tobin, owner of a restaurant in Hanover Street in District Six. Just up the road from Tobin in Hanover Street was the new Bethel Institute, an initiative of the American-based AME Church, which sought to invigorate its presence in southern Africa after its merger with Mangena Mokone's Ethiopian Church in 1896. The Institute's principal was the West Indian-born Francis Gow, one of more than twenty members of the American expatriate community in Cape Town into which Peregrino was absorbed.

Peregrino made it clear that the aim of the *Spectator* was to advocate the cause of all sections of the black population: it was an organ for all 'the people who are not white' and it was published by one 'who aspires not to be white'.[5] After a few months he introduced Xhosa columns in the paper, aimed at an African audience, and hired William Mdudana as translator.[6]

'Race pride' was Peregrino's departure point. Much information about African Americans appeared in the *Spectator*, particularly the activities of the AME Church. The *Spectator* also frequently complained about cases of colour discrimination in the Cape, though Peregrino cautioned against militant action and said that British rule 'with all its imperfections ... is so far, and until something better develops, the best form of government for the black man'.[7]

Besides his newspaper activities, Peregrino dabbled in various business ventures, acted as an agent for African chiefdoms and organisations like the South African Native Congress, and regularly engaged government officials in the southern African colonies.[8] Within a year of arriving in

Cape Town he also started three of his own political organisations, namely the short-lived Pan-African Society, the Coloured Men's Protectorate and Political Association, and the Cape People's Vigilance Society, which aimed to 'foster friendly relations between all people in South Africa who are not known as white'. W.A. Roberts, a shopkeeper involved in local church and temperance matters, was made president of the last two bodies, with Peregrino the secretary. These were in effect shell organisations, though they continued in one form or another until 1910. The Society was described derisively, but not wholly inaptly, by Peregrino's opponents as consisting only of him and his 'office boy'.[9]

'Arrogant in manner', Peregrino 'was never to find a home in the ranks of the "coloured" elite in Cape Town', according to Christopher Saunders. One of the reasons was his emphasis on race and a common 'blackness', which did not sit well with some locals, and his condescension towards them. Though prominent, and part of an expatriate community that included influential churchmen and educators, F.Z.S. Peregrino remained an outsider in Cape Town society.

In 1901 the focal point in local popular politics was 'The Stone' at the top end of District Six, where regular open-air Sunday morning meetings were held to discuss the burning political issues of the day. Here, on a regular basis gathered 'some hundreds of coloured men – Kafirs, Hottentots, half castes' – 'probably representative of every race'. The prime mover behind 'The Stone' meetings was John Tobin, who besides his business activities was a leader in sporting and cultural affairs. Tobin was original in two respects. He was against imitation and proud of his identity, saying, 'The black man who is still ashamed of his race and people is still a slave.' Tobin, whose father was Irish, also had an anti-imperialist perspective, which saw Afrikaners or 'Dutchmen' as part of a future nation with black people. As for the English-speakers, 'They are the people who oppose the idea of South African people, black and white, to govern themselves, and who do not scruple to take away our rights as citizens and electors. These are our enemies.'[10]

Tobin was to stay consistent to these views, and was thus brought into conflict with similar organisations and leaders who generally adopted pro-British positions. Like Jabavu, he supported the South African Party rather than the Progressives of Rhodes and his successor, Dr Jameson, in Cape electoral politics. Like Peregrino, he was also at this stage of his career much more explicit than fellow leaders in Cape Town about the need to create alliances with other black political groupings.

Towards the end of 1902, a lay preacher in the AME Church, William Collins, and five associates decided it was time for the 'Coloured portion of the community' to start a permanent organisation which 'had as its object the unity and banding together of the coloured races in South Africa'. Twenty prominent individuals were invited to a 'large and representative meeting' held on 30 September at the Mechanics Institute in the suburb of Claremont. The idea was accepted and the new African Political Organisation (APO) came into being after a founding congress in February 1903. Tobin was elected vice-president, thereby indicating the stature he enjoyed in Cape Town, while Matt. J. Fredericks, aged 29, became the secretary, and was soon appointed on a fulltime basis.[11]

The new organisation grew quickly. By 1905 the APO claimed to have 10,000 members and its campaigns in 1909 were able to attract direct support from more than 12,000 supporters in over 50 towns throughout the subcontinent. A major focus for the new organisation was the political situation of coloured people in the Transvaal and Orange River Colony after the South African War: this accounted for its reach across colonial boundaries.

But growth was accompanied by turbulence. Differences between the APO president, Collins, and the vice-president, present from the outset, soon divided the organisation. A faction headed by Fredericks pulled off a coup at the 1905 conference, where it succeeded in expelling both Collins and Tobin. The Edinburgh University-educated medical doctor Dr Abdullah Abdurahman, newly elected to the Cape Town City Council, was brought in as president. Highly educated, already in a position of influence and fluent in English, Abdurahman became the undisputed kingpin of the organisation, together with Fredericks. With Abdurahman at the helm, the APO was to play a major part in unfolding debates about the political future of southern Africa.

From the end of the nineteenth century Africans living in the city came under increasing pressure. By the late 1890s both white and coloured proponents of segregation were insisting that they should be segregated and moved out of the city. In 1899 the government passed the Native Locations Act and the City Council identified land at Uitvlugt near Maitland 'to separate as far as possible Natives from Europeans'. Attempts to move Africans there were at first unsuccessful, but when in early 1901 an outbreak of bubonic plague hit the city, the authorities proceeded to use health regulations to forcibly move African residents to Uitvlugt. Uitvlugt (later named Ndabeni) was effectively a compound based on the Kimberley model. This attempt to segregate Cape Town's Africans became a matrix for urban control in the colony and its consequences were subsequently incorporated into legislation that led to the reordering and social engineering of space in eastern Cape towns such as Port Elizabeth and East London as well.

In response to the removals, Cape Town's Africans residents started mobilising intensely for the first time. The leader of the protests was Alfred Mangena, a teacher and evangelist, who had permission to remain in the city during the plague. Born in Estcourt in Natal, he lived for a time in the Transkei and in Johannesburg before coming to Cape Town in 1898.[12] He immediately became involved in the activities of the local elite through an introduction by the Rev. Elijah Mdolomba of the Wesleyan Church, an influential figure both locally and in eastern Cape politics.[13] Within a short while, Mangena was politically active, calling in the Cape and British press towards the end of 1899 for 'universal franchise', a radical demand at the time. By October 1901 he was the official spokesman or 'senior secretary' of striking dockworkers in the docks location, and government officials were branding him as the arch-agitator at the Uitvlugt location.[14]

By the time the removals started early in 1901, Mangena had split from Mdolomba and was living at the St Barnabas church rectory in the city centre. He taught English and Zulu at an adult night school while also studying for a teacher's qualification and saving so that he could go abroad to further his studies. Mangena's involvement with the dockworkers and the protests at Uitvlugt stimulated his interest in the law. He and other members of the Uitvlugt committee worked closely with two white lawyers recruited to defend the location's unwilling residents. Together they gave the authorities a headache through the second half of 1901 up to June 1902, when Mangena left by boat for England, cheered off by several hundred Africans.*

During the forced removals of 1901, a bitter split developed between Mangena and Mdolomba, with whom he had initially worked. It was still echoing across the oceans and assuming bitter personal dimensions six years later. Various reasons have been given for the rift, but the fact that Mangena led the protests and Mdolomba was the main African supporter of the authorities during the relocations to Uitvlugt probably best explains it. (The brand-new church and rectory built for him in the new location may explain how Mdolomba became so compromised.) The personal bitterness emanating from this rivalry surfaced in accusations by Mangena that he had left Mdolomba to join the Anglicans because 'he was a bad man, running after women', while Mdolomba accused Mangena of absconding to England with money collected during the protests.[15]

When in 1906 Mangena sensationally charged the Governor of Natal in British courts for the deaths of Zulu people in the Bambatha rebellion, the Natal authorities used Mdolomba's testimony to tarnish his name. Mangena won his court battle and sued for libel, but the pressure on him was so great that he had to return temporarily to South Africa to defend himself. Both Mangena's remarkable life and the political mobilisation of Africans in Cape Town during the early twentieth century deserve fuller attention from historians. Far from being an invisible minority, activists here were in the forefront of some of the most intense struggles in that decade.

The activism in Cape Town was also directly linked to developments in the heartland of black politics in the eastern Cape. *Izwi* reported in 1902 that an Iliso Lomzi (or Vigilance Association) had been formed in Cape Town and had affiliated itself to the South African Native Congress (SANC), becoming one of the most active branches. The Cape Town Iliso

---

* Arthur Radasi, Coke Mji, Toise B. Skenjana, William Sipika and the headmen at the Docks – Songwevu, Sigcume and Mbangeni – were other prominent leaders of the protests in Cape Town in the early 1900s. Later, D.D. Tyakwadi and Charles Mbilini, as well as 'chiefs' Fongqo and Mapassa, came to the fore in Cape Town's Iliso Lomzi.

met regularly, kept Soga and *Izwi* in East London well informed of its activities, sent delegates to several meetings of the SANC in the eastern Cape, more than 600 miles away, and supported its projects, such as the Queen Victoria Memorial College Scheme.[16] Many of its members were migrants from the eastern Cape, working temporarily in the Cape.

⬇

Despite being a small minority in Cape Town, Africans established a presence in the city that the ruling classes could not wish away. They, likewise, linked up energetically with the political activism in the eastern Cape and the moves to construct a national movement. Cape Town also saw the emergence of one of the outstanding early struggle leaders in the person of Alfred Mangena. Moreover, the city also was home to one of the founding organisations of the modern-day ANC. Thomas Zini, president of the Cape Peninsula Native Association – a 'progressive and enlightened body', which held regular, well-attended meetings every Sunday morning at 'The Stone' in District Six – was in Bloemfontein on the historic day that the South African Native National Congress was established in 1912.[17]

Cape Town remained a meeting place and melting pot of people and ideas in the first decade of the 1900s. The colourful editor of the *South African Spectator*, F.Z.S. Peregrino, maintained close links with A.K. Soga, editor of *Izwi*, and Sol Plaatje, editor of the new *Koranta ea Becoana*. Soga met with Peregrino in 1902 and Plaatje stayed at his house in Newlands for several weeks in August 1903 while accompanying a delegation of Tswana chiefs. This meeting no doubt paved the way for the formation of the South African Native Press Association in the next year.

The most significant step forward in Cape Town's politics was the emergence of the APO, the most effective black political organisation with a South African reach before Union. Generated and sustained by the betrayal of Vereeniging, it came to stretch throughout the subcontinent. Its branches in places like Bloemfontein and Kimberley gave it close links to parallel movements of the African intelligentsia. As Union loomed ever larger after 1906, the APO and the SANC, the leading African organisation, forged closer links. Like the struggles of Gandhi and the Indian communities in Natal and the Transvaal, the APO's fight on behalf of coloured communities at this time, though happening in a parallel universe, helped foster the idea of an inclusive South African nationalism.

32

Growth of the South
African Native Congress

We say this land belongs to Ndlambe even though we are being
governed by the whites. The Congress has been started so that all
black people may lodge their complaints to it. Rarabe died before
he had gathered the black nation together. This meeting is for all
blacks in South Africa. It is the mouth of the black people to the
government here and overseas.
– SANC spokesman, at meeting of the Nxaruni Iliso Lomzi, 1907

After the South African War, the eastern Cape-based South
African Native Congress (SANC), which had increasingly come to the
fore in the last years of the nineteenth century, established itself as a
fully fledged organisation. In 1906 the Cape government recognised it as
constituting 'as representative a body of advanced Cape Colony Natives as
could be found in any organised form'.[1] The SANC was in a real sense the
parent and prototype of the many organisations that emerged throughout
southern Africa in the first decade of the twentieth century, the antecedent
of both the South African Native Convention and the South African Native
National Congress, later renamed the ANC.

No sooner had peace been concluded on 31 May 1902 than the SANC
sprang to life. Its schedule showed it meant business. A meeting of the
executive was held in June; a petition embodying African hopes and
aspirations in the post-war reconstruction period was sent to the Cape
Governor; a large conference of the organisation was held at Lesseyton
near Queenstown in September, where it inaugurated a scheme for a college

for African higher education; members of the executive met Prime Minister Sprigg in the *Izwi* office in East London in December; and in February 1903 a delegation headed by the president, Thomas Mqanda, interviewed the British Colonial Secretary, Joseph Chamberlain, in Grahamstown and presented him with a lengthy petition, detailing African attitudes towards a wide range of issues.[2] The SANC started communicating with the authorities in a regular way and the government began to take it seriously. It also promoted itself vigorously as the mouthpiece or 'parliament' for black people. Delegates from branches throughout the eastern Cape attended the annual SANC conferences, which were held from 1902 onwards.[3]

Indicative of its expanding influence, the SANC by 1903 had branches in 25 districts, mainly in the eastern Cape and Transkei but also in the large towns and labour centres of Kimberley, Cape Town and Johannesburg, to which large numbers of workers from the eastern Cape heartland were streaming.[4] The Congress therefore had a wider influence than any previous organisation and new branches continued to be established. By 1908 Walter Rubusana, in his capacity as temporary secretary, put the number at 40.[5]

Though constantly expanding, its bases were fragile, as the great bulk of the African population was rural, poor, non-literate and, to a large extent, unfamiliar with western-style constitutional politics. Industrialisation was only just starting to create the stable urban populations that would form the mass base of the ANC in the mid-twentieth century. Moreover, its financial position was precarious. Lack of funds prevented the SANC from appointing permanent, salaried officials.[6] Neither did ad hoc appeals for funds in times of crisis have much effect.[7] Such was the enduring financial crisis that local members were barely able to raise enough money – usually through subscriptions, tea meetings and concerts – to keep the branches alive and send delegates to central conferences.[8] Often, hard-working leaders had to bear the costs incurred on Congress business themselves.[9]

Despite these drawbacks, the SANC was a considerable achievement. It started its own newspaper, organised regular annual conferences and executive committee meetings, and sustained links with all its affiliated branches. Each of these, no matter how small, had a life of its own. Conferences were usually attended by around 50 people, with sometimes as many as 80 or 90 from various areas. Lasting several days, they involved considerable effort on the part of branch delegates to attend. In 1907, for instance, Joel Mehlomakulu from Herschel had to apply for a week's leave from his headmanship duties from the magistrate, travel a day-long journey on horse-back to Aliwal North and then catch a train from there to Queenstown.[10] Those districts that could not attend often sent messages of support. In a very real sense, peripheral local groups were linked by Congress to a political centre or 'black parliament' with access to the Cape government.

Working downwards the other way, Congress's roots extended to the very heart of local politics in all areas of the eastern Cape. For example, the committee of the Glen Grey Iliso Lomzi in 1906 consisted of 19 people, each representing a specific location, mission station or town in the district.[11] This network of new-style politics went back at least 20 years, as we have seen. Similarly, although the East London Iliso was primarily urban-based, representatives from outlying areas in the district took part in some of its meetings and served on joint committees.[12] Even if branches were weak and inactive, the SANC had access to virtually every area in the eastern Cape. Its organ, *Izwi Labantu*, facilitated this process of penetration. Its pages abounded with Congress and Iliso notices, instructions and reports. Organisational politics in the eastern Cape was in a very real sense based on an integrated framework extending throughout the region.

While the SANC articulated wider, national views, the routine activities of the affiliated Iiliso Lomzi revolved mainly around local issues in their various areas. These differed from place to place, reflecting particular concerns. In some areas, Iiliso emerged directly from local struggles. The Cape Town Iliso Lomzi, for instance, grew out of African resistance to forced removal from the town after the outbreak of bubonic plague, and became one of the most active branches in the SANC.[13] In general, the main preoccupations of the town-based Iiliso were matters related to the 'locations' where African residents lived. The Grahamstown Iliso, for example, brought to the notice of the town council the acute shortage of water in the location, the need for sanitation facilities and the curfew regulation.[14] The East London Iliso Lomzi, for its part, concerned itself with issues such as rents and taxes, education, prostitution, water supply, roads and the position of the location superintendent.[15] This work in East London was complemented by the representations made by respected SANC leaders like Walter Rubusana, who approached the town authorities on numerous occasions on behalf of the location residents.[16]

In rural areas, on the other hand, the priorities were different. In King William's Town, the district with the biggest African population in the eastern Cape, Iliso approached the magistrate for subsidised seed during the 1905 drought, while the Glen Grey Iliso expressed concern about the operation and modification of the Glen Grey Act.[17] In addition to these practical local matters, Iiliso also busied themselves with electoral politics and a broad range of social matters. The regular use of church facilities by the Iiliso and the prominent involvement of Iliso leaders in other spheres of community action help illustrate their rootedness in local communities.

Besides the strength it derived from its local bases, one of the most stabilising features of the SANC was the continuity in leadership. In 1903, seven of the thirteen members elected to the first executive committee a decade earlier, in 1892, were still in office.[18] There was very little change in the next ten years too, the only shake-up occurring in 1906 with the deposition of the vice-president, secretary and treasurer.[19] The first president, Thomas Mqanda, remained in office for an unbroken spell of over 20 years, while the founding secretary, Jonathan Tunyiswa, had his term of office broken only for a short time in 1906, when he fell into disfavour for ignoring Congress policy.[20]

There were three vice-presidents in the 1900s: James Pelem, Nathaniel Umhalla and James's younger brother, Meshach Pelem,* who after working at the diamond fields for ten years set himself up as a prosperous businessman in Queenstown, where he operated as a labour agent, boarding-house owner and general dealer.[21] In 1903 the executive was joined by Dr Walter Rubusana, the outstanding African politician of the early twentieth century.[22]

Both the ethnic origins of the SANC leaders and the venues where SANC conferences were held underline the fact that the Congress had a predominantly Rharhabe–Thembu base. Efforts were made in the 1900s

---

* In addition to Mqanda, Tunyiswa, Umhalla and James Pelem, surviving members of the first executive in 1903 were W.D. Soga (assistant secretary), Rob Mantsayi and Stephen Xo.

to extend this by forming branches in the heartlands of the Thembu (at Engcobo and Umtata) and of the Mpondo (at Lusikisiki and Ngqeleni), as well as in eastern Cape towns and the cities of Johannesburg, Kimberley and Cape Town. Noticeably under-represented in the organisational structure and among the office-bearers were the traditional Mfengu areas in Fingoland and along the old Ciskei frontier stretching from Peddie to Oxkraal near Queenstown. While there was not much active support for the SANC in the Mfengu communities, it nevertheless had some important connections here. The Mfengu chief Ebenezer Mhlambiso from the Amatole Basin attended meetings for several years. The religious separatist Pambani Mzimba, who came from the Alice district, also supported the Congress. In the Peddie district, SANC support centred on the locally influential Ben Tele and Thomas Mqanda himself, who was prominent as a headman in local politics.[23] Both were Mfengu. Individuals crossed lines to defy 'tribal' stereotypes. It was the policy of the Congress, like its rival, Jabavu's Imbumba, to overcome narrow affiliations and promote wider African and South African identities.

The SANC drew on the support of a wide cross-section of opinion-formers and leaders in the eastern Cape.* While school notables dominated the organisation, the expressed aim was also to draw in the 'natural leaders' of the people: traditional chiefs and their 'right hands' (councillors) and headmen.[24] Though a number of chiefs did take part in Congress activities, as we have seen, their involvement was mainly indirect. School people also acted as intermediaries for the chiefs. In 1903, for instance, James Pelem used his influence with J.X. Merriman to help persuade the government to relocate the Gcaleka chief Gwebinkumbi and his supporters, who were feeling the pinch of overcrowding and land shortage.[25] As this example reveals, the 'natural leaders' and the new educated elites acknowledged their mutual roles and collaborated to protect broad African interests.

* Influential local delegates, many active since the 1880s, included David Malasi, Thomas Zwedala, Chief Somerset Mlanjeni, Mankayi Rengqe, Sol Kalipa and Timothy Makiwane (Glen Grey/Thembuland); Joel Mehlomakulu, Plaatje Eland, Jeremiah Sikiti, the veteran Shad B. Mama, Jonas Goduka and Abram Parkies (Herschel); Eben Koti, Bryce Kota, R.B. Miliwana, James Balfour (Queenstown); Calvert Matyolo, Zachariah Sokopo (King William's Town); Peter Antoni, Thomas Nweba (East London); Robert Xholla and the Rev. George Nzungu (Grahamstown); Andrew Ross, Tobias Mvula (Port Elizabeth); and D.D. Tyakwadi and Charles Mbilini (Cape Town).

Ordinary 'red people' participated in some of the Iiliso, too. They were well represented, for instance, at meetings of the Nxaruni Iliso,[26] based at the St Luke's mission station at Newlands, near East London, among the Ndlambe. The mission had been started after Chief Mhala, father of Nathaniel, gave the Anglicans permission to work among his people in 1850.[27] An SANC spokesman at one of the Nxaruni meetings expressed pleasure at seeing 'red' and 'school' people combining and took up the theme of a lost independence when he declared: 'We say this land belongs to Ndlambe even though we are being governed by the whites. The Congress has been started so that all blacks may lodge their complaints to it. Rarabe died before he had gathered the black nation together. This meeting is for all blacks in South Africa. It is the mouth of the blacks to the government here and overseas.'[28] For these people there was a clear, natural line of continuity between traditional chiefly politics and the new forms of organisational politics that emerged from the 1880s onwards. This continuity was embodied in the active political career of Ndlambe's grandson, Chief Nathaniel Umhalla, and the involvement in the Nxaruni Iliso of the headman Umvallo, who had been a leading man at Newlands since the 1850s.[29]

More than 25 church ministers were actively involved in the SANC, not surprisingly, given the mission-school backgrounds of the new-style activists and the importance of Christianity to them. There were many separatists, including heads of churches, such as Jonas Goduka, Pambani Mzimba and James Dwane. Chalmers Nyombolo (AME Church), Kleinbooi Rasmeni (Order of Ethiopia) and the long-standing recording secretary and treasurer, Eben Koti (moderator of the South African Native Baptist Association), all served on the SANC executive, together with Dr Rubusana and other mainstream church ministers.[30]

On the whole, then, the SANC embraced and accommodated an important cross-section of African public opinion in the eastern Cape. Though it did not become a powerful force in colonial politics, within African society it strove to unite into a common front disparate, unconnected local forces and it came to represent the ideas of African consciousness, assertion and unity. The constitution of the Congress set out its objective as being 'to protect the rights of the native people in such matters as (a) land tenure (b) education and religion (c) political rights (d) election of members of parliament (e) registration of voters and other matters referring to their status as British subjects'.[31] This objective it strove to achieve in all kinds of ways. In its meetings, petitions and deputations it covered the whole gamut of issues affecting Africans in the early part of the twentieth century. These included specific government measures such as the extension of the Glen Grey system; broad South African issues such as the South African Native Affairs Commission, the 1906 Natal disturbances, responsible government in the former republics, and Union; the attitudes, responsibilities and actions of the Imperial government; colonial and African politics in general; and social issues, including education.[32]

For several years the SANC's main concern was the Queen Victoria Memorial Scheme for a college or university for African higher education. This was launched at the SANC annual conference in September 1902. By assuming control of the higher education movement, which had occupied the popular imagination for several years, the SANC put itself in the forefront of 'national' politics. An 18-person-strong committee* was formed under the *Izwi* editor, A.K. Soga, and the Rev. Elijah Mqoboli, a Wesleyan minister based in Queenstown.[33] As we shall see, the African challenge in the educational field forced the Cape government to consider providing facilities for higher education for Africans so as to absorb and moderate the assertive African-led churches and social movements that had emerged.

The Queen Victoria Memorial Scheme likewise confirms the SANC's essentially African consciousness and orientation. The Congress was also much more of a national body than an adjunct of colonial politics. Electoral politics was just one of many key issues it faced. Though the SANC expressed support for the Progressives and their allies, and *Izwi* consistently maintained a highly partisan party-political line, party and electoral politics were of small concern at the SANC annual conferences. Electoral issues were left to the newspapers, local groups and leaders acting

---

* The other members of the committee were S.T. Mdliva, J.Z. Tantsi, P.S. Lusaseni, J.W. Sondlo, T. Zwedala, C. Nyombolo, S.B. Mama, W.F. Bassie, James Pelem, Plaatje Eland, E.K. Ndobe, S. Nkume, J. Tunyiswa, D. Ketse, R.B. Kota and Boyce Kota. There was also an advisory committee consisting of N.C. Umhalla, E. Mhlambiso, W.B. Rubusana, P.K. Kawa, C.C. Madosi, R. Mantsayi, W.D. Soga, W. Philip, A.H. Maci and Z. Sokopo.

in their individual capacities. The last-mentioned displayed considerable flexibility and independence. In the 1904 election, for instance, James Pelem, the SANC vice-president, who in the 1890s had been a strong supporter of Rhodes and the Progressives, worked on an expenses-paid basis for John X. Merriman, his old foe Jabavu's political champion in the South African Party, against his old colleague in Glen Grey, David Malasi.[34] The fact that other prominent SAP supporters like J.T. Jabavu's brother Jonathan were involved with the SANC at the same time strengthens the argument that the Congress was a national rather than a party-political body.[35] Though SANC leaders generally were staunch Progressives, party politics was an indirect concern of theirs. Changing governments did not dramatically alter the position of Africans in Cape society.

Congress support for both the independent education and church movements (as well as its desire to act as a representative platform for African opinion) reflected its proto-nationalist consciousness, aims and nature. While this was an organisation modelled on colonial counterparts, it sought to be independent of colonial control and its activities were not only the result of African agency, but were sustained by it. The magistrate at Lady Frere reported in a telling (probably exaggerated) way on a Queen Victoria Memorial Scheme meeting held by Dr Rubusana of the SANC in that district: 'Rev. Rubusana was the chief spokesman and, in the course of his address to the natives, stated that the time had arrived when the natives of South Africa must throw off all European control and that the aim of the natives should be that the Magistrates, Missionaries, Inspectors etc. should all be natives. With the exception of the Mt Arthur (mission) people the natives all approved of this step. A further meeting is to be held shortly, but owing to the sedition spoken at the last meeting the Missionary has refused them the use of his church.'[36]

In sum, there was a deep-seated African consciousness evident in the religious, educational and political spheres in the early years of the twentieth century, and the SANC was, organisationally, the primary standard-bearer of this tradition in southern Africa at the time.

33

Transkei organisations
and Bhunga politics

... the Natives of the Transkei, free, true, and loyal subjects of
His Majesty, have been hindered and discouraged while holding
meetings to expand civilisation amongst themselves. We have a
good sprinkling of registered voters and it is quite time we started
to help ourselves. Our Native brethren in the Colony have their
associations which are recognised by the government and we are
quite as advanced and loyal as they are.

    – Enoch Mamba, Transkei Native Vigilance Association, 1902

In the Transkeian Territories a distinct new African voice,
speaking in a more uniform way for a wider constituency, emerged during
the first decade of the twentieth century. An important reason for this was
the extension of the Council system from the five southern districts to the
rest of the Transkei. Under a proclamation of 1903 seven more districts
– Engcobo, Mount Fletcher, Mqanduli, Qumbu, Tsolo, Umtata and
Umzimkulu – were included and a Transkeian Territories General Council,
superseding the Transkei General Council, was created to accommodate
them. The Bhunga headquarters were moved from Butterworth to Umtata,
shifting the focus of Transkeian politics northwards. In the next few years
the districts of Willowvale, Elliotdale, Mount Ayliff and St Mark's were
also incorporated, thus bringing, by 1909, a total of 16 districts into a
single administrative structure, covering an area the size of Switzerland
with some 560,000 people living there.[1]

The enlarged Bhunga became an important forum for African opinion, accepted, even if through necessity, both within African society and by the authorities, particularly after 1906 when greater popular representation was allowed by making ratepayers other than headmen eligible to become members.[2] Grafted on to the local administrative structure of magistrates and headmen, which in turn had largely been grafted onto the pre-colonial system of governance, the Bhunga came to house the most influential political communicators in the areas under its jurisdiction. These included important Mfengu, Gcaleka and Ngqika spokesmen from the southern Transkei, who had been involved since the inauguration of the Council system in the 1890s, among them Veldtman Bikitsha, Menziwe Luzipho, Lambata Mgidi, Matumbu Sigidi and Kondile Tokwe. Other Council members included hereditary chiefdom leaders like the Thembu paramount Dalindyebo, Zibi of the Hlubi and the Tlokwa chief Scanlen Lehana.[3] By 1904 some ten of the 'principal tribes' of the Transkei were represented. The chief magistrate noted two years later that the General Council was developing a broader supra-tribal unity: 'while early proceedings disclosed the Council as an aggregation of tribes rather than 33 individuals, and while still the influence of tribal association and traditional leadership holds strong, yet as the time passes these characteristics stand out less boldly and members imperceptibly grow used to form their opinions with greater indifference to distinctions which are felt to be no longer radical and with distinguishing subservience to the vote of their paramount chiefs.'[4]

Although Zibi, nephew of the Natal chief Langalibalele,[5] and Lehana, grandson of Sekonyela, at first resisted the extension of the Council system to their areas, tightening colonial control left them with no other option than to participate if they wished to retain their status and local control. Considerable anti-Council agitation also took place in Mount Fletcher and the neighbouring districts of Qumbu, Tsolo and Umzimkulu,[6] but ultimately the locals had to bow to the inevitable. In its own way, the extension of the Council system heightened political feelings and stimulated constitutional politics.

Where the Council system had become established, lobby or pressure groups emerged, seeking access to the new centre of power in the Transkei. These were modelled on the prototypical organisations which had developed throughout the eastern Cape since the 1880s. They were mostly led by and articulated the interests of the educated class, who sought to counterbalance the influence of chiefs and headmen in the councils. The most conspicuous of these groups was the Transkei Native Vigilance Association, led by Enoch Mamba, an influential figure in the Idutywa district.[7] He had been a member of both the Idutywa District Council and the Transkei General Council until his dismissal as headman in 1896 for his part in attempting to have the local magistrate removed.[8]

In the early 1900s, after returning to Idutywa following an absence of some years, he began to seek a new power base and set about 're-forming' the moribund local Iliso Lomzi, which had existed in Idutywa in the mid-1890s.[9] The aim of the new Iliso was to represent Transkeian Africans generally. In November 1901 Mamba convened a meeting of Transkeian people to promote Iliso, as well as a proposed African trading company that Paul Xiniwe of King William's Town was trying to set up for eastern Cape Africans.[10] People from no less than 23 localities in the Fingoland districts and Kentani and Willowvale attended.[11] Familiar names mentioned in the newspaper report included Pato Lusaseni, Patrick Xabanisa, Joseph Mazamisa, James and Paul Madubela, and W.F. Bassie.[12] Early in 1902 Mamba and the Iliso's secretary, William Richard Ntloko, a teacher from the Nqamakwe district, made a tour of the southern Transkei to gauge public opinion and consolidate the organisation.[13] The result was that the new Transkeian Iliso or Transkei Native Vigilance Association gained branches in Butterworth, Nqamakwe, Tsomo and Kentani – all districts under the Transkei General Council at the time.[14]

Though the branches of the TNVA went by the same name, Iliso Lomzi, as those of the South African Native Congress, the two bodies had no formal ties. This was simply a common designation for local vigilance associations. The two bodies in fact clashed in 1903, when Mamba and Veldtman Bikitsha were invited to give evidence before a parliamentary committee on the Glen Grey Act. The SANC challenged their credentials and asked that it be given the responsibility of selecting witnesses on such occasions.[15] Mamba retorted in the press, 'Who are these men? Most of them live in native locations in town and want to dictate to the officials in the Transkei as to what men they think are representative ... We have no member in their congress, we do not hold that they represent us.'[16]

The vigilance associations in Fingoland appear to have been relatively active in the 1900s, certainly if the Nqamakwe Iliso was any indicator. It met regularly throughout the decade.[17] By 1910 it was confident enough to send a deputation to Umtata to demand the transfer of the local magistrate to another district.[18] Members were spread throughout the district and many were not voters. The leadership constituted an alliance* between the most influential local teachers, such as Pato Lusaseni, James Mateza and Patrick Xabanisa of Blythswood, and peasant farmers, who included several headmen.[19] One of the members was Skelewu Mbeki, father of Govan and grandfather of Thabo and Moeletsi.

The TNVA, which had 'a good sprinkling of registered voters' in its ranks,[20] sought to obtain an input for 'advanced' people in the district councils. Mamba complained that the councils were unrepresentative and dominated by headmen, who were mostly 'illiterate red heathens with no civilised aims, troubling themselves mostly about the enlargement of their own locations and their importance'.[21] He claimed that if the appointment of the councillors was in the hands of the ratepayers, rather than the headmen, a better feeling would exist in favour of the Glen Grey Act. Expanding on this, he said:

Most of the headmen were less enlightened Natives. In almost every location you will find a man who is more intelligent than the Headman, who has been better educated; and the interests of education and general progress have been neglected because these Headmen are not able to give us assistance in that direction. And so we found that we should establish an Association which would both help the Natives in the district, and teach them a little more of politics, a little more of agriculture, a little more of farming.[22]

Although Mamba tried repeatedly to gain official recognition for his body, and emphasised that the TNVA was not antagonistic to the government

---

* Among the people involved were Henry Shosha, Josiah Binase, Jacob Mvinjelwa, Mafa Mgidi, Chief R. Dudumashe and Chief Solomon Zazela, the oldest headman in the district. The first three were members of the General Council in the 1900s. Other educationists included James B. Luti, Bennie Mahlasela, J.S. Tshainca and Anthony Soyizwapi. All were prominent in the Transkei Teachers' Association. By 1910 Xabanisa had left teaching and become a prosperous farmer and entrepreneur.

or, in principle, to the Council system, it met with official hostility.[23] In the authorities' view, the Council system afforded Africans ample means of voicing their opinions and safeguarding their interests.[24]

With the extension of the Council system in 1903, the Transkeian Iliso accordingly changed its English designation from the Transkei Native Vigilance Association to the Transkeian Territories African Union (TTAU) and tried to expand into the new council districts. A meeting of a body with that name was held in the Tsomo district in April 1905 to discuss the report of the South African Native Affairs Commission.[25] In January 1906 a branch of the TTAU was started by African 'registered voters and others' in the Matatiele and Mount Fletcher districts.[26] Around the same time *Imvo* reported a successful meeting of the 'Transkeian Iliso Lomzi' in the Nqamakwe district.[27] In 1908 Mamba was still petitioning the Prime Minister on behalf of some of 'the leading and most influential Native registered voters in the Transkeian Territories'.[28] And the following year he drew a huge audience as guest speaker at a meeting of the Nqamakwe Iliso Lomzi on the subject of the Council system.[29] The organisational co-operation throughout the Transkei that Mamba initiated outside the Council system seems to have continued through to Union. It was really a continuation of the pattern of politics that had emerged in the Transkei in the 1880s and 1890s.

Eventually, Mamba and a number of important mission-educated leaders succeeded in getting the foothold they sought in the Transkeian Territories General Council. For some years after its inauguration in 1903, the Rev. Benjamin Mazwi and Simon Peter Gasa were government-nominated councillors. Then in 1904, after representations to the government,[30] Mamba was reinstated as headman and was soon back in both the District and General Council.[31] After 1906, when a more popular system of representation was introduced, influential spokesmen like Patrick Xabanisa, James Mateza and S. Milton Ntloko also gained places on the General Council. The result, the chief magistrate noted, was a definite improvement in qualifications and standards. Moreover, 'several of the new members show a quick perception of facts and principles, debating power, and a keen interest in recent administration, especially where touching questions of finance'.[32]

A delegation representing Natal Africans observed at the time that 'the comparatively well-educated and thrifty Fingoes form a constant stimulus to the more ignorant and backward Xosas, Tembus and Bacas'.[33] All the representatives mentioned here were Mfengu, and they played a leading role in the proceedings of the General Council. Xabanisa and Ntloko proposed a successful motion to grant £10,000 to the Inter-State Native College Scheme.[34] Mamba and Xabanisa also initiated a petition to the Governor, protesting about the colour bar in the draft South Africa Act.[35] In this way the boundaries between Council politics and wider constitutional politics outside became blurred. Not only did educated political figures and non-literate chiefs and headmen combine in the councils, but they also addressed the same issues as the political organisations. Moreover, a number of chiefs and headmen in the councils were involved with local vigilance associations as well. Dalindyebo was a patron of the Umtata Iliso,[36] and Tiyo Njikelana was active in the Qumbu Iliso, which had been started by 1911.[37] Once again, these are examples of the regular alliances and co-operation between the chiefdom authorities, headmen and the educated elite in the new forms of western-style constitutional politics.

Electoral politics provided another area of political activity in the Transkei. As we have seen, the region was divided into the two widely spread constituencies of Griqualand East and Thembuland. The most extensive electoral activity occurred in the latter. In 1902 the number of African voters here stood at 785 out of a total of 2789,[38] with the biggest concentration, roughly two-thirds, in the non-council districts of Cala and St Mark's in the south-west.[39] The focus of these voters was directed more towards Cape colonial politics and the organisational activities there: Cala landowners resisted all attempts to incorporate them into the Council system. They wanted instead a divisional council based on the model of those in the colony, which would recognise their private ownership of land.[40] It was only in 1925 that they were eventually incorporated into the General Council.[41]

The number of voters in the four Fingoland districts stood at 138 in 1902. All but 10 were Mfengu.[42] These voters probably formed the nucleus of the Transkeian Iliso Lomzi,[43] and it was probably on their behalf that Mamba, in 1908, requested the government to exempt Transkeian

African voters from certain laws in the same way as their counterparts in the colony proper.[44] The other 133 voters were scattered throughout this extensive constituency, which included Umtata and the coastal regions up to western Pondoland. The size of the African vote in this part of the Transkei resulted in considerable electoral interest and organisation.[45] In 1910, when delimitation under the new Union electoral system added 504 African voters from Glen Grey to the constituency, bringing the numbers of Africans to 1294 out of a total of 2846,[46] the Thembuland voters made history by returning Walter Rubusana to the Cape Provincial Council. Rubusana thus became the first, and up to 1994, the only African to hold an elected legislative position in South Africa.[47]

34

Higher education
and the future

... when we have education, I think we should have it for a certain object. If a person wants to be a teacher, he must study for that purpose, and if he wants to become anything else, he should study with that end in view. We are accused of having a little education, which is spoiling us, and yet ... even the Government has set a standard which does not enable the Native to reach that point in education which will not spoil him. And in regard to industrial education, it is only training to go and plough the ground and sow seed. Every Native knows how to plough ground, and to sow seed.
                                    – Native Vigilance Association of the
                                              Orange River Colony, 1904

After the war, the politics of reconstruction in British South Africa was guided by one clear objective: the consolidation of the various colonies into one white-ruled country. As part of this initiative, the South African Native Affairs Commission was set up to arrive at a common 'native policy' for the whole of South Africa. When its report was issued in April 1905, Africans were quick to criticise its findings. Probably the most outspoken critic was the South African Native Congress (SANC), which rejected the Commission's proposed policy of segregation. But there was also a particular reason for the Congress's hostility towards the report. In it, the Commission proposed a scheme for a central college for African higher education similar to the SANC's Queen Victoria Memorial Scheme, which had been initiated in 1902.[1] The new Inter-State Native College

Scheme got off the ground at the end of 1905, a few months after the Commission had reported, and it soon overshadowed the SANC's project. Tensions arose as a result, particularly when J.T. Jabavu, the SANC's old nemesis, assumed a leading role in the new initiative.

Although it was directed mainly by whites and backed by the Cape government, Africans from all the colonies enthusiastically supported the Inter-State College proposal.[2] On the other hand, support for the Queen Victoria Scheme remained restricted mainly to SANC supporters. They could not compete in terms of organisation and resources with their opponents, who enjoyed the patronage of influential colonial figures and the support of the government. Key organisers of the Queen Victoria Scheme were also otherwise tied down. The convener, A.K. Soga, was engaged in writing a large book on 'The problem of the relations of black and white in South Africa' in addition to editing *Izwi*; the secretary, E.J. Mqoboli, was transferred to Cape Town by his church; and Walter Rubusana was away in England for an extended period in connection with the publication of a new Xhosa Bible.[3] Though the SANC tried to counter the Inter-State College Scheme by expressing reservations about its denominational bias and claiming it had not originated among Africans, this did little to stop the momentum.[4]

The Inter-State College Scheme grew from strength to strength. Jabavu enthusiastically supported the idea and was soon involved in its implementation.[5] Acting together with his business partner James Weir, the Lovedale school authorities and local African leaders in King William's Town, he helped arrange a convention at Lovedale in December 1905 to discuss the scheme.[6] The fact that it was referred to as the Mbumba convention was more than just a passing coincidence.[7] It was attended by more than 150 delegates from all over the eastern Cape as well as Basutoland and the Transvaal. It asked the governments of the various colonies to adopt the recommendations of the Native Affairs Commission and appointed a committee to help collect funds.[8] The committee, under the chairmanship of Weir, included such political and community heavyweights as Jabavu, Isaac Wauchope, John Knox Bokwe, James Dwane and, surprisingly, in view of their SANC affiliations, Nathaniel Umhalla and Jonathan Tunyiswa.[9]

The ensuing campaign for the Inter-State Native College aroused eastern Cape society. Supported by a propaganda fund of £500, the committee, and in particular Jabavu, who became the paid travelling secretary, addressed meetings in every part of the region. Usually presided over by the local magistrate or other prominent colonists or missionaries,[10] they were attended by hundreds of people, including, on official instructions, the local chiefs and headmen in addition to the educated class.[11] Fuelled by the newspapers and churches, the higher education scheme became a primary issue among the eastern Cape school people. In the first year or so of the campaign, Africans guaranteed a total of £40,000, more than double the sum initially estimated by the organisers.[12] The level of organisation can be gauged from the fact that by 1908 'native committees' existed in 47 magisterial districts in the eastern Cape and Transkei, and that traditional bodies such as the Basutoland National Council, political organisations such as the Transvaal Basuto Committee and the Transvaal and Orange River Colony Native Congresses, and other African newspapers also gave support.[13] A second major convention was held at Lovedale in 1908, which helped further consolidate Jabavu's networks.

The co-ordinators of the Inter-State College Scheme soon tried to absorb the SANC's project. But at a special conference called in Queenstown in July 1906 to consider future strategy, the SANC decided to persevere with its own scheme, while maintaining a friendly attitude towards its rival.[14] The Congress decided on an aggressive plan of action to resuscitate its plan. The Rev. Eben Koti, general secretary of a separatist Baptist Church, replaced Mqoboli as secretary, and leading figures like Dr Rubusana travelled around the country to drum up support.[15] But the efforts were in vain. The Queen Victoria Memorial Scheme faded and quietly expired.

There were two reasons why the SANC stuck doggedly to the Queen Victoria Scheme. Firstly, the chief African proponent of the Inter-State College was the organisation's main political rival and the competition between the two schemes inevitably acquired a political dimension.[16] The rivalry also had an important ideological dimension. It became yet another battle between the more pronounced Africanist tendencies represented by the SANC and the separatist churches, on the one hand, and the moderate assimilationism represented most conspicuously by Jabavu and the old guard, including Makiwane, Wauchope and Bokwe.[17]

The SANC's support for both the independent education and church movements (as well as its desire to act as a representative platform for African opinion) reflected its proto-nationalist consciousness, aims and nature. Though modelled on colonial counterparts, it sought to be independent of colonial control and its activities were not only initiated by African agency, but sustained by it. The Congress and the separatist movements represented the same kind of expression of Africanism, in different spheres. In 1906 it was described by Isaiah Bud Mbelle, the early architect of the Queen Victoria Memorial Scheme before it was taken over by the Congress, as 'an anti-white man campaign (à la Rubusana)' and also the 'alter ego' of Ethiopianism. 'Both use mischievous propaganda,' he declared.[18]

The Inter-State educational initiative gave Jabavu a strong platform and power base, enabling him to recover from setbacks since the time of the South African War, when forced closure of *Imvo* by the military authorities had hurt him both financially and politically. He was now back leading public opinion with a scheme that captured the popular imagination and brought about the most intense mobilisation of the eastern Cape elite up to that time.

With *Imvo* in circulation again, Jabavu could resume his political role as spokesman for a section of African opinion in the eastern Cape who were loosely grouped in the Imbumba movement. Initially, Imbumba was not a formal organisation in the same sense as the SANC, though it was rather more than just the odd conference called by Jabavu when he deemed the occasion fit. There seems to have been some structure of recognised leaders who worked closely with Jabavu and provided continuity and depth. Leaders of the local groups which had been involved with the Imbumba conferences in the 1890s – men such as Isaac Wauchope from Fort Beaufort, S. Milton Ntloko from Tsomo and John Sishuba from Oxkraal – continued to be intimately involved in organisational ventures with Jabavu until after Union. Writing in 1912, 'as one connected with the

Imbumba for a number of years and holding office of its secretaryship', Ntloko mentioned that in 1905 an attempt had been made to amalgamate Imbumba and the Congress, but 'after some lengthy correspondence between ourselves the attempt resulted in status quo'.[19] Thus, a loosely constituted Imbumba group did exist, reflecting the divisions in eastern Cape African politics in an organisational form as well. Despite frequent statements by both sides about the need for unity and co-operation, the gap between the two camps remained unbridgeable and the Imbumba group under Jabavu continued on a separate course.[20]

After the war, the first major opportunity for Jabavu to position himself politically was the general election of 1904. Once again, he and his main allies advised Africans to vote for the South African Party against the Progressives, who had the support of *Izwi* and the SANC. As usual, he campaigned extensively in the field and through his newspaper. After a tour through various constituencies, no less a person than the Prime Minister, Dr Jameson, was compelled to follow in his footsteps in order to neutralise his influence. Jabavu was in fact asked by the Afrikaner Bond to stand for parliament in the Fort Beaufort constituency, but he declined the invitation, saying that he had already committed himself to a candidate in the field.[21]

The Inter-State Native College Scheme presented Jabavu with a golden opportunity to enhance his stature as the most influential missionary-educated African in South Africa. The scheme virtually became synonymous with his name and *Imvo* became its mouthpiece. On completion the College was regarded by many as *i koliji ka Jabavu* (Jabavu's college).[22] As we have seen, the scheme had both political and ideological implications. The competition between it and the Queen Victoria Memorial Scheme intensified the tussle between Jabavu and the SANC. Politically, the Inter-State Scheme's success was achieved to the detriment of the SANC. It undermined the SANC's authority and precipitated a minor crisis within its ranks. Its vice-president, Umhalla, and its secretary, Tunyiswa, were among the King William's Town people who helped Jabavu get the Inter-State College Scheme under way and they became members of the scheme's committee. For this breach of loyalty, Umhalla was voted out of office at the SANC's 1906 annual conference. He duly left the SANC and extended his co-operation with his old rival Jabavu to the political sphere. Because he was to all intents and purposes the founder of the SANC, Tunyiswa was only temporarily suspended.[23]

In the ten years it took before reaching fruition, the College Scheme remained Jabavu's main passion. Though it was becalmed somewhat from 1908, when the various colonial governments decided to leave the issue until after political unification, it gained new life once Union had come about. Further conventions of its African supporters were held at Bloemfontein in 1912 and 1913.[24] By then, African public opinion in South Africa, as well as the various African newspapers and political organisations, was hugely in favour. The scheme eventually reached fruition when the South African Native College, the present-day University of Fort Hare, was founded in February 1916.[25] From the start, Jabavu was on the governing Council and in time his son D.D.T. Jabavu became a lecturer there.[26] Fort Hare is perhaps Jabavu's most lasting and substantial memorial.

The contested higher education schemes of the mid-1900s were a sign not only of the increasing co-operation across borders among the new generation of political activists in the African communities, but also of the inexorable movement towards political centralisation in southern Africa after the war.

Two events pushed the issue of political unification to the forefront, in line with Britain's ultimate strategic goal of consolidating its control over the subcontinent and its immense mineral wealth: the issuing of the South African Native Affairs Commission report of 1905 and the granting of responsible government to the Transvaal and Orange River Colony in 1906. Within a few years the congeries of pre-colonial chiefdoms and colonial states that had emerged in the course of the nineteenth century would finally be welded together to create a new country. The formal trigger for this envisaged federation was the release of the so-called Selborne Memorandum in 1907.

PART FOUR

UNIFICATION

35

'Closer Union' and
the Queenstown Conference, 1907

When we remember that those people who are shouting so loudly
for federation are the same gentry (the capitalists) who ... strove
to upset the orderly legislation of half a century and to throw the
native franchise to the dogs ... – woe betide the people ... Unless
some miracle happens to fend off federation under their auspices,
... this will be a glorious country for corporation pythons and
political puff-adders, forced labour and commercial despotism, but
no fit place for freemen to live in.

– A.K. Soga, *Izwi Labantu*, July 1907

The initiative in transforming the concept of federation from a
vague aspiration into a concrete goal to unify the South African colonies
was taken by members of the Milner Kindergarten. This group of talented
young imperialists had been brought out by Sir Alfred Milner after the
South African War to fill key posts in the four colonial administrations, and
continued to serve under Lord Selborne after Milner's departure in 1905.
One of the group, Richard Feetham, took the first step when he argued in
a paper read in October 1906 that a definite start should be made towards
the consummation of union. He gave several reasons for this, which rested
mainly on the contention that union was the best means of consolidating
Imperial control in South Africa and ensuring economic stability.

The other Kindergarten members agreed with Feetham's analysis and gave
their full support to the Closer Union movement. Lionel Curtis resigned from
his post in government to devote himself fully to this idea. After touring the

various colonies he drew up a draft memorandum in conjunction with his colleagues, arguing the case for union. The memorandum was then handed to Lord Selborne, who shared the Kindergarten's enthusiasm. It was agreed that to have maximum effect the memorandum should be published under the authority of the High Commissioner, but to minimise the impression of Imperial interference the support of colonial politicians should be enlisted. Curtis therefore approached Dr Jameson, the Prime Minister of the Cape, who became a willing ally.[1] Accordingly, the Cape government brought to the attention of the Governor the multiplicity of problems caused by the continued division of South Africa into various colonies and recommended that he ask Lord Selborne in his capacity as High Commissioner to review the general situation in South Africa with a view to creating public awareness of the desirability of a united South Africa.[2] When approached, the governments of the other colonies concurred.[3]

In January 1907 Curtis's memorandum, modified slightly by Lord Selborne, was sent to the various colonial governments.[4] At the next session of the Cape parliament in July, the Selborne Memorandum was tabled by Jameson. This was followed by a successful motion by F.S. Malan that the Cape government should approach its counterparts in the other colonies during the recess to consider taking preliminary steps towards union.[5] Malan was a prominent member of the Afrikaner Bond, who had himself come out as a strong advocate of federation in a series of six articles in *Ons Land*, the newspaper of which he was editor.[6] The Selborne Memorandum was then published and widely distributed, and federation, the term loosely used at this stage to describe the scheme for closer union, became a burning public issue.[7]

The Selborne Memorandum played carefully on the sentiments of South African colonists. It was directed to the white inhabitants of the various colonies and emphasised that no enduring federation could be formed unless it emanated from them. Until they united they would not realise their full potential or enjoy the full freedom of self-government. Unity would bring political, economic and industrial stability. It would also help defuse what whites saw as the potentially dangerous 'native question'. 'All South Africans are agreed,' declared Selborne, 'that the native question is at once the most important and the most profoundly difficult question which confronts themselves and their children; but by the perpetuation of five or six totally different native administrations and policies, they are doing all that is in their power to make the question more grave and the problem more difficult.'[8] He did not elaborate on what form a uniform 'native policy' should take.

Though it was directed at whites, Africans were not slow to respond to the Selborne Memorandum. The various African newspapers examined the issues involved and a conference was specially convened to air opinions about federation. When the Selborne Memorandum was made public, *Ilanga* published several editorials on the question. The newspaper urged the Imperial government to refrain from handing over the Africans to a not 'very scrupulous white autocracy'. It feared that a powerful Afrikaner caucus, which could not be relied on to 'hold the scales of justice', would eventually dominate the federal parliament.[9] At the same time *Ilanga* posed the question whether Cape Africans, the only Africans in South Africa who had the right to vote, were aware of the implications of federation: 'we may ask do they know how important the matter is? Do they know what it means to them and their fellow countrymen? We should like to see evidence in the *Izwi Labantu* and *Imvo* as to the extent of their knowledge. For we fear they are somewhere in the clouds concerning it; and who shall say what their courage is when they do know?'[10]

Ilanga's fears were not unfounded in respect of *Imvo*. The latter's response to the Selborne Memorandum and the concomitant question of federation was at first strangely non-committal. Except for a few passing references, it hardly mentioned the issue until mid-October when the Cape general elections approached. Replying to reports of hostile utterances against the Cape franchise by politicians in the Orange River Colony, *Imvo* declared, 'With Federation looming large gentlemen are required [in the election] who are convinced supporters of the moderate and just Native policy of the Cape, otherwise we are undone.'[11] Shortly afterwards, *Imvo* published correspondence between F.S. Malan, one of the prime movers of federation, and John Sishuba, an influential African electoral agent for the South African Party (SAP), to counter Progressive Party election propaganda in the Transkei. Sishuba wrote to Malan that rumours were being circulated by the Progressives that the Afrikaner Bond would remove liberal allies of the Bond in the SAP, such as J.X. Merriman and J.W. Sauer, from positions of power as soon as it assumed office, and that they would install a Prime Minster who would support moves to disenfranchise Africans at the proposed inter-colonial conference on federation. Malan's own attitude to federation and his position on the franchise for Africans were also being questioned by many, Sishuba remarked.[12]

In reply Malan said that he had always been in favour of the traditional Cape 'native policy'. When the question of Closer Union was discussed he would do his best to defend the Cape franchise. In presenting these views, Malan said he was confident that he was voicing the opinion of the great majority of Bond and SAP supporters.[13]

Malan's statements were enthusiastically welcomed by Jabavu, who explained his virtual silence hitherto on the question of federation by arguing that the issue seemed to him a question of high politics, far above the level of Africans, who, whether they liked it or not, could no more affect the process than 'the proverbial fly on the wheel, trying to stop the wagon from going forward'.[14] This was a rather uncharacteristic utterance on Jabavu's part, but it was not far out in its description of the ineffectualness of Africans in being able to influence the move towards federation at that stage.

In contrast, *Izwi*, the vociferous mouthpiece of the South African Native Congress (SANC), expressed itself strongly on federation, probably more so than any of the other African newspapers. In keeping with his newly articulated socialist interpretation of events, the editor, A.K. Soga, described the federation movement as part of a grand design for a capitalist-dominated South Africa, controlled by Rand magnates. He expanded on this theme in an editorial subtitled 'People vs capitalists'.

We hear a good deal about federation and Lord Selborne is being applauded to the skies for his interesting historical contribution to the scheme, but then we remember that those people who are shouting so loudly for federation are the same gentry (the capitalists) who attempted to steal a march on the Cape Constitution to further their own ends; who set up spurious Labour Commissions; who shouted the glories of the Chinese from the housetops; and who showed us how a country could be redeemed by a Native Affairs Commission which strove to upset the orderly legislation of half a century and to throw the native franchise to the dogs, and which is driving honest white workers out to Australia and elsewhere. We feel ... sure that if federation was to come in on their pretensions – woe betide the people ... These land and other sharks hold all the public resources and utilise them as the trump card in this great game of gamble, scramble and beggar-my-neighbour which is dignified with the name of government. Unless some miracle happens to fend off federation under their auspices, ... this will be a glorious country for corporation pythons and political puff-adders, forced labour and commercial despotism, but no fit place for freemen to live in.[15]

The question of federation was raised at the annual conference of the SANC in August 1907, but owing to 'pressure of time' it was not discussed and left to the executive to handle.[16] SANC leaders like Soga and Dr Rubusana followed this up by publishing a 'Call to Conference' under the auspices of *Izwi*. In a prominent notice, the newspaper invited 62 African and (what is significant) coloured leaders, representing various interest groups in the Cape, to meet at a conference in Queenstown to decide on a united plan of action. Unity was essential to counter the forthcoming attack on the constitutional rights of black citizens in the Cape, the attempts to keep Africans in the other colonies excluded from political representation, and the unconstitutional measures used in these colonies to hold them in lasting servitude under oppressive class legislation. *Izwi* suggested that the conference frame a manifesto to which parliamentary candidates in African and coloured constituencies would be expected to adhere in the forthcoming elections, and which they would pledge themselves to apply if elected to parliament. The manifesto would deal with the matter of federation, the franchise and other issues.[17]

In the event, the Queenstown Conference, which was held on 27 and 28 November 1907, was attended by over 80 delegates from 29 towns throughout the Cape Colony.[18] The conference was a landmark in African politics for two reasons. Firstly, it was an attempt to end the factional nature of African politics in the Cape by forming a broad alliance, including all politically active Africans, to face the challenges of union. Secondly, formal co-operation with coloured politicians took place for the first time. The African Political Organisation (APO) – the first coloured political organisation of importance to emerge in South Africa – was prominently represented, having decided at its annual conference in Port Elizabeth to accept the invitation to attend.[19]

Given the gulf which hitherto had generally existed between African and coloured politicians, the joint conference of 1907 was a decisive moment in the evolution of a united black front against white domination. Previously, the APO had made clear distinctions between coloured people and Africans. Its leader, Dr Abdurahman, had himself on occasion referred to Africans as 'barbarous natives'.[20] In its vigorous lobbying for an extension of the franchise to coloured people in the ex-republics under responsible government, the APO had been content to leave Africans disenfranchised.[21] For their part, African leaders also held reservations about forming alliances with coloured people. John Dube, for instance, with his strong sense of Zulu identity, once wrote, 'I am as jealous of the purity of the black race as the Anglo-Saxon is of his.'[22] Regional separation also militated against co-operation. In time, however, common disabilities gradually drew the leaders of these communities closer. It took the shock of Vereeniging, responsible government and the threat of union to bring them together.

The Queenstown Conference was not attended by J.T. Jabavu. Once again he shunned the opportunity to join in a broad alliance with other sections of the African political elite. His refusal to co-operate brought criticism from several quarters and bitter condemnation from *Izwi*.[23] It must be said, however, that it would have required a magnanimous gesture on Jabavu's part for him to participate in a project sponsored by inveterate rivals to his newspaper, to his favoured political party and to his pet educational scheme, the Inter-State Native College. The *Izwi*–SANC group was constantly trying to undermine his personal appeal, and he their growing stature. Indeed, his failure to discern evolving trends in African politics and his stubbornness in refusing to co-operate with other African politicians would eventually lead to his political downfall.

Besides Dr Abdurahman and a number of APO members from as far afield as Cape Town, Kimberley and Port Elizabeth, the list of delegates included a large group of SANC stalwarts like Dr Rubusana, Meshach Pelem, Jonathan Tunyiswa, Thomas Mqanda and, of course, A.K. Soga.

340

Silas Molema travelled from Bechuanaland as the personal representative of Badirile Montsioa, the Rolong paramount. Other notable figures included Jonas Goduka, head of the African Native Mission Church, and S.E.K. Mqhayi, then part-time editor of *Imvo*. Apologies were received from F.Z.S. Peregrino, editor of the *South African Spectator*, and Enoch Mamba of the Transkei Native Vigilance Association, as well as P.J. Mzimba, moderator of the Presbyterian Church of Africa.[24] The Transvaal Native Congress vice-president and another delegate from the colony signalled their intention to attend and requested the convener to forward rail tickets, but did not arrive.[25]

A host of prominent Jabavu and SAP supporters followed Jabavu's lead in rejecting the 'Call to Conference'. They included John Sishuba, Simon Sihlali, Isaac Wauchope and Elijah Makiwane. John Tobin, Dr Abdurahman's main rival in coloured politics and a staunch supporter of the SAP, likewise ignored the call. Unavoidably, as a result the conference took on a party flavour. A large majority of the delegates were Progressive Party supporters, though a small contingent of SAP supporters did attend.[26]

When the conference proceedings opened, the law agent Daniel Dwanya was appointed chairman. The question of federation was discussed at once. After the chairman had briefly alluded to the issue, lengthy speeches were made by Soga, Dr Abdurahman, Dr Rubusana and H. McCorn, an APO delegate from Port Elizabeth.[27] Soga retraced in detail the constitutional history of the Cape and declared its non-racial provisions should be made mandatory in the federal parliament.[28] Dr Abdurahman dwelt on the desirability of a federal rather than a unitary system for South Africa. Under the latter, the sound policy of the Cape would be submerged, to the detriment of blacks.[29] Broader aspirations were reflected in Dr Rubusana's claim that the meeting represented not only the Cape Colony and Transkeian Territories, but also the Transvaal and the Orange River Colony. He also hoped the conference marked the beginning of greater unity between Africans and coloured people. While they all complained of discrimination, there had for long been a colour line between themselves.[30] After a full day's discussion, the following resolutions were unanimously adopted and forwarded to the Cape and Imperial governments and to the heads of churches in the Cape:

That this Conference of the coloured people and natives of the Cape Colony assembled at Queenstown is of the opinion that in the event of the adoption of any form of closer union of the South African colonies:

(a) Federation is preferable to unification.

(b) That form of federation should be adopted in which the Federal Parliament exercises such powers only as are specifically given to it in the federal constitution.

(c) The Cape Franchise should be the basis of the federal franchise.

(d) The basis of representation of the Federal Parliament should be the voters' list.

(e) The present so-called native territories (Swaziland, Basutoland and British Bechuanaland) should be regarded as outside Federal territory and under the protection of the Imperial Government represented by the High Commissioner for such native territories, unless or until provision shall be made for the representation of such territories in the Federal Parliament by members elected on the same basis as in Colonies forming the federation.[31]

With time pressing and the questions of education, land and labour still to be discussed, a proposal was carried to set these aside and to discuss the forthcoming elections. The conference decided that, as many black voters needed guidance, it should lay down guidelines for them by pledging its support to the party that had their best interests at heart. The delegates voted overwhelmingly to support the Unionist candidates against the SAP.[32] The Unionists consisted of an alliance of the Progressive Party and a group of independents. Attempts by the small group of SAP supporters to prevent the decision to discuss party politics were unsuccessful. The APO delegates did not take part, as they were prohibited from pledging themselves to either party before the APO annual conference at Indwe the following month decided on the matter, though on that occasion the APO also came out in support of the Unionists.[33]

While Jabavu's *Imvo* described the Queenstown Conference as a 'pantomime' with 'crusted old Progressives' as the players,[34] African newspapers in Natal and Basutoland hailed it as a historic occasion and an omen of future black unity. Both *Ilanga* and *Naledi* criticised Jabavu's attitude to the conference and said it was harmful to the African cause.[35] Dr Jameson, the Cape Prime Minister and leader of the Unionists, expressed his appreciation for the support promised by the conference to his party and reiterated his determination to stand by Rhodes's dictum of equal rights for every civilised man.[36]

In response to the Queenstown Conference, Jabavu summoned a Native Electoral Convention at Debe Nek near King William's Town on 17 and 18 January 1908. He encouraged local committees of registered voters to hold meetings to elect area delegates to the Convention, and give them a mandate so that, unlike the Queenstown Conference, which he claimed was attended by 'individuals representing nobody but themselves', the Debe Convention could be truly representative of African opinion.[37] Altogether 50 delegates and 300 observers attended the meeting. It was in effect a convention of SAP supporters, as the chairman, Isaac Wauchope, readily confirmed. The delegate from Peddie, Ben Tele, one of the few SANC–Unionist sympathisers present, accused the chairman of having misled Africans when he had invited the 'whole nation' to participate.[38] Though the question of federation was raised at the meeting, it did not form a major part of the discussions. After a number of resolutions on African education, land tenure, the question of liquor prohibition and Africans in towns, the Cape government was simply asked 'to see that the rights of natives were as far as possible secured' under federation.[39]

In his address on the subject, Jabavu took an unusual line. Far from fearing that federation might lead to the downfall of the Cape system, as many others thought, he believed it would bring positive outcomes. To his mind, only by drawing the other colonies into a union or federation with the Cape would the enlightened 'native policy' of the Cape be extended. Jabavu compared the effect this would have with 'the light which has ever chased away darkness'. Only through educative contact with the Cape system would Natal, for example, be persuaded to depart from its retrogressive policies.[40] (This was also the attitude that the official Cape delegates would take when compromising on the Cape franchise during the National Convention.)

The most important decision taken by the Debe Convention was to confirm its support for the SAP in the forthcoming elections. Jabavu declared that the best thing Africans could do was to return to parliament the likes of Merriman and Sauer, the natural successors of the great old liberals like Sir George Grey and Sir John Molteno.[41] The Convention advised all its 'constituents and friends' to cast their vote for SAP candidates.[42] As expected, the SAP won the election handsomely and Merriman, one of Jabavu's political champions, succeeded Jameson as Prime Minister. Jabavu revelled in the election results.[43]

Despite Jabavu's uncooperative attitude, the Queenstown Conference had a rejuvenating and unifying effect on African politics. Besides bringing together a host of delegates from all over the Cape, it also saw a greater degree of convergence in thinking between newspapers in the different colonies. Papers such as *Ilanga*, *Naledi*, *Izwi* and the *South African Spectator* all expressed the wish to see greater political cohesion among blacks and were therefore unanimous in their criticism of Jabavu for his refusal to co-operate in the interests of the 'nation'.[44]

After the Queenstown Conference a close exchange of thoughts began to take place and new, more uniform strategies emerged. Thus, when *Naledi* reopened the idea of a Native Press Association and called for a pan-African conference to find ways of freeing the people of Zululand from the recently extended control of the Natal government, the three other newspapers reacted readily to the proposal. *Naledi* declared:

Speaking of ties of blood, where are the *Imvo*, the *Izwi*, the *Koranta*, the *S.A. Spectator*, the *Ilanga lase Natal* and the *Naledi*? Why have they not sounded the bugle-horn and called their countrymen together to meet at some convenient place to deliberate on the advisability of petitioning the Imperial Parliament to constitute Zululand into a Native reserve like Basutoland in order to free it from the ravages of war that will always follow year after year? Are we not all Bantu and therefore of the same blood? Our cousins the Zulus cannot under the circumstances help themselves and it behoves those of us favourably placed to take up the cudgels in their behalf. There is not the time to cavil or recall the tribal feuds of days gone by. These have long gone into blessed oblivion and there remains the grim fact that the white man intends turning this into a white man's country ... Yet, we sincerely believe that if we can unite and petition the Home Government we might yet be allowed to live in this country as worthy citizens of the mighty British Empire.[45]

Izwi welcomed the idea and suggested that black newspapers should agree on some way of presenting a united front on vital issues affecting Africans. *Ilanga* published *Izwi*'s views and adopted a similar standpoint: 'Wise people have long since learned that Unity is strength. If the *Imvo* is playing the fool with so serious a question as that of uplifting the Bantu people, let us ignore it and unite our efforts in the great cause.'[46]

36

Preparations for the
National Convention

It will be harder for the more liberal ideas of the Cape Colony to
penetrate than it would be for the camel to pass through the eye
of a needle.

– *Izwi Labantu*, 5 May 1908

The impetus towards union gathered strength when the South
African Party, dominated by the Afrikaner Bond, was elected to power
in the Cape elections of early 1908. This change in government signalled
the success of a remarkable anti-Imperial reaction after the war in which
Afrikaners regained the reins of power in the space of a few years in three of
the four South African colonies. The stage was now set for the unification
of South Africa mostly on their terms.

A decision was taken to make the forthcoming inter-colonial
conference on customs and railways issues 'the starting point of a united
South Africa'.[1] The conference met in Pretoria on 4 May 1908. To avoid
differences that might arise from other matters, it was decided to place the
question of Closer Union before the conference first. On the following day
the conference resolved that 'the best interests and permanent prosperity
of South Africa' could be secured only by an early union. It was decided
that the legislatures of the various colonies should be asked to appoint
delegates to a national South African convention whose object would be
to consider and report on the most desirable form of union and prepare a
draft constitution for a united South Africa.[2]

Africans were fully aware of the importance of these developments.

Jabavu's *Imvo* described the conference as an event of momentous importance and expressed the hope that union would be in 'the broadest and most liberal spirit as possible'.[3] *Izwi*, in contrast, expressed doubts about the composition of the conference and argued, 'it will be harder for the more liberal ideas of the Cape Colony to penetrate than it would be for the camel to pass through the eye of a needle.' The newspaper warned Africans, 'Put not your trust in Princes', and urged them to protect their own interests by organising and standing up for their rights.[4]

By June 1908, as *Imvo* correctly noted, the question of Closer Union was paramount throughout the country, all other matters being of subsidiary importance.[5] Many Africans in the Cape were full of optimism for the new era that was dawning. Not only did they believe that their rights would remain untouched, but they optimistically foresaw the extension of rights similar to theirs to the northern colonies. *Imvo* observed: 'there does not appear any disposition amongst those working for the Closer Union of the South African Colonies to be either unfair or unjust to the Natives in their treatment in the Union arrangements; that the existing rights and privileges of the Natives in the Cape Colony will be safeguarded we have no doubt. We are equally persuaded that something, even though not on a par with what our Cape people possess, will be done for our Native friends in the other Colonies in the direction of securing them some form of representation in the Union.'[6]

While Jabavu's views were coloured by his loyalty to Merriman and the SAP, Cape Africans generally had reason to believe that their rights were secure: the leaders of both major political parties had declared themselves opposed to any tampering with the constitutional rights enjoyed by Africans in the Cape in any scheme for union.[7] This feeling of complacency among many Cape Africans was to last until the release of the draft South Africa Act in February 1909, when they were dealt a rude shock and galvanised into action.

Counterposed to this confidence was the open alarm shown, with good reason, by opinion-makers in other colonies and territories at the prospect of union. They had little faith that colonial statesmen would voluntarily extend the political rights of Africans. Indeed, they feared the opposite. To justify its opposition to union, *Ilanga* quoted a statement by Louis

347

Botha that if he had his way he would break up the native reserves and force Africans onto the labour market. According to *Ilanga*, this was the type of prospect union held for Africans.[8] Dube's fear of an Afrikaner-dominated union was linked to the deep suspicion of union that prevailed generally in the predominantly English colony of Natal. In the Basutoland Protectorate, *Naledi ea Lesotho* wrote several editorials on the question, which were equally suspicious.[9] Though it viewed the situation in the Cape in a favourable light,[10] it was generally hostile to the idea of Africans being governed under union according to the prevailing colonial systems. In the view of the paper, if the South African colonists had their way there would be no African franchise and no Protectorates.[11] It was especially critical of the Natal government and declared that, if the Natal system held sway at union, the disturbances that had taken place there recently would be repeated in a united South Africa.[12] As union would directly affect Africans throughout South Africa, they should not wait to see what happened, but should band together and approach the Imperial government for protection.[13]

The position of Africans in a South African union was also discussed in Britain at this time and Africans eagerly followed what was said. Activists and intellectuals were particularly interested in these views because they looked to Britain for protection, and British democratic ideals formed the essence of their political aspirations. They hoped that, in view of the fact that a union could not be obtained without the British government's consent, their rights would be protected.[14]

During May 1908 the matter was raised in the House of Commons. All the speakers in the debate spoke in favour of political representation based on the Cape system for Africans. The Under-Secretary for the Colonies, Colonel Seely, said the franchise was the key to the situation. There were many things pressing for solution: African land, African education, African rights of every kind. Given the franchise, these things would solve themselves. The feeling in the Commons was that the self-governing colonies would give Africans some form of representation. This would go a long way in reciprocating the magnanimous gesture of the Imperial government in granting the ex-republics self-government with a racially exclusive constitution.[15]

It is tragic to record that this optimism among liberal-minded people that Africans would be given political representation under union was completely illusory. The British government was involved in realpolitik and was not about to exert moral influence. Commenting on the debates in the House of Commons, Lord Selborne privately informed the Secretary of State that the views expressed by Colonel Seely and others were 'founded on a complete misapprehension'. To a man, the ministers in the Transvaal and the Orange River Colony were opposed to African representation. In holding these views, he regretted to say, they faithfully reflected the views of their constituents.[16]

As the National Convention, scheduled to meet in Durban on 12 October 1908, drew closer, Africans in the various colonies began to respond more keenly to developments. In August political associations joined the newspapers in the debate about union and well-meaning white sympathisers also entered the fray.

There were two lines of thought with regard to the Convention. Cape Africans generally were disposed to put their faith in the Cape delegates and not to interfere. The feeling in the other colonies inclined towards direct action. The Becoana Mutual Improvement Association in the Orange River Colony requested an interview early in August with the Governor, Sir Hamilton Goold-Adams, and cited as its first reason 'the position of Natives under the proposed Federation or Unification of S.A. States'.[17] The Governor granted the request soon afterwards. A delegation from the Orange River Colony Native Congress was also in attendance at the interview,[18] but they were concerned mainly with other matters.* At the meeting, and in a subsequent petition, the Free Staters informed the Governor that they wished to be allowed to express their opinion on Closer Union before the question was discussed at the forthcoming Convention. However, the Governor informed the delegates that the administration of

* The Association deputation consisted of the chairman Joel Goronyane, John M. Nyokong, Timothy Seiphimo and Jeremiah Makgothi, while the Congress was represented by the chairman Jacob Lavers, J.B. Twayi, Jan Mocher, Peter Phatlane, H.C. Msikinya and Thomas Mtobi Mapikela.

Africans lay in the hands of his ministers and proceeded to notify the Prime Minister, Abraham Fischer, about the points they had raised. Fischer met the two deputations on 6 October,[19] a few days before the Convention assembled. It is likely, therefore, that Fischer proceeded to Durban, knowing at first hand the feelings of African political organisations in the Orange River Colony on the subject of unification.

In neighbouring Basutoland, the Basutoland Progressive Association, an organisation formed in December 1907, discussed Closer Union for two days at a meeting in Maseru in August 1908.[20] The Association decided that it could not support either federation or unification until equal rights were guaranteed to all subjects of the Empire, irrespective of colour or means. It expressed the hope that Basutoland and other 'native territories' would remain outside any scheme of Closer Union, under the protection of the Imperial government.[21] Similarly, *Naledi ea Lesotho*, referring to union, declared, 'No self-respecting Native would accept any form of representation short of direct representation in the legislatures of the country'.[22]

To the developments concerning union, Africans in the Transvaal also began to respond. In August 1908 Sefako Makgatho's African National Political Union forwarded a lengthy petition to the Prime Minister, Louis Botha, listing its grievances and the reforms it wanted implemented, 'especially at this moment when the question of the Unification or the Federation of the South African colonies is on the eve of consideration, and as our interests and our future prospects will therein be involved'.[23] The petition was submitted on behalf of the Africans of the Pretoria district and a number of northern Transvaal chiefs. They asked for equal rights, protection, privileges, liberty and freedom for all British subjects. Likewise, in Natal the secretary of the Natal Native Congress, H.C.C. Matiwane, called a meeting for 15 October to discuss the Convention.[24] It was eventually held on 23 October during the sitting of the National Convention and the Congress duly requested the Natal Secretary for Native Affairs to put its views before the Convention.[25]

With less than a month remaining before the Convention was due to meet, two near-simultaneous calls were made for steps to be taken to co-ordinate black opinion and make a united appeal to the Convention. The first came on 18 September when *Ilanga* urged Africans and coloured people to send delegates from their various political organisations to Durban for the duration of the Convention. These should form a Committee of Vigilance and request that their views be heard. As the majority of people in South Africa would not be represented, it was the duty of African leaders to make representations to the Convention.[26] Clearly, *Ilanga*'s editor, John Dube, contemplated the forthcoming union with apprehension.

Ilanga's proposal for a Committee of Vigilance was followed a few days later by an appeal, circularised in the form of a letter to the African press, from Theo Schreiner for Africans to combine and petition the Convention, the Imperial government and the House of Commons, asking for their rights to be safeguarded: 'I send this letter to the Native Press in South Africa under a deep sense of duty and responsibility, in the hope that the leading men amongst the Natives, sinking all petty jealousies and ignoring all dividing lines in view of the importance of the crisis, may combine in united action so as to produce a unanimous expression of opinion such as will carry weight both with the Convention, and the Imperial Government and Parliament, and will strengthen the hands of those who are fighting the battle of justice and fair play irrespective of colour.'[27] As the issue also affected coloured people, Schreiner felt that they should unite with the Africans. Among the most important points to be included in the petition to the Convention was recognition of the 'right of the civilised Native, whether in the Reserves or elsewhere, to genuine and adequate parliamentary representation based upon a civilisation franchise'.[28]

Theo Schreiner was one of four members of a family who were to distinguish themselves in their outspoken defence of the rights of Africans in the ensuing months. He was the first member of the Cape parliament to emphasise the need to protect Africans in any scheme for union, and shortly before the National Convention he published a pamphlet attacking the much-favoured idea of separate representation of Africans, an idea given authority by the South African Native Affairs Commission.[29]

Nevertheless, the appeals by *Ilanga* and Schreiner met with a disappointing response, and only a handful of individuals eventually made formal representations to the Convention. The only significant support for the appeals came from Pambani J. Mzimba, influential head of the

separatist Presbyterian Church of Africa.[30] Both *Imvo* and *Izwi* poured cold
water on the idea. The reaction of *Imvo*, *Izwi* and Cape voters in general
was that it was the responsibility of the Cape and British governments to
safeguard and represent African interests. If Africans appealed above the
heads of their representatives to the Convention, they would be displaying
a lack of faith. These newspapers, in fact, were pointedly hostile to the idea
of any African agitation during the Convention. *Imvo*'s attitude was that

It is reasonable for the Africans of the Northern colonies to be restless; they have
always been excluded from the enjoyment of civil rights because of the antagonism
of the Europeans in those colonies, there being also no doubt that the delegates of
those colonies will enter the convention still imbued with their old and bad spirit
of antipathy towards Africans. There would be nothing wrong in the holding of
meetings by the Africans of the Northern colonies. The Cape Africans are in a
different position altogether. Their civil rights are not doubted by anyone. There is
no fear that the Cape delegates will speak for anything other than the retention of
civil rights by the Cape African, of whom they have wide experience. Any agitation
by Cape Africans at this stage would have the effect of discouraging our delegates
and also make them appear as though they are ignorant of obligation.[31]

Izwi fundamentally agreed with *Imvo*'s conclusion. In its opinion, Africans
should wait and see what stand the Cape delegates would put up. However,
any modification to or abolition of the Cape franchise by the Convention
could be taken as a sign of hostility and would justify united action by
Africans and their friends.[32] Furthermore, African spokesmen were also
mollified by the choice of delegates appointed by the Cape parliament to
represent the colony at the Convention. They included Sir Henry de Villiers,
the Chief Justice; Merriman and Sauer, Jabavu's political champions;
F.S. Malan; and W.P. Schreiner.[33] A former Prime Minister, brilliant
constitutional lawyer and ardent spokesman for Africans, Schreiner was
seen as the best man to look after African interests at the Convention. In
his election manifesto of 1907 he had come out firmly against a political
colour bar in any federation of the South African colonies.[34]

At the same time, speeches in the Cape parliament and by the delegates
seemed to confirm that Africans had nothing to fear under union. During

the last session of the Cape parliament members on both sides had made it clear that the Cape franchise should be respected.[35] In moving the adoption of the inter-colonial conference resolutions, Merriman had declared that both sides of the House were pledged to maintain up to the hilt the franchise rights of Africans.[36] Jabavu believed that one of the most important features of the parliamentary session had been 'the jealous defence by the government of Native interests'.[37] Speeches in support of the Cape franchise by Sir Henry de Villiers and the Bond leader, J.H. Hofmeyr, at a farewell party for the Convention delegates in Cape Town reinforced the belief that African interests would be protected.[38]

African hopes received a setback when Schreiner was forced to withdraw as a delegate. He had gladly accepted nomination as a Cape delegate when Merriman asked him to do so in June 1908.[39] Earlier, however, realising the political and social implications involved in the trial of the Zulu king Dinuzulu in Natal, Schreiner had agreed to defend him, expecting that the trial would be over by October or November.[40] When he realised that the two events would coincide, he asked the Natal Prime Minister to postpone the trial until later, but Moor refused.[41] Schreiner was then left with a difficult decision. He chose what appeared to be the less attractive and more idealistic alternative when he announced his resignation from the Convention on 4 September. He declared that his first duty was with the person whose defence he had undertaken, and he could not set that aside, even for the high duty of attending the Convention.[42]

Thus the one person who would most probably have fought hardest against the idea of a white unitary state was excluded from the deliberations on South Africa's future. Although in public Merriman voiced his disappointment at Schreiner's withdrawal, privately he was pleased about it.[43] Indicating signs of the compromise which would come later, Merriman wrote to Louis Botha, 'It's a very good job that Schreiner retired and it will shorten our proceedings materially. Stanford [Schreiner's replacement] is a good fellow and has seen and knows too much about natives to be an ultra-negrophile. Whatever he agrees to will be accepted by the other side.'[44] Merriman had earlier expressed his wariness of Schreiner in a letter to ex-President Steyn.[45]

Colonel Walter Stanford had vast experience in African affairs and was widely, but not unanimously, regarded as a good substitute for Schreiner by Africans and sympathetic newspapers, but he was first and foremost a civil servant, not a politician.[46] Although he would stand up for the Cape franchise at the Convention, he was not equal to the overwhelming odds he faced in opposing the viewpoints of the other colonies. All the same, it is doubtful whether even the presence of someone with the qualities of W.P. Schreiner would have significantly affected the final decisions reached by the Convention.

37

The National
Convention, 1908

Providence has drawn the line between black and white and we
must make that clear to the natives, not instil into their minds false
ideas of equality.

— General C.R. de Wet, 1908

Nine years to the day after the outbreak of the South African
War, the National Convention assembled in Durban on 12 October 1908,
thus bringing to a culmination a remarkable process of reconciliation
between Boer and Briton in South Africa.

When the proceedings got under way, Sir Henry de Villiers was
unanimously elected president and ex-President Steyn of the Orange River
Colony was chosen as vice-president.[1] Thirty-three delegates representing
the four colonies and Rhodesia attended. They included the four colonial
Prime Ministers, as well as leading government and opposition members
from each colony. Except for the opening address by the Governor of Natal,
the Imperial factor was excluded. The proceedings were entirely in the
hands of colonial statesmen. However, Sir Henry de Villiers kept in regular
contact with the British High Commissioner, Lord Selborne, to gauge the
views of the Imperial government, especially on the vital questions of the
franchise and the Protectorates, and the Imperial connection was also
emphasised by the presence of a British naval squadron in Durban for the
occasion.[2]

The first point to be discussed was the form union should take.[3] The
protagonists of a unitary system were not hard put to carry their views

against those who preferred federation. The Convention then went on to the language question. Here, the equality of the Dutch and English languages was recognised. These discussions took up the first week of the session.[4] During this first week, the vital question of the franchise for black people, a delicate matter which underlay all South African politics and which could make or break union, was raised briefly. On 19 October J.X. Merriman moved that the existing colonial franchise laws should remain as they were, to be alterable only under special clauses for changing the Union constitution.[5] Later he proposed that these conditions should be a majority of not less than three-quarters of the members of both houses of parliament sitting and voting together.[6] On the other hand, Colonel Stanford moved instead that 'All subjects of His Majesty resident in South Africa shall be entitled to franchise rights irrespective of race or colour upon such qualifications as may be determined by this Convention'.[7] Stanford, in other words, proposed that the electoral colour bar should be abolished in all the colonies, while Merriman saw the retention of the status quo in each territory as the only means of reaching an agreement satisfactory to all.

From 20 to 22 October there was intense debate on the subject. Several franchise proposals were forthcoming, but no unanimity could be reached. Opinions accorded with the traditional practices prevailing in the various colonies. Broadly speaking, the Cape delegates wished to extend, or at least preserve, the non-racial franchise of the Cape, while the opposite applied to the representatives of all three northern colonies. They were unanimous in their hostility to African participation in the political system.[8]

In opening the discussions, both Merriman and Stanford reiterated their earlier proposals. Merriman said the Cape delegates had special responsibilities towards the 'natives'. They were trustees for these people and had to guard the rights which had been granted to them and never abused. The whole matter of political rights for black inhabitants should be left as it stood until after union. Stanford declared that the franchise was the crux of the whole 'native question' in South Africa. Africans should be granted not only freedom, but citizenship. In his opinion the extraordinary advances shown by Africans in the Cape Colony during the previous century were due to a great extent to their having enjoyed the franchise. The franchise was a safety valve which provided an outlet for their grievances. Grievances were not left to simmer until they led to disorder and rebellion (a pointed reference to Natal's recent rebellion).[9]

Sir Percy FitzPatrick, who represented the opposition Progressive Party in the Transvaal, spoke next. He advocated a high franchise qualification, based on a 'civilisation test' administered by a permanent tribunal.[10] When it came to his turn, Prime Minister Moor of Natal called for a total colour bar. He felt that the white and black races in South Africa could never be amalgamated: the history of the world showed that the black man was incapable of civilisation.[11]

The first four speakers thus advocated widely differing policies towards Africans. Merriman's proposal received the most support from the speakers who followed before the proceedings of 20 October were terminated. While J.W. Sauer backed Stanford's motion, Abraham Fischer of the Free State, J.W. Jagger from the Cape and J.C. Smuts from the Transvaal spoke in favour of retaining the status quo in the various colonies.[12] Fischer declared that only a Union parliament could work out the uniform 'native policy' that everyone desired.[13] In Smuts's view, Stanford's proposals were unacceptable to the northern colonies, while Moor's ideas would be rejected by the Imperial government; the franchise should therefore be left as it stood in the various colonies until after union, when it could be amended by a simple majority in parliament.[14]

The compromise strategy of making the solution to the 'native problem' secondary to the more pressing need for union, as already decided on by Smuts and Merriman before the Convention, was beginning to assert itself. It is certain that they would have sounded out other delegates on the matter before raising it; and as they were the two dominant personalities at the Convention, the odds were that their approach would be accepted in the end.

Meanwhile, the chairman, Sir Henry de Villiers, had realised that the approval of the Imperial government was imperative for union to succeed, and for some months he had kept in touch with Imperial officials on the franchise question. As the debate entered its second day on 21 October, De Villiers informed the Convention of the conclusions he had drawn from his observations, and read a letter he had elicited from Lord Selborne on the subject. Selborne said that during a visit to England in June he had met the Colonial secretary, Lord Crewe, and other British ministers to ascertain their views. They were willing to give a free hand to South Africa on the question of union, except on two points: the African franchise and the Protectorates. In respect of the first, the Imperial government would prefer a franchise qualification that would leave the door open for Africans to qualify for full rights of citizenship in the future. Secondly, it would be best for all the 'Native territories' to be incorporated into South Africa from the start, but if the franchise question was not dealt with satisfactorily, the Protectorates would not be handed over.

De Villiers had also asked Selborne to make comments on the franchise, especially with a view to elucidating the position of the Imperial government.[15] The High Commissioner had hastened to comply. He proposed a franchise for blacks based on a laborious 'civilisation test', similar to the idea suggested by FitzPatrick. Selborne had reservations about Merriman's proposal that the status quo should be retained in every colony: 'If it succeeds in making the franchise secure to the Cape natives, it will also make it practically impossible at any time to extend the franchise to any of the natives of the Transvaal, Natal or the Orange River Colony.' He said the Imperial government was greatly concerned about the franchise question. It would be placed in an invidious position 'if a Constitution is established for South Africa which leaves no open door whatever to the franchise for the native, however civilised, or for the coloured man, however civilised'.[16] Such a constitution would lead to strong protests to the Imperial government and would raise the undesirable possibility of Imperial interference.

According to Selborne, the Imperial government interpreted clause eight of the Vereeniging peace terms to mean that the question of the African franchise would be dealt with shortly after responsible government was granted to the former republics. No more appropriate moment for dealing with this question could occur than during the National Convention. Furthermore, as the Imperial government had already informed De Villiers, the question of the franchise was closely bound to the conditions of the expected transfer of the Protectorates to the Union of South Africa. If the Cape franchise was left untouched and 'a permanent adequate door to the franchise was opened to the natives' in the other colonies, the prospects for transfer would be favourable. A closed door policy would have the opposite effect.[17]

With De Villiers's entry into the debate, delegates now knew more or less the attitude of the Imperial government, which had the final say in the matter. Nevertheless, succeeding speakers, almost without exception, stuck doggedly to the broad principles of the 'native policy' pertaining in their various colonies.[18] General C.R. de Wet touched on the fundamental attitude of the north when he said, 'Providence has drawn the line between black and white and we must make that clear to the natives, not instil into their minds false ideas of equality.'[19] For their part, the Natal delegates supported an absolute colour bar for South Africa and moved an amendment to exclude blacks from membership of both houses of parliament.[20]

With most delegates insistent in their support of the status quo, the big question became whether the Convention should formulate a uniform franchise system for South Africa or whether it should leave the franchise as it was in each colony until after union. It was now clear that, unless the latter avenue was followed, deadlock would be reached. Louis Botha put it bluntly when he said that if the view of the liberal Cape members was accepted that there should be no union before a settlement was reached, then the question of union was finished.[21] In order to reach some sort of agreement, Botha proposed that the task of framing resolutions about future 'native policy' be entrusted to a committee nominated by the various Prime Ministers. The proposal was adopted and Abraham Fischer was appointed chairman.[22] As the Convention proceedings could not be held up while the delegates waited for the franchise committee to complete its deliberations, the committee met during spare hours in the evenings and the Convention turned meanwhile to discussion of other matters.*

Sir Henry de Villiers, who had continued his consultation with Lord Selborne on the franchise issue, was able to provide the committee with important advice.[23] On 21 October he had written to Lord Selborne,

---

* The franchise committee was composed of J.W. Sauer and E.H. Walton (Cape Colony), C.J. Smythe and E.M. Greene (Natal), Percy FitzPatrick and J.C. Smuts (Transvaal), J.B.M. Hertzog and Abraham Fischer (Orange River Colony), and C.P.J. Coghlan, who was nominated by the Administrator of Rhodesia, Sir William Milton.

responding to the latter's suggestion of a 'civilisation test' and informing him of the general feeling of the Convention on the franchise for Africans. De Villiers posed three further questions on which he desired clarification. Selborne's responses on 22 October were crucial, for they cleared the way for a final settlement.

De Villiers: It seems to me extremely desirable that before any resolution is arrived at I should know whether, in your opinion, the Home Government would agree to the application of the test of civilisation to coloured persons and not to Europeans.

Selborne: I believe they would, as part of a general settlement of the franchise question in South Africa which gave an adequate permanent access to the franchise to the coloured people and natives in all the British South African Colonies.

De Villiers: I should like also to know whether, in case no satisfactory test of that kind can be agreed upon, the Home Government would agree to allow the present franchise to remain in the different Provinces until altered by the Union Parliament either with or without the proviso that such alteration shall not be allowed in regard to the qualification of coloured persons in the Cape Colony unless carried by a majority of not less than three-fourths of the members of both Houses, sitting together.

Selborne: I think His Majesty's Government would feel that they would not satisfactorily answer the question until they were aware of all the main details of the general scheme of closer union, and how each part reflected upon another, and also until they knew how far the general scheme agreed upon represented the unanimous or practically unanimous opinion of the members of the National Convention, or whether the opinion of the delegates was divided in nearly equal proportions on any of the more important parts of the scheme. I am confident, however, that in default of a general settlement of the native franchise question they would warmly sympathise with any provision securing to the Cape Coloured persons and natives that access to the franchise which they at present enjoy.

De Villiers: It is very important that I should know whether the Home Government would agree to a provision that only persons of European descent shall be eligible as Members of either House of the Union Parliament. The Cape delegates seem to be prepared to accept such a provision seeing that without it an agreement on the matter of the franchise would be almost hopeless.

Selborne: I do not think that His Majesty's Government would object to such a provision as part of an otherwise satisfactory settlement of the native franchise question.[24]

The last point of De Villiers's letter was of cardinal importance: it indicated that the Cape had already bowed to the demands of the other colonies on the matter. Indeed, Merriman had agreed to support a motion to bar black citizens from the Union parliament. Assurances from the Imperial government, the final arbiter in the matter, were now being sought.

As a result of this correspondence, De Villiers was able to inform the franchise committee that Britain would probably agree to the continuance of the discriminatory Transvaal, Orange River Colony and Natal franchise systems, and even to the exclusion of black people in the Cape from the right to sit in parliament, a right they had always enjoyed but had not yet exercised. With Britain's willingness to co-operate virtually confirmed, the constraints against drawing up a colour-bar constitution were radically reduced and fears of a royal veto of a constitution embodying differential principles diminished. Instead of actively supporting the non-racial Cape franchise system, Selborne in fact weakened the chances of its being adopted elsewhere in South Africa. Moreover, the Colonial Secretary, Lord Crewe, with whom he was in constant communication during the Convention, was not insistent on the matter. Crewe's response to Selborne's answers was that they were not at variance with the general policy of the British government, although it was perhaps inclined more in the direction of the Cape system than Selborne had made out. The main aim was union. While Crewe favoured a non-racial franchise, he said he was sensible of the difficulties of its being applied in the northern colonies.[25]

After considering the various resolutions and amendments of the Convention, and the suggestions for a qualified franchise from Lord Selborne, the franchise committee presented its report to the Convention on 2 November 1908. It was discussed the following day. The last two parts of the report, dealing with non-controversial formalities, were quickly passed, but the first two parts, concerning safeguards for existing black franchise rights and a 'European descent' provision for parliamentary eligibility, were vaguely worded and gave rise to contention.[26] It soon became clear that a long debate would ensue. The Convention decided, therefore, that the amendments and disputed sections of the report be referred back to the franchise committee with instructions that it present a report the following day.[27]

The final report received the approval of the Convention. Part I of the report recommended that no law should disqualify any persons in the Cape from the vote by reason of their race or colour only, unless it was passed by a majority of two-thirds of the members of each house of parliament. Until such a law came into being, the existing franchise qualifications in the various colonies would prevail in elections of members of the central parliament. Moreover, no registered voters in any province should be removed from the register by reason of any disqualification based on race or colour.[28] Part II was submitted in the same form as it had appeared in the original report of the previous day: 'Only persons of European descent shall be eligible as members of either House of Parliament.'[29]

After approval of the committee report, supporters and opponents of political rights for black people made a final attempt to influence the constitution being drawn up by the Convention. Stanford gave notice of a motion opposing the exclusion of blacks from parliament, but then he withdrew the notice and it was not even discussed.[30] Similarly, F.S. Malan moved that the 'two-thirds' safeguard for black voters in the Cape apply to Natal as well, but he too then withdrew his amendment.[31] The hardliners on the colour question were more resilient, and gained a final concession before the resolutions of the franchise committee were adopted. Louis Botha moved that, instead of the approval of two-thirds of the members of each house being required to disqualify Cape blacks from the franchise, the clause in question should provide for two-thirds of the total number of members of both houses of parliament, sitting together, to pass the disqualification. The amendment was agreed to.[32]

With the acceptance of the franchise committee's recommendations, the Convention virtually concluded its deliberations on the question of the franchise for blacks. The matter was again raised only briefly during subsequent discussions. This happened, for example, during the Convention's deliberations on women's rights, and on the Provincial Councils; in the latter regard it was decided that, in the Cape, membership would be open to any voter, regardless of colour.[33]

In the draft South Africa Act, which contained the final decisions of the delegates before the proposed constitution was put to the country at large, three parts – sections 25, 33 and 44 – related to the colour-bar clauses decided on by the Convention. Sections 25 and 44 dealt with the qualifications for members of the Senate and the House of Assembly respectively, and permitted only British subjects 'of European descent' to become members of parliament. Section 33 and its seven subsections provided for increases in the size of the House of Assembly in proportion to the number of European male adults, rather than the number of registered voters or adult males of all colours, in each province. Other provisions of the draft Act that concern us here were Sections 35 and 153, making provision for amendments to the constitution. The latter stipulated that the entrenched clauses of the constitution could be altered only by a majority of two-thirds of the total number of members of both houses of parliament sitting together, while the former specified as one of the entrenched clauses that no person in the Cape could be disqualified as a voter except under the aforementioned condition. Altogether there were 153 sections and a schedule dealing with the Protectorates, which was also of keen interest to African leaders and activists.[34]

In all these ways, the Convention's recommendations on the franchise question were a compromise between the Cape and the northern colonies. The latter agreed to the continuation of franchise rights for blacks in the Cape, while the Cape countenanced the continuation of the colour bar in the north and the principle that blacks should be excluded from sitting in parliament.

38

Petitioning the
National Convention

We attribute the advancement in prosperity, contentment and
loyalty, which is such a marked characteristic of the natives of
the Cape Colony, to the generous policy which has permitted
them to qualify themselves as citizens and to enjoy the privileges
of citizenship. And we submit that the same happy result may be
expected to follow the extension of the Cape Franchise to our
people throughout South Africa.

– W.P. Letseleba, Transvaal National Natives Union,
October 1909

While discussions were taking place at the National Convention
about the future of South Africa, the African people, whose destinies were
being determined, were not represented. However, nothing prevented
Africans and their sympathisers from addressing themselves to the
Convention and a number took the opportunity to do so.

On the day the Convention assembled in Durban, it had before it a
telegram from W.P. Schreiner, expressing the wish that the labours of the
Convention would advance the true welfare and union of all South Africa
and its people.[1] The following day a detailed, more urgent address was
received from J.M. Orpen, who took it upon himself to speak on behalf
of those who were without an effective voice in the corridors of power.[2]
With more than half a century of practical involvement in parliamentary
politics and colonial administration in several territories in South Africa,
Orpen was regarded as well qualified to speak on the 'native problem'. In

recent years he had endeared himself to the African intelligentsia for his liberal views on African rights.[3] Orpen had supported *Ilanga*'s appeal for African and coloured organisations to send delegates to Durban to work with white sympathisers in defending the interests of blacks. But when nothing came of *Ilanga*'s proposal, Orpen approached the Convention in a private capacity and without any mandate from others. He asked the Convention, in the interests of both black and white in South Africa, to develop some liberal scheme for granting a fair measure of representation to black people throughout South Africa, with due regard to the safeguarding of white supremacy. (Clearly, even the most sympathetic colonial advocates of African rights at that time regarded white supremacy as essential.) 'Representation is the sovereign cure for every ill,' said Orpen, quoting Charles James Fox. Without representation there could be no lasting solution to the most fundamental question in South African politics.

Orpen and the Schreiner brothers, Theo and Will, were not the only white sympathisers to act with concern for the position of Africans when the Convention sat. The Rev. J.S. Moffat wrote to the High Commissioner, Lord Selborne, expressing his concern at the approach of union, and a similar letter was directed to Sir Henry de Villiers by Sir James Rose-Innes, Judge President of the Transvaal.[4] In addition, the Anglican Bishop of Pretoria forwarded to the Convention two letters with resolutions from the diocesan and episcopal synods of the Church of the Province of South Africa, expressing the hope that union would be established on the foundations of co-operation, trust and justice towards all sections of the population.[5] Later, this concern was voiced by other church bodies as well.

The first representation to the Convention from Africans came in a letter from Charles Daniel of Imbizana, Natal. It was presented on 3 November, the day the franchise committee reported for the first time and a day before the whole franchise question was resolved.[6] Charles Daniel was a member of the Natal Native Congress, representing the Lower Umzimkulu Division on that body. His letter, dated 15 October, and directed to the Natal Secretary for Native Affairs, was written in Zulu; a translated copy was presented to the Convention. 'On behalf of all the people of Lower Umzimkulu and the Division of Ixopo and Harding', Daniel hoped that while the Convention discussed the new constitution it would resolve on a scheme by which Africans would be 'drawn into proper enlightenment' and confirmed in the exemption and franchise rights granted in principle to 'civilised' Africans in Natal in 1865. If possible, the petitioner wanted to be given the opportunity of appearing personally before the Convention so that he could present his views.[7]

The most substantial approaches by Africans to the Convention came in two petitions presented by the Transvaal National Natives Union (TNNU) in November and December 1908. Designated the successor of the Transvaal Basuto Committee, the TNNU emerged out of the perceived need for greater unity among various African groups in the Transvaal at this critical period, and it was formally constituted as an organisation at a meeting on 1 January 1909.[8] On 22 October 1908 the organisers circulated numerous copies of the petition, handsomely printed on good-quality paper, throughout the Transvaal. Because of the urgent need to get the petitions to the Convention on time, they were not circulated as extensively as desired, but within a month W.P. Letseleba, the TNNU chairman, and Z. More, its secretary, were able to forward 18 copies to the Convention. These contained the signatures of almost 2000 Africans from Johannesburg, Pietersburg, Barberton, Germiston, Standerton, Boksburg and Potchefstroom.[9] A further 16 copies were forwarded on 17 December through David Pollock, secretary of the Transvaal Native Affairs Society, an organisation founded in January 1908 'to promote the study and discussion of the South African question, with a view to enunciating and advocating a liberal, consistent and practical Native policy throughout South Africa'.[10] This channel was used to communicate with the Convention on the second occasion because the petitioners had received no acknowledgement after forwarding the first batch of petition lists.[11] The supplementary petitions were signed by 1770 people from some of the districts already mentioned as well as Vereeniging, Pretoria, Kilnerton, Marabastad, Mphahlele's Location, Saulspoort, Klerksdorp and Rustenburg. As the Convention had already adjourned for the Christmas recess, these petitions were submitted only on 11 January 1909.[12]

The petition of the TNNU was a clear indication of the anxiety of Africans, particularly those outside the Cape, at the coming union. It requested representation for Africans in the parliament of a united South Africa:

We desire to remind the Convention that the natives in this Colony have hitherto been totally unrepresented in the local Parliament, notwithstanding the fact that they contribute largely in direct taxation to the Treasury, in addition to bearing a full share of the indirect taxation through Pass-Fees, the Railways and the Customs Tariff ...

We therefore submit to the favourable consideration of your Honourable Convention our claim to be permitted to qualify for the full political privileges, such as may be granted to the European population in the Constitution you are preparing for submission to His Majesty the King, while praying that the interests of those of our people who may be unable to qualify for this Franchise may be protected by a measure of separate representation following in part the method suggested in the Report of the South African Native Affairs Commission.[13]

Among the prominent Africans who signed the petition and canvassed signatures were S.M. Makgatho and P. Maeta, chairman and secretary respectively of the African National Political Union; Chief Mphahlele, who had close ties with this body; Mangena Mokone, founder of the Ethiopian Church; and two other prominent Ethiopians, Samuel Brander and H.R. Ngcayiya. Mangena and Brander were both connected with the Pretoria-based African Political Society, while Ngcayiya was a member of the executive of the Transvaal Native Congress. Their petition was widely reported in colonial newspapers as well as *Izwi* and *Ilanga*.[14]

With a view to submitting its decisions to the Convention, the Natal Native Congress convened a special meeting in Pietermaritzburg on 23 October 1908 to discuss the franchise question.[15] The issue of representation was paramount in the minds of the delegates. In an address intended for the National Convention, Martin Lutuli (president) and Mark Radebe (secretary) declared on behalf of the NNC:

We Natives of Natal, though loyal subjects of the Crown and sharing the burden of taxation, are labouring under serious disabilities by being excluded from free access to the Franchise, and having no efficient means of making our wants known to Parliament and no say in matters regarding our most vital interests such as taxation and other things. We humbly beg, with regard to our future government, for some degree of representation in the Legislature. This would go far to remove all causes of complaint and make the Natives a more contented and devoted people under His Majesty's gracious rule.[16]

As in the TNNU petition, the NNC stressed that 'the Native population should first be placed in the fair position Natives hold in the Cape Colony'. For some reason this address was never submitted to the National Convention. Though delivered for submission, it was never tabled, perhaps because basic agreement on the African franchise had already been reached and the Natal Prime Minister simply considered it unnecessary to lay the address before the Convention.

Several petitions were also forthcoming from the African Political Organisation (APO) and various other groups representing the coloured communities.[17] The APO appealed to the Convention on behalf of all black people, reflecting the greater sense of solidarity that had developed after the Queenstown Conference of November 1907. Because the organisation extended across colonial boundaries, the APO was also able to co-ordinate coloured opinion in the various colonies more effectively than Africans had done. The Cape, the Orange River Colony and the Transvaal affiliates of the APO all sent petitions to the Convention.[18] These urged that the principle of 'equal rights for all civilised persons in South Africa' should be respected and that no colour line should be drawn in the new constitution. The extension of the Cape franchise to the other colonies would be an act of wisdom which would be in the interests of whites and blacks alike. If the status quo was maintained in the various colonies, an unworkable situation would arise when people enjoying certain privileges in one colony proceeded to another where different conditions existed.

But despite all these direct representations by Africans and their sympathisers, they had no effect whatsoever on the deliberations of the Convention. Gathered in secret conclave, and unbeknown to the country at large, the delegates had already reached finality on the matter of the franchise.

39

The Protectorates and Union

Thus we do humbly beseech thee O King! to make us easy in our minds by telling us we need have no fear, in the event of South African unification or federation, that our nation will be absorbed in any of Your Majesty's Colonies, and thereby lose our national existence and our old native laws and customs, which are so well administered by Your Majesty's representatives in Basutoland.

– Letsie of Basutoland to the King of England, 1908

The National Convention also discussed the future position of the British Protectorates or High Commission Territories in South Africa, a question narrowly related to the discussion of what role Africans should be allocated in the new political system. White colonists generally expected that Basutoland (present-day Lesotho), Bechuanaland (Botswana) and Swaziland would in due course be incorporated into a white South African state. The consummation of Closer Union was seen as an ideal opportunity to realise this expectation.[1] However, this was not to be. While the British government generally accepted that it had effectively relinquished control of 'native affairs' in the self-governing colonies, it was determined to exert itself fully in the Protectorates. These areas were still directly under Imperial control. They had come under British rule under special circumstances and the Imperial government had particular responsibilities towards the people.[2] As a specially obligated trustee, Britain decided that it would not transfer the Protectorates to a united South Africa unless firm and liberal assurances were given. Local pressure helped in making this resolve concrete.[3]

As early as May 1908 the traditional rulers in the Protectorates had expressed their apprehension at reports about union. Paramount Letsie Moshoeshoe of the Sotho asked the Imperial authorities for clarification about the place of Basutoland in the proposed scheme.[4] Similar enquiries were made by Sebele Sechele of the Kwena in Bechuanaland, and by the Queen Regent of Swaziland, Labotsibeni.[5] The Sotho felt so strongly on the subject that Letsie asked for permission to send a delegation that would convey in person the loyalty of the nation, and their fears of union, to King Edward VII.[6] The chiefs were assured that their fears were groundless and that their interests would be safeguarded by the British government.[7]

Meanwhile, the High Commissioner, Lord Selborne, had been actively involved in working out a scheme for the Protectorates once South Africa became a union. In contrast to his half-hearted defence of African political rights in the South African colonies, he exerted strong pressure on the colonial and British governments in an effort to protect the interests of the people in the Protectorates.[8] His standpoint was that it was to the advantage of both the South African and Imperial governments that the Protectorates should fall within the Union, but that, as Britain had special obligations towards these territories, the transfer should not take place until a future date, when definite safeguards for Africans in the Protectorates, embodied in the Union constitution, had been met. Selborne argued that these safeguards should include respect for the inalienability of African land, the prohibition of liquor sales, a fair distribution of custom duties and a degree of political autonomy. In respect of the last matter, Selborne wanted the Basutoland National Council to be preserved and a special commission with wide-ranging powers to be appointed in place of the High Commissioner to administer the Protectorates. In this way, the Protectorates would not be directly administered by the Union government.[9]

Selborne's scheme was put to the four Prime Ministers and to Jan Smuts at the end of October. All were unhappy about the proposals. With the exception of F.R. Moor of Natal, who thought the time was inopportune even to discuss the matter of transfer, they wished to include the Protectorates in the Union at once and were strongly opposed to any interference that would affect the sovereignty of the South African government in respect of the territories.[10]

Further negotiations ensued. On 10 December, the matter of the Protectorates was discussed by the Convention and the question was then referred to a committee consisting of De Villiers, the Prime Ministers, Sir Lewis Michell and Colonel Stanford.[11] After keeping in close touch with Selborne during its deliberations, the committee submitted its report on 17 December.[12] Though it was received with mixed feelings by the Convention, it was eventually carried with only a few minor modifications.[13]

The Convention's resolutions regarding the Protectorates were embodied in a special 25-point schedule to the draft constitution. It foresaw that the Protectorates would be transferred to the Union, but the Governor-General in Council would act as their legislative authority, enacting laws by proclamation (as in the Transkeian Territories), while the Union Prime Minister would be responsible for administering the territories.[14]

This schedule was a compromise and its effects cut both ways. While the South Africans surrendered their desire to incorporate the Protectorates immediately, their appeasing approach went a long way towards minimising the risk that Britain would veto the proposed colour bar in the new constitution for South Africa. Furthermore, the terms that Selborne had persuaded the Convention to accept in regard to the Protectorates provided an important sop to the conscience of the British government. Although Africans in the South African colonies had been left without Imperial protection, the interests of those in the Protectorates had been safeguarded.

If Africans in the colonies hoped for British intervention on their behalf, those in the Protectorates clearly expected it. As the Protectorates were directly controlled by the Imperial government, African inhabitants had every right to insist that their interests be safeguarded. Early in January, soon after the National Convention had passed its basic resolutions on the future of the Protectorates, Lord Selborne informed the principal rulers in these territories that, though at first they would remain outside Union, it was likely they would be incorporated at an early date. The chiefs all reacted adversely to this news. At meetings with the Acting Resident Commissioner of Bechuanaland, Khama, Sebele and Bathoen all expressed strong opposition to being incorporated in the Union.[15] With the exception of Khama, they also subsequently put their views in writing to the Imperial authorities, imploring Britain to honour the pledge it had given to protect them and allow them to govern themselves along traditional lines.[16] The Swazi shared similar feelings. The Acting Resident Commissioner informed Lord Selborne that the news that their country would probably be incorporated in the Union at some future date was 'repugnant' to the Swazi. It was clear that the Swazi looked upon the inclusion of their territory in any form of Closer Union as a prelude to the annexation of Swaziland to South Africa.[17]

As for the Sotho, they refused to let the subject of union rest merely with assurances from Lord Selborne.[18] Even the willingness of the High Commissioner to pay a personal visit to explain the matter was not enough to satisfy them. They wished to present their views directly to the King. In the face of this insistence, Selborne had little option but to allow a Sotho deputation to travel to Britain in January 1909 for this purpose.[19] The deputation met the Colonial Secretary, Lord Crewe, on 15 February, and three days later presented their petition to the King, asking him not to assent to the inclusion of Basutoland in any Union.[20] 'Thus we do humbly beseech thee O King! to make us easy in our minds by telling us we need have no fear, in the event of South African unification or federation, that our nation will be absorbed in any of Your Majesty's Colonies, and thereby lose our national existence and our old native laws and customs, which are so well administered by Your Majesty's representatives in Basutoland.'[21]

The reply of the Imperial government to the petition was given to the deputation by Lord Crewe at a final interview on 25 February. This embodied the principles agreed to by the National Convention.[22] Though the Sotho leaders were unable to extract the assurance that Basutoland would continue as a separate entity, to a large extent their demands in the event of incorporation were met.

As reports in *Naledi ea Lesotho* during 1908 and the resolutions of the Basutoland Progressive Association show, educated Africans in Basutoland approved of the actions of the traditional rulers. Indeed, it seems they may have played some part in the chiefly protests. S.M. Phamotse, editor of *Naledi*, informed W.P. Schreiner in July 1909 that 'Since the very first sitting of the National Convention I have been in communication with the

Paramount Chief Letsie and have had interviews with him urging him to secure the services of a legal adviser, as I was sure Basutoland would be affected by Union'.[23] Phamotse, incidentally, had close ties with African politicians in the Transvaal. Until 1908, when he returned to his native Basutoland to become the official secretary to Chief Jonathan and editor of *Naledi*, he had been one of the guiding forces behind the newspaper *Leihlo la Babathso* in the Transvaal.[24]

Indeed, Africans in the South African colonies sympathised on the whole with their neighbours in the Protectorates and identified with them in the same way that Cape Afrikaners sympathised with their compatriots in the ex-Boer republics. Given this mutuality of feeling, it is no surprise that one of the consequences of the debate about the fate of the High Commission Territories was that African leaders there would send representatives to the founding meeting of the South African Native National Congress, the forerunner of the ANC, in 1912.

40

Responses to the
National Convention, 1909

This is treachery! It is worse. It is successful betrayal, for the Act
has virtually disenfranchised the black man already.

— A.K. Soga, February 1909

The attitudes and activities of Africans on the issue of union
varied widely. In the Cape, black voters maintained their wait-and-see
attitude.[1] Once the Convention had settled down to its discussions, *Imvo*
and *Izwi* focused their attention on other matters. Nothing was heard from
the South African Native Congress. Except for odd rumours about the
Convention's proceedings,[2] which gave rise to speculative reports from
time to time, no definite news escaped the tight veil of secrecy surrounding
the Convention to give any cause for alarm. On the other hand, John
Dube in Inanda, close to where the constitutional discussions on South
Africa's future were taking place, kept the spotlight on the Convention
and the Closer Union issue in the columns of *Ilanga*. The thread of *Ilanga*'s
arguments remained the same as before: the need for representation, fear
of Afrikaner domination and heavy reliance on Imperial protection.[3]

In the Transvaal, intense political activity took place from October
to December 1908, when almost 4000 signatures were collected for
submission to the Convention, and greater co-operation developed among
activists and organisations in the colony. On 1 January 1909, a number
of political organisations, including the Transvaal Basuto Committee, the
Transvaal Native Congress and Edward Tsewu's Iliso Lomzi, formed a
united body, the Transvaal Native Union (TNU), to defend their common

interests.[4] The formation of the TNU was an important event in a colony with probably the greatest diversity of people in all South Africa. The spread of universalist ideas among Transvaal Africans was reflected in the provision that coloured people could become members and that the organisation would act on their behalf. Current political developments were clearly bringing home the need for increased organisation and united action. To work with sympathetic white colonists was also thought desirable. One of the objects embodied in the constitution of the TNU was 'co-operation with all friends of law, order, liberty and justice ... without distinction of race'.[5]

At the well attended inaugural meeting of the TNU in the Nancefield location of Johannesburg, attended by delegates from 14 towns, a central executive was elected to control the activities of the organisation. The committee consisted of a cross-section of members of the various affiliated bodies,[6] including Edward Tsewu and Jesse Makhothe.* The South African Native Congress stalwart and editor of *Izwi*, A.K. Soga, who was in the Transvaal at this time, also attended the TNU inaugural meeting. After being given a special welcome, Soga impressed on the delegates the need for unity.[7]

Understandably, Africans looked for reassurances from the Imperial authorities at this crossroads in South African history. Without a voice in the discussions on a new constitutional model for their country, they were anxious to receive some kind of guarantee from Britain, as the ultimate authority, that their interests would not be ignored. Statements by high-ranking figures in Britain raised some hope in this respect. When the Colonial Secretary, Lord Crewe, declared in November 1908 that, while the British government had left colonial statesmen to decide on the machinery for union, it had a real and distinct obligation towards the Africans, *Ilanga* commented that never in the history of the land was such an assurance more valuable, and that it was bound to have an influence on current politics.[8] In December, *Izwi* noted a similar speech by the Under-Secretary of State for the Colonies, Colonel Seely, who stated that Britain's obligations to the Africans would never be lost sight of in any final settlement.[9]

---

* Other committee members were M.R. Ruoele, J.K. Moikangoa, Z. More, E. Moeletsi, the Rev. Mvuyane and Messrs Gunuza and Monakali.

The draft South Africa Act drawn up by the National Convention was finally released to the press on 9 February 1909.[10] Although many of the details were criticised, white opinion in the Transvaal and the Orange River Colony was generally favourable. However, it was widely opposed in Natal, whose inhabitants feared being 'submerged' by their neighbours. But in respect of the provisions pertaining to Africans, the draft succeeded to a large degree in placating white colonists in the three northern colonies. Most were opposed to the principle of Africans having the franchise, but they accepted the compromise with the Cape as necessary to achieve the greater goal of union.[11] A vocal minority, however, did not. Louis Botha informed Merriman that there were some Transvalers who were quite prepared to wreck union on this question.[12]

In the Cape, with its relatively non-racial tradition, it was the proposed colour bar that caused excitement. A powerful lobby, led by W.P. Schreiner, demanded amendments to the colour bar provisions in the draft when it came before the Cape parliament.[13] When the draft was first released Schreiner was in Greytown where he was still involved in Dinuzulu's trial. His immediate reaction was that it was 'narrow, illiberal and shortsighted in conception', unjust to the black majority and did not adequately safeguard their rights.[14] He later repeated this theme in well-publicised speeches in Queenstown and Cape Town.[15] Other critics of the draft included J.G. van der Horst, editor of the *Cape Times*; the influential veteran Afrikaner Bond leader, J.H. Hofmeyr; and a number of church figures and liberal personalities, mainly in Cape Town.[16] Under Hofmeyr's influence, the Cape Town branch of the Bond strongly denounced the draft and called for a referendum in the Cape before it was passed. Its main criticism was levelled at the under-representation of the Cape in the Union parliament, the strong centralisation of powers in the Union government, and the colour restrictions and inadequate protection given to black voters by the two-thirds majority clause.[17] Hofmeyr's opposition seriously embarrassed the Prime Minister, Merriman, who feared that the 'hornet's nest' stirred up in Cape Town could jeopardise the passage of the draft.[18] When the annual conference of the Bond repeated, though more cautiously, most of the objections of the Cape Town branch, including the question of protecting black franchise rights, Merriman's concern deepened.[19]

Thus while whites in the northern colonies, with a few 'negrophile' exceptions, either accepted the franchise provisions regarding Africans or considered them too generous, a vocal minority in the Cape demanded the repeal of the colour bar sections. This group found ready allies in the majority black population, which mobilised on an unprecedented scale to demonstrate its opposition to the proposed constitution. Throughout South Africa, African newspapers, political groups and spokesmen were virtually unanimous in their condemnation of its provisions.

The response of the African press to the draft was one of undisguised hostility and all were outspoken in their criticism of the colour bar. Jabavu's *Imvo* was first to comment. It described the draft as illiberal and said it 'stereotyped vicious, flagitious and immoral colour distinctions among the King's subjects'. No opening was provided for the reasonable aspirations of the black man. The 'unreasoning and unreasonable prejudices' against Africans of the delegates from the Transvaal, the Orange River Colony and Natal had overwhelmed the Cape. While Africans were grateful to the Cape delegates for preserving their voting rights, the colour bar in parliament took away the prized guarantee of political freedom and political contentment and made the African franchise 'illusory'.[20] The franchise 'has been given with one hand and taken away with the other', *Imvo* added.[21] To alienate Africans at the very outset of union was 'very, very bad policy indeed. May our beloved country be spared from it'.[22]

John Dube's *Ilanga* warned of the threat of future violence if the constitution was implemented. *Ilanga* said Africans believed in union, but only a just 'manly Christian Union'. If racial prejudice persisted and Africans continued to be seen only as exploitable labour units, the likelihood of a future filled with 'bitter hatred' loomed ahead.[23]

As usual, A.K. Soga did not mince his words in *Izwi*. 'This is treachery! It is worse. It is successful betrayal, for the Act has virtually disenfranchised the black man already even before the meeting of the Union Parliament,

which will complete the crime by solemn vote of the two Assemblies ...
This is a replica of the treaty of Vereeniging.'[24] 'At one stroke they sweep
away the work of half a century and the dearest possessions of 20,000
voters who represent the more errant millions.'[25] *Izwi* saw the report as
part of 'a calculating and deliberate compact' to get rid of the African
vote.[26] It had been engineered in the Transvaal by the 'plutocrats', who
ruled the world and were perverting British principles, with their Afrikaner
collaborators. The plot had unfolded with the treaty of Vereeniging, the
attempts to suspend the Cape constitution, and the Randlords 'getting a
little of their own back' and reasserting their power after Africans had
defeated them in their attempts to corner the African labour market after
the war. *Izwi* said it had seen this whole plot developing a long time
previously. That was why it had called the 1907 Queenstown Conference
to discuss the question of union.[27] The Cape delegates, particularly the
Progressive leaders, had finally shown their true colours by shamelessly co-
operating in this compact. Their smirky assurances could not stand up to
their dishonesty, which could be read in the draft report. They could never
again be trusted. With such a 'pack of hucksterers and huggermuggers'
as the Cape Progressive leaders had proved themselves to be, could there
be any doubt of the result when an 'ignorant Boer member' stood up in
parliament one day to propose the abolition of the African franchise?[28]

When the *Daily Dispatch* accused *Izwi* of adopting 'an inflammatory
tone and language calculated to appeal to the worst passions of its readers',
Izwi replied that the *Dispatch* need not be afraid of its dividing blacks
against whites. This could not be more surely done than by the passing of
the 'South African Conspiracy Act' in its existing form.[29] *Izwi* warned that
blacks would never be satisfied with an inferior status. '"Equal rights for
all South of the Zambesi" is the motto that will yet float at the masthead
of this new ship of state which has been launched under the Union, and no
other will be permanently substituted while there is one black or coloured
man of any consequence or self-respect in the country, or any white man
who respects the traditions of free Government – so help us God.'[30]

41

Plans for a counter-convention

Let us meet together before it is too late. Remember what happened at Vereeniging and what was done to the black man. Let not union be brought through you Chiefs Letsie, Jonathan, Ntsane, Dalindyebo, Sandile … You also our Chiefs from Natal, Transvaal, Swaziland, Zambesi and M'Zilikazi [Matabeleland].

– Thomas Mapikela, Orange River Colony Native Congress,
March 1910

Even before the release of the draft South Africa Act, the Orange River Colony Native Congress (ORCNC) decided to act in anticipation and made plans to arrange a joint convention of Africans from throughout South Africa. The aim would be to formulate and publicise the views of the excluded on union. Immediately the draft was released, the ORCNC's plan was set in motion and promoted through private correspondence between political leaders and newspaper editors in the various colonies, and through the columns of an affronted African press. A committee of the ORCNC under its secretary, Thomas Mapikela, set about organising the convention. It was to be held in Bloemfontein, the most central venue for an inter-colonial meeting.

The decision to arrange a convention for Africans was first released in *Imvo* on 9 February, the same day the draft Act was made public. Jabavu gave the plan his full support. He said it was necessary that the 'black house' should hold a council and voice its opinion before the constitution was enacted, and, if necessary, take its grievances to London. He urged all African organisations in the four colonies to meet as soon as possible to prepare for the convention: this was scheduled to take place before the various colonial parliaments met to consider the draft Act.[1]

Within days of the release of the draft, the ORCNC organising committee circularised letters to the various regions, informing interested groups of the proposed convention.[2] In view of the threat to African interests, they appealed to all associations 'guarding the rights of the people' to prepare for a 'Pitso or Ngqu' at which South African 'native opinion' would be expressed. This applied as much to enfranchised Africans in the Cape as to those disenfranchised in the Transvaal and the Orange River Colony. Although Cape Africans would retain the franchise under the new constitution, the ORCNC predicted that the 'voteless masses of Natives in other Colonies will be utilised as an instrument by the anti-native franchise majority to disenfranchise the Cape Natives'. Only the speedy extension of the vote to the northern colonies would permanently secure the African franchise in the Cape. Thus it was important that Africans join forces as soon as possible to pursue this goal.[3]

The appeal for a national convention of Africans in Bloemfontein found a ready response. Such was the hostility to the draft constitution that the convention took place scarcely six weeks after its release. In that time political activists mobilised on an unprecedented scale. Both *Izwi* and *Ilanga* added their support to that already given by *Imvo*.[4] Urged on by the African press and political leaders, local committees from far and wide organised meetings to express African opposition to the draft and to elect delegates to the regional meetings that were being held in the various colonies. At these meetings preparations were made for representation at the central convention. *Imvo*, then celebrating its 25th year of existence, commented, 'Conferences are the order of the day among the natives of South Africa on the ugly colour line that is being imposed on them in the draft constitution. We have never known our people so united and determined to contest, constitutionally, of course, a political issue.'[5] In one issue *Imvo* reported on no less than 16 protest meetings in its vernacular columns. These ranged from Vredefort in the Orange River Colony to Kimberley in the northern Cape, Cape Town in the south and Tsomo in the Transkeian Territories.[6] African women joined in the fray as well: in

Somerset East, interdenominational prayer groups met to pray for the success of those who were opposing the draft constitution.[7]

The first colony-wide organisation to meet was the ORCNC, which held its annual congress at Winburg on 17 and 18 February 1909,[8] little more than a week after the National Convention had made its draft public. After an address by Thomas Mapikela, the initiative of the central committee in arranging a convention for Africans was put to the delegates and the idea was unanimously accepted.[9]

Subsequently, Mapikela, helped by other members of the ORCNC committee, like Elijah Tshongwana and J.S. Mocher, continued with arrangements for the convention and corresponded with Soga, Jabavu and leaders in other colonies.[10] On 5 March, Mapikela circularised a second notice through the African press. This was aimed at involving traditional leaders in the convention as well and was addressed to the *Zinkosi na Mapakati, na Manene* (chiefs, councillors and gentlemen): 'Let us meet together before it is too late. Remember what happened at Vereeniging and what was done to the black man. Let not union be brought through you Chiefs Letsie, Jonathan, Ntsane, Dalindyebo, Sandile, Gwenbinkumbi, Nqwiliso, Ngangelizwe, Njokwini, Mhlambiso, Mabandla, Bakleni, Ndhlangazi, Makawula, U'Mhalla, Siwane, Molema, Falo. You also our Chiefs from Natal, Transvaal, Swaziland, Zambesi and M'Zilikazi [Matabeleland].'[11] Shortly afterwards, the dates for the convention were fixed for 24 to 26 March. Mapikela also received official permission to hold the meeting. Prime Minister Fischer explained to Prime Minister Moor of Natal that the government had decided not to interfere, as it considered it inadvisable 'to manufacture cheap martyrs' and better to learn publicly what would be said.[12]

The other main Free State organisation, the Becoana Mutual Improvement Association, held a meeting at Thaba Nchu on 20 March, at which the provisions of the draft Act were strongly deprecated. Given the particular history of the locality, the Association sought to include Thaba Nchu and Witsieshoek in the terms of the schedule to the draft Act, which dealt with the status of the Protectorates, so that Africans' land would remain inalienable.[13]

While the initiative for inter-colonial African co-operation came from the Orange River Colony, the release of the draft Act triggered the most extensive response among Africans in the Cape. The protests were led by *Izwi* and *Imvo*. They maintained a constant clamour against the proposed colour bar, encouraging local groups to do likewise and to elect delegates to represent them at proposed regional conferences.[14] Numerous meetings were held in urban and rural areas throughout the colony, particularly in the eastern Cape. They ranged from well-reported gatherings at places like Ndabeni in Cape Town to meetings in Peddie and Keiskamma Hoek.[15] Some were attended by hundreds of people, others were small. From everywhere the message was the same: the 'nation' was opposed to the 'blot' on the constitution. In areas such as the Karoo where Africans were thinly spread, and in places where organisation was lacking, Africans took part in protest gatherings organised by the African Political Organisation, playing a major part in proceedings at Graaff-Reinet and Kimberley, for example.[16] The APO was at the helm of the concerted agitation of coloured communities against the draft constitution.

Special meetings for Africans in the eastern Cape constituencies were also held by delegates to the National Convention such as Colonel Stanford and Dr Jameson.[17] This was part of a general campaign by Convention delegates to market the draft Act to the country. In the case of Stanford, his itinerary included Butterworth, Idutywa, Umtata, Engcobo and Elliot. In each town he held meetings with whites in the mornings and Africans in the afternoons.[18] In his diary Stanford alluded to the concern among Africans about union. The Thembu paramount, Dalindyebo, was one of those present at a well-attended meeting in Umtata.[19]

At these promotional meetings the position usually adopted by the Convention delegates was that, far from endangering the Cape African franchise, the draft constitution with its two-thirds majority requirement in fact protected African interests. They felt that in due course the liberal ideas of the Cape would influence the other colonies, leading to a better dispensation for all Africans.[20] Most Africans who attended these 'sweetheart' meetings generally accepted the assurances given to them. After they had expressed concern about the 'Europeans only' clauses, and asked the delegates to do their best to have them removed, the meetings usually ended with a vote of confidence being passed in the draft Act. But not all listeners were taken in. Commenting on the speeches of delegates, *Imvo* warned that the European-descent clause would make it impossible for liberal views to prevail.[21]

What did give some hope to the protest leaders was the dissenting voices of white political and church leaders in the passionate debate taking place in colonial circles over the merits of the two-thirds safeguard and the 'Europeans only' limitation. Both *Izwi* and *Imvo* provided extensive coverage of the various views. Responding to W.P. Schreiner's powerful denunciation of the colour bar in his Queenstown speech, *Imvo* praised this 'vigorous and eloquent effort', and *Izwi* expressed the indebtedness of the Africans to Schreiner for his bold stand.[22] Reservations about the draft constitution voiced by J.H. Hofmeyr and other Afrikaner Bond members were also welcomed.[23] Similarly, when Lord Selborne spoke in favour of a more liberal solution to South Africa's race relations in Cape Town, *Imvo* said his speech gave 'intense satisfaction to Natives and friends of justice'.[24] African leaders hoped that these utterances would elicit a more critical understanding of the Convention's decisions and influence the colonial parliaments in the direction of 'eliminating the deplorable and unstatesmanlike colour bar which at present disfigures the new South African Draft Act'.[25] The anti-colour bar activists not only appreciated the opposition that white liberals expressed, but invited white sympathisers to participate in the meetings Africans held to discuss the question of union and join with them in protests against the draft Act.[26]

Against this background of African solidarity and initial support for a united African convention, it seemed there was perhaps a chance to heal the deep divisions among Africans in the Cape. This optimism soon proved misplaced. Despite the common disillusionment over the draft Act and the logic in favour of united protest action, this did not happen in the eastern Cape. Part of the reason was the suggested mechanism for selecting delegates. The feeling of the organisers of the Bloemfontein convention, and of political leaders in the Transvaal and Natal and the Cape-based South African Native Congress (SANC), was that the various delegations should be representative of the respective colonies, not of local organisations.[27] However, this attitude was not shared by Jabavu. He intended going to Bloemfontein on his own behalf and that of his large informal following. But the SANC insisted that Jabavu's King William's Town Native Association should, like other local associations, first attend the regional conference it had called in Mgwali near Stutterheim, where delegates would be elected to represent the Cape at the national convention. Only through this procedure, it felt, could a properly representative delegation be sent to Bloemfontein.[28]

As matters turned out, Jabavu attended neither the Mgwali meeting nor the one at Bloemfontein. In March he withdrew his active support for the Bloemfontein convention and proceeded to organise his own conference. The decision to do so was taken at a meeting in King William's Town on 5 March. A committee was appointed to make arrangements, consisting of Jabavu and five others.[29] The well-known Nathaniel Umhalla, who had fallen out with the SANC over his participation in the Inter-State Native College Scheme, was also involved. Notices in *Imvo* advertising the Bloemfontein convention were now dropped and replaced by similar ones summoning Africans to King William's Town.[30] The date was set for 7 April. *Imvo* used the spurious argument that the Bloemfontein venue had been decided on before the publication of the draft Act, and before it became known to what extent the rights of Africans in the Cape had been affected. In view of subsequent developments a different approach was called for. But this did not explain why *Imvo* had continued to support the idea of a conference in Bloemfontein in the weeks immediately after the release of the draft.[31]

Meanwhile, plans continued for the regional conference of the SANC. The notice convening this meeting captured the urgent and anxious mood of the times. 'We are rushing to meet so as to have the people's word before the Parliament assembles. The branches must send delegates and give their views. The places which have no branches must also send people. The people as a whole must be present so as to give advice. The house [i.e. the black people] is in danger because of the decisions of the Convention of the colonies.' The notice ended with the popular expression *Zemk' Iinkomo Magwalandini!* (There go your cattle [i.e. rights], you cowards!), first used as a call for educated Africans to mobilise politically in the late 1870s and early 1880s.[32]

The Congress's Mgwali conference lasted three days, from 17 to 19 March, and was attended by 80 delegates, among them several chiefs who had responded to a call by *Izwi*.[33] SANC stalwarts such as the Thomas Mqanda (president), Jonathan Tunyiswa (secretary), Dr Rubusana, A.K. Soga, Eben Koti and William Siyo were also present.[34] From all over the Cape and Transkeian Territories, groups attended or sent messages of support.[35]

Before discussions got under way, Dr Rubusana explained the aim of the meeting to the chiefs and councillors, saying, 'The nation must be proud of itself and stand up for its rights.' Congress wanted to be the mouthpiece of the whole nation. It wished to create the unity among Africans that Ntsikana had foretold. This theme was also developed by A.K. Soga. He thanked the chiefs for attending, as they were the natural leaders, and stressed that petty differences and jealousies should be set aside in view of the great dangers facing Africans.[36]

The conference accepted the decision of the SANC leaders to send delegates to the Bloemfontein convention rather than to the Jabavu meeting. After a lively discussion on the draft Act, Rubusana, Soga and Mqanda were delegated to attend the convention in Bloemfontein a week later.[37] Though Jabavu's name was also put forward for selection, his nomination was outvoted.[38]

Meanwhile, in British Bechuanaland, which had been annexed to the Cape Colony in 1895, the Rolong saw the proposed constitution as another threat to the autonomy they had been promised. They promptly mobilised to meet the challenge. On 27 February 1909 chiefs and headmen convened a meeting in Mafeking to consider the draft Act, with the Acting Paramount, Lekoko Montsioa, presiding. J. Gerrans, who was soon to step into the limelight for his work on behalf of the Tswana chiefs, addressed the meeting and explained the draft.[39] The meeting resolved that 'The Barolong nation cannot regard the native clauses in the Draft Constitution as giving sufficient protection to the Cape coloured franchise'. The Rolong wanted steps to be taken 'to induce the Cape Legislature to get more adequate protection for them in the Constitution'.[40]

Shortly afterwards, the matter was taken further. On 8 March Paramount Badirile Montsioa wrote to the Governor and Prime Minister, asking for clarification. Would the chiefs still be allowed to govern their people as before and was it correct that, if less than one-third of the members of parliament were not sympathetic to Africans, their vote would be taken away?[41] To the first question, the government replied that people in British Bechuanaland would occupy the same position under Union as at the present time under the Annexation Act. To the second question, the Prime Minister replied that the African franchise was sufficiently safeguarded by the draft constitution, and further that Mr Merriman felt it would be the height of imprudence for Africans to 'raise an agitation' in this respect.[42]

When the draft Act was eventually released, the Rolong took the precaution of approaching the heads of the Wesleyan missions who held in their safekeeping the official documents providing guarantees to the chiefs at the time of their annexation to the Cape. A high-ranking Wesleyan superintendent, F.J. Briscoe, sought an interview with the High Commissioner, Lord Selborne, to discuss the matter, but was informed that the proper person to approach would be the Cape Governor. Selborne said, however, that it appeared clear to him that, according to the draft Act, the Union government would inherit the responsibility of the Cape government for the reserve.[43] This answer accorded with the assurance sent to Badirile Montsioa.

Further proof of the concern felt by the Rolong about the impending union was provided by the appointment of a high-ranking delegation to attend the Bloemfontein convention. It consisted of Chief Lekoko Montsioa, Chief Silas Molema (confidant and assistant of the paramount) and T. Lefenya.[44] The absence of Solomon Plaatje, who would have been a natural choice, raises an interesting question. It has been suggested that Plaatje could have been indisposed or, more probably, was engaged on other business, recruiting labour for the mines, at a time when he was in debt from his failed newspaper venture.[45]

Although the organisers of the Bloemfontein convention initially received no reply from the Transvaal, Africans here also responded to developments at this time.[46] Noteworthy was the meeting organised by the Transvaal Native Congress (TNC) in February 1909.[47] Afterwards J.G. Kaiyana, the vice-president, wrote to Jabavu informing him that he and the general secretary, Jesse Makhothe, would be representing their organisation at Bloemfontein.[48] For some reason, however, they did not attend. It could be that the TNC was represented instead by the two delegates of the Transvaal Native Union, of which the TNC was an associate member, or by one or more of the other Transvaal delegates, whose political affiliations are unknown. The first possibility seems the most likely.

For its part, the TNU responded to the appeal by the ORCNC by summoning a meeting on 8 March to inform Africans of what was happening and discuss the draft constitution. This was held in the Nancefield location in Johannesburg and was attended by 365 people, including delegates from the Krugersdorp, Roodepoort, Boksburg, Roodekop, Evaton, Johannesburg and New Primrose branches. The proceedings were chaired by William Letseleba and the secretary, Z. More. Edward Tsewu was also prominent. The meeting strongly condemned the draft Act, and sent a report containing its main criticisms to the government.[49] It denounced the delegates of the National Convention in the 'strongest terms' for shamefully neglecting the interests of Africans, who formed the majority of the population, whose loyalty to the Empire was unimpeachable and who shouldered the greatest share of taxation in the Transvaal. The High Commissioner was asked to convey to the King the meeting's request that unification should not be allowed until the interests of the 'defenceless' Africans had been properly and adequately safeguarded.[50] The TNU also delegated Z. More and E.T. Moeletsi to represent it at the forthcoming convention in Bloemfontein.[51]

Natal was the only colony where no regional meeting was held before the convention in Bloemfontein. Although, according to Dr Rubusana, the Natal Native Congress met on 13 and 14 March, it did not convene to discuss the effects of union until April and Iliso Lesizwe Esimnyama, an offshoot aimed at involving traditionalists, did not discuss the subject until the beginning of June.[52]

In the absence of organisational activity, individuals took the lead in responding to the draft Act. Early in March a prominent member of the NNC, Abner Mtimkulu, tried to persuade the government to convene a meeting for Africans on the question of union. Writing from Dundee to the Under-Secretary for Native Affairs, Mtimkulu said, 'The men here in the north wish to have the matter of union explained to them. The government should gather together the "black race" for this purpose', as had happened the previous year, so that the government could explain new legislation.[53] He added, 'We think that this would help with regard to the prevailing opinion that the black race is being sold by the British to the Dutch.'[54]

In a similar individual initiative, an unnamed minister of religion from Natal wrote to Jabavu in the Cape on the matter of African protests against union, asking for details about the arrangements for a joint meeting. A.K. Soga, editor of *Izwi*, was also in touch with people in Natal at this time, and there were letters in *Ilanga* voicing opposition to the draft constitution.[55] *Ilanga* took the lead in opposing the South Africa Act in Natal. Its editor, John Dube, who described the newspaper as the mouthpiece of the 'voteless but not voiceless' outsiders, kept up a constant stream of comment. The 'nation' was exhorted to shake off its lethargy and unite to show its opposition to the terms of union; the 'Vukani Bantu!' call was made.[56] Up to the end of April, only one editorial in the newspaper's English columns was not devoted to the subjects of union and political representation for Africans.[57]

Dube saw the necessity of convening a meeting similar to those in the other colonies, and continually urged the NNC to organise one. He warned, *Madoda lento akusiyona ukudlala* (Gentlemen, this is no playing matter).[58] But Congress was slow in responding. Only on 19 March did it issue a notice proclaiming a 'Great Meeting' of the whole of Zululand and Natal to discuss the draft constitution and find means of co-operating with Africans in the other colonies. The meeting was set for Pietermaritzburg on 1 April.[59] Meanwhile, the chairman of the NNC, Simeon Kambule, and Dube himself would represent Natal at the convention in Bloemfontein a few days hence.[60]

42

The South African
Native Convention, March 1909

Full and equal rights and privileges, subject only to the conditions
and limitations established by law and applicable alike to all
citizens without distinction of class, colour or creed.
        – South African Native Convention, March 1909

The South African Native Convention met in a schoolroom in the
Waaihoek township in Bloemfontein from 24 to 26 March 1909. It was
a seminal event in the history of South African politics, the first occasion
on which African political leaders and the fledgling political associations
in the various colonies co-operated formally, and a major step towards the
formation of a permanent national organisation.

When the Convention began at 3 p.m. on Wednesday 24 March, the 38
delegates from the four colonies had not yet all arrived, but this did not
hamper proceedings, as the agenda for the first day's activity was restricted
to the formal opening and a large group of local people were in attendance
to witness the occasion.[1] The Cape was represented by Dr Rubusana
and A.K. Soga of the South African Native Congress, Natal by Simeon
Kambule and John Dube of the Natal Native Congress, and the Transvaal
by Z. More and E.T. Moeletsi of the Transvaal Native Union, as well as by
A. Mpinda, S. Ndima and J. Ndaba, whose affiliations were not stated.[2]

The host colony was especially well represented, with all the organisations in the Orange River Colony present. The biggest delegation was from
the body that had organised the convention, the Orange River Colony
Native Congress (ORCNC). It was led by John Mocher (president), Henry

Poho (vice-president and treasurer), Thomas Mapikela (secretary), and stalwarts such as Joseph B. Twayi and Peter Phatlane, who had been involved in organised politics since the war.[3] Joel Goronyane headed the deputation of the Becoana Mutual Improvement Association, representing the well-established Thaba Nchu landowners, together with J.M. Nyokong and Jeremiah Makgothi. Then there were the delegates of the maverick Eastern Native Vigilance Association from Bethlehem, headed by its president, Obed Mokhosi. Formerly the Bethlehem branch of the ORCNC, it formed itself into a semi-independent body around 1908, after it had lost contact with the mother body. Neither the government nor the Congress recognised this group as a separate organisation, though it continued to approach the government separately until after Union, and remained connected to the emerging national movement.[4]

The members of the executive committee of the African Political Organisation (APO) in the Orange River Colony also attended the Convention.[5] Led by N.J. Daly, they did so with the full blessing of their national president, Dr Abdurahman. He informed the organisers that he had advised APO branches that they could attend if they wished, 'for it matters not who initiates the movement as long as we attain our object'.[6] Co-operation between Africans and local APO leaders went back many years in this territory of fluid identities and ethnicities, and this step was also in keeping with the increasing contact between African and coloured politicians since the time of the 1907 Queenstown Conference.*

Despite the appeal by the convention's organiser, Thomas Mapikela, for chiefs from all the British territories to attend, the response was poor. The only chiefs present were Lekoko Montsioa and Silas Molema from British Bechuanaland.[7] The editor of *Naledi ea Lesotho*, S.M. Phamotse, and a Mr Makepe had set out to represent Basutoland at the meeting, but Letsie Moshoeshoe dissuaded them from attending when they stopped over to see him on the way to Bloemfontein.[8] The Sotho clearly had no intention of upsetting the Imperial authorities at this delicate stage in the deliberations on the Protectorate's future.

The most notable absentee was John Tengo Jabavu, whose disdain for the convention was exemplified by the one scanty report in his *Imvo*,

* The other APO delegates were A.J. Maasdorp, G. Crowder, R. Symmons and B. Vorster.

in contrast to the wide coverage it received in many other newspapers.[9] Long-standing divisions in Cape politics were once again apparent. While Jabavu and his traditional supporters in the Imbumba movement set up a separate Cape Native Convention and adopted as their main departure point the primary need to protect the Cape vote, the South African Native Congress had a clear African national orientation and identified itself with the struggles of 'rightless' Africans in the other colonies – indeed, it had shown itself since 1898 to be the main promoter of the emerging national political movement.

The chairman of the convention was Joel Goronyane of the Becoana Mutual Improvement Association. After he had briefly sketched the aims of the meeting, he introduced Dewdney Drew, member of the Legislative Council of the Orange River Colony representing African interests, who had been asked by the organising committee to open the convention.[10] Editor of the Bloemfontein newspaper *The Friend* from 1904 to 1908, Drew had earned a reputation for his pro-'native' sympathies.[11] In his speech Drew adopted a cautionary and paternalistic tone. Although he recognised that the draft Act fell short of 'equal rights for all civilised men' and limited representation for everyone else, he felt that any serious attempt to bring about amendments would only worsen the position. Despite the fact that the draft constitution deprived Cape Africans of the right to sit in parliament and failed to extend the franchise to Africans in the other colonies, Drew expressed the opinion that Africans had on the whole gained substantially from the draft Act. He concluded his speech by posing the question: What was the attitude of the Africans to be? His advice was, 'Don't compromise your principles; you are bound to ask for equal rights, but take from time to time any privileges the Government offers you, and use those privileges so as to prove yourselves fit for more.' He warned them, 'Don't expect to go far in a short time.'

Drew's speech was not in accord with the mood of the convention and his assumptions were immediately challenged. A.K. Soga rejected the principle of 'accepting the half loaf'. He continued: '[Africans] could not wait for the white man to release them from their troubles. They should struggle – constitutionally I mean. They would not get any political privileges without a struggle. If they waited as Mr Drew suggested, they would get no further ... They found that, after the trouble and expense of educating themselves and their children, the white man said "thus far and no further". Not to use their constitutional privileges to secure their rights would be a fatal mistake.'[12] Soga was supported by the chairman, Joel Goronyane, who also encouraged Africans to keep on struggling for their rights in a constitutional manner.[13] He concluded that segregation would lead to race hatred. The proceedings for the opening day were then closed.

Using the procedures followed at the National Convention as a guideline, the delegates spent most of the next two days behind closed doors discussing the draft Act and how it affected Africans. Their decisions were to be made public at a meeting on the final evening on 26 March.

The discussions proper began at 10.45 a.m. on Thursday 25 March. Joel Goronyane's position as chairman was confirmed by the meeting and Goliath Rakhatoe of the Eastern Native Vigilance Society was elected as secretary. Then the resolutions adopted by the various regional conferences were read. The South African Native Congress, the Transvaal Native Union, the Becoana Mutual Improvement Association, the Orange River Colony Native Congress and the African Political Organisation all submitted proposals.[14] Discussions ensued on the various sections of the draft Act that offended Africans. Clause 153, which embodied the provision for the disqualification of African voters in the Cape by a two-thirds majority decision of both houses of parliament, was the main focus of attention. A long discussion took place on this issue. The other three sections were the colour-bar clauses referring to 'European descent'.[15]

That afternoon it was decided to send an invitation to the delegates at a large church conference in Bloemfontein to attend the concluding meeting of the convention on the Friday evening.[16] The church meeting was busy discussing the union of the Baptist, Congregational, Presbyterian and Wesleyan Methodist churches, and was attended by leading representatives from all these denominations, including the churchman and composer J.K. Bokwe. In reply, Bokwe praised the convention in a telegram both for its temperate language and for its unmistakably clear and respectful protest.[17] Bokwe was an enormously respected figure of that time. Attached to Lovedale for many years, he had left there after a quarter of a century to become a partner with Jabavu in *Imvo* in 1898, prompted by his desire to heal the split that had opened in eastern Cape politics between the Mfengu and the Xhosa. Soon afterwards he was ordained as a minister and was posted to Ugie. He became one of the most influential men in that town, winning the confidence of all sections of the population. Known as *Umdengentonga* (The little man with a big mind), he negotiated with the Cape Education Department for a school for whites, held services for them at their own request, and virtually became town clerk.[18]

Bokwe's assessment of the tone of the convention was accurate and reflected the whole approach of his generation to politics. Their protests were respectful and temperate and framed in terms of the religious and humanitarian values absorbed from Christianity and liberal politics. They went to great lengths to prove their loyalty and their suitability to participate in politics. Nothing demonstrated this more than the speeches and resolutions at the convention, and the procedure that was followed. Proceedings started with prayers.[19] The Prime Minister of the host colony was formally thanked for giving the delegates the opportunity of holding a public meeting and exercising freedom of speech. He was asked to convey expressions of loyalty to the Governor.[20] Respectful greetings were also sent to the High Commissioner, who was asked to convey the convention's loyalty to the King.[21]

By Friday afternoon the convention had finalised two sets of resolutions on the draft constitution, which summed up the general feeling of Africans towards union. The first, embodying nine points, was concerned with the rights of Africans in the South African colonies. It criticised the decisions of the National Convention and suggested several amendments to the draft Act. The other focused on the future relationship between the Protectorates and the Union.

In the first resolution of the first set, the convention recognised that union was 'essential, necessary and inevitable', but said it should promote the progress and welfare of all British subjects in South Africa. The draft Act did not do this. The colour bar constituted a fundamental wrong and injustice. It was regretted that the franchise system of the Cape had not been extended to the northern colonies and that the principle of equal rights, which many leading statesmen had supported down the years, had been ignored. Instead, a clause should be inserted in the constitution that provided for all persons to have 'full and equal rights and privileges, subject only to the conditions and limitations established by law and applicable alike to all citizens without distinction of class, colour or creed'. The Imperial government, to which black people owed their loyalty, was bound by both fundamental and specific obligations to see that this happened. It should extend to the African and coloured people the same rights that were enjoyed under the law by those of European descent.

In its deliberations on the responsibilities of the Imperial authorities, the convention paid particular attention to the terms of the Vereeniging peace treaty. It was stated that this treaty did not abrogate the pre-war promises made by the British government to alleviate the position of black inhabitants in the republics and grant them the same rights as those enjoyed by their counterparts in the Cape. 'The Eighth Article of the Peace Treaty therefore demands to be fulfilled in the most liberal sense in relation to His Majesty's native and coloured subjects in the Transvaal and Orange River Colony, and those Colonies should be required to conform to the system of the Cape Colony with regard to the principles of the franchise as far as the native and coloured people are concerned.'

Referring to Natal, it was pointed out that after annexation the Crown had promulgated a non-discriminatory constitution, but in practice this had not been implemented, placing exceptional difficulties in the way of Africans wishing to obtain the franchise. Thus the absurd state of affairs existed that out of a million Africans in Natal and Zululand the South African Native Affairs Commission had reported that there were only two African voters in Natal. Both these people were reported to be dead.

The last four of the nine resolutions in the first set all suggested amendments to certain sections of the draft Act. In sections 25 and 44, which dealt with the qualification of senators and members of the House of Assembly respectively, the convention wanted the colour bar removed by the deletion of the words 'of European descent'. In section 33, which provided for increases in the size of the House of Assembly in proportion to the number of male adults in each province, it wanted the words 'and native and coloured voters' added to the existing 'European male adults' provision. With regard to section 35, it proposed that the franchise regulations that allowed Africans in the Cape to vote should be permanently entrenched and made unalterable. This new condition should also be written into section 153, which dealt with amendments to the constitution.

The second set of resolutions concerned the future position of the Protectorates. It is an indication of the recognition by Africans of the need to harmonise their interests and view matters affecting them along national rather than parochial lines that a stand was made on this issue, even though the Protectorates were unrepresented at the convention. Delegates believed it would be preferable for the Protectorates to remain under the direct control of the Imperial government. However, if the British government decided that it would be to the advantage of the Protectorates to transfer them, the convention would 'loyally acquiesce', but certain conditions should first be met. First, the chiefs should be satisfied with the conditions of transfer. Secondly, the conditions should be fixed before the draft Act became law. Thirdly, the transfer should not take place until the Union had adopted a 'native policy' that accorded with Imperial traditions.

In addition to the formulation of these lengthy resolutions for submission to the Imperial and colonial governments, the press and the National Convention, the South African Native Convention also made tentative moves to form itself into a permanent organisation. A president and executive were elected 'to watch the draft Act, to promote organisation, and to defend the interests of the Natives'.[22] If the draft Act was not amended by the National Convention in the direction desired, the executive was to meet to organise a deputation, and choose the delegates, to proceed to Britain so as to lay the case of Africans before the Imperial authorities. It was decided to ask W.P. Schreiner to assist them, if this became necessary.[23]

The elected officials were Walter Rubusana of the South African Native Congress (president), John Dube of the Natal Native Congress (vice-president), A.K. Soga of the South African Native Congress (secretary), Jeremiah Makgothi (assistant secretary) and Joel Goronyane (treasurer) of the Becoana Mutual Improvement Association. The rest of the executive consisted of John Mocher, Thomas Mapikela, N.J. Daly, J.M. Nyokong, P.K. Motiyane and Henry Poho (all from the Orange River Colony), Chief Silas Molema (Bechuanaland), Z. More (Transvaal Native Union) and

Simeon Kambule (Natal Native Congress).[24] The important positions given to Rubusana and Soga were in recognition of the key role played by the eastern Cape-based Native Congress in promoting the idea of a national movement since the 1890s. The 1891 Congress, building on even earlier precedents, was clearly the main intellectual and organisational progenitor of the 1909 Native Convention (and these two SANCs would, in turn, become the precursors of the South African Native National Congress of 1912).

The decisions of the convention were made public at a packed meeting on the Friday night after deliberations had been concluded.[25] Conspicuous by their absence were the delegates to the church union conference who had accepted the convention's invitation to attend but did not arrive.[26] Joel Goronyane, who was in the chair, stressed the importance of co-operation among black people. This was echoed by succeeding speakers.[27]

After Soga had read the first set of resolutions, Dr Rubusana moved that they be passed by the meeting. John Dube seconded the motion and it was adopted unanimously.[28] Rubusana then read the resolutions concerning the Protectorates, and Soga proposed that they be adopted.[29] In his speech Soga was scathing in his condemnation of the colour bar.[30] As the son of a Scotswoman and an African minister, Soga could not accept the logic of, and indeed felt personally insulted by, the 'European descent' clauses, which relegated him to an inferior position in society.[31] Soga's motion was then seconded by Chief Silas Molema, and it was passed with acclamation by the meeting.[32]

Thus ended this landmark event in the course of black South African politics. Not only had representatives from all four colonies co-operated for the first time and formed an umbrella organisation, but they had also clearly spelled out their opposition to certain terms of the proposed Union and stipulated the conditions that would have to be met to make these acceptable.

43

Jabavu and the APO
join the chorus, April 1909

The introduction of the colour line into the draft South Africa Act
is unjust to the aborigines and coloured people, is unprecedented in
the annals of the British Empire, is moreover, in the opinion of this
Conference, a grave reflection upon God who made these people,
and is therefore calculated to create discontent among them, and ...
disturb the harmony and happiness of the people of South Africa.

– Cape Native Convention, April 1909

In the month after the meeting of the South African Native
Convention in Bloemfontein, the draft South Africa Act came before the
four colonial parliaments for amendment or ratification and was then
referred back to the National Convention. All the while, Africans continued
to oppose the draft Act right up to the final session of the Convention,
and began to prepare themselves for further steps if their grievances were
not addressed. There was intense activity and preparation throughout the
month of April 1909, including two further important conferences, one
held by J.T. Jabavu, the other by the African Political Organisation.

The meeting organised by Jabavu, styled the Cape Native Convention,
met in King William's Town on 7 and 8 April 1909. It was arranged as
an alternative event to the recent South African Native Convention in
Bloemfontein, with which Jabavu's eastern Cape rivals in the South African

Native Congress had aligned themselves. The attendance register confirmed the feelings of exceptionalism that motivated Jabavu and his supporters at this time. Cape voters were the most advanced politically and, it was argued, their interests needed to be defended as a first step in protecting the constitutional rights of Africans more broadly. Some 41 delegates from 17 eastern Cape towns were present.* Emphasising the local nature of this convention, none of the main Cape urban centres – Cape Town, Kimberley, Port Elizabeth and East London – were represented. Kimberley's delegate arrived after the conclusion of the meeting, while apologies were received from Port Elizabeth.[1] Jabavu was unanimously elected president and the Rev. Elijah J. Mqoboli of Cradock was made vice-president.

In his presidential address Jabavu explained how the draft Act's unexpected infringement of the rights of Cape Africans had necessitated a conference in King William's Town rather than at the venue of Bloemfontein, as originally agreed. Once the terms of union had become clear, it was 'a question of the Cape natives doing what they could to protect their own freedom which had been attacked'.[2] He said that Africans were not opposed to the principle of union. All they were concerned about was that the political rights and privileges given to them by the British government should not be tampered with. He then described how Africans had acquired these rights. In doing so, he quoted at length from the instructions sent to the Governor, Sir George Grey, when the Cape was granted representative government in 1853: 'It is the earnest desire of Her Majesty's Government that all her subjects at the Cape, without distinction of class or colour, should be united by one bond of loyalty and a common interest, and we believe that the exercise of political rights enjoyed by all alike will prove one of the best methods of attaining this object.'[3] Jabavu said that these words 'from the lips of Her Majesty were the charter of the rights and liberties of Cape Africans'. The introduction of the colour line in the new constitution was a flagrant breach of this royal charter. All Africans wanted was that the spirit and letter in which they had been given political rights more than fifty years previously should be retained in the new constitution.[4]

* The towns were Cradock, Dordrecht, Glen Grey, Herschel, Keiskamma Hoek, King
  William's Town, Middledrift, Mount Ayliff, Nqamakwe, Peddie, Queenstown, Somerset East,
  Stutterheim, Tsomo, Victoria East, Whittlesea and Xalanga.

After the meeting had discussed the matter of union, it passed a twelve-point resolution, summing up the attitudes of the delegates. Although it resolved to discuss union only in so far as it directly affected Africans, it expressed approval of the general principle. However, the meeting deprecated the intended restriction of the political privileges which Africans in the Cape had hitherto enjoyed, and expressed regret that the National Convention had not devised some scheme whereby African taxpayers in the other colonies could have a degree of representation.[5] It acknowledged the stand taken by white sympathisers on behalf of Africans at this time. It thanked the Cape delegates to the National Convention for their efforts to maintain the rights and liberties of Cape Africans, and asked them to continue along those lines. It also thanked J.H. Hofmeyr, the Schreiner brothers, white missionaries and 'other white friends of the Natives' who had opposed the draft Act.

The meeting decided on three courses of action to fight 'to the end' the deprivation of Africans' rights. First, it would forward a petition embodying the meeting's decisions to the Cape parliament, which had assembled to discuss the draft Act, as well as to the National Convention when that body reassembled in Bloemfontein. Further, should such a step be necessary, a second petition would be sent to the Cape parliament when it met to approve the final Constitution. Secondly, it resolved to establish a Native Rights Protection Fund. Districts were to forward one guinea to the central executive to enable it to carry out its work. Thirdly, and significantly, it decided to transmit its resolutions to the executive of 'other native conferences' concerned with defending African interests, and to appoint twelve delegates to meet delegates of other conferences 'for concerted action in the prosecution of the cause'.[6] This was a clear sign that, even if Jabavu himself did not, the meeting as a whole recognised the importance of the recent South African Native Convention and the need for African unity.

⁂

On the same day that Jabavu's Cape Native Convention ended, another meeting of prominent eastern Cape Africans started in nearby East

London. Though not an overtly political gathering, it was attended by the cream of the eastern Cape's opinion-formers and discussed the draft constitution, deprecated its colour-bar clauses and drew up a petition to the British government on the matter. The meeting in question was the annual conference of the Eastern Grand Temple of the Order of True Templars, the African section in the eastern Cape of the Independent Order of True Templars. This temperance body had about 2000 members, many of whom were registered voters. Senior political figures from both the Jabavu or Imbumba camp and the South African Native Congress (SANC) were among the delegates who attended the four-day meeting: J.K. Bokwe, Elijah Makiwane (who was the Grand True Templar of the Order), Isaac Wauchope and the SANC stalwarts Walter Rubusana and Meshach Pelem.[7] Jabavu did not attend, because he was in Pietermaritzburg for a Wesleyan Church conference.[8]

Templars like Rubusana, Bokwe and Pelem were not the only supporters of the South African Native Convention who continued to work against the draft Act after the meeting in Bloemfontein. The Natal delegates, John Dube and Simeon Kambule, had returned home via Johannesburg, where they addressed a large meeting of Zulu migrants on 30 March. The two men were received with enthusiasm; the venue in Doornfontein was packed to overflowing. After they had explained the whole issue of union and reported on the Bloemfontein meeting, a collection was taken and they were presented with a gift of £2 16s 9d each. The meeting resolved that all Zulu people in Johannesburg should subscribe monthly to a fund to send delegates abroad in order to bring African disabilities under the new constitution to the attention of the Imperial authorities.[9]

Another matter which came to light at this meeting was the dissatisfaction of Zulu migrants on the Witwatersrand with the ineffectiveness of the Natal Native Congress (NNC). They complained that, while they were 'alive to all matters of the black race', they received no encouragement from Natal. They said that while they responded to matters raised in *Ilanga*, they felt the people in Natal had 'given up'. This disheartened them. The meeting was critical of certain (unnamed) people who undermined the effectiveness of 'native meetings'. It wanted the NNC to ensure that it elected men to office who were committed to the African cause.[10]

While there may have been some validity in the criticism of the NNC – it was the only organisation not to respond to the call to meet before the Bloemfontein convention assembled – it seems that old divisions in Natal politics had come to the fore again. From reports a picture of internal division, lack of communication and government harassment emerges. The meeting which the NNC subsequently held to discuss union also proved unsuccessful. Although it had been postponed from 1 to 8 April 1909 to enable Dube and Kambule to attend after returning from Bloemfontein, neither was present.[11] They and other leading men excused themselves on the grounds of illness, a transparent excuse which moved the convener, Mark Radebe, to lament, 'Does the meeting to which all of us have come today cause illness? We natives are simply injuring our cause by behaving in this way.'[12]

The position was further complicated by the interference of the Natal government, which actively discouraged chiefs and headmen from attending. The Minister of Native Affairs, F.R. Moor, had acted as early as 22 March, only three days after the NNC had announced their meeting. In a circular telegram to all magistrates, Moor instructed them to inform any Africans who made enquiries that neither permission nor authority had been obtained from the government to hold the meeting. Moreover, chiefs and headmen were not to leave their areas without first obtaining leave from the authorities to do so.[13] This step was not without effect. *Ilanga* complained that because of magisterial pressure many people had been discouraged from attending.[14] On the morning of the meeting several Africans who had travelled to Pietermaritzburg from other districts decided first to report to the Native Affairs Department for fear of being accused of 'going behind the authorities'. They were persuaded to return home.[15] The government also saw to it that an *umsetshane* (a derogatory term for a government informer) infiltrated the meeting.

During the course of the morning delegates arrived at the venue, but the opening of the proceedings was delayed because the convener and NNC secretary, Mark Radebe, was meeting *Inkosi* (the Minister or his Under-Secretary). Radebe eventually arrived at midday and advised the gathering to reassemble at two o'clock. Forty people attended, all *kholwa*. In his introductory speech, Mark Radebe explained that the meeting had been called to discuss the draft constitution, an agreement that had taken place between the white people of South Africa. Africans wished to be placed 'on a proper basis at the outset, [so that] the present tendency to regard them with suspicion, as the Europeans of Natal did, would be broken down. It was only right that all races should unite if there was to be Union, not only particular ones.'[16] Most delegates favoured holding another meeting after the views of prominent men who were not present had been ascertained. As a result, the meeting ended, only one and a half hours after it had started, without having passed any resolutions on the subject of union.[17]

Protests against the draft Act emanated from other parts of South Africa as well. In British Bechuanaland, Sol Plaatje wrote to W.P. Schreiner on 13 April 1909, asking him to publicise Rolong opposition. On behalf of the chiefs and all 'their people', Plaatje sent the greetings of the Rolong to 'the defender of Dinuzulu' and thanked him for his fearless championing of the African cause.[18] Thomas Mapikela from Bloemfontein and Isaiah Bud Mbelle from Kimberley together visited John Dube at the Ohlange Institute. In the Transvaal, Sefako Makgatho, the Pretoria-based president of the African National Political Union, wrote to the authorities requesting permission to hold a meeting with the local chiefs, whom he wished to consult on the decisions taken by the Bloemfontein meeting, but this was refused.[19] The Transvaal Native Union executive was also active. On 19 April it arranged a meeting at Nancefield in Johannesburg, where the Bloemfontein delegates gave an account of the proceedings and decisions of the convention, and the question of raising funds for a delegation to Britain was raised.[20] In the Orange River Colony, the Becoana Mutual Improvement Association convened a meeting of African and coloured people in the Thaba Nchu district on 28 April 1909, only days before the National Convention was due to reassemble in Bloemfontein. The same resolutions which the Association had taken the previous month and submitted to the South African Native Convention were put to the meeting, unanimously passed and forwarded to the National Convention for consideration.[21]

It is clear from the resolutions of the conventions of Bloemfontein and King William's Town, from the meetings held in various areas subsequently, and from the attempts to collect funds in the Cape and Natal,[22] that Africans were not prepared to accept passively a final unfavourable decision from the National Convention. They continued to oppose the draft Act right up to the final session of this body and prepared themselves for further steps if their grievances were not redressed.

After the draft Act had been made public, coloured communities throughout the colonies also organised meetings to protest against its provisions. Dr Abdurahman's APO was at the head of the protests. No less than 60 APO meetings were reported to have been held by mid-April, when the APO convened its AGM in Cape Town.[23] As we have already seen, Africans were present at some of the APO meetings, while Dr Abdurahman allowed APO members to attend the Native Convention.[24] The interests of African and coloured people had become fused. Both groups used the terms 'Native' and 'Coloured' interchangeably and in their protests no difference was made between their respective political rights.

This point was forcefully demonstrated by the resolutions of the APO conference in Cape Town, which lasted from 13 to 17 April 1909 and which was attended by delegates from more than 50 towns in the Cape, Transvaal and Orange River Colony. It criticised the draft Act in terms similar to those of the African conferences, expressed a willingness to co-operate more closely with its African counterparts, and began to make preparations to send a delegation to Britain to appeal directly to the Imperial government.[25] The APO also gave its approval to the activities of the South African Native Convention in Bloemfontein and the conference organised by Jabavu in King William's Town, and expressed its desire to form a united front with these groups. It declared that 'the time has arrived for the co-operation of the coloured races in British South Africa'. The APO executive was instructed to liaise with the executives of the African organisations to bring this about.[26] In addition, it was decided to start an APO newspaper to counteract what it felt was the bias of the colonial press.[27]

By making these preparations, the APO clearly did not expect any fundamental changes from the final session of the National Convention. Though Jabavu criticised the APO for not waiting for the final Convention report before taking the decision to send a delegation, he was making an unnecessary fuss.[28] It was obvious by then that the large majority of colonial whites were in favour of the draft Act with its colour-bar provisions, and that union would come about on their terms.

44

Appeal to the British parliament

It seemed as though the curse of the serpent has fallen on them all – on thy belly shalt thou crawl and dust shalt thou eat. I hardly know what was the most awful thing. Jameson's face, … or dear old Malan looking like a lost soul, … as they squirmed and lied, and each one gave the other away, and all gave away principle. All the while there was Abdurahman's drawn dark intellectual face looking down at them. Men selling their souls and the future – and fate watching them.

– Olive Schreiner, 8 April 1909

When the colonial parliaments met to confirm the proposals of the National Convention, all four accepted the franchise provisions for Africans. Not one of them called for amendments to the colour-bar sections in the draft Act or for a tightening of the two-thirds safeguard for the franchise for black people in the Cape.[1] In the Orange River Colony, the Transvaal and Natal, none of the parliaments had any compunction about accepting the colour bar. As Abraham Fischer, Prime Minister of the Orange River Colony, told the Legislative Assembly, 'the white man had no intention of acknowledging the black man's equality or of giving him the same rights. "The law of self-preservation" was stronger than any other.' Fischer also criticised the South African Native Convention, saying it had refused to accept the advice of Dewdney Drew, who was supposed to be trusted by them. 'How then could it be expected that they would listen to and follow other white men?' Fischer declared that the demands made by the Native Convention were the work of white agitators – 'theorists, faddists and easy-chair negrophilists' – who instilled in the minds of Africans ideas that they would never have thought of themselves. These people complicated the existence of the 'white races' in South Africa.[2]

The proceedings in the Cape parliament were a different matter. A whole line of speakers sympathised with the aspirations of the black population and opposed any tampering with the Cape franchise system.[3] Even the Cape delegates to the National Convention and others reluctant to amend the draft constitution emphasised that they supported the Cape franchise system in principle. Politicians like Merriman, Jameson and Sauer stated that, though they were opposed to the exclusion of black people from parliament, it was necessary to make this concession to preserve union.[4] They argued that there was no danger to the franchise rights of blacks in the Cape. On the contrary, they envisaged the spread of the liberal Cape system to the other colonies after union.

Though this argument was accepted by most members, it failed to pacify W.P. Schreiner, one of the strongest critics of the colour clauses. On entering the debate, Schreiner said he would be failing in his duty if he did not refer to the 'blot' on the constitution. He said the Cape Colony with its long non-racial tradition was in the position of trustee:

The rights of the coloured people should not be bartered away from any benefit which the Europeans should get. Union with honour before all things ... We must recognise our trust, and they [the other colonies] must see that they could not ask us to break it, and build Union on a treacherous foundation of sand, because we would be treacherous in the truest sense of the term if we did not provide protection for the colonial native people ... If a small number of Cape representatives in the Union Parliament were not true to their trust, and with others voted for the coloured franchise being removed, would not the rights of the native and coloured people vanish into thin air under Parliamentary sanction? ... Union without honour ... was the greatest danger any nation could incur.[5]

Throughout the session, which lasted for 18 days, Schreiner fought the colour bar point for point, introducing amendments at every opportunity. Although his arguments often evoked sympathy,[6] he was unable to carry any amendments to the colour bar or make the Cape franchise unalterable. Yet he persisted with his uncompromising defence of the non-racial Cape tradition to the end. By the time a harassed Merriman finally piloted the compromise through parliament on 15 April, Schreiner, he noted, had spoken no less than 64 times.[7]

While Schreiner and other sympathisers were fighting the colour bar in the Cape parliament, black groups also used the channels open to them in an effort to dissuade parliament from accepting the draft Act unamended. Jabavu's Cape Native Convention, the APO led by Dr Abdurahman and the Wynberg Coloured Men's Political Organisation, all exerted their right of petition to protest against the draft Act.[8] Abdurahman also followed the debates from the public gallery and tried unsuccessfully to be heard at the bar of the House of Assembly.[9] In a letter to her brother, Olive Schreiner described the scene of Dr Abdurahman watching the Cape parliament acquiesce in the restriction of the political rights of black people:

It seemed as though the curse of the serpent has fallen on them all – on thy belly shalt thou crawl and dust shalt thou eat. I hardly know what was the most awful thing. Jameson's face, ... or dear old [F.S.] Malan looking like a lost soul, ... as they squirmed and lied, and each one gave the other away, and all gave away principle. All the while there was Abdurahman's drawn dark intellectual face looking down at them. Men selling their souls and the future – and fate watching them.[10]

During the sitting of the Cape parliament it was rumoured that 'a man of high position' would proceed to Britain to protest against the passing of the draft Act in the Imperial parliament if it was not amended.[11] Little imagination was needed to deduce that the person in question was Schreiner. His trenchant resistance to the draft constitution in parliament had placed him firmly in the spotlight as the central figure of dissent against the terms of union.

The black (as well as white) protest movement now coalesced increasingly around Schreiner. Both major African conferences had expressed a willingness to work with him; Jabavu and his supporters sent their petition to him to put before the Cape parliament; African newspapers described him as 'our South African Abe Lincoln'; individuals wrote to him expressing gratitude and support; and he was received with rapturous applause when he delivered an address at the opening of the annual conference of the APO, held during the parliamentary sitting.[12]

At the final session of the National Convention, which met in Bloemfontein on 3 May 1909, the matter of political rights for black people received scant attention. None of the colonial parliaments had recommended changes in this respect, and so the only time the matter arose was when petitions on the subject were tabled. There were representations from several quarters. The only petition from an African organisation at this session was that of the Becoana Mutual Improvement Association and the headmen of the Thaba Nchu district.[13] An individual petition came from John Sishuba from Kamastone in the Queenstown district, a political colleague of Jabavu's and an old supporter of Merriman.[14] There was also a weighty petition from leading churchmen from various denominations, asking the Convention to remove the colour restrictions from the draft Act. In addition, representations were made by the active and efficient executive of Dr Abdurahman's APO, the coloured voters of Wellington, and the Wynberg Coloured Men's Political Organisation.[15] All these were tabled, and the letter from the churchmen was read out on the instructions of Sir Henry de Villiers, but they made no impact whatsoever on the delegates. No discussion ensued, no amendments were moved, and the sections in the draft Act dealing with black political rights remained unaltered.[16] After almost coming to grief over the electoral issue of equal voting rights for town and country constituencies, the Convention finally reached unanimous agreement, concluded its deliberations and issued its final report on 11 May 1909.[17]

In the final step in ratifying the plans for union, the various colonial parliaments met to formally approve the revised draft South Africa Act. They were overwhelmingly in favour. In short sessions starting on 1 June

1909, the Transvaal and the Orange River Colony parliaments unanimously passed resolutions supporting the draft Act.[18] In the Cape parliament there were only two dissenting votes against a similar motion.[19] The earlier strong opposition had waned. This was due mainly to the swing by J.H. Hofmeyr and his supporters in the Afrikaner Bond in favour of the draft Act. Merriman had persuaded Hofmeyr not only to support the Act but also to become a member of the official colonial delegation to finalise the transition to Union with the Imperial authorities in Britain.[20]

However, W.P. Schreiner remained unswerving in his opposition to the colour bar. Immediately after the Prime Minister had moved that the Cape approve the draft Act in its revised form,[21] Schreiner made a final stand. He told the House that he could not accept what appeared to be a conspiracy of silence on the subject. 'There were remaining in the draft fundamental blots which, even if he stood alone, he could not hesitate to bring as clearly as possible to the notice of everybody throughout the Colony, the world, and the Parliament in England, by which means he hoped that even at the last moment some change could be effected.'[22] He said the new constitution should be one of the world's very greatest documents of liberty. Could they call this a great liberty document? He then moved as an amendment 'that this House accepts the draft Act of Union subject to the modifications necessary to safeguard the native and coloured inhabitants of this colony against discrimination on the grounds of race or colour in respect of political rights'.[23]

But the fight was lost. When Schreiner called for a division on his amendment two days later, it was defeated by 96 votes to 2. Only another former Prime Minister, the octogenarian Sir Gordon Sprigg, in almost his last public act, voted with Schreiner for his amendment.[24] The Cape parliament had agreed to abrogate its non-racial constitution for one which discriminated on grounds of colour.

The position in Natal was slightly different from that in the other colonies. Because of the strong fears about union in the colony, the Natal parliament decided to hold a referendum to test the feeling of the electorate after the National Convention had issued its final report.[25] This took place on 10 June 1909. Natal agreed by 11,121 votes to 3701 to enter the Union.[26] In a session between 16 and 18 June, the Natal parliament endorsed the will of the white electorate, which was in fact much smaller in number than the African and coloured voters in the Cape.[27]

Thus the draft South Africa Act received the support of a large majority of white colonists. Not only had every one of the 33 delegates to the National Convention concurred with the final report, but the voters or their representatives in each colony had resoundingly come out in favour. Once the four colonies had drawn up and ratified the draft South Africa Act, the focus shifted from South Africa to Britain, where the draft constitution was to be submitted for assent to the Imperial parliament.

As soon as the final report of the National Convention was released, arrangements began in earnest for W.P. Schreiner to lead a deputation to London to oppose the passage of the draft South Africa Act through the British parliament. The centre of activity was in Cape Town, where Dr Abdurahman and white opponents of the colour bar such as the Rev. Ramsden Balmforth and Dr Robert Forsyth, a Cape Town councillor, had been working in close co-operation with Schreiner.[28] They got in touch with interest groups elsewhere in the colonies. By mid-May Abdurahman had written to Jabavu and Soga and had received a reply from the latter, who said that a deputation to England was imperative. Within a few weeks almost all the parties involved in protesting against the colour provisions of the new constitution had written to Schreiner, asking him to act on their behalf in Britain or to work in co-operation with delegates they were sending: the APO, the South African Native Convention, the Orange River Colony Native Congress, the Transvaal Native Union, the Transvaal Native Congress, Jabavu's Cape Native Convention, and the Sotho paramount and others in Basutoland.[29] Schreiner had become the rallying point for those opposed to the draft Act.

Schreiner's campaign was launched in earnest on 14 May when he and other sympathisers drew up an 'Appeal to the Parliament and Government of Great Britain and Ireland'. This was intended to draw attention in Britain to what was seemingly now a lost cause in South Africa. They protested against the colour restrictions in the draft South Africa Act, as well as clause 35, through which black voters could in future be disenfranchised. While they recognised the necessity of compromise in matters not involving fundamental principles in bringing about union, this was an entirely different matter. They were compelled to protest against provisions that jeopardised the essential principles of free government and contradicted the traditional policy of Great Britain when conceding popular government. To enshrine the denial of human rights in a constitution was a grave injustice, which would 'eventually react with evil effect' on white South Africans.[30] This was the line of argument opponents of the draft Act would adopt in the ensuing months as the focus shifted from South Africa to London. The appeal was eventually signed by 22 prominent churchmen, politicians and local personalities.*[31]

To prepare for his trip to Britain, Schreiner also made private approaches to well-placed sympathisers there like the Radical MP Sir Charles Dilke and Ramsay MacDonald, the Labour Party secretary and MP.[32] Since the publication of the draft Act, Dilke had already taken it upon himself to interview the Colonial Under-Secretary of State and lead a deputation of Liberal and Labour MPs to the Colonial Secretary, Lord Crewe, asking them to protect the rights of blacks in South Africa. He also roused the Aborigines Protection Society to work towards this end. Dilke told Schreiner that his stand had not gone unnoticed in Britain: reports of Schreiner's views were read by the mandarins in the Colonial Office and 'everything you do aids our cause powerfully'.[33]

Schreiner's preparations caused a worried reaction in the Cape and nervousness in official quarters. Anxious lest he should succeed in causing sufficient fuss to induce the British government to make amendments to the draft Act, the Prime Minister, J.X. Merriman, took steps to forestall Schreiner's mission. First of all, he persuaded Sir Henry de Villiers to put forward his own travelling plans and leave for Britain on the same day as Schreiner. He said it was of the 'utmost importance' that De Villiers should keep an eye on Schreiner's 'mischief'.[34] Then on 16 June, the day Schreiner

* They included Sir Gordon Sprigg, Sir Bisset Berry (a former Speaker of the House of Assembly), five past and present Cape MPs, Archbishop William Carter and Dr J.J. McClure (both of whom had also signed the petition by members of the clergy to the National Convention) and the Vice-Chancellor of the University of the Cape of Good Hope and the Vice-President of the Cape Town Chamber of Commerce.

left for London, Merriman sent a memorandum to the Cape Governor, Sir Walter Hely-Hutchinson, putting the case against amendment and expressing the hope that the 'misguided' deputation would receive no encouragement from the British government.[35] Merriman declared that if the deputation succeeded in its aims, it would wreck union, lead to bitter resentment towards the Imperial government and put the white population in the Cape 'on the same plane of intolerance' on the colour question as the people in the northern colonies. Even if it did not succeed, the 'agitation, and the unwise speaking and writing which is sure to accompany it, is bound to have an evil effect on the mind of the natives, who will be taught to read into the Act of Union an attack on their rights wholly contrary to the spirit in which the act is conceived'.[36] Merriman also claimed that the Schreiner deputation was unrepresentative. He said most Africans realised that they had secured more under the draft Act than they had dared hope for. The deputation represented 'some of the more educated natives, by no means the most substantial or well-to-do of their race', who had been politically exploited.[37]

As part of his plans to neutralise Schreiner, Merriman also asked Colonel Walter Stanford, who was respected for his views on the 'native question', to influence the Cape Governor against the Schreiner delegation. In an interview with Hely-Hutchinson on 28 June, Stanford said that, although he shared Schreiner's objection to the 'blot' on the constitution, he was strongly of the opinion that the draft Act, which embodied the considered decisions of the Convention and the South African parliaments, should be accepted. His view was that present amendments would later increase the danger of an attack on the Cape franchise. On the other hand, if the colour question was left to the people of South Africa it would be in the best long-term interests of the black population. From his experience at the National Convention, he felt assured that there was 'a growing feeling and intention amongst the leading politicians in South Africa in favour of promoting the real interests of the Natives'.[38] Hely-Hutchinson supported these arguments enthusiastically. In commending them to the Colonial Secretary, he described Stanford as 'a lifelong friend of the Natives' and Merriman as a long-time defender of African rights, who had encountered considerable opposition on this score from W.P. Schreiner himself.[39] Merriman's and

Stanford's arguments made a significant impact. Their line of reasoning was to be used in Britain in the debate against amendments.

Fully aware that his stand was not supported by most whites, Schreiner offered to resign his seat in parliament before leaving for Britain.[40] However, as there would be only one more short session of the Cape parliament before union, his election committee in Queenstown persuaded him not to do so.[41] While the majority of his constituents were probably against his mission, there is no doubt what the feelings of the local African voters were. They sent him a special message expressing their support, thanking him for his courageous stand and invoking 'Divine blessing on the work of the delegation'.[42]

And so, tailed by no less a person than the president of the National Convention, Schreiner set sail for Britain, carrying the hopes of almost all black leaders and organisations in South Africa with him. He was to be joined abroad by African and APO delegates, who were in the meantime scrambling to make arrangements and raise funds.

45

Preparations for the delegation to England

There now remains nothing for Africans and their sympathisers to do but don their armour and go on with the fight to the end. The feelings of Africans have not been heeded in their own country, so now they have to take the matter further.

– J.T. Jabavu, *Imvo*, May 1909

While W.P. Schreiner had been making contacts in Britain and publicising the delegation, the African organisations that wished to send delegates to accompany him were busy preparing as well. To put into effect the resolutions they had made to take the fight to Britain, they had to raise funds from their financially pressed constituency and obtain the approval of the authorities for the trip. Finance was an ever-present problem for the early groups: they had barely enough money to run themselves, let alone send representatives abroad. Nevertheless, they were tenacious in getting down to the task.

The South African Native Convention hoped to send a delegation of 12 members. In the end there were only three with Convention connections: Dr Rubusana, Daniel Dwanya and Thomas Mapikela. Mapikela, a Native Convention executive member from Bloemfontein, was nominated and sponsored by the Orange River Colony Native Congress, which raised just under £170 for its delegation fund. Dwanya, a long-time Native Congress supporter, was sponsored by Chief Kama from Middledrift.[1]

While Rubusana and Mapikela travelled under the official mantle of the Native Convention – Dwanya may have been acting independently – it appears that the final decision about membership of the delegation was made regionally by associated groups who had managed to raise enough funds for their chosen members to go. It was not the elected Native Convention leaders themselves who decided or else A.K. Soga (the secretary) and Joel Goronyane (treasurer) would have been selected.[2] Soga probably had to stand back for Dr Rubusana because of lack of funds. This led to a bitter split between these two close political allies: Soga accused Rubusana of 'self-appointment' to the delegation and was angry about his exclusion for a long time afterwards.[3] Soga's omission also effectively ended his political career: *Izwi*, which he edited, closed down in April 1909 after 12 years and a bright voice in national politics became silent.

John Dube's position in the delegation needs some explanation. On 9 June Dube, who had been elected vice-president of the Native Convention in March, was informed by Dr Rubusana that the delegation 'of which you are one' was leaving on the 23rd and that he should wire money to cover his expenses.[4] At the time Dube was under pressure from the Natal government and white patrons of his educational institution at Inanda to withdraw completely from politics. As a result he seems to have played a double game, officially declaring that he could not be part of the delegation, but he nevertheless travelled to London with his wife at the same time and filled a behind-the-scenes role in the delegation's activities, in addition to raising funds for his Ohlange Institute.[5] But the Natal authorities had clearly succeeded in muzzling him, because he did not talk officially on behalf of the delegation or formally represent it while in London.[6]

Plans for the delegation were also set in motion in the Transvaal, where the Transvaal Native Union (TNU) started an active fundraising campaign to assist the delegation to England. It sought £750 to send five or six delegates. By the beginning of July the campaign had progressed to the stage where the TNU chairman, William Letseleba, informed the government that it had elected Chiefs J.O. More Mamogale, A.T.M. Makgatle and G.A.H. Mabala of the Kwena to lay the claims of Transvaal Africans before the British government.[7] Though a departure date was set and everything seemed finalised – the Administrator of the Transvaal wired Lord Crewe that the delegation had in fact sailed – the trip was abandoned and the delegates returned home, according to Z. More, the

TNU's secretary, because of a failure to raise enough money.[8]

As the TNU was no longer directly represented in Britain, this responsibility devolved upon the Native Convention representatives from the other colonies (and, indeed, Dr Rubusana formally visited the Transvaal and other territories to report back on his return). Instead, the Transvaal Native Congress (TNC), which does not seem to have involved itself actively in the TNU's preparations, took steps of its own in late June and requested two outstanding young South Africans who were studying law in England to act on its behalf. At its annual conference, held at Nancefield on 24 June 1909, the TNC vested Alfred Mangena and Pixley kaIsaka Seme with a mandate to represent it in London and co-operate with Schreiner, Jabavu and other delegates.[9] It was a move that would have historic consequences: both Seme and Mangena were to come to the forefront of national politics in a very short time.

Meanwhile, J.T. Jabavu was also preparing for his journey to London to join the Coloured and Native Delegation under Schreiner. Originally, *Imvo* had greeted the final draft South Africa Act with acclaim, as it was under the misapprehension, from newspaper headlines and 'vague summaries of the amendments', that the National Convention had decided to abolish the Europeans-only clauses and the provision stipulating the conditions for the disenfranchisement of Cape Africans.[10] The following week, however, *Imvo* retracted its approval in an embarrassing about-face, and reiterated its strong opposition to the colour-bar clauses. It said there now remained nothing for Africans and their sympathisers to do but don their armour and continue with the fight to the end.[11]

The Cape Native Convention elected a committee consisting of Jabavu (president), Elijah J. Mqoboli (vice-president), and S. Mloba and S. Milton Ntloko (secretaries) at its King William's Town conference in April. After the Cape parliament had given its final blessing to the draft constitution early in June 1909, the committee met and elected W.P. Schreiner to represent them and Jabavu to accompany him if the necessary funds could be raised.[12] Thus, after initially supporting the moves to form a South

African Native Convention, Jabavu had pulled out of that initiative (which was supported by his eastern Cape rivals in the South African Native Congress), appropriated the 'Convention' name and called together his traditional regional constituency instead, focusing more narrowly on the Cape franchise issue.

Though *Imvo* appealed to its readers in articles and prominent advertisements for support to send Jabavu to Britain,[13] the response does not seem to have been good. Jabavu, who had been in financial difficulties ever since the closure of *Imvo* during the South African War, had to dig deep into his own pockets to finance his trip. In his biography of his father, D.D.T. Jabavu blamed the 'heavy financial commitments' incurred by Jabavu on this and other 'national errands' for the subsequent decline of his health.[14] Before Jabavu could join the delegation, he had to provide a bank guarantee of about £150 to finance the running of *Imvo* during his absence. As he could not do so, he turned to 'friends of the cause' such as W.P. Schreiner and his brother Theo. It is not clear how Jabavu met the financial poser facing him, but in any event he sailed early in July, with Daniel Dwanya as a fellow passenger, hoping that he and the other delegates would make enough 'converts' to their views to force amendments to the constitution.[15] His actions showed the commitment of the early activists to the protection of African rights and the lengths they were prepared to go.

Although Jabavu realised that the draft Act would probably be accepted by the British government, he was confident that the delegation would receive enough support to 'bring about trouble over the European descent clause'.[16] African hopes that Britain might insist on amendments had been raised by press reports of a statement by the Under-Secretary of State, Colonel Seely, in the House of Commons on 27 May that the proposed South Africa Act would have to be redrafted in Britain and that the Imperial government would propose amendments.[17]

Jabavu and Dwanya were the last of the African delegates to leave. They were preceded by Mapikela (on 23 June) and Rubusana (29 June). On the day he left, Rubusana emphasised that 'we are not going to England as agitators, but as humble citizens of His Majesty's Colony to plead – before Lord Crewe – for the deletion of those colour clauses in the Act which should never have been allowed in the Draft Constitution'. 'It now remains for us ... to do all we can to get the Imperial Parliament to remove this blot and insult to the Native and Coloured races of this country from the Constitution. May God bless us in this.'[18]

✦

In addition to the colonies, Africans in the Transkeian Territories and the Protectorates of Basutoland, Bechuanaland and Swaziland came out in support of the delegation preparing to take the fight to London. As the time approached for the draft South Africa Act to be laid before the British parliament, various people in Basutoland approached W.P. Schreiner to represent them in Britain. They included the paramount Letsie, the newspaper editor S.M. Phamotse (representing the mission-educated grouping in the Basutoland Progressive Association) and the Rev. Edouard Jacottet, the veteran Paris Evangelical Mission Society minister who worked tirelessly on behalf of the Sotho throughout the build-up to Union.[19] Although representing different interests, Letsie, Phamotse and Jacottet worked closely together on this issue. In the end Schreiner agreed to act on their behalf.[20]

Chiefs in the Bechuanaland Protectorate responded in a similar way. When Bathoen of the Ngwaketse and Sebele Sechele of the Kwena heard that J. Gerrans, a 'friend for many years', was going to Britain for health reasons, they asked him to act on their behalf when the draft Act came before the Imperial authorities, to prevent Bechuanaland from being incorporated in the Union.[21] Gerrans then got in touch with Schreiner and himself became a member of the deputation in London.

In the Transkeian Territories, where the main African spokesmen had long been in close touch with eastern Cape organisations, activists and voters, there was also unambiguous opposition to the terms of union. The subject was the first matter discussed at the Bhunga's two-week session in June 1909. Enoch Mamba, president of the Transkei Native Vigilance Association, tabled a motion, requesting that the General Council discuss the draft Act as it affected the Transkeian Territories before the other matters on the agenda were dealt with.[22] The motion put forward by Mamba ('rather of the aggressive type of educated native whose attitude is not likely to help his people', according to Walter Stanford) was seconded by S. Milton Ntloko of Tsomo, who, as one of the secretaries elected at the Native Convention meeting in April, was at the forefront of planning Jabavu's trip to London.[23] In the end the Council approved a petition in protest against the draft Act,[24] which was then sent to Prime Minister Merriman. While reaffirming the loyalty of the petitioners, it expressed grave apprehension at the colour bar, which threatened the cherished rights of equality before the law and the franchise that Africans had always enjoyed. It requested that the colour line be expunged from the draft Act.[25]

This petition was an important development in the whole campaign by Africans against the new constitution. The Bhunga embraced 16 Transkeian districts with an African population of more than 500,000.[26] Most of the councillors were headmen nominated from their own numbers. That a body such as this – created to institutionalise 'loyal' participation in colonial life by dependent headmen – was so vocal on the draft South Africa Act spoke volumes about African feeling on the issue.

The final step in putting together the South African Coloured and Native Delegation to Britain was made by the African Political Organisation, the largest political organisation in the coloured communities, with branches in the Cape, Transvaal and Orange River Colony. The APO identified itself completely with Africans in the fight against the colour bar in the draft Act. Having given support at its annual conference in April to the South African Native Convention and the conference organised by Jabavu in King William's Town, the APO now began to organise on a large scale to send representatives to London and established contact with Schreiner and African leaders. There was a remarkable and immediate response to the call. One thousand collection cards were sent out to various districts and fundraising events such as tea meetings, concerts and dances were held. The organisers estimated that within two months at least 12,000 people had contributed to the delegation funds.[27] Later, they put the final estimate at approximately 30,000.[28] Collections were made in all four colonies and as far afield as Victoria Falls in Rhodesia. Over 20 new APO branches were formed in this climate of enthusiasm.[29]

Just over a month after the conference, the organisation brought out the first issue of its new newspaper. It was simply named the *A.P.O.* The newspaper immediately entered the fray, criticising the draft Act and exhorting coloured people (and Africans) to respond to this threat to their interests.[30] The paper became the rallying point of the whole protest movement of the coloured people. Through its pages, the rank and file were kept informed of developments when the newspaper printed letters from its readers and reported meetings, resolutions and collections by the dozen.

The next step was to finalise the names of the delegates to go to England. The APO executive decided to ask Schreiner to represent them and chose Dr Abdurahman, D.J. Lenders and Matt J. Fredericks, the APO president, vice-president and general secretary respectively, to accompany him.[31] By now Schreiner was something of a hero. The *A.P.O.* newspaper referred to him in glowing terms, and at least 50 meetings in the colonies passed resolutions thanking him for his stand and conveying their 'inexpressible joy' that he had decided to proceed to Britain on their behalf.[32]

Though the APO enjoyed the overwhelming support of coloured communities for its campaign against the Act, some of Abdurahman's political opponents were against the idea of a delegation to Britain, most notably John Tobin and F.Z.S. Peregrino, neither of whom had an organisational base to compare with Abdurahman's. While favouring equal rights for coloured people, they contended that a deputation to Britain would damage their cause. To publicise their views and undermine Abdurahman's plans, Tobin and Peregrino wrote letters to the press and made representations to the authorities.[33] In a further move, just before the departure of the government delegation for London, they handed an address, embodying their views, to one of its members, J.H. Hofmeyr, for presentation to a suitable person in Britain.[34] In their campaign, Tobin and Peregrino claimed that their own organisations were equal in stature to the APO: this was patently untrue. Nevertheless, their claims were readily used by the government delegates as a counter to the APO delegation and their views received the attention of the British government.[35]

⬇

A deputation to London was also sent by Indian communities in the Transvaal. As already explained, the political struggle of Gandhi and Indian organisations at the turn of the century was quite separate from the mobilisation described in this book. Gandhi explained that while the indigenous coloured and African people had a right to demand political rights, the first priority of the Indians, newly arrived since the 1860s, was not political rights at this stage, but their civil rights, which were constantly in jeopardy.[36] From both sides, there was little motivation for organising on common lines. Nevertheless, recognition of their common lot did bring about a degree of solidarity between African and Indian activists from 1908 onwards. *Naledi ea Lesotho*, for example, expressed admiration for the passive resistance campaign of Transvaal Indians.[37] *Indian Opinion* reciprocated and warned that whites, by discriminating against the various black groups, were 'trying almost to compel them' into forming a united front.[38] This editorial was warmly welcomed by both *Izwi* and *Ilanga*.[39]

Despite this growing recognition of joint disabilities, Gandhi and the Indian organisations did not join in the agitation against the draft Act, even though they foresaw that union would lead to a curtailment of the liberties of all 'non-whites', regarding it as a virtual declaration of war against the black population and 'a consummation devoutly to be deplored'.[40] Their struggle continued to be focused mainly on the past and present treatment of Indians, rather than on the wider issue of the future effects of union on the black population.

In the meantime, the Indian passive resistance campaign against discriminatory laws in the Transvaal had been proceeding. There was no sign to indicate any abatement in the harassment and deportation of Indians by the government. Indian leaders decided to take advantage of the presence in London of the leading Transvaal politicians, Botha and Smuts, with the colonial government delegation, to petition the British government for redress of their grievances. Two mass meetings of the British Indian Association in June 1909 approved of the idea of simultaneous delegations to Britain and India, and nominated delegates for these.[41] Four of the seven prospective delegates were promptly arrested by the government, which refused appeals for their release.[42] Nevertheless, the two delegations went ahead. Gandhi and Hadji Habib were to go to Britain and H.S. Polak to India. The Indian community in Durban, too, decided to follow the Transvaal example and send its own delegation to London. Abdul Kadir and M.C. Anglia, the chairman and secretary of the Natal Indian Congress, and two Pietermaritzburg merchants were appointed for this purpose and left for England in early July.[43]

By then, the Transvaal delegation had already departed. After a rousing send-off at the Johannesburg station by 800 cheering supporters,[44] Gandhi and Habib set sail from Cape Town on the *Kenilworth Castle* on 23 June. Their fellow passengers included John X. Merriman and several other members of the government delegation, as well as Dr Abdurahman and the APO delegates.[45] Abdurahman and Gandhi were jointly seen off by a group of supporters including W.P. Schreiner's sisters Olive and Ettie Stakesby-Lewis, both of whom had been active in opposing the draft Act.[46]

Before his departure, Gandhi commented that, although he was going to London in connection with the treatment of Indians in the Transvaal, he and Habib would interest themselves in the passage of the draft Act in Britain as well.[47] He remarked that Indians looked with despair upon the consummation of union, mainly because it was a union for whites only. He was opposed to the colour bar and noted that existing legislation concerning the movement of Indians in South Africa would remain unaltered until the Union parliament chose to modify the laws. Gandhi had no doubt that when this time arrived, matters would become worse for Indians rather than improve.[48]

There was thus a degree of mutual sympathy and co-operation between the Indian delegation and the joint deputation that was protesting against the draft Act. This fellowship was to be extended when Gandhi met Schreiner in London. The process of unification was slowly but surely drawing leaders of public opinion in various territories and across lines of colour and culture into a smaller orbit as the new nation-state with its common boundaries started taking shape.

46

The Coloured and Native
Delegation in London, July 1909

Your Petitioners apprehend that by the racial discrimination proposed in the aforesaid Bill as regards the qualification of members of the Union Parliament, the prejudice already existing in the Transvaal, the Orange River Colony and Natal will be accentuated and increased; that the status of the coloured people and natives will be lowered, and that an injustice will be done to those who are the majority of the people in British South Africa, who have in the past shown their unswerving loyalty to the Crown, their attachment to British institutions, their submission to the laws of the land, and their capacity for exercising full civil and political rights.

– Petition of the South African Coloured and
Native Deputation, 1909

The delegates from the South African colonies who proceeded to England to watch the progress of the draft South Africa Act through the British parliament arrived there by passenger ship at various intervals in July 1909. By 17 July the full complement of no less than 28 was gathered in London.

The official government delegation consisted of 19 members, including Sir Henry de Villiers and the four colonial Prime Ministers. All except one, the veteran Afrikaner Bond leader, J.H. Hofmeyr, had been members of the National Convention. Ranged against them were W.P. Schreiner and the Coloured and Native Delegation: Dr Abdurahman, Matt J.

Fredericks and D.J. Lenders of the APO; Dr Walter Rubusana and Thomas Mapikela, representing the considerable efforts of the South African Native Convention; Daniel Dwanya, sponsored by Chief Kama from Middledrift; J.T. Jabavu on behalf of the Cape Native Convention; and J. Gerrans, who represented Bathoen of the Ngwaketse and Sebele Sechele of the Kwena. There were also other South Africans indirectly involved as advisers and supporters, and both sides had their own British networks and sympathisers to draw on.[1]

The Coloured and Native Delegation drew support from humanitarian, Liberal and church groups such as the Anti-Slavery and Aborigines Protection Society, the London Missionary Society, the Quakers and the South African Native Races Committee, as well as influential individuals such as Sir Charles Dilke, the Labour Party leader Keir Hardie, Ramsay MacDonald, the Liberal MP and historian G.P. Gooch, the Liberal peer Lord Courtney and other parliamentarians.[2] Though lodged in various parts of London, members of the delegation worked in co-ordination, particularly Schreiner and the APO and Native Convention representatives. Schreiner ensconced himself at Morley's Hotel in Trafalgar Square, the APO representatives at the nearby Grand Hotel, and Gandhi at the Westminster Palace Hotel. They were all, therefore, a few short minutes' walk from Whitehall and Westminster, where they would be lobbying the Colonial Office and Parliament. But Jabavu, Rubusana, Dube and, most likely, the other African members as well could not afford hotels and were accommodated privately or in boarding houses.[3] Jabavu stayed with members of the Quaker movement for much of his time in London, and became lastingly influenced by them. The Quakers also hosted the Coloured and Native Delegation at their annual conference in Cardiff during its stay.[4]

There was much networking and contact between the various groups. Schreiner was in touch with Gandhi and Haji Habib, holding discussions and corresponding with them.[5] John Dube, in London ostensibly to raise funds for his school, attended a function held by his neighbour in Inanda; his wife Nokutela was one of those listed as having made a donation to help cover Gandhi's costs.[6] The Anti-Slavery and Aborigines Protection Society (APS) also assisted both the delegation in its work and Dube in his.[7]

Through the APS secretary, Travers Buxton, Dube met leading churchmen in England; through Schreiner, he met the Unwin family, publishers of his sister Olive's works, as well as Betty Molteno and Percy Molteno MP, children of a former Cape Prime Minister, who all became supporters.

Jointly and severally, the delegates signed letters and petitions, attended meetings, appointed a delegation secretary, Matt J. Fredericks, and decided on specific tasks for particular people.[8] Dr Abdurahman wrote of having been 'entrusted' with drawing up a petition to submit to parliament, and having to negotiate this with Jabavu, Rubusana and Schreiner.[9] But it is clear that Schreiner was the man at the centre of all these activities. A Cambridge-educated former Prime Minister who commanded the respect and attention of British audiences, he assumed the dominant role in the delegation. He was usually the main speaker at meetings, invitations to his fellow delegates were extended through him, and he used his influence to arrange private interviews for them.[10] However, this did not stop them from acting on their own initiative. They individually met with important people, addressed gatherings, and spoke to the press.[11]

The delegates were helped in their work by a number of talented young South Africans studying in Britain. They included Jabavu's son, Davidson Don Tengo, and Ismail, the younger brother of Dr Abdurahman, as well as a number of young lawyers and aspirant lawyers such as Richard Msimang, Alfred Mangena, Pixley kaIsaka Seme, George Montsioa (and also, most likely, the Zonnebloem-educated Henry Poswayo from the Transkei), who were to play an important role in the formation of a permanent National Congress three years later.[12]

D.D.T. Jabavu had been sent abroad by his father in 1903 after he was refused entry to the local Dale College in King William's Town. When the delegation arrived in 1909 he was registered at University College London, where he would receive a BA degree. Despite 'isolation and prejudice', he made the most of London, 'visiting museums, studying violin and piano and attending concerts and cricket matches'.[13] He spent eleven years abroad before finally returning to his home country during the First World War and here became a well-known educator and spokesman.

George Montsioa, from a royal line in Mafikeng, studied at Lincoln's Inn before qualifying in 1910 and marrying Dorothy Gabashane, daughter of the Ethiopian Church leader Marcus Gabashane.[14] The dapper Richard Msimang (a past student of both Ohlange and Healdtown) belonged to a family of *kholwa* from Driefontein near Pietermaritzburg. He came to England in 1904 through the channels of the Wesleyan Church and became a solicitor in London. Like the younger Jabavu, he spent nearly a decade in England, played football and 'spoke and dressed like an English gentleman' by the time he returned to South Africa. Msimang later married 'Nurse Grace' Mbelle, daughter of Isaiah Bud Mbelle.[15]

Mangena and Seme, who were delegated by the Transvaal Native Congress to act on its behalf in Britain, had both qualified as lawyers in London, with the former being admitted to the bar in July 1908 and the latter in June 1909, only a few weeks before the arrival of the delegates. At this time they were sharing digs with a number of other South Africans in a house in Fitzroy Square. Mangena was said by his housemate to be 'contemplating on his past and future dignity in an attic chamber'.[16] Both had developed an interest in Pan-Africanism while abroad and had ambitions of becoming involved in 'national' matters back home. The presence of the political leaders from South Africa in London must have been a source of great excitement to them.

Mangena had come to Britain in mid-1902 at the age of 23 after leading protests against the forced removals of Africans in Cape Town. After a year at school in London, he registered at Lincoln's Inn. He was soon involved in Pan-African affairs as a member of the African Society and, later, together with various West Africans and West Indians, the United African Association. This was the base from which he and A.G. Sawyer, a lawyer from Sierra Leone, charged the Natal Governor, Sir Henry McCallum, for irregularities relating to the execution of Africans during the Bambatha rebellion. The case brought him to the centre of public attention in Britain and South Africa. By the time he was called to the bar at the age of 29, he was already a seasoned politician.[17]

After completing an eight-year stint in America with a degree from Columbia University, Pixley Seme crossed the Atlantic and was admitted to Oxford in late 1906. He was active in the Oxford Union and Cosmopolitan Club for overseas students and maintained contacts with British humanitarians with South African links and also various African and African American scholars and intellectuals. From 1908, with the aim of being admitted to the bar, he found accommodation in London. He was involved with an African Union Society and visited the House of Commons to listen to debates.[18]

With the help of all these youthful cheerleaders, the delegates tried to win support for their cause in London by publicising its case in the press, co-operating with sympathetic groups, lobbying members of the British parliament and interviewing the Colonial Secretary. Schreiner started the campaign as soon as he arrived in England on Saturday 3 July 1909. In a statement to Reuters news agency, which appeared in the national press on the Monday, Schreiner said he had come to Britain

to try to get the blots removed from the Act, which makes it no Act of Union, but rather an Act of Separation between the minority and the majority of the people of South Africa. True Union must consider all elements, but here the principal element is not merely not considered, but from our point of view is dealt with in an actually insulting way. The coloured inhabitants are barred from the opportunity to rise and evolve naturally, which is the right of every free man in a free country. We do not base our movement upon the doctrine of the equality of all men, but upon the doctrine of the right to freedom of opportunity – equality of opportunity … The principles of justice which are associated in our minds with Great Britain and her expansive policy are violated in the proposed Act of Union.[19]

The next day *The Times* published the full text of the 'Appeal to the Parliament and Government of Great Britain and Ireland', which Schreiner had brought from South Africa.[20] Later, accompanied by a letter with the masthead of the delegation, signed by Schreiner, Rubusana, Mapikela, Abdurahman, Lenders and Fredericks, the Appeal was circularised to more than a thousand people, including all the members of the House of Commons and the House of Lords.[21]

As soon as he found his feet, Schreiner started making contact at Westminster and Whitehall. He wrote to several people, including Lord Crewe, asking for interviews, and on Wednesday 7 July he began lobbying members in the Commons.[22] Despite the delegation's strenuous attempts to rally British public opinion in favour of amending the constitution, it was unable to do so. The British public and most parliamentarians showed little interest in its mission, or indeed in the whole draft Act. Of the major British daily newspapers, only the *Manchester Guardian* supported the delegation.[23] Next to Dilke, its staunchest public champion was W.T. Stead, editor of the monthly *Review of Reviews*, who campaigned to have the discriminatory clauses removed from the constitution.[24]

Attention was also drawn away from Schreiner and his group by the presence of the official government delegation. The government delegates received preferential treatment from the British government and press, and provided Whitehall with convenient arguments for approving the draft constitution without unduly disturbing the British conscience. From the start the official delegates set out to discredit Schreiner and his party. Their line was that the Coloured and Native Delegation was doing more harm than good to blacks in South Africa, that it was not truly representative, and that union would benefit, not harm, black people.[25] According to Merriman, 'The present agitation can have nothing but the worse possible effect. It will put the clock back and upset the very friendly liberal policy manifested by those states which do not adopt the Cape policy. I think Mr Schreiner's present mission is one of the most unkind things ever done to the natives.' These arguments were largely successful, as Schreiner and Abdurahman had to concede. The latter noted despairingly, 'Our own [i.e. Cape] delegates are our worst enemies.'[26]

As for the British government, it saw no need to change its policy of non-interference in the domestic affairs of the South African colonies or of disturbing what it saw as a remarkable process of reconciliation between Boer and Briton, with its concomitant advantages, political and economic, for the British Empire. Thus, when the Colonial Secretary, Lord Crewe, met the government delegation in formal conference at the Foreign Office on 20 and 21 July, he made no attempt to induce them to accept any amendment to the colour-bar provisions: 'It is the fixed conviction of His Majesty's Government that these matters must be settled in South Africa itself ... His Majesty's Government are prepared to see the Bill through as it stands both as to franchise and as to representation.'[27] He suggested only a few small amendments to the main body of the draft constitution. As none affected principles and most were purely verbal, they were accepted without objection. He did, however, inform the delegates that the schedule dealing with the Protectorates 'stood on a different footing' from the rest of the draft. He reiterated the view of the British government that as a specially obligated trustee of the people of Basutoland, Bechuanaland and Swaziland, who had come under British rule without being conquered, Britain could not hand over the trust without taking formal securities for its observance. Two main guarantees were insisted on for the Protectorates: first, they would not be partitioned after their incorporation in the Union and, secondly, they would receive the full protection of the schedule when they were incorporated. These conditions caused some dismay among the official delegates, but were finally agreed to. They also accepted smaller amendments to almost half the clauses of the schedule.

Though the amendments in respect of the Protectorates came as some consolation to the Coloured and Native Delegation and to sympathetic British groups, their main point of concern, the colour bar in the constitution, remained. When Schreiner introduced Rubusana, Mapikela, Abdurahman, Lenders and Fredericks to Lord Crewe on the 22nd, the morning after Crewe had finalised matters with the government delegates, the Colonial Secretary received them courteously and responded sympathetically to their representations, but he could not give them any assurance that the desired amendments would be made.[28]

On the same day, Lord Crewe moved the first reading of the South Africa Bill in the House of Lords. From then on, it was plain sailing for the official delegation and the new constitution. The only debate on the draft constitution took place five days later on 27 July, when the Bill came up for a second reading in the Lords. A week later, the Bill passed the third reading without further discussion and without any amendments having been pressed to a division.[29]

When the debate took place in the House of Lords on 27 July 1909, all the South African delegates were in attendance. Exercising their right as Privy Councillors, De Villiers, Botha, Merriman and Moor sat in the chamber of the House, while the other government delegates looked on from the Official Gallery. Above, seated in the Strangers' Gallery, were Schreiner, Abdurahman, Gandhi, Jabavu, 'sitting eagerly ... with his head on the rails, watching with every nerve astrain the discussion of his people's rights',[30] and the other African and coloured delegates. Only seven peers participated in the debate in the Lords, and, of these, six were in favour of the Bill being accepted without amendments. In his speech, the Archbishop of Canterbury said that it was justifiable to impose on the black people in South Africa restrictions and limitations that 'correspond with those which we impose on our children', because the overwhelming majority would for generations to come be unfit to share equal citizenship with whites. Dr Abdurahman singled out the Archbishop's speech as 'the most hypocritical piece of humbug I ever listened to'.[31] The only member to speak against the Bill was Lord Courtney.[32]

In the time that the South Africa Bill was before the British parliament, the Coloured and Native Delegation and its British friends continued the fight, even though it was apparent that the Bill would be passed without the desired alterations. On 27 July Schreiner, Abdurahman, Jabavu and Rubusana addressed a public breakfast organised by the Anti-Slavery and Aborigines Protection Society in honour of the delegates, with John Dube and Alfred Mangena present as well.[33] Schreiner's speech was partly a reiteration of the views expressed in a long letter published in *The Times* that same morning. In it, he asked that the constitution should not be regarded as just a South African matter, and summarily passed. British principles were at stake – the majority of the population were being discriminated against 'solely on the grounds of prejudice' – and it was the duty of the British parliament to correct the violation of these principles.[34] A similar letter from Dr Abdurahman was printed in *The Times* the next day.

On 29 July Ramsay MacDonald organised a meeting of Liberal and Labour members of the House of Commons to meet the delegates. The MPs agreed to move amendments when the Bill came before the Commons. They decided to call for the elimination of the 'European descent' qualification, suggesting that it be made applicable to the Transvaal and the Orange River Colony only, and to demand the deletion of the provision allowing a two-thirds majority of the Union parliament to abolish the Cape franchise.[35] The following morning the delegates had another exchange with Nonconformist MPs at a private meeting held under the auspices of the London Missionary Society.[36]

In August, as the focus shifted to the impending debate in the House of Commons after the South Africa Bill had passed through the Lords, the delegates remained in touch with supporters like Dilke and Keir Hardie and continued to address themselves to MPs, even though they had already been warned by Dilke that no amendments would succeed in the Commons, and therefore 'what we move (if anything) depends on how it looks'.[37] The delegation received a boost when the Labour Party decided officially on 5 August to move amendments against colour restrictions in the South Africa Bill.[38] Further rounds of meetings were held with MPs on 10 and 11 August.[39]

Members of the Coloured and Native Delegation also made several further representations to the Colonial Office in August. On the 6th, Jabavu and Daniel Dwanya, neither of whom had signed the 'Appeal' or accompanied Schreiner and others to see Lord Crewe the previous month, were granted an interview with him, at Schreiner's request.[40] Lord Crewe also received a separate petition from the Natal Native Congress, which was not officially represented in the delegation at this time. In a brief telegram, the NNC requested him to do his utmost to safeguard Africans in Natal under Union and expressed its full confidence in the British government.[41] John Dube's hand was perhaps involved here.

The debate on South African union in the House of Commons took place on 16 and 19 August 1909. When it started, the House had before it a petition from the Coloured and Native Delegation. The petition repeated the whole range of grievances which had been expressed so often in numerous representations and meetings in the months since the release of the draft constitution in February 1909. It asked the House of Commons to make such amendments as would protect the existing rights held by African and coloured people, and to ensure that these rights were permanently safeguarded. The petition ended with the request that Schreiner or one of the other delegates be allowed to speak at the bar of the House, but this was refused.[42]

All that now remained was for the members of the delegation to sit through the debates as the South Africa Bill passed through the Commons without amendment. Even at this late stage they did not accept the inevitable outcome without protest. As the Bill came up for the third and final reading on 19 August, Jabavu made a last, unusual appeal in *The Times*. In a letter to the newspaper on that day, he said he accepted that the colour bar would be implemented in South Africa, but he did not want it officially to 'sully' British statutes. Like Pontius Pilate, Britain should wash its hands of the matter by erasing the colour clauses at present in the Bill but, at the same time, it should leave the way open for the South African parliament to reintroduce the clauses if it chose to do so. If Britain passed the constitution in its present form, it would legitimise colour discrimination. 'What the Imperial Parliament is being asked to sanction will be used as a precedent in future legislation against all native advance, and the Parliament will be quoted for all time as having put its seal on discrimination.'[43]

But the delegation failed to have the offending clauses in the constitution amended. The House of Commons passed the South Africa Bill on 19 August without a division. In moving the third reading of the Bill, Prime Minister Asquith said that, although it had been passed without amendment, it would be false to say that MPs wholeheartedly supported all the provisions. On the contrary, there was an 'absolute unanimity of opinion in the way of regret' that some of the clauses which dealt with the treatment of the black population and their access to the legislature had been inserted.[44] Asquith said further:

I wish before this Bill leaves the Imperial Parliament to make it perfectly clear that we here have exercised, and I think wisely and legitimately exercised, not only restraint of expression, but reserve of judgement in regard to matters of this kind, simply because we desire this great experiment of the establishment of complete self-government in South Africa to start on the lines and in accordance with the ideas which our fellow citizens there have deliberately and after long consideration come to ... It is perfectly true, the Imperial Parliament cannot divest itself of responsibility in the matters ... but if we have yielded ... it has been because we have thought it undesirable at this stage to put forward anything that would be an obstacle to the successful working of the future ... Speaking for myself and the Government, I venture to express not only the hope but the expectation ... that the views which have been so strongly given utterance to here will be sympathetically considered by our fellow citizens there. For my part I think, as I have said throughout, that it would be far better that any relaxation of what many of us, almost all of us, regard as unnecessary restrictions from the electoral rights or rights of eligibility of our fellow subjects, should be carried out spontaneously, and on the initiative of the South African Parliament, rather than they should appear to be forced upon them by the Imperial Parliament here. While we part from this measure without any … Amendment, … I am sure our fellow subjects will not take it in bad part if we respectfully and very earnestly beg them at the same time that they, in the exercise of their undoubted and unfettered freedom, should find it possible sooner or later, and sooner rather than later, to modify the provisions.

This was the line of argument that had generally been followed in debates. While most speakers expressed themselves against the principle of the colour bar, they did not wish to endanger union or retard the envisaged spread of Cape liberalism by interfering in the domestic affairs of the South African colonies.

The South Africa Bill nevertheless had a rougher passage in the Commons than in the Lords. A number of speakers in the Commons opposed the colour bar and called for amendments, including Dilke, Keir Hardie, Ramsay MacDonald, and other Liberal and Labour members. However, these MPs formed only a small minority and their opposition was overcome without much difficulty. Both the government and opposition front benches were basically agreed on the matter.[45]

Meanwhile, the Colonial Office had drafted Letters Patent for the creation of the office of Governor-General and Commander-in-Chief of the new Union.[46] With the agreement of the delegates and Lord Crewe, 31 May 1910 was agreed to as the date for the inauguration of the Union.[47] Thus, when the British parliament passed the South Africa Bill on 19 August 1909, the way was finally cleared for the unification of South Africa.

47

Birth of the new
South Africa, May 1910

No coloured man can feel happy; no coloured man, I hope, will
sing 'God save the King' on that day. I know I won't.

– Dr Abdurahman, February 1910

O nce the British parliament had sanctioned the new South
African constitution, the political excitement that had existed for months in
South African politics over union subsided. Although still dissatisfied with
the terms of union, Africans now resigned themselves to the inevitability
of a new dispensation based on discriminatory principles, and to their
powerlessness to alter the situation. Faced with the reality of union, they
began to look to see how they could best protect their interests in the
future. *Imvo*'s response to the passing of the South Africa Act emphasised
the point:

The blow has fallen, and the British Government and the House of Commons have
passed the Union Constitution Act without the amendments we had hoped for ....

The Native and Coloured people must now realise that an entirely new chapter
in South African history is opening, in which they will have to depend on themselves
and their South African European friends for the securing and maintenance of their
civil and political rights. They must become united politically and, refusing to cling
to any of the present political parties, must work for the creation of a new political
party in the State which will unite the religious and moral forces – European and
Native – of South Africa upon lines of righteous legislation, justice and fair play,
irrespective of race or colour.[1]

Naledi responded in a similar manner: 'What remains now for us, and for every Native organ and every freedom-loving Native to do, is to work for the consolidation of all blacks into one whole irrespective of nationality or creed, for we have seen that "Union is strength".'[2]

After the failure of the Coloured and Native Delegation, and all the earlier protests, to have the draft constitution amended, it might have been expected that politically active Africans would be discouraged and deflated, but this was not the case. The fact that Africans had mobilised on an unprecedented scale to protest had instilled confidence. 'Had the natives remained silent and allowed the draft Act to be passed without them uttering their word of dissent,' *Imvo* declared, then 'they would not have been worthy of their race, and deserved to be treated as children.'[3]

Far from returning home to a climate of defeatist apathy, the delegates were received with acclamation when they arrived back in South Africa. They were welcomed at the docks, treated to banquets, praised in the African newspapers and thanked for their endeavours by appreciative audiences at report-back meetings. When Schreiner, Abdurahman, Rubusana and other delegates stepped ashore in Cape Town on 21 September, they were welcomed by a Coloured Reception Committee, which included the remaining APO executive members and the Rev. F.M. Gow, a leading member of the AME Church. In an address of welcome to the delegates, the committee declared that, although the mission was regarded as a failure in some quarters, 'we feel that it has been a glorious success', which would inspire blacks to continue fighting until justice prevailed. Telegrams of appreciation from various towns were read out.[4] Two days later, the committee organised a reception in the Cape Town City Hall and the delegates were welcomed by an orchestra playing 'The Gladiator's Return' and presented with silverware gifts. The money for this welcome came from a reception fund initiated by the *A.P.O.* newspaper, to which thousands of people throughout South Africa had subscribed.[5] Rubusana, Mapikela and Dwanya were also welcomed by members of Cape Town's African community at a meeting in Ndabeni.[6] On his return Jabavu, who had remained behind in Britain on 'business matters', was given a similar reception.[7]

In the months after the delegates came home, further receptions and meetings were organised in the colonies to honour the delegates and hear about their work in Britain. Lenders reported back in Kimberley.[8] Jabavu spoke at a meeting in Port Elizabeth on his way home to King William's Town.[9] Mapikela toured the Orange River Colony.[10] Dr Rubusana, acting as the national leader which his position as Native Convention president required of him, reported back in East London and then travelled to Bloemfontein, Thaba Nchu, the Witwatersrand and Kimberley for the same purpose.[11] African women in King William's Town and Queenstown also organised banquets for the delegates.[12] In Cape Town, the APO convened another meeting to publicly honour Schreiner; and when he went to take leave of his Queenstown constituency in January 1910, the coloured and African people there presented him with an address of appreciation.[13]

Schreiner was portrayed in almost heroic proportions by black leaders and newspapers. His name was mentioned in the same breath as that of Wilberforce, and although he insisted that his co-delegates deserved an equal share of the acclaim, he was singled out for his sacrifice and work.[14] Abdurahman said every house should have in it a photograph of Schreiner next to that of the Queen.[15] Mapikela wrote that the Africans in the Orange River Colony wanted him to know that 'they shall never forget your name in their homes'.[16] Jabavu told Schreiner that 'all the honours of the fight are yours'.[17]

Clearly, political leaders in South Africa saw the delegation as a milestone in the history of organised politics and regarded it as a successful demonstration of protest against union. This was also the feeling of the delegates themselves. The line they took in the series of meetings after their return was that the mission had been a success because it made a priority of the question of black political rights in the whole unification issue. Instead of the matter being glossed over in Britain, the activities of the delegates had led the Imperial government and British parliament to register their disapproval of the colour discrimination in the new constitution, and this in turn had forced the South African government delegates to deny that they intended to restrict the rights of black people in the forthcoming union. The delegates argued that the considerable attention they had caused to be focused on the issue would help in the struggle for political equality that lay ahead in South Africa.[18]

The most significant development in the aftermath of the delegation to Britain was the attempts by Rubusana, Mapikela and others to consolidate the South African Native Convention as a permanent national organisation. At the meeting in Bloemfontein of March 1909 the Native Convention had taken tentative steps to form itself into a permanent organisation by electing an executive 'to watch the draft Act, to promote organisation and to defend the interests of the Natives'. It had subsequently sent Rubusana and Mapikela as delegates to Britain with Schreiner. While in London, the delegates had worked closely with South African students living there – Pixley Seme, Alfred Mangena and Richard Msimang – and discussions about the formation of a national political organisation for Africans in South Africa had no doubt occurred. More than a quarter of a century later, at the time of Dr Rubusana's death, Mapikela declared that 'the conversations which took place then had reference to the starting of the great African National Congress'.[19]

After their return, Rubusana and Mapikela busied themselves with Convention business. They reported back as delegates to meetings in the various colonies, sought to organise local and regional groups under the Native Convention, prepared for its second annual congress, and made representations to the colonial governments and, subsequently, the Union government. The aim was for the Native Convention to open channels of communication with the government and represent the interests of the African majority to the authorities.

Within a fortnight of Rubusana's return to the eastern Cape, he travelled to Bloemfontein, where on 11 October he and Mapikela interviewed the Governor and Prime Minister and requested permission to hold a political meeting. Prime Minister Fischer, grandfather of the struggle icon Bram Fischer, was reluctant to accede to the request, regarding Rubusana as 'exactly the class of gentry that I would debar from coming into this Colony to start agitations when our own natives do not require or do not understand what, under agitators, they are made to demand', but he relented because the Governor was in favour.[20] The meeting was held in the AME church hall. Rubusana spoke for more than two hours, and Mapikela reported back in detail to the Orange River Colony Native Congress (ORCNC) about their visit to Britain.[21] They then arranged a similar meeting in Thaba Nchu, home of the Becoana Mutual Improvement Association.[22] The Association was one of the strongest bases of the fledgling Native Convention: it had contributed funds towards Mapikela's travels and forwarded its views to him and Schreiner while the delegation was in London.[23]

After the Thaba Nchu meeting, Rubusana went on to the Transvaal where meetings had been arranged for him,[24] while Mapikela visited districts in the Orange River Colony, explaining the results of the mission to Britain and organising support on a local basis for the ORCNC and the Native Convention, two related bodies, one regional and the other national. Complaining to Schreiner that he had not had time to rest with his family since his arrival, Mapikela visited Winburg, Kroonstad, Heilbron, Viljoensdrift, Vrede, Parys, Bethlehem and Harrismith.[25] When Rubusana returned to the Orange River Colony late in November 1909, he, John Mocher and Mapikela petitioned the government on behalf of the Native Convention and the ORCNC on the question of compulsory passes for African women in municipal townships.[26] After a trip to Kimberley, Rubusana was back in Bloemfontein again in mid-December to make further representations with Mapikela on the matter of passes for women.[27]

The outcome of all these activities was that Jeremiah Makgothi, the Thaba Nchu-based Native Convention assistant general secretary, issued a notice convening the second annual congress of the Convention in Bloemfontein on 22–23 March. The purpose was for Africans to formulate and submit to the new Union parliament their views on important matters.[28] In this way they hoped to exercise an indirect influence on the legislative process. Most delegates were from the Orange River Colony, but some attended from the Transvaal, the Cape and Bechuanaland, including Rubusana, Silas Molema from Bechuanaland, J.S. Noah of the Transvaal Native Union and Sol Plaatje 'representing Johannesburg and Pretoria'.[29] No one from Natal was present. John Dube, the Convention's vice-president, was still abroad, having travelled to America after his visit to Britain; he remained there for more than a year.[30] Newspaper reports suggested another reason for the absence from Natal: a Natal government proclamation in February 1910 prohibited all chiefs and exempted Africans from attending political gatherings without the permission of the Secretary for Native Affairs.[31]

The South African Native Convention conference* was opened once again by Dewdney Drew.[32] The resolutions adopted this time reflected the change in emphasis in the approach of African political organisations after the passing of the South Africa Act. Instead of making lofty statements on matters such as the franchise, the Convention concentrated on issues that affected the everyday welfare of Africans, such as the pass laws and land ownership. The resolutions were sent to the government when the first session of the South African parliament assembled in October 1910.[33]

The conference re-elected Rubusana and John Dube as president and vice-president. The rest of the new executive consisted of Moses Masisi (treasurer), who replaced his Thaba Nchu colleague Joel Goronyane, and Jeremiah Makgothi (secretary), who took over from A.K. Soga after the latter's fall-out with Rubusana. Sol Plaatje (assistant secretary) was added to the leadership.[34]

After the conference concluded, Rubusana went straight from Bloemfontein to Port Elizabeth where he attended the APO annual conference, which was held there at the beginning of April. He was given a special welcome, and in turn conveyed the greetings of the Native Convention, saying that there should be more co-operation between coloured and African people. His views were endorsed by Dr Abdurahman in a vote of thanks. When the conference later discussed the matter of closer co-operation with Africans, the idea received much support.[35] During his visit to Port Elizabeth, Rubusana was also involved in discussions with other leading Africans, such as the newspaper editor S.E.K. Mqhayi, the Rev. Eben Bopi, Meshach Pelem and W.W. Skweyiya of Cape Town about the possibility of founding another African newspaper. *Izwi* had ceased functioning the previous year and the activists aligned to the regional

* Newspaper reports of the March 1910 meeting of the Native Convention do not provide a complete list of the delegates, but it is clear that, as in the previous year, most delegates were from the Orange River Colony. The ORC Native Congress was represented by familiar figures such as Mapikela, Peter Phatlane, John Mocher, J.S. Mocher and J.B. Twayi. The Becoana Mutual Improvement Association from Thaba Nchu was also again present. Its contingent included Jeremiah Makgothi and the Rev. Gabashane. The APO branch in the ORC again sent N. Daly as its representative.

Native Congress and the broader Native Convention clearly needed their own mouthpiece, given Jabavu's and *Imvo*'s opposition to them. But nothing came of the idea.[36]

It is clear, then, that strenuous attempts were made, by Rubusana and other Convention leaders from September 1909 onwards, to organise and unite activists around the country in the face of impending union. The *Pretoria News* reported in April 1910 that Sol Plaatje had spoken at meetings of 'The Vigilance, Pretoria' and the African National Political Union and explained that it was the aim of the Native Convention 'to combine all African organisations with a view to co-operation with the officials who will be entrusted with the administration of native affairs under the Union government'.[37] These efforts resulted in the formation in the following month of the Transvaal Native Organisation (TNO), which joined the two Pretoria organisations with the most important bodies operating in Johannesburg, namely the Transvaal Native Congress, the Transvaal Basuto Committee, the Transvaal Native Union and the 'Transvaal L. B. Committee' (probably the Iliso Lomzi of Edward Tsewu). The Transvaal's Secretary for Native Affairs noted that the TNO represented 'a considerable section of the native population principally in Johannesburg and Pretoria'.[38] The first chairman of the TNO was Sefako Makgatho, president of the African National Political Union since its formation in 1906. The long-serving Transvaal Native Congress secretary, Jesse Makhothe, became secretary.[39] The divisions in the Transvaal had seemingly been resolved and the activists involved showed their determination to continue the struggle for African rights in the new state that was coming into being. Clearly, the South African Native Convention was intended to be a permanent organisation to represent Africans on a national basis under union.

As the first Governor-General of South Africa, the British government appointed a junior cabinet minister and son of the famous Liberal Party leader of Victoria's reign, Lord Gladstone.[40] Although some African organisations would have preferred a familiar figure like Lord Selborne to fill the post, Gladstone's appointment met with general approval.[41] Referring to his political background, *Imvo* expressed joy that 'a stalwart from liberal stock' had been appointed, adding that he would have a heavy responsibility towards the Protectorates.[42] *Ilanga* hoped Gladstone would be 'an up-to-date Sir George Grey', who would do his best to repair the wrongs of the past.[43]

As the date for union approached, South African politics were dominated by the questions of who would become first Prime Minister, what the composition of his cabinet would be and on what lines the first general election would be contested. The obvious contenders for the post of Prime Minister were John X. Merriman of the Cape and Louis Botha of the Transvaal. Ex-President Steyn of the Orange River Colony would have been a strong contender, had his deteriorating health not forced him out of the running.[44]

Africans were in no doubt as to which of the two candidates they favoured. Merriman was not only the Prime Minister of the Cape, with its more liberal political system, but he had also worked closely with Jabavu, John Sishuba and other Cape voters in previous years. Botha, on the other hand, had been brought up in the tradition of republican white exclusivism. *Imvo* summed up the feelings of many on the matter when it declared: 'Bitter indeed would be the disappointment and dark and cheerless the prospect of Union to the millions of South African Natives, if at its beginning they did not have Mr Merriman as Prime Minister to inaugurate native administration on an enlightened and sympathetic basis such as has been associated with the Cape.'[45]

Once again, the tide of events moved against African public opinion. By the time Gladstone arrived in South Africa on 17 May 1910, Botha had become the overwhelming favourite. After discussions lasting several days with Lord Selborne and cabinet ministers from the various colonies, Gladstone asked Botha to form the first Union government on 22 May 1910.[46]

Imvo described Botha's appointment as a 'lamentable' beginning to Union.[47] Immediately on hearing of it, Jabavu wrote to his old political champion, Merriman, saying he had 'never felt so disappointed in politics' than when he read that Merriman had not been asked to assume office.[48]

Merriman also received letters from the annual conference of the Ethiopian Church, meeting at Lindley in the Orange River Colony, which expressed its appreciation for his past services on behalf of Africans and said his non-appointment as Prime Minister was a 'serious blow' and a 'puzzle story'.[49] John Sishuba wrote that 'the natives are awaiting the union with a great deal of anxiety' and that he hoped Merriman would continue to exert his influence in the government or parliament.[50]

Hiding his disappointment, Dr Rubusana sent Louis Botha a letter of congratulation on behalf of the South African Native Convention, claiming to represent 'the educated and leading natives' in South Africa. He informed the Prime Minister that it was 'the earnest prayer and wish of the natives of this country that you and your government may be wisely guided in the discharge of your onerous duties of the State – by Him from which all true wisdom proceeds – so that you may be able to govern the country in a way that will give some measure of satisfaction to all alike without distinction of colour, class or creed, and thus strive – in the treatment of natives especially – to maintain that righteousness alone which exalteth a nation.'[51]

Far from causing offence, however, Botha's first acts as Prime Minister in respect of 'native affairs' met with general approval. Facing behind-the-scenes pressure, Botha appointed Henry Burton, an ex-cabinet minister in the Cape parliament, as his Minister of Native Affairs.[52] Burton was a strong supporter of the non-racial Cape system and had privately been 'ill at ease' about the colour bar, which he regarded as a 'dreadful' and 'unnecessary' blot on the constitution.[53] In acknowledging the congratulations of his African constituents in Burgersdorp, Burton said, 'I hope I may be able to do some good.'[54] After his appointment, he continued to emphasise his good intentions as Minister of Native Affairs. During a visit to Dube's Ohlange Institute in Natal, he told the students: 'I know you are anxious as to what the Union government is going to do with you. I want you to know that I represent the government, that I am in charge of all the Native work in South Africa. You need not be afraid that we shall oppress you; we shall do what we can to improve your conditions; we sympathise with you.'[55]

Burton's elevation was followed by the appointment of a senior Cape Native Affairs Department official, Edward Dower, as Secretary for Native

Affairs in the Union administration.[56] African newspapers described the appointments of Burton and Dower as reassuring and favourable auguries for the position of Africans under Union.[57] Three other Cape politicians – D.P. de Villiers Graaff (Minister of Public Works), J.W. Sauer (Minister of Railways and Harbours) and F.S. Malan (Minister of Education) – were included in Botha's first cabinet. *Imvo* was particularly pleased about the appointment of Sauer, 'Mr Merriman's alter ego', and one of Jabavu's longstanding political favourites.[58] Jabavu and other supporters of the South African Native College Scheme also saw F.S. Malan's appointment to the education portfolio as a chance for the scheme to be pushed through under the supervision of a minister who was an acknowledged supporter.[59]

Almost the first act of the new ministry on the day Union was inaugurated was to authorise the release of the Zulu king Dinuzulu from jail.[60] The Prime Minister had been an ally of Dinuzulu in the 1880s. News of the king's release was received with widespread approval among Africans and raised hopes about their position in the new dispensation. John Dube, who had close connections with the King, greeted the news with delight from the United States. *Ilanga* as well as friends such as Harriette Colenso and W.P. Schreiner, whose defence of Dinuzulu had caused him to resign from the National Convention, also approved.[61] Considering his position, Dinuzulu's release by the new government had an important psychological effect at a critical time.

The inauguration of the Union of South Africa was to have been marked with pomp and jubilation but, owing to the death of King Edward VII on 6 May, there was a minimum of ceremony and festivity. The main ceremony was the swearing-in of the Governor-General, cabinet and judiciary in Pretoria. The Administrators also officially assumed office in the provincial capitals and on a local level commemorative ceremonies took place.[62] No Africans were included in the official national ceremonies. They either remained quietly aloof or, especially in the case of school children, attended the ceremonies as a matter of formality. There was no orchestrated campaign of boycott or protest against the proceedings.

Government officials reported that the bulk of the African population were hardly touched by Union Day, and were generally indifferent to the whole transition.[63]

The most negative response came from the APO, which decided to boycott any festivities and treated 31 May as a day of humiliation and prayer.[64] Dr Abdurahman said, 'No coloured man can feel happy; no coloured man, I hope, will sing "God save the King" on that day. I know I won't.'[65] Although most politically conscious Africans shared this disquiet, and some announced that they would have nothing to do with the 'jollification',[66] Africans generally took up a less aggressive position towards Union Day. Enoch Mamba declared in the Transkeian Territories General Council that, although Africans had made an unsuccessful appeal to the Crown to have the constitution changed, 'their ardour was not dampened and [they] would like to join in the general rejoicings on this day'.[67] *Imvo* identified itself completely with the advice given by W.P. Schreiner, that Africans treat this 'great and solemn' day as 'one for prayer and religious observation'.[68]

Several African groups sent messages of welcome to the new Governor-General. These included the ORC Native Congress, the Transvaal Native Organisation, the association representing the Mfengu on the diamond fields of which Isaiah Bud Mbelle was chairman, and the Ethiopian Church.[69] The address from the last body was overtly political:

We pray that your Excellency's interpretation of the Union Act in reference to the natives of South Africa may be a true, honest and liberal one; that your Excellency and his Council will show themselves strong and upright guardians of our people, especially in those provinces where we are taxed and yet have no representation in Parliament, and where laws which deal with us alone are passed by those who are not aware how they are pinching us – for, Your Excellency, the wearer of a shoe alone knows where it pinches. Such are many of the laws ... the Pass laws which are even extended to women and girls of 16 years, Squatters and Location laws which keep us like fugitives and outcasts wandering from place to place; as well as the laws preventing us from purchasing land.[70]

The signatories to the address included the moderator of the Ethiopian

Church, Isaiah Sishuba, and the church secretary, H.R. Ngcayiya, both of whom had been active for a long time in politics. Because of the political content of the message, the church had difficulty getting it accepted for presentation to the governor-general.[71] This would become a regular occurrence in future: while the government tried to shoot the messenger, African organisations would persist in conveying to it the message it did not want to hear.

48

Dr Rubusana
makes history

... a political bombshell
 – *Territorial News*, August 1910

After the inauguration of Union, attention turned towards the September general election for the House of Assembly and the Provincial Councils. The executive and judiciary had come into being, but there still was no legislature. Union would be properly consummated only once the country had its own parliament.

The elections were fought between the governing parties in the various colonies formed into a coalition loosely termed the Nationalists, who supported the Louis Botha administration, and the Unionist Party, a coalition of pro-British opposition parties under Dr Jameson. There were also candidates from the small South African Labour Party as well as a number of Independents.[1]

The 'native question' was not an election issue. In his election manifesto, Botha stated that one of the government's principles was 'the placing of the Native question above party politics, and the fair and sympathetic treatment of the coloured races in a broad and liberal treatment'.[2] The Unionists, on the other hand, propagated 'a Native policy, admitting of the treatment of questions relating to Natives, in accordance with the degree of civilisation attained by them, and with the different and local conditions under which they live and work'.[3] Neither of these election pledges indicated a definite intent on the part of the two major parties to pursue a new, more sympathetic line in 'native policy'. Although, with an eye on the black vote in the Cape, the 'native policy' sections were couched in vague and comforting language, both manifestos implicitly stood for the idea of an exclusive white nation held by most white politicians and voters.

Although a body of African opinion headed by men like Rubusana and A.K. Soga believed that Cape Africans should depart from the old pattern of voting along party lines and back candidates who supported the 'native interest', regardless of party affiliation, black voters in the Cape once again split along party lines.[4] J.T. Jabavu now carried the election banner for the Botha government with as much uncritical gusto as he had done for the South African Party.[5] His fierce disdain for the Unionists reached a new intensity, because Jameson had undermined Merriman's chances for the premiership by giving his support to Botha.[6] He had wanted the liberal Merriman as Prime Minister, but failing this he was convinced that Botha's 'best-man' government and 'fresh-start' policy, as exemplified by the release of Dinuzulu and the appointment of Burton and Dower to head the Native Affairs Department, were infinitely better than any alternative offered by the bankrupt Unionists.[7]

In contrast, the mouthpiece of the African Political Organisation was outspoken in its support of the Unionists, pungently reflected in the tags used to describe opposing candidates: 'cynic' Sauer, 'fitful' Merriman, 'ex-Meat King' Graaff.[8] The A.P.O. argued with passion that the Unionists were the only answer for the black people.[9] Black leaders, who a year earlier had been wholly united against the terms of union, were now squabbling among themselves about the merits of white politicians, who were all in general agreement about the new state.

After the election Soga wrote a long letter to *Imvo*, warning Jabavu and Abdurahman that the time had come for them to become 'Race leaders', instead of subordinating their activities and interests to loyalty towards white political parties. It was now time to build up black organisations and put black interests first.[10] Soga's approach was shared by Dr Rubusana and Sol Plaatje. Even though more inclined to the old Progressive view, Rubusana refused to back the Unionists in the election, because there were some Unionist candidates in the other provinces who did not endorse the Cape franchise. He preferred to adopt an independent line, supporting individuals with proven records of support for African political rights.[11]

Plaatje, for his part, encouraged Africans to vote for the Unionists, but his support was likewise not unconditional and he derived a great deal of satisfaction from the fact that a number of 'anti-native' candidates of both parties were defeated.[12]

In the event, the Nationalists won the election comfortably, gaining 67 of the 121 seats in the new parliament, while the Unionists won 39.[13] In the eastern Cape, where African voters were mainly concentrated, there were straight fights between Nationalists and Unionists in only two constituencies, Queenstown and Griqualand East. In East London, Colonel Crewe of the Unionists stood successfully against an Independent. Candidates were returned unopposed in Thembuland, Albany, King William's Town, Port Elizabeth South-West, Port Elizabeth Central (all Unionist) and Aliwal North (Nationalist).[14] In Queenstown, Thomas Searle (Nationalist), who had been actively supported by Jabavu, lost by 942 votes to 1156 to the veteran Progressive politician Sir Bisset Berry. A bitter Jabavu complained that the Unionists had won by raising the 'racial' (Boer vs Brit) bogy. He noted that the final voting figures coincided almost exactly with the division between English voters on the one hand and Afrikaner and African voters on the other.[15] And, indeed, the coincidence was close. In East Griqualand, where black voters comprised 20 per cent of the total, a Unionist was elected by 877 votes to the 675 of an Independent Nationalist.[16]

An event which raised as much interest as any of the contests for the House of Assembly was the candidature of Dr Rubusana for the Cape Provincial Council. This was the first time that an African had stood for a legislative position in South Africa.

The first inkling that Rubusana might enter the lists came early in August 1910, when Theo Schreiner, who was contesting the Assembly seat in the Thembuland constituency, sent a telegram to his brother Will, asking for his opinion as to whether an African voter was legally entitled to be nominated for the Provincial Council, and whether he thought such a step advisable.[17] Will replied that he saw no reason why an African should not stand.[18] Rubusana's decision to contest the seat formed part of a deliberate campaign after the delegation to Britain to mobilise Africans effectively in the face of union. Far from being, as some suggested,[19] a step to promote personal prestige, Rubusana in fact tried to get other Africans to stand as well. After visiting the Stockenstrom district, he called on Jabavu in King William's Town early in August and suggested that the latter contest the Fort Beaufort constituency for the Provincial Council. A large meeting of Africans, coloured people and a few Afrikaners in Stockenstrom, which fell in the Fort Beaufort constituency, had come out in favour of Jabavu as a candidate. When Jabavu asked for a more definite assurance, Rubusana wrote to the people involved and Jabavu was promptly contacted 'on behalf of the native voters of Stockenstrom' and invited to put his name forward. But after further communications and a trip to Fort Beaufort, where he found the idea of his candidature was 'generally applauded', Jabavu finally decided against standing.[20] Nothing could have demonstrated Rubusana's concern for the 'native interest' more than this episode. Here was a 'crusted old Progressive', to use Jabavu's words, trying to get his old SAP adversary to stand in a constituency against two white candidates, both of whom sympathised with the Unionists.

There was also talk that a third 'native representative', Dr Abdurahman, might stand in the Provincial Council elections.[21] Although he eventually decided otherwise, the rumour suggested some kind of plan, at least between Rubusana and Abdurahman, to have the leaders of the three major black political groupings in the Cape elected to the highest representative body open to them. At its annual conference, the APO even considered testing the 'European descent' clause in the constitution by putting up a candidate of mixed descent in the House of Assembly elections,[22] but in the event no APO candidate stood for the House of Assembly or the Provincial Council.

When the nomination court met on 19 August 1910, Rubusana was proposed by two of his African supporters. His opponents in the election were T.G.H. Gray, a Unionist, and W.J. Clarke, an Independent Nationalist.[23] Rubusana's decision to stand as an Independent showed that he did not intend subjecting himself to party constraints.[24] In a long speech after his nomination, Rubusana outlined his reasons for standing for the Provincial Council. He pledged that if he were returned he would work for all his constituents regardless of race, colour or creed. But his programme showed that his main aim was to take up the cudgels on behalf of the African cause in the new institutions of state. He said he was confident he would be able 'to throw some light on the vexed native question' in the Provincial Council and his list of priorities was African-orientated.

Rubusana's nomination caused a great stir. The local *Territorial News* described it as a 'political bombshell' that had created a 'demoralising and humiliating situation' for the constituency.[25] Indeed, to prevent Rubusana from being elected, Gray proposed to the other candidate, Clarke, that they should hold a plebiscite among white voters to decide which of them should retire, but this strategy was rejected by Clarke.[26]

It was obvious that Rubusana would in all likelihood emerge as winner if voting took place along racial lines. Black voters comprised 49.5 per cent of the total in Thembuland. Under the new delimitation the Elliot district had been excluded from the constituency, but the Glen Grey division,[27] with its 504 African voters, had been incorporated into it. The number of black voters was 1399 out of a total of 2846 – only 48 fewer black voters than whites.[28]

The *Territorial News* now tried to divide the black voters. It warned them that Rubusana's election would lead to the closing of the 'open door' and declared they had an absolute duty to themselves and the rest of the black voters in the Cape to prevent this from happening.[29] The pro-Unionist *Daily Dispatch,* the largest newspaper in the eastern Cape, pursued a similar line.[30] Nor did Rubusana receive any help from Jabavu, whose *Imvo* was the only African newspaper in the region. *Imvo* did not report Rubusana's candidature until early September, and then Jabavu used the editorials to take a swipe at the Unionist press for criticising an 'old devotee of the Prog cult' for standing, as well as to hit at Rubusana himself.[31] He suggested that the attitude of voters should be 'to criticise his case as if he were no black, for if they give him any advantage over the other candidates because of his colour then they run the risk of being classed with those who insist on the colour bar against them ... Let voters consider his qualifications and qualities apart from colour.'[32] This was a sound non-racial argument, but showed a lack of grace towards someone who had only recently tried to help Jabavu get a seat as well.

Rubusana was duly elected as MPC. He gained 766 (42 per cent) of the 1766 votes cast, beating Gray by only 25 ballots.[33] The only candidate present when the election returns were announced, he thanked the electors in a short speech and promised to do his best for Thembuland.[34]

Ilanga greeted Rubusana's victory in true African fashion by placing in the Zulu columns a praise poem lauding his achievement.[35] *Tsala ea Becoana (The Bechuana Friend)* and the *A.P.O.* also responded with delight, the former saying, 'there were MPCs who would look askance at Dr Rubusana, but he had nothing to fear as he was infinitely superior in intellectual capacity, educational qualifications, eloquence, common sense and manners to many of them'.[36] But even after Rubusana's victory, *Imvo* still maintained a lukewarm attitude.[37] Another sour response came from his former close political ally, A.K. Soga, who had fallen out with him when excluded from the delegation to England the previous year. Soga accused Rubusana of disloyalty to the South African Native Congress and of promoting his own self-interest by 'running in advance of his race'.[38]

Despite these unpleasant notes, there is no doubt that Rubusana's win came as a powerful psychological boost for Africans. He also immediately began to make use of a handsome salary and newly earned privilege of unlimited first-class rail travel.[39] No sooner had he returned to East London than he travelled to Natal where he met, among others, Charles Dube, acting editor of *Ilanga* in the continued absence of his brother overseas.[40] Since his return from Britain in September 1909, Rubusana had covered much ground, in more ways than one.

All that remained to complete the composition of the South African parliament after the general election of September 1910 was the announcement of the names of the eight senators nominated by the cabinet. Thirty-two members of the Senate of forty had already been chosen by the colonial parliaments in their final sessions. Four of the nominated senators (the 'native senators') were to be chosen 'on the ground mainly of their thorough acquaintance ... with the reasonable wants and wishes of the coloured races of South Africa'.[41]

In the hope of influencing the nominations, several organisations put forward the names of people they considered would best represent their interests to the government. The ball was set rolling by the South African Native Convention, which at its annual congress in March decided to ask the authorities to appoint Sir Bisset Berry (Cape), Dewdney Drew (Orange Free State), William Hosken (Transvaal) and Sir David Hunter (Natal). In forwarding these names to the Colonial Office in London, Rubusana said that these men had shown themselves to be consistent friends of the African people.[42] A few days later, the APO annual congress in Port Elizabeth ratified the Native Convention's decision.[43] The two bodies were clearly co-operating in this matter.

When it became known that W.P. Schreiner had decided not to seek a seat in the House of Assembly, both the Native Convention and the APO immediately substituted his name for that of Sir Bisset Berry on their list of favoured candidates.[44] Instead of making himself available for the Assembly or for a place on the bench, Schreiner had decided that his services would be more useful in the Senate where he could speak for all blacks, enfranchised and unenfranchised, and thus have for his constituency not merely the Cape Province but the whole of the Union.[45] Having announced his wish to be considered a senator, Schreiner became an obvious favourite. The *A.P.O.* newspaper declared that it would be a national calamity if 'our W.P.' were not nominated.[46]

Other bodies also sent in names to the government. J.T. Jabavu's group, now calling itself the Cape Native Vigilance Association, put forward the names of W.P. Schreiner, Colonel Walter Stanford, William Hay (an ex-Cape parliamentarian and editor of the *Cape Mercury*) and William Hosken.[47] Later, Jabavu requested that Hosken's name be replaced by that of Thomas Searle, the defeated Nationalist candidate in the general election for the Queenstown constituency.[48] Other candidates were promoted by the Orange Free State Native Congress and the Bloemfontein branch of the APO, by Africans in the Kamastone and Oxkraal reserve in the Queenstown district, the coloured people in Campbell in Griqualand West, the chiefs and headmen of British Bechuanaland, and the Transvaal Native Organisation.[49]

In the event, the final list of names of the eight nominated senators was announced on 13 October. The four chosen to represent black interests were W.P. Schreiner, Colonel Stanford, J.C. Krogh and F.R. Moor.[50] The choice of Schreiner was universally approved.[51] Dinuzulu spoke for many Africans when he told Schreiner, 'All my trust is in you ... May the Lord keep you and give you power fearlessly to advocate the just and equitable treatment of the Natives of South Africa.'[52] Although some sections of the African elite had reservations about Stanford's suitability, his appointment was generally popular.[53] But the nomination of Krogh, a Native Commissioner in Nylstroom in the Transvaal, who had been a member of the South African Native Affairs Commission, and of Moor, Natal's last Prime Minister and Minister of Native Affairs, met with unfavourable reactions. Moor's appointment, in particular, came in for tremendous criticism.[54] But at least 'our W.P.' was in the Senate and Africans had no doubt that he would do his best to protect their interests. With the composition of the Senate now finalised, the Union of South Africa had finally been consummated.

49

Attempts to cement unity, 1910–1911

The demon of racialism, the aberrations of the Xhosa–Fingo feud, the animosity that exists between the Zulus and the Tongaas, between Basothos and every native, must be buried up and forgotten; it has shed among us sufficient blood. We are one people. These divisions, these jealousies are the cause of all our woes and all our backwardness and ignorance today.

– Pixley Seme, October 1911

Union did not bring the 'fresh start' that African leaders had hoped for. In fact, in the new state the northern colonies predominated and essentially their interests and traditions rather than those of the Cape prevailed. In the white political arena, a vigorous segregationist movement developed around the figure of General J.B.M. Hertzog, calling for a South African 'native policy' based on that of the former republics. During the first year or so of Union, parliament passed several discriminatory laws, which indicated a shift in this direction. Statutes promulgated during 1911 included the Native Labour Regulation Act, which made breaches of labour contracts by Africans a criminal offence; the Mines and Works Act, which had the effect of restricting certain skilled jobs in the mining and engineering fields to whites; and the Dutch Reformed Church Act, which excluded black members of that church in the Cape from becoming members in the Transvaal and Orange Free State.[1]

Africans in the civil service also found themselves affected by the trend towards segregation. Increasingly, African interpreters were replaced by whites, and in some areas African workers on the railways were retrenched to provide job opportunities for poor whites.[2] These measures were all motivated by the broad principles of restricting social integration, ensuring an adequate supply of cheap black labour, and hampering African access to skills, organisation and land. All were resented by the African public.

Political leaders intensified their efforts to ensure an effective voice in the new South Africa. Denied full political representation, they tried to compensate by utilising the whole range of constitutional options available to them. They consolidated political organisation on a local and national level and established new newspapers to express African opinion more forcefully. They formed economic, social and religious bodies to promote the general advancement of African people and continued to enlist the support of sympathetic white groups and individuals. And they kept on petitioning and lobbying local authorities, the Native Affairs Department, the 'native senators' and the government. In the Cape, voters could also use their electoral influence to exert pressure on the members of the Provincial Council and parliament. The number of Africans on the voters' roll at the time of the last Cape general elections in 1907 was 8418; the total rose to 14,282 in 1921.[3]

Represented in the Senate by the 'native senators' and in the Cape Provincial Council by Dr Rubusana, Africans at first hoped that these bodies could be used as effective forums to voice their interests. However, the 'native problem' was not to be resolved in the Senate or Provincial Councils, but in the House of Assembly, where effective power lay and from which black South Africans were barred. W.P. Schreiner had accepted nomination as a senator in optimistic mood, declaring that his constituency was now the black people of the whole of the Union, not merely enfranchised voters in the Cape. One parliamentary session was enough to disillusion him. At the end of it he foresaw that the Senate, which had in essence acted as a rubber-stamp for the House of Assembly, would become a 'useless body unless it carries out its proper function of deliberation'.[4]

Rubusana was faced with similar constraints in the Provincial Council, where the focus was more on provincial and local, non-political matters. He occupied himself with such matters as the creation of a bridge across the Bashee River, East Coast fever, teachers' salaries and colour distinctions in new regulations for examinations for teachers' certificates.[5] Only one or two of these issues related specifically to the protection of African interests. Nevertheless, despite the limitations of the institutions in which they served, both Rubusana and Schreiner were able to promote African interests generally, by acting as intermediaries between Africans and the government, and by using their positions to highlight and articulate African concerns.[6]

In the absence of direct political representation in the new Union, African leaders saw the urgent need for a strong national organisation to represent African opinion and open up channels of communication with the government. Those at the head of the South African Native Convention continued with their attempts to consolidate this body into an effective, representative organisation in the post-Union period. In moves designed to make its presence felt, the Native Convention attempted to influence the appointment of the 'native senators'. It also forwarded the resolutions of its annual conference in March 1910 to the government when the South African parliament assembled for the first time in October.[7] On an organisational level, it placed notices in newspapers to publicise its existence, its office-bearers wrote to the press in support of African interests, and it arranged its third annual meeting in Johannesburg on 5 May 1911.[8]

That the proceedings of this 1911 meeting were not reported in the press provides a comment on the struggling nature of the aspirant national movement. Its regional affiliates at this time were the Transvaal Native Union, the Orange Free State Native Congress and the Natal Native Congress.[9] Rubusana remained president, but at least one new face, that of Cleopas Kunene (secretary), appeared on the executive.[10] Another newcomer to the scene was Pixley kaIsaka Seme, who had recently returned to the country after completing his legal studies in Britain. He appears to have assumed a leadership role almost at once. A few weeks after the AGM, a gathering of the Native Convention executive was held in Seme's office in

Johannesburg.[11] Reports of another meeting described the presence of 'Mr Attorney Seme, B.A., Transvaal, S.A.N. Convention (Johannesburg)'.[12] Seme's legal offices in the city centre were just across from Gandhi's. One of Seme's clerks, Selby Msimang (younger brother of Richard), recalled that when Seme was away from office on other matters, 'I would go and consult him [Gandhi] he helped me get over certain difficulties'. Seme himself spent a day in 1911 at Tolstoy Farm, where Gandhi 'told him about the passive resistance movement'.[13]

Seme's entry into the political arena was to have far-reaching consequences. It was clear by the middle of 1911 that ambitious new plans, driven by Seme, were afoot to strengthen the national movement so that it could function more effectively. An important part of them was that the organisation should include not only educated activists and intellectuals, but also chiefs – with their mass followings, their symbolic importance and their financial sufficiency. The primary business at the executive meeting in Seme's office on 17 June was 'to draw out the Constitution of the South African Native Convention'.[14] By July preparations were far advanced. Press reports made it known that 'Preliminary arrangements have been completed ... for the union of the various native associations throughout South Africa and a congress of the new organization will be held next month'.[15] But the announcement was premature. A large Native Convention meeting did take place on 7 August, but it was another preparatory meeting of the extended executive, not the founding conference of the new body.[16] At this meeting, Seme tabled a draft constitution, the preamble of which emphasised the need for a federation of existing organisations so that 'a well digested and accepted native opinion should be easily ascertainable by the government with respect to the great native problem in its various ramifications'.[17] The meeting resolved that the constitution should be printed and referred to the branches for scrutiny before the next annual meeting.

All the affiliated areas were represented on 7 August. The Orange Free State Native Congress sent John Mocher and Thomas Mapikela; the Transvaal Native Union sent William Letseleba and J. Mopela. Pixley Seme and Cleopas Kunene, both Johannesburg-based Zulu men, represented Natal. From British Bechuanaland came S.J. Molema (on behalf of

Paramount Lekoko) and Chief Silas Molema.* One of the issues discussed was the launching of a newspaper to serve as an organ for the national organisation. When Levi Mvabaza, editor of *Umlomo wa Bantu*, said he feared for the survival of his own newspaper, the delegates reassured him by replying that further newspapers would rather heighten political awareness and lead to greater enlightenment. In addition to this discussion, the executive appointed an unnamed arbitrator to try to resolve a dispute that had arisen between the Transvaal Native Union and the Transvaal Native Organisation. The meeting ended with the executive entrusting the Native Convention president, Dr Rubusana, with the task of calling the next meeting, preferably sometime in November.[18] The delegates then returned home to report back to their members.[19]

The next move came in October when Seme sent a circular to African leaders, communities and newspapers, outlining the need for unity and for a South African Native Congress to put this into effect.[20] The aim of the Congress would be to get 'all the dark races of this subcontinent to come together, once or twice a year'. Such national conferences would provide Africans with an effective platform to publicise their views on matters that affected them, enable the 'native senators' to remain in close touch with the people whose interests they represented, provide a direct and independent channel of information to the government itself, and make it easier for the government to achieve a uniform 'native policy' for the whole of South Africa. Only through such a Congress could Africans influence public opinion and the legislative process.

Seme also appealed to African leaders to cast aside personal differences: 'The demon of racialism, the aberrations of the Xhosa–Fingo feud, the animosity that exists between the Zulus and the Tongaas, between Basothos and every native, must be buried up and forgotten; it has shed among us sufficient blood. We are one people. These divisions, these jealousies are the cause of all our woes and all our backwardness and ignorance today.' By this time, Seme claimed, the movement was already known and 'in a great measure openly supported by nearly all leaders and greater chiefs of

* Local leaders included Z.J. Makgothi (Winburg), J.T. Moloi (Harrismith), J.S. Noah (Krugersdorp), Thomas Fakazi (Johannesburg), J.K. Sephaphathi (Randfontein) and S. Gompo (Nancefield). In addition to the official delegates, H.R. Ngcayiya, J. Mahlamvu and several others attended.

at least three colonies and all the protectorates'.

A caucus held in Johannesburg in November decided to summon the South African Native Congress to meet in Bloemfontein on 8 January 1912, a month later than originally planned.* It then approved a programme for the meeting, which was sent out to interested parties and publicised in the African press, together with the draft constitution.[21] It is clear that Seme and his colleagues had decided that, in expanding the functions and structure of the national organisation, they should drop the title of the South African Native Convention and form a new organisation altogether. This course of action was probably motivated by the need to make a fresh start and by the desire to involve groups, such as the Jabavu camp in the eastern Cape, that had withheld their support from the Native Convention.

In order to iron out existing differences in the Transvaal, it was also decided that the organisations in that province should hold a meeting early in December to confer on common policy in view of the forthcoming national congress. A committee was appointed to prepare a report in this regard, headed by Seme.[22] All bodies in the Transvaal were represented. The province would now be able to speak with one voice. As was demonstrated by the change of venue of Native Convention meetings to Johannesburg, the Transvaal had become the driving force behind the African national movement. This was reflected as well in the major role assigned to Transvaal-based members in the programme for the impending congress, above all to the three newly qualified lawyers, Seme, Mangena and Montsioa – supporters of the Coloured and Native Delegation to London in 1909 – who were to introduce the resolutions to constitute the new organisation.

One vital area where Seme and his colleagues lacked support for their nationalist plans was the eastern Cape. Enfranchised African voters there were still divided into two camps and tended to see their future salvation in participation in the Cape electoral system rather than involvement in an African national movement removed from the (white) mainstream of political life. The one notable link between the eastern Cape and the rest of the country in the move towards national unity was Dr Rubusana. In July

---

* Among those present were Seme, S.M. Makgatho, Sol Plaatje, J. Mahlamvu, Edward Tsewu, H.R. Ngcayiya, Chief Maama Letsie and other supporters from Basutoland.

1911 the press reported that he was expected to become president of the new 'union of various native associations throughout South Africa' then being planned. An executive of 30 members had already been agreed on, the report added.[23] But Rubusana was not actively involved in the initiatives spearheaded by Seme. Shortly after presiding at the annual meeting of the Native Convention in May, Rubusana accompanied Dalindyebo, paramount of the Thembu, on a three-month trip to Europe,[24] where he would attend the coronation of Edward VII. Rubusana was thus absent from the domestic political arena at an important stage. Nevertheless, as Seme affirmed, Rubusana was 'in complete sympathy' with the movement and subsequently attended the founding congress in 1912.[25]

While abroad, Rubusana and Dalindyebo attended the Universal Races Congress in London, along with J.T. Jabavu and his son D.D.T., who was studying in London at the time. Alfred Mangena, W.P. Schreiner and a number of other South Africans were also present.[26] Held at the end of July, the Congress sought to encourage international understanding and co-operation, particularly among white and black. Close on a thousand people attended. Jabavu was one of a long list of people invited to read papers, including W.E.B. Du Bois, Sir Harry Johnston and Sir Charles Dilke (the last two had also supported the Coloured and Native Delegation in London in 1909).[27]

After receiving the invitation, Jabavu and his associates Elijah J. Mqoboli and Ben Mazwi decided to establish an organisation that could act as the South African branch of the Universal Races Congress, and thereby keep Africans in South Africa in touch with sympathetic and enlightened international opinion. They proposed a meeting of all interested parties for this purpose.[28] In order to enlist the support of political leaders in the north, Mqoboli went to the Witwatersrand and addressed meetings in Johannesburg, Boksburg and Germiston.[29] Feelers were also put out to stalwarts of the rival eastern Cape-based South African Native Congress like Dr Rubusana and Meshach Pelem.[30] In the end, however, the conference – held in King William's Town in May 1911 – turned out to be yet again a meeting of Jabavu's traditional supporters, and the South African Races Congress, inaugurated in March of the following year, did not last long.[31]

In effect, Jabavu's new-style Imbumba was set up as a counter-weight to Seme's proposed Congress. Whether intentional or not, both initiatives gained momentum from May 1911 onwards, both held meetings in Johannesburg about the same time, and officials from the two sides corresponded with each other. Jabavu and his supporters were one of the many groups to respond to Seme's circular on 'Native Union'. Writing to Seme as 'an admirer of your scheme', Jabavu's associate Ben Mazwi expressed support for the idea of African unity in principle, but sought various assurances. Was the proposed Congress in any way connected with 'the Bloemfontein Convention established in 1909' and the Cape Ingqungqutela (South African Native Congress), and what terms would Seme suggest for the amalgamation of Imbumba with the new body?[32] Seme replied that the proposed organisation was neither under the auspices of the 'Bloemfontein Convention', which was 'perhaps a voice towards this direction', nor was it connected with the South African Native Congress or any other body. As regards the terms of amalgamation, Seme said that he personally wished to see all existing organisations come together in a loose federation as members of one great household under a mother Congress and speaking in one voice. Not until this was done would African views be properly considered. However, Seme could offer no terms for amalgamation: 'it would be an unwarranted presumption on my part even to think that I have any honours to distribute in connection with a matter so sacred and so entirely in the hands of the Native people of this Great Country. All that I can say is that the Imbumba ye Zizwe has an opportunity to make its own terms with the people. ... I must call for your patriotic and united support, and if you do this you have nothing to fear in the hands of a grateful people.'[33] He and his co-organisers promptly followed up this correspondence by putting Mazwi's name down on the programme for the proposed congress.

Besides these developments in the field of organisational politics, indications of growing African unity in the post-Union period manifested themselves in other spheres as well. Efforts were made to set up additional newspapers to educate, mould and represent African public opinion, and establish economic and religious organisations to encourage co-operation and promote African interests. These activities reflected a general desire to unite and strengthen the African voice in the face of white unity and intransigence.

In June 1910, at the same time that the new Union of South Africa was taking its first steps, a Thaba Nchu-based African syndicate started the weekly *Tsala ea Becoana* (The Bechuana Friend). *Tsala* appeared regularly for two years and built up a circulation of several thousand and consistent revenue from advertising. Edited by Sol Plaatje and published in Kimberley, the newspaper's columns were in English and Tswana. Like the other African-controlled newspapers, it aimed to influence African opinion, represent African interests and act as a channel through which government proclamations and policy could be conveyed to Africans.[34] Controlling interest in the syndicate that owned *Tsala ea Becoana* was held by Thaba Nchu landowners, including Joel Goronyane, W.Z. Fenyang, John Nyokong and Jeremiah Makgothi. Most, if not all, of them were prominent in national politics. *Tsala*'s shareholders also had close connections with the South African Native Convention. Thomas Mapikela and J.T. Jabavu were the two syndicate members from outside Thaba Nchu.

Undoubtedly, part of the stimulus in starting the newspaper was provided by the unification of South Africa and the need for an effective African voice in the new Union. The Thaba Nchu landowners also feared that, if white farming interests in the Orange Free State went unchallenged, their already precarious land rights and land security would be threatened. As they were denied political representation, a newspaper was one of the most effective means of political expression open to them.

The establishment of *Tsala* may have been part of a broader plan to extend the African press throughout South Africa. It was one of four newspapers launched in rapid succession. In the year or so after the first issue of *Tsala* appeared, *Mochochonono* (The Comet) was started in Maseru, while *Motsoalle* (The Friend), soon afterwards to become *Moromioa* (The Messenger), and *Umlomo wa Bantu* (The Mouthpiece of the People) were begun in Johannesburg. *Motsoalle* was a Tswana–Pedi weekly edited by Daniel Letanka. The editors of the Xhosa–English *Umlomo* were Saul Msane and Levi Mvabaza, who described the paper's policy as 'the unifying of all African tribes into one people, and further to improve and update the education of the African children'.[35]

Another attempt to promote African interests and unity, this time in the economic sphere, was made by Alfred Mangena, after his return from Britain in 1910. One of his first ventures was to form the African Brotherhood and Commercial Co-operation Society, an organisation 'expressly established for the political protection, Commercial encouragement and Unification of the Dark Races' of the subcontinent.[36] The Society aimed to organise Africans into a body which could provide funds for commercial undertakings, educational expansion and 'brotherly help' among members. It would also be concerned with politics – 'the very life and existence of every one, and therefore ... the deciding factor in a people or a nation's life'. The headquarters were to be in Pretoria, with branches countrywide. The Society intended to work in close co-operation with other African bodies and start a newspaper to promote the principles of the scheme. Whether or not it got off the ground is unknown. A short-lived newspaper, the *African Native Advocate*, started by Mangena and Sefako Makgatho in 1912, with A.K. Soga as editor, may have resulted from this enterprise.[37]

Around the time that Alfred Mangena was busy with his initiative, moves were also afoot in Christian church circles to bring together African ministers in a national organisation for the first time. In September 1910 a conference, attended by about 40 churchmen from the established as well as separatist churches, was held in Queenstown to deal with the interdenominational church conflict that for many years had been a factor in African life.[38] A follow-up conference took place in Bloemfontein in October 1911. Here, African churchmen formally organised themselves into the Interdenominational Conference of Native Races in Africa. Its first president was the Rev. Simon Peter Sihlali, who had also been first president of the pioneering Imbumba Yama Nyama three decades previously. Starting with the vice-president, the Rev. Benjamin Dlepu, also a prominent member of the original Imbumba, the executive members of the new church body read like a who's who of politics. They included Eben Koti and T.B. Soga, Ben Mazwi, J.K. Bokwe, I.G. Sishuba, and Thomas Mapikela, John Mocher, J.Z. Tantsi and Joseph Twayi, all of the Orange Free State Native Congress.[39]

While some saw the formation of the Interdenominational Conference as 'Colour Bar no. 2' and an unnecessary provocation to the establishment General Missionary Conference, which had roughly the same aims and interests, others felt that this degree of interdenominational co-operation among Africans was not in fact enough and that steps should be taken to establish a 'National Church for the Natives of Africa'. Supporters of this scheme included political figures such as H.R. Ngcayiya and Levi Mvabaza. Predictably, Africans who belonged to the established churches were against the suggestion.[40]

In the field of education, the movement for a central South African Native College continued now that the various colonies had come under a single authority. At the end of September 1910 a deputation led by the principal of Lovedale, J. Henderson, interviewed the Minister of Education about the possibility of government support for the scheme. Besides Jabavu, the most prominent African supporter of the scheme, the deputation included Joel Goronyane, Thomas Mapikela and Sol Plaatje.[41] A third convention of supporters of the South African Native College Scheme was held in 1912, this time in Bloemfontein, so that more people from the north could attend. Once again, well-known political figures such as Seme, Jabavu, Mapikela, and Martin Lutuli and Abner Mtimkulu of the Natal Native Congress were present. Several political bodies were directly represented. On the recommendation of Seme, the convention decided to approach the various political organisations officially for support in collecting funds and promoting the scheme.[42]

Thus, at every level, the educated elite in the early 1910s were mobilising and reaching out in solidarity across old territorial boundaries until, finally, they were ready to establish a 'Native Parliament' in the new whites-only Union of South Africa.

50

The South African
Native National Congress, 1912

Chiefs of royal blood and gentlemen of our race, we have ...
discovered that in the land of their birth, Africans are treated as
hewers of wood and drawers of water. The white people of this
country have formed what is known as the Union of South Africa
– a union in which we have no voice in the making of laws and
no part in their administration. We have called you therefore to
this Conference so that we can together devise ways and means of
forming our national union for the purpose of creating national
unity and defending our rights and privileges.

– Pixley kaIsaka Seme, 8 January 1912

A large number of chiefs or their representatives and the leaders
of local and regional political organisations converged on Bloemfontein on
8 January 1912 to attend the historic conference convened by Pixley Seme
to discuss the formation of a new national organisation for the African
people. Upwards of 60 delegates participated in the four-day event, which
would be remembered as a landmark in the history of politics in South
Africa and the continent as a whole.[1] They came from all over the new
Union of South Africa and the adjoining Protectorates and represented a
wide cross-section of public opinion.

For the first time, traditional leaders co-operated enthusiastically with
the educated activists on an inter-territorial basis. Several paramount
chiefs were represented directly or indirectly, the strong Sotho contingent
being the most notable. Letsie was represented by Chief Maama, Philip

Modise (his personal secretary), and half a dozen followers; while minor chiefs attended on behalf of Bathoen Gaseitsiwe of the Ngwaketse in the Bechuanaland Protectorate and the Rolong chief Lekoko. Chiefs Mohlaba from the Soutpansberg, Ramaube from Middelburg, and Mopedi and Ntsane of Witsieshoek were also present.

The Transvaal was the province best represented, with no less than 25 delegates. This was indicative of the activity that had taken place in the Transvaal in planning the conference. A number of leaders who had been active in the earliest Transvaal organisations were present, including Edward Tsewu, Sefako Makgatho, H.R. Ngcayiya and D.D. Tyakwadi, as well as emerging figures such as Pixley Seme and Levi Mvabaza. Besides the more prominent Johannesburg and Pretoria personalities, there were local leaders from places such as the Soutpansberg, Middelburg, Zebediela and Potgietersrus.

The representatives from the Orange Free State were headed by the OFS Native Congress president, John Mocher; the secretary, Thomas Mapikela; and several executive members such as Henry Poho from Winburg. While members of the Eastern Native Vigilance Association from Bethlehem were present, for some unknown reason the big names of the Becoana Mutual Improvement Association from Thaba Nchu – like Joel Goronyane, J.M. Nyokong, Jeremiah Makgothi and Moses Masisi – did not attend.

Another absentee was John Dube of Natal, the reason given being 'pressing educational and editorial calls'. During a recent visit to Johannesburg to collect funds for his Ohlange Institute, Dube had met Seme and other prominent Zulu people and arranged to send his brother Charles as a Natal representative.[2] The only other delegate from Natal was Chief James Majozi, who had helped establish both the Natal Native Congress and the *Ipepa lo Hlanga* newspaper a decade earlier.

Dr Walter Rubasana, the respected South African Native Congress leader and now high-profile member of the Cape Provincial Council, was the most notable eastern Cape delegate, and one of only a few from that area. He had not been actively involved in the immediate prelude to the conference, as he was away overseas with Dalindyebo of the Thembu (who was reputed to have sent a herd of 100 oxen to the founding conference). But Rubusana was in sympathy with the plans and, indeed, largely responsible for this great show of unity. His persistent efforts since 1909 as president of the South African Native Convention to promote unity throughout South Africa were crucial to the building of a national movement. The veteran eastern Cape and South African Native Congress activist Daniel Dwanya was another noteworthy participant. Rubusana's and Dwanya's careers were in many ways a golden thread linking together key moments in eastern Cape politics, beginning with the very first organisations, the campaign against *Tung' umlomo* in 1887 and the formation of the original South African Native Congress in 1891. This pioneering Native Congress, as well as the South African Native Convention of 1909–11, was really the direct predecessor of the national body now being formed.

From the western Cape came Thomas Zini, president of the Cape Peninsula Native Association.[3] The northern Cape delegates were Sol Plaatje, N.S. Motshumi and James Ngcezula from Kimberley. Plaatje (*Tsala ea Becoana*) was one of four newspaper editors present. There were also *Ilanga lase Natal*'s Charles Dube, Levi Mvabaza of *Umlomo wa Bantu* and F. Monyakuane, editor of the *Naledi ea Lesotho*. Monyakuane was one of several people from Basutoland who attended in addition to the representatives of Chief Letsie; some of them came on behalf of the Basutoland Progressive Association.[4]

Following his own precedent, J.T. Jabavu did not make an appearance, but there were mitigating factors – he had arrived back in Cape Town from Britain only two days before the conference began. The organisers were hopeful that Jabavu would lead his Cape supporters in the South African Races Congress into the new national organisation.[5] Ben Mazwi, the secretary, was included as leader of one of the conference's discussion topics, and the vice-president, E.J. Mqoboli, was elected as chaplain-in-chief of the new body,[6] but reports do not confirm whether they actually attended.*

When the conference began on the morning of Monday 8 January, John Mocher, the veteran Bloemfontein leader and president of the Native Congress of the host province, was in the chair. The opening ceremony

---

* Others who attended were P. Mosehle, E. Moeletsi and E. Chake from the Transvaal; Peter Phatlane (Bloemfontein), Obed Mokhosi (of the Eastern Native Vigilance Association in Bethlehem), S.T. Mdliva (Burgersdorp) and Chief Mokgalagadi of the Ngwaketse.

was conducted by the Revs. Tsewu, Mantsayi, Tantsi and Rose (the last a white Bloemfontein minister, who expressed the hope that the proposed constitution would be amended to make provision for white auxiliary members).[7] After prayers, the discussions got under way with a speech by Pixley Seme, the convener of the conference.

Chiefs of royal blood and gentlemen of our race, we have gathered here to consider and discuss a theme which my colleagues and I have decided to place before you. We have discovered that in the land of their birth, Africans are treated as hewers of wood and drawers of water. The white people of this country have formed what is known as the Union of South Africa – a union in which we have no voice in the making of laws and no part in their administration. We have called you therefore to this Conference so that we can together devise ways and means of forming our national union for the purpose of creating national unity and defending our rights and privileges.[8]

He said it would be difficult to bring about national unity, as 'this is the first time that so many elements representing different tongues and tribes ever attempted to co-operate under one umbrella in one great house', but the formation of the Congress was the first step in solving the so-called native problem, and it was sure to help the advancement of the African people, who had hitherto been separated by tribal jealousies. The different associations formed in the past had been ineffective because they did not co-operate. Congress would unite the separate bodies to work for the good of all. Speaking in the Pan-African language of the religious separatists, Seme said it seemed that the hour had come when 'Ethiopia would stretch forth her hands unto God, and when princes shall come out of Egypt'. He foresaw that the co-operation of the Protectorates would enhance the influence of the Africans in the Union, while conversely the Protectorate chiefs would benefit from the experience and constant contact the latter had with 'European civilisation' when they made representations to the authorities.[9]

At the end of his speech, Seme formally moved that 'the delegates and representatives of the great native houses from every part of South Africa here assembled should form and establish the South African Native

National Congress'.[10] Chief Joshua Molema seconded the motion, and was followed by several chiefs as well as by Dr Rubusana, who 'supported the motion in a powerful speech which was loudly cheered'. The speakers all emphasised the need for co-operation, Chief Maama's exhortation being, 'Let them go forth and tell their people that the South African races are one.' The motion was then put to the vote and passed unanimously as the delegates stood and cheered.[11]

Not all the delegates were satisfied with the name of the new organisation. Sol Plaatje, supported by Chief Joshua Molema, felt that it should have a distinctive African name. He favoured something like *Imbizo Yabantu* (Bantu Congress), which had been suggested by Cleopas Kunene in a letter to the conference. Plaatje felt that yet another 'Congress' in addition to the numerous commercial, political and agricultural congresses and councils found throughout South Africa would confuse people, while a new name like *Imbizo Yabantu* would give the organisation a distinct identity. Kunene pointed out that *imbizo* was a word that occurred in nearly all African languages in South Africa. As 'we are Abantu', Africans should not 'approach the matter from a European's point of view, but from a native's'. However, the conference rejected the suggested departure from the title originally recommended.[12]

Once the Congress had been formally established, the next business was to approve a constitution and elect the office-bearers.[13] The constitution received the general approval of the conference, though initially it was not accepted, as there were differences over the question of financial contributions from the local branches.[14] The objects of the Congress were clearly stated in the draft constitution. They were:

(a) The promotion of unity and mutual co-operation between the Government and the Abantu Races of South Africa.
(b) The maintenance of a central channel between the Government and the aboriginal races in South Africa.
(c) The promotion of the educational, social, economic and political elevation of the native people in South Africa.
(d) The promotion of mutual understanding between the Native chiefs and the encouragement in them and their people of a spirit of loyalty to

470

the British crown and all lawfully constituted authorities, and to bring about better understanding between the white and black inhabitants of South Africa.

(e) The safeguarding of the interests of the native inhabitants throughout South Africa by seeking and obtaining redress for any of their just grievances.[15]

The election of the president took place next. A committee of 18 – consisting of three members from each of the six main regions present – had been tasked with finalising arrangements. It submitted the names of three people – Edward Tsewu, Sefako Makgatho and John Dube – to the conference. The outcome was that Dube was elected in absentia by a large majority.[16] Various reasons have been offered as to why the 41-year-old Dube was chosen and not the respected Dr Rubusana, who was very much the elder statesman. One view is that the delegates were expressing their solidarity with the Natalians in their sufferings during the recent Bambatha rebellion.[17] Another view is that it was necessary to achieve the greatest possible degree of unity, and Rubusana's election would have been anathema to Jabavu's supporters in the Cape. It has also been argued that Dube's election was intended to show that African political activity should no longer be centred on the Cape,[18] where Africans were relatively privileged in being able to exercise the vote. The most likely reason is that Rubusana was simply not available for election. Had he been, he would surely have become one of the seven vice-presidents or been elected to another executive position, but this did not happen. Instead, in a move that clearly reflected the esteem in which he was held, Rubusana was made an honorary president, the only 'commoner' to be accorded the honour along with 22 chiefs, including Dinuzulu, who had recently returned from banishment.[19] The 'nobles' were to form the Upper House of the new 'Native Parliament', which would advise and guide the 'Executive Commoners'. Clearly, the organisers aimed to draw the modern and traditional elites into a broad national alliance, including those in the Protectorates. According to Seme, it was in this respect that the Congress differed essentially from anything that had been attempted before.[20]

Unlike the election of the president, where the candidates were nominated by a special committee, nominations for the other positions of office in the executive commons came from the open conference. Seven vice-presidents were elected, the positions being distributed as widely as possible on a regional basis. They were Sefako Makgatho, president of the Transvaal Native Organisation; William Letseleba, president of the Transvaal Native Union; John Mocher, president of the Orange Free State Native Congress; Simeon Kambule, a past president of the Natal Native Congress, who had also been on the first executive of the South African Native Convention; Thomas Zini, president of the Cape Peninsula Native Association; Philip Modise, secretary to Paramount Letsie of Basutoland; and Chief Silas Molema, personal representative of the Rolong paramount Lekoko.[21]

There remained open the important positions of the secretaries and treasurers who would effectively run the organisation in conjunction with the president. Sol Plaatje was nominated as general or corresponding secretary 'at the instance of the Native Lawyers who convened the movement', while Seme himself was entrusted with the work of treasurer and another British-trained lawyer, George Montsioa, was elected as the other secretary.[22] Thomas Mapikela was voted in as junior treasurer to Seme.

After the elections, the conference went on to discuss various topics. Eleven papers were read by leaders who had previously been given the responsibility of introducing each of the topics. Makgatho spoke about the 'Black Peril' – a moral panic among whites about the threat of imminent attack by Africans, including sexual assaults on white women. Plaatje introduced the issue of labour; Philip Modise tackled segregation; Levi Mvabaza and E.T. Moeletsi discussed the pass laws. Finally, Thomas Mapikela and Edward Tsewu, who had successfully taken the Transvaal government to court as head of the Landowners' Association, tabled the crucial land and 'squatter' issues.[23] Conference showed particular concern about the growing restrictions on access to land by Africans. It was decided that a deputation should be sent to wait upon the Minister of Native Affairs and request the withdrawal of the Native Settlement and Squatters Registration Bill of 1911, which debarred African syndicates from buying land.[24]

After discussion on these social issues and burning political topics, the conference appointed a committee under the chairmanship of Dr Rubusana to draft a set of resolutions embodying the views of the Congress so that they could be brought to the attention of the government and the general public. Once the resolutions had been finalised – including one dealing with the position of women – the proceedings of the conference were closed by Philip Modise, who had taken over the chair from the second day. He thanked those who had attended or sent messages of support, and expressed satisfaction at the earnestness with which the people viewed closer union. He said that more than half a century previously Chief Moshoeshoe had met Shaka, 'the mighty King of Zulus', Faku of the Mpondo, and Sekhukhune in the northern Transvaal, and also sent envoys to the chiefs of Bechuanaland, urging them to unite. Moshoeshoe did not live to see his dream realised, but the delegates to Congress could rest assured that union among black communities in South Africa was now almost an accomplished fact. He wished them to return home and tell their people that they were identified with different tribal names and dialects just as the different trees in the woods were known by different names; but the delegates could safely claim that they were now trees of one and the same forest.[25]

Thus was born the oldest living liberation movement on the African continent and one of the oldest political parties in the world – exactly 50 years after Tiyo Soga and his contemporaries had first begun articulating their ideas in *Indaba*.

Conclusion

We have been distinguished by the world as a race of born gentlemen
… and by the gentleness of our manners (poor though we may
be, unlettered and ill-clad), and by the nobility of our character
we shall break down the adamantine wall of colour prejudice and
force even our enemies to be our admirers and friend.
– Manifesto of John Dube, SANNC president, 1912

This book has revealed a tradition of African participation in
constitutional politics in South Africa that goes back 150 years, much
further than is generally supposed. While, conventionally, most accounts
of African nationalism or protest politics in this country start with the
foundation of the ANC (or the SANNC, as it was then known) in 1912, the
ANC itself has a deep history that stretches back well into the nineteenth
century, when the early constitutional politics that this book has described
first took root. Three decades before Union, within a few years of the
launching of the proto-Afrikaans newspaper *Die Patriot* and the formation
of the Afrikaner Bond – both landmark events in the history of Afrikaner
nationalism – Africans, too, had formed a Bond, or Imbumba, of their own
and an organ for 'Native Opinion'. Thousands of Africans also possessed
the vote in the eastern Cape and participated enthusiastically in electoral
politics, holding the balance of power in several constituencies. These first
generations of activists and intellectuals placed great store by the rule of
law and were highly skilled in the procedures of constitutional politics.

An impeccably proper constitutional approach was, indeed, their main strategy in seeking to prove to the colonial ruling classes their fitness to hold political rights. Herein lay both their greatest strength and, ultimately, their greatest weakness.

Understanding the twentieth-century struggle for democracy and ANC politics requires this deeper historical context. For two of the major strands in ANC thinking and policy during the course of the 1900s – Africanism and non-racialism – first found expression and became the subject of debate, particularly as to the correct balance and relation between the two, in the pre-1912 period. It was the early activists and intellectuals who first articulated both the liberatory potential of a focused African nationalism and the universalist ideas of 'non-racialism' in an African context. If the test for the relevance of political concepts is that they have a meaning in and make a difference to people's lives, this book shows that the ideas of 'the founders' indeed gave shape and a unique African content to political strategies located in the lived experiences of Africans before 1912. Their indigenous tradition of constitutionalism was to influence South African politics for generations to come.

The movement based on the new-style politics took shape in four phases before 1912. In the first, 'aspirational' phase from the 1860s to the 1880s, Africans organised and expressed themselves within prototypical structures controlled by or close to white missionaries. The second phase commenced in the 1880s, when activists started forming independent political organisations and mouthpieces, separate from and critical of the missionaries, to express African opinion within the broad discourse of colonial politics. Increasingly disillusioned by the gulf that opened between the promises of the missionaries and the realities of colonial life, this generation adopted new weapons of struggle. The bodies they founded often used strongly assertive Africanist language and encompassed pan-southern African goals. The process of mobilisation in the 1880s, which saw nearly 10,000 Africans qualifying as voters, provided the nascent national movement with its original base.

The third phase in the growth of a national political movement occurred in the 1890s. Ideological differences within the new politics came to the fore, as the style of politics expanded across territorial boundaries in the subcontinent. Different strategies and strands of thought became evident. On one hand, there were those with a more individualist, class-based approach, concerned with individual advancement within colonial society for Africans who had the requisite credentials to qualify as 'civilised'. On the other hand, there were those with a more African-oriented, 'national' approach, who gave organisational expression to their vision in the early South African Native Congress. In the 1890s the Congress and its supporters created alliances with an exploding 'Ethiopian' movement of religious separatist churches, in which African Christians challenged the entire notion of white domination. This 'marriage' allowed the political movement to take off across southern Africa, connecting pioneering eastern Cape organisations with initiatives in regions where, for historical reasons, colonial-style political groupings still did not exist or had not yet reached the same level of development.

The fourth phase of consolidating a unified national movement in politics occurred between 1902 and 1912, when Africans became part of 'British' South Africa and found themselves brought together in a single nation-state, as Britain took control of the whole subcontinent. In this decade, political organisations similar to those in the eastern Cape spread rapidly in other regions. At the same time, the fiery religious separatist movement, which had so alarmed colonial governments, started subsiding as a focus of popular resistance. Once political organisations sprang up after 1902 in places where they had not been allowed to operate before – the Orange River Colony and Transvaal (and, to a lesser extent, Natal) – the Ethiopian churches reverted to a more conventional religious role and increasingly deferred to the incipient Congress movement in respect of the political struggle. Finally, in 1912, in response to the National Convention and formal Union, Africans came together to form, first, the South African Native Convention and, then, the South African Native National Congress to protect and advance African rights in the new South Africa.

⬇

Far from being naïve, timid, conservative and collaborationist – 'black Englishmen' engaged solely in deferential politics – as many later critics and detractors have caricatured them, the early constitutionalists pursued realistic political strategies and goals and, at the same time, were deeply African in nature and outlook. They need to be seen, if they are to be properly understood, as Africans profoundly aware of their colonial context, sensitive to and constrained by the social and economic forces operating on and around them, and involved at various levels in a continuing dialectic between change and continuity. As James Campbell has noted in the context of religious separatism, despite the often self-deprecating language the school people employed to get ahead, there was an 'iron belief in African capacity' among them.

At the same time, the people who participated in the new western forms of politics were closely tied to their communities, local contexts and activities outside the work of the mission school and church, much more so than has been realised. Their stylised protocols and forms of communication, the respectful language seen in a petition to the Queen or a meeting with the Governor, did not constitute the totality of their lived experiences, character and views. Organisational politics, like 'popular' politics, were nuanced and directly connected to daily life and broader issues. The new-style activists called frequently on 'the nation' in matters of high politics, and just as readily worked with chiefs, helped illiterate washerwomen in urban 'locations', supported teachers involved in disputes over education, opposed forced removals or became involved in local struggles over land rights. They often paid a high price for their activism, including being dismissed from government positions, having their newspapers closed down and even being charged with treason.

The early organisers tried to act as spokesmen for all classes of Africans and routinely sought the support of chiefs for their endeavours. The chiefs were prayed for in the new organisations and the educated elite wrote praise poems in their honour in the missionary newspapers. Even after being educated and christianised, the school people did not surrender their identities as Africans but proudly carried them into the new colonial era, even while being uncompromisingly Christian. People like Isaac Wauchope, described as a 'royalist' despite his growing up 'beyond the authority of

Xhosa chiefs', often wrote proudly of their pre-colonial history and links. Wauchope drew constantly on African narrative imagery in his writing and used his clan praise name, Silwangubo ('He fights with the blanket, protecting his fist') as a pen name. He could recite his family history in the finest Xhosa tradition.[1] Jeff Opland's book on the great literary figure and 'poet of the nation', S.E.K. Mqhayi, illustrates the same point exactly: the roots of the new politics ran deep into the African past; the school people did not start on a blank slate with the missionaries.[2]

Just as many of the new intellectuals and activists retained respect for African culture and authority, chiefs became involved with them in the new politics, even if there was an inherent tension in the relationship between the two sets of leaders. Though the strategies of the educated class may have differed from those of chiefs holding on to the last vestiges of independence, the aims of the two often overlapped, especially in seeking to protect African interests against expanding white domination and in building new alliances. Many chiefs sent their sons to be educated by the missionaries so that they could use the new knowledge in the context of the chiefdom to respond to the challenges brought by conquest and incorporation. They employed African secretaries literate in English and the new ways, sometimes even before the loss of formal independence. In respect of the new forms of politics, the Great Places of the chiefs were an important source of popular legitimacy and resources, both human and financial. Chiefs and their sons were often in the forefront in setting up and then leading the early organisations. Many of the elites of the past era, therefore, reproduced themselves in the new.[3] Finally, as colonialism tightened its grip on both previously independent chiefly authorities and the emerging educated class, blocking opportunities and pushing them into precarious social and economic positions, old and new leaders worked together to start new newspapers, petition government and, eventually, in 1912, form the ANC itself.

The early intellectuals and activists were political innovators, responding in courageous, often contradictory ways to the challenges of their times. As one scholar has noted, 'they journeyed back and forth across vast political, cultural and personal chasms' to engineer new discourses and paths in politics. They were not involved in western-style politics in a narrow, imitative sense but as part of a dynamic African response to the new colonial milieu, with all its opportunities, challenges and restraints. The actions and aspirations of the first generations, shaped by their time and place, were realistic, often insightful and forward-looking. But their political strategy – informed by a value-system based on the *ubuntu* of pre-industrial African society, the Christian faith and mid-Victorian political liberalism – was eventually overtaken by the great changes that swept through South Africa in their lifetimes. Chief among these were the mineral revolution and the establishment of the Union, which killed the prospects for a liberal political system in South Africa. Though some of the pioneering politicians shifted into conservatism in their later years, persisting with the project of evolutionary constitutionalism and political moderation when it was already doomed to failure, we must recognise them as pathbreakers in their day. They provided the base from which the twentieth-century 'struggle' was launched, and their ethos, ideas and actions continued to inform the national movement in important ways in the changing contexts and phases of struggle throughout the century. To typify these early generations as a hopelessly compromised, dependent petty bourgeoisie, or a class of black Englishmen who were somehow not real Africans, is to miss completely the nuance and drama of their lives and the major contribution they made in shaping modern South Africa.

From being a colonial society that initially promised greater involvement for an emerging middle class showing 'civilised' qualifications, South Africa became a country that consciously closed down opportunities for Africans and sought to control them aggressively in order to secure the greatest amount of labour at the cheapest cost. Unlike the industrialised countries of western Europe, for instance, which gradually opened up their political systems to incorporate the underclasses, South African government policy consciously stunted the growth of a black middle class after 1910. The lid on the socio-economic pressure-cooker was welded down rather than lifted (until the build-up of steam blew it off in the last two decades of apartheid). This gave rise to new forms of political response and struggle after Union, including class-based worker protests; the agrarian populism of the Industrial and Commercial Workers' Union; Marxism; and, from the 1940s onwards, intensifying forms of militant struggle such as passive resistance, non-violent mass action, armed struggle and urban uprisings, based on an uncompromising demand for universal franchise. Yet these subsequent changes in the direction of politics do not make less important the contribution of 'the founders' to the long-term political development of South Africa.

⇓

In 1984, in the conclusion to my book *Vukani Bantu!*, I wrote: 'For several generations the early political elite and its prototype organisations and strategies were to influence the direction of African politics in South Africa. Indeed, some of the early leaders – Dube, Makgatho, Gumede, Seme, Mapikela and Selope Thema – whose entries into politics are described in this book, were active and influential until as late as after the Second World War. Later leaders, like J.S. Moroka, Albert Luthuli, D.D.T. Jabavu and Z.K. Matthews, were often closely related to the early leaders, and generally retained the latter's basic commitment to democratic non-racialism, although they adopted different strategies in line with changed circumstances.'[4]

Since 1984, the line of continuity – which some doubted three decades ago or saw as an ahistorical attempt to glorify an uninterrupted narrative of struggle – has become even clearer. The political traditions and intellectual concerns of the early school people remained remarkably intact, at least until the 1950s, influencing future leaders (even with the radical ruptures in context) right through the years of armed struggle and exile to democracy. Moreover, inter-generational political memories and family lineages have proved remarkably persistent. Both direct descent and other forms of association have been crucial in establishing such continuities.

A number of ready examples exist of the connections between the first generations and the present to illustrate this point. The leaders of South Africa's new democracy, established in 1994, were still part of a direct line that reached back to the earliest politics. Nelson Mandela himself spoke of how his political consciousness as a young man had been stimulated by a mesmerising performance by the 'poet of the nation', S.E.K. Mqhayi (of *Izwi* and the early SANC). A grandson of Mqhayi is Barney Pityana, one of the founders of the Black Consciousness movement and the first head of the Human Rights Commission in democratic South Africa. Mandela's successor as President, Thabo Mbeki, was in turn the son of the urbane intellectual and activist Govan Mbeki and grandson of the pious Skelewu Mbeki – he said grace even when he drank a glass of water – who was involved in the Native Vigilance Association in Nqamakwe in the early 1900s.[5] Other cabinet members could also claim a similar lineage. Ngconde Balfour is a descendant of Robert Balfour, who attended the very first class at Lovedale in 1841 and who contributed to *Indaba* in the 1860s. Naledi Pandor's great-grandfather was the composer, Lovedale notable and one-time co-editor of *Imvo Zabantsundu*, the Rev. John Knox Bokwe. Her grandmother, Frieda Bokwe, was the first African woman to earn a degree at a South African institution, and her grandfather, Z.K. Matthews, proposed the idea of the Freedom Charter. Her father, Joe Matthews, was also an ANC leader in the 1950s and 1960s, before joining the Inkatha Freedom Party and becoming a cabinet minister after 1994.

Examples of these genealogical connections between past and present abound outside cabinet. Dr Albertina Luthuli, a member of parliament, is the daughter of Chief Albert Luthuli, who himself grew up in the house of his uncle Martin Lutuli, secretary to Dinuzulu in the 1880s and a founder of the Natal Native Congress in 1900. Archie Gumede, co-president of the United Democratic Front in the 1980s and a member of the ANC negotiating team at the Groote Schuur talks in 1990, was the son of Josiah Gumede, another early Natal activist and, later, ANC president.[6] George Wauchope, one of the senior leaders of the Azanian People's Organisation, who died in exile because he refused to apply for amnesty to the Truth and Reconciliation Commission, was the grandson of Isaac Wauchope.[7] Thumi Molefe, who became the 'first lady' of the North West Province after 1994, is the granddaughter of Sol Plaatje. Mavuso Msimang, one-time director-general of the Department of Home Affairs, is the grandson of Richard Msimang and grand-nephew of Selby Msimang, who were both present at the founding meeting of the ANC in 1912.[8] Public figures such as the journalists and commentators Xolela Mangcu and Nikiwe Bikitsha, the church leader Malusi Mpumlwana and the head of the Nelson Mandela Museum, Khwezi Mpumlwana, are also descendants of people who have appeared in these pages. And we still need to find out if it is just a coincidence that Chief Isaac Mkize became first president of the Natal Native Congress 112 years ago and that Dr Zweli Mkhize is currently premier of the KwaZulu-Natal province, or that Mark Radebe was the NNC's first secretary and that Minister Jeff Radebe from the Natal ANC is currently a senior cabinet minister in the national government.

All these examples are proof of the depth and resilience of the political and intellectual traditions attached to the earliest activists, who laid the foundations for the freedom struggle in South Africa. These traditions, together with the accompanying intellectual capital, survived for generations in durable and deep-rooted networks, through multiple transitions and adaptations, to impact on the present. When Adekeye Adebajo described Nelson Mandela and Thabo Mbeki as 'anglophiles' in his assessment of their presidencies, he was in a shorthand way identifying these two products of the nurseries at Healdtown and Lovedale with the best traditions of British political thought and the politics of universalism, inclusive nationalism and human rights, which lay at the heart of the 'school tradition', the subject of this book.[9] In time, the politics and approach of the first generations were fundamentally affirmed by the negotiations that led to democracy in South Africa in 1994 and the adoption of a new constitution in 1996. The constitutional dispensation that then came into being was nurtured in many ways by their ideas and goals, although the role of this deep indigenous tradition of constitutionalism is something that is scarcely known about (or claimed as a legacy by the ANC) today.

The country has come a long way since 1912 and the contribution of the ANC in this turn-about has been immense. The organisation led one of the great moral campaigns of the twentieth century. With Mandela at its head, it had by 1994 become a global symbol of freedom and a dignified African universalism. It was the ANC that led South Africa to constitutional democracy after the appalling experiences of colonialism and the decades of apartheid. The founders would surely have been proud of the new ship of state. It was with some justification that Nelson Mandela, standing at the grave of John Dube on the occasion of the first democratic elections in 1994, could declare, 'Mission accomplished, Mr President.' The form, content and inspiration of South Africa's new democracy were, indeed, not unlinked to the politics dealt with in this book.

As we enter the second decade of the twenty-first century, it can be argued that there has been a break with the consciously shaped project of 'modernity' followed by the ANC and its leaders in the twentieth century. The ANC conference at Polokwane in 2007 arguably signalled the ending of old hegemonies and patterns within the ANC and 'struggle politics' that stretched back to well before 1912. For one thing, the traditional balance of the ANC as a broad multi-class organisation, concerned with creating the broadest possible front, was to some extent disturbed: an indication of this was the decision of a million (mainly middle-class) people who subsequently voted for the breakaway Congress of the People in 2008. Secondly, a long period of dominance by the eastern Cape in the intellectual and political leadership of the ANC came to an end. It is unlikely, after Polokwane, that the eastern Cape will recover its intellectual and political influence in determining the direction of the governing party and the country – the time when educational institutions in this province produced 80 per cent of matriculants in South Africa is, in any case, long gone. The ANC's leaders and members today represent a broad set of interests whose primary inspirations are not necessarily inclusive nationalism and constitutionalism. While the ANC continues to speak in terms of the 'tradition' of the organisation to explain the way it works, its intellectual trajectory today as well as its voice is different in important ways from the past. For one thing, fuelled by the reality of continuing racialised economic inequalities and vestiges of colonial arrogance, core policies such as non-racialism have come under challenge.

The way the ANC develops, as it heads towards its twentieth year in power, will be the topic of other books, but one can say here that the current national mood is one of uncertainty. For a troubled decade now, deep divisions and a discourse of anger have characterised internal ANC politics. Combined with high levels of corruption among the political classes and non-delivery in critical areas by local authorities and central government, this has had a negative, often paralysing effect on much-needed transformation agendas and the building of a national consensus. Critics have started to question the ANC's commitment to upholding the constitution it co-wrote. Economic inequalities remain deep-seated and intractable, causing a fundamental rethinking of direction. The optimism and vision of the 'rainbow nation' honeymoon period have been replaced by grinding contestations and sometimes mediocre displays of realpolitik. Nevertheless, despite this organisational instability and the enormous social and economic challenges South Africa still faces, the ANC has created a profound legacy in its 100 years of existence.

It took an immense sacrifice and effort over a long time by the oppressed to bring democracy to South Africa. Hopefully, this book may contribute towards a proper recognition of this fact, help overcome the ignorance that still prevails about this country's rich history, and also inspire us to deepen the democracy we have inherited. Many lessons to be learned from the past remain: none more so than the injunction by the early activists to 'Shoot with the pen' and seek constitutional and inclusive ways for developing a society that places a high value on human dignity. The founders and their story remain, therefore, as relevant today as ever.

Notes

Introduction

1 As told by Camagu Soga in J.W. Lewis jnr, 'Oom Paul se veearts', *Die Burger*, 6.1.2007.

2 On the incorporation of Africans into colonial society, see, for example, S. Forman and A. Odendaal (eds.), *A trumpet from the house tops: The selected writings of Lionel Forman* (Cape Town and London, 1992), UWC Mayibuye History Series no. 7, pp. 18-26.

3 I.W.W. Citashe to the editor, *Isigidimi*, 1.6.1882. The translation of this quote is from A.S. Gerard, *Four African literatures: Xhosa, Sotho, Zulu, Amharic* (Berkeley, 1971), p. 41. The writer of the letter later changed his surname and is best remembered as Isaac Wauchope.

4 Constitution of the Republic of South Africa, Act 108 of 1996.

5 R.S. Levine, *A living man from Africa: Jan Tzatzoe, Xhosa chief and missionary, and the making of nineteenth-century South Africa* (New Haven, 2011), p. 3.

6 Only white men could vote in the Boer Republics and the British colonies in southern Africa in the period covered by this book, except in the Cape Colony, where black men also qualified for a limited franchise based on educational and property qualifications. (Technically, Natal also provided for black men to vote, but in practice it is believed that only two people in this category were ever allowed to register.) Universal adult franchise was not yet the norm internationally either. For example, at the turn of the century, women in Europe and America still did not have the vote. In South Africa, white women received the vote only in 1930. During the apartheid period, all black South Africans were disenfranchised in South Africa. The first time all South African citizens were allowed to vote was with the advent of democracy in 1994.

7 See A. Odendaal, 'The development of African organisational politics in South Africa, with particular emphasis on the responses of Africans to the process of unification, 1899–1910' (MA, University of Stellenbosch, 1980); A. Odendaal, 'African political mobilisation in the eastern Cape, 1880–1910' (PhD, University of Cambridge, 1983); A. Odendaal, *Vukani Bantu! The beginnings of black protest politics to 1910* (Cape Town and Totowa, NJ, 1984).

8 For the sake of clarity and to avoid confusion with other early groupings (such as the South African Native Congress or SANC), I will refer generically to the ANC, even when the organisation was still known as the SANNC. The only exception is the chapter on the actual founding of the SANNC in 1912.

9 See review by T.R.H. Davenport in *Social Dynamics*, 10, 2 (1984) and dustjacket of *Vukani Bantu!*

10 See, for example, R. Ross, A.K. Major and B. Nasson (eds.), *The Cambridge History of South Africa*, 2, *1885-1994* (Cambridge, 2011), pp. 141-2, 145, 148, 196-8, 202, 204; D. Oakes (ed.), *Reader's Digest illustrated history of South Africa: The real story* (Cape Town, 1989), pp. 208-9, 277-91; T.R.H. Davenport and C.C. Saunders, *South Africa: A modern history* (Johannesburg, 2000); H. Giliomee and B. Mbenga, *Nuwe geskiedenis van Suid-Afrika* (Cape Town, 2007), pp. 179-80, 208, 235-

6; S. Dlamini, 'ANC centenary: Forward to a new era of liberation', *Cape Times*, 6.1.2012; H. Hughes, *The first president: A life of John Dube* (Cape Town, 2011); P. Limb, *The ANC's early years: Nation, class and place in South Africa, 1912–1940* (Pretoria, 2010). The prolific Jeff Opland, whose books include the path-breaking *S.E.K. Mqhayi: Abantu Besizwe. Historical and biographical writings, 1902–1944* (Johannesburg, 2001) and *Isaac Williams Wauchope: Selected writings, 1874–1916* (Cape Town, 2008), edited with Abner Nyamende, acknowledged that 'African political mobilisation' 'forwarded' his studies on early Xhosa literature 'by three years or so'. Another scholar, Les Switzer, borrowed largely from the PhD dissertation for Part 2 of his *Power and resistance in an African society: The Ciskei Xhosa and the making of South Africa* (Madison, 1993), but, unfortunately, Switzer's book, now frequently quoted by scholars working on late nineteenth and early twentieth century nationalism, did not adequately reflect the debt it owed to this source.

11 J.T. Campbell, *Songs of Zion: The African Methodist Episcopal Church in the United States and South Africa* (Chapel Hill, NC, 1998), p. xi.

12 Levine, *A living man from Africa*, p. 5.

Chapter 1: The crucible of colonialism

1 Quoted in A. Odendaal, 'Liberalism and the African National Congress' (Paper presented at Conference on Liberalism in South Africa, Houw Hoek Inn, 30 June – 3 July 1986).

2 D. Landes, *The wealth and poverty of nations: Why some are so rich and some so poor* (London, 1998), pp. 62-3, 427-30.

3 'Mnguni' [Hosea Jaffe], *Three hundred years* (Goodwood, 1982), p. 19.

4 See for example B.M. Magubane, *The political economy of race and class in South Africa* (New York, 1979), pp. 193-4; A. Adu Boahen (ed.), *Africa under colonial domination 1880–1935*, Unesco General History of Africa, 7 (London, 2003), ch. 2.

5 J. Carnes, *Us and them: A history of intolerance in America* (New York, 1996), pp. 60-1.

6 B. Rostron, 'Colonial cartography prevails', *Sunday Independent*, 25.6.2006. See also A.

Odendaal, 'The hundred years war: Brown balls, bronzed colonials and the persistence of colonial biases in 21st century rugby cultures' (Conference on Afrikaners, Anglos and Springboks, 1906–2006, London, 25 September 2006).

7 D.R. Rutman, *American Puritanism: Faith and practice* (Philadelphia, 1970), p. 4.

8 Quoted in C. Crais and P. Scully, *Sara Baartman and the Hottentot Venus: A ghost story and a biography* (Johannesburg, 2001), p. 3.

9 Quoted in J.P. McKay, B.D. Hill and J. Buckler (eds.), *A history of Western society, 2, From absolutism to the present* (Boston, 1983), p. 930. On the battle, see Adu Boahen, *Africa under colonial domination 1880–1935*, pp. 41-2.

10 J. Hari, 'The two Churchills', *New York Times Book Review*, 15.8.2010, p. 12.

11 M. Hardt and A. Negri, *Empire* (Cambridge, Mass., 2000), p. xv.

12 W.D. Hammond-Tooke, *Command or consensus: The development of Transkeian local government* (Cape Town, 1975), pp. 23-4.

13 Magubane, *The political economy of race and class in South Africa*, pp. 193-4; Hardt and Negri, *Empire*, p. xii.

14 Cory Library, uncatalogued Church of England material (Diocesan archive no. 222): St Matthew's SPG mission Keiskamma Hoek, Visit of the Lord Bishop of Grahamstown and a short account of the mission, May 1884, p. 8.

15 Levine, *A living man from Africa*, pp. 31, 11, 15, 19, 38-9, 48, 51-2, 61-2.

16 Ibid., p. 38.

17 J.C. Wells, *Rebellion and uproar: Makhanda and the great escape from Robben Island, 1820* (Pretoria, 2007), p. 13.

18 Levine, *A living man from Africa*.

19 Wells, *Rebellion and uproar*.

20 CA, 3/KWT, no. 2/1/42: G.E. Nzungu to mayor and town councillors, King William's Town, 29.3.1909.

21 D. Williams, *Umfundisi: A biography of Tiyo Soga 1829–1871* (Lovedale, 1978), pp. 19-21, 46-8, 60, 83-4.

22 K.A. Hobart Houghton, 'The problem of Bantu education in South Africa' (Paper read before the annual meeting of the South African Association for the Advancement of Sciences, Grahamstown, 1908), p. 4; M.

Wilson and L. Thompson (eds.), *A history of South Africa to 1870* (Cape Town, 1980), p. 261.

23 C. Bundy, *The rise and fall of the South African peasantry* (London, 1979), pp. 40-3.

24 Ibid.

25 R. Archer and A. Bouillon, *The South African game: Sport and racism* (London, 1982), p. 26.

26 J. Stewart (ed.), *Lovedale past and present: A register of two thousand names* (Lovedale, 1887), between pp. 32 and 33.

Chapter 2: Africans in a colonial order

1 J.M. Lonsdale, 'Some origins of nationalism in East Africa', *Journal of African History*, 9, 1 (1968), 120-1; Hammond-Tooke, *Command or consensus*, pp. 77-9, 91.

2 Editorial notes, *Imvo Zabantsundu*, 8.12.1884.

3 R.A. van Diemel, 'In search of freedom, fair play and justice: Josiah Tshangana Gumede, 1867–1946. A political biography' (PhD, University of the Western Cape, 1997), p. 33.

4 N. Mandela, *Long walk to freedom: The autobiography of Nelson Mandela* (London, 1996), p. 7.

5 Bundy, *The rise and fall of the South African peasantry*, pp. 34-5.

6 C. Bundy, 'The emergence and decline of a South African peasantry' (Contemporary Southern African Studies Research Papers, 2, Witwatersrand University, 1978), p. 39.

7 J.M. Coetzee, *Stranger shores: Essays 1986–1999* (London, 2001), p. 340.

8 M.W. Spicer, 'The war of Ngcayecibi (1877–1878)' (MA, Rhodes University, 1978), p. 239.

9 Hammond-Tooke, *Command or consensus*, pp. 23-4.

10 On Shepstone and his policy, see J. Guy, *The view across the river: Harriette Colenso and the Zulu struggle against imperialism* (Cape Town, 2001), pp. 34-8.

11 J. Hodgson, *Ntsikana's 'Great Hymn'* (Cape Town, 1980), pp. 1-2; Gerard, *Four African literatures*, pp. 27-8; Wilson and Thompson, *A history of South Africa*, pp. 256-7. See also J.B. Peires, *The house of Phalo: A history of the Xhosa in the days of their independence* (Johannesburg, 1982), ch. 5.

12 Cape of Good Hope Constitution Ordinance, 3 April 1852, Articles 8–10.

13 N. Mostert, *Frontiers: The epic of South Africa's creation and the tragedy of the Xhosa people* (London, 1992), pp. vii-viii.

14 Wilson and Thompson, *A history of South Africa*, pp. 243, 260-1; T.R.H. Davenport, *South Africa: A modern history*, 2nd edn (Johannesburg, 1978), p.101.

15 T.R.H. Davenport and K.S. Hunt, *The right to the land: Documents on southern African history* (Cape Town, 1974), document 67, pp. 41-2.

16 Grondwet van de Zuid-Afrikaansche Republiek, February 1858, Art. 9.

17 See H.J. van Aswegen, 'Die posisie van die Nie-Blankes in die Oranje-Vrystaat, 1854–1899', *South African Historical Journal*, 5 (Nov. 1973), pp. 41-60.

18 P.S. Landau, *Popular politics in the history of South Africa, 1400–1984* (New York, 2010).

Chapter 3: Tiyo Soga and voices from the 1860s

1 *Kaffir Express*, 1.5.1871, p. 4.

2 Veldtman Bikitsha to the editor, *Kaffir Express*, 1.9.1874.

3 C2-69, 'A petition of certain inhabitants of Wittebergen native reserve'; A9-70, 'Petition of inhabitants of Wittebergen native reserve'.

4 *Kaffir Express*, 1.12.1870, p. 3; 'Intlanganiso', *Isigidimi sama-Xosa*, 1.10.1871; *Kaffir Express*, 1.4.1872, p. 3 and 6.9.1873, pp. 4-5; 1.10.1872; 6.9.1873, pp. 4-5; 1.8.1875, p. 2 and 1.9.1875, pp. 2-4; 1.7.1875, p. 6.

5 See, for example, S.Trapido, 'African divisional politics in the Cape Colony, 1884 to 1910', *Journal of African History*, 9, 1 (1968), pp. 82-6.

6 Williams, *Umfundisi*, pp. 33-4.

7 Ibid., p. 55.

8 Ibid., chs. 7 and 9. See also D. Williams, 'Tiyo Soga', in C.C. Saunders (ed.), *Black leaders in southern African history* (London, 1979), pp. 132-41.

9 J.A. Chalmers, *Tiyo Soga: A page of South African mission work* (Edinburgh, 1878), p. 435.

10 *Indaba*, Oct. 1864, pp. 424-6.

11 *Indaba*, June 1864, pp. 353-4.

12 Ibid.

13 'Defensor' to the editor, *King William's Town Gazette*, 11.5.1865, quoted in Williams, *Umfundisi*, pp. 96-7.

14 Williams, *Umfundisi*, pp. 97, 128.
15 See ibid., ch. 8.
16 V. Bickford-Smith, 'African nationalist or British loyalist? The complicated case of Tiyo Soga', *History Workshop Journal* (20 January 2011), pp. 2, 11, 17-19.
17 J.H. Soga, *The South-Eastern Bantu (Abe-Nguni, Aba-Mbo, Ama-Lala)* (Johannesburg, 1930), pp. viii-ix.
18 CA, CMT 3/640, no. 73: A2/993/05, A.H. Stanford to SNA, 20.5.1905, enclosing J.H. Soga and J. April to W. Gordon, 8,5,1905; Odendaal, *Vukani Bantu!*, pp. 41-2, 178.
19 *Indaba*, Sept. 1862, p. 29; June 1863, p. 176; Sept. 1864, pp. 412-13.
20 *Indaba*, Aug. 1862, pp. 9-11.
21 Williams, *Umfundisi*, p. 112.
22 *Indaba*, Sept. 1864, pp. 408-9.
23 See ch. 34 below.
24 *Indaba*, May 1863, pp. 154-5; July 1863, pp. 186-7; Feb.1864, p. 299.
25 *Indaba*, Jan. 1863, p. 92; May 1863, p. 155.
26 *Indaba*, April 1863, pp. 140-1.
27 Cory Library, MS 16 299: Lovedale enrolment list, 1841; *Indaba*, Dec.1864, pp. 454-6; Jan. 1865, pp. 474-6.
28 Stewart, *Lovedale past and present*, pp. 253, 375, 367; Obituary, *Isigidimi*, 1.10.1887, p. 77; Obituary, *Imvo*, 29.10.1896.
29 Cory Library, MS 16 299: Lovedale enrolment lists, 1841–1869.
30 See J. Peires, 'Introducing John Parkies' (History Colloquium, Rhodes University, September 2011), pp. 5-7, 9.
31 Ibid., p. 4.

Chapter 4: The first generation of activists, 1870s
1 S.M. Brock, 'James Stewart and Lovedale: A reappraisal of missionary attitudes and African response in the eastern Cape, South Africa, 1870–1905' (PhD, University of Edinburgh, 1974), pp. 20-1.
2 Cory Library, MS 16 299: Lovedale enrolment lists, 1841–1869.
3 Wilson and Thompson, *A history of South Africa*, p. 265.
4 Cory Library, MS 15 082: Healdtown Register Book, pp.18-19.
5 Cory Library, MS 16 299: Lovedale enrolment lists, 1870–1879.
6 My thanks to Jeff Peires for this information. See M. Poland, *The boy in you* (Cape Town, 2008), pp. 49-57.

7 Editorial, *Kaffir Express*, 1.10.1870.
8 J.K. Bokwe, 'Struggle of the native press', p. 171.
9 Stewart, *Lovedale past and present*, pp. 22, 163.
10 Editorial, *Kaffir Express*, 1.10.1870.
11 Editorial, *Kaffir Express*, 1.5.1872.
12 Ibid. See also *Supplement to the Kaffir Express*, 1.2.1872 and 1.3.1873; *Isigidimi*, 1.9.1872 and 1.6.1873; Editorial, *Kaffir Express*, 1.7.1873; 'Summary of native correspondence', *Kaffir Express*, 6.11.1873.
13 J.M. Vimbe to the editor, *Isigidimi*, 1.4.1871 and 1.3.1873; N. Mantsayi to the editor, *Isigidimi*, 1.5.1872; W.J. Ntsikana Gaba to the editor, *Isigidimi*, 1.6.1872, 1.7.1872 and 1.8.1872; N. Mzimba and S.P. Gasa in 'Summary of native correspondence', *Kaffir Express*, 6.11.1873; 'An example to all natives', *Kaffir Express*, 1.6.1873; and 'The natives at the diamond fields by Gwayi Tyamzashe', *Kaffir Express*, 1.8.1874.
14 K.N. Boza to the editor, *Isigidimi*, 1.4.1871, 1.10.1871, 1.6.1872 and 1.11.1872; 'A native on the hut tax and education', *Kaffir Express*, 1,10.1871; N. Falati to the editor, *Isigidimi*, 1.3.1873; 'Isigidimi samaxosa siyahlwelwa', *Isigidimi*, 1.8.1871; 'Iratshi aliveliswa yimfundo', *Supplement to the Kaffir Express*, 1.2.1872; B. Sobikwa to the editor, supplement to *Isigidimi*, 1.3.1873; B. Sobikwa in 'Summary of native correspondence', *Kaffir Express*, 6.11.1873; 'Isicoto esikulu', *Isigidimi*, 4.2.1871; P.K. Masiza to the editor, *Isigidimi*, 1.4.1871; 'Kaffir beer', *Kaffir Express*, 1.7.1871; 'A native on ukulobola', *Kaffir Express*, 1.4.1872; 'Application for a surgeon for the Transkei', *Kaffir Express*, 1.10.1871; 'Imitshato ne parti', *Isigidimi*, 1.12.1871; P. Rwexu to the editor, *Isigidimi*, 1.6.1873; I.W. Citashe to the editor, *Isigidimi*, 1.9.1874.
15 Opland and Nyamende, *Isaac Williams Wauchope*, pp. xix, 11-13.
16 Gerard, *Four African literatures*, pp. 35-6.
17 'Umxosa', *Isigidimi*, 4.1.1871. For Kokela's second letter, see 'Umxosa', *Isigidimi*, 1.3.1871.
18 'Fundani Makowetu' to the editor, *Kaffir Express*, 4.2.1872.
19 'Umxosa', *Kaffir Express*, 1.4.1871; 'The Kaffir Express', *Kaffir Express*, 4.2.1871.
20 Editorial, *Kaffir Express*, 1.5.1872.

21 Editorial, *Kaffir Express*, 1.9.1871.
22 Editorial, *Kaffir Express*, 1.7.1873; editorial, *Christian Express*, 1.5.1876.
23 *Annual Report of the Society for the Propagation of the Gospel 1871*, pp. 6-7. See also 'Annual meeting', *Kaffir Express*, 1.6.1872.
24 *Christian Express*, 1.5.1876, pp. 10-11.
25 Government notice no.436, 1871 in CA, NA 171.
26 CA, NA 171: E. Judge to SNA, 31.10.1873.
27 Jesse Shaw to the editor, *Kaffir Express*, 1.6.1872 and 1.7.1872.
28 'Lovedale literary society', *Kaffir Express*, 2.11.1874.
29 J.L. McCracken, *The Cape Parliament, 1854–1910* (Oxford, 1967), pp. 71-2; S. Trapido, 'White conflict and non-white participation in the politics of the Cape of Good Hope, 1853–1910' (PhD, University of London, 1970), p. 261; *Kaffir Express*, 1.9.1874.
30 CA, NA 454, Letters Received, file no. 467, Ecclesiastical: Rev. J. Reid to SNA, 30.9.1873.
31 *Blue Book for the Colony of the Cape of Good Hope 1878*, p. A5.
32 G27-74, BBNA 1874, pp. 5-6. This report also appeared in *Kaffir Express*, 1.9.1874, pp. 6-7.
33 Stewart, *Lovedale past and present*, p. 289.
34 J.T. Jabavu to the editor, *Isigidimi*, 1.5.1879.
35 The first two became the first Africans to be ordained as ministers in South Africa in February 1871. See R. Hunt Davis, 'School vs blanket and settler: Elijah Makiwane and the leadership of the Cape school community', *African Affairs*, 78, 310 (1979), p. 16.
36 Spicer, 'The war of Ngcayecibi', pp. 157-8.
37 Bundy, *The rise and fall of the South African peasantry*, pp. 40-1; Bundy, 'The emergence and decline of a South African peasantry', pp. 67-77.
38 See chs. 19 and 20 below.
39 Wilson and Thompson, *A history of South Africa*, ch. 5.
40 S. Burman, *Chiefdom politics and alien law: Basutoland under Cape rule, 1871–1884* (London, 1981), pp. 148-61.
41 Spicer, 'The war of Ngcayecibi', pp. 157-61.
42 *Christian Express*, 1.8.1879.
43 Spicer, 'The war of Ngcayecibi', p. 119.
4 Ibid., p. 244.
45 See, for example, CA, HA 777, no. 160: Petition of Chief Mabandla and others to House of Assembly and petition of Bogo and others to House of Assembly [1879]; CA, HA 778, nos. 15 and 38: Petition of Paramount Chief Letsie and others to House of Assembly and petition of Gilbert Chalmers Sigcina and 250 others to House of Assembly [1880].
46 'Imbumba', *Isigidimi*, 16.2.1884.
47 'Disarmament', *Cape Argus*, 10.12.1878.
48 See, for example, editorial, *Christian Express*, 1.7.1876.
49 Quoted in 'Who was Paul Nkupiso?', *Christian Express*, 1.3.1878.
50 Quoted in *Christian Express*, 1.7.1878, pp. 7-8.
51 See 'Who was Paul Nkupiso?', *Christian Express*, 1.3.1878; *Christian Express*, 1.7.1878, pp. 1-2, 7-8.
52 'Her Majesty's subjects no. III and VI', *Christian Express*, 1.10.1880 and 1.3.1881.
53 CA, 1/TAM 9/4, no. 650: G.M. Theal to CC King William's Town, 11.7.1881.
54 I.W.W. Citashe to the editor, *Isigidimi*, 1.6.1882. The translation of this quote is from Gerard, *Four African literatures*, p. 41. See Opland and Nyamende, *Isaac Williams Wauchope*, pp. xix-xxviii for Wauchope's biography.

Chapter 5: 'Deeper than his civilisation'

1 See C. Saunders, 'Through an African's eyes: The diary of Nathaniel Umhala', *Quarterly Bulletin of the South African Library*, 34, 1 (1979); Mostert, *Frontiers*, pp. 1229-30; J. Hodgson, 'A history of Zonnebloem College, 1858–1870: A study in church and society' (MA, UCT, 1979).
2 See A. Odendaal, *The story of an African game: Black cricketers and the unmasking of one of cricket's greatest myths* (Cape Town, 2003), ch. 2.
3 J. Hodgson, *Princess Emma* (Johannesburg, 1987), p. 46.
4 J. Hodgson, 'Cape Town as a cradle of black writing', in C.C. Saunders, H. Phillips and E. van Heyningen (eds.), *Studies in the history of Cape Town*, 4 (Cape Town, 1981), p. 14.
5 Ibid., p. 9.
6 Hodgson, 'A history of Zonnebloem College', pp. 8-10.
7 See, for example, Mandela, *Long walk to freedom*, pp. 18-27.

8 Hodgson, *Princess Emma*, pp. 50-1.
9 Hodgson, 'Cape Town', p. 11.
10 Ibid., p. 53.
11 Hodgson, 'History of Zonnebloem College', p. 453.
12 Ibid., pp. 17-18.
13 J. Hodgson, 'Zonnebloem College and Cape Town, 1858–1870', in C.C. Saunders (ed.), *Studies in the history of Cape Town* (Cape Town, 1979), p. 10.
14 Hodgson, 'History of Zonnebloem College', p. 82.
15 Odendaal, 'African political mobilisation', p. 14.
16 Hodgson, 'History of Zonnebloem College', p. 76.
17 Odendaal, *The story of an African game*.
18 'Grand cricket match', *Queenstown Free Press*, 4.11.1870. My thanks to Janet Hodgson for giving me this reference.
19 Ibid.
20 Ibid.
21 Ibid.
22 Hodgson, 'History of Zonnebloem College', pp. 82-3.
23 Saunders, 'Through an African's eyes', p. 26. Umhalla's diary, which appeared as an exhibit at his trial, was published by the *Cape Mercury* and is reproduced with this article. Hereafter it is referred to as Umhalla diary.
24 Umhalla diary, 13.1.1878; 9.1.1878; 15.1.1878.
25 Ibid., especially 16 and 19.1.1878.
26 Ibid., 20-1, 26, 26, 28-9 January 1878; 7-9, 11-2, 18, 20, 24-5, 28 February 1878; 1 and 12 March 1878.
27 Ibid., 21.1.1878.
28 Ibid., 26 and 28.1.1878; 9 and 25.2.1878; 20.2.1878; 8 and 18.2.1878; 21.2.1878; 7.3.1878; 21.1.1878; 23.1.1878; 31.1.1878.
29 Quoted in Saunders, 'Through an African's eyes', pp. 29.
30 P.E. Scott (ed.), *Mqhayi in translation* (Grahamstown, 1976), p. 24.
31 Saunders, 'Through an African's eyes', pp. 27-8.

Chapter 6: *Isigidimi* and the Native Educational Association

1 See 'Parliamentary discussion on Kaffir prisoners', *Christian Express*, 1.8.1879.
2 S.B. Mama to the editor, *Isigidimi*, 1.12.1879; *Christian Express*, 1.8.1879.
3 J.T. Jabavu to the editor, *Isigidimi*, 1.5.1879 and 1.2.1880.
4 S.P. Sihlali to the editor, *Isigidimi*, [1880], cutting in possession of the writer.
5 For Jabavu's views, see J.T. Jabavu to the editor, *Isigidimi*, 1.5.1879, 1.2.1880 and 1.7.1880; 'Ntengo' to the editor, *Isigidimi*, 1.12.1880.
6 D.D.T. Jabavu, *The life of J.T. Jabavu, editor of Imvo Zabantsundu* (Lovedale, n.d.), pp. 12-13.
7 Rhodes House, APS papers, C139/1: J.T. Jabavu to F.W. Chesson, 6.5.1880.
8 For example, J.T. Jabavu to the editor, *Somerset Advertiser*, printed in *Cape Argus*, 10.12.1878.
9 Cory Library, MS 15 281: J.T. Jabavu to Rev. A. Brigg, 23.9.1879.
10 See, for example, Rhodes House, APS papers, C139/1-18: J.T. Jabavu to F.W. Chesson, 1880–1887.
11 Rhodes House, APS papers, C 139/2: J.T. Jabavu to F.W. Chesson, 18.5.1881.
12 Ibid.
13 'Imbumba yama nyama', *Isigidimi*, 1.9.1881.
14 See, for example, constitution of the Imbumba Yamanyama political organisation, *Isigidimi*, 1.10.1883.
15 'M.P.' to the editor, *Isigidimi*, 1.3.1883; 2.4.1883; 2.7.1883; 1.10.1883.
16 'Ingxoxo engemfundo', *Isigidimi*, 1.9.1883; Editorial notes, *Isigidimi*, 1.10.1883.
17 J.M. Pelem to the editor, *Isigidimi*, 18.7.1883 and 1.9.1883; I.W. Wauchope to the editor, *Isigidimi*, 1.4.1882; 'Wauchope and co.' to the editor, *Isigidimi*, 1.6.1883; I.W. Wauchope to the editor, *Isigidimi*, 16.8.1883.
18 'Hadi Waseluhlangeni' to the editor, *Isigidimi*, 1.2.1884.
19 Cory Library, uncatalogued Church of England material (Diocesan archive no. 222): St Matthew's SPG mission Keiskamma Hoek, Visit of the Lord Bishop of Grahamstown and a short account of the mission, May 1884, p. 11.
20 My thanks to Jeff Peires for this information on Gawler. See also R. Martin papers, H.A.C. Hewitt to R. Martin, 17.9.1971 for reminiscences of him.
21 'Native Teacher's Association', *Kaffir Express*, 1.12.1875; 'Intlanganiso yo manyano nge mfundo', *Isigidimi*, 1.8.1885; NLSA, Bokwe papers, vol. 1: Native

Educational Association constitution [1882], pp. 68-9 and J.K. Bokwe to J.W. Gawler, 28.10.1882.

22 See, for example, Jesse Shaw to the editor, *Kaffir Express*, 1.3.1873; editorial notes, *Isigidimi*, 1.11.1882; editorial notes, *Imvo*, 23.2.1887; advertisements, *Isigidimi*, 1.8.1879 and *Imvo*, 3.11.1886.

23 'Intlanganiso yo manyano nge mfundo', *Isigidimi*, 1.8.1885.

24 See, for example, 'Intlanganiso yo titshala e-Bofolo', *Isigidimi*, 1.8.1882; 'Imanyano nge-ncubeko', *Isigidimi*, 1.2.1883.

25 NLSA, Bokwe papers, vol. 1: J.K. Bokwe to J. Shaw, 11.8.1882, p. 59 and J.K. Bokwe to W. Philip, 11.9.1882, pp. 62-3.

26 For one example, see NLSA, J.K. Bokwe papers, vol. 1: J.K. Bokwe to J.T. Jabavu, 15.6.1888, p. 352.

27 'Intlanganiso yo manyano nge mfundo', *Isigidimi*, 1.8.1885.

28 Ibid.

29 Editorial notes, *Imvo*, 21.1.1887.

30 See Hunt Davies, 'School vs blanket and settler', p. 28.

31 See, for example, C.C. Saunders, 'The new African elite in the eastern Cape and some late nineteenth century origins of African nationalism' (University of London, Institute of Commonwealth Studies, Collected Seminar Papers on the Societies of Southern Africa in the 19th and 20th Centuries), 1, pp. 48-9.

32 For the main reports of the NEA meetings between 1881 and 1887, see 'Intlanganiso yo titshala e Burnshill', *Isigidimi*, 1.8.1881; 'Intlanganiso yo titshala', *Isigidimi*, 2.1.1882; 'Intlanganiso yo titshala e-Bofolo', *Isigidimi*, 1.8.1882; 'Umanyano nge-ncubeko', *Isigidimi*, 1.2.1883; 'Umanyano ngemfundo', *Isigidimi*, 18.7.1883; 'Umanyano nge mfundo', *Isigidimi*, 16.1.1884; 'Umanyano ngemfundo', *Isigidimi*, 1.8.1884; Umanyano ngemfundo', *Imvo* and *Isigidimi*, 2.2.1885; 'Intlanganiso yo manyano nge mfundo', *Isigidimi*, 1.8.1885; 'Ibandla le mfundo', *Imvo*, 13 and 20.1.1886; 'Umanyano nge mfundo', *Imvo*, 18.8.1886; 'Umanyano ngemfundo', *Imvo*, 13.7.1887; and 'Intlanganiso yo manyano nge mfundo', *Isigidimi*, 1.8.1887.

33 NLSA, Bokwe papers, vol. 1: Native Educational Association constitution, pp. 68-9.

34 'Intlanganiso yo titshala e-Bofolo', *Isigidimi*, 1.8.1882.

35 'Umanyano nge mfundo', *Isigidimi*, 16.1.1884.

36 'Umanyano nge mfundo', *Isigidimi*, 1.2.1884; 'Umanyano ngemfundo', *Isigidimi*, 1.8.1884.

37 'Umanyano nge mfundo', *Isigidimi*, 1.2.1884.

38 Editorial notes, *Imvo*, 21.1.1887.

39 Editorials, *Imvo*, 26.1.1885 and 2.2.1885.

40 R. Robinson and J.A. Gallagher with A. Denny, *Africa and the Victorians: The official mind of imperialism* (London, 1961), p. 1.

41 N.C. Umhalla to the editor, *Izwi*, 24.6.1902. See also editorials, *Imvo*, 21.7.1886 and 4.8.1886.

42 Editorial notes, *Imvo*, 8.12.1886; 'Umanyano ngemfundo', *Imvo*, 21.1.1887; 'Revised constitution of the Native Educational Association', *Imvo*, 6.7.1887.

43 'Revised constitution of the Native Educational Association', *Imvo*, 6.7.1887; 'Intlanganiso yo manyano nge mfundo', *Isigidimi*, 1.8.1887.

44 'O titshala nentlanganiso yabo e Monti' and 'Ikomfa' yo titshala', *Izwi*, 16.1.1906.

45 'Umanyano nge mfundo', *Imvo*, 13.1.1898.

46 Editorial notes, *Imvo*, 30.3.1885; Cory Library, MS 15 082: Report of the Healdtown Training Institution, 1881. See also editorial notes, *Imvo*, 30.3.1885 and 'Healdtown Wesleyan Teachers' Association', *Imvo*, 27.4.1885.

47 Jabavu, *The life of John Tengo Jabavu*, p. 15.

48 'Inyatelo kwicala lokukanya', *Isigidimi*, 2.1.1882; 'Engqushwa: Umanyano lo dodana', *Isigidimi*, 15.4.1884.

49 Reports by secretary, *Isigidimi*, 15.10.1883 and 15.4.1884; 'Imizamo ngohlanga', *Imvo*, 8.4.1885; Editorial notes, *Imvo*, 13.4.1885.

50 'Imumba entsha', *Isigidimi*, 1.9.1884.

51 'Intlanganiso yase Ngqushwa', *Imvo*, 10.6.1885.

52 'An honest member' and 'Mr J. Rose-Innes, MLA, Engqushwa', *Imvo*, 7.4.1886; J. Rose-Innes to S.B. Mama, 14.2.1887 in H.M. Wright (ed.), *Sir James Rose-Innes: Selected correspondence (1884-1902)* (Cape Town, 1972), pp. 51-2.

53 Wright, *Sir James Rose-Innes*, J. Rose-Innes to P.J. Mzimba, 2.5.1887, pp. 57-8.

54 'An honest member', *Imvo*, 7.4.1886; J.

Rose-Innes to S.B. Mama, 14.2.1887 in Wright, *Sir James Rose-Innes*, pp. 51-2.
55 S.N. Mvambo to the editor, *Isigidimi*, 16.1.1884.
56 Editorials, *Imvo*, 22.12.1884 and 9.3.1885.
57 'Intlanganiso yama Mfengu e Macfarlan', *Isigidimi*, 1.4.1885; Radebe Mtimkulu to the editor, *Imvo*, 8.4.1885; 'Native Association', *Imvo*, 20.4.1885.
58 Ibid.
59 CA, 1/TAM 7/9: no. 57, Under-SNA to CC King William's Town, 9.4.1885; CA, NA 203: Copy, C.A. King to CC King William's Town, 27.4.1885.
60 Editorials, *Imvo*, 27.4.1885, 4.5.1885 and 18.11.1885. For the views of the colonial press, see 'Mabandla's case', *Imvo*, 4.5.1885 and editorial notes, *Imvo*, 11.5.1885.
61 'Mabandla's case', *Imvo*, 27.5.1885; CA, NA 450: Report re Bovani Mabandla by R.J. Dick, 5.8.1885.
62 CA, NA 450: no. A/158, Under-SNA to CC King William's Town, 18.8.1885; Editorial notes, *Imvo*, 2.9.1885; 'Palpable injustice', *Imvo*, 28.10.1885; CA, NA 450: Report from C.A. King to CC King William's Town, 19.9.1885.
63 'Cruel despotism', *Imvo*, 2.4.1886.
64 CA, NA 181: Special magistrate Middledrift to CC King William's Town, 7.3.1879; CA, NA 181: Statements by William Shaw Kama and Huba Zibi, enclosures C and G in report from C.A. King to CC King William's Town, 19.9.1885; and postscript to C.A. King to CC King William's Town, 27.4.1885.
65 CA, 1/TAM 9/7: R.J. Dick to 'Sir', 12.6.1891.
66 Ibid.

Chapter 7: Imbumba Yama Nyama, 1882
1 J.K. Bokwe, 'Ntsikana and his hymn', *Christian Express*, 1.5.1876, pp. 14-15.
2 'Imbumba yamanyama', *Isigidimi*, 1.3.1884.
3 'Imbumba yomfo ka Gaba', *Isigidimi*, 1.11.1882.
4 A.T. Wirgman, *Storm and sunshine in South Africa* (London, 1922), p. 55.
5 Ibid.
6 'Intlanganiso yomanyano', *Isigidimi*, 18.7.1883.
7 I.W. Wauchope and five others to Rev. D. and Mrs Mzamo, *Isigidimi*, 17.9.1883.

8 'Imbumba yomfo ka Gaba', *Isigidimi*, 1.11.1882.
9 'Imbumba', *Isigidimi*, 16.2.1884.
10 Burman, *Chiefdom politics*, p. 64.
11 Editorial, *Christian Express*, 1.12.1881.
12 'Izimiselo ze "Mbumba"', *Isigidimi*, 1.10.1883.
13 Editorial notes, *Isigidimi*, 1.11.1882.
14 Editorial notes, *Isigidimi*, 1.5.1883.
15 'Intlanganiso yomnyaka' by I.Wauchope, *Isigidimi*, 1.1.1883.
16 CA, NA 478: Petition of Stempe Jonas and Pakasi Andries to J.C. Sprigg, 24.8.1878.
17 Editorial, *Kaffir Express*, 1.9.1871.
18 G8-83, BBNA 1883: I.W. Wauchope to A. Wylde, 22.12.1882, p. 68.
19 Editorial notes, *Isigidimi*, 1.11.1882.
20 G8-83, BBNA 1883: I.W. Wauchope to A. Wylde, 22.12.1882, p. 68.
21 See, 'Imicimbi ye "Mbumba"', *Isigidimi*, 17.12.1883; 'Imbumba', *Isigidimi*, 16.2.1884.
22 'Intlanganiso yomanyano', *Isigidimi*, 18.7.1883.
23 'Ibandla le Tiyopia', *Isigidimi*, 1.10.1884; 'Intsika ya temba', *Isigidimi*, 1.8.1881.
24 News snippet, *Imvo*, 23.3.1885; 'Umanyano lwa Besutu', *Imvo*, 10.9.1896.
25 Odendaal, 'African political mobilisation', pp. 64, 284-5.
26 'Imbumba yomfo ka Gaba', *Isigidimi*, 1.11.1882; 'Intlanganiso yomnyaka' by I. Wauchope, *Isigidimi*, 1.1.1883.
27 J.M. Maurice, *Centenary souvenir with history of the Independent Order of True Templars (IOTT) 1875–1975* (Cape Town, n.d.), p. 5; 'To-day's telegrams', *Imvo*, 27.4.1898.
28 'Ingxelo yabatunywa base Lovedale', *Isigidimi*, 1.5.1883.
29 See 'Amatempile e Rafu', *Isigidimi*, 16.5.1884 for the first six conference venues.
30 Report by Isaac Wauchope, *Isigidimi*, 1.8.1881; 'Ezivela Kubabalelani', *Isigidimi*, 1.2.1880; 'Amatempile e Rafu', *Isigidimi*, 16.5.1884; 'Intlanganiso enkulu yabazili benene e-Rini, *Isigidimi*, 1.5.1883; 'Ingxelo yabatunywa base Lovedale', *Isigidimi*, 1.5.1884.
31 'Intlanganiso ye Mbumba', *Isigidimi*, 18.7.1883; 'Imbumba yamanyama', *Isigidimi*, 1.8.1884; CA, NA 787, no. 38: Petition of the residents of the Native Strangers Location to the Legislative

Assembly (1883).

32 'Imbumba yamanyama', *Isigidimi*, 1.8.1884.

33 'Intlanganiso ye "Mbumba"', *Isigidimi*, 18.7.1883.

34 'Umanyano e Colesberg', *Isigidimi*, 1.12.1882.

35 'Utyelelo luka hon. T.C. Scanlen e Colesberg', *Isigidimi*, 1.5.1883.

36 Report of conference, *Christian Express*, 1.9.1883; 'Intlanganiso ye "Mbumba"', *Isigidimi*, 18.7.1883.

37 J. Ngaba to the editor, *Isigidimi*, 17.9.1883.

38 B.B. Kota to the editor, *Isigidimi*, 1.9.1883; S.N. Mvambo to the editor, *Isigidimi*, 16.1.1884; 'Imbumba', *Isigidimi*, 16.2.1884.

39 *Isigidimi*, 16.2.1884; 'Imbumba yamanyama', *Isigidimi*, 1.8.1884.

40 Editorial notes, *Isigidimi*, 16.1.1884; 'Imbumba yamanyama', *Isigidimi*, 1.8.1884.

41 'Intlanganiso yomanyano', *Isigidimi*, 18.7.1884.

Chapter 8: New organisations in Thembuland

1 For historical background to the creation of the Glen Grey district, see G12-87, BBNA 1887: District of Glen Grey, historical sketch by G.M. Theal, pp. 15-24.

2 D.T. Malasi and R. Kawa to J.T. Jabavu, *Isigidimi*, 1.7.1884; 'Imbumba yamanyama', *Isigidimi*, 1.8.1884.

3 'Otitshala bela Batembu', *Imvo*, 27.5.1885; see also 'I concert e Fransberg', *Isigidimi*, 15.10.1883 and D.T. Malasi to Superintendent of Education, *Imvo*, 10.6.1885.

4 Jabavu, *The life of John Tengo Jabavu*, p. 9; CA, NA 399, no. 39: H.S. Barton to SNA, 17.6.1877; CA, NA 400, no. 226: H.S. Barton to Sir Bartle Frere, n.d. and H.S. Barton to SNA, 29.7.1878; J. Peires, 'Introduction' (draft manuscript on Kawa and his work, 2011), pp. 1-3.

5 Pers. comm. by Jeff Peires, November 2011.

6 SANA to F.W. Chesson, 1884, reprinted in *Imvo*, 5.4.1899.

7 'Ukukula kwe "Mbumba"', *Isigidimi*, 2.6.1884.

8 G12-87, BBNA 1887: District of Glen Grey, historical sketch by G.M. Theal, p. 24.

9 'Ebatenjini', *Isigidimi*, 1.9.1883; 'Isililo saba Tembu', *Isigidimi*, 15.10.1883; 'Kwa Bangindlala', *Isigidimi*, 15.10.1883.

10 'Kwa Bangindlala', *Isigidimi*, 15.10.1883.

11 'Ebatenjini', *Isigidimi*, 1.9.1883.

12 CA, NA 404, no.271: J.M. Pelem to SNA, 21.9.1883; 'Kwa Bangindlala', *Isigidimi*, 15.10.1883; CA, NA 404, no. 292: J.M. Pelem to SNA, 23.10.1883.

13 'Kwa Bangindlala', *Isigidimi*, 15.10.1883.

14 Ibid.; CA, NA 405, no. 221: R. Kawa and T. Zwedala to SNA, 11.11.1884; CA, NA 484: Memorial of residents of the Tembu location district of Glen Grey to the Governor, n.d.; CA, HA 806: Petition of Tembus and others residing in or adjacent to the Tambookie Location in the district of Glen Grey, [1888].

15 H. Vanqa to the editor, *Isigidimi*, 1.7.1884.

16 'Native Association', *Imvo*, 20.4.1885.

17 Editorial notes, *Imvo*, 23.2.1885.

18 Trapido, 'White conflict and non-white participation', pp. 290-2.

19 G12-87, BBNA 1887: District of Glen Grey, historical sketch by G.M. Theal, pp. 24-5.

20 CA, NA 433: Meeting between the Hon. J.A. de Wet and the Tambookies located in the Glen Grey district at Lady Frere on 27 November 1885.

21 See, for example, the case of headman Mbovane Mabandla below. For African reactions to De Wet's statements, see editorials, *Imvo*, 16.2.1885 and 6.1.1886.

22 G12-87, BBNA 1887: District of Glen Grey, pp. 25-6.

23 UG10-13: Report of the Native Affairs Department for the year ended 31 December 1911, p. 24.

24 E.J.C. Wagenaar, 'Thembu responses to European control, 1865–1885' (chapter in unfinished dissertation).

25 he emergence of this stratum of 'progressive farmers' is described in Bundy, *The rise and fall of the South African peasantry*, pp. 92-5.

26 CA, NA 628, no. 2044: C.J. Levey to CMT, 28.11.1895.

27 Wagenaar, 'The extension of colonial and British control over the Thembu people, 1872–1885', n.p. (chapter in unfinished dissertation).

28 Editorial notes, *Imvo*, 3.11.1884.

29 Editorial notes, *Imvo*, 16.3.1885.

30 Wagenaar, 'Thembu responses to European control', n.p.

31 Thanks to Jeff Peires for his help in explaining the reordering of these Thembu lands.

32 Bundy, *The rise and fall of the South African peasantry*, p.72.

33 *Christian Express*, 1.6.1879, p. 6.

34 Ibid. See also editorial, *Isigidimi*, 1.6.1879.

35 NLSA, Sir Bartle Frere papers, MSB 197, item 80: C. Levey to private secretary to Governor, 16.8.1880.

36 'E-Batenjini', *Isigidimi*, 15.10.1883; 'Cala-Ebatenjini', *Isigidimi*, 16.2.1884 and 15.3.1884; 'Abalimi lwase Batenjini', *Imvo*, 16.2.1885.

37 'Abalimi lwase Batenjini', *Imvo*, 16.2.1885. For a list of members, see 'E-Batenjini', *Isigidimi*, 1.10.1883.

38 Wagenaar, 'Thembu responses to European control', n.p.

39 CA, NA 405, no. 57: J. Hemming to SNA, 24.3.1884, enclosing petition of the headmen of district of Cala; CA, NA 203, C. Levey to CMT, 4.9.1885, enclosing petition of the headmen of the district of Cala [1884].

40 CA, NA 751, no. 1218: no. 50/10712, Under-Secretary for Agriculture to SNA, 18.1.1898.

41 Ibid.

42 'Umanyano lwase Batenjini', *Imvo*, 1.12.1886 and 27.4.1887; CA, NA 751, no. 1218: no. 50/10712, Under-Secretary for Agriculture to SNA, 18.1.1898.

43 'Umanyano lwase Batenjini', *Imvo*, 1.12.1886 and 27.4.1887; CA, NA 751, no. 1218: no. 50/10712, Under-Secretary for Agriculture to SNA, 18.1.1898.

44 CA, HA 806, no. 98: Petition of the natives living in the Xalanga district [1888].

45 See, for example, the resistance of the Xalanga landowners to Caleb Jafte of Qumbu. CA, NA 550, no. 858: Petition of M. Rengqe and 82 others to CC Cala, 4.7.1906.

46 For example, CA, NA 486: Memorandum, N. Tile, 20.10.1884.

47 CA, NA 433: Meeting between the SNA and the Tembus proper under Dalindyebo, Umtata, 3.12.1885.

48 CA, NA 486: Memorandum, N. Tile, 20.10.1884.

49 C.C. Saunders, 'Tile and the Thembu church: Politics and independency on the Cape eastern frontier in the late nineteenth century', *Journal of African History*, 11, 4 (1970), pp. 555-6.

50 B. Sundkler, *Bantu prophets in South Africa* (London, 1961), p. 38.

51 CA, NA 486: Memorandum, N. Tile, 20.10.1884.

52 Saunders, 'Tile and the Thembu church', p. 569.

53 See, for example, Jabavu's stout attempts later in the decade to protect Mpondo independence.

54 Wagenaar, 'Thembu responses to European control', n.p.

55 Editorial notes, *Imvo*, 26.1.1885.

56 Saunders, 'Tile and the Thembu church', p. 561.

57 Mandela, *Long walk to freedom*, pp. 24-5.

Chapter 9: Mobilising along the Kei

1 A. 12-73, Report of the Select Committee on Native Affairs: Memorandum by Mr Orpen upon the Fingo and other locations in the Transkei, pp. 42-3.

2 CA, NA 516, no. 353: Sir Walter Currie's address to the chiefs and headmen of the Fingoes, 21.8.1865.

3 Obituaries, *Christian Express*, 1.8.1910, p. 127 and *Imvo*, 26.7.1910.

4 'A Fingo society' and 'Ingxowa yesitili sa mamfengu', *Imvo*, 1.12.1884.

5 G8-83, BBNA 1883, pp. 138-9; G3-84, BBNA 1884, p. 103.

6 'Transkei Teachers' Association', *Imvo*, 19.5.1886.

7 'Ititshala zase Transkei', *Imvo*, 9.5.1888; 'Ititshala zase Transkei', *Imvo*, 11.1.1889.

8 Joel J. Madubela to the editor, *Isigidimi*, 1.4.1884.

9 'Otitshala', *Imvo*, 24.11.1884.

10 See, for example, 'Otitshala e Gcuwa', *Imvo*, 11.11.1885; 'Umlisela no mtinjana eGcuwa', *Imvo*, 17.2.1886; 'Umlisela nomtinjana eGcuwa', *Imvo*, 23.6.1886; 'Impi entsha yase Transkei', *Imvo*, 3.11.1886.

11 'Pumlisela eGcuwa', *Imvo*, 11.11.1885.

12 'Umlisela nomtinjana eGcuwa', *Imvo*, 17.2.1886.

13 'O titshala eGcuwa', *Imvo*, 13.4.1885.

14 'Pumlisela nomtinjana eGcuwa', *Imvo*, 23.6.1886.

15 CA, 1/IDW 6/1/4/1: George Pamla's statement.

16 'Umanyano ngemfundo', *Imvo*, 15.1.1887.

17 'Intlanganiso yolutsha eGcuwa', *Imvo*, 11.5.1887.

18 Editorial notes, *Imvo*, 10.8.1887.

19 CA, CMT 2/68: Report of M. Blyth, 1887, quoted in S.J.R. Martin, 'Political and social

theories of Transkeian administrators' (MA, UCT, 1978), pp.19-20.

20 'Transkeian rule', *Imvo*, 24.6.1887.

21 'Umanyano nge mvo zabantsundu', *Imvo*, 26.10.1887.

22 'Intlanganiso ya pesheya kwe Nciba', *Isigidimi*, 1.11.1887.

23 Stewart, *Lovedale past and present*, p. 80.

24 Obituary, *Cape Argus*, 5.3.1904.

25 'Umteto omtsha we voti e Transkei', *Isigidimi*, 2.1.1888.

26 Ibid.

27 'A.G.' to the editor, *Imvo*, 27.6.1887.

28 'Umteto omtsha we voti e Transkei', *Isigidimi*, 2.1.1888.

29 'Umanyano nge mvo zabantsundu', *Imvo*, 26.10.1887; 'Intlanganiso ya kwe Nciba', *Isigidimi*, 1.11.1887.

30 For his description of the new Ngqika boundaries and the way the land was apportioned, see A. Gontshi to the editor, *Isigidimi*, 1.6.1885.

31 *Isigidimi*, 15.8.1884 and 1.12.1884; 'Ama Ngqika pesheya kwe Nciba', *Isigidimi*, 2.2.1885.

32 For some details of his farming activities, see his speech in 'Ama Ngqika pesheya kwe Nciba', *Isigidimi*, 2.2.1885.

33 Ibid.

34 CA, NA 405, no. 133: A. Gontshi to SNA, 23.7.1884, and enclosure F. Tyali and N. Sandile to SNA, 23.7.1884.

35 'A.G.' to the editor, *Isigidimi*, 1.10.1885.

36 Williams, *Umfundisi*, pp. v, 76-8, 87-8, 112-13.

37 'Intlanganiso ye nqubelo pambili yama Ngqika', *Isigidimi*, 1.9.1887; 'Intlanganiso yo manyano nge mfundo', *Isigidimi*, 1.8.1887.

38 For a pen sketch of Nzanzana Mqhayi, see Scott, *Mqhayi in translation*, p. 9.

39 Mqhayi, *Abantu besizwe*, ed. J. Opland, pp. 114-20.

40 For example, Umhlangaso J.S. Faku to the editor, *Imvo*, 4.11.1885 and 12.5.1886.

Chapter 10: Using the ballot box

1 McCracken, *The Cape Parliament 1854–1910*, p. 71.

2 Cape House of Assembly debates, 15.6.1887, p. 68.

3 For the extension of the franchise to the Transkeian Territories, see C.C. Saunders, 'The annexation of the Transkeian Territories', *Archives Year Book* (Pretoria,

1978), pp. 130-7.

4 Editorial notes and 'Ontsundu e parlamente', *Isigidimi*, 1.12.1881; 1.6.1883.

5 Jabavu, *The life of John Tengo Jabavu*, p. 18.

6 M. Jantjies to editor, *Isigidimi*, 17.12.1883.

7 See Odendaal, *Vukani Bantu!*, pp. 246-51.

8 J.T. Jabavu open letters, *Isigidimi*, 16.11.1883 and 1.2.1884.

9 J.T. Jabavu open letter, *Isigidimi*, 16.11.1883.

10 J.T. Jabavu open letter, *Isigidimi*, 1.2.1884.

11 Brock, 'Stewart and Lovedale', pp. 247-8; see also NLSA, Bokwe papers, vol. 1: J.K. Bokwe to Mrs Watson, 3.3.1884, pp. 166-9.

12 B.A. Tindall (ed.), *James Rose-Innes, Chief Justice of South Africa, 1914-1927* (Cape Town, 1949), pp. 52-3.

13 Cape House of Assembly debates, 15.6.1887, p. 68.

14 V. Mqingwana, 'The role of John Tengo Jabavu in Cape elections, 1884–1914' (draft PhD, Rhodes University, 1982).

15 McCracken, *The Cape Parliament*, p. 73.

16 Editorial notes, *Isigidimi*, 1.2.1884.

17 J. Gundwana to the editor, *Isigidimi*, 15.3.1884.

18 Editorial notes, *Isigidimi*, 1.4.1884.

19 Rhodes House, APS papers, C 139/5: J.T. Jabavu to F.W. Chesson, 18.8.1884.

20 'Notes on current events', *Imvo*, 20.9.1888.

21 For the results, see 'Imbuto yesibini ye palamente', *Isigidimi*, 1.3.1884.

22 'Imbumba yamanyama', *Isigidimi*, 1.8.1884.

23 'Ezovoto e Hewu', *Isigidimi*, 17.9.1884; CA, HA 803, no. 12: Petition of the natives residing in Oxkraal and Kamastone locations (1887).

24 See, for example, editorial notes, *Imvo*, 17.2.1886; 'An honest member', 'Amalungelo etu' and 'Mr. J. Rose-Innes, M.L.A., Engqushwa', *Imvo*, 7.4.1886; 'Mr Innes M.L.A. e Dikeni', *Isigidimi*, 1.2.1887.

25 Editorial notes, *Isigidimi*, 1.3.1884.

26 Trapido, 'White conflict and non-white participation', pp. 113, 115.

27 L.D. Ngcongco, '*Imvo Zabantsundu* and Cape "native" policy, 1884–1902' (MA, Unisa, 1974), p. 27; Brock, 'Stewart and Lovedale', p. 250.

28 Editorial, *Imvo*, 26.5.1885.

Chapter 11: Launch of the 'national newspaper',
1884

1 B. Kwaza to the editor, *Isigidimi*,
15.3.1884.
2 A.C. Jordan, *Towards an African literature*
(Berkeley, 1973), p. 92.
3 'Kuba balelani', *Isigidimi*, 1.5.1884.
4 'Imbumba yamanyama', *Isigidimi*,
1.8.1884.
5 Brock, 'James Stewart and Lovedale',
p. 223.
6 Ngcongco, '*Imvo* and Cape "native"
policy', p. 27.
7 Editorial notes, *Isigidimi*, 16.2.1884.
8 Brock, 'Stewart and Lovedale', p. 260.
9 NLSA, Bokwe papers, vol. 1: J.K. Bokwe to
R.W. Rose-Innes, 6.7.1885, pp. 214-15.
10 Jabavu, *The life of John Tengo Jabavu*, pp.
17, 20.
11 Ibid., pp. 61-2.
12 R.W. Rose-Innes's tribute at Jabavu's
funeral, quoted in Jabavu, *The life of John
Tengo Jabavu*, pp. 20-1.
13 For the co-operation between Richard
Rose-Innes and Jabavu in the 1884 election,
see editorial notes, *Isigidimi*, 16.2.1884 and
1.3.1884.
14 Jabavu, *The life of John Tengo Jabavu*,
pp. 20-1. 'Ezase Somerset', *Isigidimi*,
1.10.1884; CA, NA, 405: J.T. Jabavu to
'Sir', 8.8.1884; Rhodes House, APS papers,
C139/5: J.T. Jabavu to F.W. Chesson,
18.8.1884.
15 Advertisement, *Isigidimi*, 1.10.1884, p. 8.
16 Brock, 'James Stewart and Lovedale', p.
261.
17 For example, H. Mvimbana to the editor,
Isigidimi, 1.6.1882.
18 A. Gontshi to the editor, *Isigidimi*,
2.1.1882.
19 Stewart, *Lovedale past and present*, p. 80.
20 Jabavu, *The life of John Tengo Jabavu*, p.
23; see also 'Ukubuliswa kuka Mr. Xiniwe
e Bhayi', *Imvo*, 20.7.1887; advertisement,
Imvo, 3.8.1887.
21 'Natives and hotels', *Imvo*, 13.6.1894;
Imvo, 30.5.1894.
22 For lists of the *Imvo* agents, see '*Imvo*
Zabantsundu, amagosa', *Imvo*, 3.11.1884;
'Amagosa "e Mvo"', *Imvo*, 1.9.1886.
23 Quoted in editorial notes, *Imvo*,
3.6.1.1885.
24 Ibid.
25 For a discussion of this, see Brock, 'James
Stewart and Lovedale', pp. 135-9.

26 Rev. W.J.B. Moir, quoted in editorial notes,
Imvo, 9.3.1885.
27 Editorials, *Imvo*, 4.5.1885 and 8.7.1885.
28 'Lovedalian' to the editor, *Imvo*, 18.6.1885.
29 Brock, 'James Stewart and Lovedale', p.
137.
30 For opinions of the colonial press, see
Imvo, 17.11.1884 and 29.12.1884; NLSA,
Bokwe papers, vol. 1: J.K. Bokwe to R.W.
Rose-Innes, 6.7.1885, p. 214.
31 '*Imvo* and Lovedale', *Imvo*, 8.4.1885; 'The
candid monitor', *Imvo*, 19.8.1885.
32 Jabavu, *The life of John Tengo Jabavu*,
p. 21.
33 For details of Gqoba's background and his
writing, see Stewart, *Lovedale past and
present*, pp. 82-3; Gerard, *Four African
literatures*, pp. 36-9; *Christian Express*
report, quoted in *Imvo*, 4.1.1889.
34 'Abaxhasi be Mvo', *Imvo*, 18.1.1888.
Other subscribers from the Transkei
included chiefs Lebenya and Zibi and the
Mfengu leader Veldtman.
35 Umhlangaso J.S. Faku to the editor, *Imvo*,
12.5.1886.
36 'Tembu address' and 'The government and
the Tembu nation', *Imvo*, 5.11.1891.
37 CA, NA 433: Meeting between SNA and
the Tembus proper under Dalindyebo at
Umtata, 3.12.1885.
38 Editorials, *Imvo*, 28.7.1886, 8.9.1886,
17.11.1886, 24.11,1886, 1.12.1886,
15.12.1886.
39 'Ntlola-Yo-Hlanga' to the editor, *Imvo*,
15.1.1887, translated and quoted in Jabavu,
The life of John Tengo Jabavu, p. 27.
40 See, for example, 'Impawana', *Imvo*,
26.10.1887.
41 'Amagosa', *Imvo*, 3.11.1884.
42 For example, '*Imvo* e Komani', *Imvo*,
6.4.1887; 'Intlanganiso' notice, *Imvo*,
10.8.1887; '*Imvo* kwa Daliwe', *Imvo*,
13.10.1886; *Imvo*, 19.10.1887; '*Imvo*
1885', *Imvo*, 12.2.1895; '*Imvo* e Bayi',
Imvo, 4.8.1886.
43 Jabavu, *The life of John Tengo Jabavu*, p.
21.
44 CA, NA 1049: J.T. Jabavu to SNA,
1.3.1888.
45 Jabavu, *The life of John Tengo Jabavu*, p.
21.
46 Report of Sakuba wedding, *Imvo*,
27.10.1886; 'Nants' into', *Isigidimi*,
1.12.1887.

47 Report of Soga wedding, *Imvo*, 5.9.1889.
48 Editorial, *Imvo*, 3.11.1886.

Chapter 12: The Union of Native Vigilance Associations, 1887
1 *Imvo*, 25.8.1886 and 1.9.1886.
2 J.M. Pelem letters, *Imvo*, 27.10.1886 and 8.12.1886.
3 Boyce Mama letter, *Imvo*, 22.12.1886; N.C. Umhalla letter, *Imvo*, 1.12.1886; P.S. Lusaseni to the editor, *Imvo*, 24.11.1886.
4 Editorial notes, *Imvo*, 30.12.1886.
5 N.C. Umhalla to the editor, *Izwi Labantu*, 24.6.1902.
6 Ibid.
7 'Union', *Imvo*, 4.8.1886.
8 Editorial notes, *Imvo*, 8.12.1886; 'Umanyano ngemfundo', *Imvo*, 21.1.1887; 'Revised constitution of the Native Educational Association', *Imvo*, 6.7.1887.
9 'Umanyano ngemfundo', *Imvo*, 21.1.1887.
10 'Umanyano ngemfundo', *Imvo*, 13.7.1887.
11 For the early history of African cricket in the eastern Cape, see A. Odendaal, 'Some forgotten South African cricket history', *South African Cricketer*, 1 (1983), pp. 29, 34.
12 Cape of Good Hope, Act no. 14 of 1887.
13 'The petition of the South African natives to the Queen', *Imvo*, 10.8.1887.
14 T.R.H. Davenport, *The Afrikaner Bond: The history of a South African political party, 1880–1911* (Cape Town, 1966), pp. 121-2.
15 Editorial, *Imvo*, 23.3.1887.
16 Editorial, *Imvo*, 8.6.1887.
17 'Elipezulu notung' umlomo', *Imvo*, 24.8.1887; 'Abatunywa baba Tembu', *Imvo*, 21.9.1887.
18 CA, HA 803, no.12: Petition of the natives residing in the Oxkraal and Kamastone locations (1887).
19 'Native address to Capt. Brabant, M.L.A., C.M.G.', *Imvo*, 7.9.1887.
20 'Ibhunga lama lungelo abanyuli', *Imvo*, 25.5.1887; 'Iliso lomzi ontsundu wase Qonce', *Imvo*, 27.7.1887; 'Iliso lomzi ontsundu', *Imvo*, 14.9.1887.
21 CA, HA 804, no. 114: Petition of the native inhabitants of the district of King William's Town (1887).
22 'Native address to Capt. Brabant, M.L.A., C.M.G.', *Imvo*, 7.9.1887.
23 Editorial, *Imvo*, 20.7.1887.
24 'Iliso lomzi ontsundu wase Qonce' and 'Native Vigilance Association', *Imvo*, 27.7.1887.
25 Ibid.
26 Editorial notes, *Imvo*, 27.7.1887.
27 See D. Dawkins to F. Makwena, *Imvo*, 7.9.1887; Editorial and F.J. Newton to F. Makwena, *Imvo*, 30.11.1887.
28 'Utung' umlomo eBhayi', *Imvo*, 28.9.1887.
29 R. Edgecombe, 'The influence of the Aborigines Protection Society on British policy towards black African and Cape Coloured affairs in South Africa, 1886–1910' (PhD, University of Cambridge, 1976), p. 58.
30 'Elipezulu notung' umlomo', *Imvo*, 24.8.1887.
31 For details of the wider campaign against the Act, see Edgecombe, 'Aborigines Protection Society', pp. 49-50, 57-9, 62-76; Trapido, 'White conflict and non-white participation', pp. 296-9.
32 Rhodes House, APS papers, C139/10: J.T. Jabavu to F.W. Chesson, 28.3.1887.
33 For example, Rhodes House, APS papers, C139/11-18: J.T. Jabavu to F.W. Chesson, July to Sept. 1887; APS papers, C153/154: J.T. Jabavu to R.N. Fowler, 2.7.1887; and C139/14-15: J.T. Jabavu to F.W. Chesson, 6 and 15.8.1887.
34 Rhodes House, APS papers, C139/16: J.T. Jabavu to F.W. Chesson, 29.8.1887.
35 'Isaziso esikulu', *Imvo*, 31.8.1887.
36 'Ingqungqutela yabatunywa', *Imvo*, 28.9.1887.
37 'Qondani inguqulo yosuku', *Imvo*, 14.9.1887.
38 For a full report of the conference, see 'Intlanganiso enkulu yamahlelo', *Imvo*, 12.10.1887.
39 'U Mr J. Rose-Innes, M.L.A., Engqushwa', *Imvo*, 7.4.1886; 'Umanyano lwamafama antsundu Engqushwa', *Imvo*, 23.6.1892.
40 'Intlanganiso ye native teachers' association yase Transkei', *Isigidimi*, 1.6.1887; 'Imbumba eliliso lomzi ontsundu', *Imvo*, 2.11.1887.
41 'Imizi yabantsundu', *Imvo*, 28.6.1888; 'Lesseyton', *Imvo*, 30.9.1885. Sondlo was also the *Imvo* agent at Lesseyton.
42 Report of deputation to town council, *Grocott's Penny Mail*, 8.4.1904.
43 'I Bhayi no nyulo', *Imvo*, 21.9.1887.
44 'Umanyano nge mvo zabantsundu', *Imvo*, 26.10.1887; 'Intlanganiso ya pesheya kwe Nciba', *Isigidimi*, 1.11.1887.

45 A. Gontshi to the editor, *Imvo*, 9.11.1887.
46 See Jabavu's comments on Gontshi's letter, *Imvo*, 9.11.1887 and 'Kumafilisofi ase Transkei', *Imvo*, 16.11.1887.
47 'Intlanganiso enkulu yamahlelo', *Imvo*, 12.10.1887.
48 Ibid.
49 Ibid.
50 Rhodes House, APS papers, C139/19: J.T. Jabavu to F.W. Chesson, 28.11 1887.

Chapter 13: Vigilance Associations challenge *Tung' umlomo*

1 See, for example, his trip to Herschel, *Imvo*, 16, 23 and 30.11.1887 and 'Intlanganiso yamahlelo', *Imvo*, 26.10.1887; 'Icebo kumzi ontsundu', *Isigidimi*, 3.9.1888.
2 'Umanyano nge Mvo Zabantsundu', *Imvo*, 26.10.1887.
3 N.C. Umhalla to the editor, *Imvo*, 6.12.1887.
4 'The Rev. Charles Pamla and the premier', *Imvo*, 4.1.1888.
5 Editorials, *Imvo*, 4.1.1888 and 15.2.1888. A lively response to Pamla's actions occurred in the *Imvo*'s correspondence columns; see, for example, *Imvo*, 4.2.1888.
6 J. Rose-Innes to J.T. Jabavu, 31.10.1887 in Wright, *Selected correspondence*, p. 62.
7 Editorial and F.J. Newton to the Native Committee, enclosing H.T. Holland to H. Robinson, *Imvo*, 30.11.1887; Rhodes House, APS papers, C139/19: J.T. Jabavu to F.W. Chesson, 28.11.1887.
8 Bundy, *The rise and fall of the South African peasantry*, pp. 149, 158.
9 'Kwindlela eya Egqili', *Imvo*, 16 and 23.11.1887.
10 J.M. Tshangela to J.T. Jabavu, *Imvo*, 28.9.1887; 'Imbizo Egqili', *Imvo*, 23.11.1887; 'Imbizo yesibini Egqili', *Imvo*, 30.11.1887.
11 'A peep at Herschel', *Imvo*, 23.11.1887. For response to Jabavu's comments on the situation, see 'Summum Bonum' to the editor and editorial notes, *Imvo*, 21.12.1887.
12 Bundy, *The rise and fall of the South African peasantry*, ch. 5; C. Bundy, 'Peasants in Herschel', in S. Marks and A. Atmore (eds.), *Economy and society in pre-industrial South Africa* (London, 1980), pp. 208-25; W. Beinart, 'Amafela ndawo enye (the diehards): Rural popular protest and women's movements in Herschel district,

South Africa in the 1920s' (unpublished paper, 1982), pp. 4-5.
13 'E-Gqili', *Imvo*, 8.4.1890.
14 CA, NA 753, file no. 128: Minutes of meeting with SNA held at Herschel, 13.10.1908.
15 'E-Gqili', *Imvo*, 8.4.1890; J. Gundwana to the editor, undated *Imvo* cutting in possession of the writer.
16 Beinart, 'Amafela ndawo enye', p. 13.
17 See, for example, the response of the Hlubi in respect of the Mehlomakulus in 'Herschel', *Imvo*, 12.9.1894.
18 T.K. Mayisela to the editor, *Imvo*, 14.9.1898.
19 'E-Gqili', *Imvo*, 8.4.1890.
20 'Peep at Herschel', *Imvo*, 23.11.1887.
21 'Intlanganiso yotitshala Egqili (Herschel)', *Imvo*, 29.11.1888, 4.1.1889, 11.4.1889 and 17.10.1889.
22 'Imbumba Eliliso e Herschel', *Imvo*, 2.8.1888.
23 See, for example, editorial notes, *Imvo*, 4.1.1888.
24 'The boers and the blacks', *Imvo*, 18.1.1888; Edgecombe, 'Aborigines Protection Society', p. 79.
25 See, for example, 'Kubangenisa-magama', *Imvo*, 9 and 16.11.1887. For several months the registration issue was the main preoccupation of *Imvo*.
26 'Ngongenisa magama', *Imvo*, 21.12.1887; see also 'Eze zitili ngezitili', *Imvo*, 23.11.1887.
27 For example, *Imvo*, 11.1.1888.
28 'Queenstown', *Imvo*, 15.2.1888.
29 Editorial notes, *Imvo*, 11.1.1888.
30 McCracken, *The Cape Parliament*, p. 73.
31 Editorial notes, *Imvo*, 15.2.1888.
32 Report by D.T. Malasi in 'Ngongeniso-magama', *Imvo*, 21.12.1887.
33 Editorial notes, *Imvo*, 11.1.1888.
34 Editorial notes, *Imvo*, 4.2.1888.
35 Editorial, *Imvo*, 22.2.1888; editorial notes, *Imvo*, 4.1.1888 and W.F. Lance to the editor, *Imvo*, 11.1.1888; editorial notes, *Imvo*, 15.2.1888.
36 J. Rose-Innes to J.T. Jabavu, 30.1.1888 in Wright, *Selected correspondence*, p. 68.
37 There appear to have been unspecified irregularities in the collection of these funds. See, for example, N.C. Umhalla to the editor, *Izwi*, 24.6.1902; postscript to S.T. Plaatje to the editor, *Izwi*, 12.8.1902.
38 Trapido, 'White conflict and non-white

participation', pp. 131, 246; Edgecombe, 'Aborigines Protection Society', p. 81.

39 Editorial notes, *Imvo*, 14.3.1888.

40 Trapido, 'White conflict and non-white participation', p. 246; Edgecombe, 'Aborigines Protection Society', p. 81.

41 'Ivoti yabantsundu e Qonce', *Imvo*, 15.1.1888.

42 Trapido, 'White conflict and non-white participation', p. 133.

43 'Ivoti yase Gqili', *Imvo*, 15.11.1888.

44 Compare, for example, 'Isimo sonyulo kwi zitili nge zitili', *Isigidimi*, 1.11.1888 and 'Abantsundu ne voti', *Imvo*, 8.11.1888.

45 Editorial and 'Ivoti yabantsundu e Qonce', *Imvo*, 15.11.1888.

46 Open letter from E. Makiwane, *Imvo*, 1.11.1888; '"The colonel" and Rev. Makiwane', *Imvo*, 8.11.1888 and E. Makiwane to the editor, *Imvo*, 15.11.1888; 'Ivoti kwa Kama', *Imvo*, 25.10.1888; 'Lifile ilizwe', *Isigidimi*, 1.11.1888; W.K. Ntsikana to the editor, *Imvo*, 22.11.1888. For Umhalla's defence, see N.C. Umhalla to the editor, *Imvo*, 13.12.1888.

47 'Ivoti e Komani', *Imvo*, 1.11.1888.

48 'Ukonakala kwe voti' e Komani', *Imvo*, 22.11.1888.

49 Reports of meetings, *Imvo*, 13, 20 and 27.6.1889.

50 'Intlanganiso ye pasi', *Imvo*, 20.6.1889; editorial and reports, *Imvo*, 25.7.1889.

51 Editorial and 'notes of current events', *Imvo*, 11.7.1889.

52 Trapido, 'White conflict and non-white participation', p. 247.

Chapter 14: 'A Native Bill for Africa'

1 L. Ntsebeza, *Democracy compromised: Chiefs and the politics of land in South Africa* (Cape Town, 2005), pp. 64-9. The quote is from p. 65.

2 See, for example, the numerous editorials on the Glen Grey Act between July and December 1894; editorial and 'Iliso Lomzi wase Qonce', *Imvo*, 1.8.1894; Model petition to 'Her Most Gracious Majesty the Queen in Council', *Imvo*, 15.8.1894.

3 Editorial, *Imvo*, 29.8.1894, for example.

4 Edgecombe, 'Aborigines Protection Society', p. 98.

5 'The premier and "*Imvo*"', *Imvo*, 8.8.1894.

6 For the emergence of the Thembu Association, see Odendaal, 'African political mobilisation', p. 150.

7 See, for example, 'The registration in Wodehouse', *Imvo*, 12.12.1889; 'Amabango evoti e Dordrecht', *Imvo*, 23.1.1890; Notice issued by Malasi, *Imvo*, 22.10.1891; Editorial notes, *Imvo*, 24.12.1891 and 28.1.1892; 'Iduli lonyulo', *Imvo*, 17.8.1898; NLSA, Merriman papers, 1903, no. 264: J.M. Pelem to J.X. Merriman, n.d.

8 CA, MA 215: Copy of letter from D.T. Malasi to the editor, *Imvo*, 1892.

9 CA, NA 215: Resolutions of meeting at Agnes, 5.3.1892, signed by J. Mahonga.

10 CA, NA 215: Copy of letter from D.T. Malasi to the editor, *Imvo*, 1892.

11 CA, NA 215: Resolutions of meeting held at Xonxa, 3.3.1892, signed by E.G. Mahonga; Resolutions of meeting at Agnes, 5.3.1892, signed by J. Mahonga. For the report-back meeting of the deputation, see 'E Glen Grey', *Imvo*, 12.5.1892.

12 CA, NA 215: Copy of letter from D.T. Malasi to the editor, *Imvo*, 1892.

13 CA, NA 215: D.T. Malasi to chairman, Glen Grey Commission, 12.5.1892; Statement by Malwa and 21 other headmen to RM Lady Frere, 1892.

14 CA, NA 215: Statement by Malwa and 21 other headmen to RM Lady Frere, 1892; J.M. Pelem, D.T. Malasi and K. Sibeko to SNA, 24.6.1892.

15 'The Glen Grey Act', *Imvo*, 3.6.1897; 'Topics of the week', *Imvo*, 28.11.1898.

16 CA, HA 838, no. 45: Petition from D.T. Malasi and others, Sept. 1898; W.D. Hammond-Tooke, 'The Transkeian council system, 1895–1955: An appraisal', *Journal of African History*, 9, 3 (1968), p. 460.

17 The location boards consisted of three members elected by the landholders subject to the consent of the Governor. The number of people in the district involved in the elections averaged around 1500.

18 'Glen Grey politics', *Imvo*, 29.8.1895; Bundy, *The rise and fall of the South African peasantry*, p.128.

19 'Intlanganiso yotitshala e Glen Grey', *Imvo*, 7.1.1897; 'I Glen Grey teachers', *Imvo*, 27.1.1898; 'Ititshala zase Glen Grey', *Imvo*, 15.2.1899. For minutes of more than 50 meetings of the District Council, see CA, NA 528, file no. 526.

20 Cape of Good Hope, Proclamations and Government Notices relating to the Transkeian Territories: Proclamation no.

352 of 1894, pp. 1-9 and Proclamation no. 319 of 1898, p. 34.

21 CA, 1/NQA, Nqamakwe District Council letters received, 1894–5: Minutes of meeting held at Nqamakwe on 29.9.1894 by Major Elliot and the headmen and people of Butterworth, Nqamakwe and Tsomo districts; 'Mr Rhodes in Fingoland', *Imvo*, 26.3.1895.

22 CA, NA 775: J. O'Connor to CMT, 7.3.1895.

23 'Umteto ongeniswe e Transkei', *Imvo*, 24.10.1894; 'Intlanganiso e Transkei' and 'The agitation in the Transkei', *Imvo*, 8.1.1895; 'Uluntu e Transkei', *Imvo*, 29.1.1895 and 26.2.1895; 'Ipitso kwa Ngqwaru', *Imvo*, 19.3.1895; editorial and 'Current opinion', *Imvo*, 23.5.1895; 'Uluntu e Transkei', *Imvo*, 6.6.1895; 'Editorial notes', *Imvo*, 20.6.1895; 'The week', *Imvo*, 4.7.1895; CA, PM 251: William Nojiwa and others to SNA and Prime Minister [1894/5]; CA, CMT 3/192: Campbell Kupe and others to CMT, 15.12.1894, 14.1.1895 and 4.4.1895; CA, NA 775: Translation of C. Kupe and others to Native Affairs Department, 29.12.1894; CA, HA 827, nos. 372, 477, 491, 504-6: Petitions to House of Assembly [1895]; 'The Transkei deputation', *Imvo*, 18.7.1895; CA, NA 775: J. O'Connor to CMT, 7.3.1895.

24 See also 'The agitation in the Transkei', *Imvo*, 8.1.1895 and 'Mr Rhodes in Fingoland', *Imvo*, 26.3.1895.

25 See also, for example, the meeting of 'leading natives' from Queenstown, Glen Grey and Xalanga which investigated the idea of setting up an independent, nondenominational school in order to give their children an education equal to that of whites: 'Topics of the day', *Imvo*, 4.4.1894.

26 'Elipezulu no Tung' umlomo', *Imvo*, 24.8.1887.

27 'Queenstown', *Imvo*, 15.2.1888.

28 'Elipezulu no Tung' umlomo', *Imvo*, 24.8.1887.

29 'Editorial notes', *Imvo*, 11.1.1888; 'Eze zitili ngezitili', *Imvo*, 4.2.1888; 'Iliso Lomzi e Hewu', *Imvo*, 23.8.1888; 'Iliso Lomzi ontsundu', *Imvo*, 21.3.1893; and 'Iliso Lomzi ontsundu wase Hewu', *Imvo*, 21.6.1893.

30 There were no fewer than 26 Sishubas on the local voters' roll in 1903.

31 See Iliso notices signed by Nukuna, *Imvo*, 10.8.1887, 5.7.1888, 27.9.1888, 13.12.1888, 28.2.1889 and 5.9.1889.

32 Details collated from Iliso reports, *Imvo*, 24.8.1887, 23.11.1887, 21.12.1887, 15.2.1888, 19.7.1888, 9.8.1888, 11.10.1888, 1.11.1888, 4.7.1889, 3.10.1889, 26.2.1891; *Queenstown Free Press*, 5.1.1894.

33 CA, NA 774, schedule no. 73: Memorandum by Under-SNA, 9.8.1894; H. Mtombeni to RM Queenstown, 31.3.1894; and petitions of Joshua Sishuba and others and P. Matshoba and others to Prime Minister, 1894.

34 CA, NA 569, file no. 1147: Inspector of native locations to CC, 4.12.1902; and J.A. Sishuba to Inspector of native locations, 16.3.1901.

35 See, for example, 'Intlanganiso yase Lesseyton', *Imvo*, 5.3.1891; 'Reports of native conference', *Queenstown Free Press*, 5.1.1894 and *Imvo*, 5.1.1894.

36 'Iliso Lomzi kwa Ndlovukazi' and Jabavu open letter, *Imvo*, 26.2.1891; D. Dwanya to the editor and editorial, *Imvo*, 5.3.1891. Jabavu resorted to the unusual step of explaining his side of the story in an open letter to the people of Batenjini, Thembuland.

37 See chs. 15 and 16. Other indicators were Jabavu's differences with Nathaniel Umhalla and Charles Pamla, and the two camps that existed at Herschel.

38 *Imvo* gave extensive coverage to these two contests.

39 CA, GH 35/84: Return showing numbers and race of registered voters in the electoral division of Tembuland, 26.9.1902.

40 'The Indwana address', *Imvo*, 8.10.1891.

41 'Imbumba Eliliso Lomzi Ontsundu', *Imvo*, 2.11.1887.

42 UCT, Stanford papers, BC 293, B259: Umgudhlwa and others to Colonial Secretary, 15.4.1884; P.D. Tshacila to the editor, *Isigidimi*, 1.5.1884.

43 For politics in Engcobo, see also, for example, 'Inqubo ngomteto', *Imvo*, 7.11.1894; 'Engcobo petition', *Imvo*, 2.1.1895.

44 Report by T.N.M., Clarkebury, *Imvo*, 21.12.1887.

45 'Abatembu ne komkulu labo', *Imvo*, 11.12.1890; 'Umanyano lwa Batembu', *Imvo*, 18.12.1890. Among the party of

more than fifty people were Hans Matsolo, D.T. Malasi, S. Kalipa, M. Rengqe, T. and K. Poswayo and J. Sondlo.

46 'Umanyano lontsundu', *Imvo*, 15.3.1899; 'Umanyano lwabavoti', *Imvo*, 15.2.1899; 'Native political conference' and 'Intlanganiso Emqekezweni', *Imvo*, 8.3.1899; 'Umanyano Emqekezweni', *Imvo*, 29.3.1899; 'Elokuvusa ngoManyano', *Imvo*, 19.6.1899.

47 Editorial, *Imvo*, 27.11.1899.

Chapter 15: The South African Native Congress, 1890–1891

1 'Intlanganiso ye conference', by J. Tunyiswa, *Imvo*, 12.9.1889.

2 'Intlanganiso entsha' by 'Omnye wekomiti', *Imvo*, 14.8.1890.

3 N.C. Umhalla to the editor, *Imvo*, 16.12.1887; 'Ingxoxo ka Mr Mhalla', *Imvo*, 19.12.1889.

4 'Ingqungqutela yomzi ontsundu', *Imvo*, 8.5.1890.

5 Notice signed by J. Tunyiswa, *Imvo*, 26.6.1890.

6 Report by J. Tunyiswa, *Imvo*, 5.6.1890.

7 Report by J. Tunyiswa, *Imvo*, 31.7.1890.

8 'Ngentlanganiso entsha', *Imvo*, 24.7.1890 and 31.7.1890; 'Ngentlanganiso' and 'Ngentlanganiso entsha', *Imvo*, 14.8.1890; 'Ukuchitwa kwemvisiswano' and 'isikalazo sabadlala', *Imvo*, 4.9.1890.

9 'Intlanganiso entsha' by 'Omnye wekomiti', *Imvo*, 14.8.1890; 'Ingqungqutela yomzi ontsundu', *Imvo*, 8.5.1890; 'Intlanganiso egama liyi ngqungqutela', *Imvo*, 11.2.1892.

10 'Isigqibo se komiti ngentlanganiso entsha' by J. Tunyiswa, *Imvo*, 5.3.1891. An English version, translated by Umhalla, appeared in *Cape Mercury*, 5.9.1891.

11 For example, '*Imvo*', *Imvo*, 17.12.1891.

12 J. Tengo Jabavu to 'Zihlobo ezitandekileyo', *Imvo*, 17.12.1891.

13 'Intlanganiso egama liyi ngqungqutela', *Imvo*, 11.2.1891.

14 See also 'Iliso Lomzi ne ngqungqutela', *Imvo*, 14.1.1892; 'Ukugwetywa kwenyamakazi', *Imvo*, 11.2.1892.

15 'Intlanganiso egama liyi ngqungqutela', *Imvo*, 11.2.1892.

16 Ibid.

17 Postscript to letter from 'Omnye wekomiti', *Imvo*, 14.8.1890; 'Ngentlanganiso kwakona', *Imvo*, 28.8.1890.

18 'Ababhaleli be ngqungqutela', *Imvo*, 21.10.1902.

19 'Ngentlanganiso entsha', *Imvo*, 24.1.1890.

20 For the frosty relations between Rhodes and Jabavu, see, for example, 'Mr Rhodes illogical' and 'The premier and "*Imvo*"', *Imvo*, 8.8.1894.

21 Editorials, *Imvo*, 20.12.1893, 29.12.1893, 10.1.1894, 17.1.1894, 24.1.1894, 7.2.1894 and 2.5.1894.

Chapter 16: 'The Congress' versus 'The Union'

1 'Ukuvuswa komzi', *Imvo*, 7.1.1892; Comments on SANC's Queenstown conference, *Imvo*, 27.7.1898.

2 Jabavu, *The life of John Tengo Jabavu*, p. 48.

3 See, for example, comments made by Richard Kawa, Duncan Makohliso and the *Comet* newspaper (Maseru) in Jabavu, *The life of John Tengo Jabavu*, pp. 59, 144, 152.

4 'Ingqungqutela' notice by J. Tunyiswa, *Imvo*, 28.6.1893 and 5.7.1893; 'Ingqungqutela', notice by J. Tunyiswa, *Imvo*, 11 and 25.4.1895.

5 'Ukudukiswa komsebenzi', *Imvo*, 5.7.1893; 'Impawana', *Imvo*, 26.7.1893.

6 J.M. Pelem to C.J. Rhodes, 2.4.1895, quoted in Trapido, 'White conflict and non-white participation', pp. 321-2.

7 'Ingqungqutela nepepa elitsha', *Imvo*, 5.11.1891; 'Umfiliba wengqungqutela', *Imvo*, 3.12.1891; 'Isibane (lenye)', *Imvo*, 10.12.1891.

8 'Ipepa ndaba lo Zwi Labantu', *Izwi*, 21.8.1906.

9 Cory Library, unclassified Rubusana papers: W.B. Rubusana to C.J. Rhodes, 12.5.1900, n.p.

10 S.A. Allen, 'Mr Alan Kirkland Soga', *Coloured American Magazine*, 7, 2 (1904), pp. 114-16. My thanks to Bob Edgar for this unusual reference.

11 J. Peires, 'Introduction' (draft manuscript on Kawa and his work, in preparation, 2011), pp. 1-3.

12 'Ipepa ndaba lo Zwi Labantu', *Izwi*, 21.8.1906.

13 Jordan, Vilakazi, D.D.T. Jabavu, Gerard, Kuse and Opland quoted in P.E. Scott (ed.), *Samuel Edward Krune Mqhayi 1875–1945: A bibliographic survey* (Grahamstown, 1976), pp. 11-12, 33, 35-6.

14 Scott, *Mqhayi in translation*, pp. 27-8. See,

for example, his praise poem in honour of Rubusana when he was elected to the Provincial Council in 1910, 'O Vulindlela', *Imvo*, 6.12.1910.

15 For a collection of Mqhayi's writings, see Opland and Nyamende, *Isaac Williams Wauchope*, pp. xviii-xix, xxix, xxxiii, xxxv. See also Scott, *Mqhayi in translation*, pp. 27-8; J.A. Calata, 'Isikumbuzo sika Ntsikana Ongcwele', p. 4; J. Opland, 'Praise poems as historical sources', in C. Saunders and R. Derricourt (eds.), *Beyond the Cape frontier: Studies in the history of the Transkei and Ciskei* (Cape Town, 1974), pp. 1-37.

16 'Rubusana, Walter Benson' in *Dictionary of South African biography*, 2, p. 608.

17 The *Izwi* files before 1901 have been lost, but the surviving ones make this clear.

18 For example, editorial notes, *Imvo*, 12.7.1886; editorial, *Imvo*, 8.6.1887; J.T. Jabavu to the editor, *Cape Mercury*, reprinted in *Imvo*, 30.8.1898.

19 For some random examples, see editorials *Imvo*, 9.2.1888, 16.5.1889, 5.12.1889 and 19.1.1893.

20 Davenport, *The Afrikaner Bond*, pp. 184-5.

21 For example, J.T. Jabavu to the editor, *Cape Mercury,* reprinted in *Imvo*, 30.8.1898; 'Ministerial manifesto', *Imvo*, 13.7.1898; 'The native vote', *Imvo*, 20.7.1898.

22 Jabavu, *The life of John Tengo Jabavu*, p.126.

23 'Native congress', *Queenstown Representative and Border Chronicle*, 27.7.1898; 'Congress of progressive natives', *Queenstown Free Press*, 25.7.1899.

24 For example, editorial, *Imvo*, 21.9.1898.

25 For example, 'Topics of the day', *Imvo*, 8.6.1898; 'Abantsundu noSauer', *Imvo*, 17.8.1898.

26 Editorial notes, *Imvo*, 20.7.1898; 'Topics of the day', *Imvo*, 8.6.1898; 'Abantsundu noSauer', *Imvo*, 17.8.1898.

27 Notice convening Imbumba, *Imvo*, 6.7.1898; 'Iliso Lomzi', *Imvo*, 27.7.1898.

28 'U Mr Merriman nabatunywa', *Imvo*, 13.7.1898.

29 For the meeting which appointed the two delegates, see 'Unyulo olubanzi', *Imvo*, 27.7.1898.

30 Trapido, 'White conflict and non-white participation', p. 335.

31 'E.L. Qwelane', *Imvo*, 17.8.1898.

32 Over a long period Ngqase featured regularly as a spokesman in Dordrecht. See, for example, 'Glen Grey politics', *Imvo*, 28.8.1895; 'Intlanganiso enkulu', *Imvo*, 13.4.1909.

33 M.A.S. Grundlingh, 'The parliament of the Cape of Good Hope, with special reference to party politics, 1872 to 1910', *Archives Year Book for South African History* (Pretoria, 1969), p. 263. A new eastern Cape constituency, Cathcart, was created.

34 Editorial, *Imvo*, 4.9.1899; 'Imbumba Eliliso Lomzi', *Imvo*, 4.9.1899.

35 Odendaal, 'African political mobilisation', pp. 204-5.

36 For details of Jabavu's organisation and support, see ibid., pp. 180-1, 221-2.

37 CA, NA 432: W.R. (?) to E. Niland, 5.7.1906, enclosing report of Captain Veldtman's speech at the Healdtown jubilee demonstrations.

38 CA, CMT 3/550, no. 2/10: Fingo Emancipation Day, report of deputation to Governor, 29.6.1907.

39 CA, NA 1055, no. 54: Copy of circular from SNA, 23.10.1907.

40 Report of Fingo day at Peddie, *Imvo*, 30.6.1908.

41 CA, NA 432: W.R. (?) to E. Niland, 5.7.1906, enclosing report of Captain Veldtman's speech at Healdtown jubilee demonstrations.

42 'Fingo Emancipation Day' and 'Veldtman's Day', *Izwi*, 17.12.1907; 'A word in season', *Izwi*, 11.2.1908; CA, CMT 3/550, no. 2/10: A.H. Stanford to SNA, 22.9.1908 and RM Idutywa to CMT, 12.12.1907.

43 CA, CMT 3/550, no. 2/10: no. 2907/32, A.H. Stanford to SNA, 4.12.1907, enclosing report of meeting between Chief Magistrate and RM Umtata, and deputation under Chief Dalindyebo.

44 For reports of the celebrations in the various areas, see 'Umhla wama Mfengu', *Imvo*, 26.5.1908, 2.6.1908, 9.6.1908, 16.6.1908 and 23.6.1908; 'Fingo day', *Imvo*, 30.6.1908.

45 'Umhla wama Mfengu', *Imvo*, 2.6.1908; 'Fingo Day', *Imvo*, 30.6.1908; see also CA, GH 35/264 no. 321: RM Peddie to SNA, and enclosed addresses.

46 G.E. Nzungu to 'Manene nama nenekazi akowetu', *Izwi*, 6.10.1908.

47 CA, 3/KWT 2/1/2/42: G.E. Nzungu to mayor and town councillors, King William's

Town, 29.3.1909; Notice issued by Nzungu, *Izwi*, 9.3.1909.

48 'Urahla Ka Ntsikana', *Izwi*, 16.4.1909.

49 C.W. Manono, 'Ethnic relations in the Ciskei', in N. Charton (ed.), *Ciskei: Economics and politics of dependence in a South African homeland* (London, 1980), p. 105; 'Ciskei and "independence"', *Sunday Tribune*, 29.11.1981.

50 C. van Onselen, 'Reactions to rinderpest in southern Africa 1896–97', *Journal of African History*, 13, 3 (1972), pp. 473-88; Bundy, *The rise and fall of the South African peasantry*, pp. 119-22.

51 For further details, see ch. 34 below.

52 This is a point made by Trapido, 'White conflict and non-white participation'. For the voting numbers in 1903, see South African Native Affairs Commission Report [SANAC] 5, Minutes of Evidence, Annexure 2, p. 8.

53 For further details, see ch. 34 below.

Chapter 17: The 'Believers' and the British in Natal

1 The word *kholwa* is problematic. Heather Hughes has pointed out that it was used to categorise Christian Africans as almost a separate 'tribe' in segregated Natal. She uses 'insiders' and 'outsiders' instead to make the distinction between Christian and non-Christian. But *kholwa* is useful as a descriptive term if the word is understood in a nuanced way.

2 Quoted in V. Erlman, *Music, modernity and the global imagination: South Africa and the West* (New York, 1999), pp. 138, 134-5, 139.

3 Ibid., p. 139.

4 Hughes, *First president*, pp. 57-61.

5 E.H. Brookes, *White rule in South Africa, 1830–1910: Varieties in governmental policies affecting Africans* (Pietermaritzburg, 1984), pp. 44-5.

6 Charter of Natal (Letters Patent, 15 July 1865), especially articles 11-12.

7 Law no. 11 of 1864: Law for relieving certain persons from the operation of Native Law (*Natal Government Gazette* no. 921, 4.10.1864).

8 Act no. 11 of 1865.

9 SANAC 1, para. 430, p. 93; para. 20, p. 4.

10 SANAC 3, Evidence of G.A. de R. Labistour, para. 19,359, p. 98.

11 D. Welsh, *The roots of segregation: Native policy in colonial Natal, 1845–1910* (Cape Town, 1971), p. 240.

12 See, for example, *Ipepa lo Hlanga*, 14.9.1900 (Zulu original); *Ilanga lase Natal*, 19.2.1908.

13 Erlman, *Music, modernity and the global imagination*, p. 139.

14 Guy, *The view across the river*, p. 160.

15 Van Diemel, 'In search of freedom, fair play and justice', pp. 36-8 (the quote is on p. 38).

16 *Inkanyiso lase Natal*, 1.6.1894.

17 M. Marable, 'African nationalist: The life of John Langalibalele Dube' (PhD, University of Maryland, 1976), p. 39.

18 D. Attwell and D. Attridge, *The Cambridge history of South African literature* (Cambridge, 2012), pp. 214-15; Marable, 'African nationalist', p. 39.

19 *Inkanyiso*, 25.5.1894.

20 *Inkanyiso*, 1.6.1894.

21 Attwell and Attridge, *The Cambridge history of South African literature*, pp. 214-15.

22 P. la Hausse de Lalouviere, *Restless identities: Signatures of nationalism, Zulu ethnicity and history in the lives of Petros Lamula (c.1881–1948) and Lymon Maling (1889–c.1936)* (Pietermaritzburg, 2000), p. 157.

23 NA, SNA 1/1/296, Letters Received, file no. 1596/1902: Simeon Kambule and three others to Colonial Secretary, 11.5.1896; *Inkanyiso*, 6.7.1894.

24 See *Imvo*, 15.12.1888; 5.6.1890.

25 'Intlanganiso enkulu yama Wesile', *Imvo*, 17.4.1890; 'Ibandla lama Wesile', *Imvo*, 19.3.1891.

26 Quoted in Marable, 'African nationalist', p. 81.

27 Van Diemel, 'In search of freedom, fair play and justice', pp. 44-51.

28 Marable, 'African nationalist', pp. 83-4.

29 'Black supremacy', *Natal Witness*, 13.4.1901.

Chapter 18: Bloemfontein, 'Black Mountain' and Basutoland

1 Editorial, *De Express*, 10.2.1893.

2 Constitutie van den Oranjevrijstaat, 10 April 1854, 1866, Art. 1.

3 Van Aswegen, 'Die posisie van die Nie-Blankes in die Oranje-Vrystaat', p. 43.

4 T. Keegan, *Colonial South Africa and the origins of the racial order* (Cape Town, 1996), pp. 171, 180; Landau, *Popular politics*, pp. 114-15.

5 Van Aswegen, 'Die posisie van die Nie-Blankes in die Oranje-Vrystaat', pp. 41-60.

6 OFSA, Town Council, Bloemfontein, Mayor's Minutes, 1.9.1896 to 31.8.1897, p. 5; Vrouwen van huishouders der lokatie van Bloemfontein to President M.T. Steyn, 2.10.1899 (Framed illuminated address, Onze Rust, Steyn family farm, Bloemfontein).

7 Editorial, *Imvo*, 25.4.1894.

8 K. Schoeman, 'Some notes on blacks in the Orange Free State during the nineteenth century', *Quarterly Bulletin of the National Library of South Africa*, 56, 3 (March 2002), pp. 113-15.

9 *Imvo*, 21.1.1891. For an earlier letter from Somngesi, see *Imvo*, 5.11.1885.

10 W.N. Somngesi to the editor, *Cape Mercury*, January 1892 (*De Express*, 2.2.1892).

11 Campbell, *Songs of Zion*, p. 164.

12 Ibid., pp. 121-2.

13 Ibid., p. 160; Landau, *Popular politics*, p. 174.

14 C. Murray, 'Dispossession and relocation in the Thaba Nchu district: A proposal for a regional study in the eastern OFS' (Centre for African Studies, UCT, Africa Seminars, 16 September 1981), p. 5.

15 OFSA, GS 2027, file no. R2246/99: J.D. Goronyane, Y.M. Masisi, J.M. Nyokong to State President, 6.4.1899, p. 137; 12.4.1899, pp. 140-2.

16 Murray, 'Dispossession and relocation in the Thaba Nchu district', p. 7.

17 E. Kuzwayo, *Call me woman* (Johannesburg, 1985), pp. 59-63.

18 Editorial, *Imvo*, 25.4.1894; Hobart Houghton, 'The problem of Bantu education in South Africa', pp. 14-15.

19 Landau, *Popular politics*, p. 249.

20 Cory Library, Unclassified Rubusana papers: W.B. Rubusana to J. Wardlaw Thompson, 30.3.1900.

21 For full details of the tour, see C. Bolsmann, 'The 1899 Orange Free State football team tour of Europe', *International Journal of the History of Sport*, 28, 1 (January 2011), pp. 81-97; C. Bolsmann to A. Odendaal, pers. comm., 12 July 2011.

22 See Odendaal, *Vukani Bantu!*, pp. 54, 56-7, 75, 116, 168, 233, 268, 270.

Chapter 19: Diamonds and the expansion of political networks

1 J. and J. Comaroff, *Of revelation and revolution: Christianity, colonialism and consciousness in South Africa* (Chicago, 1991), 2, pp. 90-2.

2 P.T. Mgadla and S.C. Volz (eds.), *Words of Batswana: Letters to Mahoko a Becwana, 1883–1896* (Cape Town, 2006), p. 351.

3 'Chief Khama, April 1923', in F. Wilson and D. Perrot (eds.), *Outlook on a century: South Africa 1870–1970* (Lovedale and Johannesburg, 1972), pp. 19-20.

4 Mgadla and Volz, *Words of Batswana*, pp. xv, xxxiii.

5 G. Tyamzashe, 'Life at the Diamond Fields', August 1874, in Wilson and Perrot, *Outlook on a century*, pp. 19-20.

6 M. Rall, *Peaceable warrior: The life and times of Sol Plaatje* (Kimberley, 2003), pp. 18-25.

7 For a detailed discussion of the social life and activities of the black elite in Kimberley, see B. Willan, 'An African in Kimberley', in S. Marks and R. Rathbone, *Industrialisation and social change in South Africa* (London, 1982), ch. 9 and B. Willan, *Sol Plaatje: South African nationalist, 1876–1932* (Johannesburg, 1984), ch. 2. This chapter, like so much subsequent writing on Sol Plaatje and Kimberley, is based largely on Willan's pioneering work.

8 Rall, *Peaceable warrior*, p. 35.

9 D.B. Coplan, *In township tonight! South Africa's black city music and theatre* (Johannesburg, 1985), p. 40.

10 Willan, 'An African in Kimberley', pp. 250-2.

11 'Ibala labadlali', *Imvo*, 26.8.1897.

12 Willan, 'An African in Kimberley', pp. 252-4.

13 Ibid., p. 257.

14 Cory Library, MS 10 108, Sprigg Collection: Address to Sir Gordon Sprigg by the Coloured inhabitants of Griqualand West, 24.11.1892; R. van der Ross, *The rise and decline of apartheid* (Cape Town, 1986), p. 12.

15 Willan, *Sol Plaatje*, p. 47.

16 A.P.O., 18.12.1909; S.G. Millin, *Cecil Rhodes* (South Africa, 1952), p. 221; Willan, *Sol Plaatje*, pp. 51-3; Van der Ross, *The rise and decline of apartheid*, p. 13.

17 I.D. Difford, *The history of South African rugby football (1875–1932)* (Cape Town,

1933), pp. 27-28; A.C. Parker, *The Springboks 1891–1970* (London, 1970), pp. 7-8. For a profile of Frames, see Difford, *The history of South African rugby football*, p. 703.

18 T. Partridge and F. Heydenrych (eds.), *The 1990 Protea cricket annual of South Africa* (Johannesburg, 1990), p. 32.

19 J. Comaroff and B. Willan, with S. Molema and A. Reed (eds.), *The Mafeking diary of Sol T. Plaatje* (Cape Town, 1999), p. 11.

20 'A Rhodes Cup', *Imvo*, 29.7.1897.

21 'Ibala labadlali', *Imvo*, 26.8.1897.

22 D. Harris to I. Bud M'Belle, 1.11.1897, reproduced in *Imvo*, 2.12.1897.

23 Odendaal, *The story of an African game*, pp. 60-1, 76-83.

24 K. Shillington, *Luka Jantjie: Resistance hero of the South African frontier* (London, 2011), p. 163.

25 G.M. Gerhart and T. Karis (eds.), *From protest to challenge: A documentary history of African politics in South Africa, 1882–1964, 4 (Political profiles, 1882–1964)* (Stanford, 1977), p. 126.

26 G12-04, BBNA 1903, p. xii; U17-11, BBNA 1910, p. 61.

27 *Statistical Register of the Cape of Good Hope, 1909*, p. 15.

28 SANAC 4, Evidence of S.T. Plaatje, paras. 37,729 and 37,748, pp. 269-70.

29 TA, PM 36, file no. 81/2/1909: Confidential memorandum on the administration of native affairs in British Bechuanaland, E. Dower, 14.5.1909, pp. 1-5.

30 For example, CA, NA 566, Correspondence Files, file no. 1090: Native unrest at Morokweni, 1902–05: D.H. Moberley to Officer Commanding, Cape Mounted Police, Vryburg, 30.12.1904; CA, NA 752, Correspondence Files, file no. 718: Papers relating to the administration of native affairs in Bechuanaland, 1896–1912, no. D8/530/04, RM Mafeking to SNA, 20.8.1904.

31 *Mafeking Mail*, 12.2.1903.

32 Historical Papers, University of Witwatersrand Library, Silas T. Molema and Solomon T. Plaatje papers, Aa 3.6.1, Legal Documents: Memorandum of agreement entered into between G.N.H. Whales and S. Molema, Mafeking, 5.9.1901; Aa 3.6.2, Correspondence: Statement, G.N.H. Whales, 31.8.1901; T.D. Mweli Skota (ed.), *The African Yearly Register* (Johannesburg, 1931), p. 205.

33 Historical Papers, University of Witwatersrand Library, Silas T. Molema and Solomon T. Plaatje papers, A 3.6.2, Correspondence: S. Minchin to S. Molema, 26.11.1906; De Kock & De Kock to S. Molema, 6.11.1914.

Chapter 20: Gold and a new nationalism

1 See J.S. Berg (ed.), *Geskiedenis atlas van Suid-Afrika: Die vier noordelike provinsies* (Pretoria, 1998), p. 57; C. Villa-Vicencio and R. Grassow, *Christianity and the colonisation of South Africa* (Pretoria, 2009), 1, pp. 103-4.

2 Villa-Vicencio and Grassow, *Christianity and the colonisation of South Africa*, 1, pp. 109-10.

3 See B. Mbengwa and A. Manson, 'People of the dew': A history of the Bafokeng of Phokeng-Rustenburg region, South Africa, from early times to 2000 (Johannesburg, 2010), pp. 41-53.

4 Campbell, *Songs of Zion*, p. 117.

5 Ibid., p. 116.

6 See, for example, letters from M. Mokone to the editor, *Isigidimi*, 1.1.1883 and 2.4.1883.

7 Liezl Kruger has analysed letters from Wesleyan fieldworkers in both church and state archives.

8 K. Beavon, *Johannesburg: The making and shaping of the city* (Pretoria, 2004), pp. 8-9.

9 Campbell, *Songs of Zion*, pp. 121, 145.

10 J.J. Fourie, 'Die koms van die Bantoe na die Rand en hulle posisie aldaar, 1886–1899', *Argiefjaarboek vir Suid-Afrikaanse Geskiedenis* (Pretoria, 1983), pp. 247-9.

11 Beavon, *Johannesburg*, p. 68.

12 Coplan, *In township tonight!*, pp. 43-50.

13 Fourie, 'Die koms van die Bantoe na die Rand', pp. 257.

14 Ibid., p. 263; see also pp. 264-5.

15 Campbell, *Songs of Zion*, p. 147.

16 Fourie, 'Die koms van die Bantoe na die Rand', p. 247.

17 See for example, CA, NA 1131: W.S. Ndima and 50 others to Cape Government Labour Agent, 10.8.1898.

18 List of grievances attached to M. Mokone resignation letter, 1892, quoted in Campbell, *Songs of Zion*, p. 118.

19 Quoted in ibid., p. 118.

20 Ibid., pp. 103, 117-19.

21 Sundkler, *Bantu prophets*, p. 39.

22 Campbell, *Songs of Zion*, pp. 160, 187-90; Landau, *Popular politics*, p. 174.
23 Campbell, *Songs of Zion*, pp. 121-5.
24 S. Dwane, *Ethiopianism and the Order of Ethiopia* (Cape Town, 1999), pp. 20-4.
25 SANAC 2, Evidence of Rev. J. Dwane, para. 9695, p. 708.
26 E. Roux, *Time longer than rope: A history of the black man's struggle for freedom in South Africa*, 2nd edn (Madison, 1964), pp. 88-9; CA, GH 35/84, Subject Files, file no. 31, Ethiopian Movement and Episcopal Native Church of South Africa, 26.3.1901–14.9.1904: J.C. Hartzell to J.G. Sprigg, 14.2.1902.
27 Roux, *Time longer than rope*, pp. 88-9.
28 CA, GH 35/84, Subject Files, file no. 31, Ethiopian Movement and Episcopal Native Church of South Africa, 26.3.1901–14.9.1904: Minute, no. 1/411, Ministers to Governor, 2.12.1901.
29 Campbell, *Songs of Zion*, pp. 135-7.
30 Coplan, *In township tonight!*, p. 43.
31 N. Parsons, *A new history of southern Africa* (London, 1985), pp. 210-11; Campbell, *Songs of Zion*, p. 137.
32 'Rev. E. Tsewu's plaint', *Imvo*, 4.2.1897; 'Rev E. Tsewu's case', *Imvo*, 25.2.1897; 'Deposition of Mr Tsewu', *Imvo*, 5.8.1897; 'An injudicious pamphlet', *Imvo*, 9.12.1897.
33 CA, GH 35/84, file no. 31: Copy of memorandum by SNA, 25.11.1902; CA, NA 745, file no. 243: Presbyterian Church of Africa, Printed report of 1910 annual synod by P.J. Mzimba, pp. 6-7.
34 R.H.W. Shepherd, *Lovedale South Africa: The story of a century, 1841–1941* (Lovedale, n.d.), p. 245; J. Wells, *Stewart of Lovedale: The life of James Stewart* (London, 1919), pp. 294-6.
35 CA, GH 35/84, file no. 31: Minute no. 1/411, Ministers to Governor, 2.12.1901.
36 See, for example, S. Marks, *Reluctant rebellion* (Oxford, 1970), p.76.
37 Cory Library, Lovedale Collection, MS 7512: Extract from journal of D.D. Stormont, 12.10.1899.

Chapter 21: The emergence of a national movement
1 Campbell, *Songs of Zion*, pp. 152-3.
2 Saunders, 'Tile and the Thembu church', pp. 555-61.
3 'Abatembu ne komkulu labo', *Imvo*, 11.12.1890; 'Umanyano lwa Batembu', *Imvo*, 18.12.1890.
4 Reports by N. Tile, *Imvo*, 28.9.1887 and 26.10.1887; N. Tile to editor, *Imvo*, 12.10.1887.
5 'Yehi' intlekele', *Izwi*, 26.3.1907; 'Ingqungqutela la yomzi ontsundu', *Izwi*, 17.7.1906; letter from J.M. Ncakeni in 'Alitshonanga lingenancaba', *Izwi*, 10.12.1907.
6 Fieldwork undertaken by W. Beinart, Queen Elizabeth House, Oxford, 1982.
7 Saunders, 'Tile and the Thembu church', pp. 555-61.
8 Department of Historical Papers, Witwatersrand University Library, CPSA papers: AB 867/A a 1.2, F.W. Puller to 'My dear Lord', 19.12.1902.
9 'Utyelelo ku Ndlovukazi', *Imvo*, 18.1.1888; 'Inqubo yelizwi', *Imvo*, 5.2.1895; reports of Wesleyan synods, *Imvo*, 1.2.1899.
10 Department of Historical Papers, Witwatersrand University Library, CPSA papers: AB 867/A a 1.2, Memorandum by Bishop of Grahamstown, 12.4.1903.
11 T.D. Verryn, *A history of the Order of Ethiopia* (Pretoria, 1972), p. 23: SANAC 2, Evidence of Rev. J. Dwane, para. 9751, 9753, p. 714.
12 Dwane, *Ethiopianism and the Order of Ethiopia*, pp. 16-17.
13 'Elder Dwane e Melika', *Imvo*, 24.9.1896.
14 Switzer, *Power and resistance in an African society*, pp. 185-6.
15 CA, NA 754, file no.243: no. 1/685/65, Assistant CMT to SNA, 30.3.1907.
16 For example, CA, NA 700, file no. 2814: CMT to SNA, 22.9.1899.
17 Cory Library, Lovedale Collection, MS 7152c: 'The work of the past five months', report by D.D. Stormont.
18 CA, NA 544, file no. 759: Names of natives who met at King William's Town on 27 June last under the designation of 'The Native Congress'.
19 NLSA, Merriman papers, 1903, no. 285: J. Jolobe to Merriman, 9.12.1903.
20 NLSA, Schreiner papers, 1906, no. 1040: copy of telegram from Innes to Tengo Jabavu, 26.4.1906
21 NLSA, Schreiner papers, 1906, no. 1041: R.W. Rose-Innes to W.P. Schreiner, 27.4.1906, and enclosures.
22 Odendaal, 'African political mobilisation', pp. 154-5.

23 CA, NA 754, file no.243: Presbyterian Church of Africa, Printed report of 1910 annual synod by P.J. Mzimba, p. 6.

24 CA, NA 700, file no. 2814: W.E. Stanford to C.P. Crewe, 27.8.1903 and J.W. Stirling to RM Qumbu, 3.11.1904.

25 Skota, *The African yearly register*, p. 146.

26 'The late Rev. P.J. Mzimba: an appreciation', by Elijah Makiwane, *Christian Express*, 1.8.1911.

27 Campbell, *Songs of Zion*, pp. 157-9.

28 Ibid.

29 Ibid.

30 Ibid.

31 Ibid.

32 Ibid.

33 Department of Historical Papers, Witwatersrand University Library, CPSA papers: AB 867/A a 1.3, copies of correspondence, W.M. Cameron to SNA, 14.5.1903 and 6.7.1903; SNA to W.M. Cameron, 27.5.1903; W.M. Cameron to Archbishop of Cape Town, 2.9.1903.

34 Department of Historical Papers, Witwatersrand University Library, CPSA papers: AB 867/A a 1.2, Memorandum by Bishop of Grahamstown, 12.4.1903; 'The Middle Drift case', *Cape Mercury*, 12.5.1903.

35 'The Middle Drift case', *Cape Mercury*, 12.5.1903.

36 Department of Historical Papers, Witwatersrand University Library, CPSA papers: AB 867/A a 1.3, W.M. Cameron to Archbishop of Cape Town, 27.7.1903 and 17.12.1903.

37 Odendaal, 'African political mobilisation', pp. 185-6.

38 Switzer, *Power and resistance in an African society*, p. 395.

39 Cory Library, Unclassified Rubusana papers, W.B. Rubusana to Rev. J. Wardlaw Thompson, 3.03.1900.

40 'Abamnyama be ORC ne Transvaal', *Izwi*, 17.6.1902.

41 Karis and Carter, *From protest to challenge* 4, pp. 81-2.

42 'Uchuku e Boksburg, Transvaal', *Izwi*, 18.11.1902; TA, SNA 226, file no. 2019/04: Memorandum on native meetings by Acting Commissioner for Native Affairs, 2.9.1904, p. 125; CA, NA 544, file no. 759: J.M. Makhothe to SNA, Transvaal, 20.6.1904.

43 'Nge ngqungqutela', *Izwi*, 21.2.1902; Cory Library, Unclassified Rubusana papers, W.B.

Rubusana to Rev. J. Wardlaw Thompson, 3.03.1900; N.C. Umhalla to editor, *Izwi*, 24.6.1902; 'Abanyama be ORC ne Transvaal', *Izwi*, 17.6.1902; Report of convenor, Queen Victoria Memorial, *Izwi*, 7.8.1906; 'Nge ngqungqutela', *Izwi*, 21.2.1902; 'Imvisiswano', *Imvo*, 4.11.1902; 'Mzi wase Natal', *Izwi*, 26.8.1902; 'Ezase Natala', *Izwi*, 21.2.1902; 'Kwizizwe zase Natal', *Izwi*, 9.12.1902; Report of convenor, Queen Victoria Memorial, *Izwi*, 7.8.1906.

44 Campbell, *Songs of Zion*, p. 181.

Chapter 22: Women in the struggle

1 See, for example, J. Wells, *We have done with pleading: The women's 1913 anti-pass campaign* (Johannesburg, 1991), pp. vii-viii; F. Meli, *A history of the ANC: South Africa belongs to us* (Harare, 1988), pp. 50-2.

2 C. Walker, *Women and resistance in South Africa* (Cape Town, 1991), pp. 33, 142-3, 194-5, 233.

3 H. Bradford, 'Women, gender and colonialism: Rethinking the history of the British Cape Colony and its frontier zones, c.1806–1870', *Journal of African History*, 37 (1996), pp. 351-3, 355-6, 370. The quote is from p. 356.

4 This chapter follows on my recent research and writing on the neglected history of women's participation in the (socially constructed) 'gentleman's game' of cricket. See, Odendaal, *The story of an African game*, pp. 48-9, 127-9; A. Odendaal, '"Neither cricketers nor ladies": A short history of women's cricket in South Africa, 1850–2005' in *Women's Cricket World Cup 2005 South Africa* (Brochure published by the IWCC and UCBSA, 2005), pp. 6-9; A. Odendaal, K. Reddy and A. Samson, *The Blue Book: A history of Western Province cricket, 1890–2011* (Johannesburg, 2012), chs. 7 and 11; A. Odendaal, '"Neither cricketers nor ladies": Towards a history of women and cricket in South Africa, 1860s–2000s' in S. Cornellissen and A. Grundlingh (eds.), *Sport past and present in South Africa: (Trans)forming the nation* (London, 2012), pp. 114-35. This chapter was originally presented as a paper at a colloquium at Stellenbosch University in 2008 and as an article in *International Journal of the History of Sport*, 28, 1 (January 2011).

5 These quotes are from N. Erlank, 'Gendered reactions to social dislocation and missionary activity in Xhosaland 1836–1847', *African Studies*, 59, 2 (2000), pp. 205-7. My thanks to Natasha Erlank for her support and guidance in dealing with this topic.

6 For a pioneering study on gender in sport, see J.A. Mangan and R.J. Park (eds.), *From fair sex to feminism: Sport and the socialization of women in the industrial and post-industrial eras* (London, 1987).

7 K.E. McCrone, 'Play up! Play up! And play the game! Sport at the late Victorian public school', in Mangan and Park, *From fair sex to feminism*, p. 99.

8 Ibid., p. 104.

9 See J. Hargreaves, 'Victorian familism and the formative years of female sport', in Mangan and Park, *From fair sex to feminism*, pp. 134-5, 137, 141.

10 See also N. Erlank, 'Gendering commonality: African men and the 1883 Commission on Native Law and Custom', *Journal of Southern African Studies*, 29, 4 (December 2003), pp. 943-7.

11 Hodgson, *Princess Emma*, pp. 122, 133, 138, 164.

12 Ibid., pp. 176-80.

13 Cory Library, uncatalogued Church of England material (Diocesan archive no. 222): St Matthew's SPG mission Keiskamma Hoek, Visit of the Lord Bishop of Grahamstown and a short account of the mission, May 1884, p. 10.

14 A. Mager, *Gender and the making of a South African Bantustan: A social history of the Ciskei, 1945–1959* (Cape Town, 1999), p. 201.

15 *Isigidimi*, 1.10.1884.

16 'Elipezulu notung'umlomo', *Imvo*, 24.8.1887.

17 CA, HA 808, no. 113: Petition of native women, King William's Town district, July 1889.

18 'Izimiselo ze kroki', *Isigidimi*, 16.6.1884.

19 See report in *Isigidimi*, 1.5.1884.

20 'Izimiselo ze kroki', *Isigidimi*, 16.6.1884 and 1.5.1884; Archer and Bouillon, *The South African game*, p.101.

21 'Izimiselo ze kroki', *Isigidimi*, 16.6.1884

22 'Ibala labadlali: ibhola eBhayi', *Imvo*, 18.1.1888.

23 Hughes, *First president*, pp. 59, 69, 97, 164.

24 For more on Maxeke's life, see Campbell, *Songs of Zion*, pp. 277-94.

25 D. Killingray to A. Odendaal, pers. comm., 11.12.2011, with notes on 'Kinlochs'. My thanks to David Killingray for sharing the information on Alice Kinloch with me. He, in turn, wishes to acknowledge the help of Robin Kinloch.

26 Ibid. Alice Knloch was described as 'coloured' and her husband Edmund Ndosa Kinloch was a Zulu.

27 I. Geiss, *The Pan-African movement* (London, 1974), pp. 177, 180.

28 D. Killingray to A. Odendaal, pers. comm., 11.12.2011.

29 CA, 3/ELN 115, file no. 105: D. Rubusana and S. Mafongqo to D. Rees, 27.3.1899, and related correspondence.

30 See M. McCord, *The calling of Katie Makanya* (Cape Town, 1995).

31 J.M. Pelem letter, *Imvo*, 27.4.1885; 'Umtshato', *Imvo*, 5.9.1899; 'Umtshato e Xesi', *Imvo*, 29.7.1885; Skota, *The African yearly register*, p. 18.

32 Jabavu, *The life of John Tengo Jabavu*, p. 16.

33 J. Millard, 'The iron hand in the velvet glove' (undated paper, Department of Church History, Unisa), pp. 15-16; A. Nauriya, 'Gandhi and the founders of the ANC' (draft paper), p. 21; see also, 'Umanyano lwamakosikazi ase Afrika', *Izwi*, 17.9.1907; 'Umanyano lwabafazi be Transvaal ne Natal', *Izwi*, 9.3.1909.

34 'Queen Victoria Memorial: Memorandum to the Coloured Women of South Africa', *Izwi*, 14.1.1908.

35 CA, 3/ELN 453, file no. 5: W.B. Rubusana to the mayor, 6 and 14.8.1908, and related correspondence.

36 'Neglectful town councils', *Izwi*, 18.8.1908.

37 'Kwa Komani ama 400 abafazi', *Izwi*, 1.9.1908.

38 D. Gaitskell, M. Maconachie and E. Unterhalter, 'Race, class and women's activism in South Africa, 1910–1960' (Paper for the Study Project on Women in South African History, n.d.), p. 2.

Chapter 23: Black economic empowerment

1 Bundy, *The rise and fall of the South African peasantry*, pp. 15-17.

2 See L. Callinicos, *Gold and workers* (Johannesburg, 1981).

3 S. Trapido, 'The friends of the natives', in

Marks and Atmore, *Economy and Society*, pp. 254-5.

4 A. Gontshi to the editor, *Isigidimi*, 2.1.1882.

5 'Intlanganiso yomanyano', *Isigidimi*, 18.7.1883.

6 'Ibandla le Tiyopia', *Isigidimi*, 1.10.1884.

7 'Umanyano lwabasebenzi', *Imvo*, 5.11.1891.

8 See ch. 8 above.

9 'Ibandla la balimi lakwa Kama', *Imvo*, 22.2.1884; Editorial notes, *Imvo*, 17.11.1884; 'Amafama antsundu ase Kubusi', *Imvo*, 4.5.1885; 'Abalimi base Ngcobo', *Imvo*, 13.4.1885; 'Umanyano lwamafama antsundu Engqushwa', *Imvo*, 23.6.1892.

10 'The African and American Working Men's Union', *Imvo*, 28.5.1891; George Ross to 'Mzi wakowetu ontsundu', *Imvo*, 10.12.1891.

11 'Umanyano lwabasebenzi', *Imvo*, 5.11.1891; 'Abatunywa babarwebi e Kimberley', *Imvo*, 28.2.1892; 'I Qonce ne manyano lwase Bhayi', *Imvo*, 10.3.1892; George Ross to 'Mzi wakowetu ontsundu', *Imvo*, 10.12.1891.

12 'The African and American Working Men's Union', *Imvo*, 21.4.1892.

13 'The African and American Working Men's Union', *Imvo*, 15.9.1892.

14 'Umanyano lwaba sebenzi', *Imvo*, 16 and 23.2.1893.

15 'Umanyano lwase Bhayi', *Imvo*, 14.7.1892.

16 'Indaba e Bhayi', *Imvo*, 27.10.1892; 'The African and American Working Men's Union', *Imvo*, 15.9.1892; 'Umanyano lwaba sebenzi', *Imvo*, 16.2.1893.

17 'Indaba e Bhayi', *Imvo*, 27.10.1892; 'The African and American Working Men's Union', *Imvo*, 15.9.1892.

18 'Umanyano lwabasebenzi', *Imvo*, 5.11.1891.

19 Statement of the AAWMU, quoted in R.L. Kwaza to the editor, *Imvo*, 19.12.1894.

20 'Umanyano lwase Bhayi', *Imvo*, 11.4.1895.

21 See 'African and American Working Men's Union', *Imvo*, 10.4.1906; 'Isaziso', *Izwi*, 15.10.1907; 'Ipepe lendaba *Imvo*', *Imvo*, 13.4.1910.

22 'Abatunywa babarwebi e Kimberley', *Imvo*, 28.8.1392; 'Iliso Lomzi e Bhayi', *Imvo*, 26.2.1891.

23 'Umanyano lwabasebenzi', *Imvo*, 5.11.1891.

24 'The African and American Working Men's Union', *Imvo*, 28.5.1891.

25 George Ross to 'Mzi wakowetu ontsundu', *Imvo*, 10.12.1891.

26 Ibid.

27 'Umanyano lwabasebenzi', *Imvo*, 5.11.1891.

28 'Isikumbuzo soman yano', *Imvo*, 29.3.1893.

29 'Umanyano lo msebenzi', *Imvo*, 22.8.1894.

30 F. Makwena to the editor, *Imvo*, 15.9.1892; M.D. Foley and N. Mbambani to the editor, *Imvo*, 1.12.1892; 'E Bhai', *Imvo*, 5.9.1894; 'Umanyano lwa Besutu' and 'Basuto Pioneer Trading Co.', *Imvo*, 10.9.1896.

31 'Basuto Pioneer Trading Co.', *Imvo*, 10.9.1896.

32 See, for example, 'Gobelityeni' to the editor, *Imvo*, 19.5.1892; and G. Ross to the editor, *Imvo*, 23.6.1892.

33 'Ezase Qonce', *Imvo*, 21.11.1895.

34 'Intlanganiso ngamashishini', *Imvo*, 16.1.1896; 'Umanyano ngamashishini', *Imvo*, 16.4.1896; 'Umanyano' lwe mhlaba no kurweba', *Imvo*, 3.9.1896.

35 'Umanyano ngemihlaba', *Imvo*, 28.5.1896; 'Umanyano lwemihlaba eba Tenjini', *Imvo*, 18.6.1896.

36 'Transkei Pioneer Company', *Imvo*, 17.8.1898.

37 'The Ark of Refuge Society' and 'Impawana', *Imvo*, 15.8.1895.

38 Fourie, 'Die koms van die Bantoe na die Rand en hulle posisie aldaar', p. 257.

39 South African Native Races Committee (ed.), *The Natives of South Africa* (London, 1901), p. 19.

40 Report of farmers' congress, *Izwi*, 28.5.1907.

41 For example, South African Native Races Committee, *The Natives of South Africa*, pp. 57-8.

42 CA, NA 1148: Copy of memorandum by Prime Minister on report of departmental commission to institute an enquiry in certain districts of the colony in connection with the occupation of land by natives in areas other than those set apart for them and with certain associated subjects (1908).

Chapter 24: Playing the white man at his own game

1 On this, see Willan, 'An African in Kimberley', pp. 241-2, 248-52.

2 Shepherd, *Lovedale South Africa*, p. 508.

3   For a detailed discussion of this topic, see A. Odendaal, 'South Africa's black Victorians: Sport and society in South Africa in the nineteenth century', in J.A. Mangan (ed.), *Pleasure, profit, proselytism: British culture and sport at home and abroad, 1700–1914* (London, 1988).

4   'Ibala labadlali', *Imvo*, 8.10.1891.

5   'Umdlalo we krikiti', *Isigidimi*, 15.3.1884.

6   Paper read by Elijah Makiwane to the United Missionary Conference, *Imvo*, 19.7.1888.

7   'Ibola e-Monti', *Isigidimi*, 15.10.1883.

8   'King William's Town NCC vs. E. London NCC', *Isigidimi*, 16.1.1884.

9   'Ibala le cricket', *Imvo*, 19.1.1885.

10 W.M. Luckin, *The history of South African cricket, including the scores of all important matches since 1878* (Johannesburg, 1915), p. 19; 'Cricket tournament', *Cape Mercury*, 3.1.1885. The four teams participating were Port Elizabeth, King William's Town, Kimberley and Cape Town.

11 'Amangesi nabantsundu', *Imvo*, 2.3.1885.

12 Editorial notes, *Imvo*, 2.3.1885.

13 Editorial notes, *Imvo*, 16.2.1885; 'Ibola e Komani', *Imvo*, 9.12.1885; 'Ibala laba dlali', *Imvo*, 21.12.1887.

14 Quoted in 'Imvo Zabantsundu', *Imvo*, 22.12.1884.

15 Quoted in *Imvo*, 9.3.1885;

16 'Cricket', *Cape Mercury*, 24.3.1885; 'Amangesi nabantsundu', *Imvo*, 23.3.1885.

17 'Natives and cricket', *Imvo*, 9.3.1885.

18 'Editorial notes', *Imvo*, 3.11.1884.

19 See, for example, 'Ibali labadlali', *Imvo*, 23.11.1887.

20 'Ixesha le bhola, 1889', *Imvo*, 17.10.1889.

21 'Eze bola', *Isigidimi*, 15.8.1884.

22 'Kubadlali bola', *Isigidimi*, 1.11.1884.

23 Editorial notes, *Imvo*, 28.2.1889.

24 Marks and Rathbone, *Industrialisation and social change*, pp. 248-9.

25 'A sound mind in a sound body', *A.P.O.*, 15.1.1910.

26 See, for example, 'Ibala labadlali', *Imvo*, 26.3.1886; 'Ibala labadlali' and 'Ukuzigcobisa', *Imvo*, 26.9.1889 and 21.9.1889; 'Ibala labadlali', *Imvo*, 18.2.1897; 'Intenetya e Qonce', *Imvo*, 18.12.1897; 'Ukuzigcobisa', *Imvo*, 21.8.1898 and 11.9.1899.

27 'Ibala labadlali – i Jabavu Cup', *Imvo*, 16.12.1897.

28 Reports of frontier CC meetings, *Imvo*, 13.10.1892, 17.10.1894, 29.8.1895, 10.9.1896 and 21.9.1898.

29 Editorial notes, *Tsala ea Becoana*, 16.12.1911.

30 Paper read by Elijah Makiwane to the United Missionary Conference, *Imvo*, 19.7.1888; *Imvo*, 12.4.1888; 'Izimiselo ze Kroki', *Isigidimi*, 16.6.1884.

31 'Union Football Club', *Imvo*, 7.5.1891.

32 See, 'Rugby in the eastern Cape', *Work in Progress*, 17 (1981).

33 J. Peires, '"Facta non verba": Towards a history of black rugby' (History Workshop paper, Wits University, 1981), p. 1; P. Dobson, *Rugby in South Africa* (Cape Town, 1989), p. 201.

34 B. Ngozi, 'History and development of non-white rugby in South Africa' (Unpublished source book, n.d.): 'Port Elizabeth black rugby', 'Black rugby in Port Elizabeth, 'Orientals Rugby Football Club' and 'History of Spring Rose Rugby Football Club', n.p.

35 'Ibala labadlali', *Imvo*, 18.1.1888.

36 'Ibala labadlali', *Imvo*, 13.1.1898.

37 'Ibala labadlali', *Imvo*, 7.1.1897.

38 A. Desai et al., *Blacks in whites: A century of cricket struggles in KwaZulu-Natal* (Pietermaritzburg, 2002), pp. 127-9.

39 Match report, *Inkanyiso yase Natal*, 5.1.1894.

40 'Imidlalo', *Izwi*, 22.10.1907.

41 National Archives, Pretoria, NA 765, Correspondence Files, F130, 1907–1911: RM Bethulie to Acting SNA, 16.2.1911.

42 'Colour and sports', *Tsala ea Batho*, 19.8.1911.

Chapter 25: Part of a global dialogue

1   Mostert, *Frontiers*, p. xvii.

2   Ibid., p. xvii.

3   H. Crampton, *The sunburnt queen* (Johannesburg, 2004), pp. 307-15.

4   M. du Preez, *Of warriors, lovers and prophets: Unusual stories from South Africa's past* (Cape Town, 2004), pp. 7-13.

5   See, for example, Crais and Scully, *Sara Baartman and the Hottentot Venus* and R. Homes, *The Hottentot Venus: The life and death of Saartjie Baartman* (Johannesburg, 2007).

6   R. Christiansen, *The visitors: Culture shock in nineteenth-century Britain* (London, 2000), pp. 176-7.

7 R.T. Vinson and R. Edgar, 'Zulus abroad: Cultural representations and the educational experiences of Zulus in America, 1880–1945', *Journal of Southern African Studies*, 33, 1 (March 2007), p. 43.

8 For a detailed account of the delegation's trip, see Levine, *A living man from Africa*, pp. 123-57.

9 Ibid., p. 154.

10 Shillington, *Luka Jantjie*, pp. 188-9

11 Editorial notes, *Imvo*, 3.11.1884.

12 McCord, *The calling of Katie Makanya*, p. 34.

13 Ibid., p. 37.

14 Coplan, *In township tonight!*, pp. 54, 55-7.

15 McCord, *The calling of Katie Makanya*, pp. 54-5.

16 For full details of the tour, see McCord, *The calling of Katie Makanya*, chs. 4 and 5; Erlman, *Music, modernity and the global imagination*, pp. 13-14.

17 Erlman, *Music, modernity and the global imagination*, p. 135.

18 Ibid., pp. 134-7; quote from p. 137.

19 Ibid., pp. 134-5; Van Diemel, 'In search of freedom, fair play and justice', pp. 39-43.

20 Williams, *Umfundisi*, p. 31.

21 Soga, *The South-Eastern Bantu*, p. xiii.

22 As told by Camagu Soga in J.W. Lewis jnr, 'Oom Paul se veearts', *Die Burger*, 6.1.2007.

23 Soga, *The South-Eastern Bantu*, pp. xi-xv.

24 Ibid., p. xi.

25 Campbell, *Songs of Zion*, pp. 254-5.

26 Ibid., pp. 255-8.

27 Ibid., pp. 255-6.

28 Ibid., p. 262.

29 CA, GH 35/84, file no. 31: G.B. Carr to J. Chamberlain; Memorandum of an interview between H.W. Just of the Colonial Office and the Rev. P.J. Mzimba and the Rev. Damane of the Native South African Presbyterian Church, n.d. (enclosures to Cape of Good Hope no. 256, J. Chamberlain to Officer Administering the Government of the Cape of Good Hope, 31.12.1901); Memorandum, SNA, 25.11.1902 (enclosure to Minute no. 1/591, Ministers to Governor, 2.12.1902).

30 Campbell, *Songs of Zion*, p. 256.

31 Ibid., p. 134.

32 Hughes, *First president*, pp. 65-71.

33 R. Ottley and W.W. Weatherby, *The Negro in New York: An informal social history, 1626–1940* (New York, 1969), pp. 169-73.

34 CA, GH 35/84, Subject Files, file no. 31, Ethiopian Movement and Episcopal Methodist Church of South Africa, 26.3.1901–14.9.1904: D.D. Stormont to Governor, Cape Colony, 1.10.1903, enclosing 'Ethiopian Movement among the Native Churches of South Africa'.

35 See, for example, 'Iharabo zomhleli', *Imvo*, 26.1.1893; reports of trip to Bulawayo and Kimberley, *Imvo*, 11, 18 and 25.11.1897 and 21.12.1897; 'Kwa Mzilikazi', *Imvo*, 4.9.1899 and 2.7.1901.

36 The author intends to deal with this subject in further work.

37 'Notes on a visit to Scotland', *Imvo*, 19.5.1892.

Chapter 26: The South African War, 1899–1902

1 *A.P.O.*, 18.12.1909; Millin, *Rhodes*, p. 221.

2 House of Commons Parliamentary Debates, 4th series, Commons, 87, col. 271, 19.10.1899. I am grateful to Bill Nasson for providing me with this and the ensuing footnote.

3 Parliamentary Debates, House of Lords, 88, col. 257, 1.2.1900.

4 Cd 547, Further correspondence relating to affairs in South Africa, 1901: no. 37, Sir Alfred Milner to Chamberlain, 9.1.1909 (and enclosures), pp. 34-5.

5 Sir Alfred Milner to Chamberlain, 23.2.1898 in C. Headlam (ed.), *The Milner Papers* (London, 1931), 1, pp. 220-4.

6 For example, *Izwi*, 13.8.1901; 21.2.1902.

7 *Izwi*, 21.2.1902.

8 *Izwi*, 13.8.1901.

9 'A distinguished South African native', *Lagos Standard*, 8.6.1904. I am grateful to Ian Phillips for this valuable reference.

10 See, for example, the articles headed 'Boer atrocities', *Izwi*, 27.8.1901; also 3.9.1901, 20.8.1901, 21.2.1902.

11 *Izwi*, 13.8.1901.

12 L.D. Ngcongco, 'Jabavu and the Anglo-Boer War', *Kleio*, 11, 2 (Oct. 1970), pp. 7-8, 11-12, 16, 18.

13 *Natal Mercury*, 8.6.1900.

14 'The kaffir football team', *Pastimes*, 7.10.1899, p. 279.

15 F.W. Unger, *With 'Bobs' and Kruger* (Philadelphia, 1901), pp. 165-7.

16 M.G. Bidwell, 'Pen pictures of the past' (MS reminiscences, typescript in possession of Mrs Joan Hurly, Bloemfontein).

17 L.S. Amery (ed.), *The Times history of the war in South Africa 1899–1902* (London, 1900-9), 6, p. 595.
18 Editorial, *Imvo*, 16.10.1899.
19 Ngcongco, 'Jabavu and the Anglo-Boer War', pp. 8-11.
20 Ibid., pp.12-15.
21 Bill Nasson, *The South African War, 1899–1902* (London, 1999).
22 CA, NA 445: nos. 1038 and 1186, telegrams from CMT to SNA, 27.10.1899 and 4.11.1899; CA, NA 791: Copy, RM Butterworth to CMT, 28.10.1899; J.N.J. Tulwana to the editor, *Imvo*, 28.5.1900; P. Warwick, *Black people in the South African War, 1899–1902* (Cambridge, 1983), pp. 116-17. For Jabavu's reaction to the SANC meeting, see 'The native attitude', *Imvo*, 28.5.1900.
23 Ngcongco, 'Jabavu and the Anglo-Boer War', pp. 12, 16-17.
24 '*Imvo* R.I.P.', *Izwi*, 27.8.1901.
25 M. Wilson and L. Thompson (eds.), *The Oxford history of South Africa* (Oxford, 1971), 2, p. 326.
26 CA, GH 35/93, Correspondence Files, file no. 37, Arming of natives, 22.9.1901–8.1.1902: Minute, no. 1/326, J.G. Sprigg to Governor, 14.10.1901.
27 S.B. Spies, *Methods of barbarism* (Cape Town, 1977), p. 154.
28 D. Denoon, *A grand illusion* (London, 1973), p. 18.
29 General Cronje to Colonel Baden-Powell, 29.10.1899, cited in T. Pakenham, *The Boer War* (London, 1982), p. 398.
30 B. Nasson, '"These natives think this war to be their own": Reflections on blacks in the Cape Colony and the South African War 1899–1902' (Institute of Commonwealth Studies, The Societies of Southern Africa in the 19th and 20th Centuries, 8.5.1980), p. 8.
31 CA, NA 550, Correspondence Files, file no. 879, Alleged unrest amongst natives in the Colony and the Transkeian Territories, 1902: RM East London to SNA, 30.8.1902.
32 CA, GH 35/210, Subject Files, file no. 195, Bronze medals to natives in the South African War, 11.5.1904–19.1.1906: Minute no. 1/613, Ministers to Governor, 13.10.1905.
33 Van Diemel, 'In search of freedom, fair play and justice', pp. 53-8.
34 Spies, *Methods of barbarism*, p. 155.
35 Ibid., p. 279.
36 W.K. Hancock and J. van der Poel, *Selections from the Smuts papers* (Cambridge, 1966–73), 1, June 1886 – May 1902 (no. 169, J.C. Smuts to W.T. Stead, 4.1.1902), p. 485.
37 Spies, *Methods of barbarism*, p. 345.
38 Ibid., pp. 227, 262.
39 Campbell, *Songs of Zion*, pp. 165-7.
40 Nasson, 'These natives think this war to be their own', pp. 5-7.
41 J.D. Kestell and D.E. van Velden, *The peace negotiations* (London, 1912), p. 204.
42 CA, GH 35/93, Correspondence Files, file no. 37, Arming of natives, 22.9.1901–8.1.1902: Minute, no. 1/326, J.G. Sprigg to Governor, 14.10.1901.
43 Cd 528 (1901), Papers relating to negotiations between Commandant Louis Botha and Lord Kitchener (no. 10, telegram, Kitchener to Broderick, 20.3.1901), p. 6.
44 CA, GH 35/68, Subject Files, no. 9, Peace Negotiations, 12.4.1902–21.1.1903: Copy of agreement between Lord Kitchener and Lord Milner on behalf of British government and representatives of the South African Republic and the Orange Free State on 31.5.1902 (Vereeniging). See also Cd 1096 (1902), Correspondence respecting terms of surrender of the Boer forces in the field (Appendix, Draft agreement), p. 12; and Cd 1163, Further correspondence relating to affairs in South Africa, July 1902 (enclosure in no. 55, Kitchener to Broderick, 1.6.1902), pp. 155-6.
45 NLSA, Merriman papers, 1906, no. 60: M.T. Steyn to Merriman, 7.3.1906.
46 For example, TA, GOV 1012, Correspondence Files, file no. 50/35/1906, Questions affecting the native subjects of His Majesty the King: Petition compiled by the executive of the Transvaal Native Congress, n.d., p. 10.
47 Denoon, *A grand illusion*, p. 5.
48 Pakenham, *The Boer War*, pp. xiv, xvii, 573.

Chapter 27: New politics in the Transvaal

1 Odendaal, *Vukani Bantu!*, ch. 3 and pp. 74-5, 107-9, 117.
2 A1-03, Cape of Good Hope, Minutes of Custom Union Conference opened at Bloemfontein on 10 March 1903, pp. 7, 9-11.

3   CA, NA 625, file no. 1988: CC to SNA, 24.10.1903, enclosing *Koranta ea Becoana* editorial, 21.10.1903.
4   SANAC 1, paras 43,247, pp. 94-7.
5   Spies, *Methods of barbarism*, pp. 67-8. See, for example, SANAC 4, Evidence of J.B. Mama and J.B. Makue, paras. 42,055-8, pp. 646-7; and evidence of S. Mulota, S. Makapan, D. More, K. Seboch, Malukutu, D. Mogale, H. Selon, A. Mohatle, paras. 42,816, 42,821, pp. 716-17; S. Trapido, 'Landlord and tenant in a colonial economy: The Transvaal 1880–1910', *Journal of Southern African Studies*, 5, 1 (October 1978), p. 45.
6   TA, SNA 354, General Correspondence, file no. 1162/07: Report of pitso held at Wolhuters Kop Farm, Boschfontein no. 381, Rustenburg district, 9.9.1903.
7   Transvaal Colony Papers, vol. 204, 2, Report of the Transvaal Labour Commission: Evidence of General Louis Botha, para. 1198, p. 718.
8   TA, SNA 333, General Correspondence, file no. 2868/06: Rev. F. Briscoe to J.S. Marwick, 30.10.1906, p. 127.
9   Cd 3528, Further correspondence relating to affairs in the Transvaal and Orange River Colony: Transvaal Native Affairs Department annual report for the year ended 30 June 1906 (enclosure to no. 24, Governor to Secretary of State, 28.1.1907, p. 88).
10 SANAC 4, Evidence of S. Mulota, S. Makapan, D. More, .K. Seboch, Malukutu, D. Mogale, H. Selon, A. Mohatle, paras. 42,123, 42,126, p. 651.
11 See, for example, G4-04, Reports of delegates together with correspondence relating to visit of native representatives from the Colony proper and the Transkeian Territories to Johannesburg to enquire into the conditions of labour and the treatment accorded to native labourers employed on the Rand mines, 1903, pp. 12, 22.
12 Spies, *Methods of Barbarism*, pp. 304-5; TA, GOV 1012, Correspondence Files, file no. 50/35/1906, Petition compiled by the executive of the Transvaal Native Congress, n.d., p. 10; T. Pakenham, *The Boer War*, p. 573.
13 TA, SNA 226, General Correspondence, file no. 2019/04: Memorandum, Native meetings, Acting Commissioner for Native Affairs, 2.9.1904, p. 124.
14 Cory Library, MS 16291/D, Lovedale class list, 1889; 'The Free Church', *Imvo*, 27.7.1898; TA, SNA 250, file no. 459/05, Petition of W. Mpamba and five others to Lieutenant Governor (1905).
15 Campbell, *Songs of Zion*, p. 151.
16 TA, SNA 250, General Correspondence, file no. 459/05: no. 555/1613/05, Commissioner for Native Affairs to Lieutenant Governor, 9.5.1905 (postscript to letter of 8.5.1905), p. 86. TA, SNA 226, General Correspondence, file no. 2019/04: S.L. Molisapoli to Native Commissioner, Pietersburg, 29.4.1904, p. 122.
17 TA, SNA 114, General Correspondence, file no. 622/03: P.A. Masibi and 16 others to Native Commissioner, Northern Division, 4.3.1903, pp. 7-9; Minute, Assistant SNA to SNA, 18.3.1903; no. 1081/03, SNA to General Manager, CSA Railways, 3.4.1903, pp. 10-11; Telegram, Sir G. Lagden to General Manager, Railways, Cape Town, 15.5.1903; copy, SNA to Native Commissioner, Northern Division, 18.5.1903, p. 21; W.W. Hoy to SNA, 22.5.1903, 27.5.1903, and 3.6.1903, pp. 24-6; TA, SNA 123, General Correspondence, file no. 937/03: Translation (free) of the Zoutpansberg Native Vigilance Association: Manifesto, n.d., p. 148.
18 P. Rich, 'African farming and the 1913 Natives Land Act: Towards a reassessment' (University of York, CSAS, Collected Papers 4), pp. 78-80.
19 TA, SNA 226, General Correspondence, file no. 2019/04: Copy of the minutes of a meeting of the TNVA, 1.7.1904, p. 116. The date of this document should read 1.7.1903. See also *Leihlo la Babathso*, undated title page (enclosure to TA, SNA 250, General Correspondence, file no. 459/05, p. 80); L. Switzer and D. Switzer, *The black press in South Africa and Lesotho* (Boston, 1979), p. 54.
20 TA, SNA 250, General Correspondence, file no. 459/05: S.L. Molisapoli to Native Commissioner, Pietersburg, 14.2.1905, p. 74.
21 TA, SNA 226, General Correspondence, file no. 2019/04: S.L. Molisapoli to Native Commissioner, Pietersburg, 22.8.1904, 29.8.1904 and 4.9. 1904, pp. 118-19, 122 and 127-8; Memorandum, Native meetings, Acting Commissioner for Native Affairs,

2.9.1904, p. 125; and W. Windham to Native Commissioner, Northern Division, 9.9.1904, p. 115; TA, SNA 250, General Correspondence, file no. 459/05: S.L. Molisapoli to Native Commissioner, Pietersburg, 14.2.1905, pp. 74-5; Native Commissioner, Northern Division to S.L. Molisapoli, 23.2.1905, p. 76; J.C. Coghlan to Native Commissioner, Northern Division, 3.3.1905, p. 77; and petition of W. Mpamba and five others to Lieutenant Governor, Transvaal Colony, n.d. (enclosure to J.C. Coghlan to Native Commissioner, Pietersburg, 2.5.1905; p. 81), pp. 82-3.

22 *Zoutpansberg Review*, 3.3.1905.

23 TA, GOV 1012, Correspondence Files, file no. 50/35/06: The constitution of the Native Congress, Transvaal Colony, n.d. (enclosure to no. 2693/06, SNA to private secretary, Acting Lieutenant Governor, 14.6.1906); TA, SNA 226, General Correspondence, file no. 2019/04: Memorandum, Native meetings, Acting Commissioner for Native Affairs, 2.9.1904, p. 125; *Transvaal Government Gazette*, 11.12.1903.

24 Cory Library, MS 16 291/D: Lovedale class list, 1897.

25 *Ilanga*, 14.6.1907. For details of the Isivivane scheme, see the papers in NA, SNA 1/1/371, Letters Received, file no. 1806/07.

26 Karis and Carter, *From Protest to Challenge* 4, p. 104.

27 TG2-08, Mining Industry Commission, Minutes of evidence with appendices, Part 4, Evidence of J.M. Makhothe, para. 20,732, p. 1451.

28 TA, GOV 1012, Correspondence Files, file no. 50/35/06: The constitution of the Native Congress, Transvaal Colony, n.d.

29 TG2-08, Mining Industry Commission, Minutes of evidence with appendices, Part 4, Evidence of J.M. Makhothe, paras. 20,879-85, p. 1451.

30 SANAC 4, Evidence of Paulus Molatje and others (Basuto Committee), and Msane and Kumalo (Native Compound Managers), paras. 44,338-46, 44,352-53, 44,359, 44,365, 44,366, pp. 853-5.

31 TA, SNA 339, General Correspondence, file no. 2417/06: Secretary, Transvaal Basuto Committee to SNA, 25.4.1907, p. 88; and no. 1452, SNA to Native Commissioner, Central Division, 26.4.1907.

32 TA, SNA 296, General Correspondence, file no. 3626/05: P. Malatye and W.P. Letseleba to J. Mamohale, 24.11.1905 (enclosure to W.P. Letseleba to SNA, 27.11.1905, p. 36), pp. 30, 33-4 (Sotho original plus English translation).

33 TA, SNA 272, General Correspondence, file no. 1686/05: W.P. Letseleba to SNA, 22.6.1905, pp. 134-5 (Sotho original plus English translation); no. 739/05, SNA to W.P. Letseleba, 29.6.1905, p. 136; W.P. Letseleba to SNA, 4.7.1905, pp. 139-40; no. 646/05, J.S. Marwick to SNA, 7.7.1905, pp. 137-8.

34 CAD, GG 1158, no. 50/35: E. Tsewu to Governor-General, 24.11.1910; CAD, GG 1162, file no. 51/256: E. Tsewu to High Commissioner for South Africa, 1.1.1913; TA, SNA 272, General Correspondence, file no. 1686/05: no. 646/05, J.S. Marwick to SNA, 7.7.1905, p. 137.

35 Denoon: *A grand illusion*, pp. 110-20; Campbell, *Songs of Zion*, pp. 153-4.

36 Denoon, *A grand illusion*, p. 110.

37 TA, HC 17, Miscellaneous Despatches, file no. 86, Natives Transvaal: W.B. Rubusana and H. Sylvester Williams to Colonial Office, 14.11.1905 (enclosing 'Native's Protest against Registration of Property'); TA, HC 17, Miscellaneous Despatches, file no. 86, Natives Transvaal: Transvaal no. 119, Earl of Elgin to Earl of Selborne, 22.2.1906.

38 TA, SNA 272, General Correspondence, file no. 1686/05: no. 646/05, J.S. Marwick to SNA, 7.7.1905, pp. 137-8. For more on Tsewu's struggles, see Campbell, *Songs of Zion*, pp. 152-3.

39 Cd 3250 (1906), Transvaal Constitution, 1906, Letters patent and instructions relating to the Transvaal; and Swaziland Order in Council: Appendix 1, Telegram, no. 1, Earl of Elgin to Earl of Selborne, 31.7.1906, p. 39.

40 Cd 2823, Letter of instructions to the chairman of the committee appointed to enquire and report upon certain matters connected with the future constitution of the Transvaal and Orange River Colony (F. Graham to Sir J. West Ridgeway, 21.3.1906), pp. 3-4.

41 CO 879/106, African (South) no. 853, Confidential, Report of the committee appointed to enquire and report upon certain matters connected with the future

constitution of the Transvaal and Orange River Colony, Part 1, Transvaal, Appendix H: List of persons and associations interviewed by the committee in the Transvaal, pp. 43-9.

42 CO 879/106, African (South) no. 853, Confidential, Report of the committee appointed to enquire and report upon certain matters connected with the future constitution of the Transvaal and Orange River Colony, Part 1, Transvaal, pp. 29-35; and Part 2, Orange River Colony, pp. 1, 10.

43 Cd 3250 (1906), Transvaal Constitution, 1906, Letters patent and instructions relating to the Transvaal; and Swaziland Order in Council; Cd 3526 (1907), Letters patent and instructions relating to the Orange River Colony.

44 Denoon, *A grand illusion*, p. 108.

45 TA, HC 17, Miscellaneous Despatches, file no. 86, Natives Transvaal: Sir G. Lagden to Colonial Office, 3.10.1905; *Imvo*, 18.4.1905; 25.4.1905.

46 TA, SNA 274, General Correspondence, file no. 1850/05: Notes of proceedings, Deputation of natives of the Transvaal to the Governor and Lieutenant Governor, Pretoria, 28.7.1905. The original handwritten address contains the insertions and signatures.

47 TA, GOV 1012, Correspondence Files, file no. 50/35/1906, Petition compiled by the executive of the Transvaal Native Congress, n.d., pp. 3-16.

48 TA, SNA 408, General Correspondence, file no. 258/06: S.M. Makgatho, P.T. Maeta, P. Msane and others to Sir Godfrey Lagden, 16.1.1906, p. 4; Minute, Sub-Native Commissioner, Pretoria, 25.6.1906, p. 6.

49 TA, SNA 333, General Correspondence, file no. 2868/06: no. 1040/06, Acting Sub-Native Commissioner, Pretoria to Native Commissioner, Central Division, 4.10.1906, p. 100; TA, SNA 407, General Correspondence, file no. 2392/1908: Constitution of the African National Political Union, August 1906, pp. 151-4; Karis and Carter, *From Protest to Challenge* 4, p. 68.

50 TA, SNA 408, General Correspondence, file no. 258/06: Acting Sub-Native Commissioner, Pretoria to Native Commissioner, Johannesburg, 29.1.1906, pp. 10-11; TA, SNA 408, General Correspondence, file no. 258/06: Acting

Sub-Native Commissioner, Pretoria to Native Commissioner, Johannesburg, 29.1.1906, pp. 10-11; TA, SNA 320, General Correspondence, file no. 1642/06: Native Commissioner, Central Division to SNA, 12.5.1906.

51 TA, SNA 333, General Correspondence, file no. 258/06: P.T. Maeta to Sub-Native Commissioner, Pretoria, 28.9.1906, p. 123; no. 1040/06, Acting Sub-Native Commissioner, Pretoria to Native Commissioner, Central Division, 4.10.1906, p. 100; and Rev. J.F. Briscoe to Assistant SNA, 30.10.1906, p. 127.

52 TA, SNA 250, General Correspondence, file no. 459/05: Account of meeting held by the Native Vigilance Association, 7.6.1905, p. 95; S.L. Molisapoli to Native Commissioner, Pietersburg, 18.5.1905, p. 89; TA, SNA 226, General Correspondence, file no. 2019/04: Copy of minutes of meeting of the Native Vigilance Association, 1.7.1904 (enclosure to S.L. Molisapoli to Native Commissioner, Pietersburg, 29.8.1904, p. 122), pp. 116-17.

53 TG16-10, Transvaal Native Affairs Department annual report for the year ended 30 June 1909, Appendices 1 and 2, pp. 57-8; *Statistics of the Transvaal Colony for the years 1904-09*, p. 188.

54 TA, SNA 334, General Correspondence, file no. 2868/06: Pitso of natives held at Hammanskraal, 6.12.1906, pp. 2-16; TA, SNA 250, General Correspondence, file no. 459/05: Circular issued by the Transvaal Native Vigilance Association to Chiefs, 19.5.1905 (enclosure to no. Z361/05, Native Commissioner, Northern Division to Sub-Native Commissioner, 20.5.1905, pp. 90, 93), pp. 91-2 (Sotho/Pedi original plus English translation).

55 *Indian Opinion*, 6.3.1909, p. 104.

Chapter 28: New politics in the Orange River Colony

1 *Bloemfontein Post*, 31.1.1901.

2 Orange River Colony, Native Affairs Commission, Report, n.d., pp. 3-4 (enclosure to CA, NA 1149, Circulars Received Miscellaneous, Native Affairs Commission (Cape) of 1910, Reports and Memoranda 1909–12).

3 *Bloemfontein Post*, 13.3.1903.

4 Ibid.

5 Ibid.

6   SANAC 1, para. 70, p. 13.
7   J.C. Taljaard, 'Die naturelle-administrasie van die stad Bloemfontein' (MA, University of Stellenbosch, 1953), pp. 13-15.
8   R.E. van der Ross, 'A political and social history of the Cape Coloured people, 1880–1970' (MS, UCT), Part 4, Document 6, p. 1.
9   OFSA, NAB 7, file no. 79/9/05: P.H. Gresson to Advisor on Native Affairs, Bloemfontein, 9.9.1905.
10 SANAC 4, Evidence of Revs. Mpela, Kumalo and others, paras. 39,126-7, p. 368.
11 Ibid., paras. 39,127-42, p. 368.
12 Ibid., paras. 39,156-7, 39,162-70, pp. 369-70.
13 Ibid., para. 39,170, p. 370.
14 Ibid., para. 39,162-3, p. 370.
15 Ibid., paras. 39,157, 39,173-5, pp. 369-70; TA, HC 18, Miscellaneous Confidential Despatches, file no. 86, ORC Natives: D.W. Drew to J. Bryce, 19.3.1906.
16 SANAC 1, Appendix A: Comparative digest of laws affecting natives, p. A2.
17 SANAC 4, Evidence of Revs. Mpela, Kumalo and others, paras. 278-82, p. 379.
18 OFSA, NAB 10, file no. 180/06: J.Q. Dickson to E. Tshongwana, ORC Native Congress, 9.8.1906. Tshongwana later became secretary to Paramount Chief Marelane of the Mpondo.
19 SANAC 4, Evidence of J. Goronyane and J.M. Nyokong, para. 38,020, p. 293.
20 Switzer and Switzer, *The black press in South Africa*, p. 54. *Naledi* was edited by Simon Phamotse, ex-Lovedale, and was founded by the Tlale family. See B.B.J. Machobone, *Government and change in Lesotho, 1800–1906: A study of political institutions* (New York, 1990), pp. 112-13.
21 *Naledi ea Lesotho*, 3.7.1908.
22 See the copies of *Naledi ea Lesotho* in the Johannesburg Public Library.
23 CO 879/106, African (South) no. 853, Confidential, Report of the committee appointed to enquire and report upon certain matters connected with the future constitution of the Transvaal and Orange River Colony, Part 1, Transvaal, Appendix H: List of persons and associations interviewed by the committee in the Transvaal, p. 2426.
24 OFSA, CO 886, Colonial Secretary's Correspondence, file no. 667: Revised

constitution of the Orange River Colony Native Vigilance Associations, 22.10.1907 (enclosure to no. C.2094/07, J.Q. Dickson to private secretary, Governor, 5.11.1907), p. 1.
25 OFSA, CO 886, Colonial Secretary's Correspondence, file no. 667, Minute (annotated), Sir H. Goold-Adams to Superintendent of Native Affairs, 17.11.1907, n.p.
26 Ibid.
27 Karis and Carter, *From protest to challenge* 4, p. 74; T. Mapikela to the editor, *Imvo*, 19.3.1896; 'Free State', *Imvo*, 26.6.1899.
28 'Iliso lomzi', *Izwi*, 3.9.1901. NLSA, W.P. Schreiner papers, 1912, no. 2034: E. Tshongwana to W.P. Schreiner, 11.6.1912; Odendaal, *Vukani Bantu!*, p. 58.
29 OFSA, CO 886, file no. 667: Schedule to revised constitution of the Orange Free River Colony Native Vigilance Associations, 22.10.1907, p. 39.
30 OFSA, G 110, file no. 441/2 (part 2): no. 172, R.B. Allason to Secretary of State, 12.10.1908, pp. 2-6; TA, HC 131, Unclassified, file no. 170, Native Delegations: J.M. Titley to Prime Minister, Orange River Colony, 11.11.1908; and Minute no. 1403/2, Ministers to Governor, 18.11.1908.
31 OFSA, G 91, file no. 292/1: Petition from the ORC Native Congress executive committee to the King, 14.9.1908; OFSA, G 109, file no. 444/1: Resolutions, executive committee ORC Native Congress, Waaihoek, 29.8.1908 (enclosure to T.M. Mapikela to Sir H. Goold-Adams, 29.8.1908); OFSA, G 91, file no. 292/3: Statement, N.J. Daly and W.J. Fourie to Governor, 3.9.1908, pp. 161-3; OFSA, G 109, file no. 444/1: Copy of resolution, Becoana Mutual Improvement Association (enclosure in letter to Advisor, Native Affairs, Bloemfontein, 12.9.1908, pp. 165-6), pp. 168-9.
32 OFSA, GS 2027, file no. R. 2246/99: J.D. Goronyane, Y.M. Masisi, J.M. Nyokong to State President, 6.4.1899, p. 137.
33 Landau, *Popular politics*, pp. 158-9.
34 SANAC 4, Evidence of J. Goronyane and J.M. Wyokong (Nyokong), paras 37,987-38,046, pp. 291-5.
35 SANAC 4, Evidence of J. Goronyane and J.M. Nyokong, paras 37,993-6.

36 See TA, HC 131, Unclassified, file no. 170, Native Deputations: no. 146/09, C.A. Bailie to private secretary, Governor, 16.2.1909; Petition from J. Goronyane and four other delegates of the Barolong resident in Thaba Nchu to Governor, and Petition from J.D. Goronyane and five others on behalf of the native farm owners and headmen, Thaba Nchu district, to Governor (enclosures to Advisor, Native Affairs to private secretary, Governor, 27.8.1908).

37 'Bloemfontein Native', *Methodist Churchman*, 9.9.1903, p. 149. My thanks to Bob Edgar for this reference.

38 Odendaal, *Vukani Bantu!*, pp. 168-9.

39 Campbell, *Songs of Zion*, pp. 176-7.

40 Ibid.

41 Odendaal, *Vukani Bantu!*, pp. 168-9.

42 OFSA, G 110, file no. a/444/1: Minute no. 1278/2, Ministers to Governor, 19.2.1909; no. 2, Earl of Crewe to Officer Adminstering ORC, 6.1.1910.

Chapter 29: The Natal Native Congress

1 *Natal Mercury*, 8.6.1900.

2 'Natal natives voice', *Natal Mercury*, 8.6.1900.

3 'Natal Native Congress', *Natal Mercury*, 8.6.1900. See also SANAC 3, Evidence of M. Lutuli, paras. 32,255-6, p. 868.

4 Welsh, *The roots of segregation*, pp. 245-6.

5 SANAC 3, Evidence of M. Lutuli, paras. 32,202-9, pp. 865-6.

6 'Natal Native Congress', *Ipepa lo Hlanga*, 6.7.1900.

7 Ibid.

8 NA, SNA 1/4/8, Confidential and Semi-Official Correspondence, file no. 146/1900: Minute, Under-SNA to SNA, 8.5.1900 (the correct date of this minute is probably 8 June as the meeting had not yet taken place on the date mentioned); SANAC 3, Evidence of H.C. Shepstone, para. 19,247, p. 90.

9 'Black supremacy', *Natal Witness*, 13.4.1901.

10 SANAC 3, Evidence of H.C. Shepstone, para 19,248, p. 90.

11 NA, SNA 1/4/14, Confidential and Semi-Official Correspondence, file no. 22/15: Minute, Under-SNA to Minister of Justice, 25.5.1905; and N.E. Earle to Chief Commissioner of Police, 16.10.1905.

12 NA, SNA 1/4/14, Confidential and Semi-Official Correspondence, file no. C.22/05: Under-SNA to Minister of Native Affairs, 19.10.1905.

13 NA, PMO 9, Cabinet, Minutes of Meetings, Native Affairs, 1904–10: Schedule of papers for consideration of ministers, no. 154, 21.11.1905; CAD, GG 1160, file no. 50/107: SNA to private secretary, Governor-General, 26.6.1911.

14 'Dube, John Langalibalele', *DSAB* 3, p. 242; Switzer and Switzer, *The black press in South Africa*, pp. 38-9.

15 Switzer and Switzer, *The black press in South Africa*, pp. 38-9.

16 *Natal Witness*, 13.4.1901.

17 Attwell and Attridge, *The Cambridge history of South African literature*, pp. 217-19; *Izwi*, 5.6.1906; Marks, *Reluctant rebellion*, p. 73.

18 For a more detailed and informed analysis of African politics in Natal in the first decade of the 20th century, and Dube's role, see Hughes, *First president*, chs. 5 and 6.

19 Ibid., pp. 106-7, 168-9.

20 Ibid., pp. 107-8, 126.

21 Marks, *Reluctant rebellion*, pp. xv-xvi.

22 J. Lelyveld, *Great soul: Mahatma Gandhi and his struggle with India* (New York, 2011), pp. 38-42.

23 Marks, *Reluctant rebellion*, p. 365.

24 *Ilanga*, 4.5.1906.

25 See *Izwi*, 5.6.1906.

26 *Ilanga*, 4.5.1906; *Izwi*, 5.6.1906; Marks, *Reluctant rebellion*, pp. 332-3.

27 Hughes, *First president*, pp. 126, 131, 142-3.

28 Welsh, *The roots of segregation*, pp. 311-12; Marks, *Reluctant rebellion*, pp. 76, 308-9, 328-32.

29 'Address delivered by John L. Dube, Principal of the Ohlange Industrial School at the opening of a new building', *Ilanga*, 29.11.1907; *A.P.O.*, 17.5.1913.

30 Cited in *Izwi*, 5.6.1906.

31 Ibid.

32 S. Marks: 'The ambiguities of dependence: John L. Dube of Natal', *Journal of Southern African Studies*, 1, 2 (April 1975), p. 180; Marks, *Reluctant rebellion*, p. 75.

33 NA, SNA 1/1/348, Letters Received, file no. C.2675/06: Minute, Minister of Native Affairs to Prime Minister, 21.8.1906.

34 NA, SNA 1/4/20, Confidential and Semi-Official Correspondence, file no. C135/07: Report of what took place at a meeting of natives, kolwas and others, held at Ladysmith, 23.7.1908.

35 NA, SNA 1/4/20, Confidential and Semi-
Official Correspondence, file no. C135/07:
List of names expected to attend a meeting
to be held at Ladysmith on 23 July 1908
(enclosure to Z. Masuku to Under-SNA,
18.7.1908); J.T. Gumede to Magistrate,
Ladysmith, 13.7.1908; NA, SNA 1/1/410,
Letters Received: Minutes of the meeting
of 'Iliso Lesizwe Esimnyama' held at
Enyunyudu, 22.9.1908 (enclosure to N.T.
Gule to Magistrate, Dundee, 24.9.1908).
36 Hughes, *First president*, pp. 126-7.
37 Ibid., p. 143.

**Chapter 30: Gandhi and the Natal Indian
Congress**
1 B. Pachai, *Mahatma Gandhi in South Africa*
(Johannesburg, 1969), p, 9; A. Desai and
G. Vahed, *Inside Indian indenture: A South
African story, 1860–1914* (Cape Town,
2010), pp. 358-9.
2 Lelyveld, *Great soul,* pp. 38-42.
3 Ibid., p. 12.
4 J. Adams, *Gandhi: Naked ambition*
(London, 2010), p. 79.
5 Ibid., pp. 83-7.
6 Desai and Vahed, *Inside Indian indenture,*
pp. 336-7.
7 J.J. Doke, *M.K. Gandhi: An Indian patriot
in South Africa* (New Delhi, 1994), pp.
70-1.
8 See Hughes, *First president.*
9 Lelyveld, *Great soul,* pp. 18-19.
10 Adams, *Gandhi,* p. 90.
11 P.F. Power: 'Gandhi in South Africa',
Journal of Modern African Studies, 7, 3
(1969), p. 445.
12 *The Friend,* 20.2.1909.
13 Cd 5363, Further correspondence relating
to legislation affecting Asiatics in the
Transvaal: no. 40, M. Khan to M. Gandhi,
19.7.1909, pp. 31ff.
14 Editorial, *Indian Opinion,* 28.8.1909.
15 See Hughes, *First president,* pp. 107-11.
16 *Izwi,* 14.1.1908.
17 *Izwi,* 18.2.1908.
18 Lelyveld, *Great soul,* ch. 3.
19 Nauriya, 'Gandhi and the founders of
the ANC'. My thanks to Anil Nauriya
for sharing with me his valuable research
material and insights.
20 Editorial, *Indian Opinion,* 17.10.1908.
21 Lelyveld, *Great soul,* p.13.
22 Nauriya, 'Gandhi and the founders of the
ANC', pp. 2-6, 9.

23 *Naledi,* 3.7.1908.
24 Editorial, *Indian Opinion,* 1.8.1908.
25 *Indian Opinion,* 12.9.1908, p. 419.
26 Editorial, *Indian Opinion,* 29.5.1909.
27 See Nauriya, 'Gandhi and the founders
of the ANC', pp. 6-21 and Hughes, *First
president,* p. 111.

Chapter 31: Cape Town and post-war politics
1 S. Field (ed.), *Lost communities, living
memories: Remembering forced removals in
Cape Town* (Cape Town, 2001), p. 16.
2 V. Bickford-Smith, 'Protest, organisation
and ethnicity among Cape Town workers,
1891–1902', *Studies in the history of Cape
Town* (Cape Town, UCT, 1994), p. 90.
3 See A. Davids, 'Politics and the Muslims of
Cape Town: A historical survey', *Studies in
the history of Cape Town,* 4 (Cape Town,
UCT, 1984), esp. 175-6, 185-94.
4 SANAC 2, Evidence of F.Z. Peregrino,
paras. 3922-5, 3970, 4014, pp. 317, 323,
326.
5 See the advertisements that appeared
regularly in *Izwi;* for example 13.8.1901,
17.9.1901, 5.10.1901, 19.11.1901,
11.2.1902.
6 SANAC 2, Evidence of F.Z. Peregrino,
paras. 3966-70, p. 323. Extant copies
of the *Spectator* cover only the period to
December 1902. However, the newspaper
continued, albeit irregularly, until 1909.
7 C.C. Saunders, 'F.Z.S. Peregrino and the
South African Spectator', *Quarterly Bulletin
of the South African Public Library,* 32, 3
(March 1978), pp. 82-7.
8 *Izwi,* 13.8.1907.
9 Saunders, 'F.Z.S. Peregrino', pp. 82-7;
A.P.O., 12.3.1910.
10 Report by A.D.D. in *South African News,*
28.11.1903.
11 This section on the APO is drawn from
the works of G. Lewis, *Between the wire
and the wall* (Cape Town, 1984) and Van
der Ross, *The rise and decline of apartheid*
(Cape Town, 1986).
12 For a profile of Mangena, see Skota, *The
African yearly register,* p. 43.
13 'E Kapa', *Imvo,* 5.12.1898 and 'E Kapa',
Imvo, 8.2.1899.
14 C. Saunders, 'The creation of Ndabeni:
Urban segregation and African resistance
in Cape Town' (African Seminar, Collected
Papers, Centre for African Studies, UCT,
1978), p. 179.

15 Ibid.; D. Killingray, 'Significant black Africans in Britain: The formative years before 1912' (Unpublished paper, 2011). I am grateful to David Killingray for generously sharing his research with me.

16 For example, 'I Kapa ne ngqungqutela', *Izwi*, 15.1.906; L. Soha to the editor, *Izwi*, 23.10.1906; 'An excellent photograph', *Izwi*, 6.11.1906; Snippets on C.P. Mbilini and M.T. Fongqo, *Izwi*, 23.4.1907; 'Ezase Kapa', *Izwi*, 7.5.1907; 'E Kapa', *Izwi*, 6.8.1907 and 24.9.1907; 'Iliso lomzi e Kapa', *Izwi*, 31.2.1907 and 9.6.1908; Reports of QVM scheme, *Izwi*, 16 and 23.12.1902; 'I Kapa ne ngqungqutela', *Izwi*, 15.1.906; 'U-Mbilini kwa Gompo', *Izwi*, 20.8.1907.

17 *Imvo*, 24.10.1911; 31.10.1911; 14.11.1911; *A.P.O.*, 21.10.1911.

Chapter 32: Growth of the South African Native Congress

1 CA, GH 35/85, file no. 31: Prime Minister's minute no. 1/363, 1906, including memorandum by SNA. For a more detailed treatment of the SANC and its branches than this chapter provides, see Odendaal, 'African political mobilisation', pp. 192-220.

2 CA, NA 544, file no. 759: Meeting at King William's Town; 'Ingqungqutela e Xonce', *Izwi*, 8.7.1902; Petition of British subjects in Cape Colony to Sir Walter Hely-Hutchinson, *Izwi*, 19.8.1902; 'Intlanganiso ye South Africa Native Congress', *Izwi*, 14.10.1902; 'The premier interviewed', *Izwi*, 9.12.1902; *Grahamstown Journal*, 17.2.1903.

3 At Lesseytown near Queenstown in 1902, at Macubeni in the Glen Grey district in 1903, at Grahamstown in 1904, at an unknown venue in 1905 (there are no extant *Izwi* files for this year), at Queenstown in 1906 and at Wartburg near Stutterheim in 1907. An exception was 1908, when no conference was held. Though they were resumed again after that, no regular reports survive owing to the closure of the SANC's mouthpiece, *Izwi*, in April 1909.

4 CA, NA 544, file no. 759: W.B. Rubusana to R.B. Howe, 7.5.1906.

5 CA, CMT 3/640, file no. 73: W.B. Rubusana to W.T. Brownlee, 7.11.1908.

6 'The South African Native Congress', *Izwi*,

17.7.1906; 'The congress at Wartburg', *Izwi*, 13.8.1907.

7 'Abatunywa e Kapa', *Izwi*, 8.12.1908; 'Abatunywa bokuya e-kapa', *Izwi*, 19.11.1908.

8 'Iliso lomzi e Nxaruni', *Izwi*, 16.7.1907.

9 Report of convenor, Queen Victoria Memorial, *Izwi*, 7.8.1906.

10 CA, NA 739, file no. 356: J. Mehlomakulu to Inspector of native locations, 25.11.1907 and CC Herschel to SNA, 26.11.1907.

11 CA, NA 431: CC to SNA, 23.5.1906, enclosing J. Nama to 'Sir'. This Iliso was probably an extension of the old Thembu Association.

12 'Iliso lomzi e Monti', *Izwi*, 27.2.1906; 'E Monti', *Izwi*, 24.9.1907; 'Iliso lomzi', *Izwi*, 22.10.1907.

13 Reports of QVM scheme, *Izwi*, 16 and 23.12.1902. For the links between Alfred Mangena, the main figure in the resistance, and the Iliso, see C.P. Mbilini and A.T. Sannie, letters to the editor, *Izwi*, 6.8.1907; 'E Kapa', *Izwi*, 24.9.1907 and A. Mangena to the editor, *Izwi*, 15.10.1907.

14 CA, 3/AY, 1/1/1/13-14: Grahamstown Town Council minute books, 4.7.1900, 28.11.1900, 5.12.1900, and 31.7.1901 I am grateful to Rose-Marie Sellick of Rhodes University for these details.

15 See, for example, CA, 3/ELN 453, file no. 5: 'Abantsundu ne rafu zedolopu' in copy of *Izwi*, 7.9.1905 and extracts from minutes of meeting of the location committee of the town council on 13.12.1907; CA, 3/ELN 924, file no. 7: Report by C.A. Lloyd, 27.9.1913; 'I konvenshoni ne Monti', *Izwi*, 13.2.1906; 'Iliso lomzi lase Monti', *Izwi*, 25.12.1906.

16 For just a handful of examples, see CA, 3/ELN 453, file no. 3: W.B. Rubusana to town council, 7.1.1901; CA, 3/ELN 115, file no. 105: Report on alleged ill-treatment of natives by police, Assistant RM to Mayor, East London, 14.6.1901; 'Neglectful town councils', *Izwi*, 18.8.1908; CA, 3/ELN 453, file no. 5: W.B. Rubusana to Mayor, 25.2.1910.

17 CA, 1/TAM, file no. 7/38: Peter Kawa and others to R.J. Dick, 4.5.1905; CA, NA 431: Somerset Mlanjeni and Henry Vanqa to Prime Minister, 24.8.1905, and enclosures.

18 Compare names in 'Intlanganiso egama liyi ngqungqutela', *Imvo*, 11.2.1892 and CA,

NA 544, no. 759: W.B. Rubusana to R.B. Howe, 7.5.1906.

19 'Amacapaza nge ngqungqutela', *Izwi*, 15.5.1906.

20 'Peculiar tactics', *Izwi*, 15.6.1906.

21 'Pelem brothers and co', *Imvo*, 3.3.1898; notices advertising Pelem as labour agent, boarding-house owner and general dealer, *Izwi*, 6.11.1906.

22 The other SANC executive committee members in 1903 were Attwell Maci, a teacher and chairman of the village management board at Peelton, the Rev. William Philip from East London, the Rev. Peter Kawa, who had been prominent on the newly renamed Native Educational Association for a decade, and four lesser-known names, Bikani Soga, Booi Bovana, S. Mfama and Peka Nopondo. Most of them had been involved in the Congress from the start. A.K. Soga and the Rev. Elijah Mqoboli were co-opted members of the executive at this stage. Subsequently elected before Union were the Rev. Chalmers Nyombolo, the Rev. Kleinbooi Rasmeni and Samuel Krune Mqhayi, the renowned Xhosa writer.

23 See, for example, CA, NA 552, file no. 920: Memorandum by SNA on the extension of the provisions of the Glen Grey Act to the division of Peddie, 15.5.1903.

24 'Ingqungqutela', *Izwi*, 4.6.1907; 'Ikomfa yabantsundu e Blomfanteni', *Izwi*, 23.1.1909.

25 NLSA, Merriman papers, 1903, no. 264 and 214: J.M. Pelem to Merriman, n.d. and 31.10.1903.

26 'Iliso lomzi e Nxaruni', *Izwi*, 7.5.1907, 21.5.1907 and 17.9.1907.

27 L.A. Hewson, 'A study of missionary societies in South Africa' (Unpublished paper, Rhodes University, 1957), pp. 92-3.

28 'Iliso lomzi e Nxaruni', *Izwi*, 17.9.1907.

29 At the instigation of the Ndlambe clan living around Berlin, Umhalla, regarded as their chief, was appointed as headman by the government in 1899. See CA, NA 789: schedule no. 639, SNA to Prime Minister, 21.9.1899; R.J. Dick to Acting CC King William's Town, 13.6.1899 and N.C. Umhalla to J.X. Merriman, 6.7.1889; and CA, NA 785: schedule 272, enclosure N.C. Umhalla to R.J. Dick, 11.8.1898.

30 Odendaal, 'African political mobilisation', p. 186.

31 CA, CMT 3/640, file no. 73: W.B. Rubusana to W.T. Brownlee, 7.11.1908; 'Imigaqo ye ngqungqutela yabantsundu', *Izwi*, 4.6.1901.

32 CA, NA 544, file no. 759: Telegram from Native Congress to Prime Minister, 2.7.1903; 'The Congress at Wartburg', *Izwi*, 13.8.1907; Odendaal, *Vukani Bantu!*, pp. 66-7, 69, 77-9, 97-101, 162-3; 'South African Native Congress', *Izwi*, 17.4.1906; 'Congress resolutions', *Izwi*, 20.8.1907.

33 Report of convenor, Queen Victoria Memorial, *Izwi*, 7.8.1906. The other members of the executive committee were S.T. Mdliva, J.Z. Tantsi, P.S. Lusaseni, J.W. Sondlo, T. Zwedala, C. Nyombolo, S.B. Mama, W.F. Bassie, James Pelem, Plaatje Eland, E.K. Ndobe, S. Nkume, J. Tunyiswa, D. Ketse, R.B. Kota and Boyce Kota. There was also an advisory committee consisting of N.C. Umhalla, E. Mhlambiso, W.B. Rubusana, P.K. Kawa, C.C. Madosi, R. Mantsayi, W.D. Soga, W. Philip, A.H. Maci, Z. Sokopo and A. K. Soga.

34 NLSA, Merriman papers, 1903, no. 264: J.M. Pelem to Merriman, n.d.

35 NLSA, Merriman papers, 1903, no. 61: J.J. Jabavu to Merriman, 27.3.1903.

36 CA, NA 432: Confidential, C.R. Chalmers to Native Affairs Department, 12.9.1906.

Chapter 33: Transkei organisations and Bhunga politics

1 A2-09, Report of the Select Committee on Native Affairs: Appendix C, Memorandum from the secretary to the Native Affairs Department relating to local government in native areas in the Transkeian Territories and in the Colony proper.

2 Hammond-Tooke, 'The Transkeian council system', p. 464. At first this applied only to the surveyed districts of Butterworth, Tsomo and Nqamakwe where individual land tenure had been introduced. In 1913 it was extended to include the unsurveyed districts.

3 For lists of councillors, see CA, NA 628, file no. 2043: First meeting of the Transkeian Territories General Council held at Umtata on 26 to 29 August 1903; CA, NA 651, file no. 2368: List of native members of Transkeian Territories General Council for 1904 and 1906; CA, NA 1026: Minute, Ministers to Governor, May 1909, and enclosure; 'Ibhunga elikulu', *Imvo*,

26.4.1910.

4 CA, NA 652, file no. 2368: Extract from chairman's report on proceedings of General Council session in 1906.

5 G36-07, BBNA 1906, p. 51.

6 W. Beinart, 'Conflict in Qumbu: Rural consciousness, ethnicity and violence in the colonial Transkei, 1880–1913', *Journal of Southern African Studies*, 8, 1 (1981), p. 107; CA, HA 852, no. 270: Petition from J.K. Keswa and 1557 others to House of Assembly (1905).

7 For a profile of Mamba and his role in Idutywa politics, see C. Bundy, 'A voice in the big house: The career of headman Enoch Mamba', *Journal of African History*, 22 (1981), pp. 531-47.

8 'An unpopular magistrate' and editorial, *Imvo*, 12.12.1895; CA, NA 675, file no. 2352, Under-SNA to CMT, 20.4.1896.

9 CA, NA 527, file no. 510: E. Mamba to CMT, 11.4.1902.

10 'Umanyano lwama Afrika ngamashishini', *Izwi*, 10.12.1901.

11 Ibid.

12 Ibid.

13 CA, NA 527, file no. 510: W.T. Brownlee to CMT, 12.12.1902.

14 CA, NA 604, file no. 1638: Minutes of the Transkei General Council, 28.2.1903 and following days, pp. 8-9.

15 CA, NA 544, file no. 759: Telegram, Native Congress to Prime Minister, 2.7.1903.

16 SANAC 2, Evidence of E. Mamba, para. 14,202, p. 1041.

17 See for example, CA, NA 533, file no. 620: J. Ndiki and A. Soyizwapi to General Council, 22.2.1902; CA 1/NQA: I. Dudumashe and two others to Nqamakwe Divisional Council, 25.1.1902 and S. Zazela and P.S. Lusaseni to Nqamakwe District Council (1904); CA, NA 501, file no. A130: S. Mzamo and six others to RM Nqamakwe, 4.3.1905; Notice by J.J. Mateza, *Imvo*, 18.1.905; CA, NA 706, file no. 2880: J.J. Mateza to RM Nqamakwe, 24.1.1906; CA, 1/NQA: J.S. Tschainca and four others to District Council, 24.11.1906; Report, *Imvo*, 17.3.1908; 'Amanqaku ese Fingoland', *Imvo*, 21.9.1909.

18 CA, NA 755, file no. 924(i): Minutes of meeting held at Umtata on 7.9.1910 by the CMT with a deputation from the Nqamakwe district and copy of memorandum by RM Nqamakwe on complaints made by deputation to CMT, n.d.

19 CA, CMT 3/550, file no. 2/10: Telegram, no. 263, CMT to SNA, 26.6.1907.

20 CA, NA 527, file no. 510: E. Mamba to C.C. Silberbauer, 27.10.1902.

21 CA, NA 527, file no. 510: E. Mamba to CMT, 11.4.1902.

22 SANAC 2, evidence of E.Mamba, para. 14,088, p. 1033.

23 CA, NA 527, file no. 510: E.Mamba to CMT, 11.4.1902 and E.Mamba to C.C. Silberbauer, 27.10.1902.

24 CA, NA 527, file no. 510: W.G. Cumming to Prime Minister, 29.11.1901 and W.G. Cumming to CMT, 7.12.1901.

25 Report of meeting, *Imvo*, 9.5.1905.

26 CA, NA 430: S.H. Malunga and two others to RM Mount Fletcher, 9.11.906; G36-07, BBNA 1906, p. 51.

27 Report of meeting, *Imvo*, 9.5.1905.

28 CA, NA 750, file no. 170: SNA to Prime Minister, 4.9.1908; CA, NA 1008: SNA to E. Mamba, 25.2.1909.

29 CA, CMT 3/640, file no. 73: Translation of 'Amanqaku ese Fingoland', *Imvo*, 21.9.1909.

30 CA, NA 675, file no. 2552: E.Mamba to Prime Minister, 22.10.1904.

31 CA, NA 675, file no. 2552: RM Idutywa, to SNA, 24.10.1904 and 24.11.1904; CA, NA 526, file no. 509: SNA to Assistant CMT, 5.4.1906.

32 G24-08, BBNA 1907, p. 43.

33 A9-08, Report of a deputation sent by the Natal government to enquire into the working of the Council system and the system of individual land tenure in the Transkeian Territories, p. 6.

34 Jabavu, *The life of John Tengo Jabavu*, p. 81.

35 Transkeian Territories General Council, Proceedings and Report of Select Committees at the session of 1909, annual reports and accounts for 1908 and estimates of revenue and expenditure for 1909-10, pp. xix-xx, lxix-lxx.

36 CA, CMT 3/640, file no. 73: V. Zidlele to chairman, Umtata District Council, 25.1.1908.

37 CA, CMT 3/640, file no. 73: V. Zidlele to chairman, Umtata District Council, 25.1.1908; 'Iliso lomzi e Qumbu', *Imvo*, 5.1.1911.

THE FOUNDERS

38 CA, GH 35/84: Return showing numbers and race of registered voters in the electoral division of Tembuland, signed by chief clerk to CMT, 26.9.1902.

39 Ibid.

40 A2-09, Report of the Select Committee on Native Affairs, Appendix C, p xxxi. St Mark's 'somewhat reluctantly' was brought into the Council system in 1909.

41 Hammond-Tooke, 'The Transkeian council system', p. 463.

42 CA, GH 35 /84: Return showing numbers and race of registered voters in the electoral division of Tembuland, signed by chief clerk to CMT, 26.9.1902.

43 For a list of the names, occupations and places of residence of the Fingoland voters, see Cape of Good Hope, *List of persons residing in the electoral division of Tembuland whose names have been registered in the year 1903*, pp. 1-25.

44 CA, NA 750, file no. 170: SNA to Prime Minister, 4.9.1908.

45 For example, G12-04, BBNA 1903, pp. 56, 58.

46 *The Province of the Cape of Good Hope Official Gazette*, 26.7.1910, p. 459.

47 For full details, see Odendaal, *Vukani Bantu!*, pp. 246-51.

Chapter 34: Higher education and the future

1 SANAC 1, para. 342, p. 72. For details of the Queen Victoria Memorial Scheme, see *Izwi*, 17.4.1906; 17.7.1906; 7.8.1906.

2 CA, GH 35/127, Subject Files, file no. 217, Inter-Colonial Native College (Lovedale), 23.12.1905–13.8.1908: Minute, no. 1/785, Ministers to Governor, 23.12.1905; *Christian Express*, 1.5.1908.

3 Report of convenor, Queen Victoria Memorial, *Izwi*, 7.8.1906. Soga's book was intended to help the scheme. For details, see 'Prospectus', *Izwi*, 30.10.1906.

4 *Izwi*, 30.1.1906; 24.4.1906; 17.7.1906.

5 For the full record of the scheme, see M.O.M. Seboni, 'The South African Native College, Fort Hare, 1903–1954: A historical-critical survey of its development and an assessment of its influence on the education of the non-European races of South Africa in general, but of that of the southern Bantu in particular, together with suggestions for future developments' (Unisa, 1979).

6 Ibid., pp. 10-18.

7 Jabavu, *The life of John Tengo Jabavu*, p. 102.

8 Reports of convention, *Imvo*, 5.1.1906.

9 'I konvenshoni', *Imvo*, 16.1.1906.

10 Seboni, 'The South African Native College, Fort Hare', pp. 14, 36, 42.

11 See, for example, 'Peddie meeting', *Imvo*, 631906; 'Native gathering at Alice', *Imvo*, 20.3.1906; 'Idutywa meeting', *Imvo*, 15.5.1906.

12 CA, GH 35/217, Subject Files, file no. 211, Inter-Colonial Native College (Lovedale), 23.12.1905–13.8.1908: Cape of Good Hope, no. 64, Sir W. Hely-Hutchinson to Earl of Elgin, 27.2.1907; D.E. Burchell, 'African higher education and the establishment of the South African Native College, Fort Hare', *South African Historical Journal*, 8 (Nov. 1976), pp. 74-5.

13 *Christian Express*, 1.5.1908; OFSA, CO 941, Colonial Secretary's Correspondence, file no. 1193: T. Mtobi Mapikela to Under-Colonial Secretary, 28.1.1909; Fort Hare University, Rev. John Lennox papers: 'Programme of the Lovedale native convention', 1–3.7.1908.

14 A.K. Soga to K.A. Hobart Houghton and K.A. Hobart Houghton to A.K. Soga, *Izwi*, 7.8.1906.

15 Report of executive committee meeting, *Izwi*, 7.11.1908.

16 See, for example, '*Imvo* and native congress', *Izwi*, 8.5.1906.

17 Seboni, 'The South African Native College, Fort Hare', p. 61.

18 University of Fort Hare, Correspondence re establishment, 1906 and 1908: I. Bud Mbelle to K.A. Hobart Houghton, 30.10.1906.

19 S. Milton Ntloko to the editor, *Imvo*, 14.1.1912.

20 Report of conference, *Imvo*, 26.3.1912.

21 Trapido, 'White conflict and non-white participation', pp. 358, 475.

22 Jabavu, *The life of John Tengo Jabavu*, p. 81.

23 'Amanqaku nge ngqungqutela', *Izwi*, 1.5.1906; 'Peculiar tactics', *Izwi*, 15.6.1906; 'Amanqaku nge ngqungqutela', *Izwi*, 15.5.1906; 'Ingqungqutela kwa Komani', *Izwi*, 24.4.1906; 'Amacapaza nge ngqungqutela', *Izwi*, 15.5.1906; *Izwi*, 30.6.1908; Reports of meetings, *Imvo*, 9.3.1909 and 13.4.1909.

24 *Christian Express*, 16.1.912, pp. 88-9; 12.1.913, p. 23.

522

25 Unisa, D.D.T. Jabavu collection, 47 no. 12: 'South African Native College, report of the opening of the college, 8–9 February 1916'.
26 Jabavu, *The life of John Tengo Jabavu*, p. 58.

Chapter 35: 'Closer Union' and the Queenstown Conference, 1907
1 L.M. Thompson, *The unification of South Africa* (Oxford, 1960), pp. 61-4, 67.
2 CA, GH 35/238, Subject Files, file no. 247, Federation, 29.11.1906–16.2.1909: Minute no. 1/816, Ministers to Governor, 28.11.1906.
3 Ibid., Lord Selborne to Sir H. McCallum, 21.12.1906; South Africa no. 87, H. Goold-Adams to Earl of Selborne, 24.12.1906; LG 90/87, P. Duncan to Earl of Selborne, 27.12.1906; Natal no. 436, H. McCallum to High Commissioner, 29.12.1906; and High Commissioner no. 261, W.H. Milton to Earl of Selborne, 29.12.1906.
4 Ibid., Confidential, Lord Selborne to Governor, Cape Colony, 7.1.1907.
5 *Cape Hansard*, 1907, pp. 83, 227-8.
6 *Ons Land*, 30.8.1906; 1.9.1906; 6.9.1906; 8.9.1906; 11.9.1906.
7 CA, GH 35/238, Private secretary, High Commissioner to private secretary, Governor, Cape Colony, 13.8.1907.
8 Ibid., Confidential, Lord Selborne to Governor, Cape Colony, 7.1.1907.
9 *Ilanga*, 10.5.1907; 12.6.1907; 19.7.1907; 2.8.1907.
10 *Ilanga*, 2.8.1907.
11 *Imvo*, 15.10.1907.
12 J.A. Sishuba to the editor, *Imvo*, 29.10.1907.
13 F.S. Malan to J.A. Sishuba, *Imvo*, 29.10.1907.
14 *Imvo*, 7.1.1908.
15 *Izwi*, 16.7.1907.
16 *Izwi*, 13.8.1907.
17 *Izwi*, 8.10.1907.
18 *Izwi*, 10.12.1907.
19 'The APO: Its origins and progress', *A.P.O.*, 19.6.1909.
20 R.E. van der Ross, 'The founding of the African People's Organisation in Cape Town in 1903 and the role of Dr Abdurahman', *Munger Africana Library Notes*, Feb. 1975, pp. 21-2.
21 Ibid., pp. 23-4.
22 *Ilanga*, 5.12.1905.
23 *Izwi*, 22.10.1907; 17.12.1907.

24 *Izwi*, 10.12.1907.
25 J.G. Kaiyana to A.K. Soga, *Izwi*, 10.12.1907.
26 *Imvo*, 17.12.1907.
27 *Queenstown Daily Representative and Free Press*, 28 and 29.11.1907.
28 The main details of A.K. Soga's speech were published in editorial form in the *Izwi*, 3.12.1907.
29 Dr Abdurahman's address was reported in detail in *Izwi*, 10.12.1907.
30 *Queenstown Daily Representative and Free Press*, 29.11.1907.
31 Ibid.; P. Walshe: *The rise of African nationalism in South Africa* (London, 1970), p. 20, drawing on a loose history of the African National Congress by James Calata, mentions that an African conference discussed federation at the same time that the National Convention of 1908/9 was in session. It is probably the 1907 Queenstown Conference that he is referring to.
32 *Queenstown Daily Representative and Free Press*, 30.11.1907.
33 'The APO', *A.P.O.*, 19.6.1909.
34 *Imvo*, 3.12.1907.
35 *Ilanga*, 25.10.1907 and 13.12.1907. The views of *Naledi ea Lesotho* were cited in *Izwi*, 14.1.1908.
36 H. Southern Holland, private secretary, Prime Minister to secretary (Coloured and Native Conference), 18.12.1907, in *Izwi*, 24.12.1907.
37 *Imvo*, 14.1.1908; *Izwi*, 21.1.1908.
38 *Izwi*, 21.1.1908 and 28.1.1908; *Imvo*, 4.2.1908.
39 *Imvo*, 21.1.1908; 4.2.1908.
40 *Imvo*, 7.1.1908.
41 *Imvo*, 7.1.1908.
42 *Imvo*, 21.1.1908.
43 *Imvo*, 28.1.1908, 11.2.1908 and 26.3.1908.
44 For example, *Naledi*, 3.1.1908 (cited in *Izwi*, 14.1.1908).
45 Cited in *Izwi*, 10.3.1908.
46 *Ilanga*, 3.4.1908.

Chapter 36: Preparations for the National Convention
1 Thompson, *Unification*, pp. 29-30, 79-82, 89.
2 TA, HC 130, Unclassified, file no. 170: South Africa Confidential, Lord Selborne to Earl of Crewe, 8.5.1908; CA, GH 35/238,

Subject Files, file no. 238, Federation, 29.11.1906–16.2.1909: Confidential copy, J.X. Merriman to Sir W. Hely-Hutchinson, 5.5.1908; A1-08 Cape of Good Hope, Resolutions on the subject of Closer Union of South Africa passed at the meeting of the Inter-Colonial Conference on 5 May 1908.

3 *Imvo*, 5.5.1908.

4 *Izwi*, 5.5.1908.

5 *Imvo*, 2.6.1908.

6 *Imvo*, 19.5.1908.

7 UG54-37, Report of Commission of Inquiry regarding Cape Coloured Population of the Union, p. 224.

8 *Ilanga*, 29.5.1908.

9 *Naledi*, 24.4.1908; 22.5.1908; 5.6.1908; 3.7.1908.

10 *Naledi*, 3.7.1908.

11 Ibid.

12 Ibid.

13 *Naledi*, 24.4.1908; 22.5.1908.

14 *Imvo*, 19.5.1908; *Izwi*, 30.6.1908; *Ilanga*, 5.6.1908; 18.9.1908.

15 *The Star* (Johannesburg), 6.6.1908.

16 CO 879/97, African (South) no. 897, Confidential, South Africa, Further correspondence (1908) relating to affairs in South Africa: no. 168 (Confidential 2), High Commissioner to Secretary of State, 1.8.1908, pp. 283-4.

17 TA, HC 131, Unclassified, file no. 170, Native deputations: J.D. Goronyane to the Adviser, Native Affairs, Bloemfontein (stamp of Governor's Office, 5.8.1908).

18 TA, HC 131, Unclassified, file no. 170, Native deputations: T. Mtobi Mapikela to the Native Adviser, Bloemfontein, n.d.

19 Orange River Colony, Native Affairs Commission, MS documents, T.M. Mapikela to Under-Colonial Secretary, Bloemfontein (enclosure to CA, NA 1149, Circulars Received Miscellaneous, Native Affairs Commission (Cape) of 1910, Reports and memoranda, 1909–12).

20 See 'Constitution of the Basutoland Progressive Association', *Izwi*, 14.1.1908.

21 *Izwi*, 11.8.1908.

22 Cited in *Christian Express*, 1.10.1908.

23 TA, SNA 407, General Correspondence, file no. 239/08: Petition from the African National Political Union to the Prime Minister of Transvaal Colony, August 1908, pp. 134-42; cited in *Christian Express*, 1.10.1908.

24 *Ilanga*, 2.10.1908 (translation in NA, SNA 1/1/412, Letters Received, file no. 2999/08).

25 NA, SNA 1/1/415, Letters Received, file no. 3272/08: M.S. Radebe to SNA, 5.11.1908 (enclosing address to the South African Closer Union Convention in Durban assembled, signed by M. Lutuli, chairman, and M.S. Radebe, assistant secretary, on behalf of the Natal Native Congress).

26 *Ilanga*, 18.9.1908.

27 *Izwi*, 22.9.1908; *Ilanga*, 25.9.1908; *Christian Express*, 1.10.1908.

28 Ibid.

29 OFSA, G1 10, file no. a/441/1: Article on separate representation by T.L. Schreiner and K.H.R. Stuart, 7.8.1908, pp. 18-21. See also T.L. Schreiner to the editor, *Cape Times*, n.d. (cited in *Ilanga*, 23.10.1908) for his views on 'Native Reserves and Closer Union'.

30 *Izwi*, 29.9.1909.

31 *Imvo*, 6.10.1908.

32 Ibid.

33 Minutes of Proceedings with Annexures (Selected) of the South African National Convention held at Durban, Cape Town, Bloemfontein, 12 October 1908 – 11 May 1909.

34 NLSA, W.P. Schreiner papers, 1907, no. 1145A: Holograph draft of a speech by W.P. Schreiner, Queenstown, 1907, n.p.; *Imvo*, 5.11.1907.

35 *Cape Hansard*, 1908, pp. 38-48; Cape Legislative Council debates, 1908, cols. 35-49.

36 *Cape Hansard*, 1908, p. 41.

37 *Imvo*, 22.9.1908.

38 *Imvo*, 13.10.1908.

39 NLSA, W.P. Schreiner papers, 1908, no. 1287: J.X. Merriman to W.P. Schreiner, 18.6.1908 (with holograph copy of Schreiner's reply to Merriman).

40 E.A. Walker, *W.P. Schreiner: A South African* (Cape Town, 1969), pp. 277-9.

41 NLSA, W.P. Schreiner papers, 1908, F.39: W.P. Schreiner to F.R. Moor, 18.8.1908; no. 1316: F.R. Moor to W.P. Schreiner, 22.8.1908.

42 *Cape Hansard*, 1908, p. 715.

43 NLSA, W.P. Schreiner papers, 1908, no. 1323: J.X. Merriman to W.P. Schreiner, 4.9.1908.

44 NLSA, W.P. Schreiner papers, 1908, no. 1323: J.X. Merriman to W.P. Schreiner, 4.9.1908; TA, PM 63, file no. 11/1908, General Correspondence, May 1908 to

February 1909: Private and secret, J.X. Merriman to L. Botha, 14.9.1908.

45 OFSA, President M.T. Steyn Collection, A156, Incoming Letters, no. 156/1/4: J.X. Merriman to M.T. Steyn, 14.6.1908, pp. 605-7.

46 *Izwi*, 29.9.1908 and 13.10.1908.

Chapter 37: The National Convention, 1908

1 Minutes of Proceedings with Annexures (Selected) of the South African National Convention held at Durban, Cape Town, Bloemfontein, 12 October 1908 – 11 May 1909, pp. 1-3.

2 Thompson, *Unification*, pp. 173-4.

3 The only reliable but incomplete records of the proceedings are the Convention diaries of F.S. Malan and Sir Edgar Walton, and the printed minutes, which provide only the bare outlines of the Convention's resolutions, proposals, amendments and divisions.

4 Minutes, pp. 9-21.

5 Ibid., pp. 20-8.

6 Ibid., p. 23.

7 Ibid., p. 20.

8 E.H. Walton, *The inner history of the National Convention* (Cape Town, 1912), pp. 119-20.

9 Ibid., pp. 120-1.

10 Ibid., p. 121.

11 Ibid., pp. 123-4.

12 J.F. Preller (ed.), *Die Konvensie-dagboek van Sy Edelagbare Francois Stephanus Malan, 1908–1909* (Cape Town, 1951), pp. 47, 49.

13 Ibid., p. 49.

14 Ibid., pp. 47, 49.

15 Walton, *Inner history*, p. 131; Preller, *Konvensie-dagboek*, p. 53.

16 Union of South Africa, House of Assembly, Annexures, 1910-11, South African National Convention, 1908–09, vol. 5, no. 362, National Convention Correspondence and Papers: no. 25, Confidential, Lord Selborne to Sir J.H. de Villiers, 20.10.1908.

17 Ibid.

18 Preller, *Konvensie-dagboek*, pp. 55, 57, 59; Walton, *Inner history*, pp. 133-44.

19 Walton, *Inner history*, p. 138.

20 Walton, *Inner history*, p. 146.

21 Walton, *Inner history*, p. 143; Preller, *Konvensie-dagboek*, p. 59.

22 Minutes, pp. 26-7.

23 Walton, *Inner history*, pp. 145, 150.

24 Ibid.

25 CO 879/106, African (South) no. 900, Confidential, Telegrams relating to affairs in South Africa 1908: no. 373, Secret telegram (paraphrase), Secretary of State to Lord Selborne, 27.10.1908, pp. 138-9.

26 Minutes, pp. 56-7.

27 Ibid., p. 62.

28 Ibid., p. 64.

29 Ibid., p. 64.

30 Preller, *Konvensie-dagboek*, p. 73.

31 Minutes, p. 65.

32 Ibid., p. 65.

33 Walton, *Inner history*, pp. 305-6, 209; Preller, *Konvensie-dagboek*, pp. 145, 147.

34 House of Assembly Annexures, vol. 8, no. 360, Annexures 101-88: no. 160, First Report and Draft South Africa Act, pp. 1-21.

Chapter 38: Petitioning the National Convention

1 Minutes, p. 8; House of Assembly Annexures, vol. 2, no. 359, Annexures 1-100: no. 9, Telegram, W.P. Schreiner to President, National Convention, 12.10.1908.

2 Minutes, p. 9; CA, J.M. Orpen papers, Acc. 302, vol. 8: Incomplete notes by J.M. Orpen on 'The Main Native Questions in South Africa', n.d., pp. 1-2; Karis-Carter Collection (Documentation Centre for African Studies, Unisa, Pretoria) 71/YPI: 49/1, Reel 24: J.M. Orpen to the secretary, Aborigines Protection Society, 2.7.1906.

3 For example, *Izwi*, 15.5.1906.

4 TA, GOV 1152, Correspondence Files, file no. 50/39/1908, Natives Miscellaneous Correspondence: J.S. Moffat to Earl of Selborne, 10.10.1908; NLSA, De Villiers papers, file Q, box 6: J. Rose-Innes to Sir J.H. de Villiers, 20.10.1908.

5 House of Assembly Annexures, vol. 2, no. 359, Annexures 1-100: no. 87, Bishop of Pretoria to President, South African Closer Union Convention, 23.11.1908 (enclosing resolutions of Episcopal Synod of Church of Province of South Africa, 20.11.1908); no. 88, Bishop of Pretoria to President, South African Closer Union Convention, 23.11.1908 (enclosing resolutions of Pretoria Diocesan Synod of Church of Province of South Africa, 10.11.1908).

6 Minutes, p. 57.

7 NA, SNA 1/1/413, Letters Received, file no. 3134/08: C. Daniel to SNA, 15.10.1908

(Zulu original and English translation);
Under-SNA to C. Daniel, 6.11.1908. See
also House of Assembly Annexures, vol. 2,
no. 359, Annexures 1-100: no. 71, Copy
of letter from Charles Daniel of Imbizana,
Natal, 15.10.1908.

8 TA, SNA 418, General Correspondence, file
no. 114/09: Z. More to Minister of Land
and Native Affairs, 8.1.1909 (enclosing
printed report, Meeting of the Native
Committees of the Rand Centre, held
on 1 January 1909 at Nancefield). The
association became known as the Transvaal
Native Union.

9 TA, SNA 414, General Correspondence,
file no. 3373/08: M.R. Ruoele to Rev. J.
Mphahlele, 30.10.1908 (Sotho original
and English translation); Acting Sub-
Native Commissioner, Pokwani to SNA,
2.12.1908, p. 110; House of Assembly
Annexures, vol. 2, no. 359, Annexures
1-100: no. 78, W.P. Letseleba and Z. More
to Sir J.H. de Villiers (enclosing petition).

10 House of Assembly Annexures, vol. 5,
no. 362, Correspondence and Papers:
no. 92, D. Pollock to Sir J.H. de Villiers,
17.12.1908; vol. 3, no. 360, Annexures
101-188: no. 111, Petition to the National
Convention, 22.10.1908 (enclosure to
above letter); Historical Papers, University
of Witwatersrand Library, J. Howard Pim
papers, Fa 18/4: First annual report, Native
Affairs Society of the Transvaal, 1909.
The Bishop of Pretoria, Dr Carter, who
forwarded the church resolutions to the
National Convention, was on the executive
of this Society.

11 House of Assembly Annexures, vol. 5,
no. 362, Correspondence and Papers: no.
100, D. Pollock to Sir J.H. de Villiers,
30.12.1908.

12 Minutes, p. 151.

13 House of Assembly Annexures, vol. 2,
no. 359, Annexures 1-100: no. 78, W.P.
Letseleba and Z. More to Sir J.H. de
Villiers (enclosing petition to the National
Convention, 22.10.1908).

14 Izwi, 26.1.1909; Ilanga, 29.1.1909.

15 Ilanga, 13.11.1908.

16 NA, SNA 1/1/415, Letters Received, file no.
3272/08: M. Lutuli and M.S. Radebe to the
South African Closer Union Convention
(enclosure to M.S. Radebe to SNA, 5.1
1.1908).

17 House of Assembly Annexures, vol. 2,

no. 359, Annexures 1-100: no. 45, N.
Koopman to secretary, Closer Union
Convention, 17.10.1908 (enclosing address
to the National Convention); R. Samuels
and six others, on behalf of the Wynberg
Coloured Men's Political Organisation to
the South African National Convention,
November 1908.

18 House of Assembly Annexures, vol. 2, no.
359, Annexures 1-100: no. 59, Petition
of the undersigned executive members
(A. Abdurahman and three others) of
the African Political Organisation of
Coloured people resident in the Cape
Colony to the South African National
Convention, 21.10.1908; no. 60, Petition
of the undersigned executive members (J.C.
Carelse and seven others) of the African
Political Organisation of Coloured residents
in the Colony of the Transvaal to the South
African National Convention, 27.10.1908;
no. 64, Petition of the undersigned
executive members (N.J. Daly and seven
others) of the African Political Organisation
of Coloured people resident in the Orange
River Colony to the South African National
Convention, October 1908.

Chapter 39: The Protectorates and Union

1 For example, NLSA, De Villiers papers, file
Q, box 6: Copy, Confidential, 'Mr Fischer's
criticisms, objections and suggestions',
1.11.1908; Private and Confidential,
Lord Selborne to Sir Henry de Villiers,
17.11.1908.

2 CO 879/106, African (South) no. 925,
Secret, South Africa, Secret Papers (1908
and 1909) relating to affairs in South
Africa: no. 2, Memorandum, 'Natives in
South Africa, Existing responsibilities of His
Majesty's Government', p. 5.

3 R. Hyam, 'African interests and the South
Africa Act, 1908–1910', Historical Journal,
13, 1 (1970), pp. 85-6.

4 CO 879/97, African (South) no. 897,
Confidential, South Africa, Further
correspondence (1908) relating to affairs in
South Africa: Letsie L. Moshesh to Resident
Commissioner, Basutoland, 12.5.1908
(enclosure 1 in no. 100), p. 187.

5 CO 879/97, African (South) no. 897,
Confidential, South Africa: Sebele Sechele
to Acting Assistant Commissioner,
Gaberone, 23.5.1908 (enclosure 1 in no.
151), pp. 257-8; Labotsibeni and 20 others

to Resident Commissioner, Mbabane, 28.7.1909 (enclosure 1 in no. 187), pp. 319-20.

6 CO 879/97, African (South) no. 897, Confidential, South Africa: Letsie L. Moshesh on behalf of the Chiefs and the Basutho nation to Lord Selborne, 28.9.1908 (enclosure 1 in no. 248), pp. 409-11.

7 CO 879/97, African (South) no. 897, Confidential, South Africa: Draft letter to the Paramount Chief of the Basutho, n.d. (enclosure to no. 127), pp. 219-22; Confidential, High Commissioner to Resident Commissioner, Swaziland, 24.8.1908 (enclosure 2 in no. 187), pp. 319-20.

8 Full details of Selborne's activities in this respect are found in the series CO 897/97, Africa (South) no. 897, Confidential, South Africa, Further correspondence (1908) relating to affairs in South Africa.

9 House of Assembly Annexures, vol. 5, no. 362, Correspondence and Papers: no. 25, Confidential, Lord Selborne to Sir J.H. de Villiers, 20.10.1908; NLSA, De Villiers papers, file Q, box 6: Lord Selborne to Sir J.H. de Villiers (enclosing secret memorandum in respect of Protectorates), 26.10.1908.

10 NLSA, De Villiers papers, file 2, box 6: Copy, confidential, 'Mr Fischer's criticisms, objections and suggestions', 1.11.1908; Copy, confidential, 'Mr Merriman's criticisms', 3.11.1908; Copy, confidential, Sir M. Nathan to F.R. Moor, 3.11.1908; Private and confidential, Lord Selborne to Sir Henry de Villiers, 17.11.1908.

11 Walton, *Inner history*, p. 298.

12 NLSA, De Villiers papers, file 2, box 6: Copy, confidential, unsigned (Sir J.H. de Villiers) to Lord Selborne, 15.12.1908.

13 Preller, *Konvensie-dagboek*, pp. 147, 149, 151, 153, 155.

14 House of Assembly Annexures, vol. 8, no. 360, Annexures 101-188: no. 160, First Report and Draft South Africa Act, Schedule, pp. 19-21.

15 CO 879/100, African (South) no. 927: Confidential, South Africa, Further correspondence (1909) relating to affairs in South Africa: (no. 6) Acting Resident Commissioner, Bechuanaland Protectorate to High Commissioner, 12.1.1909 (enclosure 1 in no. 12), pp. 14-16.

16 CO 879/100, African (South) no. 927:

Confidential, South Africa: Sebele Sechele to High Commissioner, 8.1.1909; Linchiwe and six others to Acting Resident Commissioner, Mafeking, 11.1.1909; Baitlotle Ikanenge to Assistant Commissioner, Gaberone, 18.1.1909; Bathoen to High Commissioner, 22.2.1909 (enclosures 1 and 2 in no. 12), pp. 59-62. See also *The Friend*, 23.2.1909.

17 CO 879/97, African (South) no. 927: Minutes of meeting at Mbabane between the Acting Resident Commissioner, Swaziland, and the Chief Regent and Swazi Council on 12 January 1909 (enclosure 1 in no. 19), pp. 27-31. See also *The State*, February 1909, pp. 118-19.

18 CO 879/97, African (South) no. 927: HC no. 1/1909, Acting Resident Commissioner, Basutoland to High Commissioner, 4.1.1909 (enclosure 1 in no. 10), p. 12.

19 CO 879/97, African (South) no. 927: Basutoland, no. 154, High Commissioner to Acting Resident Commissioner, Basutoland, 28.2.1908, pp. 12-13.

20 CO 879/97, African (South) no. 927: no. 18: Minutes of proceedings at deputation of Basuto chiefs to the Secretary of State for the Colonies, at the Colonial Office, 15 February 1909, pp. 25-7.

21 CO 879/97, African (South) no. 927: no. 15.1: Petition by Paramount Chief of Basutoland with the other chiefs and people of the Basotho nation to King Edward VII, 1908, pp. 19-20.

22 CO 879/97, African (South) no. 927: no. 23: Minutes of the proceedings at a deputation of Basuto chiefs at the Colonial Office, 25 February 1909, pp. 42-3.

23 NLSA, W.P. Schreiner papers, 1909, no. 1487; S.M. Phamotse to W.P. Schreiner, 13.7.1909.

24 This newspaper, which ceased publication in 1908, was the organ of the Transvaal Native Vigilance Association.

Chapter 40: Responses to the National Convention, 1909

1 See, for example, the editorial in *Izwi*, 27.10.1908.

2 *Izwi*, 17.11.1908; 13.1.1909; 19.2.1909.

3 *Ilanga*, 16.10.1908; 23.10.1908; 30.10.1908; 13.11.1908; 20.11.1908; 27.11.1908; 4.12.1908; 11.12.1908; 18.12.1908; 25.12.1908.

4 *Ilanga*, 29.1.1909.

5 TA, SNA 418, General Correspondence, file no. 114/09: Z. More to Minister of Land and Native Affairs, 8.1.1909 (enclosing printed report, Meeting of the Native Committees of the Rand Centre, held on January 1909 at Nancefield), pp. 51-2.
6 Ibid.
7 *Izwi*, 16.3.1909.
8 *Ilanga*, 13.11.1908; 20.11.1908; 27.11.1908.
9 *Izwi*, 15.12.1908.
10 Colonial newspapers gave full coverage to the draft Act and reported widely on reactions to it. For example, *Cape Times*, 10.2.1909; *The Friend*, 10.2.1909; *Rand Daily Mail*, 10.2.1909.
11 Thompson, *Unification*, pp. 310-15.
12 NLSA, J.X. Merriman papers, 1909, no. 44: Private and confidential, L. Botha to Merriman, 17.3.1909.
13 Thompson, *Unification*, p. 316.
14 *Cape Times,* 12.2.1909; NLSA, W.P. Schreiner papers, 1909, no. 1402: W.P. Schreiner to *The Cape*, 11.2.1909; 1909, no. 1403: W.P. Schreiner to Sir B. Berry, 11.2.1902.
15 *Cape Times*, 19.3.1909 and 27.3.1909.
16 Thompson, *Unification*, pp. 315-17.
17 Resolutions of the Cape Town Branch of the Afrikaner Bond, 17.2.1909, signed by J.H. Hofmeyr, J.A.C. Graaff, J. Michau, J. Peterson and J.G. van der Horst (*Cape Times*, 18.2.1909).
18 TA, PM 63, file no. 21/1909, Closer Union correspondence: Private and confidential, J.X. Merriman to L. Botha, 9.3.1909 and 1.4.1909; OFSA, President M.T. Steyn Collection, A156, Incoming Letters 156/1/5: no. 51, J.X. Merriman to M.T. Steyn, 24.2.1909.
19 These Bond utterances on the franchise were mainly tactical rather than based on principle. CA, F.S. Malan papers, Acc. 583, no. 5: Telegram, J.X. Merriman to F.S. Malan, (?) March 1909.
20 *Imvo*, 9.2.1909.
21 *Imvo*, 16.2.1909.
22 *Imvo*, 9.2.1909.
23 *Ilanga*, 19 and 26.2.1909.
24 *Izwi*, 16.2.1909.
25 *Izwi*, 23.2.1909.
26 *Izwi*, 16.2.1909.
27 *Izwi*, 23.2.1909.
28 Ibid.
29 Ibid.
30 *Izwi*, 16.2.1909.

Chapter 41: Plans for a counter-convention
1 *Imvo*, 9.2.1909.
2 E. Tshongwana for T. Mtobi Mapikela to the editor, *Ilanga*, 11.2.1909 (*Ilanga lase Natal*), 19.2.1909; *Izwi*, 16.2.1909; see also J.S. Mocher to J.T. Jabavu, 23.2.1909, *Imvo*, 2.3.1909; J.S. Mocher to A.K. Soga, *Izwi*, 2.3.1909.
3 E. Tshongwana for T. Mtobi Mapikela to the editor, *Ilanga*, 19.2.1909.
4 *Izwi*, 16.2.1909; *Ilanga*, 5.3.1909; *Imvo*, 16 and 23.2.1909 (advertisements).
5 *Imvo*, 23.2.1909.
6 Ibid.
7 Ibid.
8 TA, HC 131, Unclassified, file no. 170, Native Deputations: E. Tshongwana to private secretary, Governor, 2.2.1909; OFSA, CO 917, Colonial Secretary's Correspondence, file no. 933/4: E. Tshongwana to Under-Colonial Secretary, Bloemfontein, 2.2.1909.
9 *The Friend*, 27.2.1909.
10 J.S. Mocher to J.T. Jabavu, 23.2.1909, *Imvo*, 2.3.1909.
11 'Umanyano Lwaba Ntsundu', *Ilanga*, 19.3.1909.
12 NA, SNA 1/1/348, Letters Received, file no. 1048/09: Confidential, telegram, A. Fischer to F. Moor, 29.3.1909.
13 OFSA, CO 908, Colonial Secretary's Correspondence, file no. 826/14: Certified copy of a resolution passed at a meeting of the Becoana Mutual Improvement Association at Thaba Nchu on 20 March 1909 and also submitted to and unanimously approved of by a mass meeting of natives and coloured people held at Thaba Nchu on 28 April 1909 (enclosure to registered, no. 209/Q/09, RM Thaba Nchu to private secretary, Governor, 14.5.1909).
14 The files of these two newspapers in the two-month period under discussion in this chapter provide extensive evidence to substantiate these statements.
15 *Imvo*, 30.3.1909.
16 *Imvo*, 20.4.1909; CA, GH 26/109, Draft General and Confidential Despatches: Secretary, APO, Cradock branch to Governor, Cape Colony, 5.4.1909 (enclosure to Cape of Good Hope no. 80,

Governor to Secretary of State, 26.4.1909);
Indian Opinion, 13.3.1909.

17 UCT Library, Stanford papers, BC 293, D
39: Stanford diary, 3–11.3.1909, pp. 27-30;
The Friend, 16.2.1909, 18.2.1909 and
1.3.1909; *Imvo*, 25.2.1909, 9.3.1909 and
16.3.1909.

18 *Imvo*, 23.2.1909.

19 UCT Library, Stanford papers, BC 293, D
39: Stanford diary, 3, 6, 8 and 9.3.1909,
pp. 27-9.

20 *Imvo*, 9.3.1909; *Territorial News*,
13.3.1909.

21 *Imvo*, 9.3.1909 and 16.3.1909.

22 *Imvo*, 23.2.1909 and *Izwi*, 23.3.1909.

23 *Imvo*, 23.2.1909.

24 *Imvo*, 9.3.1909.

25 *Imvo*, 16.3.1909.

26 *Ilanga*, 5.3.1909.

27 J.S. Mocher to A.K. Soga, *Izwi*, 2.3. 1909.

28 Ibid.

29 *Imvo*, 9.3.1909.

30 *Imvo*, 23.3.1909 and 30.3.1909.

31 *Imvo*, 23.3.1909.

32 *Izwi*, 2.3.1909 (advertisements, Xhosa
original).

33 *Izwi*, 16.4.1909; NLSA, W.P. Schreiner
papers, 1909, no. 1424A: Resumé of the
proceedings of the South African Native
Congresses and the South African Native
Convention, n.d., 2.3.1909.

34 *Izwi*, 16.3.1909.

35 NLSA, W.P. Schreiner papers, 1909, no.
1424A: Resumé of the proceedings of the
South African Native Congresses and the
South African Native Convention, n.d.,
2.3.1909. The dates given for the meeting
(13-14 March) in this source are incorrect.

36 *Izwi*, 16.4.1909.

37 Ibid.

38 *Izwi*, 23.3.1909.

39 *The Friend*, 1.3.1909.

40 Ibid.

41 CO 879/100, African (South) no. 927,
Confidential, South Africa, Further
correspondence (1909) relating to affairs
in South Africa: Badirile Montsioa
to Governor, Cape Colony, 8.3.1909
(enclosure 1 in no. 85, Cape of Good Hope
no. 87, Governor to Secretary of State,
1.5.1909), pp. 151-2; CA, GH 15/43, Prime
Minister's Minutes: no. 1/162, Ministers to
Governor, 30.4.1909.

42 CA, NA 1008, Miscellaneous Letters
Despatched, HR 1909: SNA to Chief

Badirile Montsioa, 23.3.1909; CO 879/100,
African (South) no. 927, Confidential,
South Africa, Further correspondence
(1909) relating to affairs in South Africa:
(no. 74), Private secretary, Governor
to Chief Badirile Montsioa, 1.5.1909
(enclosure 3 in no. 85, Cape of Good Hope
no. 87, Governor to Secretary of State,
1.5.1909), pp. 151-3.

43 CA, GH 13/48, High Commissioner,
Johannesburg, Despatches: Acting General
Superintendent, Wesleyan Missions to
Imperial Secretary, Johannesburg, 3.3.1909
(enclosing S. Sheppard, Administrator
to Montsioa, 29.8.1895); no. 39, Acting
Resident Commissioner, Bechuanaland
Protectorate to High Commissioner,
9.3.1909; no. 63/6, Imperial Secretary to
Acting General Superintendent, Wesleyan
Missions, Pretoria, 13.3.1909.

44 *Ilanga*, 2.4.1909.

45 B. Willan, pers. comm., 2.9.1979.

46 J.S. Mocher to J. T. Jabavu, 23.2.1909,
Imvo, 2.3.1909.

47 *Imvo*, 16.2.1909.

48 J.G. Kaiyana to J.T. Jabavu, 22.2.1909,
Imvo, 2.3.1909.

49 TA, SNA 421, General Correspondence,
file no. 968/09: Report of a meeting held
at Nancefield Location on 8 March 1909,
under the auspices of the Transvaal Native
Union (enclosure to Z. More to Director
of Government Native Labour Bureau,
22.3.1909), pp. 94-7.

50 W.B. Rubusana describes a meeting of
the Transvaal Native Congress on 13-14
March in Nancefield to discuss the draft
Act, elect delegates and submit resolutions
to the convention in Bloemfontein, but it
is probably this meeting of the Transvaal
Native Union he refers to. The dates he gives
for this meeting are the same on which he
alleges the South African Native Congress
and the Natal Native Congress held their
regional conferences. Both these details are
incorrect. Clearly, he was generalising.

51 *Bloemfontein Post*, 27.3.1909.

52 *Ilanga*, 9.4.1909 and 11.6.1909.

53 NA, SNA 1/1/426, Letters Received, file
no. 793/09: A. Mtimkulu to Under-SNA,
6.3.1909.

54 Ibid.

55 *Izwi*, 2.3.1909; Goboza to the editor,
Ilanga, 19.2. 1909; B. Dlamini to the editor,
Ilanga, 26.2.1909.

56 *Ilanga*, 9.4.1909 and 19.2.1909.
57 *Ilanga*, 30.4.1909 and 16.4.1909.
58 *Ilanga*, 19.2.1909.
59 *Ilanga*, 19.3.1909.
60 *Ilanga*, 2.4.1909.

Chapter 42: The South African Native Convention, March 1909
1 *The Friend*, 25.3.1909.
2 TA, SNA 421, General Correspondence, file 802/09: P.M. Mosetle to SNA, 8.3.1909, p. 28; Resolution of a meeting of the Transvaal Basuto Committee, Johannesburg, 14.4.1909, p. 42. Moeletsi also belonged to the Transvaal Basuto Committee.
3 The members of the 1909 executive committee are listed in the report in *The Friend*, 27.2.1909.
4 Nehemiah Serebatse, S. Tshabalala and Goliath Rakhatoe were the other delegates from this organisation. OFSA, G 110, file no. 444/5: Petition from Eastern Branch Native Vigilance Meeting to the Governor of the Orange River Colony, n.d., pp. 55-8; and Eastern Native Vigilance Association to T.M. Mapikela, 1.3.1909, p. 61; OFSA, CO 917, Colonial Secretary's Correspondence, file no. 933/3: Minute no. 933/3, Ministers to Governor, 18.2.1909; CAD, NA 237, file no. 6500/1911/F562: Petition from Eastern Native Vigilance Meeting to the Minister of Native Affairs (enclosure to RM Bethlehem to Acting SNA, 6.4.1911); no. 3851, Acting SNA to RM Bethlehem, 21.4.1911; and A. Mofolo to E.E. Dower, 19.10.1911.
5 *Bloemfontein Post*, 26.3.1909.
6 *Izwi*, 16.4.1909.
7 *Ilanga*, 2.4.1909.
8 *Izwi*, 16.4.1909.
9 *Imvo*, 7.4.1909.
10 *The Friend*, 25.3.1909.
11 *Dictionary of South African Bibliography*, 2, Drew, Dewdney William.
12 *The Friend*, 25.3.1909.
13 Ibid.
14 *Bloemfontein Post*, 26.3.1909.
15 Ibid.
16 Ibid.
17 *The Friend*, 27.3.1909; *Izwi*, 16.4.1909 and *Bloemfontein Post*, 26.3.1909.
18 CA, NA 732, Correspondence Files, file no. 515(i), Papers relating to private native locations on Crown lands, 1906–10: SNA to Prime Minister, 7.1.1910; and personal,

E. Dower to J.K. Bokwe, 22.1.1909; Karis-Carter Collection (Documentation Centre for African Studies, Unisa, Pretoria), 2:XB 20: 96/1, Reel 9A: Biographical notes, J.K. Bokwe; *Dictionary of South African Biography*, 1, pp. 88-9.
19 *Ilanga*, 2.4.1909.
20 OFSA, CO 988, Colonial Secretary's Correspondence, file no. 1905/09: J.D. Goronyane to Prime Minister, Orange River Colony, 26.3.1909; OFSA, G1 10, file no. 448/8: Minute no. 1905, Ministers to Governor, 31.3.1909 (enclosing, J.D. Goronyane to Prime Minister, Orange River Colony, 26.3.1909).
21 TA, GOV 1206, Correspondence Files, file no. 50/17/1909: J.D. Goronyane to High Commissioner, 26.3.1909; CO 879/97, African (South) no. 927, Confidential, South Africa, Further correspondence (1909) relating to affairs in South Africa: no. 65 (no. 96), Governor, Transvaal to Secretary of State, 5.4.1909 (enclosing J.D. Goronyane to High Commissioner, 26.3.1909), p. 124.
22 *Izwi*, 16.4.1909.
23 NLSA, W.P. Schreiner papers, 1909, no. 1424A: Resumé of the proceedings of the South African Native Congresses and the South African Native Convention, n.d., n.p.
24 *Ilanga*, 9.4.1909; *Izwi*, 16.4.1909.
25 *The Friend*, 27.3.1909; *Bloemfontein Post*, 27.3.1909.
26 *Bloemfontein Post*, 27.3.1909.
27 *The Friend*, 27.3.1909.
28 *The Friend*, 27.3.1909; *Bloemfontein Post*, 27.3.1909.
29 *Bloemfontein Post*, 27.3.1909.
30 *The Friend*, 27.3.1909; *Bloemfontein Post*, 27.3.1909.
31 *The Friend*, 27.3.1909; A.K. Soga to the editor, *The Friend*, 27.3.1909, *The Friend*, 29.3.1909.
32 *The Friend*, 27.3.1909.

Chapter 43: Jabavu and the APO join the chorus
1 NLSA, W.P. Schreiner papers, 1908, no. 1477A: Newspaper cuttings, King William's Town, Cape Native Convention, n.d., pp. 1-3; *Imvo*, 13.4.1909.
2 *Imvo*, 13.4.1909.
3 *Imvo*, 1.5.1909.
4 Ibid.
5 Ibid.
6 Ibid.

7 Ibid.
8 *Imvo*, 4.5.1908 and 11.5.1908.
9 *Ilanga*, 9.4.1909.
10 Ibid.
11 *Ilanga*, 26.3.1909.
12 NA, SNA 1/4/22, Confidential and Semi-Official Correspondence, file no. C 24/09: 'Statement by Native as to what took place at Native Meeting held in Pietermaritzburg, Thursday 8th April 1909, in connection with the Draft Act of Union and other matters', pp. 5-6.
13 NA, SNA 1/1/427, Letters Received, file no. 906/09: Minute, Minister of Native Affairs to Under-SNA, 22.3.1909; and, telegram, Under-SNA to Magistrate, Umgeni Division, 22.3.1909.
14 *Ilanga*, 9.4.1909.
15 NA, SNA 1/4/22, Confidential and Semi-Official Correspondence, file no. C 24/09: Notes of a meeting between Native Affairs Department (J. Stuart) and six natives, 8.4.1909.
16 NA, SNA 1/4/22, Confidential and Semi-Official Correspondence, file no. C 24/09: 'Statement by Native as to what took place at Native Meeting held in Pietermaritzburg, Thursday 8th April 1909, in connection with the Draft Act of Union and other matters', pp. 1-3, 6.
17 Ibid.
18 NLSA, W.P. Schreiner papers, 1909, no. 1430: S.T. Plaatje to W.P. Schreiner, 13.4.1909; *Ilanga*, 30. 4.1909.
19 TA, SNA 423, General Correspondence, file no. 1238/09: S.M. Makgatho to Sub-Native Commissioner, Pietersburg, 15.4.1909, p. 30.
20 *Imvo*, 27.4.1909.
21 Union of South Africa, House of Assembly, Annexures, 1910-11, South African National Convention, 1908-09, vol. 3, no. 360, Annexures 101-88: no. 175, Petition of the Becoana Mutual Improvement Association of Thaba Nchu and headmen of the natives and coloured people resident in the district of Thaba Nchu to the South African National Convention, 28.4.1909.
22 In addition to the money collected for Dube and Kambule at the Johannesburg meeting referred to above, see, for example, the list of those who contributed in response to Dube's appeal, *Ilanga*, 30.4.1909.
23 Annual report of the African Political Organisation, 1909 (*Cape Times*, 19.4.1909).

24 CA, GH 26/109, Draft General and Confidential Despatches: Secretary, APO, Cradock branch to Governor, Cape Colony, 5.4.1909 (enclosure to Cape of Good Hope no. 80, Governor to Secretary of State, 26.4.1909); *Imvo*, 20.4.1909; *Indian Opinion*, 13.3.1909; *Izwi*, 16.4.1909.
25 *A.P.O.*, 24.5.1909; *Cape Times*, 17.4.1909.
26 *Cape Times*, 17.4.1909.
27 *Cape Times*, 17.4.1909 and 19.4.1909; *A.P.O.*, 25.5.1909.
28 *Imvo*, 20.4.1909.

Chapter 44: Appeal to the British parliament
1 Minutes of Proceedings with Annexures (Selected) of the South African National Convention held at Durban, Cape Town, Bloemfontein, 12 October, 1908–09: Appendix G, Resolutions and amendments to Draft Act adopted by the various parliaments during the sessions held in April 1909, pp. 345-9.
2 Orange River Colony, 29, Debates in the Legislative Assembly, 30.3.1909–1.4.1909, pp. 12-16; *The Friend*, 31.3.1909.
3 For examples in the first few days of the session, see the speeches of Cronwright-Schreiner, Vosloo, Greer, Searle and Alexander, in *Cape Hansard*, 1909, pp. 20, 22, 25-6, 45-6, 49.
4 *Cape Hansard*, 1909, pp. 8, 29-30, 17-19.
5 Ibid.
6 For example, the speeches by Searle and Alexander, *Cape Hansard*, 1909, pp. 45, 49. Alexander said Schreiner's first speech in the Assembly 'would live for ever in that House'.
7 NLSA, J.X. Merriman papers: Merriman diary, 7.4.1909, 8.4.1909, 12.4.1909, 13.4.1909, 15.4.1909.
8 CA, HA 864, Petitions 1909: no. 6, Petition of delegates to the Native Conference held in King William's Town to consider the Union Draft Act, n.d.; no. 4, Petition of Abdullah Abdurahman and others constituting the general executive of the African Political Organisation, n.d.; no. 7, Petition of the Wynberg Coloured Men's Political Organisation, n.d.
9 CA, HA 901, Letters Received: M.J. Fredericks to the Speaker, House of Assembly, 2.4.1909; CA, HA 913, Letter Book: no. 31, E. Kilpin to general secretary, APO, 2.4.1909.
10 O. Schreiner to W.P. Schreiner, 8.4.1909, cited in Z. Friedlander (ed.), *Until the heart*

changes: A garland for Olive Schreiner (Cape Town, 1967), pp. 109-10.

11 CO 879/100, African (South) no. 927, Confidential, South Africa, Further correspondence (1909) relating to affairs in South Africa: no. 78 (Cape of Good Hope, Confidential Parliamentary, no. 4), Governor to Secretary of State, 19.4.1909, pp. 141-3.

12 *The Argus*, 14.4.1909.

13 House of Assembly Annexures, vol. 3, no. 360, Annexures 101-88: no. 175.

14 NLSA, J.X. Merriman papers, 1902, no. 87: J.A. Sishuba to Merriman, 16.9.1902; J.A. Sishuba to the editor, *Imvo*, 21.10.1907, *Imvo*, 29.10.1907; F.S. Malan to J.A. Sishuba, 15.10.1907, *Imvo*, 29.10.1907.

15 House of Assembly Annexures, vol. 3, no. 360, Annexures 101-88: no. 174, M.J. Fredericks to National Convention, 3.5.1909 (enclosing list of APO resolutions, 13–17.4.1909); no. 167, A. Auret and F.H. Brutus to National Convention, 8.3.1909; no. 168, Petition of the Wynberg Coloured Men's Political Organisation to the National Convention, 29.4.1909.

16 Minutes, pp. 250, 256-7, 262-3.

17 Thompson, *Unification*, pp. 362-72.

18 Minutes, Appendix I, Resolutions adopted by the various parliaments approving of the Draft Act as well as addresses to the King for the authorisation of the proposed Union, pp. 355-7.

19 *Cape Hansard*, 1909, p. 172.

20 Thompson, *Unification*, pp. 389, 393.

21 *Cape Hansard*, 1909, pp. 160-2.

22 Ibid., pp. 163-4.

23 Ibid., p. 172.

24 Ibid.

25 NA, GH 1320, Copies of Secret Telegrams Despatched to Secretary of State, 7.2.1907–26.5.1910: Governor to Secretary of State, 27.5.1909, pp. 155-6.

26 Cd 5099, Correspondence respecting an Act for a Referendum in Natal on the Draft South Africa Union Act: Colony of Natal, Referendum Act, 1909, Return showing the result of the polling in each electoral district and the Colony as a whole, 12.6.1909, p. 8.

27 Minutes, Appendix I, pp. 355, 357.

28 NLSA, W.P. Schreiner papers, 1909, nos. 1446 and 1435: A. Abdurahman to W.P. Schreiner, 11.5.1909 and D.R. Forsyth to W.P. Schreiner, 22.4.1909 (enclosing Rev. R. Balmforth to D.R. Forsyth, 15.4.1909).

29 *A.P.O.*, 5.6.1909 (Appeal to Schreiner), p. 11; A. Abdurahman and five members of APO executive to High Commissioner, 16.6.1909 (cited in *A.P.O.*, 19.6.1909, p. 10); NLSA, W.P. Schreiner papers, 1909, no. 1424A: Resumé of the proceedings of the South African Native Congresses and the South African Native Convention, n.d., p. 4.; no. 1472: J. Mocher and J.T. Mocher to W.P. Schreiner, 21.6.1909; no. 1475: Typed copy of a resolution of the Transvaal Native Congress, 24.6.1909, signed J.M. Makhothe; no. 1477A: Newspaper cuttings, King William's Town, Cape Native Convention, n.d., p. 6; no. 1463: Telegram Paramount Chief of Basutoland to W.P. Schreiner, 14.6.1909; no. 1458 and 1561: Rev. E. Jacottet to W.P. Schreiner, 5.6.1909 and 8.6.1909, n.p.; no. 1487, S.M. Phamotse to W.P. Schreiner, 13.7.1909; UCT, W.P. Schreiner papers, BC 112, file 11 (6.1): W.P. Letseleba and Z. More to W.P. Schreiner, 16.7.1909; file 12 (6.5): Telegram, J.T. Jabavu to W.P. Schreiner, 16.6.1909.

30 NLSA, W.P. Schreiner papers, 1909, no. 1448: 'An Appeal to the Parliament and Government of Great Britain and Ireland', 14.5.1909.

31 Ibid.

32 UCT, W.P. Schreiner papers, BC 112, file 11 (7.1): C.W. Dilke to W.P. Schreiner, 24.5.1909.; file 12 (10.1): Ramsay MacDonald to W.P. Schreiner, 16.6.1909.

33 UCT, W.P. Schreiner papers, BC 112, file 11 (7.1): C.W. Dilke to W.P. Schreiner, 24.5.1909.

34 NLSA, De Villiers papers, file 2, box 6, Correspondence re South African National Convention and South Africa Act, 1908–11: J.X. Merriman to J.H. de Villiers, 10.6.1909.

35 CA, GH 26/109, Draft General and Confidential to Secretary of State, London: Confidential memorandum from J.X. Merriman to Sir W. Hely-Hutchinson, 16.6.1909 (enclosure to Cape of Good Hope, no. 131, Sir W. Hely-Hutchinson to Earl of Crewe, 16.6.1909).

36 Ibid.

37 Ibid.

38 NLSA, J.X. Merriman papers, 1909, no. 307: Copy of telegram, Governor to Secretary of State, 28.6.1909 (enclosure to Sir W. Hely-Hutchinson to J.X. Merriman, 29.6.1909).

39 CA, GH 26/109, Draft General and Confidential to Secretary of State, London: Confidential memorandum from J.X. Merriman to Sir W. Hely-Hutchinson, 16.6.1909 (enclosure to Cape of Good Hope, no. 131, Sir W. Hely-Hutchinson to Earl of Crewe, 16.6.1909).

40 W.P. Schreiner to Sir Bisset Berry, 9.6.1909, *Queenstown Daily Representative and Free Press*, 25.6.1909.

41 Ibid.; UCT, W.P. Schreiner papers, BC 112, file 11 (2.8): Sir Bisset Berry to W.P. Schreiner, 26.6.1909.

42 UCT, W.P. Schreiner papers, BC 112, file 11 (2.14): H. Myoli and seven others to W.P. Schreiner, 1.7.1909.

Chapter 45: Preparations for the delegation to England

1 NLSA, W.P. Schreiner papers, 1909, no. 1424A, p. 4; OFSA, G113, file no. 461/6: J. Mocher to Sir H. Goold-Adams, 21.6.1909, p. 160; *Imvo*, 6.7.1909.

2 OFSA, Gl 13, file no. 461/6: J. Mocher to Sir H. Goold-Adams, 21.6.1909, p. 160. See, for example, *A.P.O.*, 5.6.1909, p. 11 and 19.6.1909, p. 8; *Imvo*, 15.6.1909.

3 A.K. Soga to the editor, *Imvo*, 11.10.1910.

4 NA, SNA 1/1/435, Letters Received, file no. 1931/09: Telegram, W.B. Rubusana to J.L. Dube, 12.6.1909.

5 Hughes, *First president*, pp. 147-54.

6 Ibid.

7 TA, SNA 429, General Correspondence, file no. 1922/09: W.P. Letseleba to Minister of Native Affairs, 1.7.1909, p. 62; TA, PM 52, file no. 106/6/1909, Minister of Native Affairs schedules: Prime Minister's minute no. 35, J. de Villiers to Administrator, 25.6.1909.

8 TA, HC 133, Unclassified file no. 172, Natives under Union: Telegram, no. 1, Administrator to Secretary of State, 26.7.1909; TA, SNA 429, General Correspondence, file no. 1922/09: Native Commissioner, Rustenburg to SNA, 17.8.1909, p. 77; Z. More to SNA, 13.8.1909, p. 76.

9 TA, SNA 433, General Correspondence, file no. 2418/09: Resolutions of the Transvaal Native Congress annual conference, 24.6.1909 (enclosure to J.M. Makhothe to Native Commissioner, Central Division, 12.7.1909), pp. 121-4. For details of the conference, see also *Imvo*, 20.7.1909, and

NLSA, W.P. Schreiner papers, 1909, no. 1475: Typed copy of a resolution of the Transvaal Native Congress, 24.6.1909, Johannesburg.

10 *Imvo*, 11.5.1909.

11 *Imvo*, 18.5.1909.

12 *Imvo*, 15.6.1909; UCT, W.P. Schreiner papers, BC 112, file 12(6.5): Telegram, J.T. Jabavu to W.P. Schreiner, 16.6.1909.

13 See, for example, the advertisement headed 'Abatunywa Pesheya', placed by Jabavu in the Xhosa columns of *Imvo*, 22.6.1909, 29.6.1909 and 6.7.1909.

14 Jabavu, *The life of John Tengo Jabavu*, pp. 49-50.

15 *Imvo*, 6.7.1909; 22.6.1909.

16 Ibid.

17 *Cape Times*, 28.5.1909; *Imvo*, 1.6.1909.

18 Cory Library, Sprigg Collection, MS 10 108, W.B. Rubusana to Sir J. Gordon Sprigg, 29.6.1909.

19 NLSA, W.P. Schreiner papers, 1909, nos. 1463 and 1465: Paramount Chief, Basutoland to W.P. Schreiner, 14.6.1909 and 15.6.1909; no. 1487: S.M. Phamotse to W.P. Schreiner, 13.7.1909; nos. 1458, 1461 and 1470: Rev. E. Jacottet to W.P. Schreiner, 5.6.1909, 8.6.1909 and 18.6.1909; Historical Papers, Witwatersrand University Library, Lagden papers, D 1, Correspondence 1881–1908: E. Jacottet to Acting Resident Commissioner, Maseru, 29.1.1909, and E. Jacottet to Sir G. Lagden, 13.2.1909.

20 NLSA, W.P. Schreiner papers, 1909, F 85: W.P. Schreiner to Paramount Chief of Basutoland, 14.6.1909. See also T. Couzens, *Murder at Morija* (Johannesburg, 2003), pp. 304-11.

21 CO 879/100, African (South) no. 927: no. 143, J. Gerrans to Earl of Crewe, 22.7.1909 (enclosing Chief Bathoen to J. Gerrans, 18.2.1909, and Sebele Sechele and three others to J. Gerrans, 24.3.1909), pp. 254-5.

22 Transkeian Territories General Council, Proceedings and Reports of Select Committees at the Session of 1909, Matters tabled for discussion, p. iv.

23 UCT, Stanford papers, BC 293, D 39: Stanford diary, 8.3.1909, p. 29.

24 Transkeian Territories General Council, Proceedings and Reports of Select Committees at the session of 1909, Report of the Select Committee on the Draft South African Act, p. lxix.

25 CAD, NA 237, Native Affairs 1910, file no.
    1/1910/F562: Dalindyebo and eleven others
    to Prime Minister, Cape Colony, 21.6.1909
    (enclosing petition from the Transkeian
    Territories General Council to Sir Walter
    Hely-Hutchinson, n.d.).
26 A2-09, Report of the Select Committee on
    Native Affairs, Appendix C, Memorandum
    from the SNA relating to local government
    in native areas in the Transkeian Territories
    and in the Colony proper, p. xxix.
27 A.P.O., 19.6.1909, p. 7.
28 NLSA, W.P. Schreiner papers, 1909, no.
    1477: Resumé of (APO) proceedings in
    connection with the proposed South African
    Union, n.d.
29 A.P.O., 19.6.1909, p. 7.
30 A.P.O., 24.5.1909, pp. 4-5.
31 NLSA, W.P. Schreiner papers, 1909, no.
    1477.
32 For example, A.P.O., 5.6.1909, p. 11;
    19.6.1909, p. 3; 3.7.1909, p. 9; CO
    879/100, African (South) no. 129, (no.
    410), High Commissioner to Secretary of
    State, 23.6.1909 (enclosure 2 to no. 129,
    A. Abdurahman and four others to High
    Commissioner, 16.6.1909), pp. 239-40;
    no. 137, (no. 429), High Commissioner to
    Secretary of State, 30.6.1909, p. 251.
33 F.Z.S. Peregrino to the editor, Eastern
    Province Herald, 16.7. 1909; J. Tobin to the
    editor, Eastern Province Herald, 20.7.1909.
34 Cape Times, 22.6.1909.
35 Lord Crewe to J.H. Hofmeyr, n.d., cited in
    'The Stone's Startling Statements', A.P.O.,
    9.10.1909.
36 Indian Opinion, 29.5.1909.
37 Naledi, 3.7.1908.
38 Indian Opinion, 18.4.1908.
39 Izwi, 5.5.1908.
40 Indian Opinion, 12.9.1908, p. 419;
    17.10.1908; 13.2.1909, pp. 69-76.
41 Indian Opinion, 19.6.1909, p. 270 and
    26.6.1909, p. 275.
42 Indian Opinion, 26.9.1909, p. 275.
43 'A short statement of the grievances of
    the British Indians in Natal by the Natal
    Delegation', by A. Caadir, A. Bayat, H.M.
    Badat and M.C. Anglia, 10.8.1909, Indian
    Opinion, 18.9.1909, pp. 403-4.
44 Indian Opinion, 26.9.1909, p. 278.
45 The Friend, 23.6.1909; M.K. Gandhi,
    Satyagraha in South Africa (Ahmedabad,
    1928), p. 349.
46 South African News, 24.6.1909; Cape
    Times, 6.3.1909; NLSA, W.P. Schreiner
    papers, 1909, no. 1490: H. Stakesby-
    Lewis to W.P. Schreiner (enclosing Dr
    Andrew Murray's letter about the draft
    constitution), 14.7.1909. A collection of
    Olive Schreiner's articles on the question
    of Union was published in book form as
    Closer Union (London, 1909).
47 South African News, 24.6.1909.
48 Indian Opinion, 3.7.1909, p. 286.

Chapter 46: The Coloured and Native Delegation in London, July 1909

1   The Times, 17.7.1909.
2   NLSA, W.P. Schreiner papers, 1909, nos.
    1484 and 1492: Travers Buxton to W.P.
    Schreiner, 10.7.1909 and 15.7.1909; no.
    1518: R. Wardlaw Thompson to W.P.
    Schreiner, 29.7.1909; no. 1482: A.F. Fox,
    South African Native Races Committee
    to W.P. Schreiner, 7.7.1909; no. 1513: J.
    Keir Hardie to W.P. Schreiner, 29.7.1909;
    no. 1503: J.H. Wilson to W.P. Schreiner,
    23.7.1909 (enclosing printed invitation
    signed by Thos. Burt and six others, July
    1909); TA, HC 133, Unclassified, file no.
    172, Natives under Union, Delegation to
    England: A.F. Fox to Earl of Selborne,
    26.7. 1906; UCT, W.P. Schreiner
    papers, BC 112, file 11: C.W. Dilke
    to W.P. Schreiner, 6.7.1909, 7.7.1909
    and 23.7.1909; and Lord Courtney to
    W.P. Schreiner, 26.7.1909; Cape Times,
    9.7.1909.
3   This information was gleaned from
    the letterheads and addresses on the
    correspondence of the delegates.
4   Killingray, 'Significant black South Africans
    in Britain', n.p.; Jabavu: The life of John
    Tengo Jabavu, p. 112.
5   UCT, W.P. Schreiner papers, BC 112, file 12
    (3.1-3.2): M.K. Gandhi to W.P. Schreiner,
    24.7.1909 and 17.8.1909. See also The
    State, Sept. 1909, p. 257, and the cartoon
    of Schreiner and Gandhi in the Rand Daily
    Mail, 4.7.1909.
6   Hughes, First president, pp. 151-3.
7   Ibid.
8   OFSA, G 21, file no. a/35/13: Copy, Matt.
    J. Fredericks to Colonial Office, 11.8.1909.
9   A. Abdurahman to APO executive
    29.7.1909, A.P.O., 11.9.1909; NLSA,
    W.P. Schreiner papers, 1909, no. 1522: A.
    Abdurahman to W.P. Schreiner, 2.8.1909.
10 NLSA, W.P. Schreiner papers, 1909, nos.

1517 and 1522: Lionel Crewe to W.P. Schreiner, 29.7.1909 and A. Abdurahman to W.P. Schreiner, 2.8.1909.

11 A. Abdurahman to APO executive, 29.7.1909, *A.P.O.*, 11.9.1909.

12 NLSA, W.P. Schreiner papers, 1909, no. 1531: R.W. Msimang to W.P. Schreiner, 10.8.1909; *The Times*, 28.7.1909; Mapikela's statement in *Umteteli wa Bantu*, 18.7.1936, p. 2; *Imvo*, 9.11.1909.

13 For details of his stay in Britain, see C. Higgs, *The ghost of equality: The public lives of D.D.T. Jabavu of South Africa, 1885–1959* (Cape Town, 1997), pp. 16-23.

14 Killingray, 'Significant black South Africans in Britain', n.p.; Gerhart and Karis, *From protest to challenge*, 4 (Political profiles, 1882–1964), p. 96.

15 'Funeral of Mr R.W. Msimang', *Umteteli wa Bantu*, 16 December 1935, p. 3; Killingray, 'Significant black South Africans in Britain', n.p.

16 C. Saunders, 'Pixley Seme: Towards a biography', *South African Historical Journal*, 25 (1991), p. 204.

17 Killingray, 'Significant black South Africans in Britain', n.p.

18 For more details, see Saunders, 'Pixley Seme' and Killingray, 'Significant black South Africans in Britain'.

19 *The Times*, 5.7.1909.

20 *The Times*, 6.7.1909.

21 NLSA, W.P. Schreiner papers, 1909, no. 1500: W.P. Schreiner, W.B. Rubusana, T. Mapikela, A. Abdurahman, D.J. Lenders and Matt. J. Fredericks (South African Coloured and Native Delegation, 1909) to 'Sir', 21.7.1909; A. Abdurahman to APO executive, Cape Town, 29.7.1909, *A.P.O.*, 11.9.1909.

22 UCT, W.P. Schreiner papers, BC 112, file 11 (9.3): Lionel Earle to W.P. Schreiner, 8.7.1909; *Cape Times*, 9.7.1909.

23 E.A. Walker, *W.P. Schreiner* (Oxford, 1937), pp. 327-8.

24 UCT, W.P. Schreiner papers, BC 112, file 12 (19.1–19.6): W.T. Stead to W.P. Schreiner, 10.7.1909, 14.7.1909, 20.7.1909, 21.7.1909, 26.7.1909, 18.8.1909; W.T. Stead to the editor, *The Times*, 18.8.1909; *Imvo*, 24.8.1909.

25 *The Times*, 28.6.1909 (Jameson); 5.7.1909 (De Villiers); 12.7.1909 (Sauer and Merriman).

26 A. Abdurahman to APO executive,

29.7.1909, *A.P.O.*, 11.9.1909.

27 CO 879/102, South Africa, no. 933, secret 1909, July 20 and 21, Draft South Africa Union Act: South Africa Bill, Conference between delegates from South Africa and the Secretary of State for the Colonies, pp. 1-6.

28 NLSA, W.P. Schreiner papers, 1909, no. 1502: Holograph notes by W.P. Schreiner, 22.7.1909; *The Times*, 23.7.1909.

29 *The Times*, 23.7.1909; 28.7.1909; 5.8.1909.

30 *The State*, Sept. 1909, p. 257.

31 A. Abdurahman to APO executive, 29.7.1909, *A.P.O.*, 11.9.1909.

32 *The Times*, 28.7.1909.

33 Ibid.

34 W.P. Schreiner to the editor, *The Times*, 27.7.1909.

35 *A.P.O.*, 14.8.1909.

36 UCT, W.P. Schreiner papers, BC 112, file 12(18): W.B. Rubusana to W.P. Schreiner, 23.7.1909; A. Abdurahman to APO executive, 29.7.1909, *A.P.O.*, 11.9.1909.

37 UCT, W.P. Schreiner papers, BC 112, file 11: C.W. Dilke to W.P. Schreiner, 5.8.1909, 6.8.1909, 12.8.1909, 17.8.1909, 18.8.1909; NLSA, W.P. Schreiner papers, 1909, no. 1529: J. Keir Hardie to W.P. Schreiner, 8.8.1909; Walker, *W.P. Schreiner*, p. 330.

38 *The Times*, 6.8.1909.

39 UCT, W.P. Schreiner papers, BC 112, file 13: Newspaper cuttings, *The Standard*, 10.8.1909; *Imvo*, 17.8.1909.

40 Delegate report, J.T. Jabavu, London, 7.8.1909, *Imvo*, 31.8.1909; UCT, W.P. Schreiner papers, BC 112, file 11 (9.1): Lionel Earle to W.P. Schreiner, 2.8.1909.

41 CO 879/106, African (South) no. 934, Confidential, Telegrams relating to affairs in South Africa 1909: no. 168, Telegram, Officer Administering the Government of Natal to Secretary of State, 2.8.1909 (enclosing telegram, Natal Native Congress to Secretary of State, 2.8.1909), p. 65.

42 NLSA, W.P. Schreiner papers, 1909, no. 1538: W. Segal to W.P. Schreiner, 19.8.1909.

43 J.T. Jabavu to the editor, *The Times*, 19.8.1909.

44 House of Commons, Report of the Speeches on the South Africa Bill, 16 and 19 August, 1909 (reprint from the official report of 'The Parliamentary Debates'), p. 116.

45 Thompson, *Unification*, pp. 425-32. For full details of the debate in the Commons, see House of Commons, Report of the Speeches on the South Africa Bill, 16 and 19 August, 1909 (reprint from the official report of 'The Parliamentary Debates'), pp. 1-118.

46 CO 879/100, African (South), no. 161, Earl of Crewe to J.X. Merriman, 25.8.1909 (and enclosures), p. 276.

47 *The Times*, 2.8.1909.

Chapter 47: Birth of the new South Africa, May 1910

1 *Imvo*, 31.8.1909.
2 *Christian Express*, 1.10.1909.
3 *Imvo*, 6.7.1909.
4 *A.P.O.*, 25.9.1909.
5 *A.P.O.*, 9.10.1909, pp. 5-6.
6 *Imvo*, 25.1.1910.
7 UCT, W.P. Schreiner papers, BC 112, file 12(6.3): J.T. Jabavu to W.P. Schreiner, 30.8.1909; NLSA, W. P. Schreiner papers, 1909, no. 1554: J.T. Jabavu to W.P. Schreiner, 24.9.1909; *Imvo*, 14.12.1909.
8 *A.P.O.*, 23.10.1909, p. 4.
9 *Imvo*, 14.12.1909.
10 NLSA, W. P. Schreiner papers, 1909, no. 1583: T.M. Mapikela to W.P. Schreiner, 19.11.1909.
11 *A.P.O.*, 25.9.1909, p. 8; OFSA, CO 908, Colonial Secretary's Correspondence, file no. 826/16: Handwritten departmental report for the Orange River Colony Colonial Secretary, 29.11.1909; *Imvo*, 14.12.1909.
12 *Imvo*, 14.12.1909.
13 *A.P.O.*, 23.10.1909, pp. 9; 29.1.1910, p. 7.
14 *A.P.O.*, 25.9.1910, p. 7; 29.1.1910, p. 6.
15 *A.P.O.*, 9.10.1909, p. 5.
16 NLSA, W. P. Schreiner papers, 1909, no. 1583: T.M. Mapikela to W.P. Schreiner, 19.11.1909.
17 NLSA, W. P. Schreiner papers, 1909, no. 1554: J.T. Jabavu to W.P. Schreiner, 24.9.1909; UCT, W.P. Schreiner papers, BC 112, file 12 (6.1): J.T. Jabavu to W.P. Schreiner, 31.8.1909.
18 See, for example, the speeches by Jabavu to the New Reform Club in London (*A.P.O.*, 4.12.1909, p. 8) and by Schreiner when the delegates arrived back in Cape Town (*A.P.O.*, 25.9.1909, p. 7).
19 *Umteteli wa Bantu*, 18.7.1936, p. 2.
20 OFSA, CO 917, Colonial Secretary's Correspondence, file no. 933/7: Handwritten minute, Acting Colonial Secretary, 11.10.1909; Handwritten minute, A. Fischer to Under-Colonial Secretary, 11.10.1909.
21 *The Friend*, 21.10.1909.
22 OFSA, CO 908, Colonial Secretary's Correspondence, file no. 826/16: Handwritten departmental report for the Orange River Colony Colonial Secretary, 29.11.1909.
23 NLSA, W. P. Schreiner papers, 1909, no. 1486: D.W. Drew to W.P. Schreiner, 12.7.1909.
24 OFSA, CO 908, Colonial Secretary's Correspondence, file no. 826/16: Handwritten departmental report for the Orange River Colony Colonial Secretary, 29.11.1909; CO 917, Colonial Secretary's Correspondence, file no. 933/7: Handwritten minute, Acting Colonial Secretary, 11.10.1909; Handwritten minute, A. Fischer to Under-Colonial Secretary, 11.10.1909.
25 NLSA, W. P. Schreiner papers, 1909, no.1583: T.M. Mapikela to W.P. Schreiner, 19.11.1909.
26 OFSA, G1 10, file no. 444/9: W.B. Rubusana, J. Mocher and T.M. Mapikela to Sir H. Goold-Adams, 29.11.1909 (enclosing W.B. Rubusana, J. Mocher and T.M. Mapikela to Colonial Secretary, 29.11.1909), pp. 157-61.
27 *Imvo*, 14.12.1909; OFSA, Gl 10, file no. 444/0: W.B. Rubusana and T.M. Mapikela to Sir H. Goold-Adams, 18.12.1909, pp. 163-4.
28 OFSA, CO 988, Colonial Secretary's Correspondence, file no. 1905/1: 'Isaziso se Konvenshoni! Any'Amatole!', signed J. Makgothi, Feb. 1910 (plus English translation); J. Makgothi to Colonial Secretary, 22.3.1910.
29 *The Friend*, 25.3.1910.
30 Dube wrote regular reports, headed 'Lapho Kuhamba Kona u Mafuku-zela', about his travels. See, for example, *Ilanga*, 29.4.1910.
31 *Imvo*, 1.3.1910.
32 *The Friend*, 25.3.1910.
33 Historical Papers, Witwatersrand University Library, Silas T. Molema and Solomon T. Plaatje papers, Tshidi Baralong Tribal Affairs, Cc9 African National Congress: no. 1118/F374, E. Dower to South African Native Convention, 2.2.1911; *Pretoria News*, 9.4.1910.

34 'Native Convention' and 'Natives and Union, Organisation', *Pretoria News*, 9.4.1910.

35 *A.P.O.*, 9.4.1910, p. 8 and 21.5.1910, p. 9.

36 *Imvo*, 29.3.1910.

37 *Pretoria News*, 9.4.1910.

38 CAD, GG 1158, file no. 50/15: SNA, Transvaal to private secretary, Administrator, Transvaal 23.5.1910.

39 *Imvo*, 14.6.1910.

40 Thompson, *Unification*, pp. 448-9.

41 *Imvo*, 21.12.1909; TA, SNA 433, General Correspondence, file no. 1922/09: Resolutions of the Transvaal Native Congress Annual Conference, 24.6.1909 (enclosure to J.M. Makhothe to Native Commissioner, Central Division, 12.7.1909), pp. 121-4; Resolutions of meeting of Baralongs in Mafeking, 1.1.1910, *Mafeking Mail*, 5.1.1910.

42 *Imvo*, 28.12.1909.

43 *Ilanga*, 28.1.1910.

44 Thompson, *Unification*, pp. 450-2.

45 *Imvo*, 5.4.1910.

46 Thompson, *Unification*, pp. 454-5.

47 *Imvo*, 31.5.1910.

48 NLSA, J.X. Merriman papers, 1910, no. 499: J.T. Jabavu to J.X. Merriman, 23.5.1910.

49 NLSA, J.X. Merriman papers, 1910, no. 241: H.R. Ngcayiya to J.X. Merriman, 9.6.1910.

50 NLSA, J.X. Merriman papers, 1910, nos. 107 and 318: J.A. Sishuba to J.X. Merriman, 21.5.1910 and 6.7.1910.

51 Cory Library, Unclassified Rubusana papers, Letter Book: W.B. Rubusana to L. Botha, 6.6.1910.

52 CO 879/106, Africa (South) no. 952, Confidential, Telegrams relating to affairs in South Africa 1910: no. 57, Telegram, Governor-General, South Africa to Secretary of State, 1.6.1910, p. 20. See also NLSA, J.X. Merriman papers, 1910, no. 162: General Scobell to J.X. Merriman, 27.5.1910 (enclosing, telegram, Administrator to Lord Gladstone, 27.5.1910).

53 NLSA, J.X. Merriman papers, 1910, no. 20: H. Burton to J.X. Merriman, 11.2.1909.

54 Telegram, Koba to Burton, 1.6.1910 and telegram Burton to Koba, 1.6.1910, in *Imvo*, 14.6.1910.

55 *Imvo*, 25.10.1910.

56 *Imvo*, 28.6.1910.

57 *Imvo*, 5.7.1910; *Tsala ea Becoana*, 9.7.1910 and 8.10.1910.

58 *Imvo*, 7.6.1910.

59 *Imvo*, 5.7.1910; *Tsala ea Becoana*, 9.7.1910.

60 CAD, GG 1158, file no. 50/3: Minute no. 11, Ministers to Governor-General, 31.5.1910.

61 *Ilanga*, 3.6.1910; 2.9.1910; CAD, NA 288, file no. 578/1911/F727, Release of Dinuzulu: H. Colenso to L. Botha, 30.5.1910 and W.P. Schreiner to L. Botha, 30.5.1910.

62 Thompson, *Unification*, pp. 459-60.

63 See the reports of the reactions of Africans to Union by local government officials in U17-11, BBNA 1910, pp. 325-43.

64 *A.P.O.*, 4.6.1910, p. 9; see also the various branch reports in the *A.P.O.*, 18.6.1910, pp. 2-3, 5-6.

65 *A.P.O.*, 26.2.1910, p. 9; see also A. Abdurahman, 'Address to the Coloured People of South Africa', *A.P.O.*, 4.6.1910, p. 8.

66 *Imvo*, 17.5.1910.

67 Transkei Territories General Council Proceedings 1910, p. 87.

68 *A.P.O.*, 7.5.1910, p. 9.

69 CAD, GG 50, file no. 3/100 A: Telegram, Bud Mbelle to Lord Gladstone, 16.5.1910; Telegram, Mapikela. to Lord Gladstone, 16.5.1910; CAD, GG 1158, file no. 50/15: NA 1646/10/3491/10, SNA, Transvaal to private secretary, Administrator, Transvaal, 23.5.1910 (enclosing copy of an address from Transvaal Native Organisation to Viscount Gladstone, n.d.).

70 CAD, GG 1158, file no. 50/8: Minute no. 264, Ministers to Governor, 27.7.1910 (enclosing address from I.G. Sishuba and four others on behalf of Ethiopian Church of South Africa to Viscount Gladstone, n.d.).

71 CAD, GG 1158, file no. 50/8: Handwritten minute, H.J.S. to Governor-General, 3.8.1910; file no. 50/34: Handwritten minute, H.J.S. to Governor-General, 29.11.1910 and H.R. Ngcayiya to Lord Gladstone, 24.11.1910.

Chapter 48: Dr Rubusana makes history

1 Thompson, *Unification*, p. 460.

2 *A.P.O.*, 2.7.1910, p. 6.

3 Ibid.

4   *Territorial News*, 27.8.1910; A.K. Soga to the editor, *Imvo*, 11.10.1910.
5   See the editorials in *Imvo*, 9.8.1910–13.9.1910.
6   *Imvo*, 16.8.1910.
7   *Imvo*, 28.6.1910; 5.7.1910; 23.8.1910.
8   *A.P.O.*, 24.9.1910, p. 5.
9   *A.P.O.*, 2.7.1910, p. 6; 10.9.1910, p. 5; 24.9.1910, p. 5.
10 A.K. Soga to the editor, *Imvo*, 11.10.1910.
11 *Territorial News*, 27.8.1910.
12 B. Willan, 'The role of Solomon T. Plaatje (1876–1932) in South African society' (PhD, University of London, 1979), p. 101.
13 See Thompson, *Unification*, pp. 471-9 for a summary of the general election.
14 *Daily Dispatch*, 16.9.1910.
15 *Daily Dispatch*, 17.9.1910; *Imvo*, 20.9.1910.
16 *Daily Dispatch*, 21.9.1910.
17 NLSA, W.P. Schreiner papers, 1910, no. 1632: Telegram, T.L. Schreiner to W.P. Schreiner, 4.8.1910.
18 NLSA, W.P. Schreiner papers, 1910, J 16: Telegram, W.P. Schreiner to T.L. Schreiner, 5.8.1910.
19 A.K. Soga to the editor, *Imvo*, n.d.
20 *Imvo*, 23.8.1910.
21 *Imvo*, 27.9.1910.
22 *Imvo*, 30.8.1910; *Tsala ea Becoana*, 27.8.1910.
23 *A.P.O.*, 9.4.1910, p. 3.
24 *Territorial News*, 27.8.1910.
25 *Territorial News*, 27.8.1910; 3.9.1910.
26 Gray Election Committee to W. Kilfoil, Engcobo, and E. Kilfoil to Gray Election Committee, *Territorial News*, 3.9.1910.
27 *Imvo*, 16.8.1910.
28 *The Province of the Cape of Good Hope Official Gazette*, 26.7.1910, p. 459.
29 *Territorial News*, 10.9.1910.
30 See *Imvo*, 13.9.1910.
31 *Imvo*, 6.9.1910 and 13.9.1910.
32 *Imvo*, 6.9.1910.
33 *The Province of the Cape of Good Hope Official Gazette*, 7.10.1910, p. 961.
34 *Territorial News*, 24.9.1910.
35 *Ilanga*, 28.10.1908.
36 *Tsala ea Becoana*, 1.10.1910; *A.P.O.*, 24.9.1910.
37 *Imvo*, 27.9.1910.
38 A.K. Soga to the editor, *Imvo*, 11.10.1910.
39 R.W. Rose-Innes to the editor, *Daily Dispatch*, cited in *Imvo*, 20.12.1910). Rose-Innes was shocked that Rubusana could now freely use first-class railway facilities, including toilets, and expressed the fear that this would lead to a new era of the professional African politician.
40 *Ilanga*, 28.10.1908.
41 Thompson, *Unification*, pp. 478-9.
42 CAD, GG 820, file no. 23/43: Dr Rubusana to Lord Crewe, 5.4.1910.
43 *A.P.O.*, 23.4.1910, p. 7; CAD, GG 820, file no. 23/47: N.R. Veldsman to Viscount Gladstone, 26.5.1910.
44 CAD, GG 820, file no. 23/47: N.R. Veldsman to Viscount Gladstone, 23.5.1910; file no. 23/51: N.R. Veldsman to Viscount Gladstone, 1.6.1910.
45 NLSA, J.X. Merriman papers, 1910, nos. 144 and 261: W.P. Schreiner to J.X. Merriman, 26.5.1910 and 14.6.1910; Walker, *W.P. Schreiner*, p. 336.
46 *A.P.O.*, 21.5.1910.
47 CAD, GG 821, file no. 23/82: J.T. Jabavu to Viscount Gladstone, 16.9.1910.
48 CAD, GG 821, file no. 23/88: J.T. Jabavu to Lord Gladstone, 20.9.1910.
49 CAD, GG 821, file no. 23/83: J. Mocher, N.J. Daly and T.M. Mapikela to Lord Gladstone, 13.9.1910; file no. 23/61: J.A. Sishuba to Governor-General-in-Council, 9.8.1910; CAD, GG 820, file no. 23/46: S. Pieterse to Viscount Gladstone, 11.5.1910; G. Bukkuis and 115 others to Governor-General-in-Council, n.d.; Copy of petitions signed by 250 people to Governor-General-in-Council, n.d.; CAD, GG 821, file no. 23/82: D.J. Lenders and nine others to Viscount Gladstone, 13.9.1910 (and annotations); S. Plaatje to Governor-General, 13.9.1910; CAD, GG 1158, file no. 50/25: S.M. Makgatho, J.G. Kaiyana, J.M. Makhothe, E.K. Chocke and 21 others to Viscount Gladstone, n.d.
50 CAD, GG 821, file no. 23/100: Minute no. 1227, Ministers to Governor-General, 13.10.1910.
51 See, for example, *Imvo*, 18.10.1910.
52 Quoted in Walker, *W.P. Schreiner*, p. 337.
53 *Imvo*, 18.10.1910.
54 *A.P.O.*, 22.10.1910, p. 7.

Chapter 49: Attempts to cement unity, 1910–1911

1   Walshe, *The rise of African nationalism*, pp. 30-1.
2   See, for example, *Imvo*, 19.12.1911 (Editorial and 'A Native Government

NOTES

Sympathiser' to the editor, 3.11.1911);
NLSA, W.P. Schreiner papers, 1912,
nos 2023, 2034, 2037 and 2057: T.M.
Mapikela to W.P. Schreiner, 29.5.1912;
B.M. Mlamleli to W.P. Schreiner, 30.5.1912;
Copy, T.M. Mapikela to Acting Secretary
for Justice, 16.6.1912 and B.L. Mlamleli to
W.P. Schreiner, 12.8.1912.

3 McCracken, *The Cape Parliament*, p. 81;
Walshe, *The rise of African nationalism*,
p. 240.
4 Walker, *W.P. Schreiner*, pp. 336, 338.
5 Union of South Africa, Province of the Cape
of Good Hope, Minutes and Ordinances
of the First Session of the First Provincial
Council, for example, pp. xii, 9, 11-12, 17,
39, 69, 98.
6 The Schreiner and Rubusana papers
provide ample evidence of representations
made by the two men on behalf of Africans.
See Cory Library, Unclassified Rubusana
papers, W.B. Rubusana to E. Dower,
29.11.1910; W.B. Rubusana to H. Burton,
30.12.1911; W.B. Rubusana to Mayor and
members of the Town Council of Adelaide,
Cape, 29.2.1912; SNA to W.B. Rubusana,
9.10.1912.
7 Odendaal, *Vukani Bantu!*, pp. 252-3.
8 See the full-page, two-column notices in
Tsala ea Becoana, 9, 16, 23 and 30.7.1910;
and the notice issued by Jeremiah Makgothi
in *Tsala ea Becoana*, 16.4.1911 and *Imvo*,
18.4.1911.
9 *Ilanga*, 2.6.1911.
10 See the profile of Kunene in Skota, *The
African yearly register*, p. 30.
11 *Ilanga*, 2.6.1911.
12 *Imvo*, 5.9.1911. Early in 1911, Seme also
wrote a glowing biographical profile of
the SANC president, W.B. Rubusana, in
which he criticised A.K. Soga for attacking
Rubusana when he stood as a candidate
for the Cape Provincial Council. See *Imvo*,
24.1.1911.
13 Quoted in Nauriya, 'Gandhi and the
founders of the ANC' (draft paper).
14 *Ilanga*, 2.6.1911.
15 Nauriya, 'Gandhi and the founders of the
ANC', p. 13.
16 Ibid.
17 *Imvo*, 5.9.1911; Historical Papers,
Witwatersrand University Library, Silas T.
Molema and Solomon T. Plaatje papers,
Cc9 African National Congress: Printed
draft constitution enclosed in P. KaI. Seme

to Chief Silas Molema, 3.11.1911.
18 *Imvo*, 5.9.1911.
19 Mocher and Mapikela, for example,
reported back at a meeting in Bloemfontein
on 16 August. *Tsala ea Becoana*, 26.8.1911.
20 *Ilanga*, 20.10.1911; *Tsala ea Becoana*,
28.10.1911.
21 See *Ilanga*, 15.12.1911 and 12.1.1912;
Tsala ea Becoana, 23.12.1911; *Indaba
Zabantu*, 1.1.1912.
22 *Imvo*, 5.12.1911.
23 'A native union', *Indian Opinion*, 29 July
1911, as quoted in Nauriya, 'Gandhi and
the founders of the ANC'.
24 *Imvo*, 2.5.1911.
25 *Imvo*, 5.12.1911.
26 *Imvo*, 29.8.1911.
27 *Imvo*, 16.5.1911; *The Argus*, 9.1.1912.
28 See E.J. Mqoboli's statement, *Imvo*,
14.3.1911; B.S. Mazwi to the editor, *Imvo*,
21.3.1911; Notice, 'Umanyano Iwabantu',
signed by J.T. Jabavu, 15.5.1911, in *Imvo*,
16.5.1911.
29 *Imvo*, 30.5.1911.
30 *Imvo*, 16.5.1911. For Rubusana's
response, see.W.B. Rubusana to S.P. Sihlali,
24.3.1911, in *Imvo*, 9.4.1912.
31 Approximately 50 delegates from 16 towns
throughout the eastern Cape and Transkei
attended on 24 May 1911, as well as one
from Cape Town. The meeting resolved
to collect funds to send Jabavu to London
and appointed a committee to draft and
publish a constitution for the proposed
body. The committee consisted of Jabavu,
Mqoboli and Mazwi, and Messrs Mabona,
Xabanisa, Mtombeni, Ntloko and J.A.
Sishuba (secretary). The committee met
in Queenstown on 14 June to finalise the
constitution for a new Imbumba Yezizwe
Zomzantsi Afrika (South African Races
Congress). The constitution was published
in the next issue of *Imvo* under Jabavu's
signature. At the end of June 1911, he
left for Britain, from where he sent back
regular reports in English and Xhosa, which
were published in *Imvo*. The inaugural
conference of the new-style Imbumba,
originally intended for September or
October, was not held until March 1912,
probably to allow Jabavu to be present.
32 B.S. Mazwi to Pixley Seme, 3.1.1911, in
Imvo, 5.12.1911. In this letter Mazwi
refers to a meeting of 'our local Imbumba',
probably meaning the Queenstown branch,

scheduled for 14 November. There are no reports of a meeting of the full Imbumba at this time.

33 Pixley Seme to B.S. Mazwi, 9.11.1911, in *Imvo*, 5.12.1911.

34 For more details of the Tsala, see Historical Papers, Witwatersrand University Library, Silas T. Molema and Solomon T. Plaatje papers, Da 1, 6-7, 20, 22, 34 and 52 Correspondence, and Aa 3.6.1 *Koranta ea Becoana*, Legal Documents: J.D. Goronyane to Chief Silas Molema, 8.6.1911.

35 Switzer and Switzer, *The black press in South Africa*, pp. 51-3, 63.

36 CAD, PM 1/1/300, file no. 155/6/1910: A. Mangena to General L. Botha, 19.8.1910, enclosing Rules and Regulations of the African Brotherhood and Commercial Co-operation Society.

37 NLSA, W.P. Schreiner papers, 1913, no. 2122: A. Mangena to W.P. Schreiner, 9.1.1913, and enclosure; Switzer and Switzer, *The black press*, p. 28.

38 *Tsala ea Becoana*, 30.7.1910; *Christian Express*, 1.11.1910, p. 188.

39 *Tsala ea Becoana* and *Imvo*, 14.11.1911; *Christian Express*, 1.9.1911, p. 137.

40 'A Native Minister' to the editor, *Imvo*, 10.10.1911; *Tsala ea Becoana*, 17.2.1912.

41 *Tsala ea Becoana*, 8.10.1910.

42 Minutes of Third Convention of Native and European supporters of the scheme for the establishment of a South African Native College for Natives held at Bloemfontein, 2 and 3 April 1912 (*Christian Express*, 1.6.1912, pp. 88-9).

Chapter 50: The South African Native National Congress, 1912

1 The most complete list of the delegates appeared in *Tsala ea Becoana*, 10.2.1912. See also *Ilanga*, 26.1.1912; *Pretoria News*, 8.1.1912; CAD, GG 1161, file no. 50/169: Report by Phillip Mochekoane and Josias Mopedi, n.d.

2 *Ilanga*, 12.1.1912 and 2.2.1912.

3 *Imvo*, 24.10.1911; 31.10.1911; 14.11.1911; *A.P.O.*, 21. 10.1911.

4 *Pretoria News*, 8.1.1912.

5 Ibid.

6 *Ilanga*, 12.1.1912. Skota, *The African yearly register*, p. 423.

7 *Pretoria News*, 15.1.1912.

8 R.V. Selope Thema, 'How Congress began', *Drum*, August 1953, p. 4 and quoted in

Walshe, *The rise of African nationalism*, p. 34.

9 *Pretoria News*, 15.1.1912.

10 Walshe, *The rise of African nationalism*, p. 35.

11 Ibid.

12 *Tsala ea Becoana*, 17.2.1912.

13 *Ilanga*, 26.1.1912.

14 *Tsala ea Becoana*, 17.2.1912.

15 Ibid.

16 *Ilanga*, 26.1.1912.

17 Marks, *Reluctant rebellion*, p. 365.

18 Walshe, *The rise of African nationalism*, p. 35.

19 *Ilanga*, 26.1.1912.

20 See the statement by Pixley Seme in *Ilanga*, 22.3.1912.

21 *Ilanga*, 26.1.1912. My description of the first SANNC office-bearers, based on Charles Dube's report of the meeting, differs from that of Walshe, who relied on a much later, secondary account by T.D. Mweli Skota.

22 *Tsala ea Becoana*, 10.2.1912.

23 'Programme for the proposed South African Native National Congress', *Ilanga*, 12.1.1912.

24 *Ilanga*, 26.1.1912.

25 *Ilanga*, 26.1.1912; *Pretoria News*, 13.1.1912.

Conclusion

1 Opland and Nyamende, *Isaac Williams Wauchope*, pp. xviii-xix, xxix, xxxiii, xxxv. Phyllis Ntantala's description of her husband, the celebrated writer A.C. Jordan, underlines the point. He was 'a peasant in outlook, one who remained suspicious of city ways to the end of his life' yet he was 'a Classical and European scholar of literature, history and music, one who could field with the best'. To understand this apparent contradiction, she explained, 'One needs to know the roots from which such people have sprung.' See P. Ntantala, *A life's mosaic* (Cape Town, 1992). What applies to A.C. Jordan, father of the ANC intellectual Pallo Jordan, applies equally to many of the first generations of mission-educated intellectuals and political leaders whose identities were deeply felt and self-consciously nurtured.

2 See Mqhayi, *Abantu besizwe*.

3 John Gawler, the first president of the pioneering Native Educational Association

in 1879, was the grandson of Nxele
Makhanda. S.M. Makgatho was related to
Sekhukhune. Nathaniel Umhalla was the
grandson of Ndlambe. Samuel Moroka,
his classmate at Zonnebloem, was the son
of Chief Moroka of the Seleka Rolong at
Thaba Nchu. Silas Molema was part of
a royal lineage among the Tswana. Tiyo
Soga's father, a councillor of Sandile, died
in war with his king, and both Sandile and
Hintsa insisted that the western-educated
Tiyo accompany them to meetings with
colonial officials. Leaders such as J.M.
Nyokong, Walter Rubusana, John Dube
and Martin Lutuli were likewise related to
chiefs and councillors through kinship and
marriage or acted as advisers to them, and
they regularly made use of the patronage
and sponsorship of chiefs to advance their
own plans. Dube's Ohlange Institute got
off the ground because of support from
his father's close associate and kinsman,
Chief Mqhawe of the Qadi, who was a
hereditary chief. Organisations such as the
Transvaal Native Vigilance Association
and Iliso Lesizwe Esimnyama in Natal,
which actively tried to promote 'tribal'
participation and project 'tribal' grievances,
also demonstrate this point well.

4 Odendaal, *Vukani Bantu!*, p. 292.
5 Colin Bundy, *Govan Mbeki* (Johannesburg, 2012), chs. 1 and 2.
6 Van Diemel, 'In search of freedom, fair play and justice', pp. 24-6.
7 Interview with Makhenkhesi Stofile, Cape Town, 23.11.2010.
8 'Death of the late R.W. Msimang' and 'Funeral of Mr R.W. Msimang', *Umteteli wa Bantu*, 9 and 16.12.1933.
9 Adebajo, 'Where to, Africa?', *Mail & Guardian*, 23.12.2010.

Acknowledgements

The Founders is the culmination of work stretching over three decades and it was given its current shape during a sabbatical spent in the History Department at the University of Kentucky in Lexington in the United States in 2011. Consequently, I am indebted to many people and institutions, starting with my slightly bemused colleagues in the Western Province Cricket Association and the trophy-grabbing Cape Cobras, who permitted their somewhat unconventional chief executive to go off into the distant cold to write books. *The Blue Book: A History of Western Province Cricket, 1890–2011* (co-authored with Krish Reddy and Andrew Samson) and this work are the products of that sabbatical. I am grateful to colleagues on the executive and staff for their support and belief in me, and to the WPCA for giving me a contract that allowed me to pursue my love of reading and writing history alongside a job that itself has provided a rich learning experience. My thanks, particularly, to Solomon Makosana, Norman Arendse, Mohamed Ebrahim, Cyril O'Connor, John Bester, Beresford Williams, Peter Cyster, Omar Henry, Nabeal Dien, David Griqua, Anthea Alie, Evan Flint, Jasmiena Davids, Carol van Vuuren, Faeeda Emjedi and Ameena Smith, whose efficiencies have guaranteed mine.

Similarly, I owe a great debt to Professor Mark Kornbluh, Dean of Arts and Science at UKY, who found nothing strange in the idea of a CEO of a professional cricket body from South Africa coming to spend time in a History Department at an American university – indeed, he persisted until I accepted. Mark initiated the *Kentucky and South Africa: Different Lands, Common Ground* programme, and I was privileged to be part of it together with Eddie Daniels, Ahmed Kathrada, Barbara Hogan and other exemplary South Africans. Mark and Dr Mimi Behar were wonderful hosts, and they have become valued friends. Thanks also to Amy Hisel, Debbie Burton, Ted Schiatzki, Betty, Bob and Sarah Lorch, Kirsten Turner, Lauren Kientz and Steve Wrinn for their generosity and support during my stay in Lexington. Andrew Champion, IT boffin, digitised my previous work so that I could get my innings going with some quick singles. Professor Francie Chesson-Lopez and her colleagues in the History Department went out of their way to welcome this stranger into their ranks, especially my neighbours on the 17th floor such as Paul Chamberlin, Hang Nguyen, Eric Christianson, Eric Myrup, David Hamilton, James Albisetti, Jacobi Williams and Jeremy Popkin. Course colleagues Tina Hagee, John Davies, Sara Compion and my 120-strong HIS315 'Sport and Society' class of 2011 added to this feeling of family.

I also owe colleagues at the University of Missouri (St Louis) and Michigan State University a big debt for their support for my research, writing and involvement, even though I am no longer a full-time academic, especially Joel Glassman, Chuck Korr and Ron Turner at UMSL and Kurt Dewhurst, Marsha McDowell, Peter Alegi, Peter Limb and Bobby and Ursula Vassen at MSU.

In the years since my research started in 1978, I have received considerable support from many other people and institutions. Those I need to thank at Stellenbosch University are Hermann Giliomee, valued supervisor of my master's dissertation, and Professors D.J. van Zyl and D.J. Kotze. At St John's College, Cambridge, my supervisors were Professor Jack Gallagher, Dr John Iliffe and Dr John Lonsdale and my college tutor was Dr George Read, while Peter Linehan gave friendly support. Colin Webb and Christopher Saunders at the University of Cape Town gave me a 'temporary assistant junior lecturer' opportunity, which enabled me to do a research stint back home during the PhD. Burridge Spies and Ben Liebenberg offered me my first lecturing job at the University of South Africa, where Johannes du Bruyn, Lucille Heymans, Etta Lubbe, Albert Grundlingh and Greg Cuthbertson were supportive colleagues and friends.

In addition to those already mentioned, there were many others who encouraged me in one way or another during the writing of my master's and PhD dissertations: Colin Bundy, Jeremy Kriekler, Tim and Margy

Keegan, Felicia Stoch, Richard Malinga, Gordon Maputa, David Gxilishe, Tozie Gxilishe, T.D.M. Mosomathane, Wayne Hendricks, Clyde Daniel, David Brink, David Botha, Chris Aucamp, Rodney Davenport, Leonard Thompson, Thomas Karis, William Beinart, Peter Walshe, Bill Nasson, Shula Marks, Richard Ralston, Brian Willan, Stanley Trapido, Karel Schoeman, Andy Smith, Hilary Sapire, Lulu Thethiwe, Tozie Gxilishe, William Twaku, the Pelem family, Ian Brenson, Scott Optican and Peter van Ryneveld. On a personal level, Cheryl Kingwell, Laureen Simpson and Liz Offen gave me support for which I will always be grateful. Liz also typed the PhD – apparently one of the earliest completed on the big mainframe computer housed in the Metallurgy Department at Cambridge.

After the PhD and the publication of *Vukani Bantu!*, I took a detour away from my research and writing on the origins of the struggle, going on to engage more with its later 20th-century history. This was an indication of the personal journey I undertook, which included joining 'the struggle' during tumultuous years in South Africa's history, and taking up the invitation by Randy Erentzen and Professor Jakes Gerwel to teach at the University of the Western Cape. My activism and the many years at 'Bush', as it set itself the challenge of becoming the 'intellectual home of the left' in South Africa (at a time when people were being tested in deep ways personally and intellectually), were part of a defining journey in my life.

Already in 1978 I had the privilege of interviewing Selby Msimang in Pietermaritzburg, one of those present at the founding conference of the ANC in 1912. He was in his nineties at the time and his urbane dignity made a big impression on me. In the ensuing years, I was privileged to meet and learn from many other intellectuals and activists outside the universities. Being involved in a United Democratic Front area committee and organisations such as the National Education Crisis Committee and the National Sports Congress in the 1980s drew me intimately into the ideas world of the then banned ANC. Powerful events like the funeral of the Cradock Four and the million signature campaign launch in Soshanguve (where people sang *Oliver Tambo bamb' isandla sam* a mere 20 kilometres from where P.W. Botha was ensconced in the Union Buildings) brought home to me the strength of the ANC legacy. At Dakar in 1987, I met formidable ANC intellectuals such as Thabo Mbeki, Pallo Jordan, Mac Maharaj and

Kader Asmal and helped carry the luggage of Beyers and Ilse Naudé.

Six months later, I was in London on a productive sabbatical during which I produced books on Alex la Guma (with Roger Field) and Lionel Forman (with Sadie Forman). This time also led to the launch of the Mayibuye Centre at UWC. I had the privilege, too, of being drawn intimately into the South African exile community: Sadie Forman, Wolfie Kodesh, Margaret Castle and her neighbour Eleanor Kasrils made me part of their London family. Through them I was introduced to their friends and comrades such as Rica Hodgson, Ethel de Keyser, Esmé Goldberg, and Barbara and Terry Bell – strong-minded people who were not afraid to talk straight about exile icons to whom we younger people showed such deference. In London, I also worked with the remarkable Sheila Levson and Blanche La Guma, and met Essop, Meg and Aziz Pahad, Thabo Mbeki, Ronnie Kasrils, Francis Meli, Mzala, Jeremy Cronin, Sam Ramsamy, Sipho Pityana, Harold Wolpe, Tito Mboweni, John Hoffman, Howard Barrell, Garth Strachan, John Daniel, Martin Legassick and Baruch Hirson. Discussions with younger comrades from home like Khumi Naidoo, Khetso Gordon, Yvonne Muthien, Nozipho Diseko, Eliza Kentridge and my friend Jeremy Kriekler further stimulated my thinking on ANC and South African history. At the International Defence and Aid Fund for Southern Africa (IDAF), Barry Feinberg, Gordon Metz, Tony Trew, Norman Kaplan and Ramni Naidoo gave me insight into their valuable work and access to their magnificent resources, which we eventually brought back to UWC. Pallo Jordan and Aziz Pahad gave me the ANC's support for the Mayibuye project and Ronnie Kasrils, Jacob Zuma, Brian Bunting and Apollon Davidson helped me to visit Cuba and the Soviet Union. Through Pallo Jordan, I also met in Lusaka the stalwart historians Jack Simons and Ray Alexander, sitting in the shade under the big avo tree in their garden, as well as Zola Skweyiya, Larry Joseph and Barney McKay.

Jakes Gerwel and colleagues in the History Department at UWC allowed me to take a sabbatical in Britain in 1988/89, which, again, profoundly influenced the course of my career and personal development. Academic support came also from Robin Cohen, who offered me a visiting fellowship at the Centre for Ethnic Relations at Warwick University; Shula Marks, who provided shelter at the Institute for Commonwealth

Studies in London; and Bob Edgar, who hosted me at Howard University in Washington. I was fortunate to visit 11 campuses in the United States and various institutions in Sweden, Holland, Cuba and the Soviet Union.

These were exciting times during which I began to know the illegal ANC and its history well. Then, suddenly, the organisations were unbanned and the exiles returned and the final push towards democracy took place, leading to the first elections on 27 April 1994 and the Mandela era. In the run-up to, and aftermath of, the brutal, beautiful dawn of a new democracy, my work focus shifted more towards culture and archives (setting up the Mayibuye Centre), museums (helping turn Robben Island Maximum Security Prison into a national museum and a Unesco World Heritage Site), policy and legislation.

It was wonderful to be able to welcome home the exiles (many in our home, with Zohra) and, in the course of heading the Robben Island Museum, I met hundreds of ex-'Islanders', learning in a privileged way about that aspect of the liberation struggle's history. But my biggest reward in this personal and intellectual journey was coming into contact with the elders, who bore with exceptional dignity the values and traditions of a great struggle. Ahmed Kathrada became my mentor. I also sat with Nelson Mandela in his cell on Robben Island and listened to and met the gentle Walter Sisulu, Wilton Mkwayi, Govan Mbeki, Andrew Mlangeni, Raymond Mhlaba, Kwedi Mkalipi, Andimba Toivo ya Toivo, Reg and Hettie September, Fred and Sarah Carneson, Albie Sachs, Josiah Jele, James April, Brian and Sonia Bunting, Albertina Sisulu, Helen Joseph, Mama Zihlangu, Amy Thornton, Christmas Tinto, Zoli Malindi, Dennis Goldberg, Rusty Bernstein, Blanche La Guma, Walter and Adelaine Hain, Lionel Davis, Beyers Naudé, Desmond Tutu, Laloo Chiba, Indres Naidoo, Mary Benson, Wolfie Kodesh ('Jewish godfather' of my daughter) and others who personified the universalism and deep values of the struggle. These were profound personal and learning experiences that gave meaning to my entire life. Their stories (and the awareness that many history-makers were dying without having their contributions recorded) reminded me of the need to return eventually to the rich topic of The Founders.

The 1980s and 1990s were times when, in my experience, people were fully alive to ideas, values, action, and when generosity, empathy, courage and displays of deep humanity were in abundant supply. I was privileged to be touched, even if briefly, by some remarkable people, including Paul Weinberg, Liz Floyd, Yvette Breytenbach, Merrick Zwarenstein, Andrew Boraine, Jonathan de Vries, Miranda Quanashe, Willem Basson, Bennie Schereka, Lynette Maart, Patti Smith, Tony Karon, Moira Levy, Rashid Lombard, Jimi Matthews, Nyami Goniwe, Di Bishop, Gaby Shapiro, Jonathan Shapiro, Beth Silbert, Annica van Gyslwyk, Raymond Suttner, Willy Hofmeyr, Trevor Manuel, Cheryl Carolus, Bulelani Ngcuka, Dullah Omar, Barbara Hogan, Saki Macozoma, Peter Hain, Ebrahim Rassool, Ben Tengimfene, Ngconde Balfour, Cheryl Roberts, Farieda Omar, Donnie Jurgens, Marion Lacey, Moegsien Williams, Zubeida Jaffer, Gaye Davis, David and Marie Philip, Mike Kirkwood, Njabulo Ndebele, Mongane Wally Serote, Roger Jardine, Max and Elinor Sisulu, Barney Pityana, Nicki Romano, Vanessa Solomon, Lindiwe Mabuza, Barbara Masekela, June Bam, Jon Weinberg, Jonathan Berndt, Songezo Nayo, Lucien Le Grange, James April, Joe Marks, Don Pinnock, Patricia Schonstein, Omar Badsha, Allister Sparks, Kier and Maud Schuringa, Karel Roskam, Feroza Cachalia, Mohammed Seedat, Max du Preez, Dorothy Woodson, Barry Streek, Sedick Isaacs, Stone Sizani, Steve Tshwete, Rodney Davenport, Denver Webb, Dorothy Woodson, Jane Carruthers, Barney Pityana, Sandy Prosalendis, Graham Duminy, James Early, Joel Netshitenze, Jeff Peires, Francis Meli, Marcus Solomons, Christopher Merrett, Tyrone Appolis, Natsha Erlank, Rooksana Omar, Joseph Dlamini, Lucien le Grange, Crain Soudien, Breyten Breytenbach, Cornelius Thomas, Duke Ngcukana, Ciraj Rassool, David and Marie Philip, Greg fredericks, Khaya Majola, Jonathan Price, George Hallet, Phuti and Tiisetso Tsukudu, Vince Kolbe, Shafiek Morton, Mary Burton, Lavinia Crawford-Brown, Sheryl Ozinsky, Nomboniso Gasa, Alec and Jenny Boraine, Van Zyl Slabbert, Mike Savage, Bennie and Shirley Rabinowitz, Paul Yule, Glenda Kruss, Maureen Robinson, Ashwin Desai, John Young, Ebrahim Moosa, Sheik Nazeem Mohammed, Mogamad Moerat, Hassan Solomons, Roseida Shabodien, Amanda Botha, Sue Williamson, Sandra Kriel, Leon Vermeulen, Patricia Davison, Marlene and Patti Silbert, Saki Veldman, Johan Graaff, Verne Harris, Luli Callinicos, Eric Miller, Chris Ledochowski, Joan Rapp, Amy, Linda and Peter Biehl, Nondithini Dini, Thenjiwe Perhe, Rashid Omar, Michael Weeder, Vladimir Shubin, Lawson

Naidoo, Richard Calland, Johann Graaff, Archie Henderson, Stone Sizani, Makhenkhesi Arnold Stofile, Margaret Nash, Cameron Dugmore, Johnny de Lange, Alec Erwin, Gertrude Fester, Graham Abrahams, Cecyl Esau, Neville van der Rheede, Jenny Schreiner, Chris Giffard, Eugene La Guma, Leteane Monatse, Wilma van Biljon, Mare Norval, Garth and Zusy Johnson, and an extended cricket family whom I have acknowledged elsewhere. My apologies to the many people I have left out.

I have only a short paragraph left to acknowledge those at UWC, the Mayibuye Centre and Robben Island not yet named: people like Alfred Mandita, Monde Stemele, Hein Willemse, Anna Strebel, Madeleine Fullard, Khwezi Mpumlwana, Jaap du Rand, Gary Minkley, Ernest Messina, Niki Rousseau, Dominee van der Linde, Dave Scher, Ingrid Scholtz, Fanie de Jong, H.C. Bredenkamp, Chris Loff, Premesh Laloo, Patricia Hayes, Uma Mesthrie, Denise Daniels, Hamilton Budaza, Graeme Goddard, Anthea Josias, Esther van Driel, Bertie Fritz, Shanaaz and Suleiman Isaacs, Lucky Makamba, Norman Kaplan, Tholakele Nzuza, Wendy Manuel, Felicia Siebritz, Colin Darch, Mathokoza Nhlapo, Karen Chubb, Cheryl Hendricks, Cheryl Potgieter, Shirley Walters, Keith Gottshalk, Rhoda Kadalie, Milton Shain, Sandile Dikeni, Dheela Khan, Murray Michell, Wynand Louw, Niki van Driel, Jaap Durand, Kathy Kenned, Daan Cloete, Renfrew Christie, Lieb Loots, Muhamed Haroon, Stan Ridge, Julian Smith, Larry Popkas, Nic Kok, Nomonde Mbulawa, Shannon Copperfield, Victoria Matshikiza, Sobantu Stofile, Barbara Davis, Lizo Ngqungwana, Ashley Forbes, Thozama Jonas, Ruth Carneson and many others whom I wish I could name. My thanks to the Rector, Brian O'Connell, for generously overseeing an honorary professorship at UWC for me in 2001.

The bulk of the research for this book was conducted in the Western Cape Archives Depot and the National Library of South Africa in Cape Town. Here I was generously helped by people such as Arlene Fanaroff, Peter Coates, Sandy Rowolt, Mike Berning, Karel Schoeman, Marion George, Michelle Pickover, Graham Duminy and many other dedicated people who went out of their way for me. Their monastic dedication and care for history and the material from which we create narratives partly inspired me, I am sure, to start the Mayibuye Centre with its unique multimedia collections in 1991.

I also made use of the facilities at the Special Collections Department of the University of Cape Town Library, the Library of Parliament, the Carnegie Library in Stellenbosch, the Cory Library at Rhodes University, the Department of Historical Papers at the Witwatersrand University Library, the Johannesburg Public Library, the Documentation Centre for African Studies at the University of South Africa, as well as the Transvaal and Central Archives Depots in Pretoria, the Natal Archives Depot in Pietermaritzburg, the Orange Free State Archives Depot in Bloemfontein, Rhodes House, Oxford, and the British Library and Public Records Office in London. The staff at the various libraries and archives were always most helpful.

I must also acknowledge assistance received from various funding bodies and institutions, including the Human Sciences Research Council, the Centre for African Studies at the University of Cape Town, Sir Henry Strakosch Memorial Trust, Elsie Ballot scholarships, the Wilcocks bursary, the Smuts Fund in Cambridge, UWC, Michigan State University, the University of Missouri (St Louis) and the University of Kentucky.

Christopher Saunders, Pallo Jordan, Colin Bundy, Jeff Peires and Bob Edgar read parts of this manuscript and have been supportive over many years. Finally, I wish to thank Jacana Media and my editor, Russell Martin, for bringing two books to press for me in the space of seven months in the calmest possible way. Russell alarmed me at times as he cut and cleaned up with vigour, but it is a better book because of his help.

The work was finalised during the exquisite South African summer of 2011/12, when I was often at my desk as the birds woke and the sun rose to announce another day. It has been a rare privilege to be able to tackle this topic and to do this writing. Thanks to my family for their love and support throughout. My parents and my sister Louise have always been there for me. I learned to read newspapers sitting on my father's lap next to a paraffin lamp with a bad wick – and that was also the safest space I have ever known. Zohra Ebrahim and our beautiful children, Rehana Thembeka, Adam and Nadia Odendaal, are the warm centre of my life.

André Odendaal
Kenilworth
May 2012

Index

American Board of Missions 159, 165, 252

Anglia, M.C. 423

Anglican Institution, Grahamstown 237

Anglo-Zulu War (1879) 8, 40, 161, 163, 242

Antigua 221

Anti-Slavery and Aborigines Protection Society (APS) 58, 116–17, 122, 220, 244, 412, 425–6, 431

Antoni, Peter 315

Ark of Refuge Society 229

Asquith, Herbert 433–4

Association for the Advancement of the Nqika (Intlanganiso Ye Nqubelo Pambili Yama Ngqika): aims of, 92; formation of (1885), 92; members of, 119

Australia 235, 339; Australian Cricket Board, 239

Ayliff, Rev. John 16, 39

B

Baartman, Sarah 242

Balfour, James 315

Balmforth, Rev. Ramsden 411

Bambatha 19; rebellion (1906), 297–8, 308, 471; political impact of, 289, 301

Bantu Women's League 213

Bassie, W.F. 317, 321; member of BMIA, 89–90

Basuto Pioneering Trading Company 71, 228

Basutoland 34, 64, 69, 110, 141, 166, 172–4, 178, 196, 226, 239, 342, 344, 369, 373, 411, 430, 460, 463, 468

Basutoland National Council 328, 370

Basutoland Progressive Association 372, 419; formation of (1907), 350

Bathoen Gaseitsiwe, Chief 184, 186, 419, 467; representatives of, 425

Bechuanaland 18, 198, 207, 226, 341, 396, 419, 430, 439, 473

Bechuanaland Annexation Act 185

Becoana Mutual Improvement Association (BMIA) 283, 393, 409, 439–40, 467; branches of, 349;

members of, 90, 283, 391, 396; Thaba Nchu meeting (1909), 381, 403

Bekwa, William 155

Bell, Augustus 99, 106, 123

Berlin Mission Society 187, 188

Berry, Sir Bisset 412, 445, 453

Bethlehem 283, 391, 439, 467–8

Bhunga 420

Bikitsha, Captain Veldtman 87, 132, 154–5, 202, 228, 262, 320–1; associates of, 222; family of, 88

Bikitsha, Charles 89–90

Binase, Josiah 322

Bloemfontein 15, 166–9, 171, 197, 210, 213, 224, 261, 279–80, 282, 309, 331, 384–7, 393, 398, 400, 402–4, 409, 437-8, 453, 465, 468

Bloemfontein Cricket Club 179

Bloemfontein Native Vigilance Committee 279, 280

Blyden, E.W. 27

Blyth, Captain Matthew 90

Blythswood 322

Boers 9, 150, 187, 262, 355, 378, 429; Transvaal, 161, 176

Bokwe, Candlish 98

Bokwe, John Knox 31, 63, 72, 98, 127, 155–6, 222, 236, 327, 329, 393, 401, 464; background of, 151; clerk of *Kaffir Express*, 35; visit to UK (1892), 255; *Vuka Deborah*, 245

Booth, Joseph 165

Bopi, Rev. Eben 440

Botha, Louis 270, 348–9, 350, 353, 360, 376, 430, 442, 447, 448

Botlocks, Abel 174

Botswana 369

Bottoman, Thomas 61

Bovula, Nicholas 61

Boza, K.N. 36

Bradford, Helen 214

Brander, Samuel 367; background of, 193

Briscoe, F.J. 386

British Bechuanaland 185, 211, 276, 386, 391, 403, 453, 458; annexed by Cape (1895), 385; declaration of (1885), 184

British Empire 17, 78, 295, 345, 429;

McCord, Margaret 221
McCorn, H. 341
McCrone, Kathleen 215
McKay, John 72, 99
McKinley, President William 251
Mdima, Nokutela 219
Mdliva, S.T. 124, 317, 468
Mdolomba, Rev. Elijah 307–8
Mehlomakulu, Joel 123, 313, 315
Mercator, Gerhard 5
Mercury Printing Press 263
Merriman, John X. 150–1, 206, 260, 315, 318, 338, 344, 347, 353, 356–8, 376, 407, 413, 423, 429, 430, 442, 448; Prime Minister of Cape, 229, 376, 412, 420; support for J.T. Jabavu, 149, 351
Methodism 142, 148, 165, 171, 196, 289
Mfecane 297
Mfengu 20, 24, 30–1, 38, 41, 42, 64, 69, 80, 87–8, 90–1, 118, 122, 148, 151, 153–7, 180, 195, 205, 206, 237, 279, 320, 324, 394, 445; activity in Cape-Xhosa War (1877–8), 40; Bele, 41, 65; Cape Town community of, 302; Ciskeian, 17; landowning elites, 83; observation of Fingo Emancipation Day (1908), 154; settlements of, 16–17, 38–9, 65
Mgcodo, Benjamin 131
Mgidi, Lambata 91, 320, 322
Mgijima, Enoch 20
Mgwali 12, 25, 40
Mhala, Chief 46–7, 49, 316
Mhlambiso, Chief Ebenezer 61, 66, 151, 205, 228, 315, 317
Michell, Lewis 371
Middledrift 66, 141–2, 153, 195, 204–5, 208, 226, 399, 414, 425
Miliwana, R.B. 315
Milner, Sir Alfred 260, 261, 267, 335; Kindergarten, 335–6
Milton, Sir William 359
Mines and Works Act (1911) 455
Mini, Chief Stephen 164, 264, 285, 287, 292
Mji, Coke 308

Mkize, Chief Isaac 285
Mkobeni, J.M. 151
Mlanjeni, Chief Somerset 130, 315
Mlanjeni's War (1850–3) 17, 33, 195
Mloba, S. 417
Mnga, William 71
Mngqibisa, Abraham 193
Mnyanda, S.H. 151
Mocher, Jan 168, 278, 280, 282–3, 349, 381
Mocher, John 396, 440, 458, 464; executive member of president of ORCNC/OFS Native Congress, 390, 467–8, 472
Mochochonono (The Comet) 463
Modise, Philip 472, 473
Moeletsi, E.T. 375, 390, 468, 472
Moffat, Rev. J.S. 365
Mohlaba, Chief 467
Moikangoa, J.K. 375
Mokgalagadi, Chief 468
Mokgatle of the Fokeng 186, 188
Mokgatle, Bloemhof 188
Mokgatle, Paul 188
Mokhosi, Obed 284, 391, 468
Mokone, Mangena 188, 191, 192, 193, 194, 196, 198, 203, 208, 250, 274; founder of Ethiopian Church, 202, 367; head of Kilnerton Institute, 192
Molema, Chief Joshua 176, 177, 459, 470
Molema, Chief Silas 185, 386, 391, 396–7, 439
Molisapoli, Simon 272
Moloi, J.T. 459
Molteno, Betty 426
Molteno, Percy 426
Molteno, Sir John C. 135, 144, 344, 426
Momoti, W.P. 67, 72
Monde, Walter 49–50
Montshiwa Tawana 176–7, 185, 186
Montsioa, Chief Lekoko 385, 386, 391
Montsioa, George 186, 460, 472; background of, 426–7
Montsioa, Paramount Badirile 185, 341, 386
Monyakuane, F. 468
Moor, Frederick Robert 430, 454; Minister of Native Affairs, 402, 454;

Tshatshu, Chief Kote 9–10, 20, 47
Tshongwana, Elijah 282, 381
Tshwete, Isaac 141
Tsolo 79, 319–20
Tsomo 17, 87–8, 90, 132–3, 321, 323, 329, 380, 399, 420
Tsonga 188
Tswana 20, 34; *kgotla*, 48; language of, 171, 176–7, 180, 463
Tulwana, J.N.J. 147
Tung' umlomo 114, 128, 130
Tunyiswa, Jonathan 63, 106, 118, 139, 146, 317, 327, 331, 340; secretary of SANC, 142, 204, 314
Turner, Bishop Henry 170, 196; visit to South Africa (1898), 198, 252
Tuskegee Institute 251, 253
Twayi, Joseph B. 175, 238, 261, 278, 279, 280, 282, 349, 391, 440, 464
Tyakwadi, D.D. 308, 315
Tyali, Chief Feni (Fynne) 92
Tyamzashe, Benjamin 148
Tyamzashe, George 147–8
Tyamzashe, Henry 148
Tyamzashe, Peter 140, 146
Tyamzashe, Rev. Gwayi 30, 39, 107, 179, 181; arrival in Kimberley (1872), 178; background of, 35–6; member of NEA, 61; writings of, 35
Tyhume River, 31

U

Uitenhage 71–2, 96–7, 99, 126, 141, 195, 227, 246
Uitvlugt (Ndabeni) 307–8
Umhalla, Nathaniel Cyril (*usoGqumahashe*) 38, 46, 61, 69, 113, 118–19, 121, 127, 142, 145–6, 153, 155, 233, 314, 317, 327, 330, 384; background of, 50–1; capture of, 41; charged with treason, 52–5; diary of, 53–4; editor of *Izwi Labantu*, 147; family of, 39, 41, 46–7, 316; trial of, 54–5
Umlomo wa Bantu (The Mouthpiece of the People): launch of, 463; staff of, 459, 468
Umtata 315, 319, 322, 325, 382

Union for Native Opinion (Manyano nge Mvo Zabantsundu) 112; founding of (1887), 90, 93, 207; members of, 91
Union of Native Vigilance Associations, *see* Imbumba Eliliso Lomzi Yabantsundu
Union of South Africa (1910), 9, 14, 82, 89, 145, 212, 329, 410, 423, 434, 444, 447, 454
Union Rugby Football Club 237
Unionists 342, 343, 448, 449, 451; led by Dr L.S. Jameson, 343, 447
United Native Political Associations of the Transvaal 275
United Presbyterian Church 249
United States of America (USA) 180, 195–6, 206, 210, 219, 242, 247, 250–2, 444; American Revolution, 6; Civil War (1861–5), 253–4; education system of, 251; Reconstruction era, 253–4; Republican Party, 251

V

Vahed, Goolam 297
Van der Horst, J.G. 376
Van der Kemp, Rev. Johannes (*uNyengane*) 10
Vanqa, Abram 132
Vanqa, Henry 78
Vantyi, J. 151
Venda 188
Victoria East 17, 57, 61, 64, 87, 91, 96–101, 399
Victoria, Queen 245; reign of, 441
Vili, Rev. James J. 89–90, 203
Vimbe, John Muir 30; writings of, 35
Vorster, B. 391
Voters Registration Act, *see* Parliamentary Voters Registration Act
Vyavaharik, Madanjit 295–6

W

Walton, E.H. 359
War of the Axe (1846–7) 17
Warner, Rev. E.J. 77, 131, 216–17
Warren Expedition (1884) 184
Warren, W.J. 99, 126–7
Wartburg 142, 146, 153